LEGACY

LEGACY

The Natural History of ONTARIO

EDITOR-IN-CHIEF:
John B. Theberge

ASSOCIATE EDITOR AND ILLUSTRATOR:
Mary T. Theberge

ASSOCIATE EDITOR:
David Barr

ASSOCIATE EDITOR:
Theodore Mosquin

CARTOGRAPHER:
Don Bonner

SPONSORS:
Ontario Heritage Foundation
Federation of Ontario Naturalists

McClelland & Stewart Inc.
The Canadian Publishers
481 University Avenue
Toronto, Ontario
M5G 2E9

Canadian Cataloguing in Publication Data

Theberge, John B., 1940-
Legacy : the natural history of Ontario

Includes index.
ISBN 0-7710-8398-X

1. Natural history—Ontario. I. Title.
QH106.2.O5T48 1989 508.713 C89-093531-9

Printed and bound in Canada

Contents

PART FOUR
VIGNETTES OF NATURE

PART FIVE
PERSPECTIVES ON NATURE

Introduction

John B. Theberge

There is infinite beauty in a trillium, a flaming red maple tree, a loon drifting on a glassy lake.

There is wild music in the plaintive notes of a white-throated sparrow, most common bird of the boreal forest, and in the distant howl of a gray wolf floating up from some lonely lakeshore on the stillness of a summer night.

There is excitement in spring trees alive with tiny wood warblers – forest jewels – and in the fall flights of broadwing hawks in their hundreds that ride the thermals along the Erie shore.

There is natural wonder in the contemplation of the 2.9-billion-year-old rocks that make up a portion of the Canadian Shield in Ontario, and the billion-year-old fossils near the present shoreline of Lake Superior.

More than ever before, there is a hunger in our society to know about these things, the legacy of nature, the ecosystems that support us, the science-dimension for a personal philosophy. It is a hunger that, for the curious, can never be completely satisfied; the table is too richly set. But it can be appeased, and that is the purpose of this book.

The more we understand any facet of nature, the more deeply felt is our sense of beauty, excitement, and wonder. The trillium is playing out a time-tested evolutionary strategy – to leaf out and bloom down on the forest floor before the maples and beeches create so much shade that photosynthesis is retarded. The maple tree flames red because of the pigment *anthocyanin* in the vacuoles of its epidermal cells. Anthocyanin is concocted by cold weather and is unmasked after the breakdown of chlorophyll due to reduced photoperiod. The loon drifting with neck arched and head down is watching for shiners, whose population in a small lake it can significantly influence. The lake itself may have formed in a kettle depression caused by an ice block around which moraine gravels were piled as a glacier retreated ten thousand years ago.

A high-domed, arched cathedral of hardwood forest in southern Ontario or a wild pulpit of pine trees growing on a rocky point in the north, unlike their human-made counterparts are alive and functioning. They capture energy, cycle nutrients, respire, transpire, and support complex webs of living things. Whole books have been written on the molecular chain of events that occurs during photosynthesis alone! To ponder new insights into what is going on in any natural scene is to confront the mysteries of the universe expressed in a trillium, a flaming maple, a drifting loon.

This book presents the natural history of a province: an overview of nature; a distillate of the most exciting, unusual, and rare; a description of nature's best. It is written by naturalists and scientists who spend much of their time exploring whatever subject is their passion in nature. It features

Cabot Head, Bruce Peninsula.
DON GUNN

Eastern tamarack in a boreal bog.
JOHN THEBERGE

chapter-length overviews of traditional topics – bedrock, birds, fish, and forests – as well as short "science excursions" on specific subjects explored in greater depth, and short "vignettes of nature" focused on highlights and arranged geographically.

Our book has been written and illustrated to appease curiosity; to create "feelings of nature" through description, art, and photo; and to deepen a sense of beauty, excitement, and wonder. If your bookmark works its way through the book, what will emerge is an integrated and holistic sense of the physical environment and the species that play out their lives around us. Sensing that wholeness invariably heightens feelings of both time and place, of belonging, of "interconnectedness," of unfathomable beauty and design. It may even lead to an "ecological perspective" – an ethic and personal philosophy of caring and oneness with the environment, a denial of "human-centredness," a deep respect and reverence for the land and living things.

The book rides a wave of public interest in natural science; witness its popularity in television and radio, in magazines and books, and in science centres, planetariums, and museums. And the book accompanies a crest of public concern over continuing environmental deterioration in this province, North America, and the world. The disappearance of the passenger pigeon, the virgin northern hardwood forests, and the giant eastern white pine from Ontario are nothing compared with all that may disappear in the next one hundred years.

The authors share a concern that what is described in this book, when viewed one hundred years from now, is not remembered as "what used to be." That will not happen if the genuine interest in nature swelling in Canada and Ontario continues to grow. As it grows, so does our assurance of a future Ontario in which wild places and species will endure.

Part One

A SMALL PIECE OF PLANET EARTH

Global Dynamics and Ontario

Roger W. Macqueen

Over the past three decades a revolution has occurred in our understanding of the way in which the Earth works. The old ideas on fixed continental positions, based mostly on what was known of their geology, perished quickly in the flood of knowledge that has come from the ocean basins since the mid 1950s. Curiously, many pieces of evidence in support of continental drift, or *plate tectonics* as it is now known, are present on the continents but were unrecognized. What is this theory of plate tectonics? Where did it come from? And what has it to do with Ontario?

The roots of our knowledge of plate tectonics go back at least to the last century. Oceanographers discovered then that the ocean floors are, on average, about four kilometres below the surface of the ocean. In contrast, the continents average about one kilometre above the surface of the ocean. To explain the vast difference between these two levels, it was suggested, with little evidence, that the oceans are underlain by heavy rocks containing silica, iron, and magnesium, whereas the continents are made up of lighter rocks containing mainly silica and aluminium. The continents thus "float" higher than the ocean floors. This suggestion is broadly correct, but it was not until sophisticated geophysical measuring tools were invented after the Second World War that the rest of the story was discovered.

Continental drift was first suggested seriously as a concept in 1915 by the German meteorologist Alfred Wegner. He based his ideas on the symmetry of the continental margins on both sides of the Atlantic Ocean, and on the fact that as many as six different continents in the southern hemisphere contain identical fossil assemblages, glacial features, and specific rock units. Wegner's ideas were dismissed, however, because his evidence was not conclusive enough, and no one could figure out the mechanics of continental drift.

By the mid 1950s evidence was accumulating that fit into Wegner's theory. Continuity of the ridge systems was demonstrated among the mountain systems on the ocean floor, including the Mid-Atlantic Ridge and the East Pacific Rise, which stretch approximately 24,000 kilometres. Also discovered was the fact that these submerged mountains dwarf those on

Worldwide pattern of plates and directions of their movements.

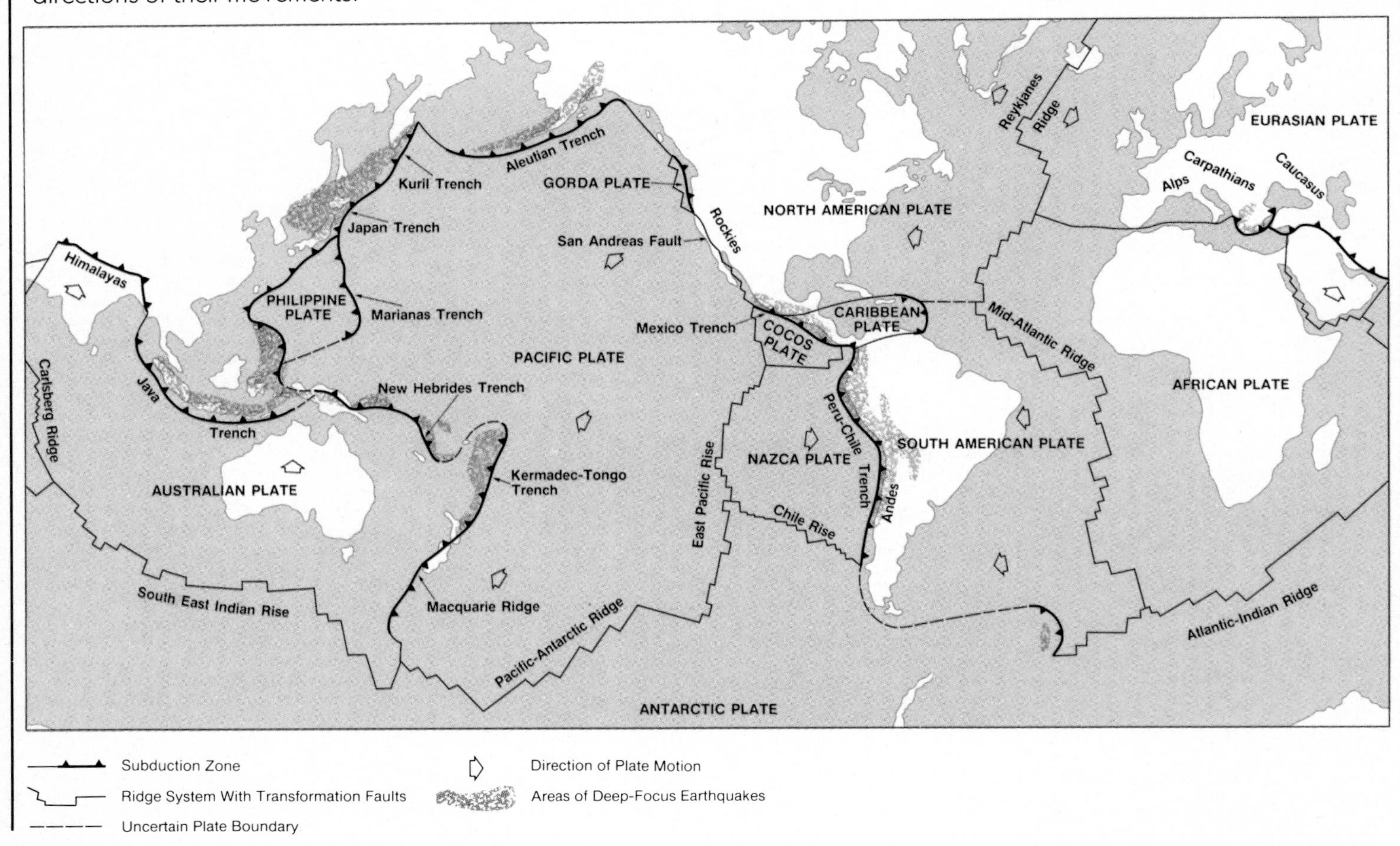

the continents. Meanwhile, on the continents, study of the orientation of iron or iron-rich particles trapped in rocks forming today showed these particles to be aligned within the Earth's present magnetic field, yet radically different orientations in magnetic field were found in old rocks. Either the Earth's magnetic field had changed – considered unlikely – or the continents had moved.

This magnetic puzzle was soon resolved. Volcanic rocks dated by radioactive decay, particularly those formed over the last 4.5 million years, showed conclusively that the Earth's magnetic field had indeed reversed from time to time. These rocks took on the magnetic field that prevailed when they were spewed out of volcanoes. We still do not know why the magnetic reversals happen, but there is no question that they do. Through painstaking work on a global scale, a "magnetic reversal scale" was established showing times of normal and times of reversed polarity.

The magnetic reversals, rather than negating the theory of continental drift, formed a key component of the evidence proving it. They showed conclusively the phenomenon of *sea floor spreading*. In this concept, new ocean crust is created from initially molten rock along the ocean ridge systems, and destroyed in ocean trench systems (later known as *subduction zones*). The continents are viewed as passive riders on ocean-floor "conveyor belts."

During the time the magnetic reversal scale was being developed, two groups of earth scientists, one in England and one in Canada, independently arrived at the same startling conclusion: if new crust really *is* created along ocean ridge systems, the record of magnetic reversals should be present in the volcanic rocks of the ocean floor. Indeed, it is, as has been shown in many thousands of kilometres of records of the Earth's magnetic field at sea. By extrapolating beyond the 4.5-million-year magnetic reversal scale (because reversals have been going on over at least the past 600 million years) it has been possible to date the ocean floors.

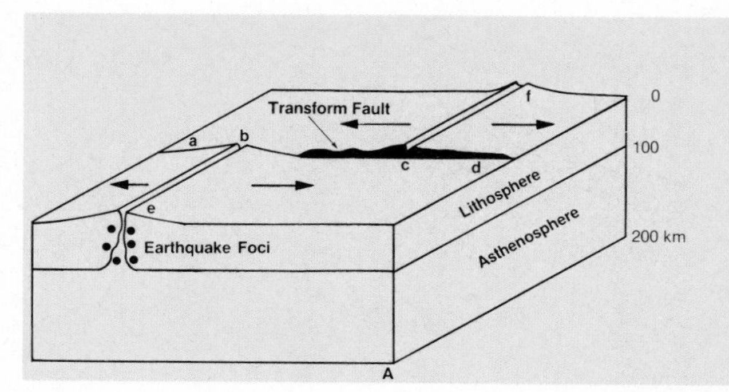

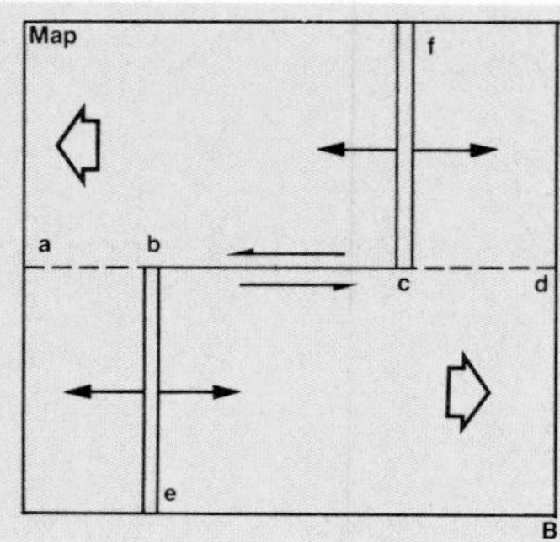

The relative movement of plates associated with ocean ridge and fracture zones. Arrows indicate the direction of movement.

Earthquakes provide more key evidence of continental drift and sea floor spreading. In the late 1950s, western nations collaborated to set up a world-wide seismic observatory network, mainly in hopes of detecting Soviet underground nuclear explosions. An unexpected by-product of this network was, and is, high-quality data on the location and depths of earthquakes around the globe. Analysis of earthquakes between 1961 and 1967 produced a striking conclusion: all *deep focus earthquakes* (those whose energy release takes place 300 to 700 kilometres below the Earth's surface) and most *intermediate focus earthquakes* (70 to 300 kilometres in depth) occur along ocean trenches, whereas *shallow focus earthquakes* (up to 70 kilometres below the surface) occur along ocean ridge systems. Taken together, more than 90 per cent of the energy released globally by earthquakes occurs along the ocean trenches and ridges.

Even more startling conclusions were revealed by systematically measuring ocean depths and amounts of heat escaping from various places on the ocean floors. The crests of ocean ridges are, on average, about two and a half kilometres below the surface of the ocean and are relatively warm. On either side of the ridges, naturally enough, the depth of the ocean increases. At the same time, the temperature of the ocean floor decreases. Thus, the crust cools, contracts, and subsides in response to loss of heat.

A curious feature of the ocean ridge system is that rather than forming a straight ridge, often pieces are offset short distances from one another. Thus, short, linear, "transform faults" are created at right angles to the ridge. These faults represent lateral slippage of blocks along the ridge and characterize most of the world's ridges.

The evidence accumulated in the 1960s, although powerful and convincing, was bolstered considerably by the *Deep Sea Drilling Project*, undertaken from 1967 to 1980. More than five hundred holes were drilled in the ocean floor at sites widely spaced over the world's oceans. Very early in this work it became obvious that the basic conclusions of sea floor spreading were correct. Sediments in the vicinity of ocean ridges are either absent or thin and young; they increase in both age and depth away from the ridges. In addition, the age of the oldest sediments, those far away from the ridges, as dated by microfossils, is about the same as the age of the underlying volcanic rocks, dated radiometrically. No rocks found anywhere on the ocean floors were older than about 180 million years. In contrast, the oldest rocks on the continents are 3.9 billion years old – about twenty times as old. This evidence was the geological icing on the geophysical cake – sea floor spreading is a fact.

Global Dynamics

What of plate tectonics? This name was coined in 1968 to convey the idea that the upper layer of the Earth forms a number of relatively rigid blocks or

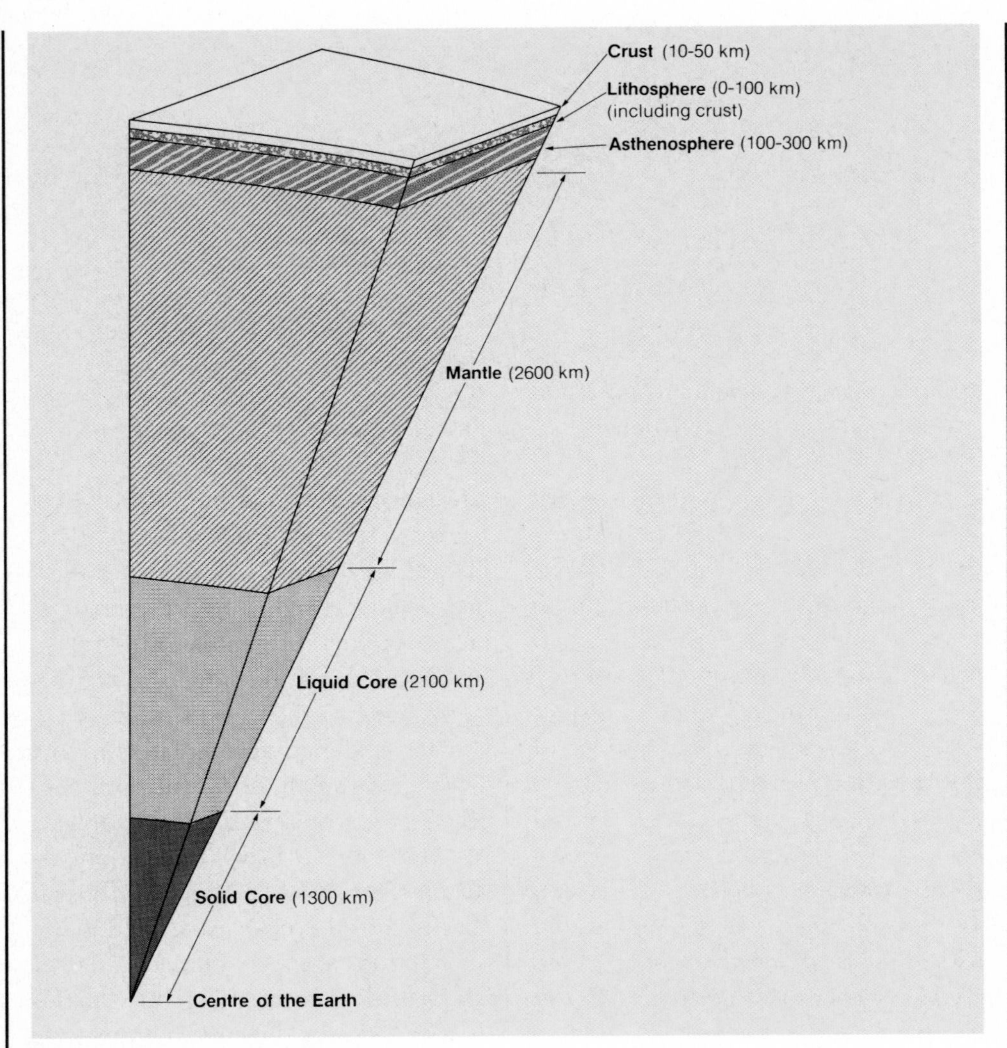

View of the Earth's interior.

plates, and that we are really dealing with not merely sea floor spreading, but the motion of these plates about the surface of the Earth. The plate margins on one side consist of zones of crustal production (the ocean ridges), and at the opposite side, zones of consumption (the ocean trenches).

In this new view of our world, the major geological zones are the *lithosphere*, the uppermost 10 to 100 kilometres of the Earth, consisting of relatively cool and rigid rocks, and the underlying *asthenosphere*, from 100 to about 300 kilometres below the surface, made up of hot, weak rocks capable of flowing. The character and geometry of these zones are known through earthquake studies, now at a very sophisticated level.

Currently six major plates are recognized: *African*, *Pacific*, *Americas*, *Eurasian*, *Australian*, and *Antarctic* – all bounded by easily recognizable margins and particularly well-defined by earthquake epicentres. In addition there are several minor plates, including the *China*, *Nasca*, and *Scotian* plates, and a variable number of even smaller plates including the *Juan de Fuca* and *Cocos* plates. These small plates are much more difficult to define, partly because their margins are not as clearly identifiable by earthquake epicentres.

On our restless Earth, plates move at rates ranging from one to fifteen centimetres per year. We have learned this from studies of the chronology of ocean-floor magnetic reversals, earthquake motions, and now the prospect of absolute measurements via laser telemetry from satellites. Unless the Earth is expanding – and most scientists believe it is not – these rates of plate motion require that some plates, such as the Americas plate, continue to grow, whereas others, such as the Pacific plate, continue to shrink. Shrinkage occurs because the forward edges of these plates are subducting below the plate margin they are being forced against.

Over the past decade the emphasis at sea has been to describe, sample, and understand plate margins, particularly those such as the Mid-Atlantic Ridge and East Pacific Rise where crust is being produced. As well, knowledge of plate motions and geometries has been refined, and study has progressed on unique features, such as the origin of the Hawaiian Islands, the sulphide vents or "black smokers" found mainly along the East Pacific Rise, and a whole host of characteristics occurring at subduction zones, such as the fate of sediments – do they subduct? Among the exciting findings from the ocean floor is our new understanding of the importance of "seawater cycling," probably the major control on the composition of seawater. At presently estimated rates, it appears that the entire volume of water in all the world's oceans is cycled in less than ten million years through newly formed, hot but cooling and contracting ocean ridge crust. This crust constitutes 23 per cent of the globe's surface.

On land the search for evidence of plate motions and processes has been most rewarding in young mountain belts such as North America's western Cordillera. There we find evidence of ancient sea floor in the form of *ophiolites* – distinctive igneous and metamorphic rocks in a stratigraphic order that is characteristic of similar rocks on ocean floors today. The marginal belts of young mountain ranges also display assemblages of igneous and sedimentary rocks characteristic of both former plate margins and continental margins. Core zones of these ranges consist of igneous and metamorphic rocks in which ancient *terranes*, sometimes known as *suspect* or *exotic terranes*, can be found. Terranes are distinct pieces of crust with unique

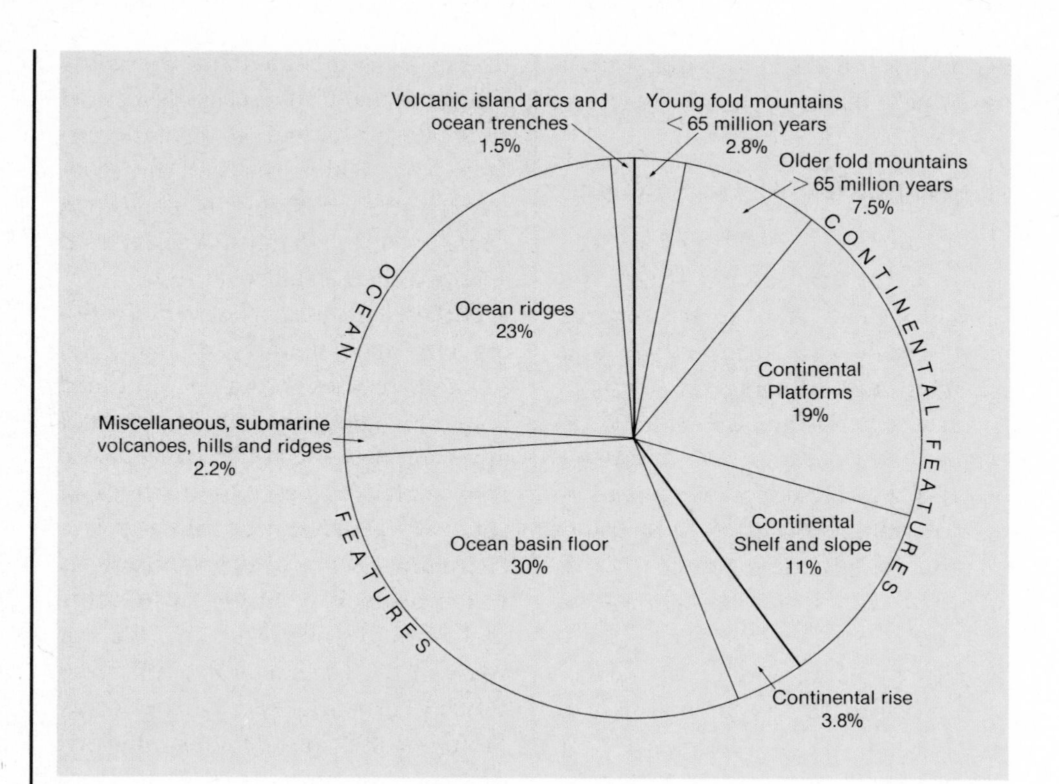

Major features of the Earth's solid surface shown as percentages of the total world surface.

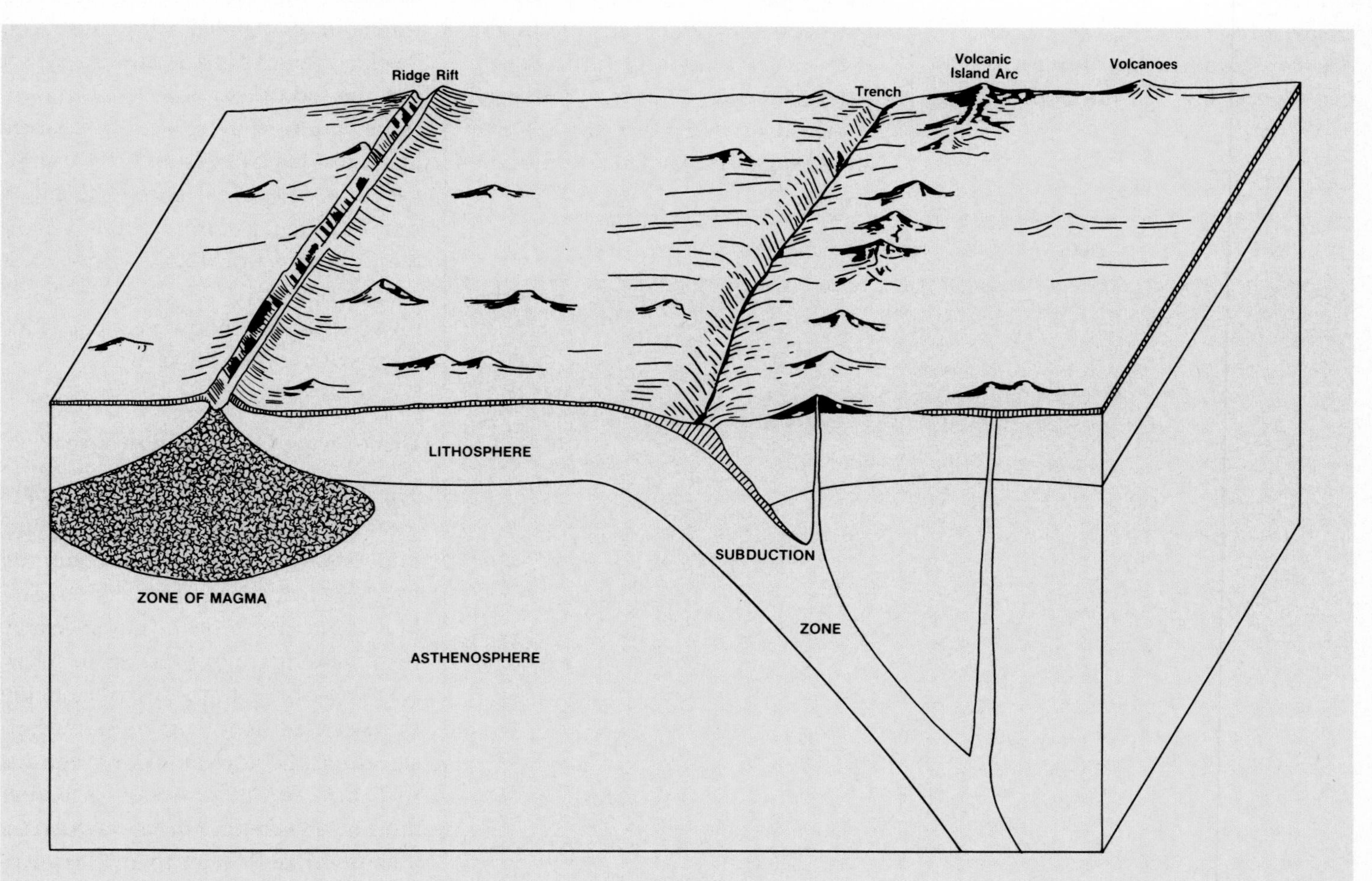

Schematic diagram showing the generation of oceanic lithosphere at an oceanic ridge, and consumption of oceanic lithosphere in an ocean trench subduction zone such as those of the western Pacific Ocean. Note that volcanic activity is associated with the subduction zone. Volcanic materials derived from different depths within the subduction zone have different compositions.

rocks, fossil assemblages, and ancient magnetic positions of the poles. Many terranes show evidence of having travelled long distances on ocean floor "conveyor belts," reaching their present positions through continental collisions along subduction zones.

It is clear that oceans have a life cycle, now known as the *Wilson Cycle* after Ontario scientist J. Tuzo Wilson, who made major contributions to our understanding of ocean dynamics. Oceans are born along new *rift zones*, such as the present Red Sea and laterally continuous East African Rift Zone; they expand, as the Atlantic Ocean is presently doing; and they die through plate consumption along subduction zones, such as appears to be the fate of the Pacific Ocean. Old mountain belts such as the Appalachians preserve evidence of ancient oceans: ophiolites that once formed as part of volcanic sea floors of extinct oceans form a distinctive belt within the Appalachians.

ss *North America*: Westward Bound

As volcanic rocks are injected into the centre of the Mid-Atlantic Ridge, the Americas plate and North America move steadily away from Europe at a maximum rate of about ten centimetres per year. At the other side of the Americas plate, Pacific Ocean crust is being consumed along a complex system of subduction zones and transform faults bounding western North and South America. The highly asymmetrical geometry of the Pacific plate, with its spreading ocean ridge system located close to continental North America, makes it clear that vast volumes of Pacific Ocean crust must have been overridden already by the Americas plate. Indeed, the structure of the American "Basin and Range" geological province in Colorado and Nevada suggests that in places the continent has overridden the spreading centre, as manifested by a widespread zone of downfaulted blocks at the surface. The lighter rocks of the continents, pushed along by the ocean conveyor belts, do not sink at zones of subduction, but slide over top.

Geological time scale.

EON	ERA	PERIOD	EPOCH	TIME SPAN (millions of years)
PHANEROZOIC	CENOZOIC	Quartenary	Recent	0 - 0.01
			Pleistocene	0.01 - 2
		Tertiary	Pliocence	2 - 10
			Miocene	10 - 25
			Oligocene	25 - 35
			Eocene	35 - 55
			Paleocene	55 - 65
	MESOZOIC	Cretaceous		65 - 135
		Jurassic		135 - 180
		Triassic		180 - 210
	PALEOZOIC	Permian		210 - 280
		Carboniferous		280 - 350
		Devonian		350 - 400
		Silurian		400 - 425
		Ordovician		425 - 500
		Cambrian		500 - 600
PRECAMBRIAN: PROTEROZOIC	HADRYNIAN			600 - 1000
	HELIKIAN			1000 - 1800
	APHEBIAN			1800 - 2500
PRECAMBRIAN: ARCHEAN	LATE			2500 - 2900
	MIDDLE			2900 - 3400
	EARLY			3400 +

If the 1970s were a decade of refining our understanding of plate tectonic processes from ocean-based data, the 1980s have been a decade of applying plate tectonic concepts to continental geology. One such application is geological/geophysical studies along a series of strips or *transects* which begin in continental interiors and continue offshore. This type of study in the Canadian and American Cordillera to the west of the Rocky Mountain Belt has demonstrated the existence of many exotic terranes which have collided with and been "welded" onto North America over a long period of time as a result of continued interaction between the Pacific and subsidiary plates and the Americas plate. The importance of such terranes in the makeup of young mountain belts world-wide was not recognized until the late 1970s. It seems clear that this process is a major means of continental growth.

Discovering Our 3-Billion-Year Past

The elegance and simplicity of plate tectonics provides a framework for understanding and interpreting the Earth. Before being able to determine how an area has been influenced by plate tectonics, however, earth scientists must be able to describe simply the types and ages of its rocks. Reconstructing a geological history requires that rocks and processes of formation must be dated either in a relative sense ("earlier than," "later than," "equivalent to") or in an absolute sense ("600 million years ago").

Geological events can be dated or ordered by observing three sequences of physical change: the fossil record of past life on Earth; the decay of radioactive elements; and magnetic attributes of rocks involving either magnetic reversals or changes in the positions of continental masses over time, relative to the Earth's north and south magnetic poles. Radiometric and certain magnetic measurements provide absolute ages. The fossil record provides relative ages, unless calibrated by the absolute ages obtained from the decay of radioactive elements. Rocks dated in these ways, and the relative positions of rock masses, provide the principal means by which earth scientists seek to understand the chronology of past events and processes. This approach has served us well and is the basis of the geological time scale.

In applying the plate tectonic framework to understanding earth history, it is often surest to proceed backwards from the present. Accordingly we can reconstruct plates, plate margins, and continental positions with some confidence for the *Cenozoic Era*, the last 60 million years of earth history, but the oldest known sea floor is *mid-Mesozoic*, up to 200 million years old. Without the existing sea floor data to work with, our global reconstructions back that far are made with progressively less confidence. For the even older Paleozoic and Precambrian eras, earth scientists must deal with magnetic indicators, fossil assemblages, ancient climatic indicators, and assemblages of sedimentary, igneous, and metamorphic rocks that in their distribution or character may resemble rock masses of modern plate tectonic settings. Although, as with all such reconstructions, many questions remain, a spectacular degree of success has been achieved in applying plate tectonic concepts to the geology of large regions as far back as the 2-billion-year-old rocks of the Slave province of the Canadian Shield in the Northwest Territories.

Plate Tectonics in Ontario

Ontario is located in the relatively stable continental interior of the North American plate; present plate margins and continental margins are located far away. Hudson Bay, although marine, is an inland sea, not an ocean. There are no mountain belts such as the Appalachians of New Brunswick, Nova Scotia, and Newfoundland, or the Cordillera of British Columbia and Alberta. Altogether, Ontario today could be regarded as relatively "immune" from plate tectonics. But was this always so?

To answer this question, we must look briefly at Ontario's geology. Precambrian Shield rocks are exposed over much of northern Ontario, but are overlain in southern Ontario and the Hudson Bay Lowlands by a thin veneer of younger Paleozoic sedimentary rocks of marine origin. These Paleozoic sediments, the youngest being *Devonian* in age (350 million years), remarkably are the youngest rocks in Ontario, with the exception of a thin Cretaceous and Mesozoic-aged succession in the Hudson Bay Lowlands. Where are all the rest of the younger Paleozoic, the Mesozoic, and the Cenozoic rocks? Possibly the Cretaceous rocks found in the Hudson Bay Lowlands were once much more widespread than they are at present, but conclusive evidence is lacking. Or perhaps rocks younger than Devonian were never deposited except as noted. Our present understanding of the behaviour of continental interior regions such as Ontario suggests that such regions have been stable and above sea level for a very long time.

More certain is that southern Ontario reflects ancient plate-controlled mountain-building processes in the Appalachians to the east and south. Sedimentary rocks laid down in the early *Ordovician* and then the early

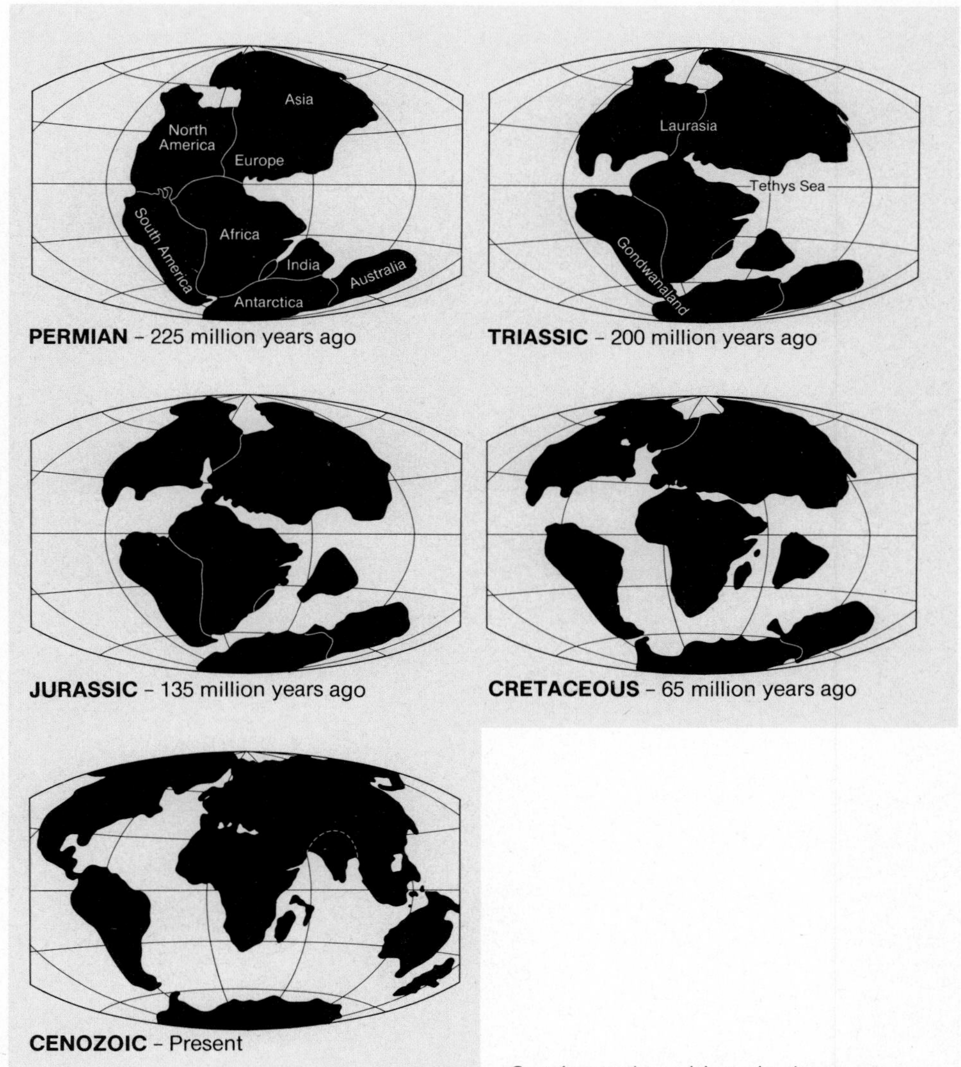

Continental positions in the past.

Devonian age consist of shales which are thought to have been formed from the westward influx of land-derived sediment eroding from distant uplifted areas in the Appalachian mountain belt. The Appalachians rose as the result of the closing of the predecessor of the Atlantic Ocean, and the impact of Europe and northern Africa against North America. The rest of the Paleozic record consists mostly of shallow-marine sediments accumulated on the margins of the ocean-filled Michigan or Appalachian basins to the west and southeast.

In general, the farther back one proceeds in the Precambrian rock record, the more strikingly different the rocks and the environments they formed in seem to be, as compared, for example, with Cenozoic environments. The youngest Precambrian rocks of Ontario are those of the Grenville province, an area of similarly aged rocks which stretches in a belt from central and southeastern Ontario to eastern Labrador. These rocks are dated radiometrically at about 1 billion years. There is evidence that they are the once deeply buried roots of old mountains after the erosion of more than twenty kilometres of formerly overlying rocks. An analogy is made with a present continental collision zone that formed, and continues to form, the Himalayas, where the lithosphere has been greatly thickened by partial subduction of the continental Indian-Australian plate beneath the Eurasian plate. Here, the highest rates of uplift and erosion in the world are occurring. Precambrian rocks of the Grenville province are thought by many geologists to be akin to the northern margin of the partly subducted Indian-Australian plate.

The oldest Precambrian rocks of Ontario, spread across much of the north, are those of the Superior province, more than 2.5 billion years old

Flat-topped mesas at the edge of the Nipigon plate. These mesas formed from the injection of molten lava into and over older sedimentary rocks some 1.1 billion years ago, all related to the collision of the Superior and Grenville continental plates. P. KOR

and belonging to the *Archean Eon*. The Superior province is a vast "sea" of granites and sedimentary rocks altered by heat and pressure, forming rocks such as gneiss, within which are linear belts of predominantly volcanic rocks. These linear belts, known as *greenstone belts*, are rich in precious metals such as gold, silver, and platinum, as well as base metals such as copper and zinc. The Abitibi Greenstone Belt of northern Ontario and Quebec is the largest greenstone belt in the world.

The greenstone belts may have formed as arcs of volcanic mountains in response to heat and pressure at subduction zones. However, the application of plate tectonic concepts to these rocks is hotly debated. All agree that current plate motions, geometries, and rates of movement are not directly applicable. It seems clear that rates of heat loss from the interior of the Earth during Archean time were two or three times those at present, and that the crust was hot, thin, and highly mobile. This probable set of conditions has led some to the view that Archean plate tectonics, if such existed, featured small, fast-moving plates, a suggestion that can be supported by the complexity and diversity of greenstone belts. But, volcanic rocks, such as those found in greenstone belts, are heavy and when poured on the surface would tend to sink within the hot, thin crust. The complexity of the structure of Archean greenstone belts the world over suggests that they may indeed have been re-arranged almost continuously as they formed. Quite the opposite happens to similar volcanic rocks today where they are extruded on the relatively thick, cool crust. The modern Hawaiian Islands provide an example: the volcanic piles constituting the Islands persist intact after extrusion, merely causing subsidence

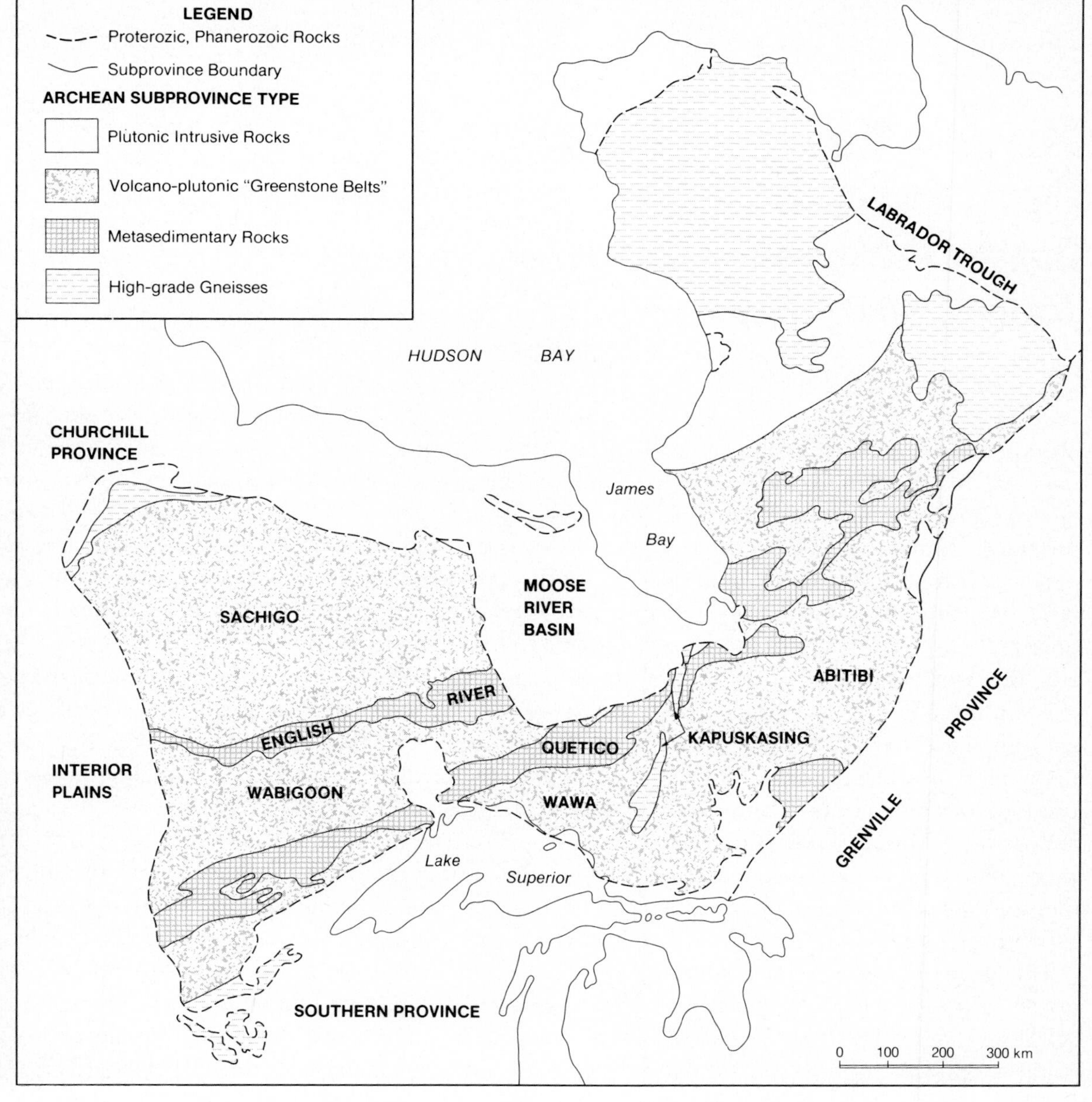

Simplified geology of the Precambrian Superior Province of Archean age, northern Ontario, Quebec, and Manitoba. Major greenstone belts such as the Abitibi, Wabigoon, and Sachigo are separated from each other by belts of metasedimentary rocks such as the English River and Quetico belts.

of the surrounding cool, relatively old and thick oceanic crust.

Questions, Questions, and More Questions

The plate tectonics framework, as scientifically and aesthetically pleasing as it is, nonetheless raises many fundamental questions. It seems clear that the Earth may be described as an enormous "heat engine," and that plate tectonics is simply a means for the Earth to rid itself of heat derived from the decay of radioactive elements deep within the lithosphere and asthenosphere. But what makes the plates move? One view holds that they move in response to some form of heat-driven convection currents in the Earth's asthenosphere and mantle, in which hot, ductile materials rise towards the surface either as plumes or rectilinear cells of some sort. In this view, the mantle drives the plates. Another view is that older parts of oceanic plates tend to sink under their own weight, pulling thinner, younger, hotter lithosphere along to eventually reach the trench and sink. In this view, the plates drive the mantle. There are proponents for each of these views, and there is some evidence that both mechanisms may operate.

How far back in time has plate tectonics operated? How variable have spreading and subduction rates been over time? What causes plate motions to occur that result in continents becoming aggregated to form supercontinents, as occurred before the present continents broke away? How do earthquakes with epicentres on the continents relate to plate tectonic processes? What bearing has plate tectonics on the origin and preservation of mineral resources? There is no shortage of challenging questions. It is safe to say that enthusiasm, scientific curiosity, and the levels of unification of various sub-disciplines of earth sciences have never been greater. Much has been learned, but much remains to be discovered.

◆ SCIENCE ◆ EXCURSION ◆

Dating Earth Processes and Features

John B. Theberge

Of fundamental interest to all natural sciences are processes of change, evolution, and their time scales. Driving this interest is a quest for a time-space perspective for ourselves in relation to other living things, our planet, and the universe. Only a few hundred years ago, no evidence existed to question guesses of the Earth's age, which varied from 6,000 to 10,000 years, based upon biblical interpretations. Scientific inquiry in physics, astronomy, and biology over the past two hundred years, however, has accumulated evidence to document a much older history for the Earth.

The geological time scale, developed and refined over the past two centuries, provides the temporal framework for dating scientific events and phenomena. The outlines of this scale began to appear with the realization that layers of rock represent specific ages and intervals of time, and sedimentary rock accumulates such that youngest is nearest the surface (unless overturned by mountain-building processes). The names for the major intervals of geologic time reflect places where rocks assigned to these different intervals were first recognized. For example *Cambrian* is derived from Cambria, the Roman name for Wales, where rocks containing earliest evidence of complex life-forms were first studied; *Devonian* is applied to somewhat younger rocks in Devon, England; *Cretaceous*, from the Latin word *creta*, for chalk, was first applied to the white cliffs on both sides of the English Channel. Accurate ages for these geologic intervals, known as *Periods*, came later, and confirmed the stratigraphic progression from young to old moving downward from the surface of the Earth.

The geological time scale for rocks of the *Paleozoic* ("ancient life"), *Mesozoic* ("middle life"), and *Cenozoic* ("modern life") eras was developed long before the use of radioactivity to provide absolute ages. Without the later calibration by radiometric means, the geological time scale provided only relative ages: for example rocks of the Devonian Period, identified by the fossils they contain, were recognized as younger than rocks of the Cambrian Period, but older than rocks of the Carboniferous or Cretaceous periods, etc. Radiometric dating provides absolute ages essential to calibrate the relative time scale so well developed through the study of fossils in the early and middle parts of the last century.

The most common methods of absolute dating of rocks involve radiometric dating through the use of a number of naturally occurring radioactive isotopes. Radioactivity, upon which these methods depend, was discovered in 1898. Its significance to heat production in the Earth was realized two years later through the work of Marie and Pierre Curie. Its first proposed use to measure geologic time was made by the British physicist Lord Rutherford in 1905, and its actual application to the geological time scale was formulated at Yale University in 1907.

Radioactivity involves processes which take place in the *nuclei* (the dense, central parts) of atoms of some elements, such as uranium. Nuclei are made up of *neutrons* and *protons*, which together give the atom its mass number. Atoms of some elements are found with different mass numbers, each of them being called an *isotope*. Uranium, for example, has two isotopes, U-235 and U-238, whose mass numbers differ by three. Both forms of uranium undergo radioactive decay caused by the loss of two types of particles: *alpha particles* (which consist of two neutrons and two protons, thus causing the mass number to decrease by four) and *beta particles* (which are high-velocity, negatively charged *electrons*). Electrons are not part of an atom's nucleus, therefore the loss of a beta particle does not change mass number. It does, however, alter the nucleus by changing one uncharged neutron into a positively charged proton. In both of these decay processes, energy is released which eventually is transformed to heat.

Four radioactive isotopes make up the principal heat-producing atoms in rock: U-238, U-235, thorium-232, and potassium-40. Each one has its own constant rate of decay, changing to a number of unstable isotopes that alter again before arriving at a stable form. Spontaneous radioactive decay of U-238, for example, leads first to thorium-234 through the loss of an alpha particle, then through twelve or thirteen other isotopes, and ends with a stable one, lead-206.

The rates of decay of these four initial isotopes have been measured by direct observation, and extrapolated to give estimates of the length of time necessary for half the atoms of parent isotopes to convert to the stable end isotope. A cross-check on this estimate can be made by reverse estimation of the time necessary for the stable isotope to double. An assumption of constant decay over time is based upon experimental evidence that neither heat, pressure, nor chemical reaction can change the rate of decay. "Half-life" is estimated, rather than the time for total conversion, because any process occurring at a constant rate theoretically never ends (or ends at time infinity). For example, a constant 2 per cent decrease in a population of animals ultimately will result in very few animals, but at any point in time, 98 per cent of that population will survive until the next point in time. Applying this to half-life in radioactive decay, half the atoms of U-238 will be converted to lead-206 after 4.5 billion years, half of those remaining after the next 4.5 billion years, half of those after the next 4.5 billion years, etc.

Important Slow-decaying Natural Radioisotopes

Parent Isotope	*Stable Daughter Products*	*Half Life (in billions of years)*
Uranium-238	Lead-206 plus helium	4.5
Uranium-235	Lead-207 plus helium	.7
Thorium-232	Lead-208 plus helium	14.0
Rubidium-87	Strontium-87	51.0
Potassium-40	Argon-40, calcium-40	1.3

Magma, as it crystalizes to a solid state either as granite under the surface or basaltic lava on the surface, fixes within it mineral compounds with very small amounts of radioisotopes. Granite fixes the most, with an average of four parts per million (ppm) of uranium, fourteen ppm of thorium, and 3.5 per cent radioactive potassium. Potassium is found in small quantities in most rock-forming minerals. Potassium/argon dating is used extensively to provide age estimates of many rocks more than 2 million years old, and has helped age early hominoid remains found in Africa.

Carbon-14 is another important radioisotope for dating any geologically young organic material, such as bone, hair, shell, charcoal, peat, and wood. It is produced continuously in the upper atmosphere by cosmic radiation bombarding atoms of nitrogen. An atom of ordinary nitrogen-14 when struck by a neutron from outer space, absorbs it and emits a proton, becoming an atom of C-14. The C-14 combines quickly with oxygen to form carbon dioxide and is diffused through the lower atmosphere where some of it is consumed by plants in photosynthesis. But C-14 is unstable, decaying back to N-14, with a half life of about 5,730 years. Thus, the ratio of C-14 to C-12, normal carbon atoms, can be compared with the ratio that existed when the plant or animal was living, and dated accordingly. The original ratio is assumed, with some evidence, to be similar to that found today.

The process of age determination from radioisotopes involves careful extraction of the isotopes. While mistakes have been made (owing to contamination by airborne lead, for example) the many thousands of determinations using different isotopes attest to the validity and accuracy of these methods. Potassium-40 is considered the most useful "general purpose" radioisotope for dating because it can be used on rocks as young as a few thousand years to the oldest rocks known. Ages from C-14 are considered least reliable, with possible errors of plus or minus 5 per cent. Minor fluctuations in cosmic radiation, or upsets in the carbon cycle occasionally cause dates that cannot be confirmed by other methods. Usefulness of carbon-dating is confined largely to the past 50,000 years.

A second means of obtaining absolute ages of rock masses, although less accurate than radiometric methods, is through study of the magnetic properties of rocks. Two properties are of interest: the polarity of particles (normal, as at present, or reversed with respect to the present), and the orientation of the particles. Dating rocks by magnetic polarity generally requires the use of other clues, commonly fossils or radiometric dates, in order to recognize which interval of normal or reversed polarity is recorded by a particular rock mass. Study of the orientation of particles in space provides a "paleomagnetic pole"; because paleomagnetic poles are known with some confidence for the Earth's main continental masses for the past 600 million years, this method can provide an approximate absolute age.

Ice cores from glaciers in the Canadian Arctic, Greenland, and the Antarctic have demonstrated sequential temperature fluctuations over time through different ratios of oxygen-18 and the more common oxygen-16. The ratios of these two isotopes have been shown experimentally to vary with temperature. Dates for changes in these ratios, while not easily derived, have been estimated from theoretical assumptions, and conform with ages obtained from other lines of evidence. As well, temperature sequences recorded in the glaciers mirror those determined in the terrestrial pollen record of the *Pleistocene Epoch*, the last two million years of Earth's history.

Tree rings of bristlecone pine in California that can live up to 6,000 years, and radii of the slow-growing rock lichen *Rhizocarpon geographicum* that grows for 5,000 years, provide measures over geologically recent intervals of time. At the other extreme of geological time, astronomical estimates of distances to stars, based upon measures of parallax, or angle, as the Earth circles the sun, are so great as to be measured in light-years. (The distance light travels in one year is about 9.6 trillion kilometres. We can look at quasars on the outer fringes of the universe whose light has taken about 15 billion years to reach us.) If astronomical estimates of motion, distance, and time were wrong, our space probes to the planets would never have landed.

Ontario in the Sweep of Continental Climate

F. Kenneth Hare

Anything but Temperate

Ontario lies in the same northern mid-latitudes (43–58 degrees N) as northern Europe or coastal British Columbia. Yet, unlike those favoured regions, Ontario's climate is anything but temperate! Instead, it displays extreme cold in winter, and formidable heat in summer. Why should this be?

The answer lies in the peculiar geography of North America with its high, wide, western mountains running from Mexico to Alaska. This formidable barrier blocks or retards the inward flow of Pacific air. Hence the continent lacks what keeps Europe temperate – a free flow of oceanic air from the west. When Pacific air does penetrate, it has been much altered by its passage over the mountains.

On the other hand, North America's northern and southern flanks are unprotected. Tropical air can flow northward from anywhere across the southern boundary of the United States, especially west of the Mississippi. This Gulf air, as it is nicknamed, penetrates as far as central and eastern Canada from time to time, giving Ontario hot, humid spells in summer. By contrast we are also open to frequent southward outbreaks of Arctic air, bringing cool relief in summer and frigid cold, for the latitude, in winter.

Ontario's climate is thus affected in all seasons by an interplay between surface airstreams of different origins: Arctic, Pacific, and tropical. Atlantic airstreams contribute occasionally, bringing mild and damp weather in winter and spring, but the dominance of the "big three" is rarely interrupted for long.

Coming with these interacting surface airstreams are several classes of storms, causing most of Ontario's rain and snow. Thus the climate is unusually turbulent, and violent weather is not uncommon. Often Ontario's climate is referred to as *continental*, but this is not accurate; much of the time the weather is dominated by moist airstreams from the Gulf of Mexico, the Pacific, or, over eastern Ontario, the Atlantic. Rarely does North America really cook up its own weather, as Siberia and inner Asia habitually do. Only in the great seasonal contrasts does the adjective *continental* justify itself for our climate. But these contrasts are really brought in by travelling airstreams. They are not generated locally by extremes of radiative heating and cooling, as the textbooks often say they are.

The adjective that does fit better is *monsoonal*. Our climate resembles that of Korea and Japan. In those countries, winter is dominated by a great outflow of northwest winds from Siberia, called the winter monsoon. So too is Ontario's winter dominated by cold northwesterlies flowing from our own Arctic, although their dominance is a little less drastic. The Asian summer is influenced primarily by the southwest monsoon, a hot, muggy airstream from the tropics just like our own Gulf air. Even the storms affecting Ontario are like those of the Far East. So we can claim to have some sort of monsoonal climate, though we rarely choose to do so! Fortunately we receive fewer tropical cyclones – hurricanes, called typhoons in the east – than does Japan. But otherwise the regimes are similar.

Far up above, overriding these surface airstreams, is the wide sweep of the circumpolar westerlies, the belt of west winds between the sub-tropics and the sub-Arctic that encircles the globe. The strong cores of these winds, which blow nine to fourteen kilometres above the Earth, are called *jetstreams*. Ontario lies below these westerlies at all times, and one or another jetstream often lies directly above us. The jets correspond roughly to the boundaries between Arctic, Pacific, and tropical airstreams, though they lie a little north of the surface boundaries. We are all familiar with these jetstreams, since jet aircraft cruise within them, often at the level of maximum wind. That is why it takes an hour longer to fly from Toronto to Vancouver than it does to fly eastward.

This, then, is Ontario's climate – governed from on high by a part of a great world-wide flow of air, the westerlies, and directly influenced by the interplay of three continent-wide surface airstreams: Arctic, Pacific, and tropical, with some assistance from the Atlantic. It has been this way, with only subtle changes, since the end of the last ice age about ten millennia ago.

Atmospheric Circulation

Air is heated by solar energy absorbed mainly at the Earth's surface, where temperatures tend to be highest. With altitude, temperatures fall until the *tropopause* is reached, an invisible surface that caps the Earth's main turbulent layer, the *troposphere*. At this height, nine to twelve kilometres in our latitudes but nearer seventeen kilometres in the equatorial belt, winds are at their strongest. Nearly all the water vapour, clouds, and storms, however, lie below. Cruising in a jet aircraft one looks down on the panorama of weather. Up there, at usual cruising altitudes, only occasionally does one fly through choppy clouds. Temperatures at this level are near −45°C to −55°C at all times of year because one is far above the main heat source, the Earth's surface.

Looking upwards from the jet, one sees a very different layer, the *stratosphere*, where almost no water vapour or cloud exists. Now temperature begins to increase with height because of abundant ozone (O_3, oxygen with three atoms in the molecule) in the layer between fifteen and fifty kilometres up. Ozone strongly absorbs solar energy, so the temperature at fifty kilometres high is nearly as warm as at ground level.

Climate, the first of all empires, is a system dependent on gigantic energy transformations. There is no likelihood that we shall soon learn to control it. Winds arise from unequal heating of the lower atmosphere over which we have no control. This occurs chiefly in four ways:

- Diurnal differences – solar heating is nil at night and strongest at midday, imposing the familiar temperature variation between night and day;
- Seasonal differences – solar heating is least when the noon sun is lowest (the winter solstice, near December 21), and greatest when the noon sun is highest (the summer solstice, near June 21 in Ontario);
- Latitudinal differences – solar heating is least at the poles and strongest at the equator because the sun's noon elevation is different. Even in the twenty-four daylight hours of June 21, the sun's elevation never exceeds 23.5 degrees at the poles;
- Ocean effect – solar heating is most effective over dark-coloured ocean surfaces, which absorb more of the sun's rays than do the light surfaces of the continents. Moreover, the oceans store the energy in summer, and release it gradually in winter, causing only small diurnal and seasonal temperature differences. In a small way the Great Lakes do this on Ontario's behalf.

These inequalities of heating translate themselves into rising and sinking convective motions of the air on all scales, from purely local "thermals," to the global overturnings of the tropics and equatorial belt. The vertical motion creates differences in air pressure, and these in turn give rise to wind systems (and vice versa). The resulting global system of winds and pressure is referred to as the "general circulation of the atmosphere."

Because these convective processes occur on a rotating Earth, the relation between wind and pressure is quite different from that suggested by simple common sense. The prejudice in our minds is to expect air to flow from high pressure to low. But the deflecting force of the Earth's rotation – the so-called *Coriolis force* – requires that in equilibrium (the *geotrophic balance*), winds blow instead along lines of constant pressure, keeping the low pressure on the left in the northern hemisphere. Hence the weather map shows great areas of high pressure about which the winds rotate clockwise, called *anticyclones*, and of low pressure, in which the motion is counterclockwise, called *cyclones*. These pressure systems, or wind patterns, themselves migrate. Ontario's succession of weather changes comes from an endless procession of anticyclones and cyclones across the province, most of them moving from the west because they are steered by the westerly wind system within which they are vast eddies.

Low- and high-pressure systems develop both in and along the margins of the three east-flowing airstreams – Arctic, Pacific, and tropical – that influence Ontario's weather. Cold and warm air masses come in contact with one another because of the different origins of the airstreams or different

Thunderhead building.
NORM LIGHTFOOT

heating and cooling effects over land and water. These interfaces are called *fronts* and commonly extend vast distances. If the edge of the Arctic airstream, or cold upper air within it, slips southward, its southern edge represents a cold front. Behind this cold front, huge clockwise-flowing eddies (highs, or anticyclones) form. The cold air subsides, and barometric pressure rises because of inflow aloft. Conversely, warm air from the Pacific, or at some seasons even the tropical airstreams from the Gulf of Mexico move northward, their northern edges representing warm fronts.

So it must have been almost since the world began, because the planet has always rotated, and the sun's power to irradiate us has not changed drastically. But the Earth's orbit fluctuates periodically, and so does the rate of spin, influencing both the length of day and the distribution of solar heating between northern and southern hemispheres in roughly 20,000-to 40,000-year cycles. The Earth's atmosphere, moreover, has evolved so as to throw a blanket around the planet. Water vapour, clouds, carbon dioxide, and ozone work to retain heat near the Earth's surface, the so-called greenhouse effect.

For millennia, the atmospheric gases have changed very little. Recently, however, we have discovered that carbon dioxide and certain trace atmospheric gases are increasing. It may be that this will be the last century in which Ontario's climate is stable.

The Seasons

January and February lie at the bottom of Ontario's temperature scale with −25°C mean daily temperatures in northern Ontario and as low as −5° in the southwest and Niagara Peninsula. Snow and ice blanket the province, although in the extreme south thaws may punctuate normal winter conditions.

For much of the winter, Arctic air covers the province, usually under the control of anticyclones moving from the northwest. Clear, cold, and sometimes windy, these Arctic anticyclones move away from us towards the Atlantic, allowing rather warmer air to creep back from the Pacific or the mid-western United States. But more outbreaks of Arctic air behind sharp cold fronts bring these mild interludes to an end. Nothing quite like these "cold highs," as they are called, was in the experience of the European settlers who came to Ontario, though they would have been familiar enough to Asian immigrants. Where the cold outbreaks cross the partially frozen Great Lakes, the warm waters create strong convection in the airstream, and heavy snow flurries are carried onshore in such places as the Bruce

Peninsula, Prince Edward County, and the Sault Ste. Marie region.

Winter storms are often violent and spectacular. They involve eastward-moving cyclones, with warmer air on their southern flanks, each followed by a renewed outbreak of Arctic air. The warm air overruns the cold along the warm front and is uplifted near and ahead of the cold front. Snow falls heavily north and east of the moving cyclone centre, accompanied occasionally by rain or freezing rain near the warm front (freezing rain comes from warm clouds that drop their moisture through sub-freezing air near the ground). The gentlest and fastest moving storms come from Alberta or the northern plains of the United States and leave only light snow behind. The severest cyclones move up from the Great Plains of the United States or the Mississippi Valley. It is this class that produces the ice storms and heavy winds to which the Great Lakes region is subject. Similar storms moving along the Atlantic coast of the United States bring even more violent ice- and snow-laden storms to Atlantic Canada.

Some winters are more severe than others; they may begin as early as November or extend into early April. The mildest, like that of 1982–83, may cause little ice to form in the Great Lakes.

In March, April, and May, temperatures climb slowly upwards. Spring is late, cloudy, and stormy throughout the province – much later, latitude for latitude, than in western Canada. Arctic airstreams seem very unwilling to let go their dominance. Fairbanks, Alaska, and Whitehorse, Yukon Territory, are both warmer than Thunder Bay in April, and Montreal is warmer than Toronto in both April and May. The thaw line creeps northwards, crossing southern Ontario in mid to late March and not reaching the Hudson Bay coast until late May. The comparison with green, resplendent Europe or Vancouver Island in this season is marked.

But in the end the sun triumphs, and the land begins to green. By late May and early June, Ontario's climate, even in the north, resembles that of northern Europe. Periods of brilliant sunshine in Arctic highs dry up the land and melt the residual ice. Navigation resumes in the Great Lakes in early April. Severe cyclonic storms continue to occur, however, often with violent contrasts – heat, humidity and thunderstorms in the south, howling blizzards in the north. Tornadoes occasionally move across the south.

In June the atmospheric pattern adjusts to the summer conditions. Warm tropical airstreams bring humid heat to the south and by the end of the

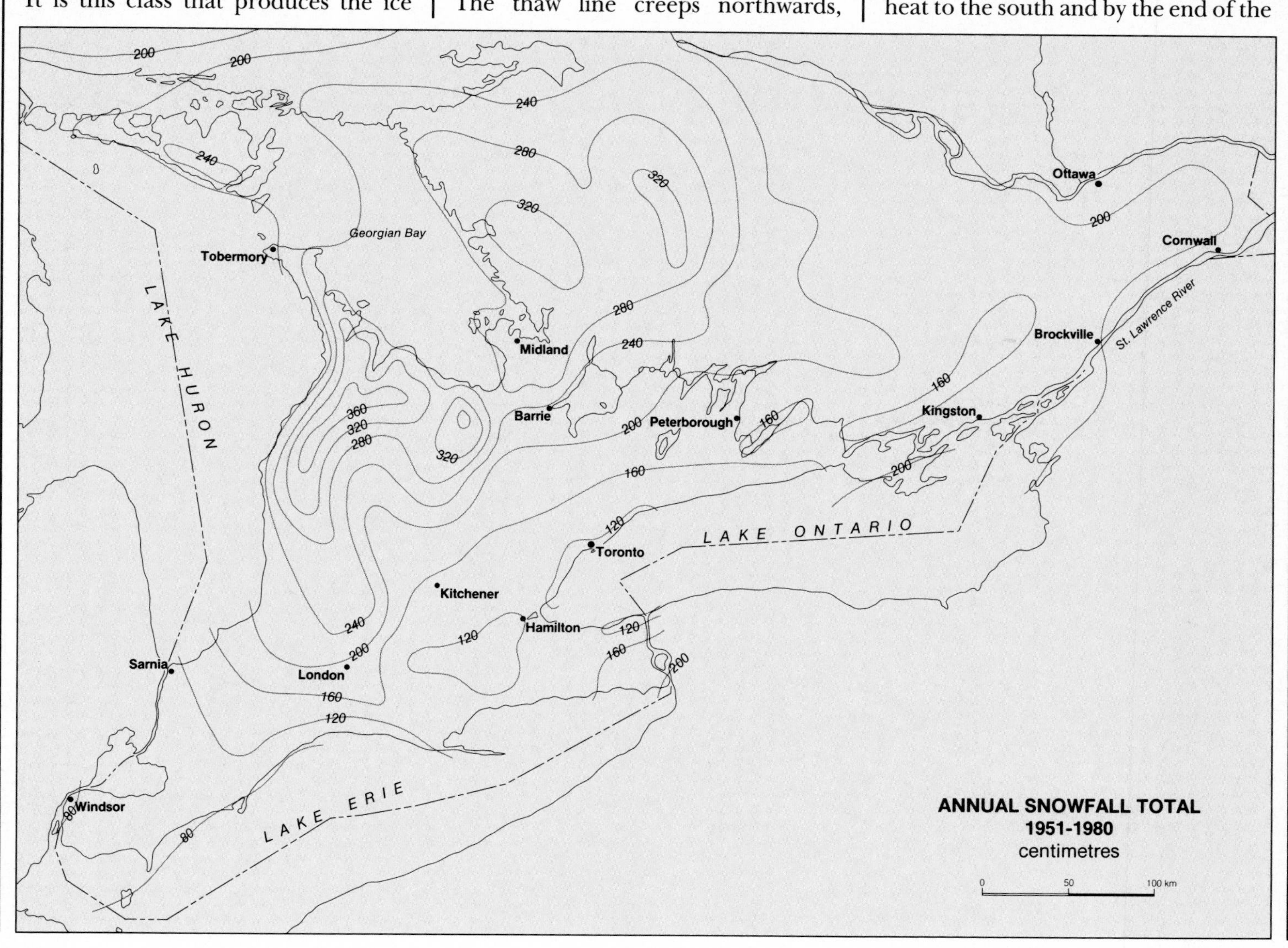

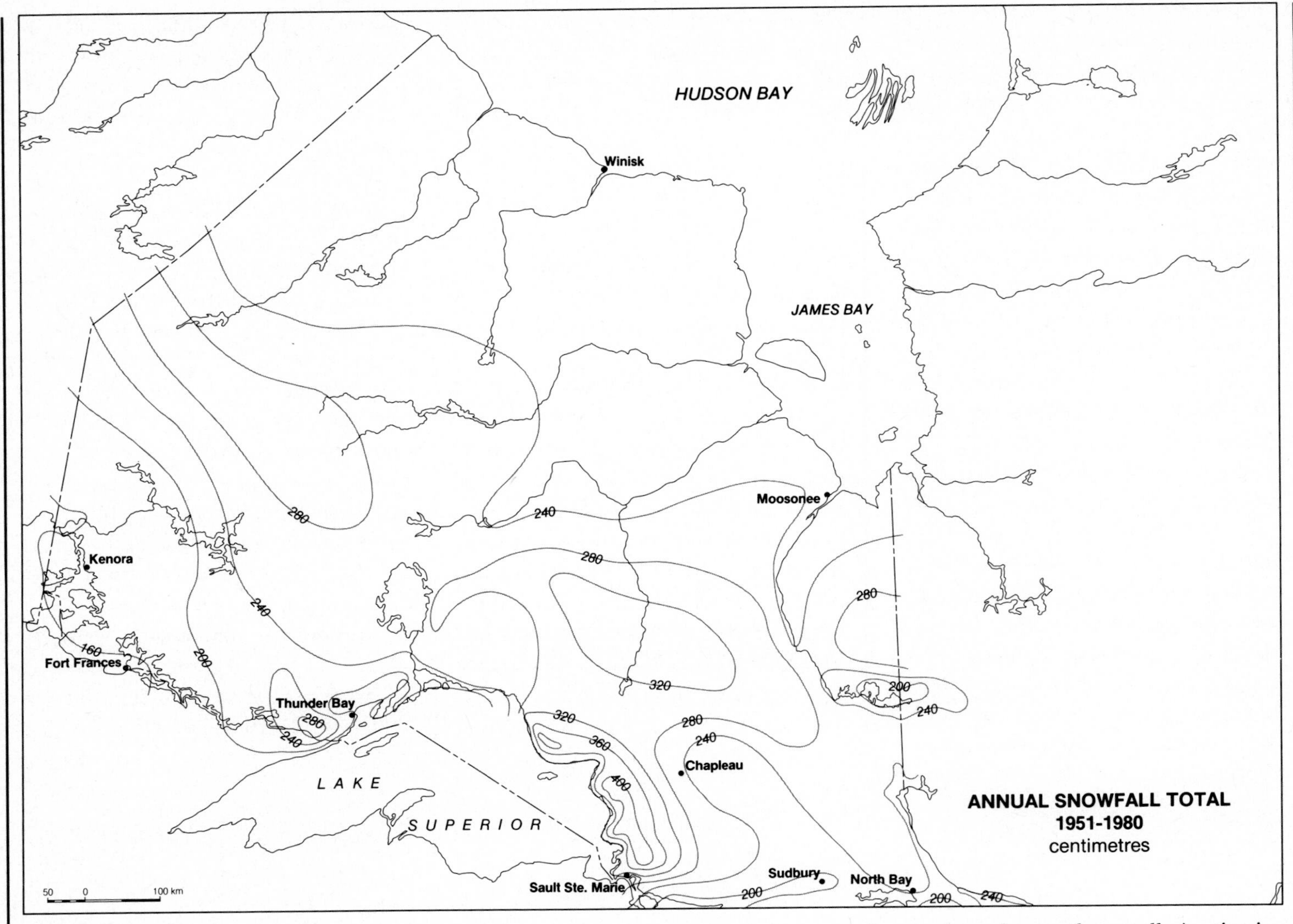

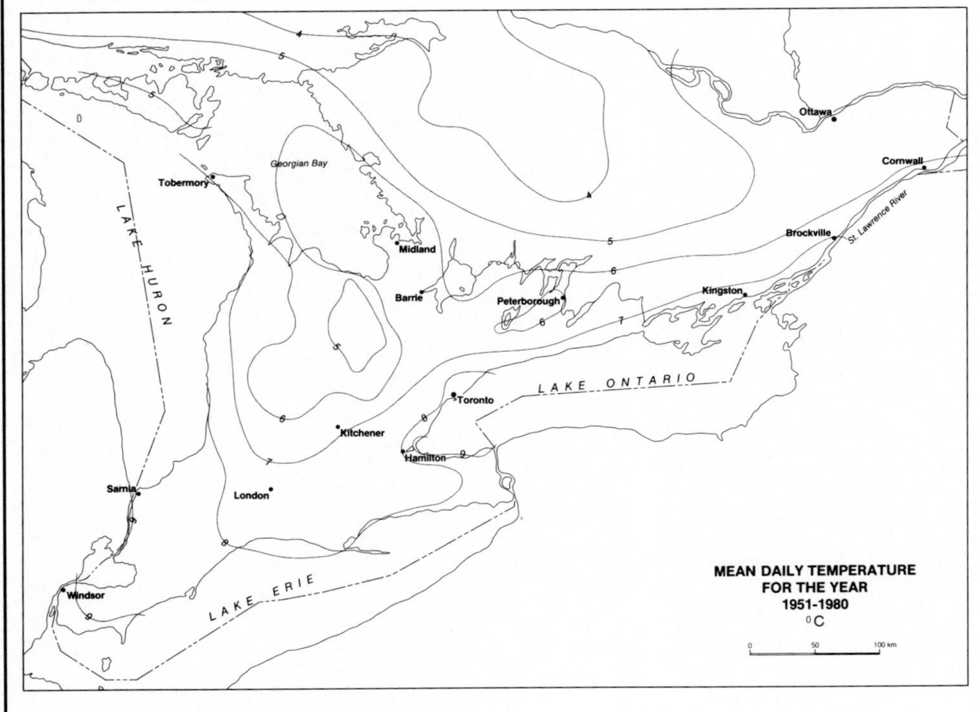

month to the north as well. Arctic airstreams appear less often. Cyclones continue to cross the province bringing cold, grey rains, but their track now lies across the north, or even across Hudson Bay. Only the cold fronts, as a rule, give significant rain to the south, coming in the form of widespread and often violent thunderstorms. The warm fronts of these summer cyclones are usually diffuse and are not associated with extensive rain.

Summer is similar in all regions except the Hudson Bay Lowlands, where cool northeasterlies off the frigid waters and thawing ice keep temperatures below 15°C on many summer days. In the south, however, summer in most areas is a season of reliable warmth, and mean daily temperatures range to above 20°C. These temperatures arise not only from the sun but from the flow of warmth from Pacific and prairie airstreams, as well as from much more humid airstreams originating in the mid-western United States, ultimately even from the Gulf of Mexico in more extreme cases. Thunderstorms are common in all areas, especially over southern and northwestern Ontario, where a significant proportion are nocturnal. Many of these night-time storms form by day just east of the Rocky Mountains and drift eastwards for twelve to eighteen hours into Ontario.

In northern Ontario, more widespread, cooler rainfalls are common in summer, brought by cyclones travelling across the region from the west. Uplift of warm air along and ahead of the cold fronts of such cyclones is another cause of thunderstorms in the south. Frost is rare but cannot reliably be neglected in the northern-most settlements even in July and August. In the south, the latest-known frosts have occurred in June; when they occur that late they do extensive damage to crops such as tobacco and field-grown tomatoes. Forest fire damage is more common in the northwest, where some thunderstorms are "dry" – rain evaporates before landing. Under such conditions, lightning strikes are a major hazard for highly flammable softwood timber.

In September and October very rapid cooling ushers in the fall. Westerly winds freshen, and Pacific airstreams become dominant. Moving anticyclones and cyclones from the west bring rapid weather changes. Thundery rains give way to the gentler, more widespread precipitation of the cool seasons. Frost reappears and occurs farther and farther south. The freeze-up of lakes and rivers, and the beginnings of snow-cover appear in the north as early as mid or late October. By November, the cyclonic storms are often intense; the strong westerlies with their jetstream cores lie right across the mid-continent at this time, whereas in winter they are farther south. The cyclones produce widespread snowfalls in the north, though rain is more usual in the south. The

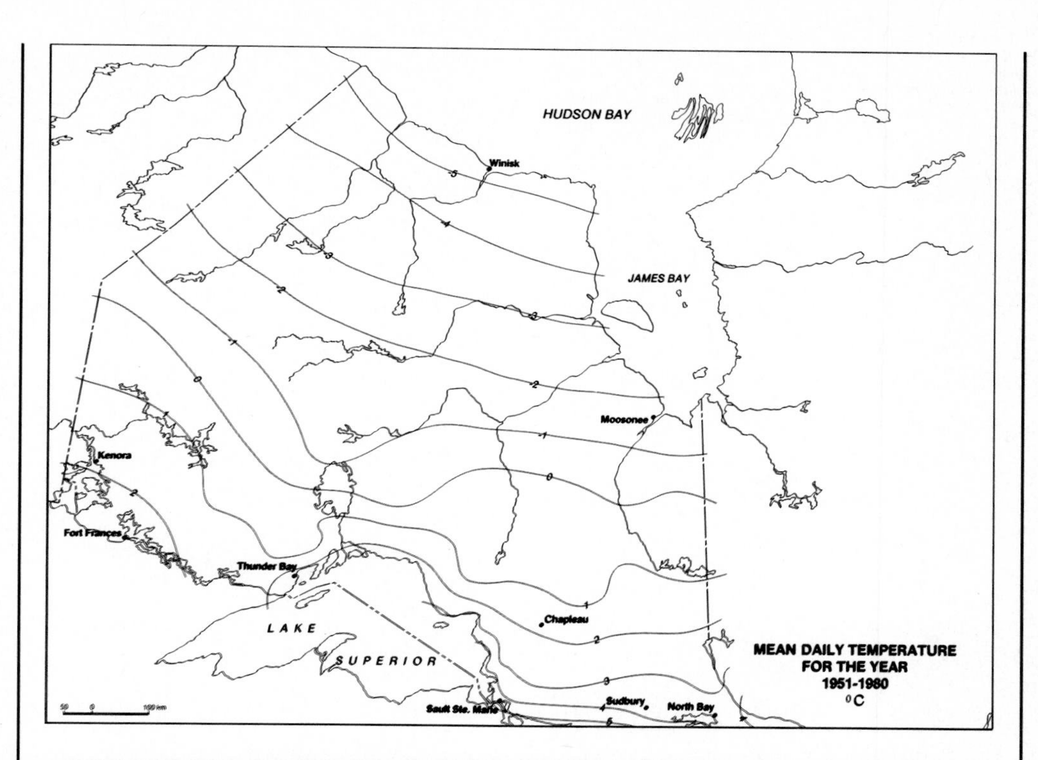

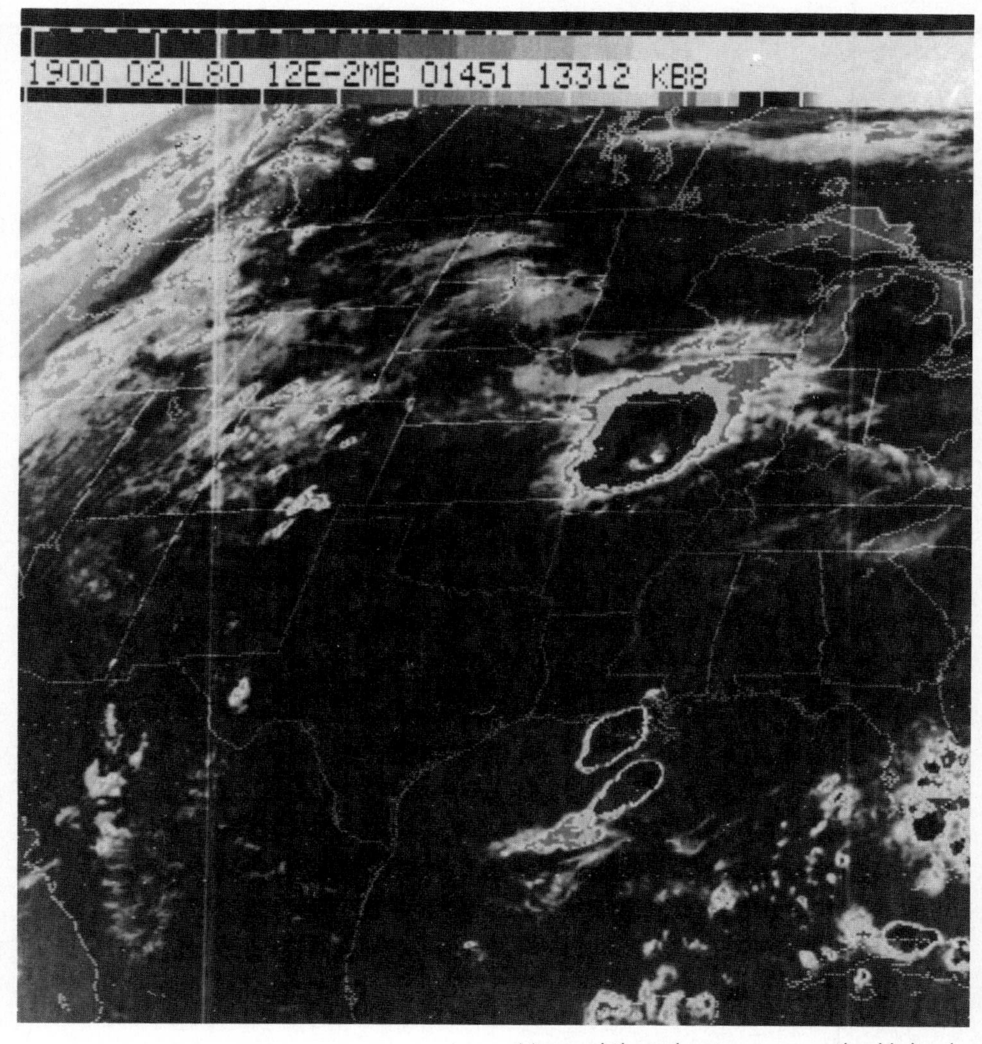

Massed thunderstorm over the United States mid-west on July 2, 1980, moving northeast towards the Great Lakes. Such storms often affect southern Ontario in summer. SATELLITE PICTURE COURTESY OF R. MADDOC

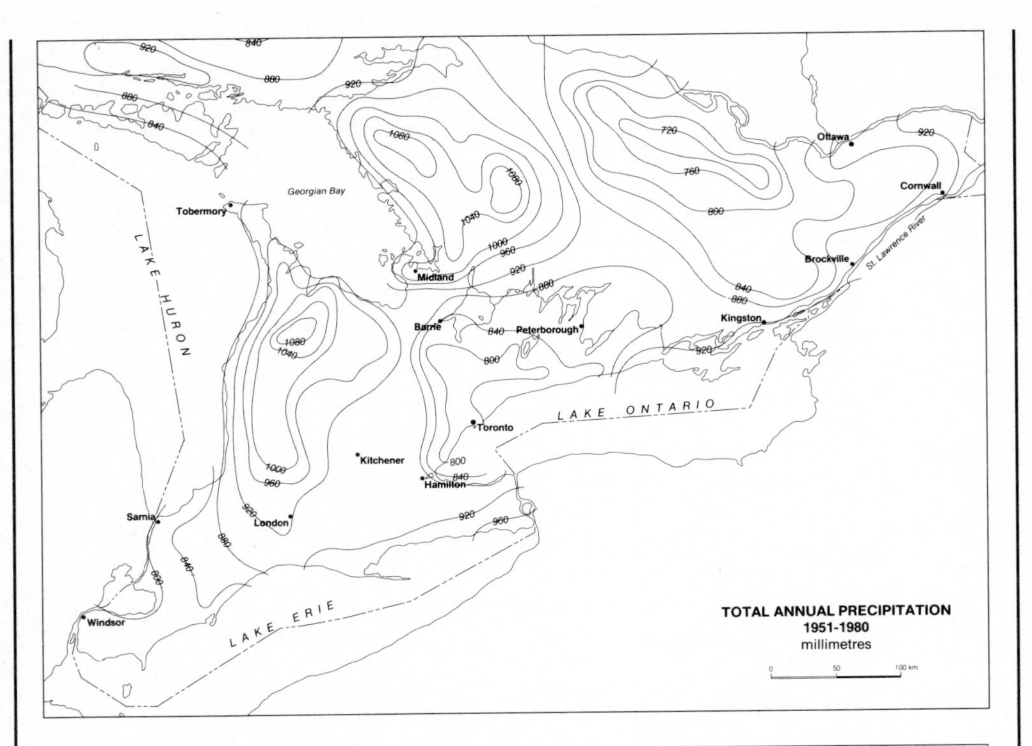

TOTAL ANNUAL PRECIPITATION
1951-1980
millimetres

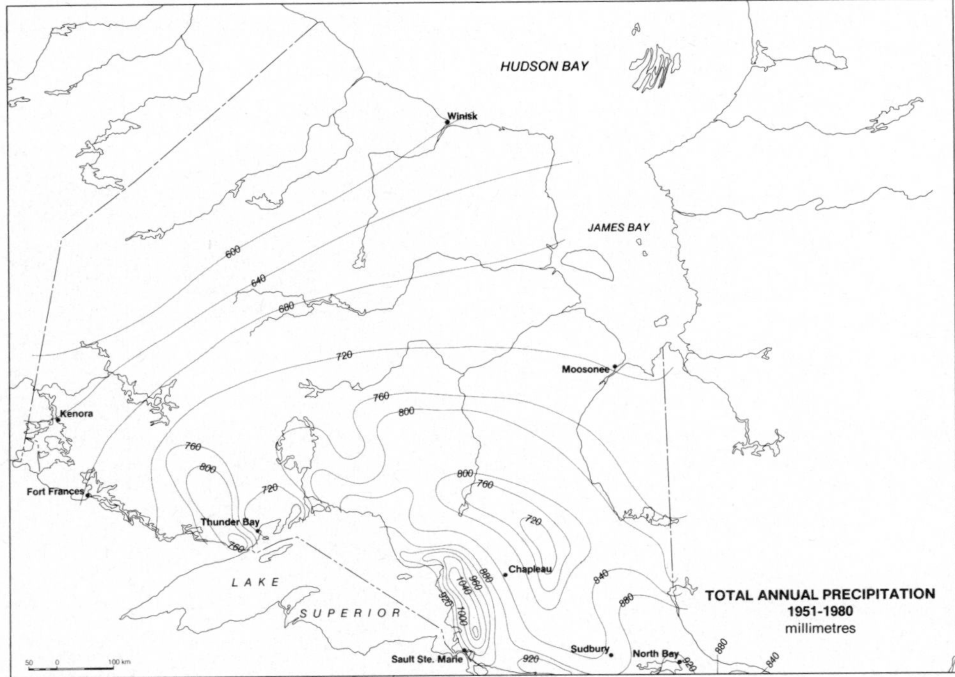

TOTAL ANNUAL PRECIPITATION
1951-1980
millimetres

severest Great Lakes storms occur in this month.

Finally in late November or early December, Arctic airstreams reappear in strength, driven by cold anticyclones moving out of the northwest. The freeze-up reaches southern-most Ontario by the end of December, and snow cover extends to most parts of the province. Winter is once again in command.

This seasonal rhythm repeats itself annually but with substantial variation from year to year. In some years, precipitation may be well below normal over large areas, though rarely the whole province. Drought is not often prolonged, but while it lasts may be quite damaging. On the whole, however, Ontario's climate is among the world's most reliable. This is because it stands very much at the crossroads of the continent's storm systems, where the two major cyclone paths, from the prairies and from the mid-west, converge, and where there is access to moist airstreams coming from several directions.

Climates of the Past

Using "proxy" records, that is, using evidence of the *effects* of climate, geologists and botanists have given us a remarkably detailed record of former climates in Ontario. The evidence used includes pollen assemblages from stratified lake-bottom sediments and peat deposits, some of which go back more than ten thousand years, almost to the time when the last ice-sheet melted, re-exposing Ontario's surface. Also crucial is the geological evidence, chiefly moraine deposits left by the ice, and the numerous abandoned lake and marine shorelines. Much has been learned by studying the succession of vegetation on the land, and beetles, whose hard parts tend to be preserved. The ability we now have to date past records by various geochemical and radioactive indicators has added precise measurement of elapsed time to an otherwise qualitative record.

These proxy records tell us that the retreat of the ice, including the exposure of the Great Lakes basin, was rapid. Initially, as the ice exposed the south about 13,000 to 12,500 years before the present (BP), the climate still must have been cool and relatively dry. But the available evidence argues for a quite rapid re-establishment of temperature and precipitation levels as high as those of today, and probably by about 8,400 years BP, a little warmer. Several of Ontario's great forest trees, most notably the white pine, were able to push well north of their present limits. There are also indications of some fluctuations in precipitation.

On the whole, however, the record confirms what is suspected from much of the rest of the northern hemisphere – the modern climate was re-established at the beginning of the Holocene (about 10,000 years BP). The controlling solar radiation and dynamics of air movement have varied little since then. In other parts of the continent a distinct mid-Holocene warm phase (8,000 to 4,000 years ago)

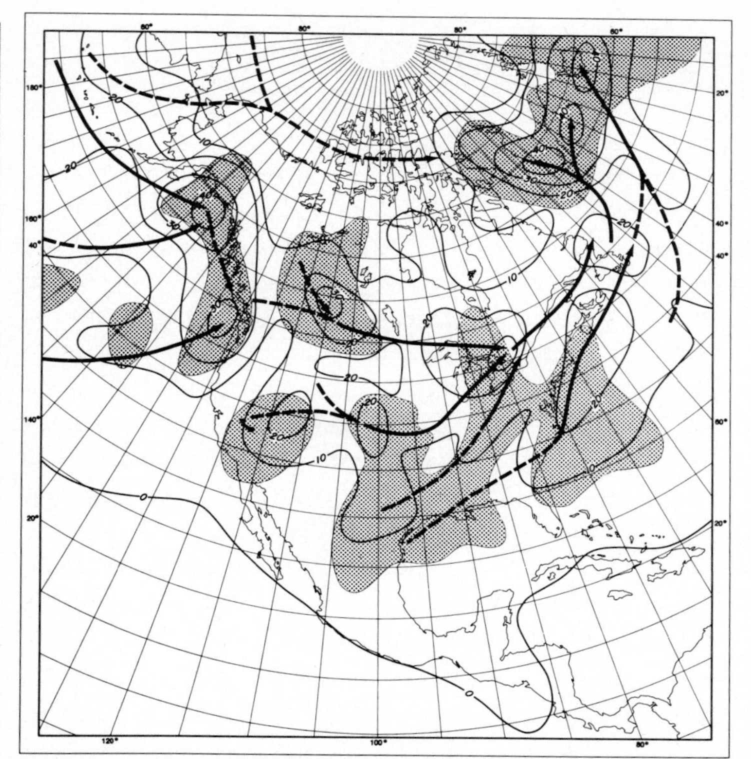

Paths often taken by cyclone centres in January. Note the convergence of two of the main paths over the Great Lakes and central Ontario. Cyclonic storms are large, and many extend 50 to 500 kilometres from their actual centres. Stippled areas show where new cyclones often form. (*F. K. Hare, modified from W. H. Klein*)

can be detected. But in Ontario, differences in temperature and precipitation that have been inferred in past millennia – for example, for the northward migration of white pine – resemble in scale those occurring between extreme years in our present climate. A remarkable fossil sequence of lake deposits excavated near Kitchener, Ontario, shows that after 8,400 BP, mean July temperatures were probably one to two degrees Celsius warmer than today's. However, this temperature is still within the range of variation of contemporary climate. Only a small shift northward of the characteristic storm tracks and jetstreams could account for the apparent warmth of the mid-Holocene millennia.

Small though we suspect climatic variations of the past ten thousand years to have been, compared with the convulsions in the preceding Pleistocene epoch, they must have been highly significant to the stability of ecosystems and the struggles of prehistoric Indian communities and European and American settlers to maintain their livelihood. There is little evidence, however, to suggest major or persistent climatic changes. Ontario's recent history has been worked out on a background of climate like that we experience today – extreme, harsh, and stimulating, yet capable of sustaining a variety of gainful activities based upon forest and soil and the vast water resources that the climate ultimately provides.

Future Climate

If the past climates have differed little from those of today, what evidence exists to argue for future climatic change in Ontario? Present opinion among professional climatologists is that dramatic changes are indeed likely within the next century, and that the beginnings of these changes are already evident.

Changes are expected because atmospheric composition is being altered by human interference. Rising carbon dioxide levels – about .4 per cent per annum – are matched by

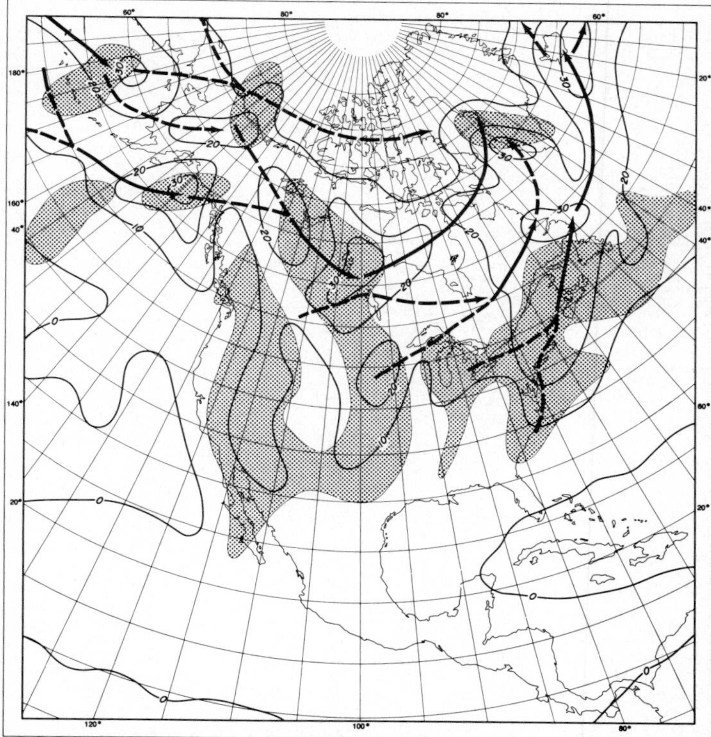

Paths of cyclone centres in July (compare with the previous map). At this time most cyclones cross northern Canada, their cold fronts affecting Ontario. (*F. K. Hare, modified from W. H. Klein*)

even more rapid increases in methane, nitrous oxide, and various synthetic gases, notably the fluorocarbons so widely used in refrigeration. All these gases are active absorbers of terrestrial infrared radiation, and hence tend to increase the "greenhouse effect." By the second quarter of the twenty-first century, an effect equivalent to a doubling of carbon dioxide, with a corresponding rise in annual temperatures of two to five degrees Celsius, seems entirely probable. Such a change clearly would be revolutionary, far bigger than anything experienced in the recorded climatic history of Ontario – bigger, in fact, than any event since the ice melted off Ontario's surface and climate rebounded to its present state. Younger people alive today will see some of the changes, unless our calculations are quite wrong.

It would benefit the province, and the nation, to be prepared to live through drastic change towards a warmer and perhaps drier world.

◆ SCIENCE ◆ EXCURSION ◆

Weather Systems

F. Kenneth Hare

As the science of climatology matures, accumulated detail of atmospheric circulation often confounds earlier, simpler models. This statement is especially true of macrodisturbances – the cyclones and anticyclones – "lows" and "highs" on the weather map. A general description of this involved topic is invariably an oversimplification, but nonetheless instructive at a superficial level in understanding North American climatic patterns that influence Ontario.

A westerly current of air (from the west) flows at ground level from about 30°N to 60°N (also at equivalent latitudes in the southern hemisphere). It extends up for ten or fifteen kilometres, and with altitude becomes stronger and wider, spanning from about 20°N to 70°N.

In this current of air there are north-south temperature and pressure gradients, with the warmest temperature and the highest pressure at 30°N. Lines of similar temperature and pressure extend parallel to the direction of flow. Air flows along constant pressure above the zone of ground friction.

The temperature and pressure gradient is, however, unstable. Because of some topographic barrier, or unequal heating of land and water, small perturbations develop and tend to amplify as they move eastward. Larger perturbations caused by great mountain barriers tend to remain more stationary and do not amplify. They are responsible for regions of standing low- and high-pressure systems, such as the Aleutian and Icelandic lows. It is the smaller perturbations, however, that develop into travelling weather systems.

The small perturbations begin as cyclonic waves. These appear on the weather map initially as "troughs and ridges" of low and high pressure. They become more and more pronounced as they move eastward until a trough becomes a counter-clockwise vortex (a cyclone, or low) and a ridge a clockwise vortex (an anticyclone, or high).

The eastward movement of the low brings in warm, moist air – which rises ahead of the low – while pulling in cold air from behind – which cuts beneath the warm air ahead. Rain or snow fall from these areas of warm air uplift; gentle precipitation ahead of the warm front, heavier and often thundery at the cold front.

The changes of pressure are actually induced, not by changes of temperature, but by the upward or downward movements of air (*uplift* or *subsidence*), because these are accompanied by net inflows or outflows of air. Behind the low, above the surface northwesterly wind, the air *subsides*, and there is general *convergence* of air through a quite deep column above it. The convergence increases the mass of air above the observer, and hence raises the surface pressure. Ahead of the low, above the area of rising warm air, there is general *divergence* of air, which depletes the mass in each column. Hence surface pressure falls.

The low-pressure vortex induces even stronger warm and cold fronts on the weather map than did the original wave. The vortex pulls warm air from the south into the southern part of the cyclone, and this air rises as it moves northeastward into, and southeastward ahead of, the advancing storm. Being warm, it rides over the cooler air but also pushes it northward at ground level – a warm front. Similarly, cold air is pulled in ahead of the storm as rising easterlies north of the centre, and this air is drawn southward behind the centre – a sharp cold front.

These travelling fronts, together with their associated high- and low-pressure systems, driven by the westerlies aloft, provide most of the daily variation in weather to which we are accustomed.

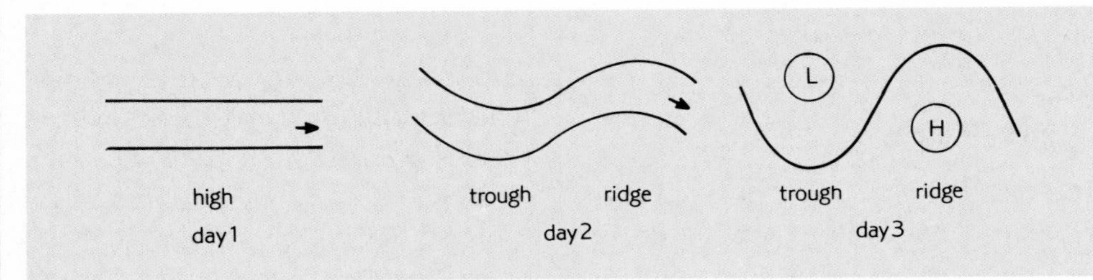

Development from an eastward flow of air of a cyclonic wave developing into high and low pressure cells.

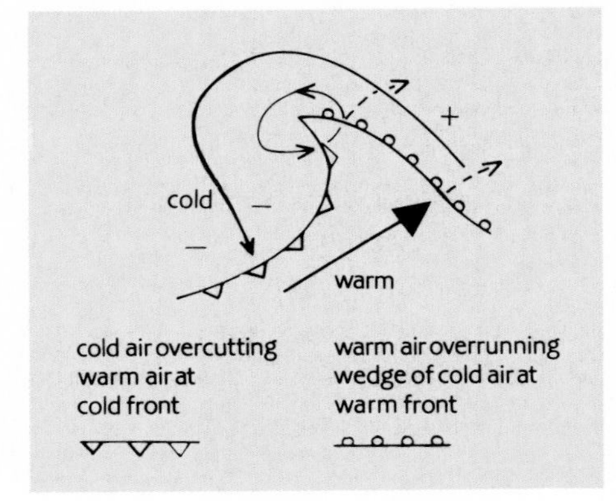

Temperature distribution in the cyclone (low pressure cell).

Ontario's Biota in Space and Time

John B. Theberge

On a May day, when a warm onshore wind bends the beach-edge willows guarding the outlet of Oshawa's famed Second Marsh, the trees will be full of birds. So will the marsh, with wrens chattering and coots scolding, and flocks of teal, pintails, and mallards dabbling along the cattail fringes. And so will the beaches, where tiny sanderlings and least sandpipers scurry erratically about.

Here, or in any similar wild place left along the north shore of Lake Ontario or Lake Erie, a good day's birding will produce 140 species or more. That represents about one-quarter of all species known to breed in Canada.

But, along the James Bay coast on a similar May day, or in June when all the migrants are back, a hike across the tundra flats with their lingering snow patches, and through the wet sedge marshes is much less productive. The best bird list you could expect here is much shorter, perhaps only one-third the number of species seen farther south.

Leave Ontario and travel to the bottomlands and red rock cliffs along the Rio Grande in south Texas. Here the vegetation is rich and the sun hot – and birds are plentiful. You could easily double Ontario's best bird list.

There is a pattern across North America, a gradient from few species to many, north to south. It is found not only in birds. In the tiaga forests of Polar Bear Park on the shore of James Bay, only three or four species of trees raise their stunted crowns into the cold wind. In contrast, an upland woodlot in Ontario's northern hardwood forests consists of perhaps ten different tree species. Only a short distance south, however, Point Pelee's Carolinian forest contains almost three times that number.

Across North America there are similar patterns in birds, plants, mammals, reptiles, amphibians, and insects. Moreover, the north-south pattern is not the only one. More species of almost everything are found in the west than in the east. More variability in numbers of species occurs in areas adjacent to one another in the west than in the east. Fewer species live on islands and peninsulas.

These patterns have been the subject of considerable scientific speculation and inquiry. Are they evidence of different rates of evolution? Migration? Past cataclysmic disturbances? A host of theories exist. But one fact is clear. More than chance is operating to dictate the diversity of biota in any one place. The richness of living forms to which we are accustomed in Ontario fits into an orderly continental arrangement.

A Piece of the Nearctic Realm

Biogeographers divide the world into six "realms" on the basis of differences in the proportion of various Orders of living things. Ontario is part of the Nearctic Realm, which covers

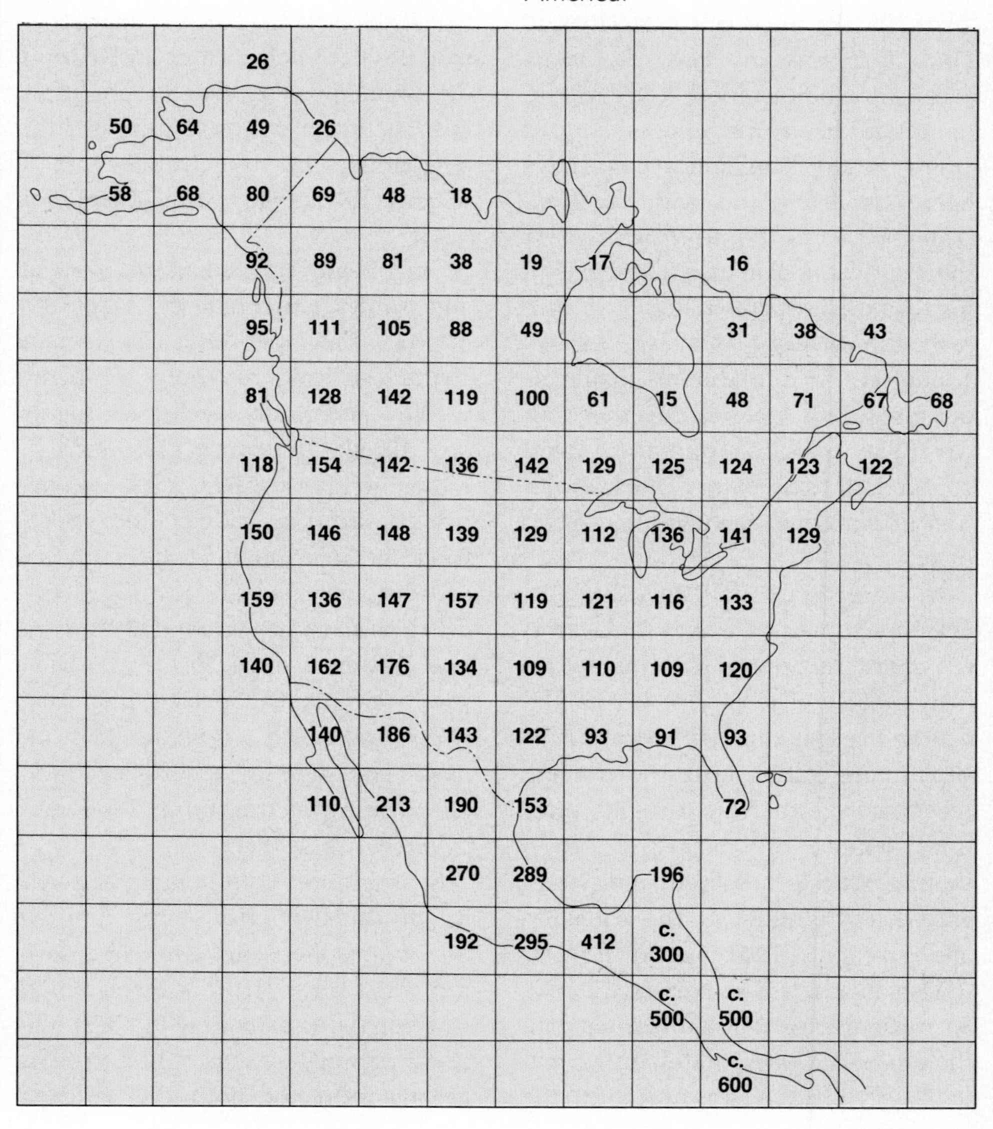

Pattern in the number of breeding birds in equal size blocks across North America.

all of North America. The Nearctic Realm is characterized by its large number of vertebrate families, especially its rich variety of reptiles and placental mammals. This richness reflects the warm Eocene, 50 million years ago, when North America, especially northern Canada, provided a centre for the evolution of these two groups. Among conspicuous mammals that evolved here are mule and white-tailed deer, black and grizzly bear, wolf, coyote, fox, and snowshoe hare.

This "home-grown" variety in species was enriched by periodic land bridges connecting the Nearctic Realm with the Palearctic Realm (Europe and Asia north of the Himalayas). From the east, at times, northern Canada was joined to Greenland and Scandinavia. From the west, at times, Alaska was linked across the Bering Strait with northern Russia. Our fauna was enriched with many species, including moose, elk, caribou, mountain sheep, and, of course, man.

For the last 15 million years we have been connected, too, with the Neotropical Realm (South America) via the Isthmus of Panama. The Neotropic formerly was dominated by marsupials, the earliest mammals to evolve. It hosted few placental mammals because South America, together with Australia, split off from the united continental mass before much evolution of placental mammals had taken place.

In the Nearctic and Palearctic, however, marsupials were later replaced as the more successful placental mammals evolved. The success of the placentals prevented any significant marsupial immigration northwards along the Central American isthmus after that connection emerged. Even though many placental mammals migrated south, only two, the armadillo and porcupine, migrated north to establish themselves in North America. Armadillos expanded no further than the southern United States, but porcupines spread all the way north into the boreal forest, even beyond the Arctic Circle in Alaska, Yukon, and the Mackenzie Valley.

Patterns in Productivity

Environments with many species characteristically are highly productive. More solar energy is captured and forged by photosynthesis into green plants. More plants mean more food available for herbivores. More herbivores can support more carnivores. As a result, productive ecosystems have the greatest *biomass*, or weight of living things.

But why should productive ecosystems also have the most species? One explanation is that productive ecosystems, with greater numbers of individuals, generate more competition. The evolutionary antidote to competition is specialization. Competing individuals can "sidestep" one another if they develop their own exclusive food or habitat preferences. So, any gene change favouring specialization in a competitive environment will confer a selective advantage to the animal that has it.

One need only compare tropical and tundra environments to see the effects of competition. The tropics characteristically are home to many species, and these species are highly specialized. On tropical grasslands, in Zimbabwe, for instance, nineteen species of grazers live side by side, each a food and micro-habitat specialist. In contrast, on Canada's northern tundra, there are two large grazers, caribou and musk-oxen. Both eat a wide variety of plants. Species inhabiting Arctic and north temperate environments tend to be less specialized, capable of eating many different foods and living in diverse places.

Setting the continental patterns in productivity from up high in the troposphere are the east-flowing jetstreams. They induce broad weather patterns below, establish climatic parameters, and in the process greatly influence both the diversity and productivity of life in Ontario. And that productivity varies greatly. For example, a species-rich deciduous forest in relatively warm southern Ontario may produce 1,200 grams of plant tissue per square metre per year. This level of production mirrors climate in a belt extending northwest across the aspen parklands of the northern prairies, and east into the Maritime Provinces. Almost as productive, although cooler and less diverse, is the boreal forest of northern Ontario. The boreal forest achieves its surprisingly high productivity because of the efficiency of the cool/temperate-adapted conifers that roll to the seemingly endless horizons. Productivity on the northern tundra, however, drops sharply. With its perennially frozen soils and short period for photosynthesis, the tundra's production may be only one-tenth that of boreal or hardwood forests.

Diversity and Disturbance

Despite the obvious relationship between species diversity and productivity, so evident in a comparison of northern and southern Ontario, some troublesome questions about the continental patterns remain. For example, species diversity of mammals in the Canadian Arctic was much greater during the Pleistocene Era than now, with climates no warmer. To account for this, one theory holds that the repeated glaciations sweeping across the land may have periodically killed off species in the north. In contrast, southern environments have been more constant over longer periods, allowing more species to survive.

What is bothersome about that theory, however, is the role of the *glacial refugia*. The glaciers did not cover everything. They left ice-free refugia in the eastern high Arctic, interior Alaska and Yukon, and various high-mountain plateaus. Populations of species that survived there were isolated from one another, and the geo graphical isolation so imposed is one

White trilliums. LARRY LAMB

of the pre-conditions for the development of new species. Indeed, variation at the subspecies level is found today in moose, caribou, sheep, and a few other species that lived in different refugia during the last glacial period. In those cases, wholly different species did not evolve supposedly because the period of isolation was too brief. In contrast, species that could travel over ice, such as polar bears and arctic foxes, today do not show this variation caused by isolation. Thus, repeated glaciation may have been simultaneously a destroyer and creator. Either species adapted or they perished.

The West-East Pattern

Neither differences in productivity nor constancy of environments help explain why western North America displays more diversity of birds and mammals than does the east. But what is striking about the mountainous west is its physical variability. Altitudinal gradients result in temperature extremes between the top and the bottom of a single mountain that in the east would require you to travel from Baffin Island's icecap to extreme southern Ontario. As well, climate often is very different on north-facing and south-facing mountain slopes at the same altitude, resulting in a cool, moist forest just around the slope from a hot, arid grassland. Consequently, many habitats and niches exist for species in close proximity to one another.

Ontario's mountains are old and ground down. No doubt the diversity of species living here today would be greater if the mountains were still here.

Patterns over Time

Not only does Ontario's biota fit into geographical patterns, but into patterns in time. The distribution and abundance of plants and animals in Ontario has never remained constant very long. Like coloured glass in a kaleidoscope, living things in our mid-continent location fall into a spatial pattern in the slow turn of time, always distinct, but always part of a grand design.

Range shifts and expansions are common, often reflecting changes in local or regional climates, alterations in environments, or even just the slow spread of pioneering genotypes within species. Thus, species that genetically are not sufficiently different from others may meet, breed, and possibly create hybrids. Hybrids are common among some salamanders, they occur between Ontario's two species of

Scarlet tanager. DON GUNN

toads, and are found so frequently in butterflies that one is left questioning the distinctiveness of many species. In contrast, many bird species which have spread into Ontario in the last fifty to one hundred years have remained distinctive. Examples are cardinals, mockingbirds, and western meadowlarks, which can be distinguished from eastern meadowlarks chiefly by their song.

Range shifts may alter species not only through hybridization, but through resultant competition. One important ecological axiom, known in the textbooks as *Gause's Principle*, is that no two species can occupy the same niche indefinitely. When they compete, one or the other will move away or become extinct. The house sparrow and European starling, both introduced from Europe, have overlapped with hole-nesters such as the eastern bluebird and red-headed woodpecker, contributing to drastic declines in both these native species across eastern Canada. A historic spread of the red fox may have contributed to the near-disappearance of the gray fox in Ontario. In the confined environment of Long Point, jutting out into Lake Erie, there is evidence that coyotes recently may have displaced red foxes.

These recent changes in species are minor compared with those that have occurred over geologic time. What is now Ontario has hosted a panorama of species that marched onto the life stage on prompt from genetic and environmental cues. Since species evolve over time, one might expect more species to be alive today than ever before. But Ontario hosted more species of mammals a million years ago. Its diversity of birds was greatest in Tertiary times, 10 million years ago. Although many species marched onstage, most of them marched off again.

Nothing larger than unicellular organisms lived in Ontario, or anywhere, for the first 4 billion years of the Earth's existence. Evolution seemed permanently stalled at the barrier of cellular co-operation. The diversity of unicellular life may have been great, but about these organisms little is known. Some of them still can be found today petrified in the rock along part of Lake Superior's north shore, frozen in time for the past 1.5 billion years.

Only about 600 million years ago, multi-cellular organisms first appeared. In the Cambrian Period, trilobites dominated the shallow seas that covered most of southern Ontario. Corals and brachiopods became abun-

Eastern chipmunk. DON GUNN

dant with them for a time. Primitive forests of spore-bearing trees dominated in Ontario sometime between the appearance of the first land plants 425 million years ago and the first seed tree trunk found in 350-million-year-old shales at Kettle Point. Seed-bearing gymnosperms completely replaced spore-trees 200 million years ago, as reptiles became the dominant large animal Class. But then, 65 million years ago most of the reptile species left abruptly. Replacing them was an explosion of mammalian species. The number of flowering plants expanded; grasses appeared, and very recently, man.

How would today's biota be characterized by paleontologists of the future? They would record that for the first time in the evolutionary record, remarkably, one single species suddenly came to exert a profound impact on the whole planet, creating in places a hitherto-unknown environment which it populated in great abundance. Viewed over the scale of geologic time, this human era featured a near-cataclysmic impoverishment of biota – with at least one species becoming extinct per day. Coincident with the extinctions was the appearance of a host of new human-made chemicals permeating air, water, and land.

But while man is unique, cataclysmic events are not. In fact, they are common, a major determinant of patterns over time. Sudden world-wide extinctions have occurred with a periodicity of approximately 26 million years, generating theories of meteor or comet impacts as we travel through the *Oort Belt* – a current focus of astronomical research. Many of these sudden extinctions were dramatic: two in the Devonian Period 360 and 340 million years ago, the first of which resulted in 142 of 148 species of corals becoming extinct, and the second causing wholesale extinction of shallow marine organisms; the Permian extinction, greatest of them all, 225 million years ago, in which 95 per cent of all marine species died out; the Triassic, 195 million years ago, when 400 genera of the sea-dwelling ammonites, representing almost all of them, ceased to exist; and the end of the Cretaceous, 65 million years ago, which spelled the demise of the dinosaurs as well as a large proportion of all plankton and marine life.

Characteristically, extinctions were followed by periods of relatively rapid speciation – life on the rebound. After the second Devonian extinction, conifer trees first appeared and reptiles evolved from amphibians. After the Cretaceous extinction, mammals radiated into many new forms. No satisfactory explanation exists for the extinction-speciation correlate, although speculation is abundant. New species may inhabit vacant niches, surviving because of a freedom from competition. Or, if glaciers appeared after extinctions, geographic barriers may have isolated populations and allowed for gradual re-shuffling of genes over time. Supporting this premise is the observation that most of the major extinctions were characterized by periods of low sea levels that may have resulted from cooler temperatures and consequent larger icecaps.

However, for major sudden radiations of new species to occur, something must drive an increased rate of genetic mutation, the chance appearance of new forms to try their hand at survival. If the causes of sudden extinctions, such as an increase in radiation, also caused increased mutagenic effects, the relatively sudden appearance of new species after extinctions may be more comprehensible. No current theory provides such an explanation.

In natural environments, the sum is greater than the parts. Each individual, regardless of species, does nothing more than attempt to survive and leave genes to the future. To do this, some exploit new environments, some stay in old ones, some change to better fit the environment, and, either gradually or suddenly, some die out.

No species but ours can be aware of the patterns in space and time to which they contribute and into which they fit. Yet the patterns in living things exist. They do so because living things are but the animate form of biogeochemical cycles and energy flow – sunlight to heat. The patterns represent successful adaptations to the variability in the biosphere, the thin shell capable of supporting life that makes our planet unique.

Part Two

PROVINCIAL PERSPECTIVES

Foundations of the Land
Bedrock Geology
R. J. Davidson

Ontario's rocks reveal close to 3 billion years of earth history. Like the pages in a book, they describe the events that have shaped the province. The stories behind these events are outlined by the geological time scale, from the Precambrian through the Paleozoic to the Mesozoic eras. These stories revolve around ancient volcanic eruptions, rising mountains, eroding continents, changing sea levels and the accumulation of marine sediments.

Beneath Ontario, and indeed much of North America, lies a vast expanse of hard Precambrian rock, the foundation of the continent. Buried in the Hudson Bay region by a mantle of younger rock, it climbs to the surface and is exposed across most of Ontario as the Canadian Shield. This Shield rises to more than 450 metres above sea level near the continental divide and then descends below Lake Superior and passes under the lower Great Lakes where it is again buried by younger rock.

In Ontario, the Canadian Shield is made up of four distinctive structural provinces, named Superior, Southern, Churchill, and Grenville. Each has a very different story to tell. These structural provinces, with three relatively flat lowlands, make up the province's seven major geological regions. The first chapter of Ontario's bedrock story begins in the Archean Eon with the creation of the Superior structural province. It begins when the planet was very young.

Archean-age volcanic rocks, some of the oldest in Ontario, exposed near Potter's Mine, Munro Township. These rocks are part of an ancient sequence of lava flows which display a "spinifex" texture caused by the rapid cooling of extruded molten lava.
R. J. DAVIDSON

Archean Eon

All rocks greater than 2.5 billion years old were created during the oldest period of earth history, the Archean Eon. Rocks formed in the Early Archean record the evolution of a thin discontinuous crust on the Earth's outer surface. This crust was uplifted and eroded on at least two occasions during ancient periods of mountain-building, called the *Uivakian* and *Wanipigowan orogenies*. These orogenies are recorded in scattered places in northwestern Ontario by igneous rocks with radiometric dates exceeding 2.9 billion years.

Then, closer to 2.7 billion years ago in the Late Archean, the Earth's primitive crust was penetrated by volcanoes and buried by thick sequences of volcanic and sedimentary rocks. The volcanoes spread lava from a series of east-west-trending volcanic island arcs. Over time, these arcs were eroded and their sediments deposited into basins along their margins. These alternating island arcs and sedimentary basins form the linear volcanic and sedimentary belts that distinguish the Superior structural province.

The volcanic arcs, also known as *greenstone belts*, supply the gold, silver, copper, zinc, and other metals that fuel the mining camps at Timmins, Kirkland Lake, Wawa, and Red Lake. The sedimentary belts contain some of Earth's oldest fossils, once colonies of primitive bacteria and algae. Finally, the volcanic and sedimentary rocks were intruded, uplifted, and deformed by massive igneous rocks during the *Laurentian orogeny*, 2.7 billion years ago, and again during the *Kenoran orogeny*, 2.5 billion years ago.

By the end of the Archean Eon, the islands and basins had consolidated into a large, stable, mountainous continent surrounded by seas.

Silicated "feather joints" in Archean meta-sedimentary rocks at Beaverhouse Lake, Quetico Provincial Park. These raised structures are thought to be tension cracks, or joints, which have been filled with a silica-rich solution. The resulting hard quartz stands out above the softer, easily eroded sediments. R. J. DAVIDSON

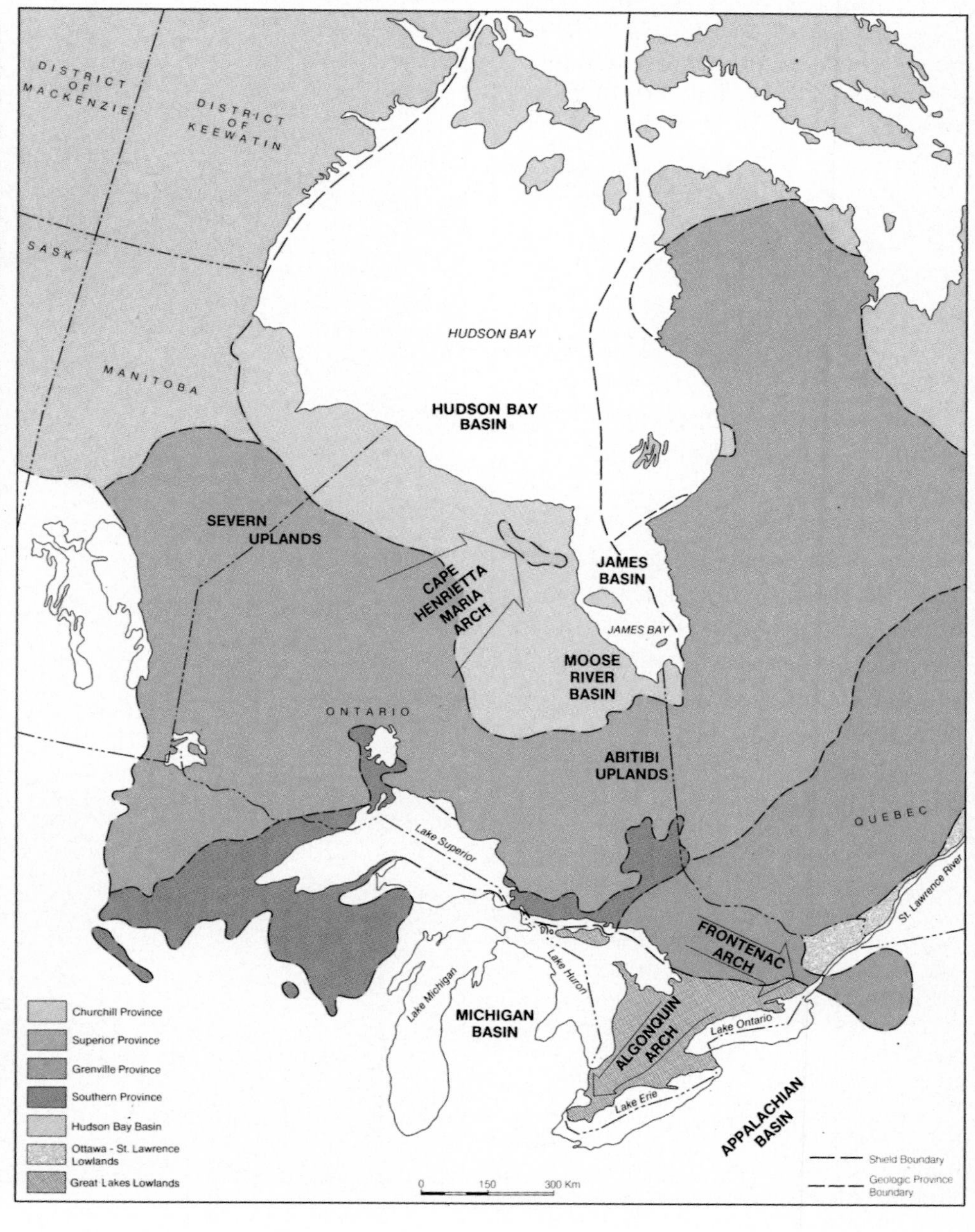

The geological regions of Ontario. Shades of brown are all Precambrian in age (more than 600 million years old), the oldest being rocks of the Superior Province; shades of grey are all more recent Paleozoic, or to a very limited extent, Mesozoic rocks.

The Proterozoic Eon – Aphebian Era

A long period of erosion, called the *Eparchean interval*, marked the beginning of the Proterozoic Eon, 2.5 billion years ago. Over the next 500 million years, the continent Laurentia and its Algoman Mountains were reduced to an expansive, flat, low-lying, bedrock plain. Today, this surface is part of the Severn and Abitibi uplands and is noted for its diverse drainage systems that follow the patterns etched into the bedrock by years of erosion. Many of these features can be seen while exploring the trails, rivers, and lakes of Pukaskwa National Park, as well as Opasquia, Woodland Caribou, Quetico, Missinaibi, Lake Superior, and other provincial parks.

But more significant for the structure of Ontario as we know it today, between 2.5 and 1.8 billion years ago the rocks of the southern structural provinces accumulated alongside Laurentia's southern and eastern margins. These rocks remain as the Huronian, Animikie, and Whitewater groups. At the same time, rocks of the Churchill province accumulated along the northern margin.

Oldest of these rocks, deposited off Laurentia's southeastern shores, are conglomerates laid down by ancient

Large boulder, or "dropstone," in the middle of the picture, dropped from an iceberg into soft, fine-grained Huronian sediments located near Elliot Lake. This feature provides evidence for the presence of glaciers some two billion years ago. R. J. DAVIDSON

rivers as sands and gravels some 2.5 billion years ago. Today these Huronian conglomerates are famous for their uranium ore mined at Elliot Lake.

Successively younger Huronian sediments record the multiple advance and retreat of continental glaciers and marginal seas. This sedimentation ended about 2.1 billion years ago with the upwelling, or intrusion, of the *Nipissing diabase sills*. These sills are tabular masses of igneous rock which were injected from below into planes of weakness in older Huronian sediments. North of Lake Huron, these sediments and sills have been

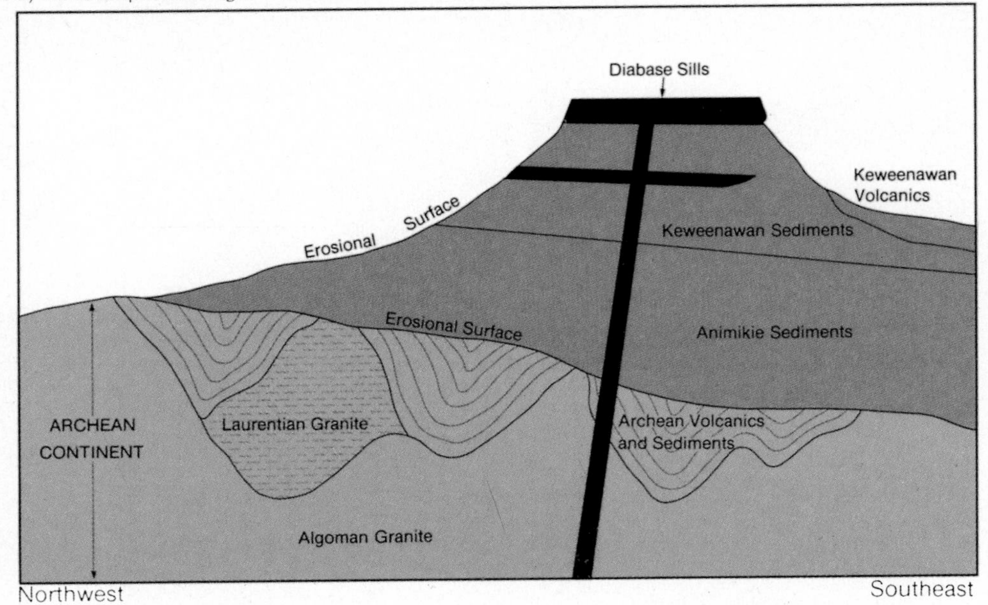

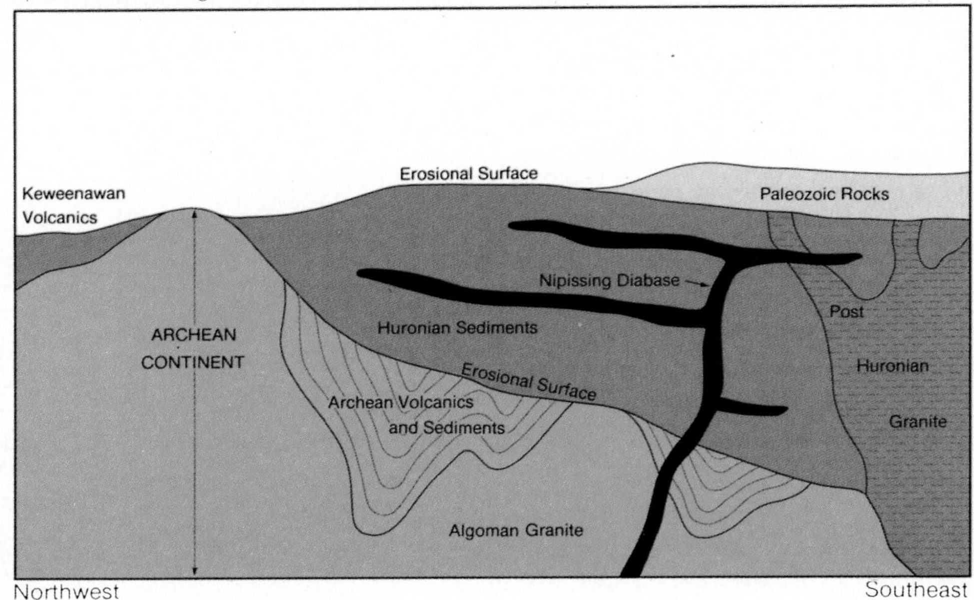

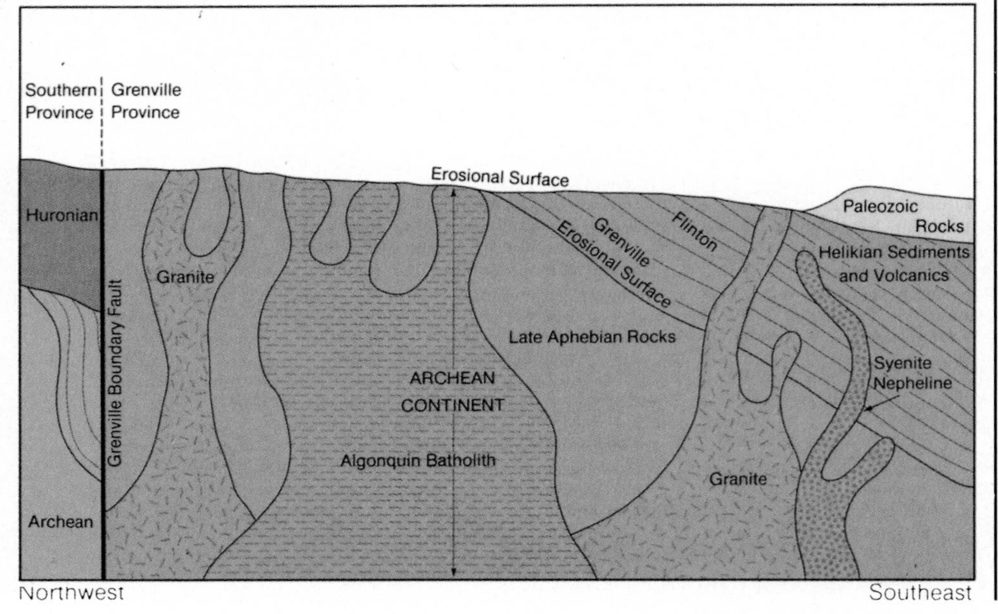

Relationships of Ontario's Precambrian rocks as cut-aways in three locations. Colour coding follows the previous map. Maps a) and b) show how the old Archean Continent (Superior Province) was buried by younger sediments in the region that is now the Southern Province (see previous figure). Map c) shows the interface between the Southern Province and the younger Grenville Province which, to the south, is buried by even younger Paleozoic rocks.

folded and faulted into the Penokean Hills, characterized by the rugged terrain of Mississagi Provincial Park, and the magnificent white LaCloche Mountains of Killarney Provincial Park. North of Sudbury, they form the Cobalt plain which is displayed in Lady Evelyn–Smoothwater Provincial Park by Maple Mountain and the Ishapatina Ridge, Ontario's summit, 750 metres above sea level.

Off Laurentia's southwestern shores, the Animikie group was deposited on rocky beaches and in calm, offshore waters. Its conglomerates, cherts (flints and silaceous rock), shales, and limestones can be seen from Gunflint Lake in LaVerendrye Provincial Park, northwest to Kakabeka Falls Provincial Park and the north shore of Lake Superior. The Animikie's lower chert beds at Schreiber Channel Provincial Park are renowned for their abundant, well-preserved mounds of blue-green algae. These sediments were buried about 1.7 billion years ago by carbonate-rich shales eroded from Laurentia's surface and laid down into a deep, marginal sedimentary basin by turbid water currents. The rocks are well displayed in road cuts north of Sibley and along the Pidgeon River in LaVerendrye Provincial Park. About 1.1 billion years ago, the Animikie sediments were pierced by thick, tabular, igneous sills and dikes. In the past 1 billion years, the Kaministiqua River and its predecessors have shaped these layered rocks into a series of steep valleys, talus slopes, cliffs, and plateaus called the Port Arthur Hills.

Farther east, the rocks of the Whitewater group collected in the Sudbury basin about 1.8 billion years ago. These rocks have been the subject of much debate. Their oldest volcanics and sediments may have been formed from explosive volcanic eruptions, or they may be rocks fragmented and deposited in the aftermath of a meteorite impact. The basin's elliptical shape and the presence of impact features called *shattercones* on its periphery also support the meteorite theory. Overlying silty sediments may be shallow offshore deposits, or the subaqueous infilling of the crater by material suspended by the meteorite impact. Turbid submarine currents then filled a subsiding basin with coarse sandy sediments, and the basin's outer edge was intruded by molten igneous rocks about 1.7 billion years ago. This intrusion, which is mined for its nickel at Sudbury, may have been initiated by the impact and fracture of the Earth's crust by the meteorite.

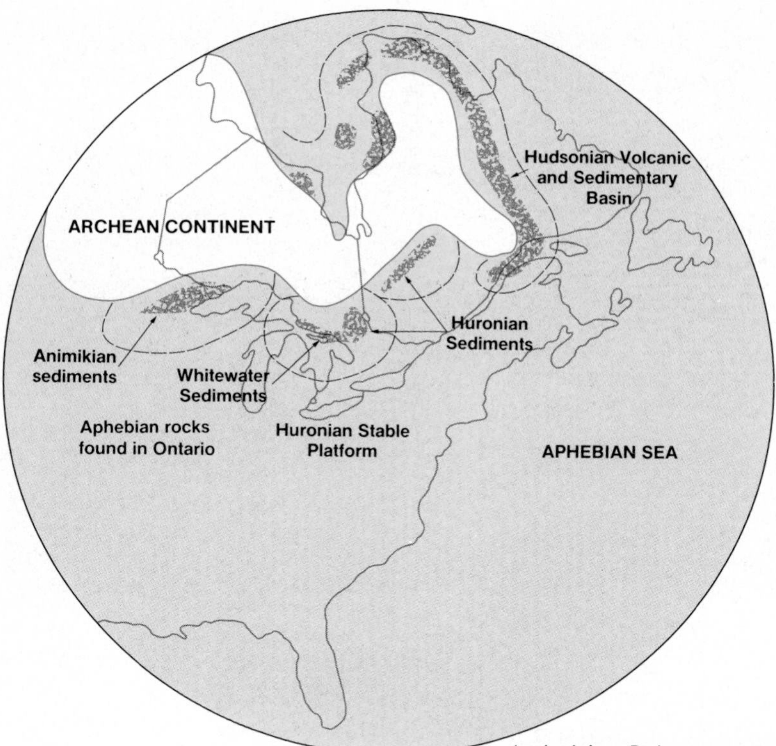

Aphebian Paleogeography (2.5 to 1.8 billion years ago). Shades of blue indicate areas under water; white areas are above water.

At the end of the Aphebian Era, Laurentia's northern margins were uplifted during the *Hudsonian orogeny*. The construction of the Hudsonian Mountains was accompanied by erosion and the accumulation of sedimentary and volcanic rocks in basins off the continent's eastern and northern shores. A small portion of these rocks outcrop in the Hudson Bay region at Sutton and Nowashe lakes and in Polar Bear Provincial Park. Here, the northern basin was filled about 1.8 billion years ago with magnesium-rich limestones, called *dolostones*. This infilling was followed by uplift and the accumulation of coarse fragmented sediments in shallow water, and then down-warping with the deposition of iron-rich silts and sands in deeper water. These sediments were then intruded by sills of molten igneous rocks to create the northwest-trending Sutton Hills which rise more than 180 metres above the surrounding lowlands.

The Proterozoic Eon – The Helikian Era

By the Helikian Era, beginning 1.8 billion years ago, Laurentia was a large, stable continent. Far off its southern shores, possibly hundreds of kilometres off at first, on what today is the Atlantic Ocean, volcanoes spread lava across the sea floor towards the continent. At the same time, sediments eroded from volcanic islands were deposited into marginal seas. Eventually, continental drift caused the continent and the sea floor to collide at Laurentia's margin, pushing a vast range of mountains skyward and forcing the sea floor down into deep submarine trenches. These mountains

Glacial ice scouring on bedrock of the Grenville Province. A. G. MCLELLAN

were built in several stages during the *Grenville orogeny* between 1.8 and 1 billion years ago. The mountains and associated erosion, sedimentation, and volcanism are now recorded by the rocks of the Grenville structural province which stretches across central Ontario, Quebec, and Labrador.

Helikian sediments and volcanics about 1.3 billion years old are found today from the St. Lawrence River north to Renfrew, Bancroft, and Haliburton. They include the mixed volcanics and sediments, including sandstones, shales, and limestones of the Grenville supergroup. These rocks were intruded by massive igneous rocks, deformed, and uplifted about 1.2 billion years ago. This was accompanied by erosion and the deposition of the conglomerates, sandstones, shales, and limestones of the Flinton group about 1.1 billion years ago. These highly metamorphosed rocks are prized by mineral collectors for their numerous diverse and well-formed mineral specimens. These rocks and minerals can be observed in outcrops along the many roads traversing the Frontenac arch and in Charleston Lake, Frontenac, Silent Lake, Egan Chutes, Petroglyphs, Bon Echo, Murphy's Point, and other provincial parks.

Helikian Paleogeography (1.8 to 1 billion years ago).

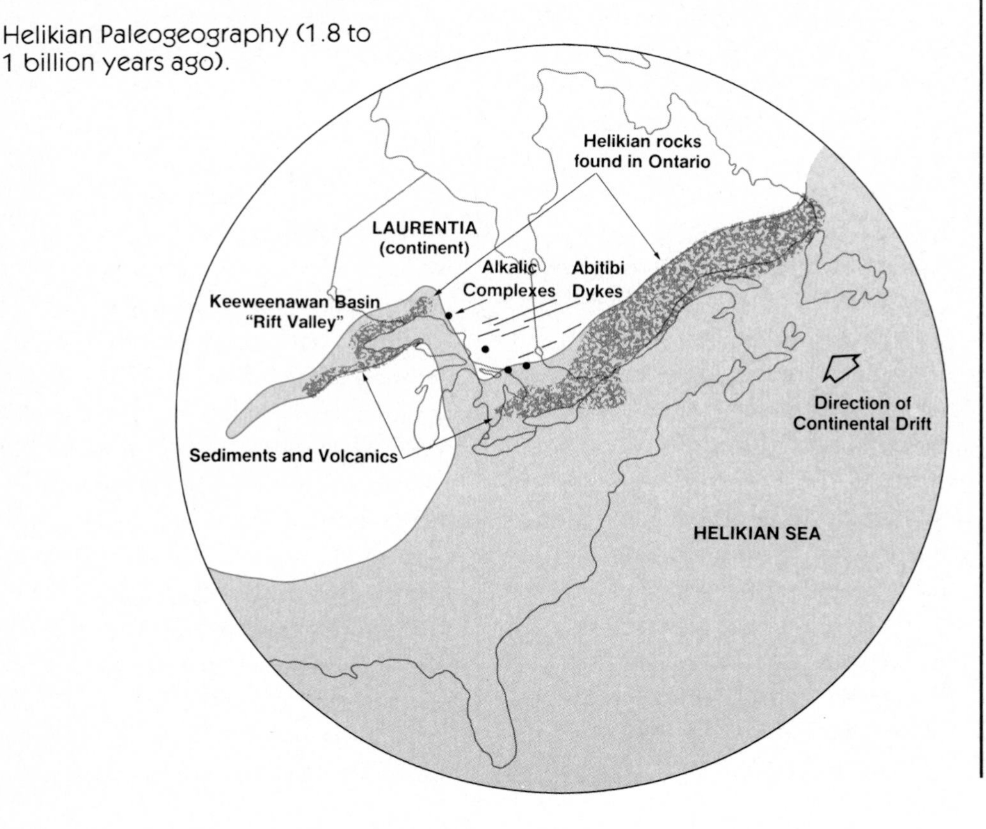

The construction of the Grenville Mountains culminated about a billion years ago. In the meantime, erosion has removed the mountains and exposed the ancient crust on which they were built. This crust is made up of deformed sedimentary rocks of Aphebian age and a variety of igneous rocks including the 1.4- to 1.5-billion-year-old *Algonquin batholith*. This batholith is a huge body of granitic rock that formed deep within the Earth and that has since moved towards the Earth's surface. These older rocks now form the Algonquin uplands and may be seen south of the French, Mattawa, and Ottawa rivers in Algonquin Provincial Park and along the coast of Georgian Bay. The northern boundary of the Grenville structural province and the position of the ancient continental margin are now marked by the Grenville boundary fault, which stretches from south of Killarney northeast to Lake Timiskaming.

The subduction of the sea floor and building of the Grenville Mountains was accompanied by the creation of a great rift valley in the Lake Nipigon and Lake Superior basins. This rift was filled with the rocks of the Keweenawan supergroup between 1.4 and 1 billion years ago. The oldest Keweenawan sandstones, shales, and limestones can be seen in Sibley Provincial Park and on the shores and islands of Black and Nipigon bays in Lake Superior. The deposition of these sediments was interrupted about 1.1 billion years ago by the intrusion of sills across and between the flat-lying sediments. These thick, tabular sheets of igneous rocks form the spectacular flat-topped mesas and deep canyons of the Nipigon plain which is characterized by the prominent Sleeping

Head of the well-known "Sleeping Giant" mesa near Thunder Bay, taken from the Sibley Peninsula. P. KOR

Giant and Nor'westers near Thunder Bay. The rift was later filled with shales, sandstones, and thick volcanic flows. The repetitive nature of these rocks provides the ridge and swale pattern that dominates the Black Bay peninsula, Isle Royale, and Michipicoten Island.

The Paleozoic Era

In the Paleozoic Era, the Canadian Shield was eroded, submerged beneath advancing seas, and buried by thick marine sediments. These sediments were deposited over a brief period of geological time 600 to 210 million years ago. The Paleozoic Era includes Cambrian, Ordovician, Silurian, Devonian, Carboniferous, and Permian periods, which, in turn, are divided into Upper (youngest), Middle, and Lower (oldest) segments. Only rocks of Upper Cambrian to Upper Devonian age have been found in Ontario. In the Mesozoic Era, the construction of the Appalachian Mountains and the emergence of low land in eastern North America forced the westward migration of the sea. As the sea retreated, Paleozoic rocks were exposed to the elements and stripped from much of the Canadian Shield. This erosion continued into the Cenozoic Era, about 60 million years ago, and persists to this day.

Today, remnant Paleozoic rocks are preserved in small pockets on the surface of the Canadian Shield and more extensively in the Hudson Bay, Great Lakes, and Ottawa–St. Lawrence lowlands. These lowlands contain distinctive sedimentary basins separated by arches of Precambrian rocks. The Hudson Bay Lowlands are divided into Hudson and James basins by the Cape Henrietta Maria arch. The Great Lakes Lowlands are separated into Michigan and Appalachian basins by the Algonquin arch, and the Ottawa–St. Lawrence Lowlands are isolated from the Great Lakes Lowlands by the Frontenac arch. All three lowlands expose progressively younger rocks as you travel away from the Shield, and towards the centre of their basins. This characteristic striped pattern is caused by the shape of the Precambrian surface, the inclined position of the younger rocks on the outer edge of the Shield, and by the millions of years of erosion that have planed the tilted ends off these rocks.

The Cambrian and Lower Ordovician Periods: Ontario's oldest Paleozoic rocks were formed in the Upper Cambrian as sand- to boulder-sized materials. They were eroded from Laurentia's surface and deposited into marginal seas. These events are recorded in Lake Superior Provincial Park and at Sault Ste. Marie by the Jacobsville sandstone. In the Lower Ordovician, the sea moved inland across the continent. The first evidence of this marine transgression is illustrated in the Ottawa–St. Lawrence

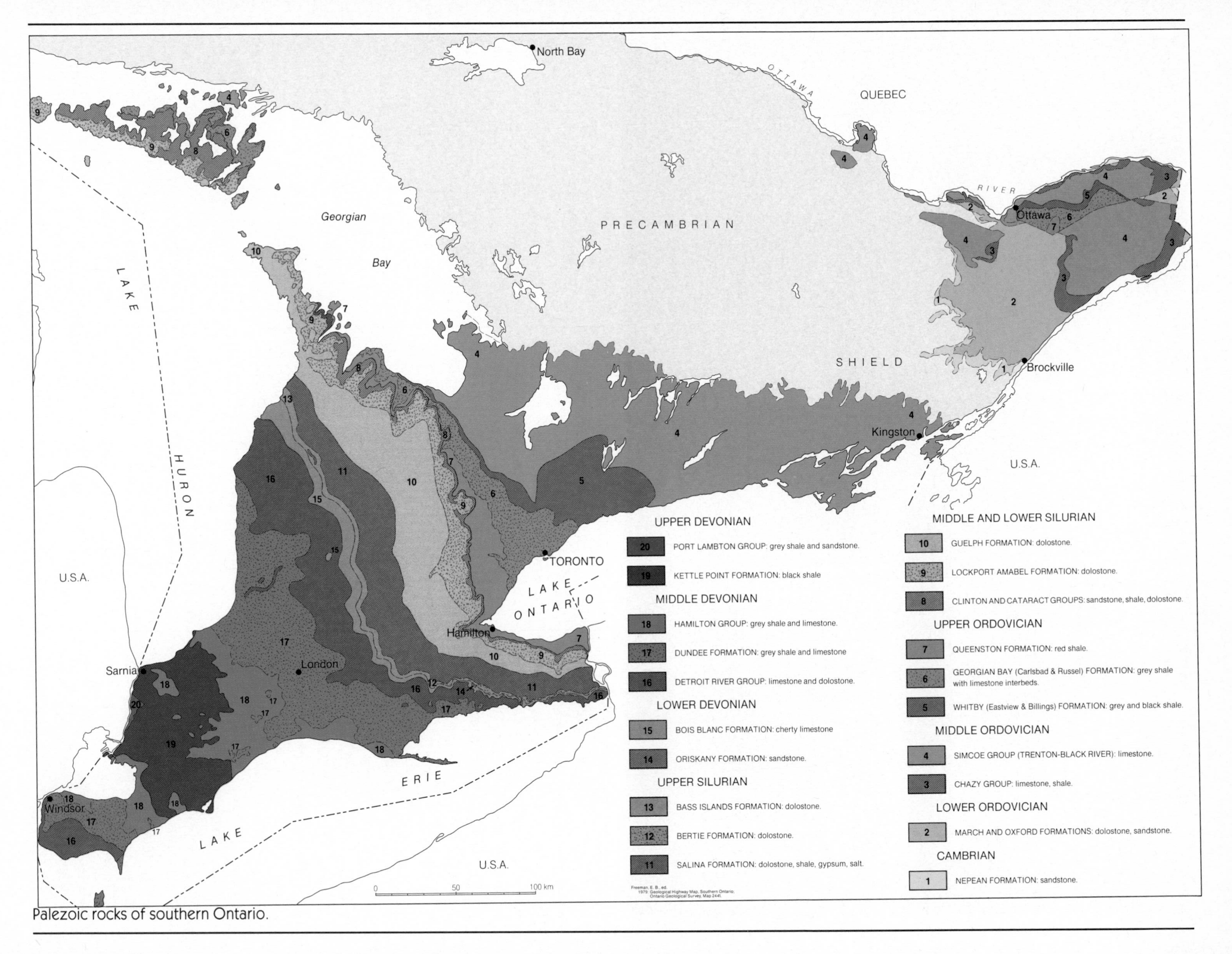

Palezoic rocks of southern Ontario.

Lowlands by the Nepean, March, and Oxford formations near Ottawa. In southeastern Ontario, these sediments reach thicknesses of up to 200 metres. The Nepean sandstone was deposited in near-shore, beach, and dune environments and provides the first record of Paleozoic life in Ontario. This sandstone is an attractive building stone, used in many of Ottawa's most impressive structures including the Parliament Buildings. The March and Oxford dolostones were later deposited in a shallow embayment on the southern edge of the continent. These dolostones are characterized by their distinctive conodonts, brachiopods, and gastropods. (Details of these and other invertebrate life forms are described in another chapter, "Vistas of Time, Rocks, and the World of Invertebrate Fossils").

The Middle Ordovician Period: Warm, shallow seas continued to advance northwest across Laurentia, depositing shales and limestones on top of older rocks. More than 300 metres of these sediments are recorded in the Ottawa–St. Lawrence and Great Lakes lowlands. On the east side of the Frontenac arch, these sediments form the Rockcliffe, St. Martin, and Ottawa formations. West of the arch, they are called the Shadow Lake, Gull River, Bobcaygeon, Verulam, and Lindsay formations. The Gull River stone, or "Kingston limestone," is one of Ontario's most attractive and widely used building stones. It was spread beyond the Kingston area by early sailing ships using it for ballast. All these rocks illustrate the proliferation of a wide variety of life forms, including brachiopods, cephalopods, molluscs, and trilobites and the appearance of colonial bryozoans, rugose corals, and graptolites in Ontario's fossil record.

The Upper Ordovician Period: The entire continent of Laurentia now lay submerged beneath advancing seas. The only lands above water were the newly formed Taconic Mountains, forerunners of the Appalachian Mountains. Shallow, muddy waters extending northwest from the base of these mountains were soon filled with up to 550 metres of shales belonging to the Whitby, Georgian Bay, and Queenston formations. These sediments dominate the Lake Ontario and Georgian Bay region of the Great Lakes Lowlands and outcrop sporadically in the Ottawa–St. Lawrence Lowlands. The red shales of the Queenston formation are especially visible in the Niagara Gorge and at the base of the Niagara Escarpment. The blue-grey Georgian Bay shales out-

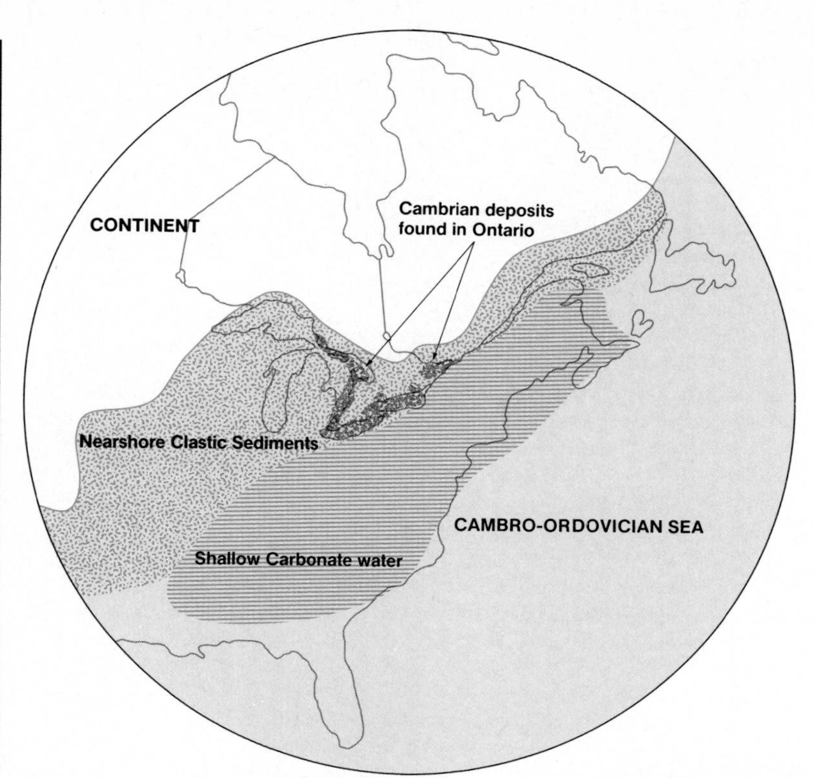

Upper (late) Cambrian to Lower (early) Ordovician Paleogeography (about 500 million years ago).

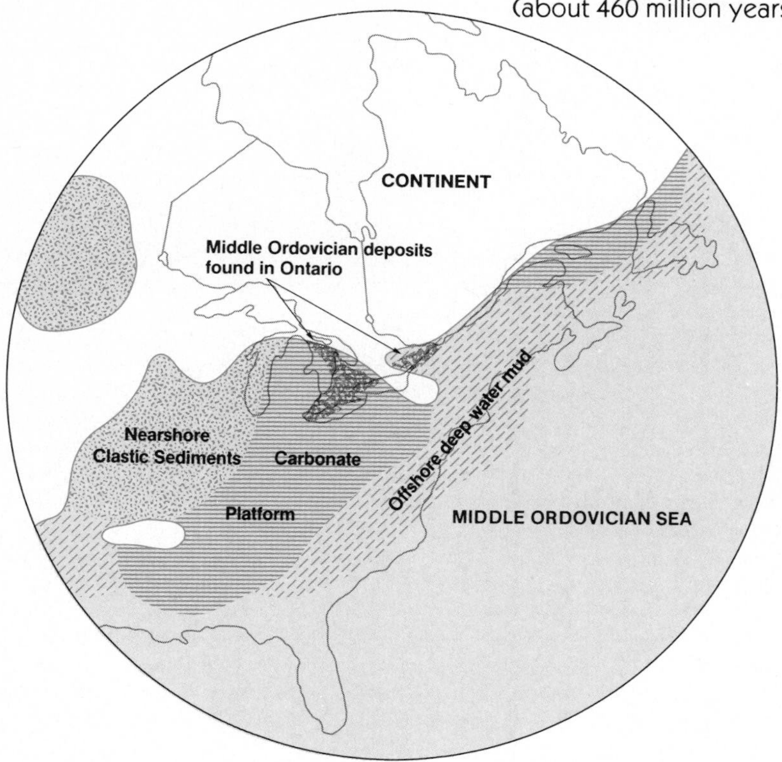

Middle Ordovician Paleogeography (about 460 million years ago).

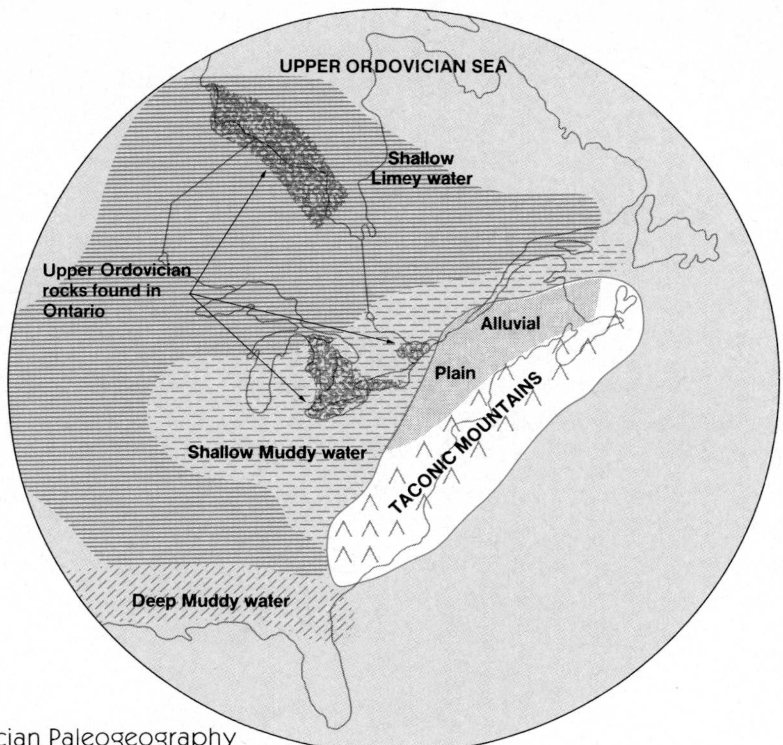

Upper Ordovician Paleogeography (about 420 million years ago).

cropping at Toronto along the Humber and Credit rivers have been mined and made into bricks at the Don Valley Brickworks to construct many of Toronto's finest homes and other buildings. Far to the north, in the Hudson Bay Lowlands, more than 130 metres of limestones belonging to the Portage Chute, Surprise Creek, Caution Creek, and Chasm Creek formations accumulated in shallow, limey seas. These murky Upper Ordovician seas were habitat for numerous bryozoans, graptolites, brachiopods, peleycpods, ostracods, cephalopods, and trilobites.

The Lower Silurian Period: The sea advanced east across the waning Taconic Mountains, depositing sands, silts, and muds in southwestern Ontario and limey sediments over the rest of the province. This marine transgression is recorded in the Great Lakes Lowlands by the Whirlpool sandstone, Manitoulin limestone, Power Glen shales, Cabot Head shales and dolostones, and Grimsby sandstone. The Whirlpool sandstone takes its name from the whirlpool in the Niagara River south of Rock Glen Park; its light colour provides a striking contrast with the older red Queenston shale immediately below. This rock once was a prominent building stone, used to construct Ontario's Legislative Building and Toronto's Old City Hall. The Whirlpool, Power Glen, and Grimsby formations were restricted to the Appalachian basin by the Algonquin arch. At the same time, the Manitoulin and Cabot Head formations accumulated on and to the north of the arch in the Michigan basin.

These Lower Silurian sediments reach a thickness of 155 metres in the Appalachian basin, 31 metres over the arch, and 62 metres in the Michigan basin. In the Hudson Bay Lowlands, the 45-metre-thick Severn River limestone was deposited in shallow water. In the early Silurian sea, graptolites, cephalopods, and trilobites became less prominent, while corals, bryozoans, brachiopods, and ostracods flourished.

The Middle Silurian Period: Calcium-rich sands, silts, and muds were deposited into the expanding sea. Close to the shore of the Taconic Mountains, fine sediments settled to the bottom of a shallow muddy sea. Offshore, barrier and pinnacle reefs accumulated, and sediments precipitated in shallow, limey waters. These seas are recorded in the Great Lakes Lowlands by more than 130 metres of sandstones, shales, limestones, and dolostones of the Clinton group and by the Lockport and Guelph formations. The Clinton and Lockport beds can be seen in the upper cliffs of the Niagara Escarp-

Lower to Middle Silurian Paleogeography (about 410 million years ago).

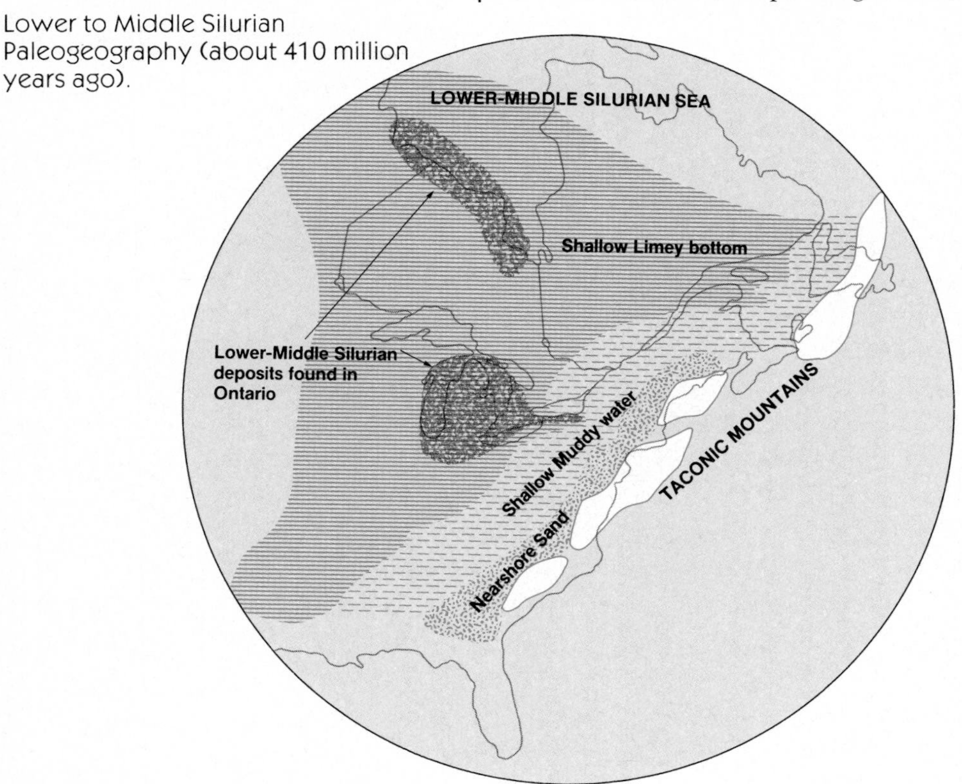

ment from Niagara Falls to Dundas, while the Lockport's "Amabel Member" dominates the escarpment north of Waterdown. The Amabel limestone, or marble, is one of Ontario's most popular building and decorative stones. The same rocks are also recorded in the Hudson Bay Lowlands by up to 150 metres of limestones and dolostones belonging to the Ekwan and Attawapiskat formations. These sediments contain rich fossil assemblages dominated by corals, bryozoans, ostracods, and brachiopods.

The Upper Silurian Period: The development of extensive organic reefs and the subsidence of the sea floor was followed by the deposition of saline sediments within confined basins. In the Great Lakes Lowlands, the Appalachian and Michigan basins were filled with more than 500 metres of salts, anhydrites, gypsum, shale, and limestones belonging to the Salina and Berti-Bass Islands formations. The Salina beds are mined for gypsum near Hagersville and for salt at Windsor and Goderich. To the north, in the Hudson Bay Lowlands, more than 250 metres of sandstones, siltstones, shales, and dolostones of the Kenogami River formation were deposited into broad shallow seas. The saline nature of these Upper Silurian seas provided a most unsuitable habitat for marine life.

The Lower Devonian Period: This period witnessed the creation of a low-lying continent and the temporary withdrawal of the sea from much of Ontario. The rise and fall of this continent in the Great Lakes Lowlands is marked by the near-shore Oriskany sandstone and marine Bois Blanc limestone formations. Their combined thickness in the Appalachian basin is less than 20 metres, while the Bois Blanc is more than 60 metres thick in the Michigan basin. The transition from sea to land, and back to sea again, is illustrated in the Hudson Bay Lowlands by more than 100 metres of limestones, dolostones, sandstones, and shales of the Stooping River and Sextant formations. The continental Sextant beds are noted for their fossil land plants, while the Oriskany, Bois Blanc, and Stooping River beds are noted for their prominent large brachiopods and rugose corals, and their less prominent bryozoans, ostracods, cephalopods, and trilobites.

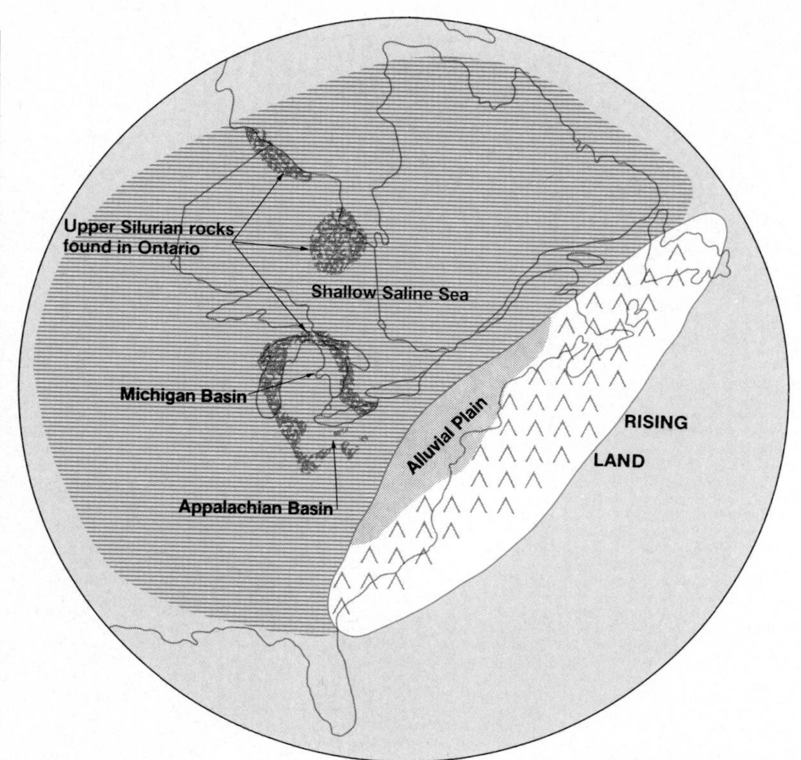

Upper Silurian Paleogeography (about 400 million years ago).

The Middle Devonian Period: Shallow seas had re-advanced across the continent, creating stable carbonate platforms and complex organic reefs. These seas are recorded in the Great Lakes Lowlands by the Onondaga, Detroit River, and Dundee limestones and dolostones, and in the Hudson Bay Lowlands by the Kwataboahegan,

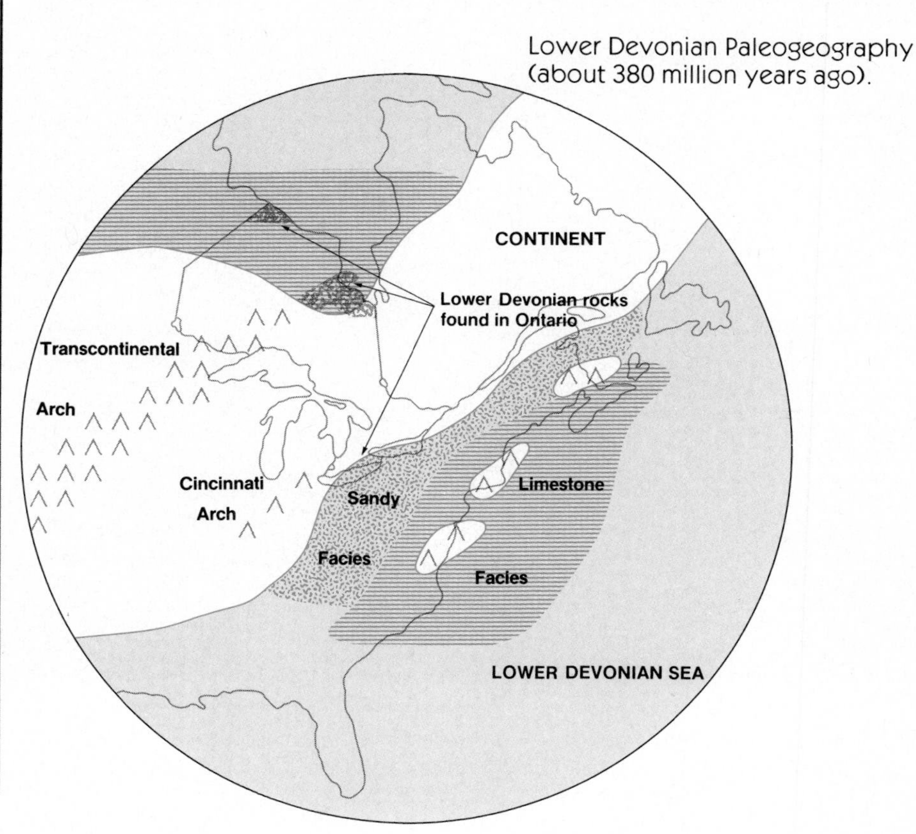

Lower Devonian Paleogeography (about 380 million years ago).

Cliff showing Kettle Point formation on Georgian Bay southwest of Grand Bend. In the foreground is a "kettle" that has rolled out of the eroding dark shales. Kettles, made of limestone, are round structures built by a sequential chemical growth process that is not fully understood. LARRY LAMB

Moose River, and Murray Island limestones. At the end of the Middle Devonian, the old Taconic Mountains once again began to rise from the sea. These renewed mountains, now called the Acadian Mountains, were then eroded, and a mixture of shales and limestones was deposited across Ontario. In the south, the Algonquin arch and Appalachian and Michigan basins were blanketed by the Hamilton formation, while in the north, the Williams Island formation was laid down in the James basin. In the Great Lakes and Hudson Bay lowlands, respectively, Middle Devonian sediments reached thicknesses of more than 250 and 420 metres. These sediments preserve abundant stromatolites, rugose corals, brachiopods, and lesser amounts of peleycpods, gastropods, crinoids, trilobites, fish, and other animals.

The Upper Devonian Period: This period was dominated by the uplift of the Acadian Mountains where the Appalachians now stand. From the base of these mountains, plains and deltas were constructed towards the sea. Farther offshore, shales were deposited into shallow muddy waters. These offshore sediments are recorded in the Great Lakes Lowlands by the rocks of the Kettle Point and Port Lambton shale formations and in the James Bay basin by the Long Rapids shale formation. These marine sediments are characterized by distinctive conodonts, brachiopods, and by abundant plant spores.

The Mesozoic Era

During the Mesozoic Era, some 210 to 60 million years ago, the area now occupied by North America was transformed from an expansive sea to a vast continent. The late Paleozoic and the early Mesozoic, or Triassic Period, was dominated by the construction and erosion of the Appalachian Mountains along the continent's east coast. The construction of these mountains and

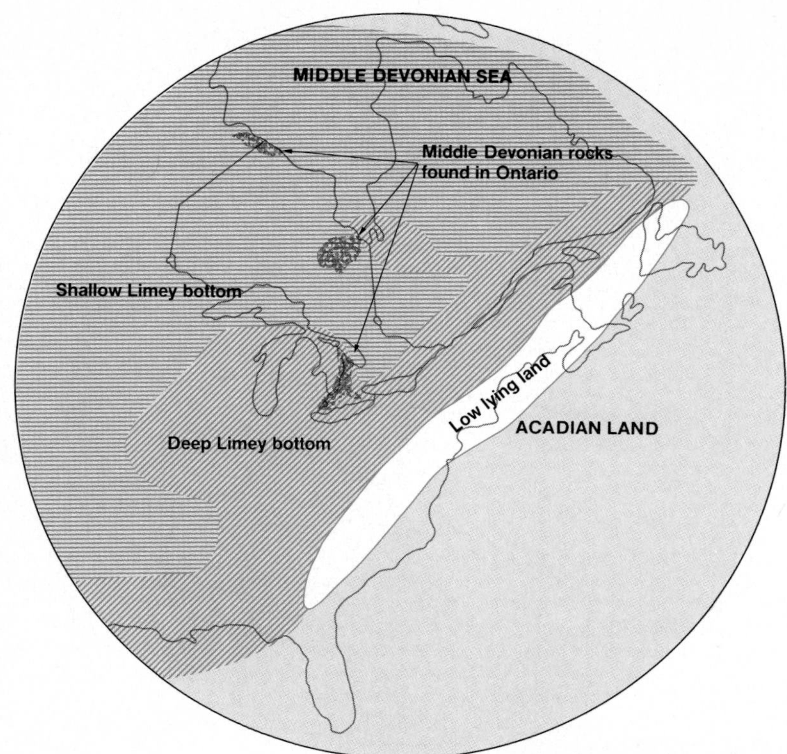

Middle Devonian Paleogeography (about 370 million years ago).

the closing of the Atlantic Ocean was initiated about 250 million years ago in the late Paleozoic, when North America collided with land that today is Europe and North Africa. At the same time, lowlands rose across all of Ontario and across much of central North America. Far to the west, offshore volcanic islands emerged from the sea where the Rocky Mountains now stand. In the succeeding Jurassic Period, a rift began to separate America from Europe and North Africa about 180 million years ago, creating a new Atlantic Ocean. Seas between the low, eastern lands in North America and the western volcanic islands deposited marine sediments over much of the Canadian prairies and the

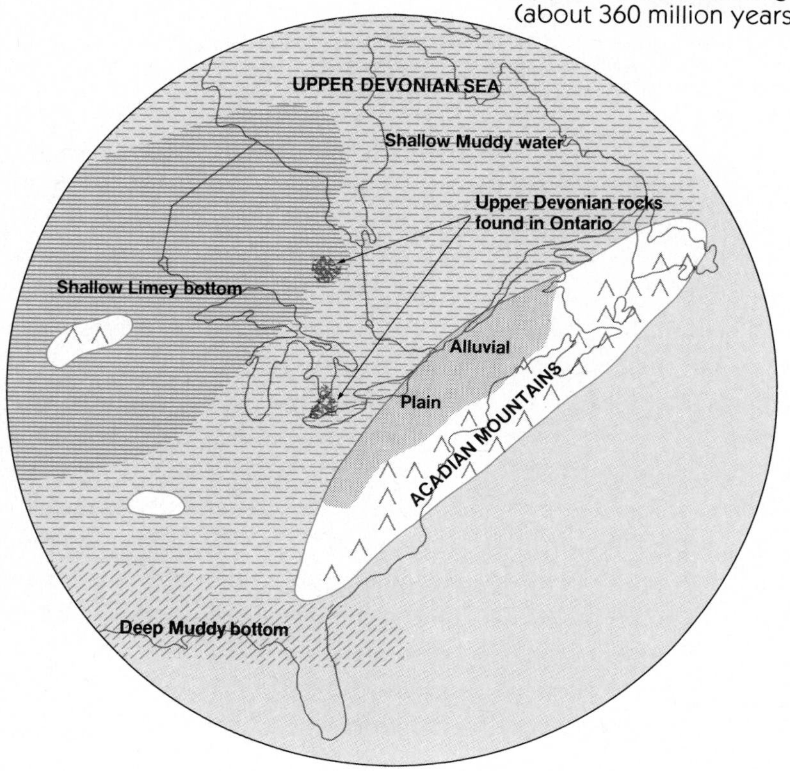

Upper Devonian Paleogeography (about 360 million years ago).

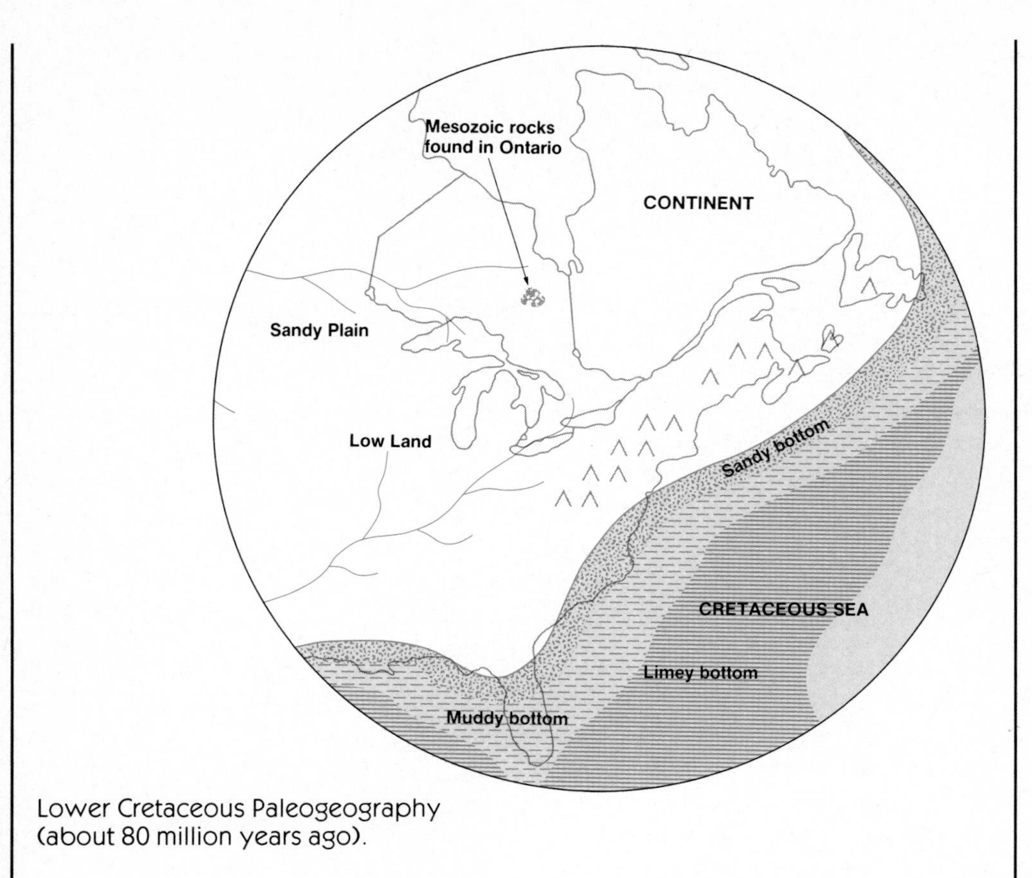

Lower Cretaceous Paleogeography
(about 80 million years ago).

central and western United States. In the late Mesozoic, or Cretaceous Period, the Atlantic continued to expand, the Cordilleran Mountains replaced the western volcanic islands, the intercontinental sea retreated, and the new continent of North America was born.

Most of Ontario was above the seas during the entire Mesozoic Era. The only evidence of the dramatic events of the surrounding enlargement of the continent is the deposition of the Mattagami soft coals, silica sands, and fire clays in the James basin. These sediments record the presence of the low Cretaceous continent and its evolving plant life. The Mesozoic, and indeed the Cenozoic right up to today was a time of erosion rather than burial. Because of this long period of erosion, the Precambrian foundation of the continent and the ancient Paleozoic deposits lie largely unmasked at Ontario's surface to reveal the geological handiwork of the ages.

• SCIENCE • EXCURSION •

Rock Cycle

John B. Theberge

Nothing is immutable, not even rocks, Earth, or the universe. But they change slowly in the scale of human time. Even the 2.9-billion-year-old granites on the Precambrian Shield were once magma inside the Earth and they will be sediments in the sea a very long time from now.

The rock cycle is in slow gear, except for hot spots – volcanoes and oceanic ridges. Nonetheless, cycle it is. Most fundamental is *basaltic magma*, seething in the Earth's liquid mantle, oozing from oceanic ridges, spewing from volcanoes. It cools on the Earth's surface as ocean floor, or coats the sides of volcanoes and flows to the valleys below. Now basalt rock, it consists of about half silicon dioxide. Silicon, forming 28 per cent of the Earth's crust, is the second most common element, after oxygen at 46 per cent. The silicon dioxide in basalt is tied up in more complex forms as the mineral called *plagioclase feldspar* (a mineral is a combination of elements; a rock is a mixture of minerals). Plagioclase feldspar occurs in both a sodium variety, $NaAlSi_3O_8$, and a calcium variety, $CaAl_2Si_2O_8$. These, and other forms of feldspar, are the most common minerals of the Earth's crust. They are all aluminium silicates, taking advantage of aluminium, the third most common element in the crust at 8 per cent.

Basalt also contains about 10 per cent iron and magnesium oxides, as well as a mixture of silica with calcium, magnesium, or iron. With no quartz mineral, it is dark or black in colour. Normally a hard, fine-grained rock, it may also occur as a cindery form, having been affected by volcanic gases during its formation.

Basalt is the most common volcanic rock, but there are others. Rhyolite is lighter coloured and contains quartz. Obsidian, or natural glass, has the same chemical composition as rhyolite but cooled more quickly. Pumice, too, is chemically the same but is sponge-like, having formed while full of gases.

Basaltic magma, then, is the source of volcanic rock. Another form of magma exists, however, called *granitic magma*. It is the source of granite rock, the stuff of continents. It is less dense than basalt, hence is responsible for continents riding on top of basalt "conveyor belts," and for their staying "afloat" across zones of subduction. Granitic magma forms in part directly from basaltic magma, through the settling by gravity and early crystallization of iron, magnesium, and the compounds of silica mixed with calcium, magnesium, iron, and plagioclase feldspar. What is left is granitic magma, with about 70 per cent silicon dioxide (compared with 50 per cent in basaltic magma), but only 2 per cent iron and magnesium oxides (compared with 10 per cent). It is an acidic rock, whereas basalt is basic.

This igneous magma does not extrude or erupt onto the surface but is exposed as cooled-off, solid rock after the erosion of overlying rock. Its crystals, in consequence of this slow cooling, are larger. In this slower cooling, quartz, the pure form of silicon dioxide, usually forms. Quartz comes in very small or very large crystals, and, with other minerals, may form ornamental stones such as amethysts, garnets, jasper, agates, and many others.

Granite, the most common igneous rock, consists of about 60 per cent potassium feldspar known as *orthoclase* ($KAlSi_3O_8$), 30 per cent quartz, and usually some sheet-like micas which are also oxides of aluminium and silicon. Granites are light coloured – greys or pinks depending upon the amount and type of feldspar and its mineral content.

Another igneous rock is *diabase*, which is more like basalt in that it has no quartz, is rich in iron and plagioclase feldspar, and is basic rather than acidic. It is classed as igneous, however, because of its coarse crystals, the result of slow cooling before being exposed by erosion of overlying rock, rather than being extruded onto the surface as lava.

Igneous magma may form not only from basaltic magma, but from a redevelopment of magma from metamorphic rocks deep in the cores of mountains. Heat and pressure may make these existing rocks molten again. This process may account for *batholiths* of igneous rock, the exposed cores of ancient mountains now standing up above the relief of the rest of the landscape.

Sedimentary rocks are formed by erosion or dissolution of existing rocks. Shale is most common worldwide, making up about 40 per cent of all sedimentary rocks. Shale consists primarily of clays mixed with some fine-grained quartz and hardened into rock. Clays that contribute to shale, or remain in soil, all consist of aluminium silicates in very fine particles that are water resistant. They originated primarily from granite rocks as the weathering products of feldspars.

Other sedimentary rocks, most notably limestone, or calcium carbonate, precipitate out of a dissolved state in water and settle to the bottom. Limestone may crystallize in seawater due to changes in temperature or pressure, or contact with other minerals. It may also form from the shells of marine organisms such as corals, molluscs, and certain protozoa. Dolomite is magnesium-impregnated limestone, and is more weather-resistant, hence its place as caprock at Niagara Falls and much of the Niagara Escarpment. Gypsum, a calcium sulfate, is an evaporate from water, as is common salt.

Metamorphic rocks are pre-existing rocks that have been altered by heat and pressure without melting. The parent rock becomes plastic but not molten. Metamorphic rocks may exhibit different mineral contents or chemical compositions from their parent.

Metamorphism may be partial or complete. If partial, relics of the parent rock may still be visible as banding, or even as fossils. For example, one of Ontario's most abundant metamorphic rocks, called *gneiss*, has a banded structure that survived its metamorphism from sandstones and other sedimentary rocks. In this case, metamorphism recrystallized the mineral present in the original layers, but did not destroy the layers. Other gneisses, from igneous rock, recrystallize and form layers of quartz, feldspar, and mica, as well as new minerals such as hornblendes. Other metamorphic rocks of sedimentary origin are: slate (from shale), marble (from recrystallized limestone), and quartzite (from sandstone).

Thus, the four major rock types – volcanic, igneous, sedimentary, and metamorphic – transform into one another in a slow dance over vast periods of time.

Glacial Landforms

R. J. Davidson

Drumlin east of Cambridge. Its streamlined shape reflects the direction of ice movement with the steep slope pointing in the direction of the origin of the glacier. IAN MCKENZIE

On their travels back and forth across Ontario, the continental glaciers scoured the Earth's surface and built enduring surface landforms out of glacial drift – the sediment laid down by ice. This glacial drift averages twenty-five to thirty metres in depth over southern Ontario's bedrock. On its surface are moraines, drumlins, eskers, kettles, kames, and a variety of outwash features that together represent the footsteps of the glaciers.

Moraines are hilly landforms and broken topography of a variety of shapes and sizes. They consist of unsorted glacial drift, or *till*, made from ground-up rock ranging from house-sized boulders to microscopic particles of clay. *Ground moraines* are vast, wrinkled sheets of glacial till which were deposited beneath the glacier. *End moraines* are linear ridges of glacial drift deposited along the sides or at the terminus of the glacier lobes. An *interlobate moraine* consists of two end moraines deposited side-by-side by the margins of two adjacent glacier lobes.

Many of the moraines of southern Ontario surround "Ontario Island," the high land that was ice-free during the Mackinaw Interstadial and Port Huron Stadial, 13,000 to 12,000 years ago. This land lay between the Huron and Erie-Ontario glacial lobes. These lobes pushed east and southeast, and

Esker, marking a stream within the glacier, Esquesing Township. NIAGARA ESCARPMENT COMMISSION

north and northwest respectively to build moraines at their margins.

Drumlins are long, "whale-backed" hills, often occurring over broad areas, each drumlin with a similar orientation. Drumlin formation is associated with ground moraines. Drumlins formed with, and in the direction of, the glacier's movement, by the gouging action of ice on the sides of the forming drumlin and the plastering of glacial till on top. The oldest drumlin field, between Guelph and Orangeville, was formed by the northwest advance of the Erie-Ontario ice lobe during the Port Bruce Stadial, 14,000 years ago. The rich fields of drumlins across Northumberland, Peterborough, and Victoria counties formed later from minor northward advances of the Ontario lobe that occupied what is now the area of Lake Ontario. All together there are more than four thousand drumlins in southern Ontario.

Eskers look like abandoned railway embankments. They were formed from melt-water streams carrying gravels and sands in crevasses or tunnels in the ice. When the ice melted, the streambed of gravel was simply dumped on top of the land. Eskers are most common north of Stratford and of Peterborough, and in association with drumlins from Belleville to Lindsay.

Kames and kettles are often found in association with esker ridges. *Kames* are cone-shaped hills formed by a waterfall of sediment-laden melt-water falling through crevices in the glacier, or over its lip, or formed in some other partially defined way at the base of the glacier. *Kettles* are circular depressions created by ice-blocks left stranded and buried by moraine material as the glacier retreated. When the ice melted, the surface sediments collapsed. Most of these places today are small, circular lakes or bogs.

At the glacier's margin, melt-waters carved channels, filled spillways with sand and gravel, and built outwash plains and terraces. Proglacial lakes formed in front of the retreating glacier. While the northern shores of these lakes were bounded by the glacier, the southern shores were carved into the glacial sediments. As the glaciers retreated, a succession of shorelines and drainage outlets were created. Many of these lakes are noted for their varved (mineral-mottled) clays, with repetitive layers of thin clay and thick sand illustrating the winter (clay) and summer (sand) accumulation of sediments within the lake. Like growth rings of a tree, these seasonal couplets can be used to trace the local history of the lake and the retreating glacier.

A kame – a conical hill built by glacial melt-water falling from an ice-lip – at Baden Hills near Waterloo. LARRY LAMB

Other outwash features include deltas built up from glacial melt-water, and flat plains where standing water behind ice-dammed lakes laid down thick beds of fine clay sediments.

These, with other less common glacial landforms, form the basis of the topography of southern and, in places, northern Ontario.

The Wrinkled Surface
Surficial Geology
R. J. Davidson

Part A: Moulded by Ice

Ontario's surface features are the product of its pre-existing bedrock topography and the constant modification of this topography by natural elements. The landscapes created by these elements can be traced back to the Tertiary Period, from 63 million to 1 million years ago. This time was marked by the uplift of North America, the construction of the Rocky Mountains, the development of vast inland lakes at the base of these mountains, and by the creation of extensive badlands, canyons, and river systems. In Ontario, the Niagara, Onondaga, Red Rock, and other escarpments were forming. The Canadian Shield was stripped of its Paleozoic and Mesozoic bedrock cover and, as a result of this erosion and weathering, great volumes of gravel, sand, silt, and clay were produced, just as in earlier erosional periods. But this time the erosional debris was not buried and pressured into stone. It has remained on the surface, to be pushed around by ice, wind, and water, where it creates the "surficial geology" on top of the bedrock.

Tertiary Rivers

During the long Tertiary Period, a complex network of rivers spread out across the land. The greatest of these, the Laurentian River, passed over and eroded the soft shales occupying the basins of Lake Michigan, Lake Huron, Georgian Bay, Lake Simcoe, and Lake Ontario on its way to the St. Lawrence River and the Atlantic Ocean. Major tributaries joined the Laurentian through Saginaw Bay to Lake Huron, and from Lake Erie through the Erigan valley, while smaller tributaries flowed through now-buried bedrock valleys in the Wingham, Walkerton, Ipperwash, and Dundas areas. As the river system matured, drainage from Lake Erie shifted eastward from the Erigan valley at Short Hills Provincial Park to form the Niagara River, Gorge, and Falls. In the river's headwaters, runoff was largely responsible for the creation of the Niagara Escarpment, Ontario's most spectacular and well-known surface feature.

In the Pleistocene, the last 1 million years, these river valleys and escarpments were accentuated by multiple advancing and retreating glaciers, and in many places they were buried by more than one hundred metres of glacial sediments. This landscape evolution continues today as wind, water, and gravity help carve Ontario's escarpment ridges and Great Lakes drainage system.

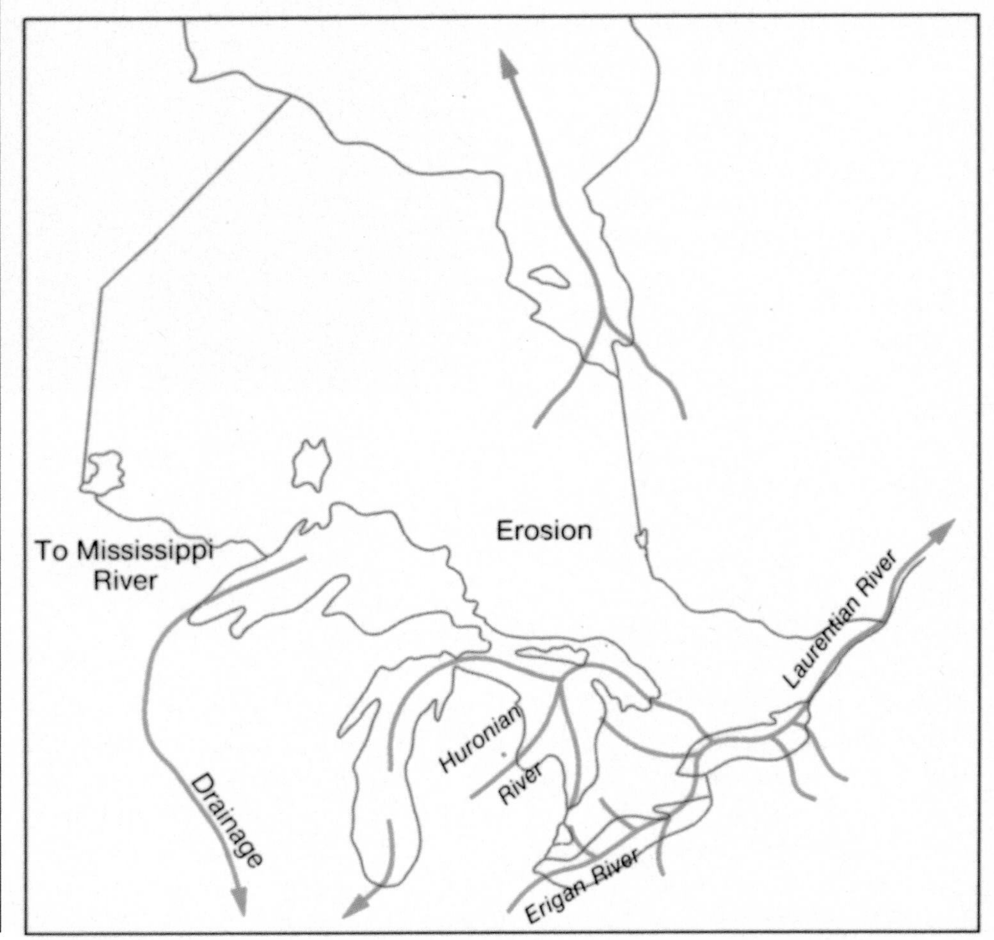

Tertiary Rivers (63 million to 1 million years ago).

Early Glaciation – Illinoian

The first evidence of glaciation in Ontario is marked by the occurrence of glacial deposits called *till*, consisting of gravel, sand, and clay. Ontario's oldest tills are found resting on the bedrock surfaces at Toronto and in the Moose River basin. These tills were most probably deposited during the *Illinoian glaciation* more than 120,000 years ago.

At Toronto, the Illinoian-aged York till may be observed at the Don Valley Brickyard in East York, in a railway cut near Woodbridge, and from time to time within excavations at construction sites in the city. The most noteworthy of these occurrences, however, is the one at the Brickyard. This locality is recognized by the international scientific community as the benchmark for this rare deposit. It is also the only place where the York till can be seen in association with older bedrock and younger surface sediments.

In the Moose River basin, three tills separated by two proglacial lake deposits have been observed within the eroded banks of the Missinaibi, Pivabiska, and Soweska rivers, along Coal Creek, and at a few other scattered localities. This multiple sequence of glacial sediments probably represents minor advances and retreats of the ice front in the western portion of the basin. The occurrence of one till in the eastern portion of the basin suggests the long-standing presence of the glacier. The Illinoian tills and proglacial lake deposits of the Moose River basin may be observed and studied within nature reserve zones in the Missinaibi River Provincial Park.

The Illinoian Glaciation (about 120,000 years ago).

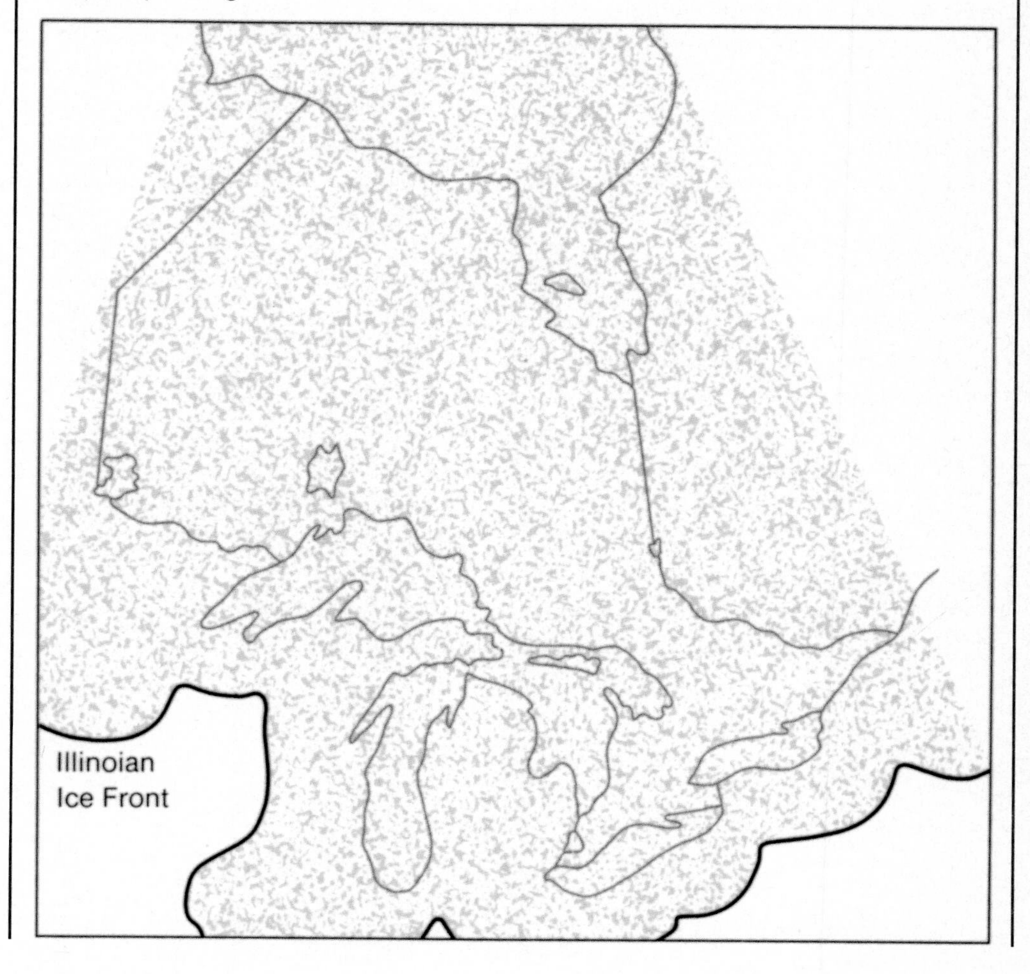

Sangamonian Interglaciation

The Illinoian tills exposed at Toronto and in the Moose River basin are both overlain by nonglacial sediments. This fact suggests the retreat of the continental glacier and the return of warm weather. The resulting temperate, terrestrial environment, the Sangamonian interglacial, occurred over 75,000 years ago.

The most famous nonglacial sediments in Ontario, and perhaps North America, are those found at the Don Valley Brickyard. Here, up to eight metres of stratified clays, silts, and sands from the Don formation have produced more than seventy species of fossil plants, including the remains of tree trunks, branches, and perfectly preserved leaves. The Don formation has also produced more than forty species of clams and snails and parts of giant beaver, groundhog, deer, bison, and bear. Carolinian plant species like black oak, shagbark hickory, osage orange, basswood, sycamore, black cherry, hop hornbeam, and pawpaw suggest a much warmer climate. Further, a number of clam species have been found that presently inhabit the Mississippi River and Gulf of Mexico, suggesting a direct link between the Lake Ontario basin and the gulf coast.

These sediments and fossils have been the subject of almost one hundred years of observation and study by scientists, educators, and students from all over the world. They have provided a focus for Pleistocene studies and have helped to shape our understanding of North America's glacial history.

In the Moose River basin, nonglacial sediments are found in the banks of the Missinaibi, Mattagami, Abitibi, Little Abitibi, and other smaller rivers and creeks. These sediments, which have been named the Missinaibi formation, trace the retreat of the Illinoian glacier and the subsequent inundation of marine seas over a land depressed by the vast weight of the glacier. They also record the rebound of the land causing a recession of the sea and development of an ancient river system, as well as the evolution of an extensive boreal forest, and finally the deposition of cold fresh-water lakes prior to the onslaught of the Wisconsinan continental glacier. Localities recording the details of these events are protected within nature reserve zones in Missinaibi River Provincial Park.

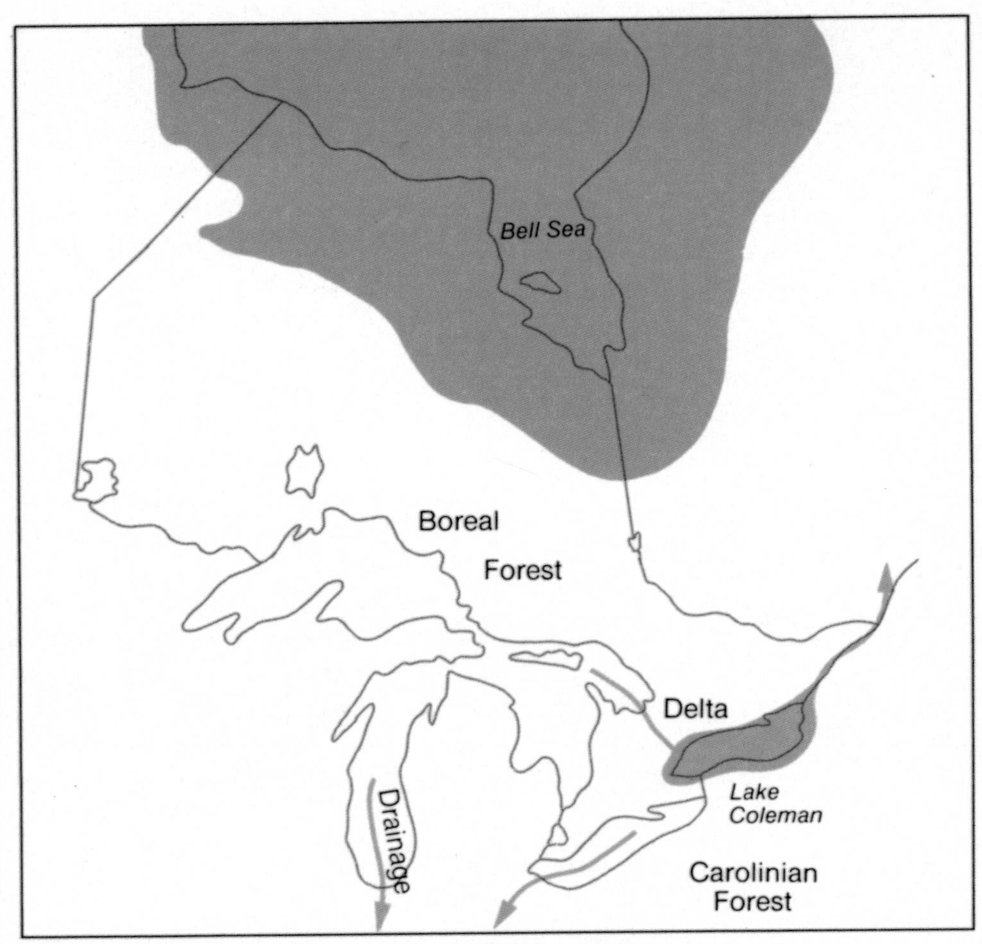

The Sangamonian Interglacial (about 120,000 to 70,000 years ago).

The Last Great Glaciation – Wisconsinan

Ontario's landscape is dominated by one of the world's most spectacular collections of glacial features. The complex history of these features has been painstakingly pieced together over the last 150 years by the Geological Survey of Canada, the Ontario Geological Survey, various state geological surveys, and independent university researchers. Their efforts have culminated in the systematic organization of Ontario's glacial features based upon the successive advances and retreats of the last great Wisconsinan glacier. This glaciation has been divided into early and late cold substages separated by a relatively warmer middle substage. These substages have been divided into stadials and interstadials and, in turn, into phases and intervals to denote successively smaller advances and retreats of the ice.

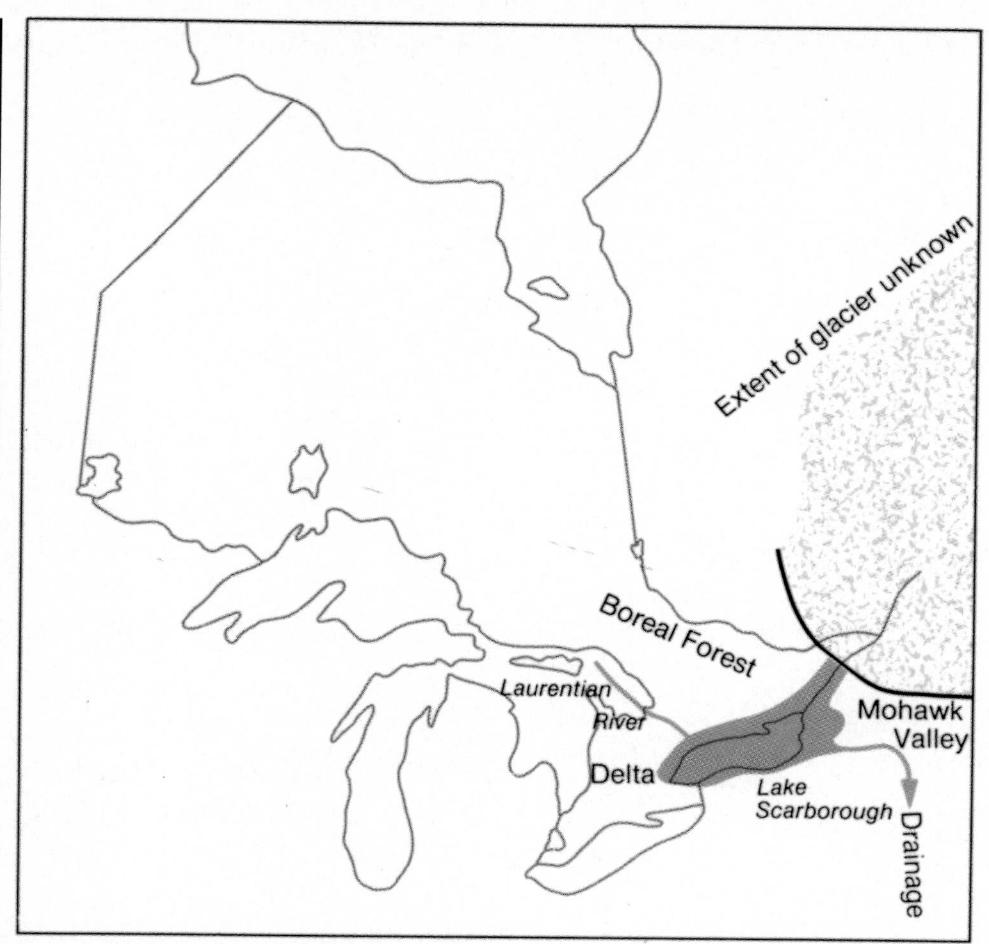

The Nicolet Stadial (about 70,000 years ago).

NICOLET STADIAL

The first evidence of Wisconsinan glaciation in Ontario is recorded by till in the St. Lawrence Lowlands and by a large delta in Lake Ontario's western basin. These sediments were deposited more than 70,000 years ago during the Nicolet stadial. At this time, the advancing glacier blocked the St. Lawrence River, deposited the Beçancour and Johnsville till, and forced water back into the Lake Ontario basin creating proglacial Lake Scarborough. This lake probably overflowed and drained south through the Mohawk valley. Rivers flowing into Lake Scarborough through the Laurentian valley deposited extensive deltaic sediments, including the numerous remains of clams, snails, insects, and the abundant pollen from black spruce, tamarack, balsam fir, sweet gale, wild strawberry, and many other boreal plants. These species suggest a climate about 6°C cooler than that of today. The deltaic sediments, called the Scarborough formation, are well exposed at the Scarborough Bluffs, the Don Valley Brickyard, and at the Woodbridge railroad cut.

ST. PIERRE INTERSTADIAL

The Nicolet stadial was followed by the St. Pierre interstadial about 67,000 years ago. By this time, the St. Lawrence River had been freed of glacial ice, and the Great Lakes once again drained to the sea. Lake Scarborough gave way to an unnamed low-level lake about six metres below present Lake Ontario. In the lake's western basin, rivers cut and filled valleys in the Scarborough delta with sediments, the remains of bison, elk, black bears, and musk-oxen, and pollen from pine, spruce, birch, oak, various grasses, and ferns. The river sediments are called the Pottery Road formation and may be observed at the Don Valley Brickyard and at some locations along the Scarborough Bluffs. These and related sediments at St. Pierre, Quebec, indicate that the temperature was 2°C to 4°C colder than it is today.

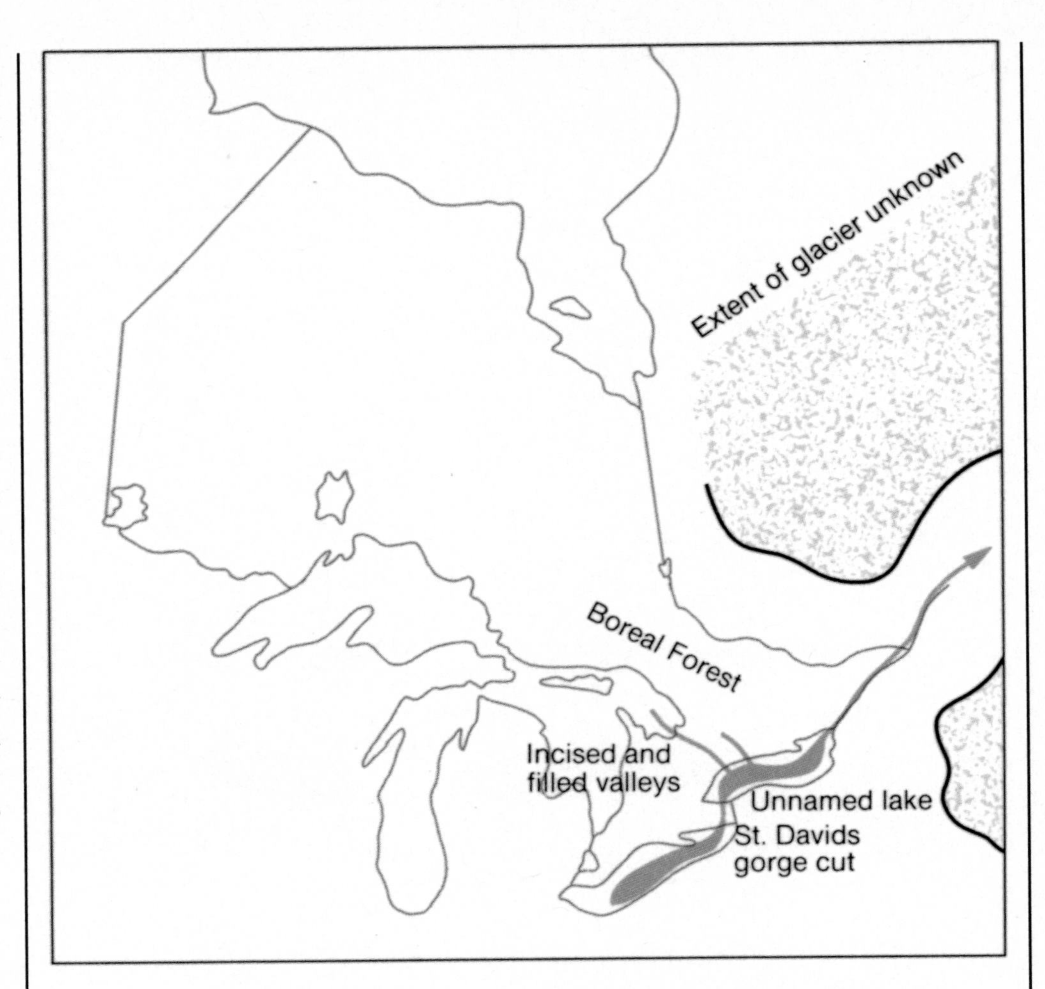

The St. Pierre Interstadial (about 67,000 years ago).

GUILDWOOD STADIAL

The St. Pierre interstadial ended about 55,000 years ago with a major re-advance of the ice front during the Guildwood stadial. The Wisconsinan glacier moved southward covering all of Ontario and many parts of the north-central United States. In Ontario, the advance is traced by the Sunnybrook till exposed at the Scarborough Bluffs and in the river valleys near Toronto, as well as a sequence of buried tills in Waterloo County, the Canning till along the Nith River, and the Lower Bradtville till in the shore-cliffs near Port Talbot. The Guildwood stadial represents the maximum advance of the Early Wisconsinan glacier.

The Guildwood Stadial (about 55,000 years ago).

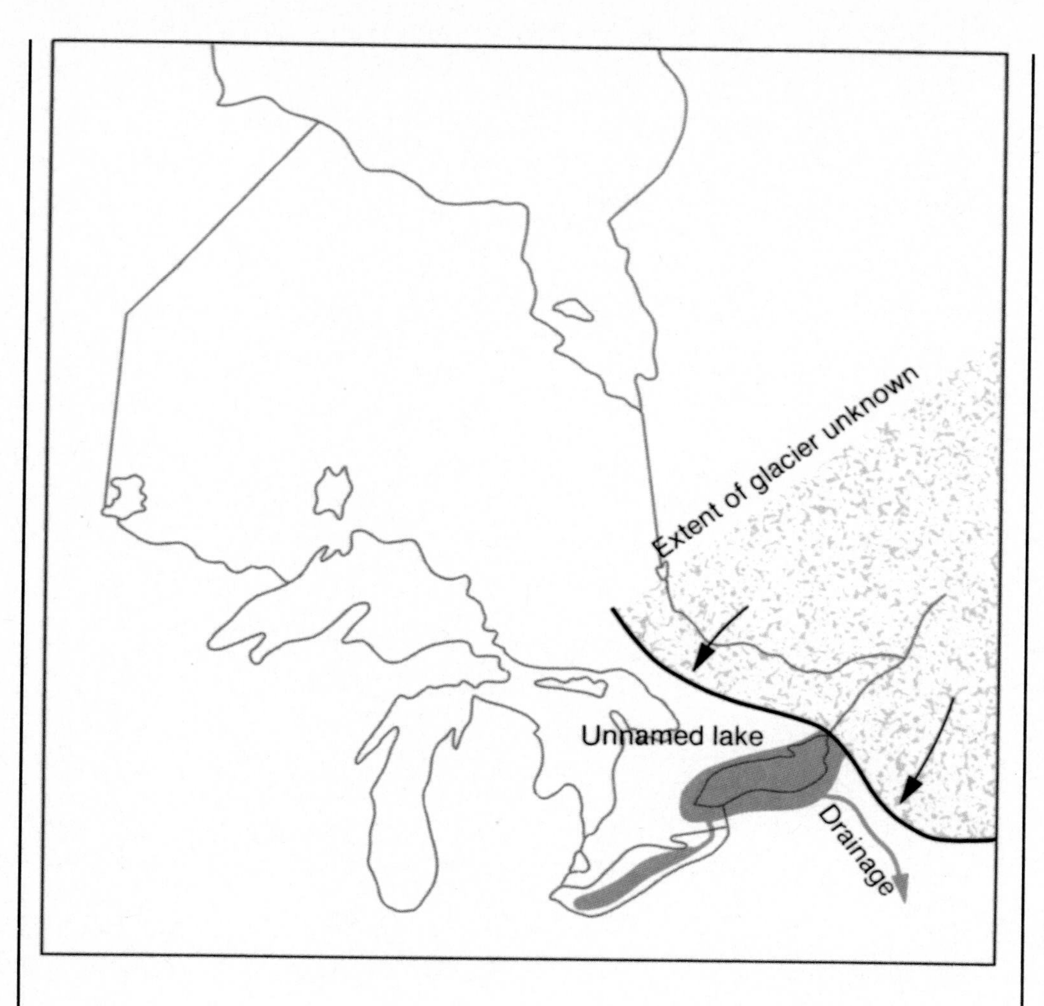

PORT TALBOT INTERSTADIAL

A major retreat of Guildwood ice occurred between 48,000 and 36,000 years ago during the Port Talbot interstadial. This recession occurred in three stages. An early warm interval is recorded by green lake clays exposed in the Erie shore-cliffs near Port Talbot. A middle cold phase is recorded by the Dunwich till north of Lake Erie and associated varved (stratified) clays in the Erie shore-cliffs. A late warm interval is also recorded in the Erie shore-cliffs by lake silts, beach gravels, and peat. The Port Talbot sediments, called the Tyrconnell formation, are rich in pollen from jack pine, black spruce, white spruce, birch, willow, and alder. The major difference between the two warmer intervals is the relative absence of oak from the late interval.

The Port Talbot Interstadial (about 48,000 to 36,000 years ago).

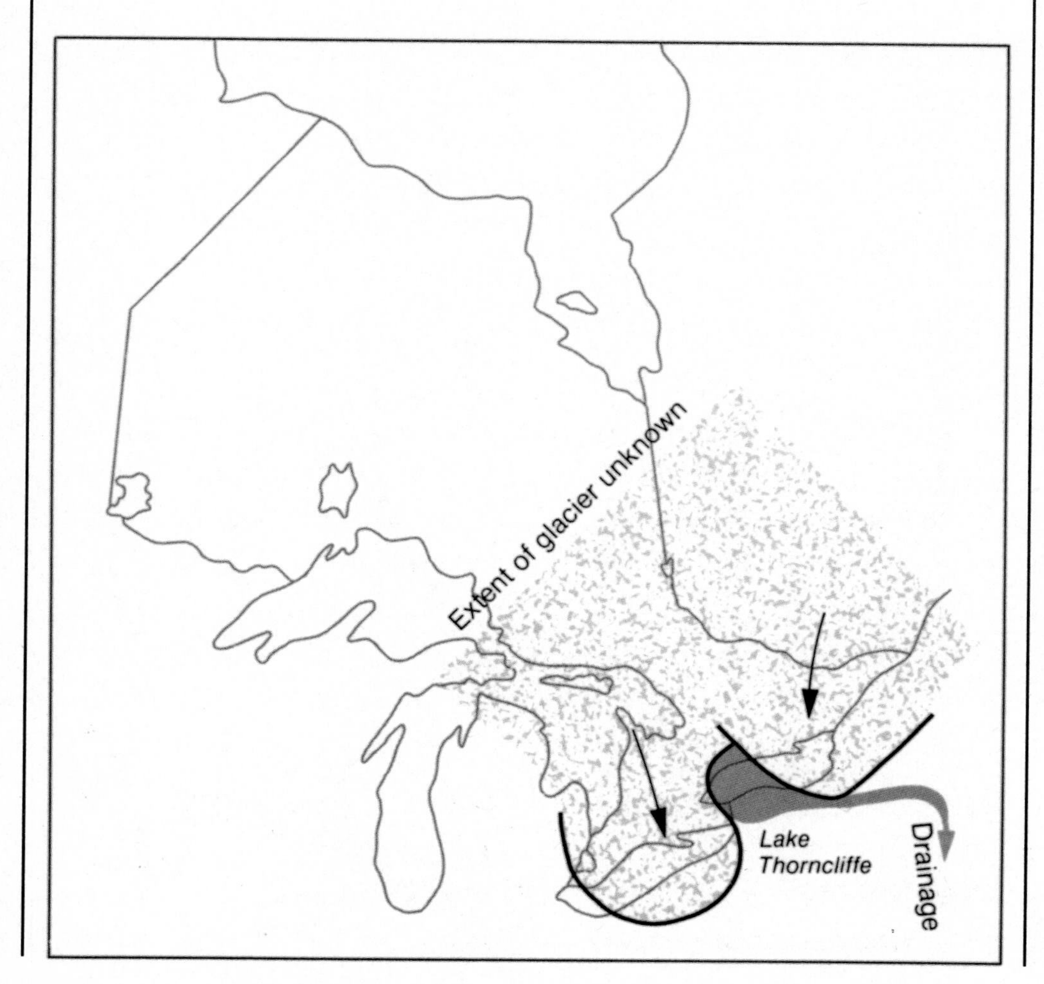

CHERRYTREE STADIAL

The Port Talbot interstadial was terminated by the re-advance of ice between 35,000 and 28,000 years ago during the Cherrytree stadial. Cherrytree ice covered most of Ontario and parts of the north-central United States. This re-advance is marked by the Southwold till in the Lake Erie shore-cliffs and the Conestoga till in the Region of Waterloo. It is also recorded in river valleys and shore-cliffs near Toronto by the Seminary and Meadowcliffe tills and the lake sediments of the Thorncliffe formation. These lake sediments contain few fossils but have provided boreal pollen, ostracods, molluscs, and the remains of grizzly bear and woolly mammoth.

The Cherrytree Stadial (about 35,000 to 28,000 years ago).

PLUM POINT INTERSTADIAL

The Cherrytree stadial gradually gave way to the warm climate of the Plum Point interstadial about 27,000 years ago. Again, the ice front retreated in stages. An early interval is recorded near Plum Point on Lake Erie by frost wedges in the Dunwich till and by the oxidation of the till's upper surface. It is represented at the Scarborough Bluffs by a sequence of massive and varved proglacial lake clays. A middle phase is recorded in the Scarborough Bluffs by a thin water-lain clay till. A late interval is also recorded at the Scarborough Bluffs by proglacial sands and varved clays. Near Plum Point, this interval is marked by the beach sands and gravel of the Wallacetown formation. The sediments at Plum Point are devoid of fossils, while at Scarborough a few fossils are found.

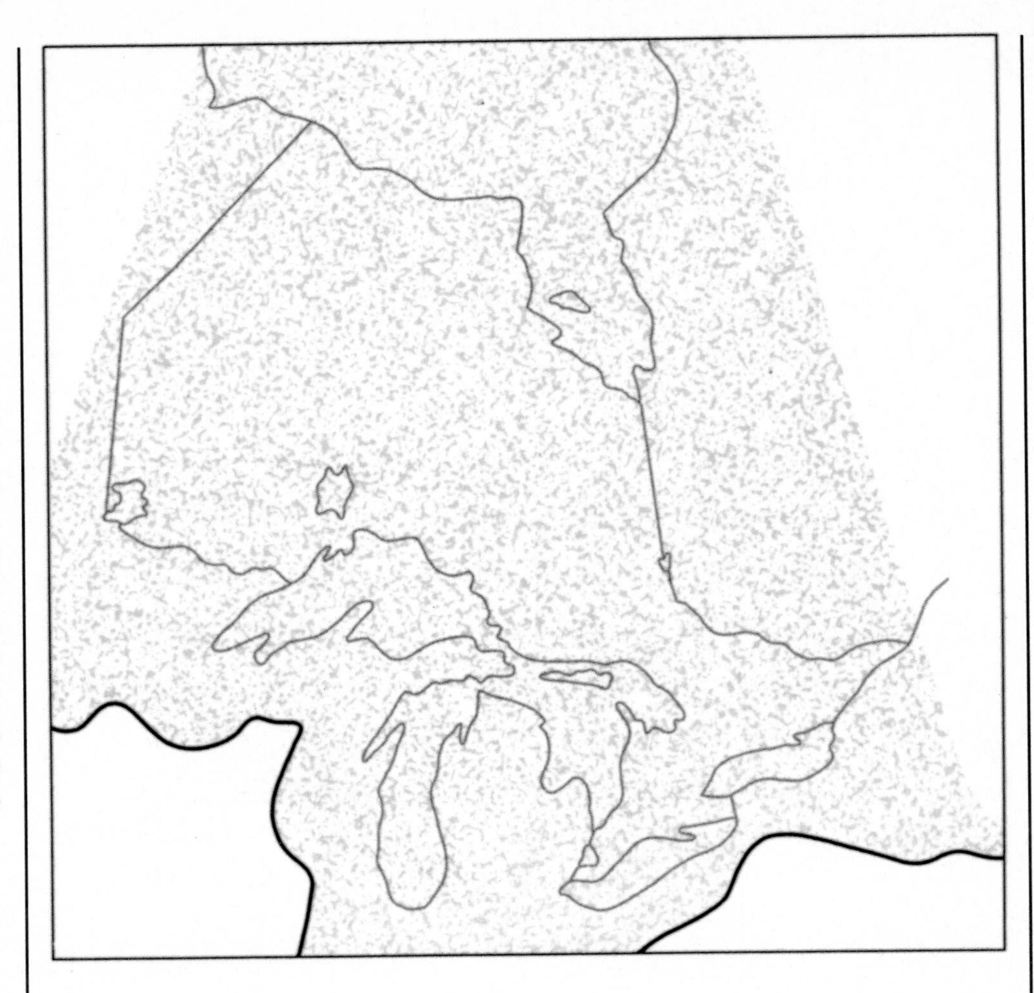

The Plum Point Interstadial (about 27,000 years ago).

NISSOURI STADIAL

The maximum southern advance of the Wisconsinan glacier occurred during the Nissouri stadial about 20,000 years ago. Re-advancing ice engulfed all of Ontario, Michigan, and parts of Wisconsin, Illinois, Ohio, Pennsylvania, and New York. In the St. Lawrence–Great Lakes Lowlands, Nissouri ice deposited the Gentilly till in the St. Lawrence valley, Leaside till at Toronto, and the Catfish Creek till at the stadial's benchmark in Nissouri Township, near London. The Catfish Creek till is also found in the core parts of the Blenheim, St. Thomas, and Dorchester moraines.

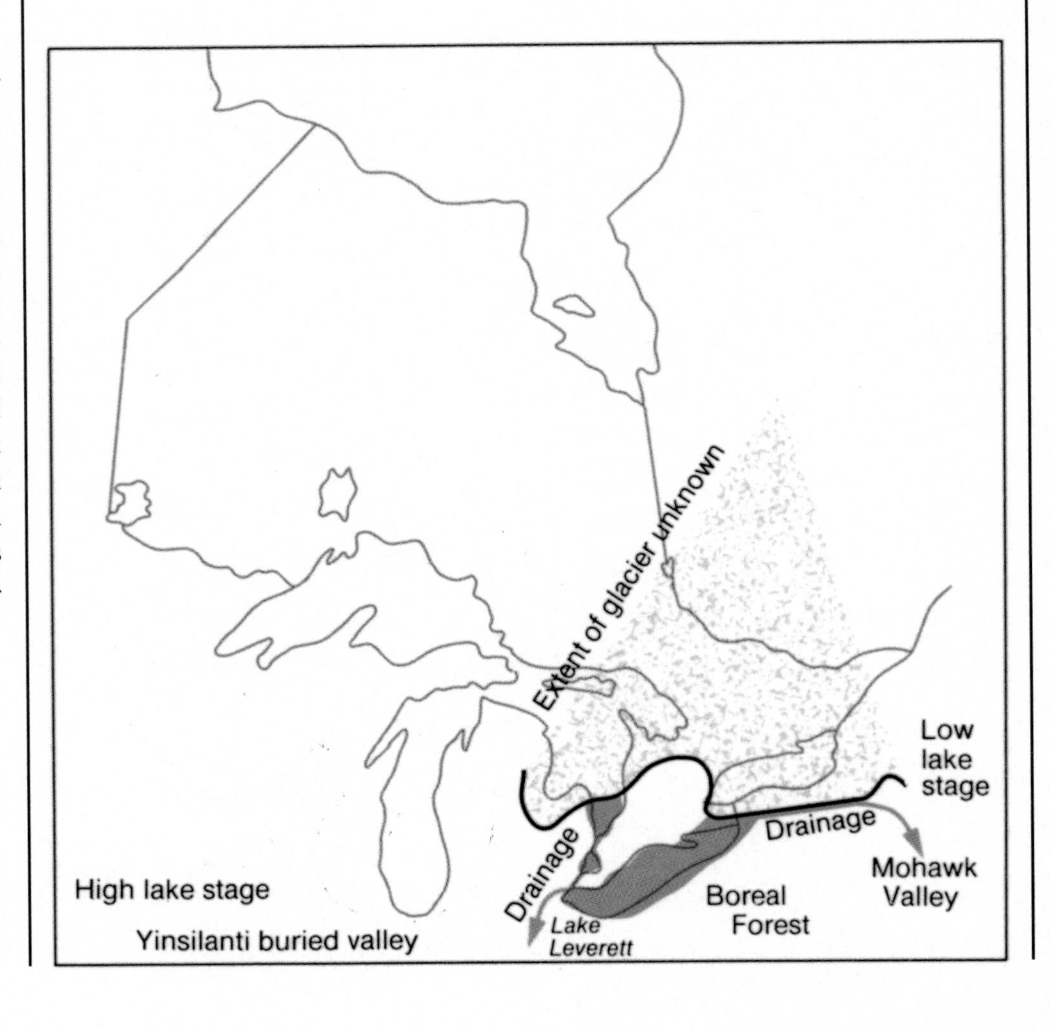

The Nissouri Stadial (about 28,000 to 23,000 years ago).

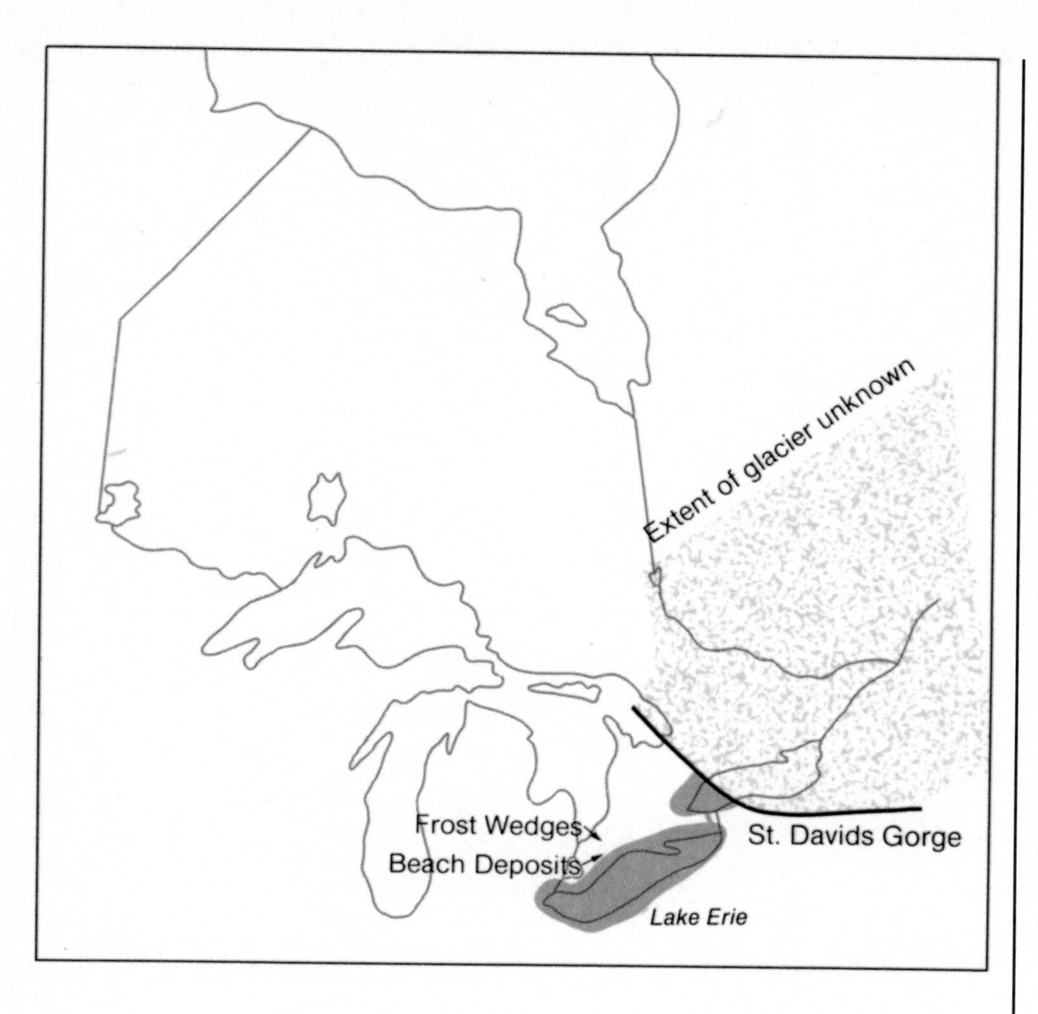

ERIE INTERSTADIAL

The retreat of Nissouri ice was followed about 15,000 years ago by the warmer climate of the Erie interstadial. At the interstadial's benchmark in the Lake Erie shore-cliffs, well-developed beach gravels and offshore lacustrine sands are found on top of the older Catfish Creek till. The lake responsible for these sediments, Lake Leverett, was three to four metres higher than Lake Erie and probably drained eastward. Beach deposits from a higher level of Lake Leverett have also been found to the north, near Sparta and London. This higher lake reached an elevation of 285 metres above sea level and may have drained west across Michigan through the now-buried Ypsilanti valley. Pollen retrieved from lake sediments at Wildwood Lake near St. Marys indicate a forest cover of pine, spruce, birch, alder, and oaks.

The Erie Interstadial (about 15,500 years ago).

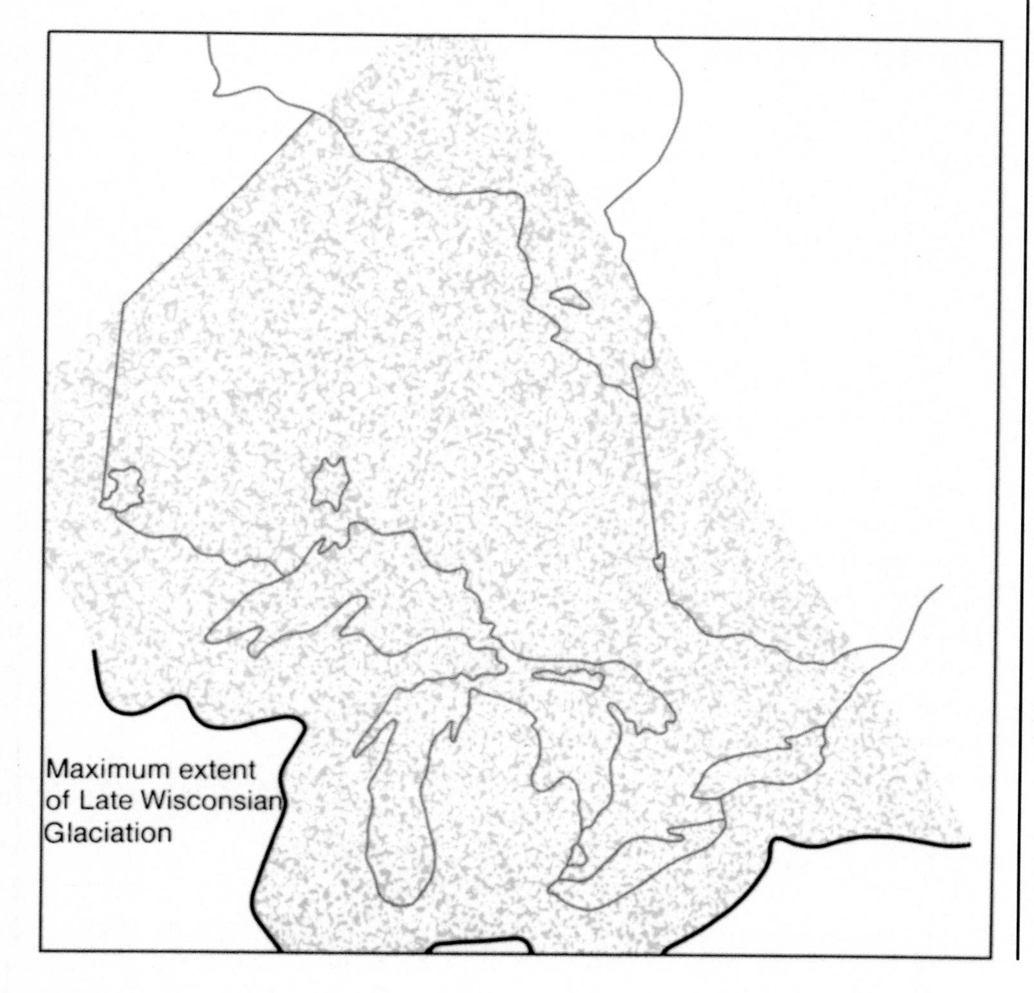

PORT BRUCE STADIAL

The Erie interstadial lakes were consumed about 14,000 years ago by ice re-advancing during the Port Bruce stadial. Rather than solely a re-advance of ice from the north, glaciers centred in the Lakes Erie, Ontario, Huron, and Georgian Bay basins expanded outward to cover all of Ontario and parts of the north-central United States. Each glacier deposited a unique set of tills and end moraines. From the northern edge of the Erie ice, the Port Stanley till and the Ingersoll, St. Thomas, Norwich, and Tillsonburg moraines were deposited. The north side of the Ontario basin ice deposited the Maryhill and Wentworth tills, parts of the Oak Ridges moraine north of Toronto, and the Paris, Galt, and Moffat moraines.

The Port Bruce Stadial (about 14,000 years ago).

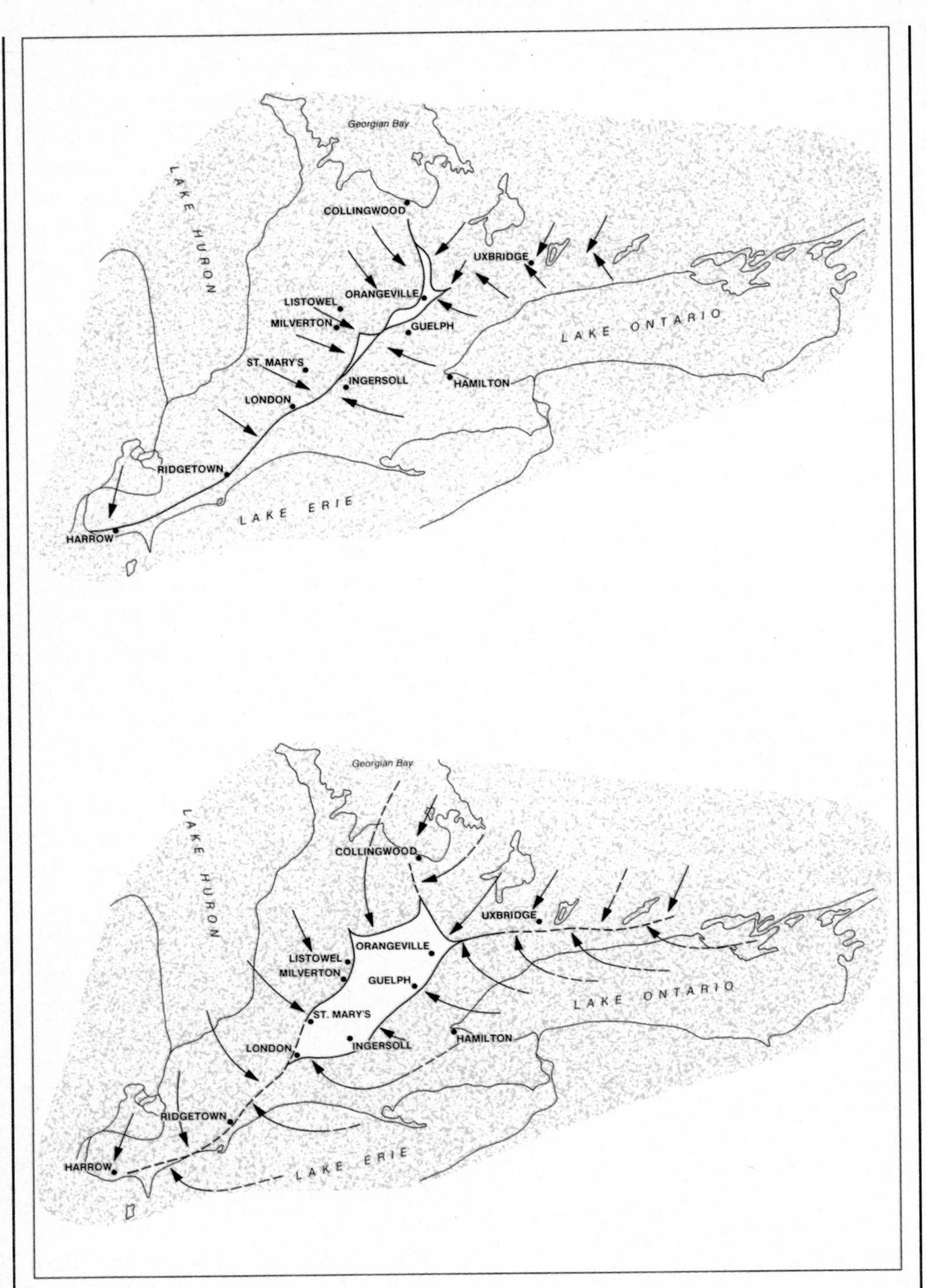

The upper map shows how the re-advance of ice during the Port Bruce Stadial came from the proto Great Lakes basins. Then, at the beginning of the Mackinaw Interstadial, the ice split across the higher central part of southern Ontario (melting back faster than it advanced), gradually opening to expose "Ontario Island."

South-moving ice from the Lake Simcoe basin laid down the Newmarket till and Singhampton moraine. East- and south-advancing Huron – Georgian Bay ice laid down the Stirton, Tavistock, Mornington, Stratford, Wartburg, Elma, and Rannoch tills and formed the Macton, Milverton, Mitchell, Lucan, Dublin, and Seaforth moraines. The tills and moraines of the Port Bruce stadial also display an impressive array of associated glacial landforms including eskers, kettles, kames, and outwash deposits.

The early retreat of the Port Bruce ice was also marked by the formation of proglacial lakes Maumee I, II, and III in the Erie basin.

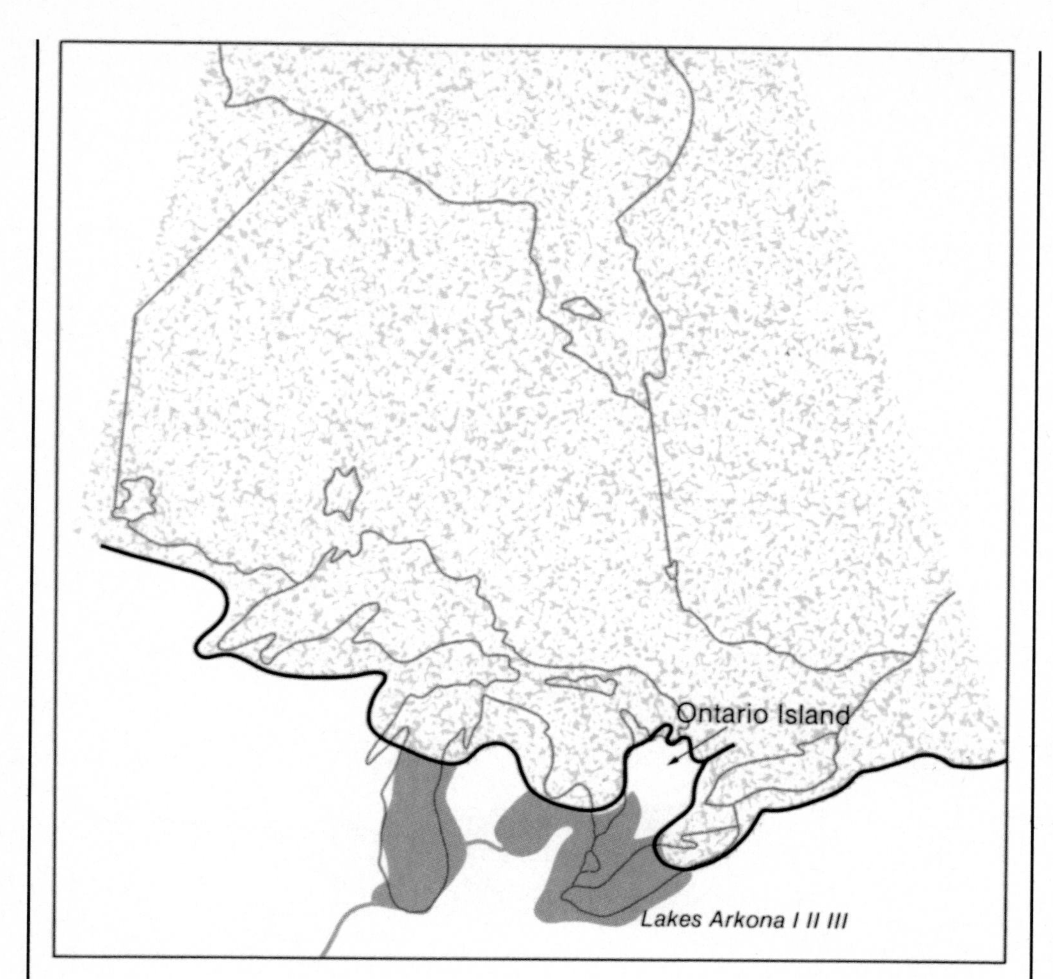

MACKINAW INTERSTADIAL

The final retreat of Port Bruce ice back toward the lake basins occurred about 13,000 years ago during the Mackinaw interstadial. This recession was marked by the creation of Ontario Island, a land base totally surrounded by lakes and glaciers. Ontario Island formed first as a split between ice-lobes, which then widened to expose a dome of relatively higher land. Ontario Island today is ringed with the moraines that were built during this and the previous period. At this time, a warm climate caused the disintegration of the ice mass and the deposition of parts of the Oak Ridges and Orangeville moraines. High-level lakes returned to the Erie basin. Lakes Arkona I, II, and III and Lake Ypsilanti carved and deposited a series of shorelines into and on top of the freshly deposited tills and moraines.

The Mackinaw Interstadial (about 13,000 years ago).

Moraines of southern Ontario today.

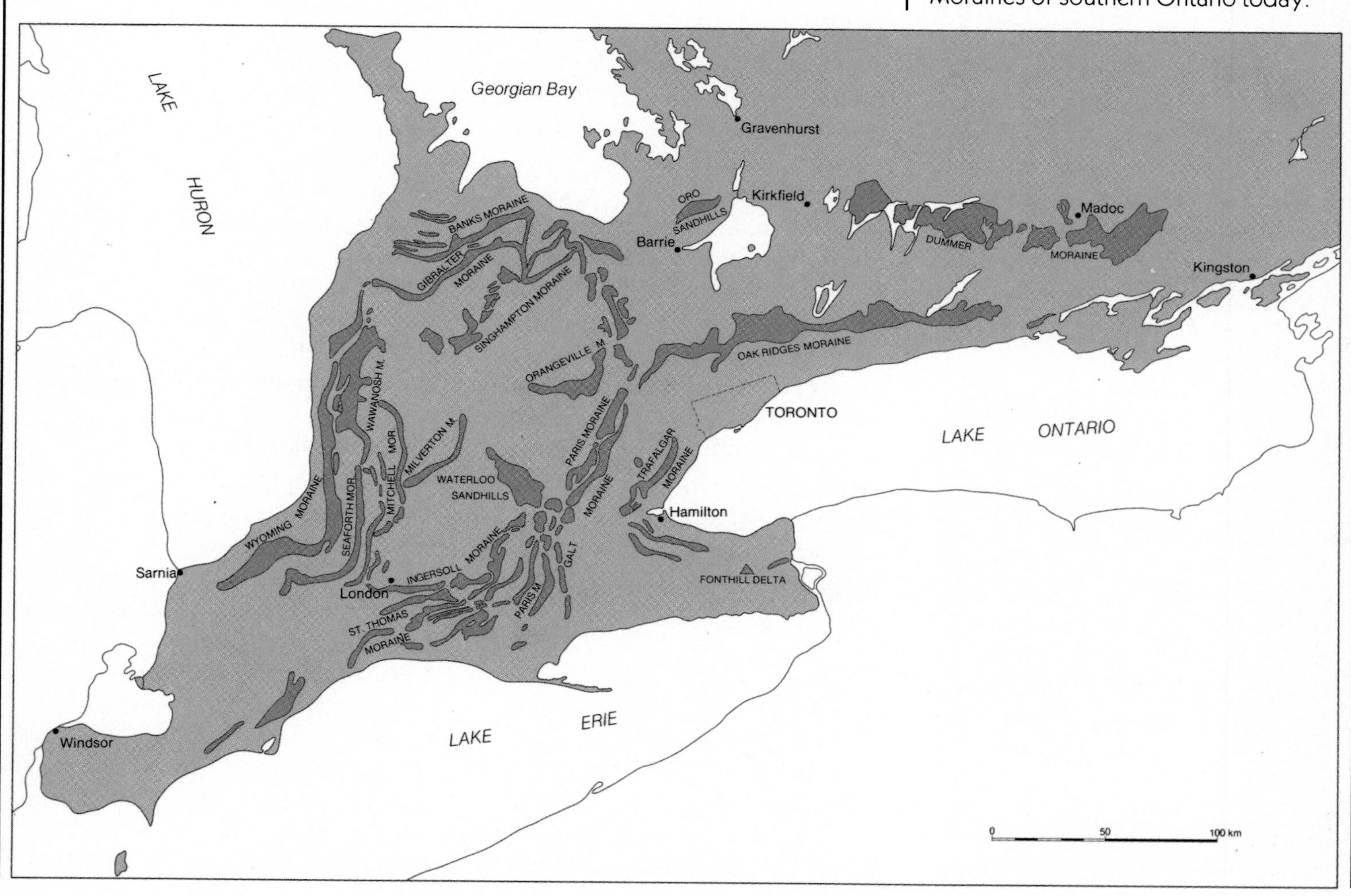

The Port Huron Stadial (about 12,900 years ago).

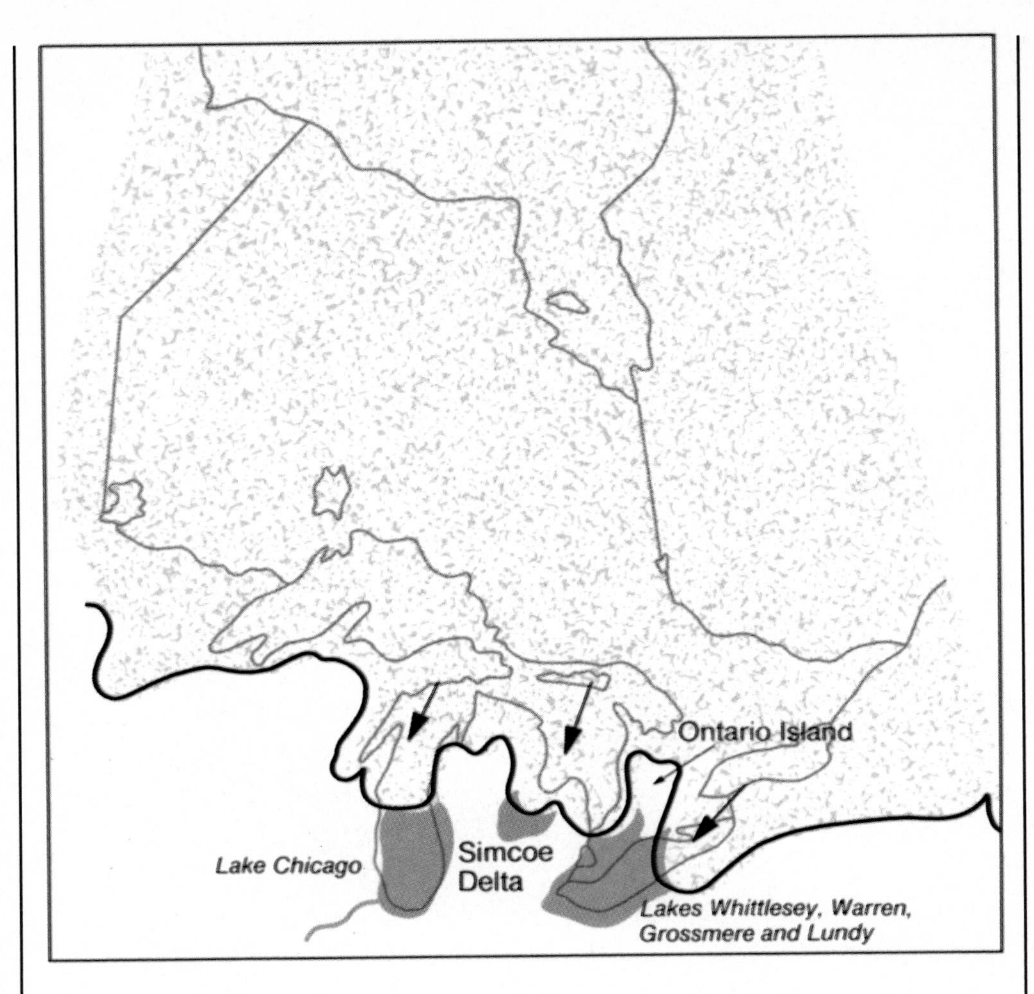

PORT HURON STADIAL

The Mackinaw interstadial was short-lived as cold climate prevailed and Port Huron stadial ice re-advanced about 12,900 years ago. Again, ice moved out of the lake basins toward the centre of Ontario Island. An early phase deposited the St. Joseph's till and Wyoming moraine in the Huron basin; a silt till and the Walkerton and Gibraltar moraines in the Georgian Bay basin; and the Halton till and Niagara Falls, Crystal Beach, Palgrave, and Waterdown moraines in the Ontario basin. This period of deposition was followed by the retreat of ice back into the lake basins. North of the Oak Ridges moraine, melt-waters were trapped between the glacier and the moraine, creating the Schomberg ponds. In the Erie basin, rising water levels formed proglacial lakes Whittlesey, Warren I and II, and Wayne. A late phase saw Georgian Bay ice deposit a silty clay till and the Banks and Williscroft moraines. Lake Simcoe ice then advanced over the Schomberg ponds and deposited the Kettleby till, while Lake Ontario ice moved south to deposit the Vinemount moraine and north to deposit the Gooseville moraine. In the Erie basin, proglacial lakes Warren III, Grassmere, and Lundy were formed.

NORTH BAY INTERSTADIAL

The retreat of Port Huron ice between 11,840 and 8,100 years ago saw the deglaciation of southern Ontario and much of the northwestern and northeastern portions of the province. This period of warmer climate was marked by the rapid retreat of the continental glacier across the Canadian Shield. Deglaciation was dominated by warm intervals separated by several minor cold phases.

Two Creeks Interval: This early warm interval saw the ice retreat from the Ontario basin to the Oak Ridges moraine exposing the Peterborough and Quinte drumlin fields, eskers, kames, outwash, crevasse fillings, and glacial ponds. Proglacial Lake Iroquois eroded shore-cliffs and deposited prominent beaches, spits, and forelands in the Ontario basin. In the Huron basin, early Lake Algonquin formed at the foot of the retreating ice. This lake drained south through an outlet at Port Huron to early Lake Erie, Lake Iroquois, and the Mohawk valley. Ice moved north to Kirkfield between 11,500 and 11,200 years ago, where a new outlet lowered early Lake Algonquin by draining its waters across the Kawarthas to Lake Iroquois.

Kirkfield Phase: Re-advancing ice then closed the Kirkfield outlet and raised the lake level about 11,200 years ago to form main Lake Algonquin. This cold phase may correlate to the Greatlakean stadial which has been well documented in Wisconsin and Michigan, but appears to be absent in Ontario. The deposition of the Bass Lake, Lake Simcoe, and Dummer moraines, the inundation of the Champlain sea into the Ottawa–St. Lawrence Lowlands, and the lowering of Lake Iroquois to Lake Frontenac may have occurred at this time.

North Bay Interval: The warm North Bay interval saw the ice recede farther across Algonquin Park, creating new outlets and lower levels in Lake Algonquin. These outlets are well displayed in Algonquin Park, while spectacular shorelines associated with the lower lakes can be seen in Awenda and Waubaushene Beaches provincial parks. In Lake Superior's western basin, proglacial Lakes Keeweenaw and Duluth were formed in succession, while proglacial Lake Agassiz began to form near Lake of the Woods.

Algonquin Phase: This cold phase between 11,000 and 10,100 years ago slowed the glacier's northward retreat. This phase is marked by a

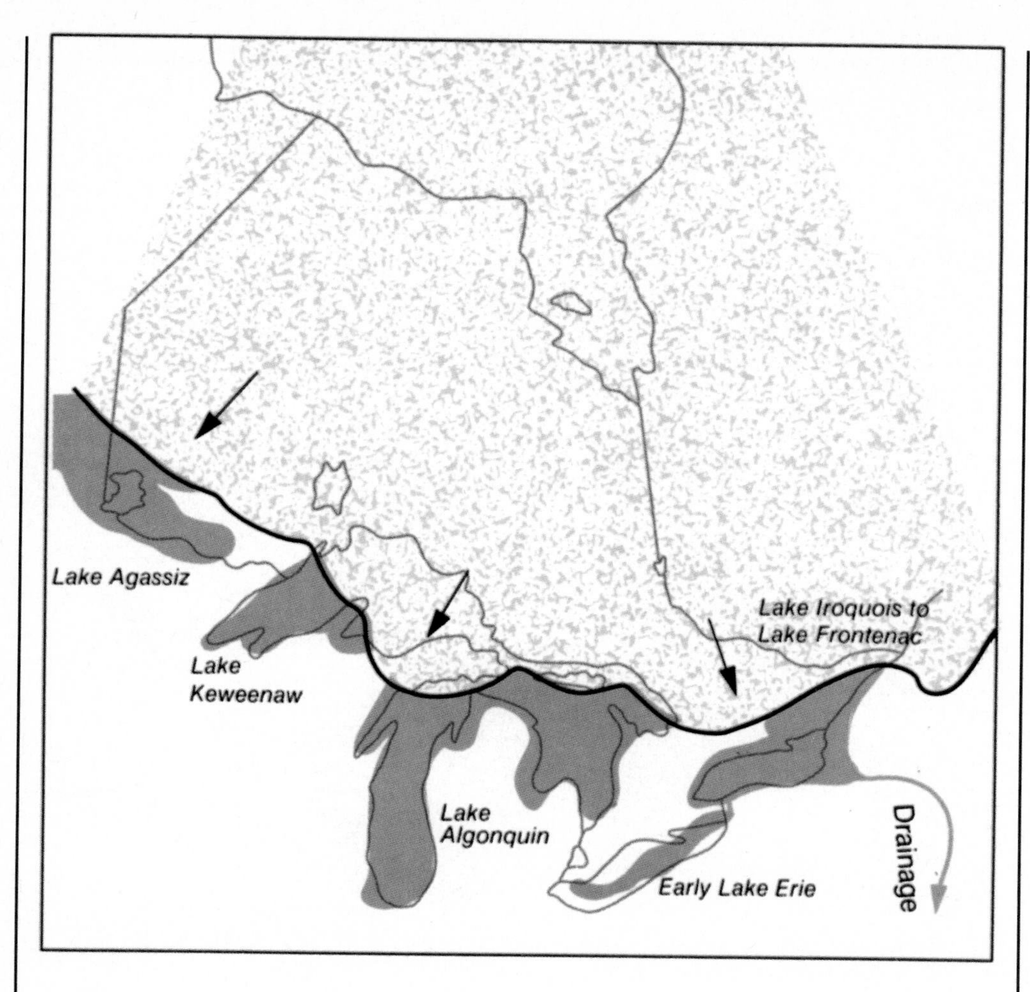

The North Bay Interstadial, Kirkfield Phase (about 11,200 years ago).

discontinuous ridge of moraines that stretches across northeastern Ontario into Michigan and then northwest across Lake Superior to Woodland Caribou Provincial Park. In the northeast, the Cartier moraines, associated proglacial lakes, spillways, and deltas were formed along the shores north of Lake Algonquin. In the northwest, the Dog Lake, Hartmann, Brûlé Creek, and Eagle-Findlayson moraines were deposited into proglacial Lake Agassiz. In the Superior basin, melt-waters carved the Kakabeka spillway and deposited the Kaministiqua delta into Lake Beaver Bay. This spillway is illustrated by an impressive gorge and falls cut at Kakabeka Falls Provincial Park, while the flat surface of the delta provides the modern-day site for the city of Thunder Bay.

Timiskaming Warm Interval: Again, the glacier retreated north, exposing a scoured and moulded bedrock surface and depositing shallow, discontinuous, sandy, stony tills; eskers, kames, kettles, and outwash; and other ice-disintegration features. This interval was dominated by proglacial Lakes Barlow-Ojibway, Nakina, Kelvin, and Agassiz. These lakes formed at the foot of the northward-retreating ice and eroded and deposited shorelines along the southern heights of land. Lake Barlow-Ojibway's features can be observed across the northeast with spectacular examples of the lake's sediments being seen at Kap-Kig-Iwan, Frederickhouse Lake, and North Driftwood River provincial parks. Lake Kelvin shorelines can been seen at West Bay Provincial Park, while the sediments, shorelines, and outlets of Lake Agassiz may be observed at Butler Lake, Opasquia, and Ouimet Canyon provincial parks.

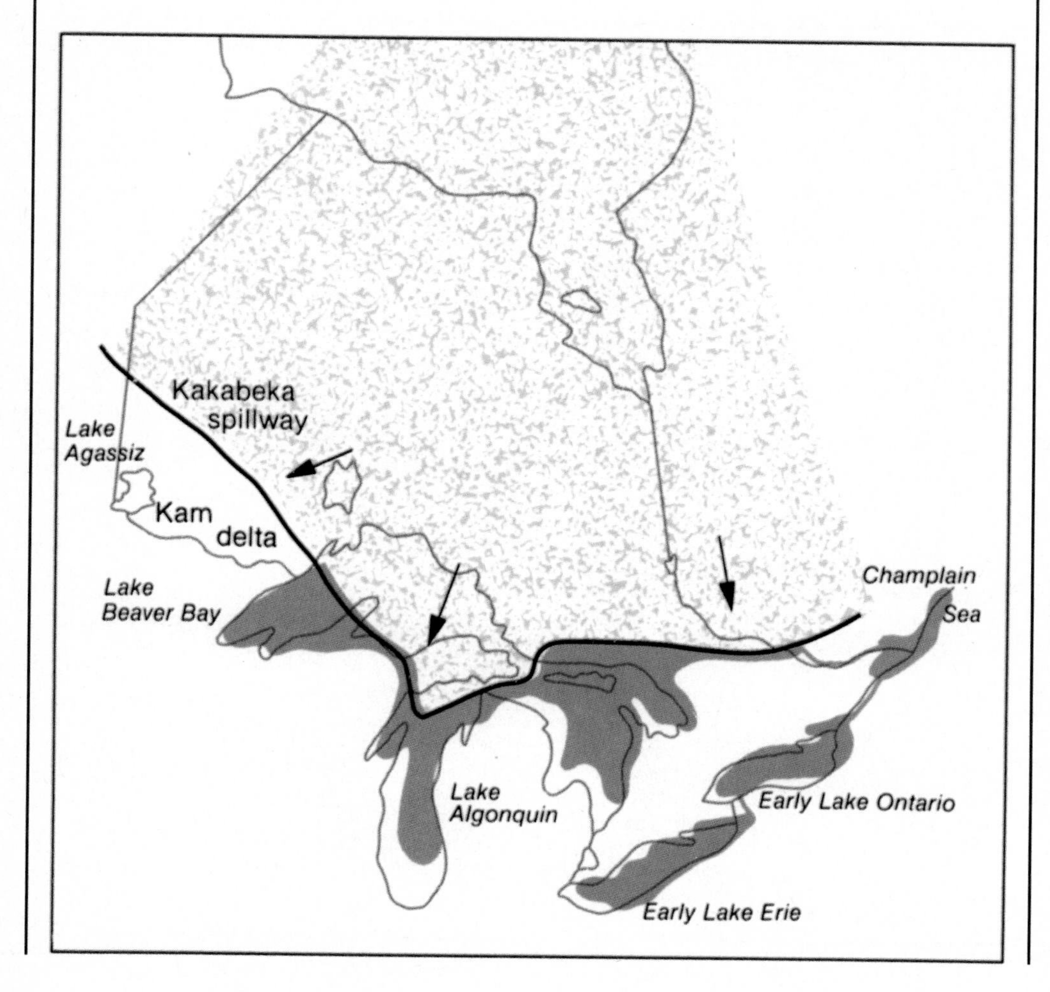

The North Bay Interstadial, Algonquin Phase (11,000 to 10,100 years ago).

The North Bay Interstadial, Nakina Phase (about 9,000 years ago).

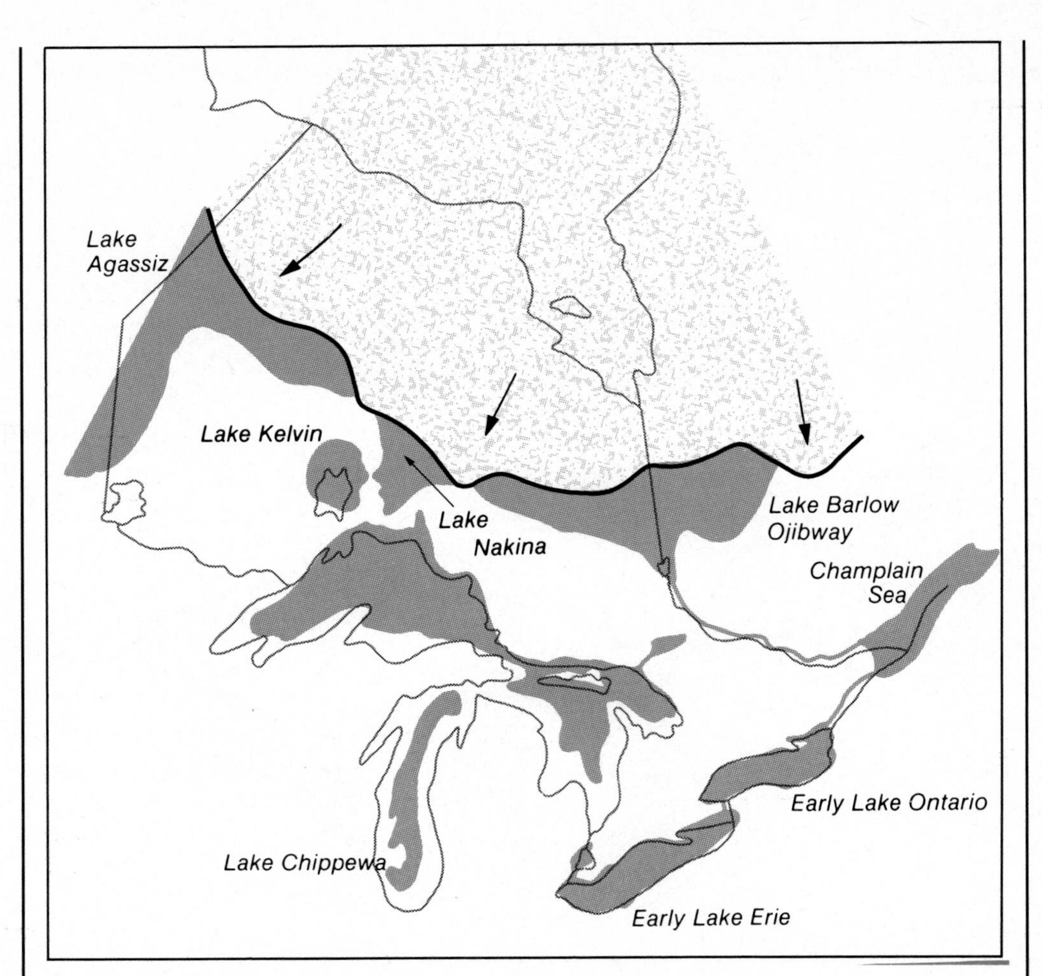

Nakina Phase: Yet another cold phase in the ice's northward migration was marked by the Frazerdale, Arnott, White Otter, Nakina, and Whitewater moraines. In the Lake Superior basin, Lakes Minong and Houghton formed shorelines along Superior's northern and eastern shores. Lake Agassiz continued to swell in the northwest, depositing vast lake sediments and cutting a complex sequence of shorelines. In the lower Great Lakes, low water levels dominated the Michigan and Huron basins, while rising water levels created modern Lakes Erie and Ontario.

DRIFTWOOD STADIAL

The rapid retreat of the continental glacier across the Canadian Shield was halted for the last time during the Driftwood stadial. This re-advance was postulated to explain the widespread occurrence of a clay till over the varved clays of proglacial Lake Barlow-Ojibway. An excellent example of this relationship may be observed in Brunswick House Lake Provincial Park. The Driftwood stadial is also recorded by two distinct sets of striae and drumlin orientations and by two small end moraines north of Smoothrock Falls. The Cochrane till can be observed in North Driftwood River Provincial Park near the confluence of the Abitibi River. The widespread deposition of clay till on top of preexisting glacial landforms has given rise to an interesting mantled or *palimpsest* topography. The till-covered eskers, kettles, and kames of Greenwater Lake and Little Abitibi River provincial parks provide excellent examples of this phenomenon.

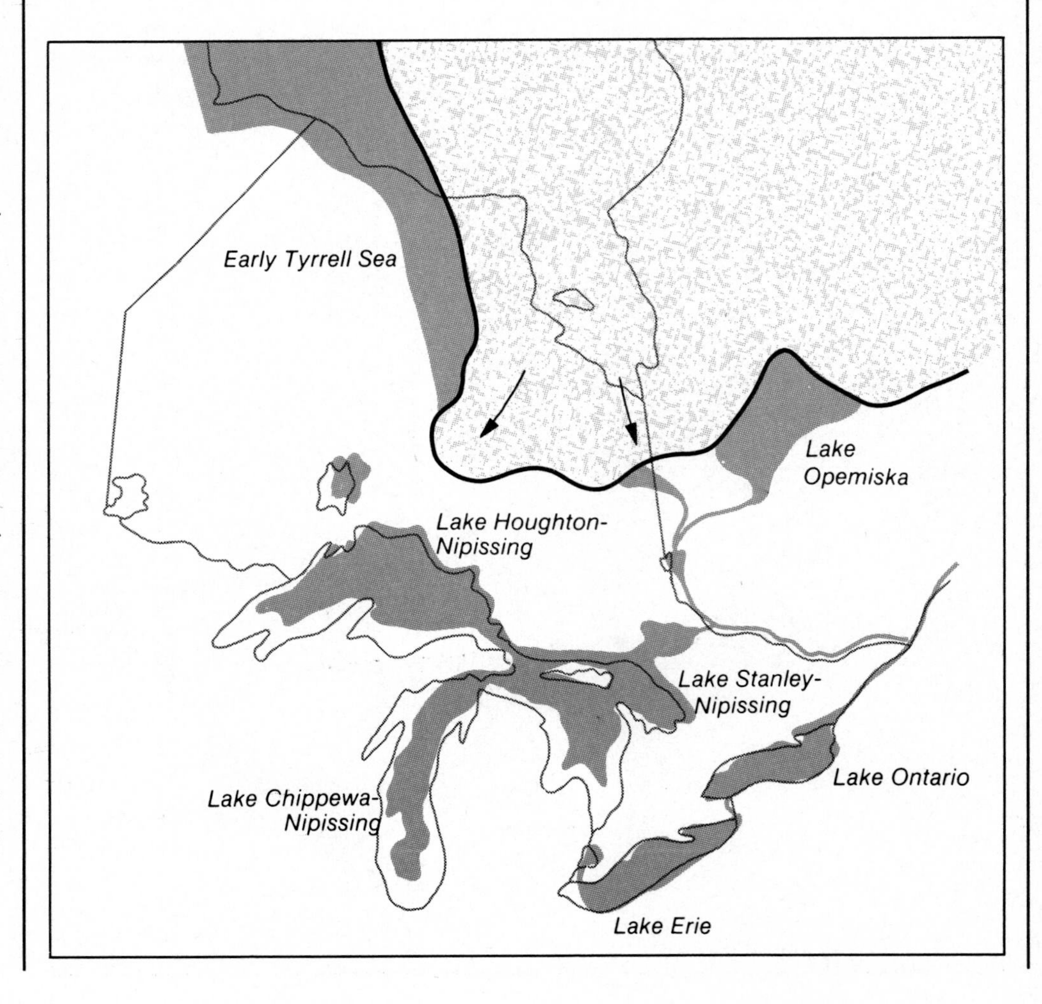

The Driftwood Stadial (about 8,200 to 8,100 years ago).

Glacial Lake Agassiz beach ridges cut into and deposited on the flanks of the Sachigo Hills in far northwestern Ontario. These strands mark the successive positions of Lake Agassiz's rapidly changing water levels. R. J. DAVIDSON

Part B. The Present Interglacial

In the fourteen thousand years since the last glacier covered the entire province, the ice mass moved northward, advancing and retreating, gradually giving way to the warmer conditions we experience today. As the influence of this last great continental glacier waned, the emerging landscape was once again reshaped. Gravity moved rock and soil down slopes. Running water eroded river basins and deposited deltas, fans, and plains. Sinking water etched the bedrock surface and dissolved subterranean caverns. Standing water carved coastlines, and winds moved materials from these coasts inland to create dune fields. Collectively, these actions reshaped Ontario's post-glacial landscape into the diverse and dynamic physiography that characterizes Ontario today.

Mass Wasted Landforms

Mass wasted landforms are common to all areas of the province. They result from the massive gravitational downslope movement of rock and soil. At first, movement occurs gradually; however, once it has reached a critical point it can occur abruptly, sometimes endangering human life and property.

On rock surfaces, common mass wasted forms include cliff faces, bedrock crevices, crevice caves, rockslides, talus slopes, and boulder aprons. These forms are commonly found on flat, jointed, bedrock surfaces with steep slopes. They are well displayed along the length of the Niagara Escarpment, in the Port Arthur hills near Thunder Bay, and at countless localities throughout the Canadian Shield. Spectacular examples of mass wasted forms in rock environments can be seen at Mono Cliffs, Cabot Head, Cyprus Lake, Lake Superior, Ouimet Canyon, and other provincial parks.

In areas with soils, common mass wasted forms include earthflows, mudflows, slumps, and landslides. These forms are commonly found where thick, saturated, clay soils have been eroded by rivers, waves, or the thoughtless actions of man. Such areas are found on the north shores of Lakes Erie and Ontario and along rivers in the Haldimand clay plain. The most spectacular of these environments, however, are found in the Ottawa–St. Lawrence Lowlands. Here, thick clays deposited by the Champlain Sea have been dissected by the many small rivers draining into the Ottawa and St. Lawrence rivers. The steep unstable slopes created by these rivers are noted for their landslides. The most spectacular of these is found near the village of Lemieux.

Farther north, in the Hudson Bay Lowlands, the effects of mass wasting are controlled by extreme temperatures and the lack of significant relief. Here, the freezing and thawing of water in the pore spaces of rock and soil are actively creating a variety of features: patterned ground consisting of circular "moats" of rock; solifluction ridges where surface soil slips on the sides of hills like icing on the sides of a cake; thermokarst lakes formed where permafrost has melted and the soil eroded away; and conical ice-cored hills called *pingos*. Many of these features are found commonly in Polar Bear Provincial Park.

Fluvial Landforms

Ontario's vast and varied landscapes have given rise to a diverse network of drainage basins and fluvial (water-carved) landforms. The distinctive character of the Great Lakes–St. Lawrence Lowlands, Hudson Bay Lowlands, and the Canadian Shield have each produced a unique assortment of river systems.

In the Great Lakes–St. Lawrence Lowlands, relatively short rivers with small drainage basins have developed on glacial landforms and limestone plains. In the headwaters of the Beaver, Nottawasaga, Credit, and other rivers along the Niagara Escarpment, impressive waterfalls, plunge pools, gorges, and potholes have formed. Spectacular and scenic examples of these features can be seen at Elora Gorge and Niagara Falls. The lower reaches of these and other rivers such as the Grand, Thames, Don, Rouge, and Ganaraska have cut through easily eroded glacial materials, carving dendritic drainage basins with numerous small ravines, springs, streams, cut banks, channel fill, point bars, meanders, oxbows, and floodplains. Other rivers developed on limestone plains such as the Bonnechere, Moira, Salmon, Indian, Trent, and Ottawa often follow pre-existing bedrock topography and structural trends. The waters flowing through these channels often play an active role in the creation of subterranean caverns.

In the Hudson Bay Lowlands, the dendritic patterns of the Severn, Winisk, Ekwan, Attawapiskat, Albany, Moose, and other rivers radiate out from estuaries on the coast, across flat ancient and recent marine sediments, to their rugged headwaters in the Canadian Shield.

The Canadian Shield displays a wide

range of drainage systems including dendritic, annular, radial, centripetal, and rectangular patterns. In almost all cases, these patterns are shaped by bedrock composition or pre-existing topography. Contributing to the myriad of drainage patterns observed on the Shield are easily eroded bedrock layers, folds, faults, joints, elliptical masses of igneous rock, the configuration of glacial landforms, and even meteorite impact structures. The dominant Shield drainage pattern, however, is one of numerous lakes and ponds linked to each other by narrow outlets and small streams. The linkages from lake to lake are often marked by overflows, rapids, or waterfalls. Many of the lakes and ponds are isolated and support a variety of bogs and other wetlands. Many of these drainage patterns are believed to be pre-Paleozoic in age. The mouth of the French River, for example, may be the remnant of a large delta that once drained a prominent ancient river. The Shield also contains some the province's best contemporary deltas. These include the Mississagi delta on the north shore of Lake Huron and the Gravel River delta on the north shore of Lake Superior.

Karst Landforms

Karst landforms, or features dissolved into carbonate-rich bedrock, are poorly developed in Ontario. This can be attributed to the action of glaciers eroding and burying the bedrock surface and to the relatively short period of time since glaciation that karst processes have been permitted to actively modify the landscape. Still, many fine examples of both surface and subsurface karst forms may be observed in the province.

Surface karst forms are found on limestone and dolostone plains. Some of the best developed dolostone plains occur along the south shore of Manitoulin Island and on the Bruce Peninsula. Good examples of limestone plains may be observed at Cardin, Napanee, and Smith's Falls. These flat expanses of sparsely vegetated open bedrock pavement contain a variety of interesting features. The most abundant feature is *karren*, a general term used to describe the pitting, grooving, and channelling of the bedrock surface. The top of the Niagara Escarpment at Cabot Head and the south shore of Manitoulin Island contain fine examples of karren. Some of the larger forms found on these plains may include sinkholes, karst windows, and natural bridges. *Sinkholes* are large circular depressions caused by sinking water and the collapse of surface debris. When subsurface streams are observed at the bottoms of sinkholes they are called *karst windows*. Good examples of these larger features are found at Wodehouse Creek where it enters the Beaver Valley, and others have been reported from Gypsum Mountain and the Attawapiskat River in the Hudson Bay Lowlands.

The most common subsurface karst landform is the cave. Caves may be classified as *vadose*, those formed above the water table; *phreatic*, those formed below the water table; or *collapse*, those formed by the collapse of rocks from the walls of other caves. A variety of features including passages, rooms, chambers, waterfalls, scalloped bedrock, stalactites, and stalagmites are common to all cave forms. While Ontario's caves are immature, due to the effects of glaciation, there are several interesting ones, including St. Edmund's Cave, Bonnechere Caves, and Moira Cave.

Marine and Lacustrine Landforms

Many splendid examples of marine and lacustrine (lake-made) landforms can be observed along the coasts of Ontario's Great Lakes, countless lesser lakes, and Hudson Bay.

Near-shore landforms such as shore-cliffs, sea caves, arches, and flowerpots have been formed by the erosive actions of waves and currents. Magnificent shore-cliffs have been carved into the glacial sediments at the Scarborough Bluffs and Lake Erie. Similarly, bedrock cliffs have formed on the eastern and northern shores of the Bruce Peninsula and the northern shore of Manitoulin Island. The Bruce Peninsula and Flowerpot Island, in particular, are noted for their spectacular sea caves, and flowerpots. The rugged north shore of Lake Superior also displays sea caves, arches, and numerous other intricate erosional features. The Sea Lion in Sibley Provincial Park, Devil's Tower in Lake Superior Provincial Park, and the wave-sculptured rocks in Neys Provincial Park are just a few examples of these features.

Depositional forms such as beaches, spits, tombolos, barriers, and forelands can be observed on most lakes. The most common shoreline features are *beaches* made up of fringes of sand, gravel, cobbles, and boulders at the water's edge, and *spits*, which are ridges of sand attached to the mainland at one end. *Tombolos*, a more complex landform, are sandspits joining bedrock islands to the mainland. Tombolos may be simple, like those at Rock Point and Point Abino, or they may display a complex network of spits and islands such as the tombolo at Presqu'ile Provincial Park. *Barriers* are spits attached to the mainland at both ends. Spectacular examples of barriers on the Great Lakes include those found at Sandbanks Provincial Park and at Burlington Beach. *Forelands* are low-lying fringes of sand, gravel, cobbles, and boulders that protrude lakeward. Long Point, Rondeau, and Point Pelee parks are fine examples of forelands.

Aeolian Landforms

The cold deserts associated with the retreat of the Wisconsinan glacier and the temperate deserts found along the Great Lakes coast provide Ontario with a rich assortment of aeolian (wind-caused) landforms. Cold desert landforms include loess fields constructed from wind-blown sand, and a complex variety of parabolic dune forms. Excellent examples of these landforms have formed on proglacial lake beds and deltas north of Lake Erie near Simcoe, in proglacial lake beds at Esker Lakes Provincial Park, along the Pipestone River, and at numerous other locations across the Canadian Shield.

Coastal desert landforms include wind-sculptured sands, semi-circular depressions called *blowouts*, prominent transverse foredunes, and one or more secondary inland dune ridges. The largest and most distinctive coastal dune systems have formed at right angles to prevailing winds at the heads of circular bays. The dunes at Wasaga Beach, Pinery Provincial Park, and the Sand River in Lake Superior Provincial Park have developed in this way. Other dune systems have formed at right angles to prevailing winds on top of extensive barriers at the mouths of bays and rivers, such as at Sandbanks Provincial Park, Wolfe Island in the eastern basin of Lake Ontario, and at Sable Island Provincial Park at Lake of the Woods. Coastal dune systems have also developed on tombolo bars at Presqu'ile Provincial Park, Point Abino, and on large, sandy forelands at Long Point, Point Pelee National Park, and Rondeau Provincial Park.

Earthen Blanket
The Soils of Ontario
Doug Hoffman

After the cosmic bulldozers drew back from Ontario they left a desolate, devastated, biologically barren landscape. But it was a varied one: high piles of sand and gravel in some places, smooth rolling hills in others, flat clay plains, sand plains, till plains, and bare scoured rock.

For ten thousand years or so, this surface was worked over, first only by wind, rain, frost, snow, and ice, then by rootlets and rhyzoids and acids secreted by plants, then by burgeoning populations of soil organisms: bacteria, fungi, nematodes, protozoans – unicellular and multicellular – up to earthworms, shrews, and moles.

Today we think of this surface, except where the bedrock is still exposed, as soil or dirt. But soil is far from "dirt." Ten thousand years have worked their magic and created a chemical and biological factory in this surface metre of staggering importance. All living things depend upon its functioning. Here atoms change bonds from one molecule to another. Here electric potentials develop around particles that allow nutrients to be absorbed by plants. Here specific genera of bacteria capture nitrogen and transform it to usable forms. If those bacteria were gone, terrestrial life on Earth would go too.

Seven of Canada's nine Orders of soils are found in Ontario: Podsolic, Luvisolic, Brunisolic, Gleysolic, Regosolic, Crysolic, and Organic. These Orders differ from one another because of environmental factors such as climate, vegetation, or their parent material. Parent materials may consist of sand, clay, silt, or gravel, and vary in origin, some with a high proportion of limestone and others formed mainly from granitic rock. The glaciers may have left them as only a thin veneer a few centimetres thick over bedrock, or as fifty-metre-deep deposits called till. Or water may have deposited them as outwash plains, deltas, or ancient lake beds.

These parent materials over time gave rise to different soils largely because they influenced the speed and extent of water percolation. Water movement in soils is important because it carries with it soluble ions of various elements and compounds. This movement results in distinctive layering of most soil into *horizons*.

Variations in horizons provide the major feature used to classify soils. Each horizon has a letter designation: O for organic; A for a mixture of organic and mineral, often with a loss through leaching of clay, iron, and aluminium; B for an accumulation of some combination of minerals, silicates, clay, and humus; C for the parent material relatively unaltered by water percolation or mineral accumulation or loss. Sub-horizons often are found as intermediates between major horizons. Differences in colour, and to some extent texture, characterize the different horizons.

The source of all soil is rock, ground up and pulverized by ice, water, wind, heat, freezing, and thawing over time. Much of Ontario is composed of granitic bedrock. This bedrock is rich in minerals, particularly iron, potassium, and aluminium, whereas the limestones and shales that form the bedrock in southern Ontario are composed mainly of calcium and magnesium. The softer limestones weather more readily than the hard granites, resulting in soils – and vegetation – that are quite different.

Podsolic soils are the most extensive in the province. Their location coincides mainly with the acidic, hard, granitic rocks of the Precambrian Shield. During glacial times the ice moved slowly back and forth over the bedrock grinding, crushing, and depositing rock materials over the countryside in the form of rugged moraines and rolling plains consisting of "glacial till" – boulders, gravels, sands, clays, and silts. The thickness of deposits over bedrock varies considerably. In most cases it is relatively thin, and the

Typical Podzolic soil with a dark organic surface layer, a leached, grey zone (A horizons), and an orange-brown zone of accumulation (B horizon) which can be divided into an upper, more intensely coloured area of iron accumulation and a lower, slightly less iron-rich area. The lowest layer, below thirty-six inches, is pale grey parent material typical of the original soil before time and water had stratified it (C horizon).
DOUGLAS HOFFMAN

underlying bedrock often appears in places at the surface.

Ice-transported materials were not the only ones upon which Podsolic soils developed. Water-deposited materials formed flat outwash plains of non-calcareous sands and gravels, which also provided the proper medium for the development of Podsolic soils.

Acidic conditions cause the movement of iron, aluminium, and humus in the soil, and develop the soil profile. Rain and melting snow provide the moisture which percolates through the surface, carrying the soluble bases out in the drainage water and moving other compounds to lower positions. This process is common to soil development everywhere, but is intensified in Podsolic soils where the more acidic parent material is derived from igneous rocks low in soluble bases. Podsolic soils attain their bright reddish and yellowish colours from the accumulation of iron and aluminium oxides in the B horizon, and this characteristic distinguishes them from other soil orders.

Soils of the *Luvisolic Order* are recognized mainly by the accumulation of clay in the B horizon. They are most common throughout southern Ontario but may occur anywhere in the province where the parent materials contain significant amounts of calcium and magnesium carbonates. A difference exists between those Luvisolics located in the south and those occupying the more northerly clay belt, because of the difference in mean annual soil temperature. The colder temperatures of the Luvisolics around New Liskeard, Dryden, and Thunder Bay produce soils with a very thin surface horizon, while the warmer soil temperatures in southern Ontario result in soils with thick surfaces. Luvisolic soils occur on many different landforms. Usually they are found on ground moraines, but they also occur on recessional moraines, drumlins, outwash plains, lacustrine plains, and as windblown deposits called *loess*.

Vegetation on Luvisolic soils in southern Ontario is typically hardwood, because soil there is less acidic than on the Precambrian Shield. Carbonates and other bases are plentiful in glacial till derived from limestone, dolomite, sandstone, and shale, which prevent acid conditions from building up. Acidity is low, as well, without the contribution of decaying coniferous needles. In the more northern parts of the province, however, softwoods predominate on the Luvisolic soils. Jack pines are common on the drier sites, and aspens occupy places with intermediate drainage.

Brown colours – dark surfaces underlain with brown subsoil, are the main characteristic of the *Brunisolic soils*. They are scattered throughout the province with the largest areas located in Lanark, Leeds, Grenville, Dundas, Stormont, Glengarry, and

Typical Luvisolic soil but in this case the wide, upper zone demarks the depth of cultivation and the wide, grey zone is the leached zone (A horizons). The dark brown band from thirty-seven to forty-two inches is the zone of accumulation (B) but, diagnostic from a podzolic soil, here it contains a high content of clay rather than iron or aluminium that has leached from above. Below forty-two inches are two types of parent material, one more gravelly and the other more sandy, indicating water-washing of this original glacial till (C horizon). DOUGLAS HOFFMAN

Brunisolic soil with a thin surface organic layer and no zone of eluviation. The parent material here is a light grey sand. DOUGLAS HOFFMAN

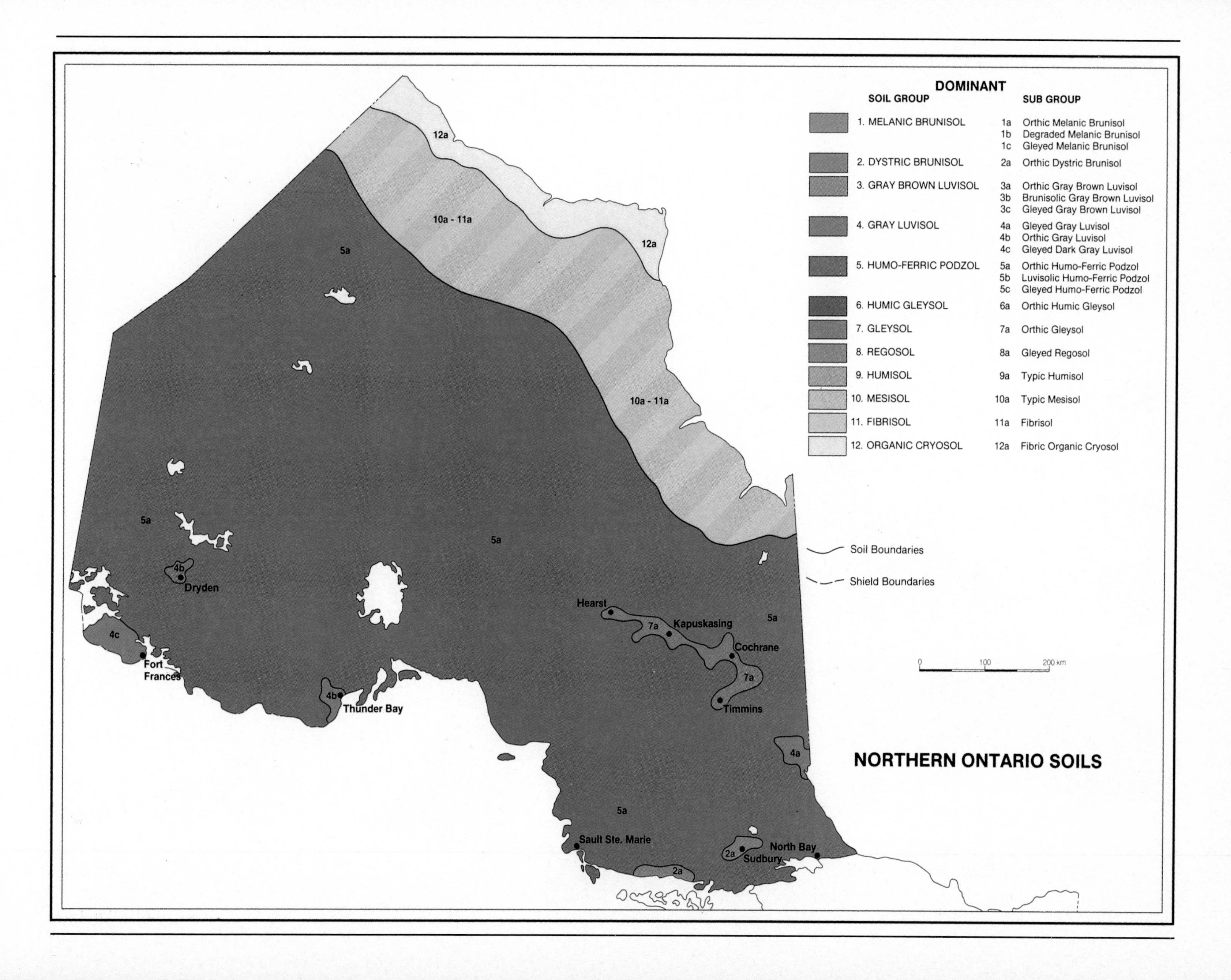
NORTHERN ONTARIO SOILS
DOMINANT
SOIL GROUP
SUB GROUP
1. MELANIC BRUNISOL
1a Orthic Melanic Brunisol
1b Degraded Melanic Brunisol
1c Gleyed Melanic Brunisol
2. DYSTRIC BRUNISOL
2a Orthic Dystric Brunisol
3. GRAY BROWN LUVISOL
3a Orthic Gray Brown Luvisol
3b Brunisolic Gray Brown Luvisol
3c Gleyed Gray Brown Luvisol
4. GRAY LUVISOL
4a Gleyed Gray Luvisol
4b Orthic Gray Luvisol
4c Gleyed Dark Gray Luvisol
5. HUMO-FERRIC PODZOL
5a Orthic Humo-Ferric Podzol
5b Luvisolic Humo-Ferric Podzol
5c Gleyed Humo-Ferric Podzol
6. HUMIC GLEYSOL
6a Orthic Humic Gleysol
7. GLEYSOL
7a Orthic Gleysol
8. REGOSOL
8a Gleyed Regosol
9. HUMISOL
9a Typic Humisol
10. MESISOL
10a Typic Mesisol
11. FIBRISOL
11a Fibrisol
12. ORGANIC CRYOSOL
12a Fibric Organic Cryosol
Soil Boundaries
Shield Boundaries
0
100
200 km
12a
10a - 11a
5a
4b
Dryden
4c
Fort Frances
4b
Thunder Bay
Hearst
7a
Kapuskasing
Cochrane
Timmins
4a
Sault Ste. Marie
2a
Sudbury
North Bay

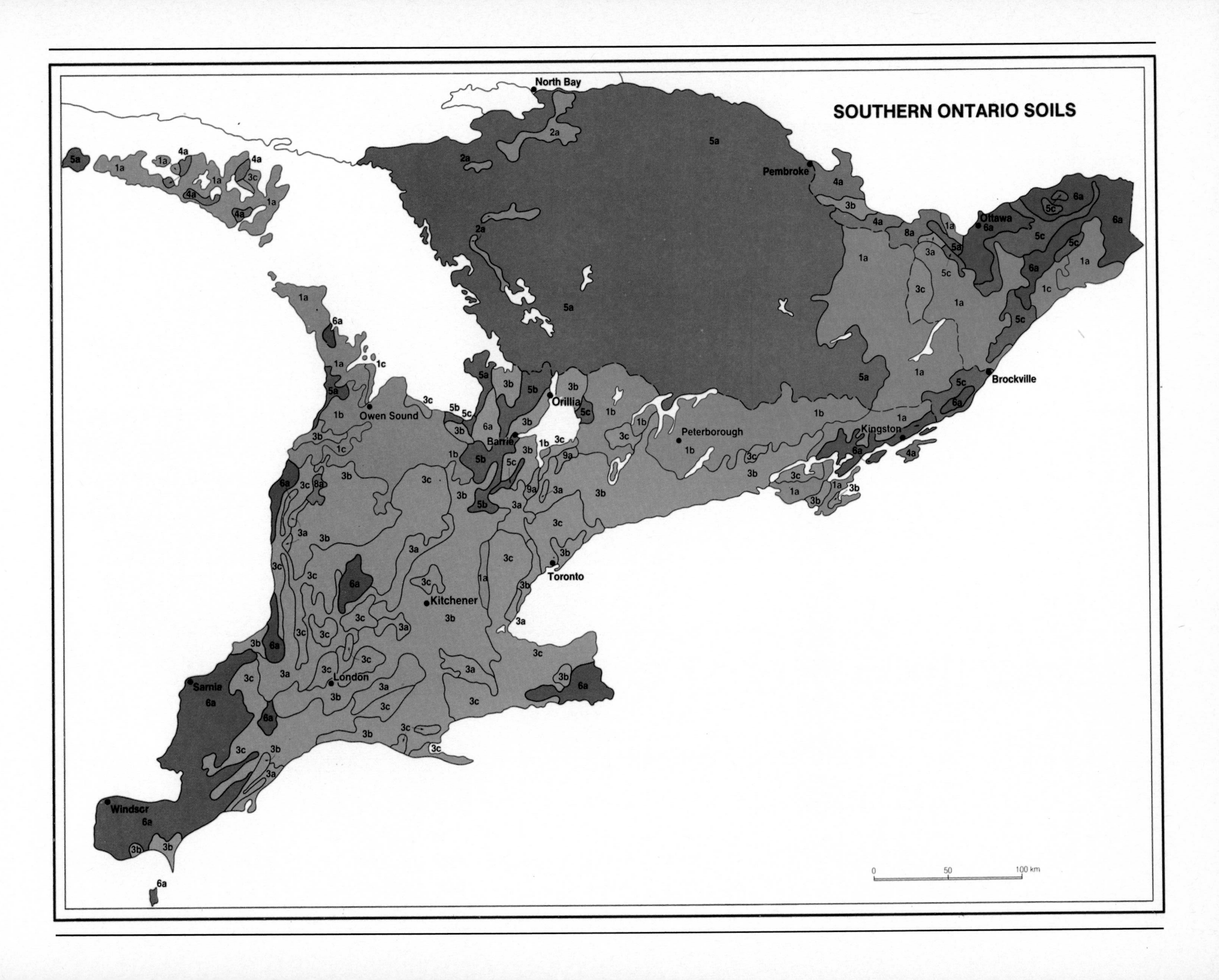
SOUTHERN ONTARIO SOILS
North Bay
Pembroke
Ottawa
Brockville
Kingston
Peterborough
Orillia
Barrie
Owen Sound
Toronto
Kitchener
London
Sarnia
Windsor
0
50
100 km

the more northerly parts of Bruce, Grey, and Victoria counties. In these places they are generally associated with ground moraines and drumlins. Presumably because they are young the Brunisolics show little horizon differentiation. Brunisolic soils include some that are calcareous to the surface and very slightly leached and others that are strongly acid and weathered to a considerable depth. In addition some have thin surface layers while others are thick.

Brown soils such as Luvisolics grow predominantly hardwoods where soil materials originate from calcareous bedrock. Brunisolics in the Shield also may support the growth of hardwoods, but with a much higher proportion of softwoods such as red and white pines.

All mineral (non-organic) soils that remain saturated for most of the year are placed in the *Gleysolic Order*. They occur in association with all of the other orders but occupy the level and depressed sites in the landscape. They are characterized by thick dark surface horizons and drab grey subsoils. The grey subsoils are often spotted with red or yellow blotches called mottles, sure evidence of wet conditions within the soils. Gleysolic soils make up a large part of Essex, Kent, Lambton, Carleton, Prescott, Russell, and Glengarry counties. They also occur in large tracts in the Great Clay Belt extending from Cochrane to Hearst, a distance of 215 kilometres.

The vegetation that grows on Gleysolic soils is predominantly adapted for moist soils and the cool microhabitat conditions of lowlands: hemlock, yellow birch, black ash, and other wetland species.

Organic soils develop in marshes, swamps, bogs, and fens – wherever there is an extremely reliable and stable water supply. Under such conditions, dead and dying vegetation accumulates because a lack of oxygen prevents decomposition. To be considered an Organic, a soil must contain at least 30 per cent organic matter

Dominant Soil Orders, Groups and Subgroups in Ontario and Their Major Characteristics

SOIL ORDER	SOIL GROUP	SOIL SUBGROUP	PARENT MATERIAL	MAJOR CHARACTERISTICS
BRUNISOLIC				No marked movement of clay, humus, iron, or aluminium from **A** horizon to **B** horizon.
	Melanic Brunisol	Orthic Melanic Brunisol	Very calcareous till, outwash, and deltaic	Same as above with a dark-coloured **A** horizon more than 10 cm thick.
		Degraded Melanic Brunisol	Deposits from limestone	Same as above with a thin leached layer.
		Gleyed Melanic Brunisol		Same as above but with distinct mottles*.
	Dystric Brunisol	Orthic Dystric Brunisol	Non-calcareous till, outwash, and lacustrine deposits from igneous and metamorphic rocks consisting mainly of quartz	Same as above with a dark-coloured **A** horizon less than 10 cm thick.
LUVISOLIC				Marked movement of clay, humus, iron, and aluminium from the **A** horizon and their accumulation in the **B** horizon.
	Grey-brown Luvisol	Orthic Grey-brown Luvisol	Calcareous fine-textured till and lacustrine deposits from limestone and dolostone	Same as above with a dark coloured **A** horizon more than 5 cm thick.
		Brunisolic Grey-brown Luvisol	Calcareous medium- and coarse-textured till, outwash, and deltaic deposits from limestone and dolostone	Same as above with brown layer immediately below the surface.
		Gleyed Grey-brown Luvisol	Calcareous fine-, medium-, and coarse-textured till, outwash, deltaic, and lacustrine deposits from limestone and dolostone.	Same as above with mottles*.

and extend to a depth of more than forty centimetres. Depths vary considerably. Where old ponds, streams, and other sinks in the landscape are filled in with the debris from trees, shrubs, grasses, and mosses, depths of thirty metres and more are common. In other places, especially in the north, expanses of organic materials may be only one or two metres thick over a mineral layer.

Organic soils vary in their stages of decomposition from those called *fibric*, in which the plant materials are readily recognized, to those called *humic*, in which the original form of the plant can no longer be identified. Three stages of decomposition – fibric, mesic, and humic – form the basis of their classification. The most extensive areas of peatlands are found in the far northern reaches of the province. Many small areas occur in other parts of Ontario, but most cover too small an area to be mapped at a provincial scale.

Regosolic soils are found where recent landslides or flooding have occurred, where the climate is dry and cold, or where the parent materials are nearly pure quartz sand. Regosolics are most commonly found in the floodplains of streams and rivers. The largest area of these soils occurs along the Ottawa River around the city of Ottawa.

Crysolic soils are those where permafrost remains close to the surface, found in Ontario along the northerly edge of the Hudson Bay Lowlands. They may look the same as many of the organic and mineral soils previously described, but because of the presence of permanently frozen subsoil, they have been placed in a separate Order. Little is known about the Crysolic soils in Ontario except that they normally consist of forty centimetres or more of fibrous organic material with permafrost near the surface.

Life in the Soil

When a soil profile is viewed in the field, few of the plants and animals

SOIL ORDER	SOIL GROUP	SOIL SUBGROUP	PARENT MATERIAL	MAJOR CHARACTERISTICS
	Grey Luvisol	Orthic Grey Luvisol	Calcareous fine-textured till and lacustrine deposits from limestone	Same as above with a dark-coloured **A** horizon less than 5 cm thick.
		Gleyed Grey Luvisol	Same as above	Same as above with mottles*.
		Gleyed Dark-grey Luvisol	Same as above	Same as for other luvisolics with mottles* and dark-coloured **A** horizon more than 5 cm thick.
PODZOLIC				Marked movement of clay, humus, iron, and aluminium from the thin organic and **A** horizons. Accumulation of humus, iron, and aluminium in the **B** horizon.
	Humo-ferric Podzol	Orthic Humo-ferric Podzol	Non-calcareous, medium- and coarse-textured till, deltaic, and outwash deposits	
		Luvisolic Humo-ferric Podzol		Same as above. Some clay accumulation in a second **B** horizon.
		Gleyed Humo-ferric Podzol		Same as above with mottles*
GLEYSOLIC				Have features indicative of periodic or prolonged saturation with water. Horizon colours are usually drab grey with bright reddish or yellowish mottles*. They commonly occur in association with other soils listed in this table.
	Humic Gleysol	Orthic Humic Gleysol	Calcareous fine-, medium-, and coarse-textured deposits from limestone and dolostone	Dark-coloured **A** horizon more than 10 cm thick.

SOIL ORDER	SOIL GROUP	SOIL SUBGROUP	PARENT MATERIAL	MAJOR CHARACTERISTICS
	Gleysol	Orthic Gleysol		Dark-coloured **A** horizon less than 10 cm thick.
ORGANIC				Composed mainly of organic debris such as mosses, sedges, leaves, and twigs. Most are saturated with water for long periods.
	Humisol	Typic Humisol	Well-decomposed mosses, sedges, etc.	
	Mesisol	Typic Mesisol	Moderately decomposed mosses, sedges, etc.	
	Fibrisol	Typic Fibrisol	Slightly decomposed mosses, sedges, etc. Sphagnum often predominates	
REGOSOLIC				Weakly developed. Horizons are commonly indistinct.
	Regosol	Gleyed Regosol	Calcareous and non-calcareous materials of fine, medium, and coarse textures	
CRYSOLIC				May have horizons resembling those of soils of the Brunisolic, Regosolic, Gleysolic, or Organic orders. Permafrost occurs within one metre of the surface.
	Organic Cryosol	Fibric Organic Cryosol	Slightly decomposed mosses, sedges, etc.	

*Mottles are an indication of retarded drainage.

active in the soil are seen. Some animals such as earthworms and woodchucks leave ample evidence of their burrowing activities, but others, especially those less than 0.2 millimetres in size, called *microfauna*, engage in activities much more difficult to assess with the human eye. Similarly, very small plant organisms make their habitat in soil, but their presence is seldom noted because of their size. Yet both plants and animals harboured in soil have important effects on various soil characteristics.

The numbers and health of earthworms depend upon conditions in the soil. The common earthworm survives best in moist, loosely packed soil containing a thick layer of organic matter and covered with litter. These conditions are most often met in the Gray-Brown Luvisols, Melanic Brunisols, and the Humic Gleysols. Earthworms are well-known soil mixers. Their burrowing, along with the passage of soil through their bodies, carries soil from the surface to depths of two or three metres and back up again.

Many other large soil animals survive best in soils with abundant organic matter. Millipedes prefer humus and rotting plants, easy chewing for their rather weak mouth parts. Ants and termites obtain most of their food above ground level so they have little to do with the decomposition of organic remains. They live in the soil for protection from predators and weather. Their greatest function is bringing soil particles to the surface that may be useful for plant growth. Ants may occur anywhere in the province on any of the various soils, but termites limit themselves to places where the winters are not too harsh.

The most important and most numerous of the soil dwellers are micro-organisms, those too small to be seen by the naked eye. Most micro-organisms function as decomposers and include such groups as protozoa, fungi, and bacteria.

Protozoa are single-celled organisms that depend upon the thin film of water surrounding soil particles and the tiny channels of capillary water trapped in the pores of the soil. They are more abundant in upper parts of the soil profile, feeding primarily on bacteria which are also most abundant in the upper soil layers, feeding in turn on organic matter. Much is unknown about soil protozoa, especially their effect on soil. Some may increase the rate and efficiency of nitrogen fixation by bacteria, and thereby be vitally important to soil fertility.

Soil fungi are just as abundant as soil bacteria. Most soil fungi are *saprophytes*; they live on dead or dying organic material. As a result they perform essential roles in the decomposition of organic matter. Their main sources of food are the more resistant organic molecules common to plants. Cellulose, lignin, and starch are resistant to bacterial composition but are easily decomposed by fungi. The distribution of soil fungi depends on food supply, moisture content, and oxygen concentration. They flourish in moist conditions and can adapt to situations where oxygen is low. However, they will not survive where oxygen is non-existent. Thus, soils that are wet most of the year or permanently frozen will contain few or no fungi. Soil fungi will likely be negligible in Gleysolic and Crysolic soils.

Bacteria are the most important members of the soil community. They occur in all soils but vary in numbers according to environmental conditions. For example, bacteria flourish better in basic than in acidic soils. They are important in recycling many elements, especially nitrogen, which is essential to all green plants. Some species have the ability to remove free nitrogen from the air and form nitrogen compounds that can be absorbed by plants. These nitrogen-fixing bacteria are found in nodules on the roots of legumes such as clover, beans, and peas, as well as free-living in the soil. Some bacteria can decompose insecticides and other organic poisons that man releases into the environment.

Changes in Ontario's Soils

Left without human interference, all of Ontario's upland soils would eventually become Podsolics due to the leaching out of soluble bases. Lowland soils likely would revert to Organics if allowed to return to their natural state. However, both man and nature conspire to change soil character. Man's role today is much more extensive than that of nature.

Cultivation removes the O horizon of a soil, mixing it with the A horizon. If no net loss of humus resulted, cultivation would not destroy natural soil productivity. But the most drastic effect of man on the soils of southern Ontario is erosion. Freshly ploughed, slopes are subject to both sheet and gully erosion that wash humus to the low field corners or to surface streams, and speed up leaching of nutrients to soil depths below the reach of roots. Because humus provides surfaces for mineral exchange with rootlets, its loss drastically reduces soil fertility.

The common antidote to loss of natural soil fertility is to lace the land with chemical fertilizers. Such additions can have profound effects on soil chemistry, soil pH, and soil animals. Part or all of the remaining soil profile is lost, with the result that physical conditions deteriorate; soil particles become compacted and their blocky structure is destroyed.

Continuous cultivation leads to more rapid decomposition. Discing, harrowing, and other farm operations introduce more oxygen into the soil, resulting in an increased rate of oxidation. The organic soils of the Holland Marsh may be subsiding at the rate of about three centimetres a year.

Conservation practices can help. Contour ploughing, strip cropping, crop rotation, additions of organic material, and appropriate use of chemical fertilizers, pesticides, and herbicides can do much to maintain agricultural land in good condition.

Soils are also altered by drainage of wetlands. Removal of water from a swamp or a bog allows oxygen to enter the spaces between soil particles, and, just as on cultivated land, the organic component of the soil is oxidized. As well, much soil has been removed or paved over in urban environments.

In northern Ontario, both forestry and forest fires have had pronounced effects on soil. Clear-cutting on slopes results in soil erosion. Nutrients, especially nitrogen, are more easily removed from the soil and washed to nearby rivers and streams. Soil is compacted by heavy machinery, and profiles destroyed by skidding logs. Chemical sprays have reduced soil life. Fire, more common with intensive human use of the forests, often burns the organic soil layer, and resultant ash is blown or washed away.

Fire, on the other hand, can increase soil productivity, speeding up the nutrient cycles by unlocking nutrients stored in boles and limbs of trees. Wood ash is particularly high in phosphorus, which significantly increases regrowth. Conversely, nitrogen is often less available after a series of burns, and poor growth is a result. In addition, there is a decrease in micro-organisms immediately after a fire, although many times they will recover quickly.

Human activity has increased soil productivity in other ways. The introduction of grasses and legumes into what was once a forested southern Ontario has resulted in thicker soil surface layers on lands used for pasture or hay. Evidence also exists that surface Podsolic and Brunisolic soils have been improved by increased earthworm populations in such districts as Muskoka, Parry Sound, and Nipissing. Perhaps fishermen have contributed to worm populations in the north by casting their bait aside once their fishing holiday is over.

Soil Conservation

How we value and how we conserve our soils depends upon our willingness to give them legal protection from exploitation and mismanagement. If we consider soils as nothing more than real estate then we will continue to abuse them.

Good soils grow everything best – agricultural crops, forests, wildlife – because for nutrients, the non-living and living parts of ecosystems are one continuum. The richest soils – the Luvisolics, Brunisolics, and Gleysolics – are found in southern Ontario; the soils of the Shield in central and northern Ontario are primarily thin, acid, and stony. Thus, only a little over 2 per cent of the province is considered Class I for agriculture, about the same amount is Class II, and about 3 per cent is Class III. This 7 per cent constitutes all of Ontario's prime agricultural lands.

Ontario's soils have been ten thousand years in the making. Projections have been made that, with current rates of erosion, in forty years all the topsoil on agricultural lands in the province may be gone. Then, a risky dependence on imported or artificial fertilizers will have to replace natural fertility. Acid precipitation poses another threat. All living things depend ultimately on the soil. If we destroy the productivity of our soils, at stake is much of the diversity of nature.

◆ SCIENCE ◆ EXCURSION ◆

Springtails: Agents of Change

David Barr

Ontario's most populous animal species is not a bird or mammal; it's not a resident of fresh-water lake or Arctic sea, nor a creature of the air. Instead, it is certain to be a member of the soil fauna, and it might very well be an invertebrate group known as springtails, member of the Order Collembola.

Collembola are tiny, six-legged arthropods (related to lobsters, spiders, and insects) which look a lot like insects although they may be only distantly related to them. More important than their evolutionary relationships is the incredible abundance of Collembola in soils. The population estimates are almost unbelievable, ranging from about twenty-five thousand per square metre to over 10 million per cubic metre! And they occur in all Ontario soils, from Pelee Island to the high Arctic, as well as around the rest of the world, from rock crevices in the Antarctic to hot sands in the Mojave Desert. The only other Ontario animal populations that even come close in numbers and ubiquity are also soil invertebrates: the mites, nematodes, and enchytraeid worms.

As might be expected with such a numerous animal, Collembola are also very small, averaging less than two millimetres in length. They come in two basic varieties. The most familiar one has a short, rounded body, long antennae, and the remarkable ability to jump distances of twenty to fifty times their own length. These are the so-called springtails, and to the extent that they are noticed by most of us at all, are the tiny, blackish, jumping "bugs" that occasionally show up in the soil around house plants.

Although a full inventory of the Ontario species of Collembola has not yet been completed, we know the province is home to at least several hundred different kinds. Many can be distinguished without the aid of magnification, especially if a handful of fresh, fertile soil is spread out on a piece of white cloth. While most are coloured in retiring browns and greys, some species are a brilliant orange, green, purple, or blue.

Late fall emergence of springtails in Backus Woods, southwestern Ontario.
MARK STABB

Springtails are especially visible when they jump with the aid of their forked tail. The tail is flexed to fold under the body where it is held in place by a peculiar peg-like structure projecting below the abdomen. Energy is stored when the tail is latched beneath the body and released when the catch is slipped. The sudden straightening of the tail propels the animal forward two to five centimetres at a bound.

Springtails are found primarily in the surface layers of the soil where the air spaces between soil particles are large enough to accommodate their relatively long legs and antennae. But a second kind of Collembola is found in the deeper layers of the soil. These are also insect-like animals, but longer and more cylindrical than springtails, clearly segmented, and with short stubby legs and antennae. The springing organs of these subterranean creatures are reduced so that they are primarily crawlers. Even their eyes may be lost, for they normally inhabit the deeper soil where air spaces are smaller and light seldom penetrates.

Whatever their appearance or favoured soil microhabitat, most Collembola feed primarily on plant material. It may be the filamentous threads of fungae weaving through the soil; it may be living higher plants or bits of dead leaves and twigs that litter the soil; it may be microscopic soil algae and yeasts. Most Collembola are *saprophages* – they feed on dead organic matter such as carrion and animal faeces. A very few, however, are carnivores and prey on microscopic soil invertebrates or insect eggs. In turn, Collembola are fed upon by other invertebrate carnivores in the soil, such as some beetles, mites, and pseudoscorpions.

Like many insects, Collembola have a high reproductive potential. Males and females do not even need to find each other for fertilization, because the males simply deposit small, stalked packets of spermatozoa throughout their environment. Females then pick up the sperm packets wherever they find them and are fertilized. Eggs are laid in batches of 5 to 100 each, and when they hatch within a few weeks, the young are miniature versions of their parents. The young feed on the same rich food sources as the adults and can grow quickly. In as little as six weeks, they will become sexually mature and begin reproducing.

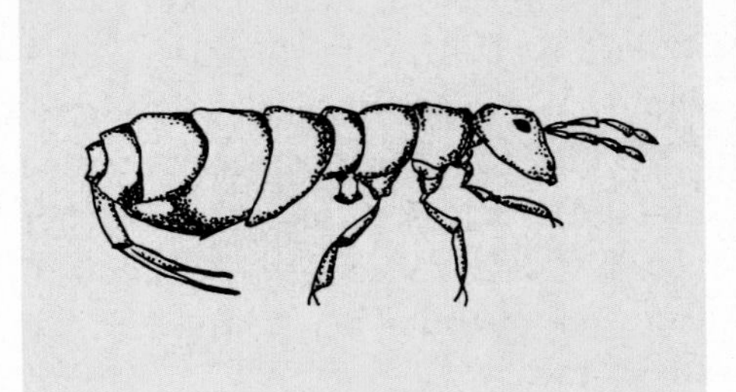

Elongated springtail.

Although Collembola are dependent on a high relative atmospheric humidity of 90 per cent or more, which is characteristic of the air spaces within moist soil, they can survive markedly unfavourable conditions too. They can lie dormant beneath frozen soil in winter. During prolonged drought, they can enter a state of torpidity called *diapause* and survive for up to eighteen months without feeding. Collembola populations are greatly reduced when soils are disturbed by ploughing, but bounce back quickly after seeding.

Globular springtail.

But what do Collembola actually do for the soil? Fertile soil is a complex medium. When first derived from finely divided rock, it is barren and nearly lifeless. Only the hardiest of plants can survive. With time, however, soil productivity increases due to the progressive integration of organic materials produced by plants and animals. When organisms die, their organic material is added to the soil and supplies the chemicals which nourish plant growth and provide complex organic compounds that bind fertile soil particles together.

But dead vegetation such as leaves and twigs do not simply dissolve into the soil on their own. In their original state, they are actually rather resistant to attacks by fungi and bacteria. Only after *comminution*, the process of being ground up into hundreds of thousands of minute particles, do these rich organic materials become vulnerable. This "processing" prepares the litter for attack by those micro-organisms which will complete its breakdown to simpler elements.

Collembola are agents of this processing. They are primarily *detritivores*, feeding on relatively unchanged organic materials. With countless millions of tiny jaws, they reduce it to a finely ground base for fungal and bacterial growth. Together with the detritivorous mites, Collembola are one of the major forces releasing organic material and redistributing it in the soil. Other organisms, like earthworms, may do the same job, but by their sheer numbers, Collembola hold pride of place in the health of Ontario soils.

Hardy Pioneers
Lichens of Ontario
Irwin M. Brodo

Among the aspects of the north that contribute strongly to Ontario's special feeling of "wilderness" is its abundance of lichens–festooning the spruces, colouring the rocks, carpeting the forest floor. Ironically, most people travelling through northern Ontario overlook lichens, noticing instead the trees and rocks they grow upon; those who spend their lives in southern Ontario rarely have an opportunity to see any lichens at all.

Lichens often are ignored because they are so unlike other kinds of plants. In fact, strictly speaking, they are not plants at all, but fungi and microscopic algae growing together in composite structures. The integration is so complete that until little more than one hundred years ago, scientists regarded them as a separate plant form.

This *symbiotic* or mutually beneficial partnership is such a successful way of life that 18,000 to 20,000 species of fungi live as lichens. We have about 700 or 800 species in Ontario. Of these, about half are little more than crusts, tightly covering bark, rock, or soil, which cannot be removed without taking their substrate with them; these are the *crustose lichens*. The others are either more or less flat, leafy forms called *foliose lichens*, or three-dimensional, cushion or hair-like forms called *fruticose lichens*.

Lichens can be grey, green, yellow, orange, or red. They can be fringed and delicate, or lumpy and lobed. They can be so small that they actually live within the upper layers of a rock with only their fruiting bodies poking out. The only feature they all have in common is their means of obtaining nutrition – the fungus-alga partnership.

Because lichens actually are comprised of two organisms, each lichen has two names, one for the alga and one for the fungus. To make things less complicated, lichens are referred to only by the name of their fungal component. The assumption, true in the vast majority of cases, is that each lichen is caused by a different species of fungus. Identifying a particular species of foliose or fruticose lichen can often be done by eye or with a hand lens. Naming crustose lichens almost always involves examining the fruiting bodies and spores of the fungus under a microscope.

Something about the process of being a lichen makes it possible for many species to form special chemical compounds found in no other organism, the so-called lichen substances. Strange to say, although these compounds have many uses for man, we are not entirely sure of their use for lichens themselves. Some are used as antibiotics for humans, some in dyeing wool, some in the perfume industry, and a few for poisoning wolves (in Europe, not Ontario!) Because these substances are often characteristic of individual species and are fairly easy to demonstrate and even isolate, they are also used to help in lichen identification.

Lichens most often reproduce simply by fragmentation. A piece containing both fungal and algal components will begin growing on any suitable substrate. Each particle may contain just a few algal cells wrapped in fungal tissue. Specialized fragments, such as powdery *soredia* or tiny outgrowths called *isidia* have evolved in many species making this asexual fragmentation method of reproduction extremely effective.

Although it is obviously more efficient for both organisms in a dual relationship like a lichen to reproduce at once, the lichen components can also reproduce independently. The algae multiply within a lichen asexually and become spread when a lichen breaks apart and the alga escapes the partnership. Lichen algae can live independently, but the fungal partners can only survive as lichens. The lichen fungi form sexual spores, usually in cup-shaped or flask-shaped fruiting bodies. These spores are dispersed by wind or water and can germinate on a suitable substrate. If the germinating fungus encounters precisely the right species or even race of alga, it will form a new lichen. That a lichen fungus should encounter its own particular alga sounds like a chancy business, but it apparently happens all the time in nature. In fact, fertile crustose lichens probably use this reproductive route most of the time.

Lichens are especially interesting for two reasons. First, they seem to have a penchant for growing in extremely inhospitable places, such as on bare, sun-scorched rocks, tree bark or twigs, old wood, and barren, thin soil. Secondly, lichens are very sensitive to most types of air pollution, especially sulphur dioxide, the princi-

Two types of lichen fruiting bodies: isidia and soredia.

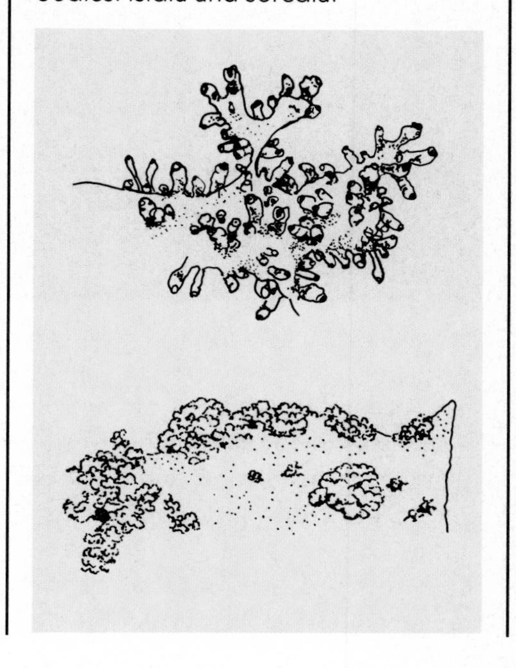

Map lichen (*Rhizocarpon geographicum* group) on a granite boulder in Pukaskwa National Park.
JOHN THEBERGE

A community of six lichen species in the Waterloo Region: soldier cap lichen (*Cladonia cristatella*) is red, among which is brown *Cladonia gracilis* and the yellow cups of *Cladonia pleurota*. The grey, single stalks in centre right are *Cladonia bacillaris*. The branched, grey lichens along the bottom are reindeer moss (*Cladina rangiferina*), and the similar-looking but yellow lichen in the bottom corner is *Cladina mitis*.
JOHN THEBERGE

pal source of acid rain. These two unique properties are related. Unlike most plant forms, lichens can live on the moisture in the air. In other words, they do not need roots and thus are free to grow on hard, impenetrable surfaces. The green or blue-green algae within lichens provide all the nutrition the fungus partner needs, with enough left over for the algae themselves. When the air is dry, the lichens dry out and become dormant. If any moisture becomes available, however, even during the winter, they will begin growth again. Lichens, therefore, are very independent.

Unfortunately, lichens have to pay for this independence. They grow extremely slowly, most of them less than two to four millimetres per year. Because they absorb moisture from the air, they also absorb the acids dissolved in atmospheric water; they have no filtering mechanism. Since they do not drop leaves in the fall or discard diseased parts, these poisons accumulate. Soon, even under relatively low levels of air pollution, the algae in the lichen are weakened or killed, and the partnership is dissolved. Within weeks, the lichen decays and disappears. That is why so few lichens are seen in Ontario's urban centres.

Ontario is, however, still one of the most lichen-rich provinces. In one locality near the north shore of Lake Superior, over one hundred different species were once collected within a few hours. The reasons for this unusual diversity and abundance of lichens are the diversity in microhabitats and the moist, clean air. The firs and spruces host one set of lichens on their bark and branches; other species are found on the pines; still others live on poplars, maples, cedars, and other trees. Each rock type supports its own species of lichens, and those rocks located mostly in the shade have different species from those in the sun. The lake and stream shores display others, some forming bright orange or white spots on rocks splashed by water, and some forming very distinct black zones just above the water level. Bare, sun-lit soil always exhibits dozens of species of fruticose lichens such as *Cladonia*, but also less noticeable crustose species. Thus, each microhabitat sustains a characteristic lichen flora.

From north to south, the lichen vegetation changes dramatically. On the tundra fringing Hudson and James bays, lichens are among the most conspicuous forms of life. The bright yellow-green map lichen (*Rhizocarpon geographicum*) forms almost circular patches on exposed boulders. Their slow growth, less than one millimetre per year, has been used to date glacial features and artifacts in the north, and there is evidence that some large patches may be thousands of years old.

A particularly striking aspect of an Arctic landscape is the presence on the flat tundra of brightly coloured boulders covered with orange-red patches of *Xanthoria elegans* and *Caloplaca*, blue-grey *Physcia* species, and yolk-yellow *Candelariella*. These boulders serve as perches for snowy owls or gulls, and so their surfaces are well fertilized. This lichen community, responding to the unusual abundance of nitrogen in the notoriously nitrogen-poor Arctic soils, has parallels growing on calcium-rich substrates such as caribou bones and musk-oxen skulls which also dot the Arctic landscape.

In the sub-Arctic and northern boreal zones, the reindeer lichens, species of *Cladina*, cover the exposed ground with an almost closed mat over the one-third of the entire region not consisting of water or closed forest. These lichens and some similar fruticose species comprise the main winter diet of woodland caribou. Few other animals are able to utilize the largely insoluble carbohydrates, low proteins, and sparse fats available in this material.

Xanthoria elegans on limestone, Bruce Peninsula. LARRY LAMB

Farther south, in the southern boreal zone, spruce and fir trees are draped with various hair lichens: the black *Bryorias* and the yellow-green *Alectorias* and *Usneas*, also eaten by caribou and sometimes white-tailed deer. Branches are covered with the

Cladina stellaris forming a deep mat in a jack pine forest, Pukaskwa National Park. JOHN THEBERGE

Usnea cavernosa in Sibley Provincial Park. DON GUNN

abundant *Hypogymnia physodes*, a curious species without a common name that has lobe-tips that burst open exposing masses of granule-like soredia.

A whole new set of lichens can be found in the northern hardwood zone, where sugar maple and white pine are first encountered. Whereas about 80 per cent of the boreal and tundra lichens in Ontario are found in comparable regions of Europe and Asia, the northern hardwood forest lichens are most characteristic of North America. This flora repeats itself in similar forests on the east coast and down the Appalachian Mountains. The huge lungwort (*Lobaria pulmonaria*) is one species characteristic of old, mature maples and birches from eastern Lake Superior to Fundy National Park in New Brunswick. In recent years, however, it has been all but eliminated from southern Ontario due to habitat reduction and air pollution. The lichens of the deciduous forests along the Lake Ontario shore, with their southern affinities, have largely disappeared.

Lichens, then, are our first indicators of a deteriorating environment. The challenge is whether or not we will heed their warning. If we don't, it is doubtful that there will be any significant lichen vegetation left in accessible parts of Ontario in twenty-five to fifty years.

OPPOSITE
Lungwort (*Lobaria pulmonaria*) on a yellow birch. Because of its sensitivity to air pollution, this lichen is fast disappearing. SHARON GOWAN

Mystical Kingdom
Ontario's Forest Fungi
Sheila C. Thomson

Early man was baffled by the sudden appearance of mushrooms on the forest scene, and by their equally mysterious disappearance, sometimes for years. As a consequence, fungi, like other puzzling phenomena of nature, were surrounded with superstition, myth, and miraculous healing properties. Even to this day, fragments of this fungi folklore still hang on.

Much of the aura of mystery surrounding fungi stems from their "invisible" nature. In the forest, fungi consist of fine thread-like growths, masses of microscopic filaments embedded in the tissue of the host plant, or permeating the soil and duff. Until the fungus happens to produce a fruit-body – perhaps in the form of puffball or mushroom – it is virtually invisible to the casual eye. (The term *mushroom*, strictly speaking, refers only to one particular family of fungi that have gills, but in common practice it is applied to all conspicuous, fleshy fungi.)

Traditionally, fungi have been classed as part of the plant kingdom. As do the mosses and other lower plant forms, the fungi reproduce by spores rather than seeds. Nevertheless, modern thinking removes them to a separate kingdom of their own.

Fungus spores, usually single cells, are microscopic in size. It would take about 150 typical mushroom spores to form a chain one millimetre long. Being microscopic, the spores eluded even the sharpest eyes of early searchers, who were puzzled to find no sign of seeds in these strange plant-like growths. Fungus spores are produced, often in astronomical numbers, within structures called *fruit-bodies*. It is the fruit-body of a fungus that we are seeing when we discover a morel in the spring woods, or a big bracket shelving out from the trunk of a tree. A fruit-body is not the fungus plant itself, any more than a milkweed pod is the milkweed plant itself. A milkweed pod – or a rose hip, or pine cone – is the counterpart of the fruit-body in the fungus world. The different forms assumed by fungus fruit-bodies identify them and provide clues to their relationships with one another, and thus to a classification.

In spite of the great diversity of showy fungi in Ontario's forests, almost all belong in one or other of two large groups: the *basidium fungi* (Basidiomycetes) and the *ascus fungi* (Ascomycetes). These two groups are distinguished by beautifully clear-cut but microscopic characters. The microscope enables us to see the elegant organization of the spore-bearing surface. An acquaintance with the two terms, *ascus* and *basidium*, will provide a better understanding of the functioning of fruit-bodies, even though the cells in question are microscopic and thus beyond easy visual grasp.

Two types of fungi fruiting bodies: basidiospore and ascospore.

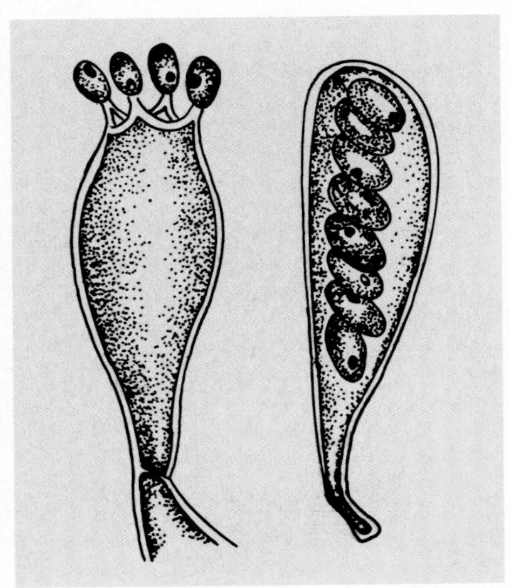

Basidiomycetes, such as the mushrooms, produce their spores on a compact layer of special cells called *basidia*. A typical basidium is an elongated club-shaped cell with four prongs at its tip, each prong bearing one external spore. At maturity, the spores are shot from the prongs of the basidium. On the other hand, Ascomycetes, including cup-fungi and their relatives, produce their spores inside special cells called *asci*. A typical ascus is a sausage-shaped sac enclosing a row of eight spores. The spore-bearing surface of cup-fungi and other Ascomycetes is a tightly-packed layer of these sacs, somewhat resembling a layer of upright test tubes. At maturity, Ascomycetes release their spores by exploding them forcibly into the air, blowing open the hinged lid or other aperture at the top of each microscopic sac.

Fungi in the Forest Community

Lacking the green chlorophyll of leafy plants, and thus the means to manufacture their own food, the fungi have turned an apparent handicap to advantage by feeding on material manufactured by other organisms. Many fungi exist as parasites on living plants or animals, often causing disease and decay. The familiar honey mushroom, for example, is a harmful parasite, aggressively attacking and damaging its host tree.

Surprisingly, many fungi co-exist in complete harmony with their respective host organisms. Lichens are the classic example of mutually beneficial partnerships between fungi and green plants, in this case algae. Some flowering plants, too, are actually dependent upon a fungus partner for their well-being. Some wild orchids require the presence of certain fungi in the soil in order to germinate and grow. Some mushrooms and many boletes associate themselves with certain tree species, without harm to the tree. In such cases, the microscopic filaments of the fungus plant in the soil form an intricate association with the fine rootlets of the tree, a *mycorrhizal* (fungus-root) association which benefits both tree and fungus.

A large number of fungi, however, simply feed on dead organic material. These are the great re-cycling agents of forest ecosystems, constantly breaking down plant and animal material and returning it to the soil. No doubt fungi play a variety of less obvious roles in the forest as well, interacting with other organisms in unsuspected ways. Although much has yet to be learned, it is certain that the fungi play a vital role in the complex inter-relationships that keep forest communities dynamic and healthy.

Fungus Names

Lack of common names and the unwieldiness of their scientific names presents a major stumbling block to familiarity with even the most common forest fungi. We find it difficult to remember names – *Tremella mesenterica*, for example – which do not impart some image to our minds. Witches' butter, on the other hand, a simple folk name for the same yellow jelly fungus that grows on rotting logs, will stay with us forever. Luckily, most of the big families of fungi, such as the puffballs and the cup-fungi, are easily recognized and named by anyone who takes a critical look at the fruit-bodies.

In spite of a demonstrated need for common names for fungi, without the internationally accepted rules for those unpronounceable scientific names, the science of mycology – the study of fungi – would be in utter chaos.

Basidiomycetes

The Polypore Family

Perhaps the most familiar Basidiomycetes are the large woody brackets, often called fairy-steps, that shelve out from the sides of tree trunks and stumps. These brackets are the polypore (many-pored) fungi. Close examination of a mature bracket's underside will reveal that it is covered with minute pore-like openings through which the microscopic spores are shed. Bracket fungi always position their fruit-bodies so that the pored surface faces down, since the spores, which are released from the basidia into vertical columns inside the bracket, depend on gravity for their eventual escape to the open air. As the hundreds of thousands of spores in a large polypore drop free, even the slightest air current will carry them away. In very still weather, a mass of brown spore powder sometimes can be found on top of a bracket. These spores were shed by the bracket immediately above in the cluster and provide a rare opportunity to see and feel these minute cells. Polypore fruit-bodies are woody or leathery in texture, and some kinds remain actively growing for many years.

Several common polypores are easy to recognize. Turkeytails are small,

Sulphur polypore (*Polyporus sulphureus*) on a red oak near Ottawa.
H. A. THOMSON

thin, and leathery, appearing in great clusters on old stumps and logs. Their fan-shaped brackets are beautifully banded in greys and browns. Anglers are familiar with the thick birch polypore or fisherman's fungus. This is a smooth, rounded, pale grey or brownish bracket, common on birch trees, with a surface soft enough that loose fish hooks can be embedded in it for storage.

Some common polypores are richly coloured. The stalked woody hemlock bracket, mahogany red, has a lacquered sheen as if freshly varnished. Another beautiful species, the sulphur polypore, grows on hardwoods and has no look-alike. It is a startling sight to come upon a big cluster of its brilliant yellow or orange brackets pushing out from the side of a tree trunk. When young and tender, this polypore is delicious to eat, well deserving its common name, chicken-of-the-woods.

Apart from decorating the forest trees, what role do polypores play in forest ecosystems? To the forester, the answer is simple. They are feeding on the tissue of the invaded tree, degrading or ruining the wood for commercial purposes. From the standpoint of forest ecology, however, polypores are active agents for change and renewal. Polypore spores tend to invade a tree at an open wound, perhaps where a branch has broken off. The germinating spore sends a network of fungus filaments through the tissue of the host tree, gradually causing rot. As decay progresses, the tree weakens, so that it is the first to fall under the stress of wind storms or heavy snows. In the sunny glade thus created, other organisms move in to take advantage of the changing habitat. Tree seedlings needing sunlight get a start. Other plants, growing slowly in shade, grow faster with the added light and begin to produce flowers. Eventually the decaying log itself provides habitat for a whole community of animals and plants: deer mice, red-backed salamanders, beetles, ants, mosses, lichens, mushrooms, and slime moulds.

The Mushroom Family

Wild mushrooms come in a fascinating array of shapes, sizes, colours, and textures. However, all have one feature in common. On the undersurface of the mushroom cap is a series of blades, called *gills*, which radiate spoke-like from the stalk to the cap margin. Mushroom spores are released from basidia into the spaces between the gills. Gravity carries the spores down to open air below the cap, for dispersal on passing air currents.

A typical mushroom fruit-body is umbrella-shaped, with a central stalk topped by a hemispherical cap. From this basic shape, many variations have evolved so that a mushroom cap may be conical, shell-shaped, bell-shaped, funnel-shaped, or irregular – but as long as its spores are borne on the gilled under-surface of the cap, it is still a mushroom.

Mushroom fruit-bodies can vary in size from a few millimetres to many centimetres across. One of Ontario's largest mushrooms, the big white horse mushroom of pasture land, has been known to reach a diameter of almost thirty centimetres. By contrast, some delicate forest species raise a thread-like stalk only two or three millimetres high, topped by a minuscule cap, so that it takes very keen eyesight to make out the tiny gills that are the hallmark of a mushroom. Between these two extremes can be found every possible size and stature.

Most mushroom fruit-bodies last only a few days. In a good mushroom season the mushroom hunter can walk the same path through a woods week after week discovering new mushrooms on each occasion. While many kinds of mushrooms fruit dependably year after year in suitable habitat, other kinds rarely form fruit-bodies. Several years may elapse between fruiting seasons for some rarely collected mushrooms.

An ever-expanding underground mushroom colony sometimes reveals its size and shape by the position of fruit-bodies which it periodically sends to the surface at its outer perimeter. Occasionally, in unobstructed grassy areas, one may find a complete circle of mushrooms. The fruit-bodies subsequently disappear, leaving only a mysterious ring of discoloured grass, the fairy ring of folklore. In wooded areas, large arcs rather than circles of mushrooms are sometimes found, the colony being distorted by tree roots and other obstructions.

It is unfortunate that we lack an adequate vocabulary to describe mushroom odours. Many mushrooms have an odour distinctive enough to be used as a diagnostic characteristic. A small marasmius mushroom, smelling strongly of garlic, is used in soups. One woodland agaricus is as fragrant as vanilla. A nippy odour of chlorine distinguishes a whole group of little bell-shaped mycena mushrooms. The fruity apricot fragrance of the edible chantarelle is well known to mushroom hunters. Other kinds of mushrooms are noted for smelling of almonds, raw corn, bitter nuts, fish, even mouse urine! Cataloguing the odours of the wild mushrooms in your favourite woodland is one way of getting to know them better.

Wild mushrooms, like wild berries, are surely meant to be eaten. The difference in flavour between a wild mushroom and the commercial kind can be as great as that between a freshly picked sun-ripened peach and a canned peach. A large number of wild mushrooms are edible and delicious. Some are distasteful, mildly poisonous, or deadly. Our knowledge of edible and poisonous mushrooms has come down to us over the centuries through painful experimentation by country folk. The trial-and-error method can prove unpleasant, even disastrous. It is worth repeating the old warning that no rule of thumb is safe when deciding on the edibility of a wild mushroom. There are too many poisonous kinds, too many different chemical substances involved. Unless you are familiar enough with a wild mushroom to know it by name, you do not know it well enough to eat. Fortunately, excellent mushroom handbooks are on the market today. Certainly, no one should attempt to collect wild mushrooms for food unless he or she can recognize the innocent-looking but deadly poisonous death angel. A number of other kinds are almost as virulent.

The Puffball Family

Some of the more intriguing designs for spore dispersal have evolved among the puffballs and their kin. The familiar puffballs of meadow and woodland are comparatively simple fruit-bodies, essentially globes or pear-shaped cases containing a mass of spores. The most primitive method of spore release among the puffballs is simply the cracking of the outer wall when the fruit-body is mature. Some puffballs are able to scatter their spores farther afield by breaking free from the parent plant and rolling to new locations, carried along by wind or other agents. Many common puffballs have a large pore that opens at the apex of the ball when the spores are mature. Spores are puffed out and carried on the wind when the puffball is struck by a large raindrop, or trampled by a passing animal, or squeezed by a child who wants to see it puff.

Some of the earthstars, which are actually puffballs with a double outer case, are able to raise their fruit-bodies slightly above the ground for spore dispersal, standing on tiptoes, as it were. How do they manage this feat? The outer of the two layers of the puffball case splits into petal-like segments, which curl outward to produce the characteristic star pattern. They then proceed to curl downward, their tips pressing against the ground and acting as legs which raise the central spore-bearing case into position for spore dispersal.

The curious stinkhorns also belong in the puffball family, and in fact they first appear above ground in puffball-like cases called *eggs*. As a stinkhorn develops, it bursts out of its egg and

The beautifully ornamented spore case of the puffball *Lycoperdon*.
H. A. THOMSON

Earthstars are elegant puffballs. Here the apical pore through which the spores are shed is clearly visible.
H. A. THOMSON

Splash cups of the bird's nest fungus *Cyathus striatus*. Three cups contain spore pellets that have not yet been ejected. H. A. THOMSON

sends up a stout stalk, cone-shaped at the top. At this stage of development, several of the stinkhorns are very attractive, one displaying a beautiful rose-coloured stalk, another bearing a delicate, lacy white veil. Not for long can their beauty be admired, however! On the apical cone there develops a foul-smelling slimy matrix filled with the maturing spores. Attracted by the disgusting odour of rotting flesh, carrion insects gather in the slimy mass and carry away stinkhorn spores in the slime which adheres to them.

Most fascinating of all this family are the little bird's nest fungi. Growing in small groups on twigs, wood chips, or soil, the largest approach the size of a thimble. The smallest are only a few millimetres across. When mature, each tiny cup (the "nest") opens to display its clutch of hard little pellets (the "eggs"). The nest, little splash-cups, are the open fruit-bodies, while the eggs are pellets of mature spores. In some species, the splash-cups are shaped with such mathematical precision that a large raindrop landing in the cup can eject the pellets of spores to a distance of one or two metres! In some, the pellets are coated with an adhesive substance so that they stick firmly to whatever vegetation they strike. They are dispersed when the dead leaves fall and blow to new locations. An elegant refinement to this spore-dispersal mechanism has been evolved by some species. Attached to each pellet of spores is a cobweb-fine filament coiled up in a storage pocket until the pellet is sent flying from the cup. When the adhesive end of the filament strikes a blade of grass, it sticks and holds. The flying pellet of spores is pulled up short, its momentum causing it to twirl round and round the grass blade on the end of its filament. Here it remains, firmly attached to the vegetation. Browsing animals now join the dispersal team, feeding on the vegetation and dispersing the spore capsules in their dung.

Other Eye-Catching Basidiomycetes

Not every umbrella-shaped fruit-body turns out to be a mushroom. Boletes look for all the world like stout little mushrooms until one checks the undersurface of the cap to find a layer of soft tubes instead of gills. This group of fungi includes the famed edible boletus and many other prized edible species, along with several poisonous kinds. Most boletes that appear to be growing in soil are in fact growing in intimate association with the root system of a tree, having struck a biological bargain that benefits both tree and fungus in the acquisition of nutrients.

Hydnums, too, can resemble mushrooms, but the spore-bearing surface of a hydnum fruit-body is covered with a layer of spiny teeth. Even some stalked polypores mimic the umbrella shape of a mushroom, but the pored under-surface of the cap, and the woody texture of the whole fruit-body will identify a polypore, whatever its shape.

Numerous other showy Basidiomycetes inhabit Ontario's forests, including beautiful coral fungi, jellycaps, horns-of-plenty, and the delightful little earth-tongues, to mention only a few. All are engaged in interacting with other organisms and competing for a niche in the forest community.

Scarlet cup, an Ascomycete, sends up its fruit-body very early in the spring.
JOHN THEBERGE

Eyelash cup decorates the trunk of a fallen tree. H. A. THOMSON

Orange-peel fungus near Ottawa.
H. A. THOMSON

Ascomycetes – The Cup-Fungi

Sooner or later the mushroom seeker will discover cup-fungi growing in a woodland. The fruit-bodies of cup-fungi are miniature bowls, saucers, or discs. These ascomycetes are often inconspicuous in colour, or so small as to escape notice, but the woods abound with them. Several common cup-fungi are strikingly attractive. The beautiful scarlet cup is found in April, when the woods are still wet from melting snows. It grows attached to fallen hardwood twigs that lie half buried in damp, black humus. The interior of the opening cup displays a surface of blood-red velvet, the richest red in all the colourful world of fungi. Another eye-catching cup-fungus is the orange peel. Its saucer-shaped fruit-bodies are often found in summer growing scattered along old logging roads in sandy soil. A first impression on seeing the ground strewn with splashes of orange is that a careless hiker has scattered his orange peelings here. The green-staining cup, colouring the wood of its host tree a deep bluish-green, puts out charming little blue-green discs, attracting attention by their unusual colour. The eyelash cup is an attractive and very common little cup-fungus growing on damp, rotting wood. Each scarlet-orange saucer is rimmed with a fringe of black bristles, the eyelashes.

Spring-fruiting morels and the false morels are close relatives of the cup-fungi, differing essentially in the stalked form of the fruit-body, and the pitted or convoluted spore-bearing surface. Less common but always a delight to come across are stalked goblets and little saddle fungi, some with beautifully fluted stalks, but always in muted colours.

The cup-fungi and their relatives are Ascomycetes. In contrast to Basidiomycetes, they tend to have the spore-bearing surface uppermost, or

at least outermost, since the spores are exploded forcibly into the air from the spore sacs or asci. In cup-fungi, the phenomenon of spore discharge can actually be observed with the naked eye, in spite of the microscopic size of the spores. When a fruit-body is fully mature, a slight change of air pressure may be enough to trigger spore discharge. Moving a few damp leaves from around a cup-fungus, or blowing on its surface, may be enough to cause a sudden puff of spores. An unexplained little puff from leaf litter or a mossy log is often a clue to the presence of a ripe cup-fungus, saddle, or perhaps morel.

Fungus Habitat

Most fleshy fungi thrive in cool, moist situations. A wooded area after a rainy spell in early autumn is the ideal hunting ground for fungi, and the less the woodland has been tidied up by man, the greater the number of fungi that will be found in it. Black spruce forests of northern Ontario may produce great numbers of fungi, but the variety of species will of course be limited to those kinds adapted to the uniform habitat of this forest type. An old hardwood forest, or mixed forest that has been left undisturbed for a long time can bring forth a great profusion of strange and colourful fruit-bodies.

It is almost impossible to convey, to those who have never experienced it, the reality of an old forest during one of those rare seasons when weather patterns trigger a tremendous fruiting of fungi. The hidden world of fungi bursts onto the forest scene in an astonishing display of brilliantly coloured fruit-bodies – cinnamon, yellow, lavender, rose, flaming orange, parrot green, scarlet, as well as all the softer browns and greys. In such a season, it is unforgettable to explore a rich forest on a crisp fall day, making discovery after discovery of fungus forms never before encountered: corals and jellies, funnels and earth-tongues, saddles, shells, clubs, and goblets. Delicately beautiful or strangely grotesque, they excite a sense of wonder and delight that seldom can be experienced in today's technical world.

Coral fungus of the forest floor.
H. A. THOMSON

Hundreds of different fungus species inhabit the forests, unlocking the nutrients in trees, enriching the soil, parasitizing some plants and animals, enabling others to thrive, competing, co-existing, biodegrading. Are they good or bad, friend or foe to the forest? Neither good nor bad, the fungi are a natural, vital, dynamic, and essential part of the forest community.

OPPOSITE
The common fly agaric, colourful but poisonous. H. A. THOMSON

Mycorrhizae: Symbiosis in the Soil

Mark Stabb

Mushrooms, puffballs, stinkhorns, cup-fungi – the spore-producing structures we know as fungi – are merely the pinnacles of a much larger biomass of fungal threads called *hyphae*. The combined weight of this hyphal system may equal two metric tons per hectare, especially in the boreal forest where fungi can be the main instigators of litter breakdown. However, these threads are more than just janitors of the forest. Fungal hyphae are, in fact, silent partners with the roots of many of our best-known flowering plants, shrubs, and trees in the uptake of water and vital nutrients like nitrogen and especially phosphorus. These partnerships are called *mycorrhizae* (literally, fungus-roots).

Fungal hyphae and minute root hairs of plants form a network of feeding appendages throughout the soil. Often they come in contact with one another. If two species are compatible, the fungus hyphae may become so closely entwined with the plant roots that a symbiotic relationship, approaching the creation of a new entity, results. Just as fungi co-operate with algae in the creation of lichens, so fungi link with plant roots in the creation of mycorrhizae.

Mycorrhizal phenomena were unearthed more than one hundred years ago, but only now are we beginning to comprehend this widespread process and its implications. Far from being an anomaly in nature, scientists now believe that mycorrhizal associations might be expected to occur in 90 per cent of all higher plants, from ferns to fir trees.

Fungi can associate with roots either externally or by penetrating the rootlet cells. Fungal threads, about one-half the diameter of fine human hairs, can wrap the root hairs in a sheath, flush with or probing between the root's epidermal cells. These *ectomycorrhizae* are common to coniferous trees such as pine, spruce, and tamarack, and are found also on members of the birch, beech, and willow families. Forests of these species are adorned with many ectomycorrhizal fungi, including many of the gilled mushrooms such as the poisonous fly agaric, and almost all of the Family Boletaceae (which exhibit pores instead of gills) such as the edible old man of the woods (*Strobilomyces floccopus*) and king bolete (*Boletus edulis*).

Ecto- and endomycorrhiza showing the difference in their relationship with a plant root hair.

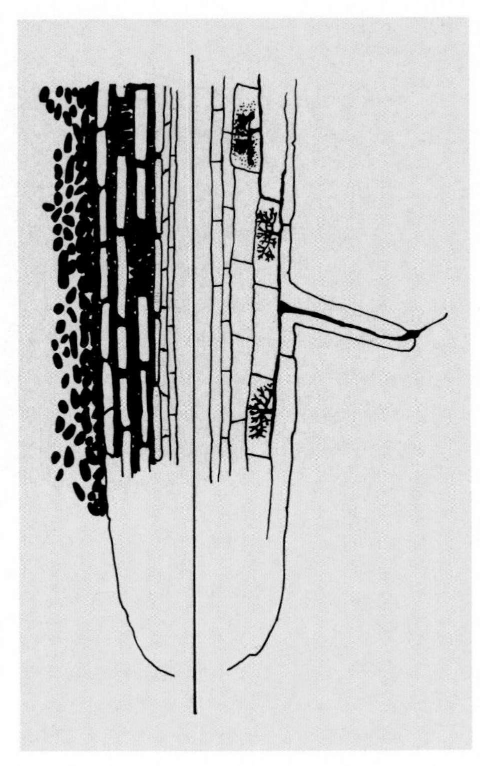

Orchids, heaths, maples, walnuts, grasses, and many crop plants have an even more intimate relationship with fungi. They are prone to *endomycorrhizal* connections in which the hyphae actually penetrate the root and branch out within the epidermal cells, where they exchange elements and water even more effectively than ectomycorrhizae. Endomycorrhizal associations are more common than ectomycorrhizal associations, but they are much more difficult to characterize and study. The few groups of fungi that have been isolated from endomycorrhizae are not known to form fruiting bodies for sexual reproduction. Lacking conspicuous fruiting bodies, their presence in the forest is not easily detected. In fact, these fungi are so committed to mycorrhizal relationship that often they will not grow in the absence of their host plant.

Clusters of coral-like branches associated with roots often indicate endomycorrhizal "infection." Endomycorrhizae give rise to roots that appear stubby, differing greatly from the conventional image of roots that decrease in diameter as they extend away from the trunk. In an extreme case, a non-photosynthetic group of orchids called coralroots derives its name from the mycorrhizae that make plant life possible without chlorophyll.

In most plants, the sugary products of photosynthesis appear to have stimulated the evolution of mycorrhizal fungi. Scientists have tagged plant sugars with small radioactive doses to follow the carbon compounds in plant tissues. A large proportion of the radioactivity later was found to be concentrated in the mycorrhizal fungus. Laboratory research has indicated that normally about 10 per cent of the products of photosynthesis are supplied to mycorrhizal fungi for their services to the host plant.

Why do fungi link up with roots? We know that fungi are quite capable of obtaining energy from sugar derivatives and other carbon compounds in dead organic matter. Evidently a microscopic community revolves around the carbon resources in the soil, with fungal hyphae being just one of many competitors for soil nutrients. The strategy of clinging to or penetrating roots allows fungi direct access to a competitor-free source of readily usable sugars.

Micro-organisms such as nitrogen-fixing bacteria have taken a similar approach to avoiding competition through their incorporation in the root nodules of plants like alders. There the bacteria have unhindered access to the resources of alder roots, and the alder obtains vital nitrogen compounds through this association. The alliance has made alder one of our most hardy plants, able to withstand tremendous water and nutrient deficiencies. Many mycorrhizal plants can survive these same soil stresses and are better at coping with disease, soil acidity, or salinity than are non-mycorrhizal plants.

In some ways, mycorrhizal fungi benefit their host plants by acting as extensions of the plants. Hyphae linked with roots greatly increase the surface area of potential absorptive tissues and quite possibly act as physical barriers to potential disease organisms. Some fungi are also inherently better than plant roots at acquiring nutrients from infertile soils.

As research is uncovering this underground story, previously unknown interactions with mycorrhizae are being postulated. Northern flying squirrels are known to eat large quantities of fungi, especially fungi that grow and fruit beneath the forest floor. Alaskan Indians knew this hundreds of years ago and evidently would not eat flying squirrels because they ate "dirt." "False" truffles, Ontario relatives of the edible European varieties, are good examples of these subterranean-fruiting fungi that are known to be mycorrhizal. Present-day observers have collected faecal samples from northern flying squirrels which, when cultured in laboratories, prove to contain viable spores of fungi. This discovery has led some ecologists to believe that flying squirrels and other fungal gourmets are important dispersal agents for mycorrhizal fungi. Thus it is possible that some mammals may enable forests to recycle nutrients more efficiently.

Research is also pointing to new industrial applications for mycorrhizae. Applied ecologists realize the mycorrhizae help plants handle environmental stresses and are seeking to make use of mycorrhizal knowledge in mine-tailing reclamation, nursery development, and forest operations. In time we may come to recognize mycorrhizal fungi as unexpected allies in our quest for sound environmental management.

Botanical Relics
The Primitive Plants of Ontario
Theodore Mosquin

What are primitive plants? Are any found in Ontario? If so, how many? What do they look like, and where do they grow?

Botanists consider plants to be primitive if they still possess today the same key characteristics which were present in their ancient ancestors, 250 to 400 million years ago. On that basis, it may surprise even the curious observer of nature that, excluding algae, fungi, and lichens, Ontario hosts more than five hundred different species of primitive plants.

Just why key characteristics of some plants, particularly reproductive structures, have survived practically unchanged for eons of time is a scientific puzzle. One theory states that such plants arrived early at near-perfect physical and physiological adaptations. Once perfection was attained, natural selection could hardly act to alter them further. Many of these plants are the botanical equivalent of the coelacanth, an ancient fish discovered in deep waters off the coast of Africa some years ago. Such life forms, whether animal or plant, are truly living fossils.

An outstandingly successful primitive feature of the plant word, one which originated in the Silurian Period some 380 million years ago, is the reproductive propagule called a *spore*. Many kinds of Ontario plants have retained the spore as their primary means of reproduction. While familiar plants such as wildflowers, grasses, and deciduous and coniferous trees reproduce by seeds, the ferns, horsetails, club mosses, true mosses, and liverworts reproduce by spores.

From Woodsias to Maidenhair and Cinnamon Fern

Along the edge of a red maple swamp, one often comes upon great stands of cinnamon or ostrich ferns. Crouched amongst the giant fragrant fronds, the trees and sky shut out, one is transported to another time – an ancient tropical world some 150 million years ago, full of primeval beauty and ruled by dinosaurs. Then, ferns as tall as

Cinnamon fern in Rondeau Provincial Park. P. A. WOODLIFFE

a three-storey house dominated the great virgin swamps of the world. Walking through a fern forest today, it is easy to imagine tracking or being tracked by some huge reptilian monster.

When tracing the history of any one of Ontario's fern species, one confronts vast spans of time, shifting continents, the origin of birds, mammals, and all flowering plants as well as extinctions on a massive scale. Both the giant ferns and the giant reptiles were at their zenith simultaneously, in the Mesozoic Age. The Mesozoic is not recorded in any detail in Ontario because of the near-complete absence of rocks from that time. But since Ontario's climate then was tropical or subtropical, conditions undoubtedly were suitable for both these forms of life. Fossil imprints of fern stems, spores, and giant fronds from elsewhere show that except for size, some ferns have changed little over the ages.

In ferns, flowers as well as seeds are absent. Instead, each plant produces millions of tiny spores which look very much like brown dust. Indeed, one of the best ways to identify a fern species is to take careful note of the location and manner in which the spores are produced. In some species, such as the wood ferns, woodsias, cliff-brakes, spleenworts, polypody, bracken, and others, the spores develop in small brownish spots, streaks, or rusty mats on the underside or edges of their green fronds. But in the cinnamon, sensitive, and ostrich ferns, special fronds are devoted exclusively to spore production. Other ferns, such as the royal and interrupted, have fertile leaflets at the top or in the middle of the frond, while still others, such as the adder's tongue and grape ferns, have a main spore-bearing stalk on which only one leaf grows.

Ferns also spread by a variety of vegetative means. Bracken, for example, owes its success to tough, long, horizontal rhizomes often extending twenty to thirty centimetres underground. Bracken is the best known and the most widely distributed of all Ontario ferns, thriving not only on the acid soils of the Precambrian Shield but on calcareous sites such as in Wellington and Lanark counties. Not only is it widespread in Ontario, but it is one of the world's most successful plants, found all around the northern hemisphere as well as in Australia, South America, and South Africa. What cottager, woodland gardener, or hiker has not been confronted from time to time with a waist-high jungle of bracken?

As autumn approaches, the yellow fronds of bracken colour the floor of the north woods. It deserves our full admiration not only for its success, but its beauty. And for mice, snowshoe hares, chipmunks, and other small mammals, it provides a protective canopy from sharp-eyed avian predators.

Interrupted fern in Algonquin Provincial Park. JOHN THEBERGE

Other Ontario ferns that spread by underground rhizomes are the sensitive, hay-scented, ostrich, and polypody, while one, the bulblet fern, can establish a new plant by disseminating the tiny green bulblets which grow along its fronds. The walking fern develops plantlets on its leaves where they touch the ground.

On a world scale there may be as many as ten thousand fern species, most of them growing in the tropics or subtropics. Many species unfortunately are being exterminated by human pressure. Forty-five species live in Ontario, a conservative estimate, some with more than one recognizable variety. Not all botanists agree on these numbers, however, because in a typical woodlot some individual ferns which appear to be virtually identical may not be. Different numbers of chromosomes, or other obscure characteristics that can only be determined by microscopic or chemical analysis, may create barriers to interbreeding.

Although several species of ferns usually can be found in almost any woodland, one of the best places to find them in abundance is in older forests with large, gnarled trees, extensive canopies, and varied terrain, where the natural ecosystem is still relatively intact. Ferns also thrive near springs, along ravines, and by streams or waterfalls. Many a botanist has risked his life trying to collect that just-out-of-reach fern on a steep cliff.

While bracken and polypody ferns grow well on acid soils, at least several other Ontario species prefer dry, exposed, highly calcareous substratum, usually limestone or dolomite rocks with a high pH. Among these are the walking fern, the rare purple cliff-brake, and wall rue which can be locally common on limestone ridges, cliffs, and crevices in the Bruce Peninsula and Manitoulin Island.

Even the harsh sub-Arctic climate near James and Hudson bays is home to some ferns. The alpine woodsia, the fragile fern, the fragrant shield fern,

Delicate maidenhair fern at Backus Woods, southwestern Ontario.
MARY THEBERGE

and some others occur on acid or calcareous sites. Some, like the alpine woodsia which is widespread in the Arctic, reach their southern limit of distribution along the north shore of Lake Superior. Clearly, these northern species contain as-yet-unknown adaptations to allow them to survive and thrive so far from the warm lands of their tropical ancestors.

One of the most intriguing aspects of Ontario ferns is that while some are sensitive to frost, others remain green all winter long. Thus, the fronds of the marsh fern, the maidenhair, and the bulblet fern will freeze at the slightest frost, while the polypody, Christmas fern, spinulose wood fern, marginal shield fern, and all aspleniums remain green all winter under the snow. Just how this evergreen characteristic should arise in some of our northern ferns, considering the tropical origins of their ancestors, is an interesting scientific question. The possible advantage of staying green is to allow photosynthesis to occur on warm days in the autumn, winter, or spring, but these ferns had to evolve some internal physiological mechanism to allow them to accomplish that.

Eleven species of ferns are considered rare in Ontario, and some are not found in any other province. Among the more abundant rarities are the previously mentioned alpine woodsia, the hart's-tongue fern of the Bruce Peninsula, the broad beech fern of southern Ontario, and the purple cliff-brake which has a sporadic distribution on Manitoulin Island, the Bruce Peninsula, and at several localities in the Niagara area, and near Ottawa and Kingston. Some species are truly rare while others may not be as rare as we think, due to lack of botanical exploration in some parts of the province.

One of the most elegant descriptions of fern habitat is that of the nineteenth-century writer Frances Theodora Parsons, who wrote in 1899:

> No other plants know so well how to choose their haunts. If you wish to know the ferns you must follow them to Nature's most sacred retreats. In remote, tangled swamps, overhanging the swift, noiseless brook in the heart of the forest, close to the rush of the foaming waterfall, in the depths of some dark ravine, or perhaps high up on the mountain-ledge, where the air is pure and the world wider and life more beautiful than we had fancied, these wild things are most at home.

Ground Pine, Ground Cedar, and Other Christmas Greens

Ontario's forests contain another distinct group of spore-bearing plants whose ancestors are well documented in the fossil record, and who lived as giant trees in the Carboniferous Period more than 300 million years ago. Our ten or so species, none growing higher than one or two centimetres, are known as the club mosses or ground pines. These names are very misleading; the plants are not related to either mosses or pines. They are perhaps best known to the general public from the soft evergreen Christmas wreaths available in floral shops each winter.

All our species are perennial and evergreen. They can be particularly common in boreal and transitional forests where sometimes large patches are encountered. The stems are trailing, much-branched, and covered with quite small elliptical leaves. The spores develop in mid summer at the ends of erect stems in structures called *strobili*, which look somewhat like miniature cones.

Club mosses, like ferns, are eaten by relatively few animal species. With no seeds or berries, they have no packaged energy source, except for the spore cases which, when disturbed, explode into a yellow dust. One species, the shining club moss, besides developing large spore sacs, produces bulbils, curious small bulbs that fall to the ground and propagate the species. But even this species is not sought as a food.

Today's ferns are still represented, at least in tropical environments, by giants like their ancestors, but the giant club mosses live no more. Why the giants died out but the diminutive forms survived is a mystery. To contemplate the giant club moss forests that once grew in Ontario while standing in a patch of their stunted survivors is an exercise in imagination.

Horsetails

Books on the life of Ontario's pioneers often refer to the "scouring rushes" used to clean dirty dishes and particularly intransigent cooking pots. The plants in question were actually members of the unique genus *Equisetum*, most likely the species *Equisetum hyemale*. This genus, and this species in particular, with its tough greyish-green stems, possesses almost invisible longitudinal rows of projecting silicon crystals – hence the name *scouring rush*. To demonstrate the cutting power of these crystals, just rub a stem of this species gently against the flat of your fingernail. Only two or three pulls will scrape up a small mound of fine flour-like dust.

Stiff club moss (*Lycopodium annotinum*) in Quetico Provincial Park. Sphagnum moss is in foreground.
SHAN WALSHE

Our most abundant species is probably the field horsetail which, like some ferns, bears two distinct kinds of stems. One stem is short-lived, unbranched, and without chlorophyll, and it bears a large *strobilus* or cone at its apex from which yellow wind-borne spores are released. The other stem is sterile and green and persists through the summer. Most of our species, however, bear their "cones" at the apex of a green branching stem.

A characteristic peculiar to the horsetails is their jointed stems. These can easily be pulled apart, section by section. Leaves grow in whorls only from each joint.

Like ferns and club mosses, the horsetails of Ontario had tall tree-like relatives in the Carboniferous Period whose fossil record is well-preserved.

Carpets of Green – The Mosses

Mosses are an integral part of the Earth's ecosystems; hundreds of other species of plants and invertebrates are dependent upon them or the habitats they create. There is much more to mosses than the myth that they only grow on the north side of a tree!

Because Ontario includes many *biomes* – from the deciduous forest of Point Pelee to the Arctic tundra – and because we have a temperate to cool climate, more than four hundred of the world's nine thousand or so moss species are found here.

The life cycle of a typical moss plant includes two major phases: the *gametophore* phase and the *sporophyte* phase. Sporophytes lack chlorophyll and literally grow out of the top or side of the gametophores. Thousands of gametophores packed together like matchsticks in a box make up the familiar green mossy banks and carpets seen on forest floors, rocks, or tree trunks.

Moss sporophyte growing on gametophyte.

Gametophores are only a few centimetres long and have numerous tiny green leaves. They are anchored to their substratum not by roots, but by filamentous structures called *rhizoids*. Microscopic male and female structures are found on the gametophores, either on the same plant or on different plants depending on species. After fertilization, the sporophyte phase develops *in situ*, out of the fertilized egg. Sporophytes have a very thin stalk topped by a spore-bearing rounded capsule whose shape and manner of spore release varies greatly among the different groups of mosses.

Many mosses are already growing rapidly soon after the snow melts, when spring wildflowers are at their peak. Like the early flowers, they take advantage of the sunlight and moisture availabe to them in April and May, just before the forest floor becomes heavily shaded by leaf growth. In the deciduous forests of southern Ontario, many mosses grow as *epiphytes* – they are anchored well up on the trunks or branches of trees where they can obtain nutrients from rain water, bird droppings, dead insects, decaying tree bark, and dust.

Sexual reproduction in mosses is by spores. One of the most characteristic mosses of Ontario forests is polytrichum, which looks like a miniature spruce tree only three to five centimetres high. Seven species are widely distributed in Ontario. The spores of polytrichum are so small that a single "fruit," only half the size of a raindrop, can produce more than 65 million spores!

The ecology of mosses differs from that of flowering plants in that they can grow on apparently inhospitable surfaces such as tree bark, bare rock, and barren soil. This enables them to fulfill the very important ecological role of first colonizers. Together with lichens they often become established in the harshest of exposed habitats, initiating changes in the substratum that make it suitable for colonization by higher plants.

Moss species can occupy a great variety of habitats. Some, like many ferns, prefer calcareous sites, and their distribution is governed by the location of such sites. Others may grow under water, while still others are restricted to the mounds of earth around animal burrows in the Arctic tundra.

Along the Arctic coast and in the "spray zone" on rocky headlands along the Lake Superior coastline, moss species often form dense, roundish tufts on which grow wildflowers such as saxifrages, potentillas, drabas, and pinks. This peculiar tuft characteristic appears to increase water retention, thus enhancing chances of survival. The densely packed tufts can be surprisingly diverse with up to twenty moss species per square metre, as well as a rich invertebrate fauna, which needs reliable moisture to survive.

Mosses are especially prolific in northern Ontario, with its vast boreal forests and peatlands. Here, under white spruce, balsam fir, jack pine, and white birch the ground may be clothed in a continuous carpet of velvet green. Such splendour is possible on the floor of the boreal forest because the layer of fallen conifer needles is very thin and does not cover mosses, thus allowing ample sunlight for photosynthesis. But the number of moss species in these forests can be low. Extensive carpets often contain only one species, such as, for example, the exquisitely beautiful *Hylocomium splendens*.

The peat mosses, or sphagnums, have a powerful impact on the ecology of bogs and other lowland environments, especially throughout the boreal forest. Given the right circumstances, sphagnums have the ability to grow upward continuously, year after year and century after century for tens of thousands of years. When upward growth is greater than the rate of decay at the base, then peat accumulates steadily until a balance is reached. All other small plant species present on the sphagnums must grow continuously upwards too, or their stem tips will be buried by the moss. In this manner, sphagnums have created the great bogs and peatlands of Ontario.

Over millions of years, flora and fauna have evolved that are adapted to peatland environments. The number and diversity of small invertebrate species that live in the sphagnum is surprising – one site was shown to have 145 species. A comparable non-sphagnum forested site dominated by mosses may accommodate only half that number. Included on the sphagnums may be unicellular ciliates and flagellates, as well as rotifers, nematodes, and various algae and bacteria. Many of these species can tolerate the inevitable periods of desiccation. Some graze on the mosses, others suck their juices, and yet others eat each other; a microcosm of the larger world around them.

Ontario's mosses belong to a large group of equally small plants, collectively known to scientists and naturalist as *bryophytes*. Some of these bryophytes are shaped like miniature livers and hence are called *liverworts*; others have leaves so intricate that they resemble fine lacework and are called *leafy liverworts*. These miniature plants are even more primitive than mosses but can be readily found in places where mosses thrive, because they too like shade and dampness. That the liverworts are ancient is a certainty, but as their tissues are soft, fossilization was difficult, and so their ancestry is more obscure.

Relics of the past, Ontario's primitive plants remind us that *primitive*, far from being a derogatory term, means a longevity unparalleled in the world of plants.

Adornments of the Wild
Ontario's Wildflowers
Theodore Mosquin

Wildflowers. The word conjures up many pictures, recalls many scenes: a clump of white bloodroots carpeting a corner of a maple wood, a patch of fragrant twinflowers perfuming a rocky woodland, a long magenta strip of fireweed colouring a roadside.

About three thousand different kinds of wild flowering plants grow in Ontario, including grasses and sedges, evergreen and deciduous trees, and shrubs. They fill the woods, ravines, shorelines, wetlands, abandoned fields, and wild lands across this enormous province with beauty.

One of the great mysteries about wildflowers is their marvelous diversity of shape, size, colour, and scent. Wild roses, the common roadside dandelion, and the black-eyed Susans of abandoned farm meadows all have bright flower parts radiating in a flat plane from a common centre, like miniature suns. Yet the elegant flowers of golden-orange jewelweed crowding the earthen embankments of many a beaver dam and the tiny flowers of the fragrant wild mint of damp meadows and stream banks are bilaterally symmetrical; the left side of the flower is an exact mirror image of the right. Cardinal flowers blaze scarlet in the greenery bordering gravel stream beds; tall yellow evening primroses hide the scars of old logging roads; purple harebells cling in the crevices of sheer rock cliffs. What, one wonders, were the events and forces which, over vast spans of time, produced all this variety?

The shapes and sizes and pollinating devices assumed by wildflowers are almost endless. The solitary flower of a wild blue flag in a marshy pond serves it just as well as the six to a dozen graceful flower-heads of a red columbine growing on a rocky woodland, or the hundreds of small flowers that make up the inflorescence of a goldenrod or aster blowing in a dry sunny field. Foul-smelling flowers of skunk cabbage and red trillium attract their own particular pollinators just as surely as do the fragrant perfumes of basswood and certain thistles, while many flowers, completely lacking in fragrance, have devised other ways to ensure pollination and seed set.

A number of curious adaptations of wildflowers even evoke movement. The blossoms of some flowers follow the sun as it crosses the sky each day. Some, like the yellow trout lilies, close their petals in the evening, while goat's-beard (also known as Johnnie-go-to-bed-by-noon) closes by mid-day. The laurels catapult their anthers; jewelweed seed capsules explode. And the

Blue flag iris. DON GUNN

Cardinal flower. DON GUNN

bizarre leaves of the sundews and the pitcher plant capture insects!

In contemplating these wildflower adaptations, one catches fleeting insights into the marvelously integrated natural ecosystems of Ontario, indeed of Earth itself. Each adaptation is a demonstration of what can be achieved by living things in the seemingly endless evolution of new forms of life on this planet.

Flowers co-evolved with their pollinators; consequently the two are largely dependent upon each other for survival. Many wildflowers would be unable to produce seed without their insect pollinators, while without flowers, the very survival of some pollen- and nectar-feeding bees, flies, and butterflies would be in jeopardy. In the wild, while the strategies for survival of plants allow most species to bloom for only a week or two, the blossoming of one species is rapidly followed by another so that from the first warm days of spring to the hard frosts of fall, some wildflowers are always available for their insect visitors. In turn, flowering times across the summer affect the abundance and activities of all bees, butterflies, flowerflies, and hummingbirds until the growing cold puts an end to the annual cycle.

Generally, Ontario's flora is the end product of evolution from tropical ancestry, and adaptations must be interpreted in this context. We now know that most of today's flowering plant families came into existence in the early days of dinosaurs. Gradually, over 100 million years, as the North American continent split from Africa and Europe and drifted away, more and more tropical lands came under the influence of temperate and Arctic climates, a process that is continuing today. Many tropical families evolved new species and genera with adaptations to increasingly colder lands. Most of Ontario's flora, like the flora in the rest of Canada and the northern half of Eurasia, represents the end-products of this evolution from tropical ancestors and ecosystems. Because all plants change through time, the original tropical ancestors are no longer present. In tracing the exact origins of many adaptations, fragmentary evidence is all that remains.

Red columbine. P. A. WOODLIFFE

Radial and Bilateral Symmetry in Flowers

Anywhere in Ontario one can find intriguing examples of floral adaptation wherein the symmetry of the flower has been beautifully fashioned to make possible a special relationship with select pollinators. Primitive flowers were *radially symmetrical*, that is, their petals, sepals, and stamens were arranged in two or more planes around a common axis. While primitive, this form of floral symmetry is extremely adaptive and so has been retained to modern times by numerous families and species. On the Hudson Bay coast, beautiful radial symmetry is found in the pink flowers of moss campion and the white mountain avens. In the boreal forest, pink-striped wood sorrel and wild lily-of-the-valley nestled among mosses of a shady bank have retained radial symmetry. The flowers of trilliums and bloodroot are arranged in the same way. So are the buttercups growing in vacant fields, the marsh marigolds and water lilies in the wetlands, and the blue-eyed grass of country lanes.

Most radial flowers offer virtually any visitor a ready-made landing plat-

White water lily. GARY ALLEN

Jewelweed. DON GUNN

Common wood sorrel. H. A. THOMSON

form from which open nectaries or pollen can be reached. Insects can creep around at their leisure. The flowers receive abundant visits from numerous insects with limited sensory capabilities, such as beetles, wasps, and flies.

From the radial flower has evolved the striking *bilateral symmetry* of many flowers, for example, honeysuckles, violets, mints, bladderworts, and most elaborate of all, the orchids. The two-sided configuration of these flowers is often accompanied by pleasant colours and scents. Visitors to bilateral flowers must approach from a certain direction only and must move in a particular way to reach the source of food. Nectaries are frequently concealed, and nectar-guides may entice visitors to a particular point inside the flower. Often, stamens and pistils are arranged to touch the visitor's body at particular times and spots, thus bringing about cross-pollination when the visitor goes to another flower.

The larger pollinators – bees, moths, and hummingbirds – because they fly with their heads in an upward position, provided the principal co-evolutionary force which caused bilateral flowers to evolve. Like the flight orientation of pollinating insects and birds, bilateral flowers have an "up-and-down" orientation. The more primitive radial flowers have no such requirement for special pollinators.

Bilateral flowers appear to have evolved repeatedly in many different families. The evidence for this is provided by families like the buttercups, which contain both species with radial flowers such as the delicate hepatica and species with bilateral flowers such as the delphiniums.

Even more interesting are the beautiful, compound inflorescences of the umbels in the parsley family, and those of the wild asters and sunflowers of the composite family. In the parsley family, Queen Anne's lace has pronounced bilateral flowers at the periphery of the inflorescence and radial flowers at the centre. Among sunflowers, each head is made up of dozens or even hundreds of tiny radial flowers all packed together and surrounded by a ring of bright yellow, bilateral ray flowers. The bilateral flowers at the perimeters of parsnip and sunflower inflorescences probably did not evolve in response to the flight orientation of insects; rather the entire inflorescence appears to behave functionally as a radial flower since it provides a large platform for the landing and rummaging activities of a wide range of insects.

Pins, Thrums and In Between

An ingenious floral adaptation for promoting cross-pollination is *heterostyly*. Every wildflower enthusiast should be aware of this phenomenon. To see it you must examine carefully the relative lengths of pistil and stamens. Heterostyly is easy to miss unless individual flowers are examined with care. Once you have seen it, however, your view of just what nature can accomplish with flowers will never be the same!

Hoary puccoon showing thrum flowers. POINT PELEE NATIONAL PARK, B. REYNOLDS

Buckbean. DON GUNN

Pickerelweed. DON GUNN

In the simplest kind of heterostyly, a species produces two kinds of plants. One kind of plant has flowers with long stigmas and short stamens; the other has short stigmas and long stamens. If you look directly down into the showy yellow flower of a puccoon growing on sandy areas along the shoreline of Lakes Ontario, Erie, or Huron, you will see five anthers located right at the exit of the flower (thrums) or the stigmatic tip of a pistil (pins). Thrum flowers have a short hidden pistil at the bottom of the flower while pins have short stamens at the bottom of the flower. Pin flowers must receive the pollen from thrum flowers and vice versa in order for seed to set.

Heterostyly like this, with two kinds of flowers, may be seen in the bearded white flowers of bogbean growing in sphagnum bogs and fens, in partridgeberry half-hidden beneath firs in the mixed forests of the Canadian Shield, and in the dwarf Canadian primrose that thrives in rocky crevices in the spray zone along the shores of Lake Superior.

A more complex system of heterostyly occurs with *three* different levels of anthers and stigmas. In this situation, all flowers on a plant can be one of three types: medium pistil with long and short stamens; short pistil with long and medium stamens; or long pistil with medium and short stamens. Generally, separate plants having identical pistil lengths cannot be cross-pollinated with each other; only the plants of any two different style lengths can be cross-pollinated, thus allowing seed to set.

Growing along the shores of marshes and in protected areas of small lakes is the tall blue pickerel weed. The phenomenon of heterostyly can be observed by looking at three flower types in this species and examining the relative lengths of pistils and stamens in a dozen or so plants in different locations along the shoreline. One can also look for the three different kinds of flowers in the purple loosestrife, a European species which has invaded the wetlands over much of southern Ontario. The beautifully scented trailing arbutus, common in shaded pine forests of northern Ontario, is yet another of nature's heterostyled species.

Invisible Reflected Energy of Flowers

Another interesting co-evolutionary relationship between flowers and their pollinating insects results from the ability of many pollinating insects to see ultraviolet light. It is not a coincidence that numerous flowers, especially those more advanced on the scale of evolution such as dandelions and puccoons, have acquired the ability to reflect brilliantly that portion of sunlight which is in the ultraviolet.

Bees see the world of natural greenery in various shades of grey. Against this grey background, flowers reflecting ultraviolet stand out starkly to a bee. Sit quietly in a meadow where one or two dandelions are in flower, especially when few flowers are available elsewhere in the area, and watch the passing bumblebees. From a rapid tangential flight path metres away, the bee will suddenly turn and head directly for what is to it a shining point of ultraviolet light emanating from the flower, a light invisible to humans.

Bees can also see blue-green, which in the colour spectrum of a bee is the opposite of ultraviolet. Thus, many flowers have evolved adaptations in which their floral parts *totally absorb* ultraviolet, and usually this means that the opposite colour, the so-called insect blue-green, is dominant and extremely visible from a distance.

Of course, many flowers do not rely on reflected ultraviolet or blue-green to attract their pollinators. Simple colour differences against the background, large flower size, sheer abundance of flowers, or scent all can be more important. But the presence of flower-insect interdependencies based on a range of energy invisible to us is a hint of what in the natural world may lie beyond our direct perception.

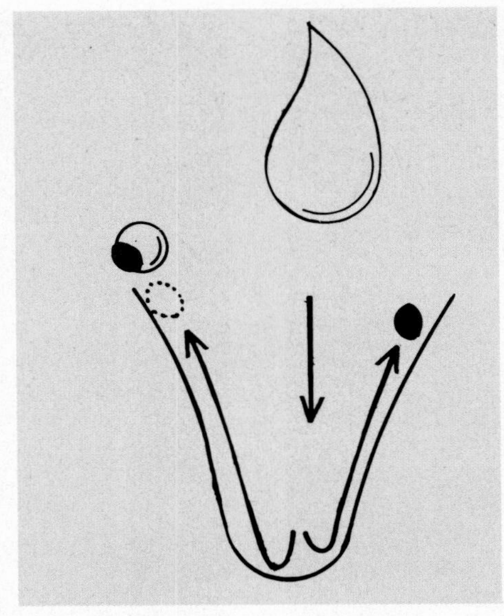

A raindrop falling into the splash-cup mechanism of mitrewort.

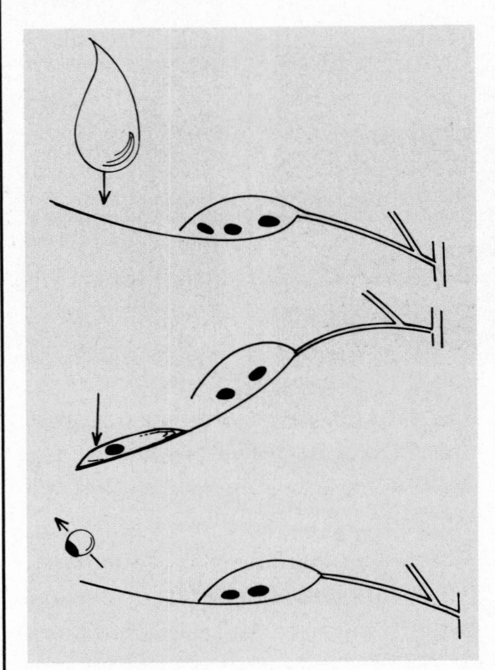

A raindrop striking the springboard mechanism of foamflower.

Splash-cups and Springboards

Many people are familiar with the obvious adaptations of certain plants for seed dispersal: the wind-blown milkweed floss, the parachutes of dandelions, or the burs of the beggar-tick. But splash-cups and springboards are methods less well known for scattering seeds.

These unique adaptations are plant responses to raindrops. Two species in the saxifrage family have perfected the splash-cup – the golden saxifrage flowering at margins of cool, vernal pools in the mixed forests of the Shield, and the mitrewort or bishop's cap with its delicate spikes of snowflake flowers found in the same woods in May. As the flowers mature, each develops into a beautifully crafted splash-cup resembling a miniature bird's nest with the tiniest of shiny black seeds in place of eggs. When a raindrop makes a direct hit on the cup-shaped "nest," the seeds are ejected to a distance of up to a metre.

A raindrop mechanism of a different type, the springboard, has evolved in another saxifrage, the lacy white foamflower, which blooms in late May down among the sugar maple seedlings of the same woodlands. Here, seed is held in a small, partially enclosed cup at the end of a tiny branch, much like a person's hand about to roll a bowling ball. When a raindrop falls on the capsule at the tip, the branch first bends down and then springs upward, casting a few seeds along with a tiny drop of water some distance from the plant.

On reflection, it should really not be surprising that raindrops, falling from overhead canopies or directly out of the sky, have had a major influence in shaping some adaptations of plants, for rain, as an ecosystem force, has been present since the beginning of life.

Catapulting Stamens

One of the most fascinating adaptations of Ontario's wildflowers is found in both the bog and sheep laurel of the heath family. One or the other of these species can be found in open sandy or boggy areas throughout the province. A good place to see them is along the Trans-Canada Highway between Petawawa and Deep River in June and July.

The pink radial flowers of laurels are shaped like porridge bowls. Each has ten stamens and a single style with a truncated stigma. However, as the flower is opening, indeed even after it is fully open, the pollen-filled anthers are not free; rather, the tip of each anther is solidly anchored in a tiny notch of the corolla bowl while the anther filament is arched outward like a bow fully drawn just before the arrow is released.

After a day or two the flower becomes fully mature, and the pollen in the anchored anthers is dry and ready to fly. At this time, nectar is secreted, and along comes the unsuspecting bee, flower-fly, or butterfly. The appropriate tickle of any of the ten arched filaments, and – wham! Once the anther is released from its notch in the corolla, it springs forth with lightning speed and throws an almost invisible cloud of mature pollen directly at the stigma. If an insect happens to be in the way, so much the better – pollen can then be carried to the next plant to effect cross-pollination.

The Mystery of the Pop Flower

Without any doubt, first prize for the most amazing of all adaptations in Ontario's wildflowers goes to the modest bunchberry or, as it is more aptly named, pop flower. This species, the only almost-herbaceous member of the dogwood family, is found from Carolinian forests to treeline and across Canada and Eurasia.

A young flowering stem is topped by four conspicuous white or light green bracts which people sometimes mistake for petals. At the centre, between the bracts, are found a dozen or so small, inconspicuous, and seemingly uninteresting flower buds bunched together. Each bud has four very tiny petals. The very odd feature of the tiny petals (not the large white bracts) is that one of them harbours a minute antenna about one millimetre long, projecting upward from the unopened flower bud. As the flowers mature, they gradually become ready to pop. When the antenna is touched ever so slightly by any object it causes the entire flower to open with lightning speed. Accompanying the small explosion is a faint wisp of pollen which is catapulted into the air above the flower by four tensioned "elbow-jointed" stamens whose anthers were already fully open and properly positioned just before the flower popped. Any insect landing on the bunch of flowers is very well dusted indeed.

This pollination method is unique in all of the plant kingdom. One can only marvel that such a singular but functionally integrated series of highly adapted structures and actions can be produced by mutation, gene shuffling, and natural selection.

To pop a pop flower you need a tiny twig sharpened to a needle point, and

Sheep laurel showing anthers cocked before release. DON GUNN

Pop flower (bunchberry) showing tiny antannae and both open and closed flowers surrounded by large, white, showy bracts. H. A. THOMSON

ideally the weather must be warm, dry, and sunny. As well, you need 20:20 vision or better.

Floral Adaptations Through the Seasons

Some of the forces which operate in natural communities and which slowly produce the marvels of evolutionary adaptation among flowers can be appreciated by imagining a trip through the landscapes of Ontario from spring to fall.

Willows are among the first species to provide copious nectar and nutritious pollen for an army of newly emerged insects, which possibly could not exist without this rich early banquet. In swamps and lowlands, among the chorus of spring frogs, large bumblebees travel to the nectar-laden female flowers and the pollen-rich male flowers, collecting food for their upcoming broods. At the same time, as they inadvertently transfer pollen to the receptive willow stigmas they are ensuring a good willow seed crop. This time of year is critical for both willow flowers and bumblebees. The willows must have pollinators when their flowers are ripe; the bumblebees benefit from an early start to raising their broods. Over a large region, an early start means thousands of additional bumblebees all summer and fall to carry out the work of pollinating other species. Thus, events occurring in early spring can have a powerful influence on other species in the regional ecosystem.

An interesting spring-flowering shrub is *Dirca*, or leatherwood, the world's most northern representative of the giant tropical family which includes the camellia. Even before the yellow trout lily is in flower, the drooping, nectar-filled flowers of leatherwood dot many a sugar maple and beech forest across southern Ontario. Several species of small, early-emerging woodland bees visit and pollinate the leatherwood flowers. It is interesting to speculate how this shrub, so far removed from the land of its tropical ancestors, has come to flower with the first burst of spring, when the last patches of winter snow are still on the ground. Perhaps this is the only season, except late fall, when potential pollinators can locate the flowers with ease among the copious greenery which comes later. A somewhat similar reason might have caused witch hazel, a large shrub of Ontario's southern forests, to produce its strap-petalled yellow flowers in late autumn, after the leaves have fallen.

Flower of the leatherwood shrub.
DON GUNN

In May and early June, dandelions, presumably introduced from Europe, provide prodigious amounts of both pollen and nectar to any and all insects. The probable outcome of such a cornucopian offering is that when dandelions are at their peak virtually all pollinators abandon other flowers, including native ones, thus reducing, perhaps even eliminating, seed set in these other species. The success of dandelions in corralling all available pollinators, in theory, gradually forces other less-competitive species to shift their flowering dates. Only by flowering earlier or later than dandelions can seed set be assured. Gradual shifts by species within a community such as this may be one of the causes for the divergence of flowering time.

In northern Ontario, the tall pink-flowered fireweed flowers so flamboyantly that it seems out of place in this cool, temperate climate. This species is widely distributed across northern Canada and Eurasia. Like no other plant across this region of short, cool summers, fireweed offers nectar in such quantity that bumblebees, night moths, butterflies, wasps, and many pollinating insects survive and maintain their own populations (as well as that of the fireweed) very well. During mid summer when fireweed is in full flower, a mobile beekeeper can take advantage of its abundance and obtain a fine pink honey for the market.

But the deeper woods are dark and offer little habitat for most bees and butterflies. What of the many woodland wildflowers which also must be cross-pollinated: the dainty white starflower, the dangling green bells of Solomon's-seal, the small woodland orchids? For the pollination of many of these species, small woodland flies and mosquitoes are important. A host of unique evolutionary relationships have developed here just as they have for the edge-of-the-woods species and those of open fields.

The asters and goldenrods, last flowers of the fall, crowd the abandoned fields and (unsprayed) roadsides of late August and September, providing pollen in great quantity. These autumn wildflowers hum with the activity of countless pollinating insects searching for food as the days grow shorter and the sun's rays more feeble. They provide the principal energy-base upon which dozens, perhaps hundreds, of insect species depend for over-winter survival.

Knowing any wildflower intimately means considering it not as an individual flower, not even as an individual species, but as an intrinsic part of a complex natural ecosystem. Relationships unimagined and yet-undiscovered abound. No living thing could exist for long without the ecosystem which is its home, which gave rise to it, and which by its very presence it helped create. Ontario's wildflowers are celebrations of the marvellous life-generating and life-sustaining interrelationships of Earth's natural ecosystems, which, over vast spans of time, gave rise to all plants and animals, including ourselves.

True Solomon's-seal. MARY THEBERGE

◆ SCIENCE ◆ EXCURSION ◆

Pollination in Ontario's Wild Orchids

Theodore Mosquin

Orchids are the most beautiful of wildflowers. Intricate shapes, delicate colours, and puzzling floral structures have made them the object of more wildflower books and articles than any other group of plants. Some people devote their lives to growing and photographing orchids and to travelling to different regions of the Earth in search of new species and varieties. The orchid family is enormous; over twenty thousand species are found around the world, most copiously in the tropics.

The forests, meadows, fens, and bogs of Ontario provide perfect habitats for some sixty native orchid species. And just like their tropical relatives, the flowers of each species, whether small or large, are novel and sometimes complex in design. Each species has a special story to tell about how it goes about the serious matter of achieving pollination.

Scientific descriptions of orchid pollination read like Alice's accounts of Wonderland; even the truth seems improbable and unreal. Just how the pollination mechanisms in orchids could originate and survive continues to fascinate the botanically curious.

First, a little botany. An orchid flower is highly modified – three petals and three sepals surround a fused column of anthers and stigma, all anchored to the apex of a capsule-like ovary. One petal (the lip or *labellum*) is fancifully modified into a slipper in the case of lady's-slippers, for example, or into a nectar-filled spur in the many species of *Platanthera*. The other two petals, as well as the three sepals, are less colourful or ornate and tend to be quite similar, although fusion of floral parts and other modifications among them differ according to species. The column at the centre of the flower, enclosed or surrounded by the modified petals and sepals, bears one stigma located nearer to the centre (base) of the flower while one or two anther sacs containing waxy masses of pollen are positioned closer to the tip of the fused column.

In some of Ontario's orchid species, the relative geometrical positions of the anthers, stigma, and modified petals force specific pollinating insects to enter and leave the flowers in a certain way, thus bringing the pollen in contact with the stigma. Others have anthers so modified that they literally lie in wait for a potential pollinator, stick fast to it, and get carried on to the next flower. Ontario's orchids seem to employ four major strategies for achieving pollination, each with many variations: enchantment, one-way passage, ambush, and self-pollination.

Calypso, Bruce Peninsula.
J. ROSS BROWN

Enchantment

Ontario's most showy orchids – the fairy-slipper (Calypso), rose pogonia, grass pink, dragon's mouth (Arethusa), and all species of lady's-slippers growing in southern Ontario, so enchant potential pollinators with their colour and scent that the flower gets pollinated for free. These orchid flowers offer no nectar reward, and the bees have no interest in the pollen. But the flowers need the bees; without them pollination is impossible. There would be no way for the pollen to move from the anthers to the stigma, which is located close to the base of the generally horizontal column. Here is how the enchantment strategy works.

In late May or June, when plants of these species begin to flower, queen bumblebees emerging from hibernation and some smaller bee species are out foraging for nectar from whatever plants happen to be flowering at the time. When the first flowers of these particular orchid species emerge, passing bees see and smell them and enter the flower in search of nectar.

Bees are among the most intelligent of insects. After several visits, a bee learns that the orchid contains no nectar whatsoever. Further, bees have an uncanny ability to distinguish one scent from another, so it takes but a few experiences to learn the futility of visiting flowers of any of these species. But, in becoming "educated," the bees pollinate some orchids. Studies have shown that from 5 to 30 per cent of flowers of these large-flowered orchid species achieve pollination in this manner, while the balance never receive insect visits and consequently bear no seed.

Grass Pink on the Bruce Peninsula.
J. ROSS BROWN

The bumblebees are the principal pollinators of the large orchids such as the showy lady's-slipper, moccasin flower, and fairy-slipper. The tiny flowers of the ram's-head and little white lady's-slipper are too small for the large queen bumblebees to enter, and these species flower in May before the smaller worker bumblebees emerge. For these orchids, other species of small bees, which can be abundant in spring, are their main pollinators, but the principle of enchantment is the same. The reward to the bee appears to be nil.

Pink moccasin-flower near St. Williams.
MARY THEBERGE

Showy lady's-slipper orchids, Middlesex County. J. ROSS BROWN

Yellow lady's-slipper orchid at Rondeau. P. A. WOODLIFFE

Hybrid small white lady's-slipper and small yellow lady's-slipper on Walpole Island in Lake St. Clair. P. A. WOODLIFFE

The One-Way Passage

Lady's-slippers have combined the strategy of enchantment with another – the one-way passage. The pollinating insect is forced to follow a single-track journey through the slipper; once in the flower it first brushes against the stigma, and then, during its escape from the slipper, brushes against the pollen-bearing anthers. After escaping, it carries pollen on to the next flower.

In lady's-slippers, the entry into the flower is the very obvious hole at the top of the slipper. Bees cannot exit through this entrance because the surface of the slipper at this spot is so perfectly waxy and slippery. The exit they use is also located at the top of the flower but right next to the spot where the flower is attached to the ovary. The exit contains a series of rough areas and hairs which appear to be specially designed to ensure that the trapped bee does indeed leave by the "right" way, precisely where the anthers are located.

But, as is so often the case in nature, there is an exception. The sparrow's-egg lady's-slipper, found in Pukaskwa National Park and in the clay belt, avoids any need for pollinating insects altogether. Its column is so modified that as the flower matures the anthers come into direct contact with the stigma, bringing about automatic self-fertilization. At Pukaskwa, virtually every flower of this beautiful species sets a full capsule of seed.

One-way passage of a moccasin-flower (pink lady's-slipper orchid).

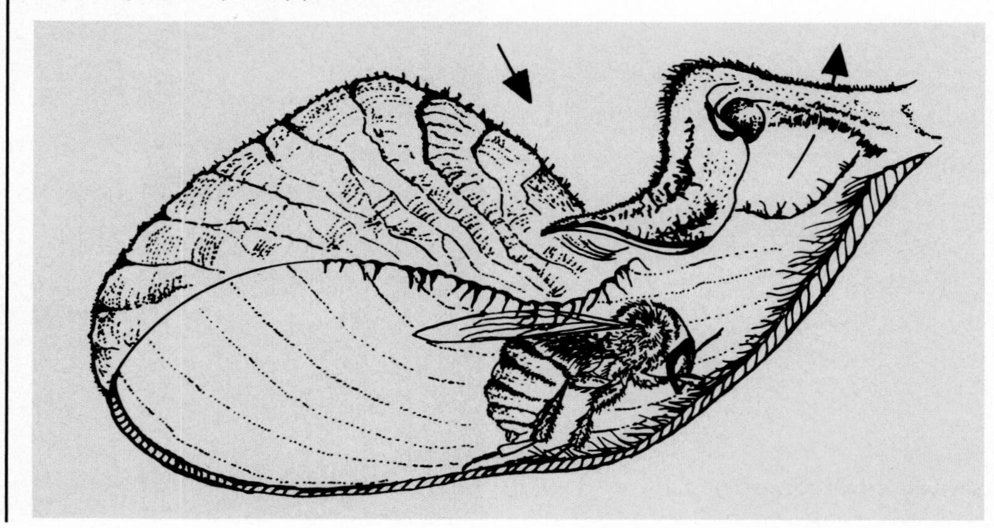

The Ambush

One of the most ingeniously crafted pollination devices in the anthers of Ontario orchids is found in nectar-bearing species. Ladies'-tresses and different species of the genus *Platanthera*, such as the white-fringed orchid, prairie white-fringed orchid, white bog orchid, and others, have developed an ambushing device known as a *pollinarium*. Pollinaria are about one or two millimetres long and made up of three parts: an expanded portion filled with a waxy mass of pollen grains, a thin middle thread called a *caudicle*, and an intensely sticky end called a *viscidulum*. All told, a pollinarium looks much like a tiny baseball bat with the "Crazy Glue" viscidulum at the thin end and the main body of the bat filled with the waxy pollen. But only the viscidulum is slightly exposed, lying in wait at the narrow entrance to the flower. An insect entering the flower for nectar usually ends up with the sticky end of the pollinarium cemented to its tongue or other parts of the head. Depending on just where the pollinarium sticks to an insect and upon the size and strength of the insect, the viscidulum may be impossible to dislodge, and the insect may go through life with one to a dozen pollinaria permanently affixed to one or another part of its body – eyes, mouth parts, legs, or back.

In areas where these orchids are found, pollinaria may be seen on flower visitors such as butterflies, bumblebees, flies, and female mosquitoes.

An important corollary to this pollination mechanism is a sticky stigmatic surface strategically located just back of the flower entrance. The stigma is so sticky that when a pollen mass comes into contact with it, the pollinarium may get broken in half when the insect withdraws; the viscidulum usually remains on the insect but the pollen mass attaches to the stigma.

I recall vividly a meadow in Lanark County one September where by actual count, some thirty-six hundred flowering shoots of nodding ladies'-tresses were in splendid flower. About fifteen bumblebees were active, gathering nectar. But every flower they probed with their long black tongues was lying in ambush with its pollinaria. Sneaking up on the bumblebees I observed the action. As the bee explored deeply into each flower for

Three pollinaria attached to the head of an *Aedes* mosquito.

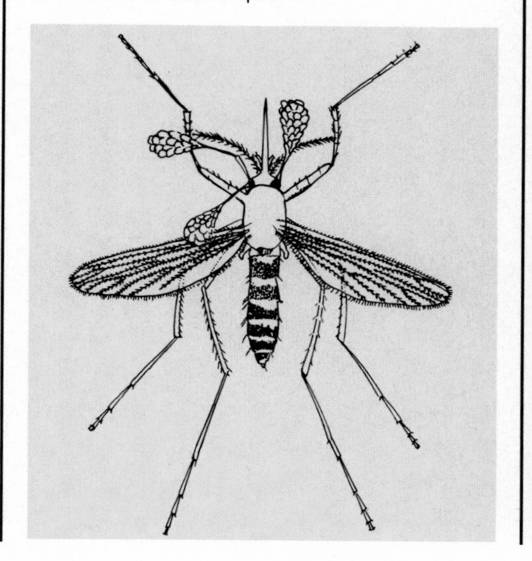

Small purple-fringed orchid, Bruce Peninsula. J. ROSS BROWN

nectar, one or two fresh pollinaria became cemented to different parts of its tongue, often directly at the tip. The bees spent considerable effort and energy attempting to remove the pollinaria with their powerful legs; obviously, the pollinaria were the source of considerable irritation. Most pollinaria fell off except for one or two which invariably remained near the tip ready for deposition on the stigma of the next flower.

One of the surprises of orchid pollination is the interest that female mosquitoes show in seeking nectar, thus helping the orchid achieve pollination. Like a blood meal, nectar may provide needed energy for egg development. Unlike bees and butterflies, mosquitoes have very long, thin, weak legs, so there is no possibility of removing the pollinaria. Thus, mosquitoes have often been seen with numerous pollinaria adhering to their heads and other body parts.

Self-Pollination

Most of Ontario's sixty orchid species have small flowers. In some of these species, pollination can take place without insect pollinators. Other species with equally small flowers are cross-pollinated, so there is no foolproof way to determine self- from cross-pollination except by very careful observation of plants grown in

Arethusa, Grey County. J. ROSS BROWN

insect-proof cages. Some species are partially self-pollinated, while retaining complex mechanisms to ensure some cross-pollination. The autumn coralroot, for example, has some permanently closed flowers which self-pollinate by direct contact between stigma and pollen. But the same plants also have some open flowers which expose reproductive parts and therefore may be cross-pollinated by visiting insects.

Some orchids have developed a means of rotating their pollen masses in a manner that moves them onto the edge of the stigma. This is the case with the helleborine, spotted coralroot, early coralroot, Loesel's twayblade, and possibly others. In the case of Loesel's twayblade, it has been found, by using a mist spray on orchids growing in a greenhouse, that raindrops play a key role in the rotation. When water drops strike the raised anther cap, they push the pollen masses around to the edge of a ridge along the stigmatic surface.

Another method of self-pollination is accomplished by bending of the *caudicle*, which is the short, thin thread of a pollinarium described previously. This method is known in the tall northern green orchid. It also occurs in the spotted orchid, introduced from Europe and naturalized in the Timmins area.

Lastly, self-pollination is achieved in some species by pollen simply dropping down onto the stigma located below. The helleborine, little club-spur orchid, and dwarf rattlesnake plantain adopt this method.

To experience the joy of discovering an orchid's deeper secrets takes patience, a hand lens, and time to travel in a very large province. It also takes a sense of respect for the wild places – woods, meadows, fens, and bogs – where orchids and their essential pollinators – native bees, butterflies, flies, and mosquitoes – together make their home.

Ontario's Trilliums

James S. Pringle and Theodore Mosquin

The trilliums that grace Ontario's woodlands represent just four species out of about fifty – all native to the northern hemisphere. Their name comes from their flower parts, which occur in threes (*tri* = three): three sepals, three petals, and one pistil comprising three carpels. Their fame in Ontario, however, comes from the place of honour which the white trillium has as our floral emblem. The soft, white petals suggest a blossom of peace and purity.

All trilliums flower in spring or, at the latest, in early summer. Their berries, produced in mid or late summer are dark red. The several seeds in each berry bear an oily appendage attractive to ants, which carry the seeds intact to their nests, thereby contributing to seed dispersal. Most trilliums finish their annual growing cycle, wither, and disappear by mid or late summer, leaving little trace of the wealth of bloom waiting to grace the woods next spring.

A curious fact about the trilliums is that they, along with such plants as the lilies, irises, and grasses, are *monocotyledons*, that is, their embryos and seedlings have one rather than two seed-leaves. Most monocotyledons have parallel-veined leaves, yet trilliums have evolved uncharacteristic broad, net-veined leaves.

The four species of trilliums growing in Ontario are the white, red, painted, and nodding. From time to time other species are reported, but these reports turn out to be based either on misidentifications or horticultural introductions. Each species has its own habitat requirements that determine its geographical range, but all grow in mature woodlands, preferring shady sites that are neither excessively dry in summer nor subject to long flooding in the spring.

The white trillium, designated Ontario's floral emblem in 1937, is the most widely distributed trillium in Ontario. It thrives in the rich hardwood forests of southern Ontario, where it comes into full flower just after the forest canopy has leafed out. On the Canadian Shield, however, its distribution is greatly restricted by the prevalence of acid soils low in calcium. In general, its northern limits are about the latitude of North Bay, although a few scattered occurrences are known farther north.

A characteristic feature of the white trillium is that at full bloom its large, snow-white petals turn pink and then slowly wither, although a rare form has pink petals from the first. Its flowers may be up to eighteen centimetres across, but they more commonly range from five to ten centimetres. A white or light yellow spider, camouflaged against the white petals, is often found lurking inside the flower, waiting to capture insects who come to it in search of food. Deer browse regularly on its buds.

White trilliums are subject to infection by mycoplasma-like organisms which are similar in appearance to bacteria without cell walls. These organisms occur in the phloem tissue and are responsible for the green stripe sometimes seen down the centre of each petal. Their more advanced manifestation is a syndrome including

A variant of the white trillium.
DON GUNN

White trillium. LARRY LAMB

Painted trillium. JOHN THEBERGE

Red trillium. MARY THEBERGE

leaf blades on long stalks, enlarged sepals, increasingly green petals, distorted stamens, and aborted pistils.

The next most common trillium in Ontario is the red trillium. It grows in rocky or other coarse-textured soils which may range from calcareous to acidic. Its petals spread widely and taper gradually, and the margins are not fluted. Ordinarily, the petals are deep purplish red, but occasionally other colour forms are encountered, most often pale yellow. The flowers of the red trillium have an unpleasant, carrion-like scent that attracts flies which may act as pollinators.

The painted trillium is a species of the spruce-fir and mixed hemlock-hardwood forests. In Ontario it grows mostly on acid soils farther north than the white or red trilliums, and it flowers a bit later in the season. Its narrow, fluted petals are white with a rose-red chevron near their base. Its leaves have a distinctive bronzy tint when young and also differ from leaves of the red and white trilliums by being stalked.

The fourth and least common species in Ontario is the nodding trillium, so called because the flower stalk curves downward so that the flower hangs below the leaves. Viewed from above, a colony of nodding trilliums in bloom gives the impression of being white trilliums that have not yet flowered. This species is most common along the north shore of Lake Superior and in parts of eastern Ontario, with only scattered occurrence across southern Ontario. It is usually found in rich, clay, bottomland soils, but not all factors restricting its distribution are understood.

The nodding trillium is rather small, and unlike the other species, has pleasantly-scented flowers with strongly recurved white petals. Perhaps the sweet fragrance has evolved to attract pollinators, since the flowers are so inconspicuous.

In much of southern Ontario, the woodlands in which trilliums grow have been greatly reduced by urban, agricultural, and other developments. Where woodlands remain, trilliums are often still present in impressive numbers. In the much-visited nature reserves near cities, however, trillium populations are often in decline because picking and trampling dam-
flowering time, a trillium has put
age the plants and compact the soil. At
nearly all its food reserves into new growth. Picking a trillium then removes virtually all its green, chlorophyll-containing tissue before photosynthesis has been allowed to make the food that later is stored over winter in the bulb for survival and new growth the following spring.

Nodding trillium. DON GUNN

Base of a giant white pine in Quetico Provincial Park. SHAN WALSHE

Latticework of Ecosystems

Ontario's Forests

Mike Singleton

There are spindly, stunted, treeline spruces in northern Ontario draped with black lichens that blow in the breeze. There are towering deciduous forests in southern Ontario with exotic-sounding species like sassafras, tulip-tree, and Kentucky coffee tree. Between these two extremes stretches a bewildering array of other forests: cathedrals of arching maples, beech, and pine, their balconies full of life; snippets of savannah reminiscent of Africa; impenetrable jungles of vine-draped elm, ash, and silver maple; vast tracts of white and yellow birch, eastern hemlock, white, red, and jack pine. There are cedar-lined valleys, oak groves...the list could run for pages.

Making sense of what at first seems like a crazy-quilt of different forest types is no small challenge. Ontario's forests are the complex product of many dynamic forces: moving continents, a global "heat engine," glaciation and nine thousand years of subsequent regrowth, as well as millions of years of plant and animal evolution. As the product of these ever-shifting forces, each of Ontario's forest types exists as a fleeting assemblage of species, here today but undoubtedly subject to vast change – natural and human-induced – in the future.

If we were able to look down from a satellite sailing high above North America, the bewildering array of forest types would meld into a broad picture. We could identify a succession of belts running from northwest to southeast across Ontario: tundra along the Hudson Bay and James Bay coasts; a broad sweep of boreal forest to the south; a great belt of mixed forests extending eastward through Quebec to the Maritimes; and finally a thin band of Carolinian hardwoods along Lake Erie's shore. To the west of Ontario lies a flat mosaic of croplands, formerly expanses of prairie. Fringing the former prairie is a thin arc of aspen parklands that just touches Ontario's border west of Kenora.

What brought about and maintains this pattern in Ontario's forests? Primarily climate, especially *effective temperature* (for plant growth), a blend of mean annual temperature, mean July temperature, length of the frost-free period, length of the growing season, and number of growing-degree days. The northwest-southeast cline in effective temperature is largely due to latitude, but also to prevailing northwesterly winds. The vast surface of Canada's northern mainland acts with the scattering of Arctic islands and quick-to-freeze channels as a nucleus for the development of cold Arctic air masses. If the air over North America stayed still, one would expect great, concentric isotherms of southward-penetrating cold. But the prevailing winds from the west and northwest deform this mass to produce a southeastward cold lobe. Hudson Bay and James Bay, influenced by this lobe, act as a frigid fist to chill the nearby landscape, to extend permafrost far southward, and to push tundra and treeline south into Ontario.

Peering down more closely from our satellite, we might notice that where the four broad vegetation belts are wide enough, subtle differences exist from east to west in each of them. The prevailing west winds flow over the mountain cordillera on the west coast of North America and as a consequence are dry when they reach the continental interior. Dried even further by warm temperatures across the prairies, the winds reach Ontario in a very wrung-out state. But, alternating with them, as described in an earlier chapter, are moister winds flowing from northwest, southwest, south, and even southeast or east. Ontario is thus at a critical juncture where airflows collide, and even a brief storm may carry considerable precipitation. The result of our position relative to the storm systems is that eastern Ontario generally receives somewhat more precipitation than western Ontario. The Great Lakes heighten this generalization, causing greater precipitation in their lee. And highland areas like the Algonquin Dome also cause a "rainshadow" effect on their eastern side. All these differences, the forests faithfully reflect.

The Significance of Site

Within each of the broad vegetational belts in Ontario are many local groupings of forest communities. In a forest, one detects these finer divisions while walking up or down slopes, or to or from lakes and wetlands. Eventually, one begins to wonder why individual tree species are growing where they are. The answer is *site*.

Site is a blend of many factors: landscape relief, slope, soil texture, nutrient availability, degree of protection from extreme chilling and ice and snow abrasion, orientation to the sun, and a host of other factors. Slope and soil texture work together to produce huge differences in moisture availability. Soils with small to mid-sized particles (clays and loams) tend to hold moisture, while sands and gravels drain water off quickly. The steeper the slopes and coarser the material, the drier the soil will be.

Slope often works with vegetation and ground water in other ways, too. Deep, nutrient-rich humus accumulates at the toe of slopes, supporting plants that demand this rich setting. Springs and swamps located there will support luxuriant growths of cedar and jewelweed. Calcareous springs, produced when slightly acid rainwater percolates over buried limestone or through sedimentary rubble, produce conditions poisonous to many plants. Here, tamarack inherits the setting, along with a host of calcium-loving plants.

The direction a slope faces often is significant to forest growth. Both soil and vegetation act as solar collectors, converting sunlight into heat. If the slope is north rather than south, the snow cover receives less incident sunlight, melts less, accumulates deeper, and lasts longer. Once exposed, the ground is much slower to warm, and the net effect is a relatively cold site.

Nearly all of Ontario's trees, and other plants too, are capable of growing over a much wider range than they actually do. Indeed, the normal range of a tree species is frequently not where growing conditions are ideal; rather, many trees grow on inferior sites, where some trait gives them a competitive advantage.

White spruce is an excellent example. It is quite capable of growing in the climatic conditions offered by every part of Ontario, from the treeline to the Lake Erie shore. It will show the most rapid, luxuriant growth just north of Lakes Erie and Ontario – provided that competition, insects, and disease are held at bay. But it is almost absent here, and only becomes a prevalent species 600 kilometres to the north. In the south, it simply cannot compete with the hardwoods.

Because both site features and competition are complex variables, forest communities do not fit neat, predetermined mixtures. There are tendencies, trends, and patterns, but the more we analyse them, the less predictable they become. The composition of trees in the forests often is influenced by very local conditions – the wanderings of squirrels to carry seeds, and insects to snip off leaders, and a host of other chance events that are part of living ecosystems.

Region 1 – Northern Boreal Forest

A tour of Ontario's forest regions should begin at treeline, just south of Hudson Bay. Right away we find that the treeline is no line at all. Instead, vast, open forests of scattered black spruce and eastern tamarack interfinger among great stretches of open muskeg, sedge marsh, and polygonal plates of *Cladonia* lichens characteristic of the tundra. Here, two great communities, tundra and forest, battle it out across a broad front of ever-shifting moisture and cold, as they have continuously for one hundred thousand years, through four successive glacial advances and retreats. Twice during the past ten thousand years, this tundra-forest interface was located farther north; during the recent Little Ice Age it fell farther south. Its location is a measure of length of current growing season, summer temperatures, and precipitation.

Black spruce trees here have a stunted appearance, often growing in small, ground-hugging clumps. The tops and windward sides of the clumps are perpetually moribund, their sensitive growing tips abraded and killed off, year after year, by wind-blasted snow. Spruces one-third of a metre high may be twenty or more years old. Trees two to four metres high, where they get that big, may have lived one hundred to two hundred years!

Southward about eighty kilometres, we find ourselves near the centre of Forest Region 1. Sub-Arctic in appearance, it is a strange, foreign-looking place. Over the region's vast area, roughly the size of southern Ontario, a spongy "living carpet" virtually blankets the ground, dominated by sphagnum mosses and fen plants where it is wet, by feather mosses and lichens where it is partially dry, and by a mixture of lichens and heaths where it is drier still. The same short, widely spaced black spruce and tamarack poke through, but they are less clumped than those farther north, and they trace elaborate patterns around the myriad bogs, fens, and very shallow lakes that abound.

Cold, flat, and wet are the operative words here. Although air temperatures may reach 32°C during the long and generally sunny days, the brief summer barely dents the cumulative effect of extended, extremely cold winters. Mean annual temperatures are well below freezing (−6° to −3°C over the region). Consequently the growing season is extremely short, the soil is permanently cold, and the permafrost is continuous, or nearly so.

With barely fifty-five centimetres of precipitation each year, this region actually receives the least rain in Ontario. But to plants, rainfall counts less than available moisture, and the landscape here is very wet. Water drains poorly because of the landscape's extreme flatness, and permafrost prevents water from percolating into the soil.

In the perpetually wet sites, where sphagnum mosses reign, time produces a waterlogged blanket of peat. Because of an acidic, oxygen-free setting just below the living sphagnum tips, plants do not decompose but become part of an enormous, growing sponge. The sponge grows both upward – on top of accumulating peat – and outward – creeping over trapped pools of open water.

This is an infant terrain, still being created. Here, isostatic rebound, occurring since the glaciers left the region, is still lifting the flat land from beneath Hudson Bay and James Bay. As the land slowly emerges from the northward-retreating shoreline, the gently moulded sea bottom appears, along with strands of successive beaches and sand and gravel bars. These beaches endure today as jumbled ridges of limestone pebbles and rocks, devoid of "fines." A few centimetres to a couple of metres in

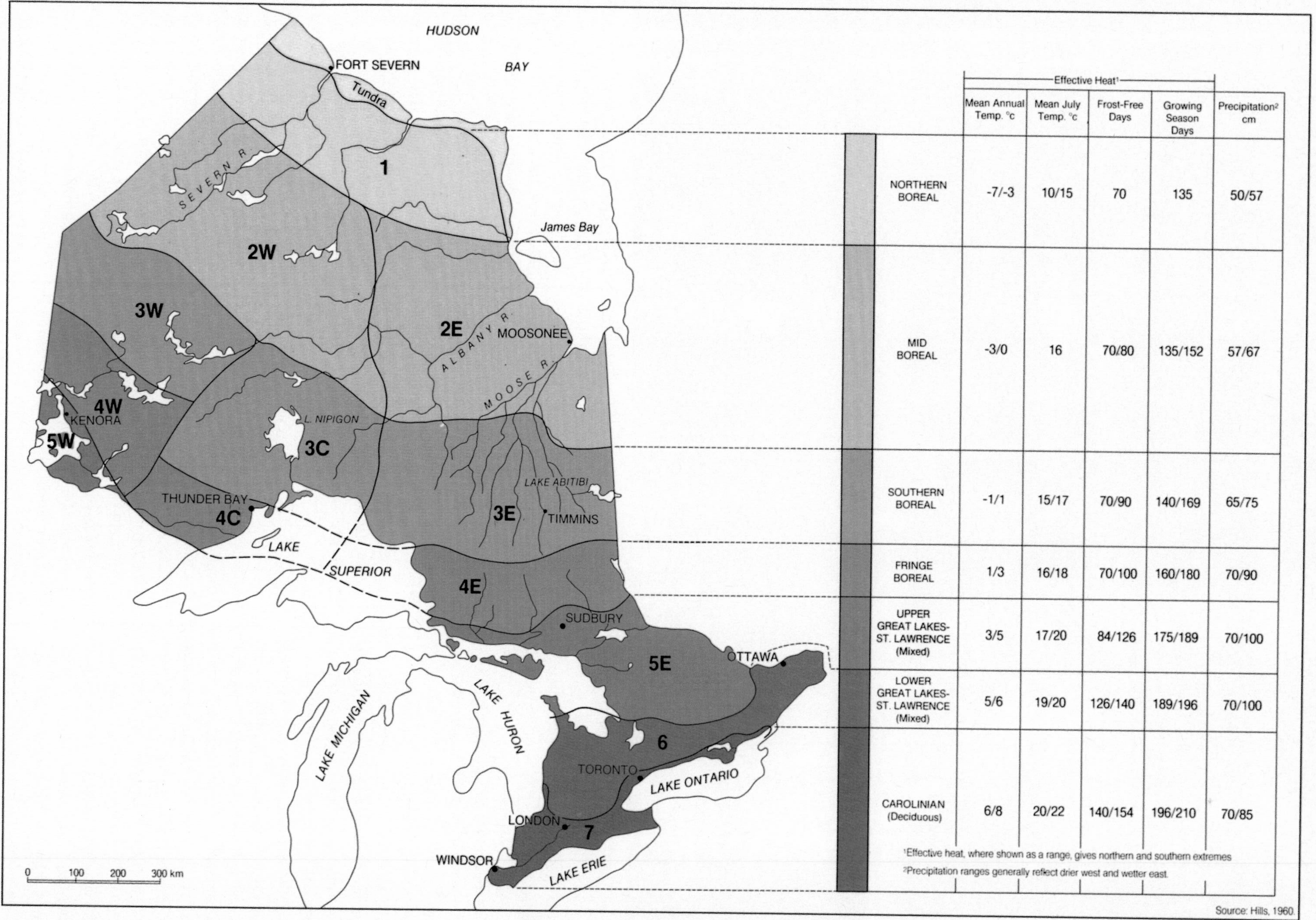

	Effective Heat[1]				
	Mean Annual Temp. °c	Mean July Temp. °c	Frost-Free Days	Growing Season Days	Precipitation[2] cm
NORTHERN BOREAL	-7/-3	10/15	70	135	50/57
MID BOREAL	-3/0	16	70/80	135/152	57/67
SOUTHERN BOREAL	-1/1	15/17	70/90	140/169	65/75
FRINGE BOREAL	1/3	16/18	70/100	160/180	70/90
UPPER GREAT LAKES-ST. LAWRENCE (Mixed)	3/5	17/20	84/126	175/189	70/100
LOWER GREAT LAKES-ST. LAWRENCE (Mixed)	5/6	19/20	126/140	189/196	70/100
CAROLINIAN (Deciduous)	6/8	20/22	140/154	196/210	70/85

[1]Effective heat, where shown as a range, gives northern and southern extremes

[2]Precipitation ranges generally reflect drier west and wetter east.

Forest regions of Ontario.

Northern boreal forest near the tundra.
HARRY LUMSDEN

height, they run for many kilometres at right angles to the land's natural fall.

The succession of stranded beaches creates special habitats. In the absence of fines, the rain that does fall upon these cobble ridges is drained off almost instantly. Here, lichens, ericaceous shrubs, and squashberry endure the drought. On the higher, south-facing and southern beaches, more southerly species creep in – stunted white spruce and a few poplars.

The beaches create another habitat too, because both the water that falls upon them and, more importantly, the "upslope" water must percolate through their calcareous framework on its way downhill. Here, the less acidic water prevents the growth of sphagnum and black spruce, and creates fens instead, where a mixture of calcareous-loving herbs survive. Along these fen-fringes and in the many spots where the calcareous underlying soil remains within the reach of roots, tamarack takes over, using, as it were, the one setting abandoned by every other tree.

Region 1's forest, verging upon being no forest at all, reflects stripped-down conditions where the differing effects of soil, moisture, acidity, temperature, wind, ice, and time are more evident than in more complex ecosystems to the south.

Region 2 – Mid-Boreal Forest

Three hundred kilometres south our forest tour has landed us in the midst of a forest region twice the size of southern Ontario. The basic pattern of the forest has not changed – pond, bog, fen, and scattered stunted trees – but there are important differences in detail. The black spruce is less stunted, in places forming a closed forest. There is also more complexity. Green and speckled alder appear as significant forest components. White birch makes its debut on hot, dry sites. Balsam poplar forms an important part of the forest in warm, moist locations. And, most important of all, on drier sites balsam fir – virtually absent in Region 1 – becomes a key forest ingredient, mingling with the more common white spruce. Sandy ridges bear mixed associations of spruce, poplar, and fir.

Nevertheless, despite more rapid tree growth, extensive, open, wet habitats are found here, just as in Region 1. The greater effective heat causes sphagnum, as well as trees, to grow more luxuriantly. The sphagnum works against trees by impeding drainage, creating pools, growing over the pools of its own creation, building up peat, and even marching uphill to drown feather moss and black spruce communities. When the trees are felled by rot, they are quickly buried and then slowly incorporated into the peat by the moss's creeping growth.

Region 2 is a wide band, crossing several physiographic regions as well as gradients in both humidity and precipitation. Just a little to the west, we see the effects of these gradients and of changing geomorphology. Most noticeably, balsam fir declines in importance, being outcompeted by white spruce. Fir prefers the moist, humid sites in the east. The extreme western end of the region is characterized by white birch, trembling aspen, and balsam poplar, all species of the aspen parklands. Changes occur in the shrubs, too, with squashberry, which requires drier sites, becoming common.

Region 3 – Southern Boreal Forest

Two hundred and fifty kilometres farther south, well to the west of Cochrane, we find the same basic ingredients – open bogs and fens, rivers and lakes, mixed spruce and fir. But there is a difference – more relief, more complexity, more maturity. It is apparent that in this southern boreal region, the marginal associations which just crept into Region 2 are "stepped up" to form major patches of the forest tapestry. The white spruce-balsam fir associations become extensive. Greater effective heat drives larger, faster-growing, denser stands of these trees and allows white and red pine to grow among them on raised, warm sites. Both white spruce and balsam fir occupy the middle ground between drought-prone sand ridges and wet soils. Thus, a theoretical dry-to-wet sequence of forest types consists of: aspen and birch to white spruce to balsam fir to black spruce (or tamarack where it is calcareous) to open, wet muskeg (or fen).

In addition to the forest stands typical of lands farther north we find a multitude of new associations: white elm and black ash in protected, warm valleys; red maple on south slopes; balsam poplar and white cedar on hilltops. The driest sites – the sandy eskers – are clothed in jack pine.

Despite the physical variety in this land, not all these stands of trees seem to fit. For instance, we might find a birch and aspen stand on a windthrown site, its high canopy rippling and rustling in the breeze. The rising understorey, just coming through the herb and shrub layer is, strangely, balsam fir mixed with a few white spruce, rather than deciduous trees to replace the now-aging canopy. The reason? Aspen and birch are shade-intolerant, requiring almost full sunlight to develop, while spruce and fir can get started in the forest's shade, patiently waiting for age to overtake their short-lived deciduous forerunners.

Nearby is a pure white spruce stand, twenty-one metres tall. Its floor is cool and dark, with a springy carpet of needles and pallid feather mosses, but unexpectedly devoid of other plant life. A dense helix of rot-resistant boughs obscures essential light and warmth from the ground, while rain water made acidic from dripping through the spruces and percolating through its needle-carpet leaches out essential nutrients from the upper soil. The product of acidic leaching is the characteristic ashy podzol soil of spruce forests, where little but spruce can endure the nutrient impoverishment.

A slope nearby is covered by a forty-year-old stand of white spruce trees, stripped of needles by spruce budworm and being recolonized by balsam fir, whereas, only a short distance away, a seventy-year-old stand of aged balsam fir is being taken over by white spruce. The explanation for these differences shows how chance events and the physiological characteristics of different species can influence forest stands. White spruce is fantastically fecund; it may produce a million seeds to a hectare in a peak year. While it can live to two hundred years, it does not reproduce until it is about sixty. Balsam fir, however, produces fewer but larger seeds, which gives seedlings a head start during their critical first year. It reproduces at just twenty years, but lives only to about seventy.

Thus, after twenty years, balsam fir is ready to reproduce, while white spruce is not, explaining the balsam fir understorey in the dead forty-year-old white spruce stand. But, when the firs reaches about sixty, they begin dying, and the long-lived white spruce then expand to fill in the gaps and hold sway – until, that is, some disturbance comes along.

Disturbance may be from spruce budworm, windstorm, logging, or fire. Fire is an integral part of the boreal forest system, and few areas of closed forest survive long without it. Started by lightning or humans, fire creates variety and recycles nutrients back into young, vibrant systems. It produces a myriad of different forest

Southern boreal forest. SHAN WALSHE

associations, depending upon dryness, forest age, availability of seed sources, and whether the fire stayed in the tree crowns or spread along the ground. Aspen trees typically come in after fire, their light seeds blown from long distances, and large areas of the southern boreal forest form a mosaic of various shades of green representing different stages of succession after fire.

This forest is not a simple progression, A to B to C. It is a composite of each species' longevity, fecundity, palatability to "bugs and browsers," nutrient needs, and moisture tolerance. It is a stage where events follow one another in an endless play – disease, fire, windthrow, drought, flood – perpetually interrupting the balance and shifting the competitive edge from one species to another.

Region 3 crosses an even broader gradient of humidity and precipitation than does Region 2, in fact, researchers have carved it into three site regions. Balsam fir, now in its real heat belt, endures all the way to the Manitoba border. But, heading west, the forest is progressively taken over by drier associations.

Region 4 – Boreal Fringe Forest

One hundred and sixty kilometres south, we find ourselves in a belt that stretches northwest from New Liskeard all the way to Red Lake. It is a region which can best be described as a tension zone between the mighty boreal forest, the Great Lakes-St. Lawrence mixed and hardwood forests to the southeast, and the prairie-parkland to the southwest. White spruce-balsam fir forests endure in cooler valleys, lowlands, and upland flats (where they mix with some pines), but black spruce and tamarack are increasingly confined to narrow rings around the myriad bogs and rivers.

An abundance of dry sites is the result of the greater relief – rolling Precambrian Shield with great rock hills and deeply faulted valleys – and greater effective heat that burns off more water, resulting in less muskeg. Together with the longer growing season, conditions exist where pines can outcompete spruce and red pine on shallow soils and exposed ridges, white pine on deeper and more water-retentive soils, and jack pine on many sites after fire.

Boreal fringe. JOHN THEBERGE

South-facing valley sides and protected uplands grow a sprinkling of sugar maple, red maple, and yellow birch. The deeper, meandering valleys often reveal an elaborate gradation of species, including everything from red pine and white pine through trembling aspen, large-toothed aspen, striped maple, and alder.

Moving westward, we see the same progressive transformation toward arid forests that was evident in Region 3. Poplar and birch, particularly, become important components of many different sites. In the extreme west, communities of bur oak, grass, and sedge, reminiscent of African savannah, appear on the hottest, driest sites. They remind us that the forests here are fed mostly by the dry, prairie air.

Upper mixed forest. LARRY LAMB

Region 5 – Upper Mixed Forest

Next, our tour takes us two hundred kilometres south. Just south of North Bay, near Algonquin Park, we find the same rolling, Precambrian Shield bedrock capped to a variable depth by a wide range of soils. But the forests are different. We have entered the top (cooler) half of a giant moisture lobe extending eastward from the Great Lakes.

From a cool, dark stand of eastern hemlock and yellow birch, one might walk uphill, through stands of sugar maple, to windswept ridges where pine and red oak sweep to the east. From this vista it is clear that some lowlands and moist, north-facing slopes are covered with hemlock and yellow birch. Hemlock produces a constant rain of acidic, long-lasting needles that accumulate as an acidic duff. Herbs, shrubs, and most trees cannot take the combined acidity and absence of light, nor can they root through the ever-thickening mat of partially-decayed needles. Most seedlings of yellow birch wither before their roots reach fertile ground. Only a few yellow birch seeds that fall on rotting logs and stumps germinate to grow among the hemlocks. Eventually, even hemlock seedlings become excluded by the thickening duff. They must await fire, which becomes increasingly more probable as the stand ages.

The sugar maple communities dominating the slopes and uplands of these northern hardwood forests are almost pure in some places, generally on sites that dry out most between summer rains. In other places they are mixed with yellow birch and basswood, especially on cooler, moister sites such as hillsides where subsurface water flows. Scattered white pines grow with the maples in moderately dry sites, and with American beech where it is hot. The high, exposed ridges are dominated by the pines, sometimes mixed with oaks.

But there is a multitude of other forest types, too. Much of the lowlands are covered with white spruce and black spruce, depending on wetness, and balsam fir. These species, dominant in the north, cling here to the cooler sites where competition from the hardwoods is less severe. Lake and stream edges are often alder-choked. Bogs are now deep-set and highly structured with rings of vegetation around them reflecting wet to dry conditions. Vast, drought-prone sand plains, like those near Petawawa, grow wave after wave of jack pine.

Everywhere, we see evidence of both logging and fire. These are man-used forests, their natural rate of disturbance by fire, insect, and wind magnified by chainsaw. Tragically, to picture what these forests were like without human influence requires imagination. Even provincial parks have failed to preserve any of these forests untouched.

After each major disturbance, if the

Changes in forest composition from the retreat of the glaciers to present in the Algonquin environment as determined from fossil pollen found in lake-bed sediment cores. Forests reflect gradual warming to very slightly higher than present temperatures 4,000 years ago, then slight cooling, then slight warming.

(a) Melting glacier leaves stranded an ice block which later melts to create a "kettle" lake.

(b) Tundra – lichens, sedges, soapberry, mountain avens, etc.

(c) Open boreal forest – lichen-moss carpet and scattered spruces, similar to Forest Region 1 today.

(d) Boreal forest.

(e) Spruce-dominated forest with red, jack, and some white pine, similar to Region 4 today.

(f) White pine becomes dominant. Red and jack pine and spruce fade.

(g) Mixed forests – hemlock-yellow birch dominate. Maple-beech on highlands, similar to Region 5 today.

(h) Oak-dominated maple-beech forest similar to Region 6 today. Temperature maximum.

(i) Mixed forests – maple-beech, hemlock, white pine.

(j) Mixed forests with white pine resurging. Increasing spruce in response to more cooling. Fading of maple, beech, hemlock especially on lowlands.

(k) Mixed forests – sharp decline of white pine. Rebounding warmer species: maple, beech, hemlock.

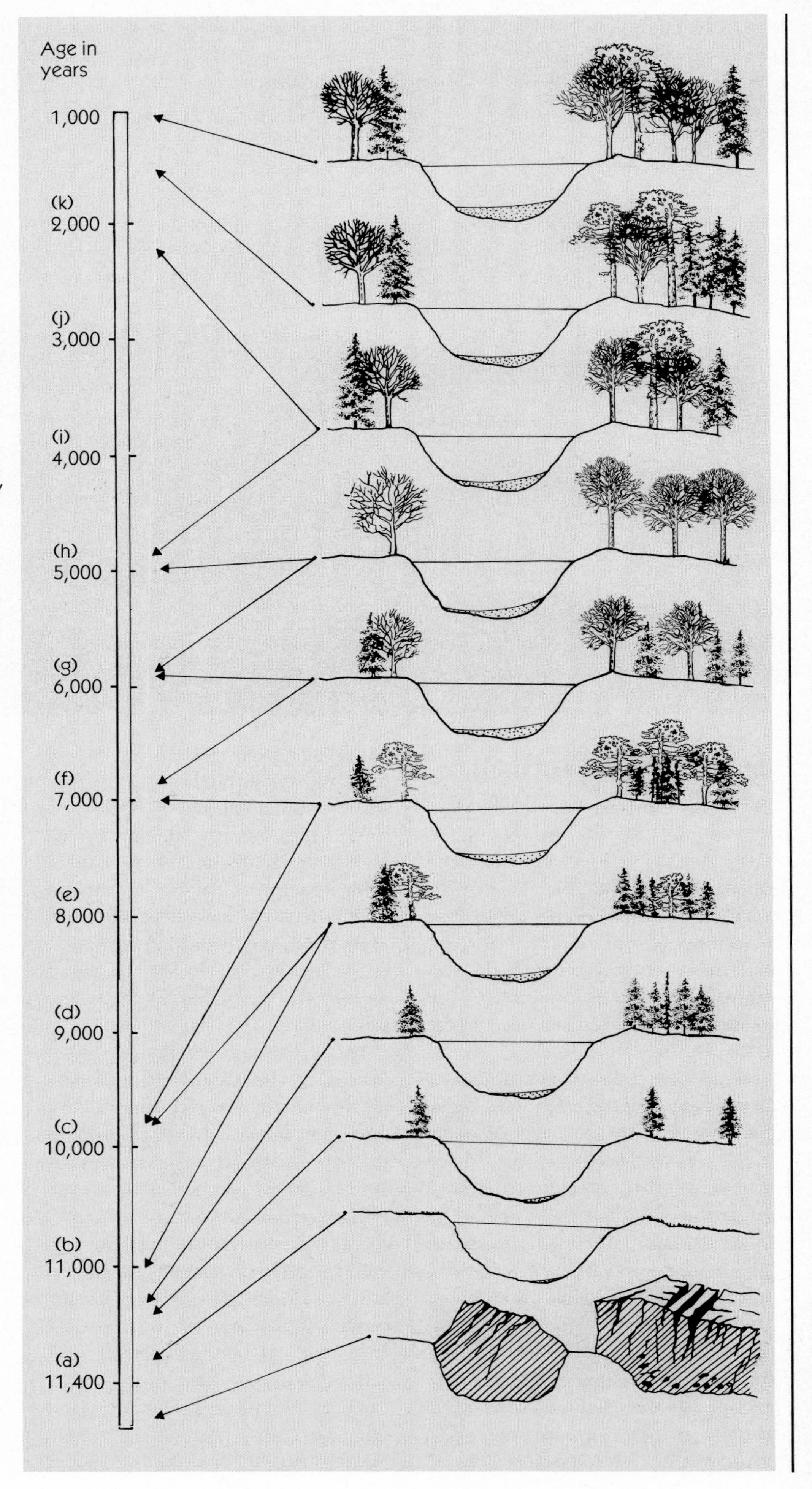

forest canopy has been sufficiently opened, poplar, white birch, and red maple along with shrubs like beaked hazel are the most common colonizers. But, just as in the boreal forest, the colonizers give way to different chains of forest succession depending on whether the site is dry, moist, wet, hot, or cool.

Nine hundred and twenty-five kilometres to the west, across Lake Superior, we are in the tension zone between boreal forest and prairie-parkland. Although technically part of the same heat belt that we just left, there is almost no resemblance in the forest. Hemlock is absent. Sugar maple and yellow birch grow close to Lake Superior but thin out to the west. In their place, we again see spruce-dominated forests, just as in Region 4, intermingled with white, red, and jack pine. But arid-loving red pine covers a steadily wider range of sites. And poplar and birch are more dominant, suggesting the arid Manitoba landscape where they win out over both spruce and humid-loving hardwoods. West of Atikokan, associations of bur oak, sedge, and grass become common.

Region 6 – Lower Mixed Forests

Next we find ourselves in the southern half of the Great Lakes-St. Lawrence forest lobe, 125 kilometres south of Algonquin on the Orangeville moraine. The landscape here is dishevelled, with patches and strips of forest on marginal agricultural land – valleys, swamps, rock outcrops – among the predominating fields. No vestigial forests survive here, either. These are places where mighty cathedrals of sugar maple and white pine rose twenty to thirty metres or more before branching into great canopies. Beneath lay three- or four-storied complexes of life, catering to a wide variety of wildlife. We will not see the like of these forests in our lifetime; they took a thousand years or more to develop.

Examining the woodlots, we recognize the dominance of sugar maple, in its prime on the more calcareous soils of southern Ontario. More American beech is mixed in on warm sites. Younger stands include more light-demanding black cherry, white ash, and basswood, most of which will disappear from the stand as it ages. Basswood, while its seedlings germinate poorly in the shade, persists in old forests because of its habit of root-sprouting. When a main stem dies, other stalks grow up to exploit the same root system. White elm once was an important component of these forests, especially on wetter sites, but most are now gone, victims of Dutch elm disease.

Downwind of the Great Lakes, summer rainfall generally arrives in five- to fifteen-day cycles. The result of this periodic watering is great fluctuations in soil moisture. Under this regime, hemlock is remnant, confined to sites with deep humus and more moisture-retentive soils.

Oaks become increasingly important on dry sites, foretelling the next shift in major tree species to occur as we move farther south. In moist areas, the slower relative growth of oaks causes them to lose out to maple and beech, but on drier sites, the oaks' equally great ability to suck water from the soil, and their waxy, thick-cuticled leaves provide them with a much greater endurance for drought, giving them a competitive edge.

Silhouettes of Ontario's three spruces: white, black, and red. Red spruce, characteristic of the Acadian forests of the maritimes, extends into eastern Ontario in the Upper Mixed Forest Zone.

While these northern hardwood forests have suffered from human exploitation, their diversity has increased, especially in young stands. Abandoned pastures come up in hawthorn, apple, blue beech, and ironwood, followed by sugar maple and the hickories. Wet stream valleys grow dense stands of white cedar. Old farm homesteads are recolonized by groves of the exotic black locust. Efforts to reclaim barren blow-sand, such as on many parts of the Oak Ridges moraine or on rock sites, have resulted in plantations of red, white, and Scotch pine, and white spruce, some used for the Christmas tree market. Even hybrid poplar has been planted extensively on abandoned farmlands.

Region 7 – Carolinian Forest

Near the town of Simcoe, another two hundred kilometres south, we land in the Carolinian zone, a narrow strip wedged along Lake Erie's north shore. Here, less than 10 per cent of the total landscape remains forested; whole counties are less than 3 per cent.

Most of the familiar species of trees are here – sugar maple, American beech, white ash, basswood, red oak, white oak. But there are additions – black walnut, butternut, sassafras, tulip-tree, pawpaw, sycamore, chin-

Carolinian forest. LARRY LAMB

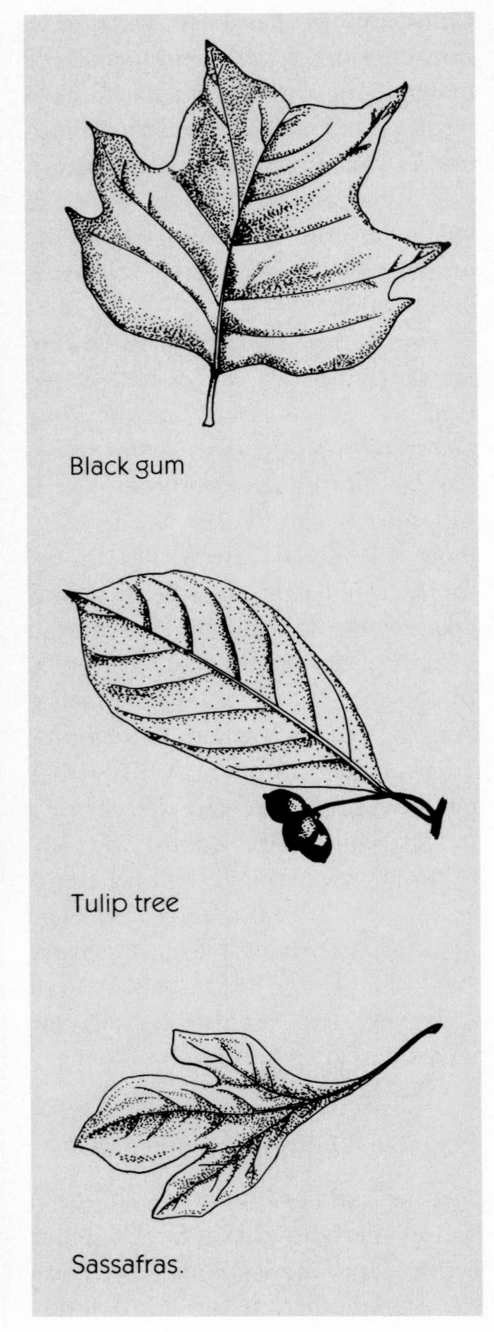

quapin oak, black oak. The diversity of tree species climbs here to seventy, more than double the number in Region 4, and twenty times that of Region 1.

Coniferous trees have all but disappeared, outcompeted by broadleaf species with their light-capturing forest crowns that help them capitalize on the greater warmth to produce more energy. A few hemlocks persist, but gone are the white spruce and the balsam fir. Around cool, isolated bogs, some black spruce and tamarack still grow, but even white pine fades, enduring only on the dry sites associated with the Niagara Escarpment and on crests of sand-ridges.

On drier sites – generally the sand plains laid down as deltas at the edge of the primordial Great Lakes – red, white, and black oak prevail over large areas, often accompanied by shagbark hickory. Locally, sassafras occurs, and you might find saplings of sweet chestnut, a major tree species all but eliminated by chestnut blight, an introduced fungus that raced through eastern North America early in this century.

Poorly drained lowlands, especially the clay plains which began as primordial lake bottoms, bear swamp forests of red maple and silver maple, as well as mixed sites of swamp white oak, black ash, and eastern cottonwood. Stands of the rare black gum survive in a few wet swales, their colonies producing vast numbers of suckers which, cypress-like, patiently await the shafts of light that signal their elders' impending demise and send them racing upwards to the canopy.

River valleys, like those of the Thames and the Grand, are characterized by both flood plains and a series of terraces, the former growing black willows, peach-leafed willows, and sycamore, the latter with magnificent stands of black walnut mixed with other hardwoods.

Many of the Carolinian tree species barely reach as far north as Ontario; the hop tree, for instance, occurs in only a few pockets hugging the Lake Erie shoreline, and the honey locust is native only at Point Pelee. Others, like sycamore and black walnut, occur over a considerable range, and some, like hackberry, are found in isolated places as much as 150 kilometres to the north. This distribution reflects not only differences in tree tolerances, but the past march of forests across the land. During a slightly warmer period five thousand years ago, Carolinian forests may have extended farther north. Remnants, in particular local hot spots, may remain.

In the hardwood-dominated forests, succession is less of a sudden, wholesale change than it is among the conifers, where entire stands can be bumped back to an earlier stage. Canopy-destroying fire rarely occurs in the humid, less flammable, leafy hardwoods. Rather, "gap-phase regeneration" takes place. The loss of a single, huge tree, or a small cluster of trees from wind, rot, or lightning, creates a minor hole in the canopy, up to half an acre in extent. The resultant sunlight reaching the forest floor allows the existing maple and other saplings to spring upward, along with light-demanding shrubs such as red elder and raspberry. Black cherry may seed in, and a few white ash. Over time, these trees race for the canopy.

Eventually, the canopy closes over once again. But, somewhere close by, the process is repeating itself. And so it goes, a towering, uneven-aged forest constantly replenishing itself.

Thus, Ontario's forests, from spindly, open spruces to rich assemblages of Carolinian species, are vibrant, living communities, lattices upon which all other species fit, triumphs of plant evolution, expressions of climate, and now of human conduct, shifting across space and time.

◆ SCIENCE ◆ EXCURSION ◆

Forestry and Ontario's Forests

Mike Singleton

From the ring of the woodsman's axe, the rhythmic sound of the crosscut saw, and the shouts of the river drivers, to the whine of a chainsaw and the grinding motors of log skidders and logging trucks, Ontario's forests have long been influenced by people.

Commercial forest operations, by their very nature, levy major disturbances on ecosystems. Such disturbances, however, are not unique. Fire, windthrow, flood, and drought are natural events that drastically alter the character of forests. These disturbances are common enough, in fact, to play a necessary role in the function of forests and the maintenance of forest and wildlife diversity. As a result of natural disturbance, most forest regions in Ontario looked like green patchwork quilts made up of different successional stages even before logging became an economic mainstay of the province.

Today, however, most of those patches are caused, or at least influenced, by man. In southern Ontario, because of forestry, agriculture, and urbanization, the towering Carolinian forests are almost gone, as are the ancient forest cathedrals of the Great Lakes-St. Lawrence forest, and the mammoth white pines. In northern Ontario, past decades of increased fire and, more recently, huge clear-cuts have greatly increased the size and decreased the age of the patches. In some large clear-cuts, soil erosion has reduced the productive capacity of the land and caused siltation of water bodies and fish spawning beds. Effective fire prevention has resulted in great accumulations of flammable limbs so that when fire does occur, its intense heat consumes much of the organic matter in the soil. Regeneration in such places has been painfully slow. Where dark green monocultures of planted red pine or spruce forests have been stripped of their natural hardwood components by spray and saw, the resulting ecological simplicity has invited outbreaks of forest pests, which in turn invite more spray and increasingly unstable conditions.

The initial effect of logging is traumatic on a forest ecosystem, but possibly no more so than fire and other major disturbances. Haul roads connect, web-like, to myriad skidder trails where logs are pulled out of the bush. Skidders crush or grind up herbs, ferns, and other plants under their indifferent tread. Lopped-off tops of trees and limbs obscure the ground. In hardwood forests perhaps 50 to 60 per cent of the trees remain after logging – a semi-open landscape instead of a forest; conifer forests normally are clear-cut.

Where clear-cuts are small, they may mirror to some extent the natural ecological conditions caused by small burns. Large clear-cuts in northern Ontario, however, dramatically change the amount of ground-water infiltration and surface moisture. Less water percolates into the soil; more runs off. The results of this altered hydrologic regime include wild fluctuations in flow – floods following rainfalls alternating with long periods when streams may dry up. Temperature and siltation increase, reducing water quality and choking spawning beds.

That we still have functioning forest ecosystems in most of Ontario is only because forests possess a remarkable regenerative capacity. Forests can and do recover where the soil is still fertile, where enough seed trees remain, and where the size of the disturbed area is not too large. The living organisms in the "net" of the soil – seeds, spores, rootlets, bulbs, rhizomes, invertebrates, and other life – may endure, ready to sprout anew. Throughout the period of recovery, the species of birds, mammals, and other populations that live there change dramatically. Animals of the mature woodland, such as woodpeckers, porcupine, and flying squirrels, decline sharply at first, but in their place, scrub-loving species take over. In the recovering forest, often the diversity of wildlife species is even higher than before. Deer, grouse, and an array of songbirds thrive in regenerating, early successional landscapes. Progressively the canopy develops again, streams recover, and the evidence of logging disappears.

About 95 per cent of Ontario's 377,000 square kilometres of productive forests are committed to forestry. Thus, the future of Ontario's forested environments depends upon wise and ecologically responsible forestry.

◆ SCIENCE ◆ EXCURSION ◆

Spruce Budworm and the Spruce-Fir Forest

Alan G. Gordon

The Spruce-Fir Stronghold

The vast North American boreal forest, or *taiga*, is characterized by few species of trees. A major portion of this forest is dominated by spruce and balsam fir. These spruce-fir forests occur not only in the boreal zone, but in isolated pockets within the Great Lakes-St. Lawrence region immediately to the south, and in related Maritime and Appalachian forests. The spruce-fir forests have occupied wide expanses of northeastern and northern North America since the Pleistocene glaciers retreated northward eight to ten thousand years ago.

Three species of spruce make up this forest. White spruce and black spruce are boreal and have the most extensive ranges of any coniferous species in North America, much greater than that of any pine. They range from the east coast of Newfoundland to western Alaska, and they may be the most abundant coniferous species in the world. In contrast, red spruce is entirely eastern in its North American distribution, ranging throughout the Appalachian Mountains, much of the Maritime Provinces, southern Quebec, and east-central Ontario. Its range has been diminished greatly by over-harvesting.

In Ontario, black spruce grows in extensive pure stands primarily on lowland wet or moist sites. White spruce grows on better drained sites, in pure stands but most often in association with trembling aspen, balsam fir, and white birch. Red spruce prefers acidic tills but avoids calcareous soils and limestone bedrock. It grows in pure or mixed stands with most other northern hardwood and boreal species.

Balsam fir, a principal associate of white spruce and red spruce, is a strong component of the spruce-fir forest in the Maritimes, Quebec, and Ontario. It also grows in extensive pure stands in parts of the Maritimes. Historical records indicate that spruce was formerly more prevalent in what are now predominantly fir areas, but it has been diminished by harvesting.

Balsam fir is a short-lived species compared to spruce and rots out much sooner. Because its wood is less dense and has a lower cellulose content, its commercial value is lower than spruce. It seeds profusely, especially as it approaches maturity. It regenerates much more aggressively than does spruce in the eastern part of its range, from Manitoba eastwards.

Spruce Budworm

Spruce budworm plays a major role in the periodic devastation and renewal of the spruce-fir forest. This insect probably has been present with spruce and fir for thousands of years, throughout the Pleistocene and perhaps as far back as the Pliocene. This fact suggests that somehow the forest has developed and used a successful strategy to get along with the budworm without our assistance for a long time. If the spruce-fir forest was ultimately unable to survive such periodic onslaughts upon itself, it would have been eliminated long ago.

Budworm moths are dull grey with spots of brown on the forewings. Wingspan is about two centimetres. They mate and lay eggs in a cluster of

Spruce budworm pupae. DON GUNN

fifteen to fifty on the underside of spruce and fir needles in July or early August. The eggs hatch in August as tiny larvae. Without feeding, the first larval *instars* (the stages between each successive moult in the developing insect) spin silken *hibernacula*, or sheltering cases, in bark or twig crevices. Here, they overwinter. In the early spring, they emerge as a second instar and mine out one or two needles before moving into developing shoots. After having fed on and destroyed the shoot, they emerge as a third instar. They increase in size through the third, fourth, fifth, and sixth instars during May and June. They feed initially on new foliage and when that is gone, they move back along the branches, feeding on older foliage. At the seventh instar stage, in June or early July, they pupate, emerging in July as moths to fly, mate, and begin the cycle again.

Most attempts to control spruce budworm have utilized chemical pesticides and, more recently, biocides such as Bt (*Bacillus thuringiensis*). This bacterium kills budworm through a complex reaction to a crystal protein which it contains. The insect larvae die from ingesting the bacterium.

Foresters and entomologists have long recognized the impossibility of trying to eliminate the budworm through spraying. They feel that controlling the population until harvesting can be accomplished is the best plan. This control involves spraying – particularly where the numbers of budworm approach epidemic levels, threatening to destroy forest stands – to temporarily reduce populations to levels where little damage occurs. This action will allow the forest to stand for another five to twenty years or more, when cutting can take place.

Origins of Outbreaks

Methods of searching for and sampling budworm populations have been improved immeasurably in recent years by techniques utilizing sex pheromones. These techniques have demonstrated that budworm is widespread at relatively constant, low levels almost everywhere throughout the spruce, fir, and spruce-fir forests.

Budworm outbreaks can, and often do, occur anywhere when low-level, local populations increase in response to the coincidence of favourable climatic and stand conditions. The spread of the budworm also may be augmented by larval movements and moth flights. Local winds and weather systems can spread budworm from areas of high concentration to distant, less-infested areas.

How Does the Forest Respond to an Outbreak?

In the life of a spruce-fir stand, a spruce budworm outbreak at some point is almost inescapable. The effects of massive defoliation proceed through the stand as an energy transfer pulse which immutably alters the development of that stand.

Long-term studies of white spruce-fir forests in northern Ontario and red spruce-fir forests in south-central and eastern Ontario are providing some remarkable information and new insights on how the forest and the budworm function together. Surprisingly, they clearly show that the perpetuity of the spruce component in such stands is actually dependent upon budworm events.

Consider a stand of relatively mature or even somewhat post-mature trees (indicated by a declining growth rate) some years *before* a budworm event. Spruce trees from ten to sixty centimetres dbh (diameter at breast height) dominate the stand. Large balsam fir have long since dropped out or been eliminated. Such a stand typically has few very large spruce trees, moderate numbers (say twenty per hectare) of immature trees between ten and twenty centimetres dbh, and fifty to two hundred small trees less than eight centimetres dbh. In contrast, none of the fir trees present would be greater than fifteen centimetres dbh.

However, beneath the larger trees, the rising (secondary) stand, which is expected to form the next mature forest, contains five hundred to fifteen hundred small fir per hectare, a ratio of fir over spruce of about 7:1, possibly going as high as 10:1 or 12:1. The young fir are growing aggressively, and as they rise in the stand, the numbers of small spruce competing with them will drop still further.

Many foresters have always expected that the spruce will somehow get through to form the next mature forest. The truth is that left to their own devices they won't. Spruce are somewhat tolerant of shade, red spruce considerably more so than white, but they are ultimately not as shade-tolerant as balsam fir. Looking at the ratios of young fir to young spruce in this forest, we can see that there are simply not going to be enough places left with sufficient light for the spruce to grow.

Enter the budworm.

Spruce budworm populations have been building up in nearby stands, and they now begin to overflow. Our stand experiences a massive budworm attack.

The overstorey is attacked first, and subsequently the rising secondary stand. The attack lasts about seven to ten years; by then all the fir except the smallest regenerating seedlings are dead. With only a few losses, the spruce remain intact in the overstorey and in what is left of the secondary stand.

What is important to the future forest is the remaining advanced-growth spruce in the secondary stand, and particular the increasing spruce regeneration. Before the outbreak, fir greatly outnumbered spruce; after the outbreak the ratio may be as low as 2:1 fir to spruce, or even 1:1 if the outbreak continues. A prolonged and active outbreak will result in high numbers of larvae competing for food. The fifth and sixth instars will be forced to spin down from the overstorey trees in search of food, and they will destroy more fir regeneration. The ratios may eventually favour spruce. In the new wave of regeneration, these spruce, having escaped the competitive embrace of the balsam fir, will be permitted once again to maintain their species' presence in the next stand.

A number of points, then, may be made about the effect of spruce budworm on the spruce-fir forest:

1) The survival rate of spruce in both the overstorey and the secondary stand is much greater than that of fir.
2) The elimination of much of the rising secondary stand releases young spruce which would otherwise have been lost through competition.
3) In a spruce-fir forest, the secondary stand making up the pre-attack understorey and dominated by rising balsam fir is not, in the end, the stand that will replace the overstorey. Rather, after attack, it is the non-apparent spruce regeneration which will develop under and replace much of the present secondary stand.
4) Since all the fir fifteen centimetres dbh and smaller have been eliminated, there will be no fir of flowering size left in the stand and, therefore, no seed production on any fir for the next twenty years. This permits the seed being produced by the remaining overstorey spruce to initiate more spruce regeneration in the openings provided by the dying fir.
5) An ancillary point is that defoliation of the fir is also transferred as an energy pulse in the form of nutrients in the larval *frass* (excrement and uneaten needle fragments). These nutrients are quickly available to existing small seedlings, many of which will be spruce. Data from ecosystem studies in spruce-fir forests also indicate that this nutrient recharge is sustained over the next several years by the disintegration and return to the forest floor of the standing dead fir boles and branches.

These five points reflect the co-evolution of spruce budworm and the spruce-fir forests – the accommodation of one to the other over long periods of time. They strongly support the hypothesis that where spruce and fir grow together, spruce budworm is an essential factor in maintaining spruce in the stand through time. The re-occurrence of spruce is dependent upon the budworm to reduce the amount of fir. The significance to forest management of this conclusion is that if the stands are sprayed with chemical pesticides or biocides to control the budworm, balsam fir is perpetuated, in turn eliminating or drastically reducing spruce in future stands.

◆ SCIENCE ◆ EXCURSION ◆

Forests Are More Than Trees

Mike Singleton

Forests, by definition, are dominated visually and in terms of biomass by trees. Forests are, however, living communities of both plants and animals interacting with one another in interdependent webs tied together by energy capture and flow, nutrient cycling, cybernetic feedback mechanisms, and a host of relationships: symbiotic, parasitic, saprophytic, and mutualistic. Indeed, trees are not the most abundant form of life in forests. In a hypothetical four-hectare Great Lakes-St. Lawrence forest, with meadow edge, one might expect to find in the following numbers:

The species drawn upon in this example come from a pool in the province of: 100 species of trees, 2,800 other vascular plants, 69 terrestrial mammals, 430 birds (breeding and migratory), 49 reptiles and amphibians, 465 mosses, and – very roughly – 50,000 invertebrates.

Group	Number of Organisms	Number of Species
Trees	5,000	25
Other vascular plants	2.5 million	200
Mammals	1,200	30
Birds	1,000	45
Reptiles and Amphibians	1,500	15
Mosses	7 million	50
Invertebrates	2,400 million	4,000

◆ SCIENCE ◆ EXCURSION ◆

Leaf Colour

John B. Theberge

The scarlet of the maples can shake me
like a cry
Of bugles going by
Bliss Carman, "A Vagabond Song"

Most flamboyant, most lavish of all natural phenomena in Ontario is the extravaganza of autumn colours. Blazing hills of red, orange, and yellow grandstand across the landscape. Flaming red maples crown the ridges, extravagant trembling aspens daub the boreal greens with gold, scarlet viburnums blush in the bogs. Like fire slowed down to last a season, the brilliance kindles, spreads, consumes, fades, and finally dies.

This outlandish display of colour is caused by the plant's molecules, and its function is basic to life on Earth. The cytoplasm that fills leaf cells is scattered with small granular-appearing bodies called *plastids*, of three types: chloroplast, chromoplast, and leucoplast. *Leucoplasts* are colourless and are chiefly important as centres for starch formation and storage. They are not relevant to leaf colour, but the other two plastids are.

Chloroplasts, usually disc-shaped, contain 1 or 2 per cent chlorophyll molecules. Because of its molecular configurations, chlorophyll absorbs all wavelengths of visible light except green, which is reflected. Chloroplasts are exceedingly complex chemical factories in which photosynthesis proceeds.

In chloroplasts, besides molecules of chlorophyll in different forms, are found related molecules called *carotenoids*. These reflect yellow, orange,

Structure of an epidermal leaf cell.

and sometimes red light. They consist of carbon and hydrogen in hexagonal configurations joined into long chains. There are two basic types: *carotenes*, which are hydrocarbons; and *xanthophylls*, which are oxygen-containing derivatives. More than seventy molecular configurations of carotenoids have been identified in the plant kingdom.

Carotenoids appear to have two functions. They trap light energy and through electron displacement provide the first step in transforming it to potential chemical energy, passing the energy on to receptor chlorophyll molecules for photosynthesis. One configuration of carotene, called *beta-carotene*, is especially efficient, transferring close to 100 per cent of light energy that strikes it. The second function appears to be the opposite – light shielding, especially by xanthophylls, to prevent photo-oxidation and hence destruction of chlorophyll pigments.

When eaten by animals, the beta-carotene molecule may split in half and take in water to form two molecules of vitamin A. If green plants stopped synthesizing carotene, animal life would not survive. The yellow and orange pigments of oranges, squash, carrots, and other vegetables are all due to carotenes.

The carotenoids also are found in *chromoplasts*, the third type of plastid, which may be disc-shaped but also may be long, spindle-shaped, or angular. Chromoplasts may be plastids from which chlorophyll has disappeared, or they may never have been green. During ripening of some fruit, such as bananas and tomatoes, chlorophyll breaks down, converting chloroplasts to chromoplasts, or revealing chromoplasts previously present but not visible, and yellow or red colours result.

In the leaves of hardwood trees, xanthophylls, more plentiful than carotenes, are primarily responsible for golds and yellows. But both types of carotenoid pigments are masked while chlorophyll is present. Chlorophyll strongly absorbs both ends of the visible light spectrum – blues and reds – but reflects green; carotenoids absorb blue and violet while reflecting red, yellow, green, and some blue which mixes to yellow. Yellow (of the carotenoids) modifies the shade of green (of the chlorophyll), but cannot replace it.

While carotenoids are responsible primarily for yellows and oranges in autumn leaves, another pigment, called *anthocyanin*, is responsible primarily for shades of red, scarlet, and purple. Anthocyanins, like carotenoids, are complex molecules. They are water soluble, and are not found in plastids but in the vacuoles of cells. A *vacuole* is a region in a plant cell bounded by a membrane and filled with watery sap. Dissolved in the water are colloidally dispersed proteins, sugars, organic acids, and anthocyanins. Their colour may vary with acidity.

Red maples, Peterborough County.
PAT SINGLETON

Anthocyanins are responsible for the purple in turnips, radishes, beets, blue and red grapes, plums, cherries, and many flowers, as well as the reds and purples in autumn leaves. Their function is not understood, but they develop so abundantly in the autumn leaves of some tree species, such as red maple, that they mask the yellow carotenoids.

Much folklore surrounds the environmental conditions that stimulate leaf colour. Some years are indeed more brilliant than others. In response to both shortening hours of daylight and lowering temperature, a separation layer of specialized cells grows at the base of the leaf stalk, or *petiole*. These cells are short, lack lignin, and form a mechanical weakness.

A corky layer of cells then forms just below the separation layer to protect the exposed cells of the twig from drying out or from fungal infection when the leaf falls. During this sealing-off process, the movement of water to the leaf is greatly restricted. Chlorophyll synthesis decreases, and existing chlorophyll molecules break down. The pectin in the cell wall of the separation layer dissolves through enzymatic action, leaving the leaf suspended by its *vascular bundles* – the circulation vessels between veins of the leaf and the branch.

Contributing to leaf fall, too, appear to be plant hormones, called *auxins*, produced in the blade of the leaf. They are organic compounds, active in minute amounts, and produced most abundantly in growing young leaves. They travel down the leaf petiole and inhibit leaf fall. In older leaves, or those stressed by too much shade or by insects, auxin production decreases, initiating the separation layer. Thus, some leaves, or whole trees may change colour prematurely, a certain indication of stress.

Differences in autumn weather influence primarily the anthocyanins – the amount of reds. Anthocyanins are stimulated both by direct light and by the accumulation of sugars from rapid photosynthesis as a result of light. So, bright autumn weather favours red colours. Often in sumacs and some trees, reds predominate on the crown and outside leaves before colouring spreads to other, more shaded leaves, because of this light effect. Poison ivy flushes red in strong light but yellow in the shade.

Low temperatures also increase anthocyanin production, colouring valley-floor trees where cool air sinks to the lowlands. However, contrary to popular belief, frosts *inhibit* leaf colour by hastening complete cell destruction and leaf fall.

Wind at the edges of woodlots may increase water stress and cause leaves to colour there first. Ridge-top trees growing on shallow soils over bedrock may experience similar stress and early colour.

Sugar maples mostly turn yellow, the predominant colour in southern Ontario. Under the influence of colder weather they are redder in northern Ontario. Most Carolinian species turn yellow: sycamore, hickories, black walnut, butternut. So do the poplars and birches in patches all through the boreal forest. Red maples, some oaks, and shrubs such as sumacs, viburnums, and dogwoods flash predominantly red. Silver maples and ash trees mix reds and yellows. Beeches mix yellows with rich brown tannin. Leaves of elms and alders normally fall green. These species differences are genetic, linked to DNA codes for pigment production. The variability itself is evidence that no one formula is best. Thus, the diversity of autumn's resplendence appears to be a pure extravagance, a superfluity of nature, but one that endows Ontario greatly with beauty.

Typical reds of staghorn sumach.
JOHN THEBERGE

Sugar maples, Lanark County.
LARRY LAMB.

◆ SCIENCE ◆ EXCURSION ◆

Evolution of Tree Species

Alan G. Gordon

Many of the tree species that currently make up Ontario's forests have come down from very ancient times. The *angiosperms*, broad-leaved flowering species commonly called "hardwoods," appeared and greatly expanded their ranges in the Cretaceous Period, 135 million to 65 million years BP (before the present), and may have originated even earlier. Several genera and perhaps even some individual species familiar to us today arose that long ago, such as certain poplars, willows, alders, birches, beeches, oaks, walnuts, sassafras, cherries, hackberry, magnolias, gums, sycamores, and tulip-tree.

The *conifers* or cone-bearing trees, commonly called "softwoods," arose even earlier, beginning near the end of the Paleozoic Era 230 million years BP, and expanding through the early and mid Mesozoic Era (Triassic, Jurassic) to have a world-wide distribution by the mid Cretaceous Period. Ancestors of the family *Pinaceae*, particularly the genus *Pinus*, the pines, were well established by the Cretaceous. On the basis of available fossils, other genera of this family – the spruces, hemlocks, firs, and larches – with species the same or similar to the species we know today, are thought to have arisen and radiated (spread) after the pines. They are therefore considered more modern.

None of the modern genera of the family *Pinaceae* necessarily arose in a straight line from an earlier-established genus such as *Pinus*. That is, the pines did not give rise to the spruces, hemlocks, or larches directly. Rather, they arose quite randomly from other branches of the family tree than the one that gave rise to *Pinus*. Most of the ancestors that gave rise ultimately to the modern species are now extinct.

The fossil record shows that spruces were present in Japan and Europe in the late Cretaceous. This and their modern distribution indicate that differentiation and radiation of this genus already had occurred by that time. Spruce fossils have been found from the early Tertiary, 65 to 55 million years BP, across what is now the sub-Arctic or the Arctic from southwestern Alaska to northwestern Ellesmere Island, southwestern Greenland, and Spitzbergen. In Greenland, not only spruce but also pine fossils have been found from this period, but neither hemlock nor tamarack apparently had evolved. The first hemlock appeared in Asia in the Eocene, 55 to 38 million years BP, and was widespread as far as western North America and China by the Oligocene Period, 38 to 25 million years BP. Tamarack first appeared in the Oligocene.

Tempering these interpretations of dates and places of origin of the *Pinacea* is the fact that not all genera are equally likely to be well preserved fossils. Those species occupying higher and drier sites, such as mountain slopes, are much under-represented as compared to those growing near swamps, silt rivers, or still lakes. When these trees fell into water, low levels of oxygen in the aqueous sediments inhibited breakdown.

About thirty-five to forty species of spruce live in the world today. These actual species did not actually appear until between 5 million and 2 million years ago. There are ten to fourteen hemlocks, thirty-five to forty firs, and eleven larches. All are found only in the northern hemisphere, and all are circumpolar. Hemlocks are the most restricted, living in North America, China, and Japan but absent from Europe in modern times, although they occurred there as late as the Pleistocene, 2 million years ago.

In early and mid Tertiary times, 65 million to about 15 million years ago, a vast, temperate forest extended over the whole northern hemisphere and across what is now the Arctic. This forest is known to have been a great, mixed, *mesophytic* forest – containing tree species that grow best under conditions of medium moisture and humidity – not unlike parts of Ontario today. These species included not only the *Pinacea* but the hardwoods: maples, beeches, oaks, tulip-tree, gums, sassafras, magnolias, hickories, walnuts, birches, ashes, and many other woody deciduous shrubs and hardwood trees.

While there are many related descendants of the trees in this great forest growing today in North America, Europe, and Asia, most of the Eurasian and North American tree species are quite distinct from each other. Remarkably, however, there are a substantial number of very similar pairs of species sharing two widely disjunct ranges: in eastern North America (the southern Appalachians to the Great Lakes, including southern Ontario), and in parts of China and Japan. This is a special flora, known as the *Arcto-tertiary flora*, reflecting its origins, in which one or two species of each genera grow in eastern North America and a second nearly identical species of the same genus grows in Asia. A few of these species pairs have proven to be genetically compatible, further indicating their common origin. This flora is important to the present-day tree species composition of Ontario, and also includes some of the associated ground flora. The white trillium, for example, has a closely related sister species growing in Japan and China and nowhere else in North America, western Asia, or Europe.

Most of the genera of trees in Ontario today originated and radiated from their place of origin before continental drift isolated North America. Twelve species of maples inhabit North America, but 115 occur in China. Consequently, maples are thought to have originated in the Asian part of the supercontinental land mass (Laurasia) and radiated from there. On the other hand, there are so many pine species in the New World, fifty-nine versus thirty-five for the Old World (the same number as exist in Mexico alone!), that there is a strong possibility that pines radiated from the North American portion of the previous supercontinent.

Many other species in all continents, however, originated after the continents separated. Two land bridges existed between North America and Eurasia: one to the east through Greenland, connecting with northern Europe, and the other, Beringia, linking northwestern North America with northeastern Asia. The first of these bridges, above water all through the Mesozoic, was available to temperate fauna and vegetation at least to the late Cretaceous, about 65 million years ago. Many of the early conifers, as well as many angiosperms, dispersed across this bridge. The second bridge, above water through the same earlier times, stayed available for dispersal of trees to less than 20 million years BP.

The land bridges were limited in their usefulness as dispersal routes, however, by climate. During much of the time they were open, the climate was tropical or subtropical, and the lowlands were occupied by broad-leaved, evergreen, tropical rain forest, even as far north as latitude 60 degrees N, our present-day sub-Arctic. There were, however, intermittent uplands on the land bridges, and strips of land still farther north with cooler, temperate climates. As well, during the enormous times involved there was some favourable climatic oscillation. At least two cooler periods afforded better opportunities for the temperate flora to disperse across the bridges: at the end of the Cretaceous and beginning of the Paleocene, and in the late Oligocene.

The land bridges help explain genetic affinities found among species separated today by ocean gaps. For example, red spruce, a species confined to eastern North America, will breed freely with Serbian spruce (*Picea omorika*), a rare species of Yugoslavia's Dinaric Alps. Both species are old, do not look alike, and have markedly different ecological requirements. The ancestors of these species have not been near one another for at least 65 million years, since the close of Beringia, yet genetically they are very close. In contrast, Norway spruce (*Picea abies*) is a comparatively recent species. It is common and wide-spread in Eurasia, and has been introduced into North America. In southern Ontario it is familiar as a windbreak around farmhouses and along farm lanes. It does not have genetic affinities outside its natural range. While it will cross with a few Asian spruces, it will not do so with any North American species.

Besides land bridges, another influence on range expansion of tree species is competition. Many species are able to grow in a given area, but few will dominate sufficiently well to persist. A fact not well appreciated is the intensity of the age-old struggle between the *gymnosperms* – conifers and their allies – and the angiosperm hardwoods, since the coming of the latter. This battle continues in the modern forest today, and man now participates influentially in it. Unfortunately the conifers continue to lose. In the Jurassic (195 to 136 million years BP) there were more genera and species of conifers than we shall ever know again.

By the middle of the Cretaceous Period, the angiosperm hardwoods, spreading quite rapidly after their recent origins, had become the dominant group of seed plants. The conifers and their relatives, which had originated much earlier and dominated until the mid Cretaceous, lost many genera and species through competition from the hardwoods. Angiosperm species today are many times more abundant in the world than the conifers and their allies. Conifers usually have become restricted by the hardwoods to more stressed sites where the hardwoods cannot easily follow. Conifers survive competition best on cold, wet, hot, and dry sites. Hardwoods generally hold the better middle ground, the mesic sites. Conifer strongholds today remain on mountain ranges at great distances from one another: the Alps, Appalachians, Rockies, Himalayas, Sierra Madre, and others. Similarly, conifers have been able to survive better in the high boreal sub-Arctic forests than have hardwoods.

One further factor, the herbivorous impact of dinosaurs, influenced forever the struggle between gymnosperm conifers and the angiosperm hardwoods, tipping the balance in favour of the hardwoods. Millions of years of conifer browsing by high-feeding dinosaurs before hardwoods evolved clearly did not inhibit the conifers, which then were at their peak numbers of species. But at the beginning of the Cretaceous Period, many of the large dinosaurs that browsed at heights of eight to fourteen metres were replaced by smaller (a few to several tons) species that browsed and cropped much lower down.

The crowns of trees that were browsed high up were mature and full. There was usually enough vegetation left for persistent growth and reproduction. However, with the switch to low-feeding dinosaurs, regeneration was eaten. When coniferous regeneration is growing in the presence of hardwood regeneration and its leaders are clipped, usually the coniferous seedlings lose their height dominance to the hardwoods and die. Young conifers today whose leaders are browsed by rabbits and deer suffer the same fate. Dinosaurs also ate hardwoods, but these are better able to survive browsing. Hardwoods can often sprout new shoots from their rootstocks, something few conifers can do.

The major consequences of evolution which we see today in the forests were accomplished long before the Pleistocene, but evolution still proceeds. It is amazing to consider, however, that of the approximately 260 tree and shrub species that now inhabit Ontario, not one was present during full glaciation only eighteen thousand years ago. Ontario was then covered entirely by ice. All these species re-advanced into the province from glacial refugia or from south of the ice, following its melting only six thousand to twelve thousand years ago.

Vistas of Time, Rock and Invertebrate Fossils

Alfred C. Lenz

Life arose early in the Earth's history. Planet Earth and our solar system condensed from interstellar matter about 4.6 billion years ago. The oldest rocks presently known on Earth date back 3.8 billion years. Even these rocks, being sedimentary, had to have formed from the long-term erosion of older rocks. In the world's oldest known rocks are microfossils of living things.

These ancient rocks, with their evidence of early life, have been found in southern Africa and western Australia. In North America, while rocks close to 3 billion years in age are common, they have been subjected to such high heat and pressure (metamorphism) that much of the original textures have been altered or lost. Nevertheless, the oldest fossils on the continent are found in Ontario. They are representatives of the same earliest living forms found on the other two continents that apparently changed little in their first billion or billion and a half years of existence.

Along Lake Superior's north shore, extending about two hundred kilometres, is the now-famous Gunflint Iron formation. These banded, dark red, iron-rich rocks, are commonly called *banded iron formations* because they are made up of thin, bright red beds alternating with those that are more iron-rich and darker, purplish-red. Motorists along the Trans-Canada Highway in the vicinity of Schreiber are treated to views of this unusually colourful rock in the road-cuts along the way.

Stromatolites in the Aphebian-age Gunflint Formation in Schreiber Channel Provincial Nature Reserve. The light-coloured rings represent accumulations of blue-green algae on darker-coloured boulders. These fossil remains were deposited in shallow coastal waters about 2 billion years ago. R. J. DAVIDSON

Included in the banding of this rock is the "Gunflint Chert," a partially crystalline quartz formed from sediments of colloidal silica settling to the bottom of a shallow sea. In settling, the silica entrapped and embedded a dazzling array of single-celled organisms in laminated mound-like structures called *stromatolites*. In spite of their antiquity, these stromatolites beautifully preserve various kinds of bacteria, cyanobacteria (sometimes called blue-green algae), and even fungus-like forms. Some organisms are unique – *Kakabekia umbellata*, for instance, consist of an umbrella-like cap, basal bulb, and slender connecting stalk. Many of the most exciting finds have been made at the base of picturesque Kakabeka Falls.

At the time these ancient rocks were formed, the Earth's atmosphere is thought to have been *anoxic*, or virtually devoid of oxygen, as it had been for the previous one or more billion years. To almost all organisms living then, free atmospheric oxygen would have been poisonous. It is commonly held that any free oxygen which might have resulted from early photosynthetic reactions became bonded to the iron-rich sediments, causing the red colour.

All of these earliest microscopic fossils are *procaryotes*, that is, simple cells without a nucleus. More advanced nucleated cells known as *eucaryotes*, characteristic of higher organisms from amoeba to man, did not appear in the rock record for about another billion years.

After the discovery of these microfossils, the Gunflint Chert locality became so well known that collectors, from professional to amateur, wanted samples, and the outcrop was in danger of disappearing. Fortunately, the area has now been protected in a nature preserve.

Somewhat younger Precambrian rocks – between 1.8 and 1.1 billion years old – contribute to the magnificent scenery between Thunder Bay and Kenora. They underlie a relatively small portion of Ontario. They are part of a vast thickness, up to 15,000 metres, of relatively flat-lying strata, which includes very thick volcanic rock interbedded with sedimentary rock. These sedimentary rocks, too, include carbonate strata consisting of spectacular stromatolites, but the rocks here are interesting in other ways as well. The sedimentary portions, though very thick, are predominantly dark red in colour, implying that by this time the Earth's atmosphere contained enough free oxygen to oxidize the iron in the rocks. These rocks, unlike the older banded iron formations, are not banded and are much more uniformly bright red. They are a part of the immense iron-ore deposits in neighbouring Minnesota and northern Michigan.

Interesting too are the stromatolites containing varying amounts of native copper. This copper was widely used and traded by the early aboriginal peoples. Geologists and biologists are unsure whether the copper minerals in the stromatolites are there because they have been concentrated through biological activities of the cyanobacteria, or simply because of the open spaces in the stromatolitic structures. A number of elements and minerals are known to be concentrated by both living bacteria and cyanobacteria.

During the vast period of time between about 1 billion and about 550 million years ago, Ontario's Shield area suffered little more than slow erosion, forming the basis of today's rounded hills and myriad lakes. The Earth, however, underwent some remarkable changes, especially biologically. The nucleus-bearing eucaryotes appeared sometime between 1.4 and 1 billion years ago, paving the way for all higher, multi-celled organisms. These did not appear until about 700 million years ago – relatively large soft-bodied animals, including "jellyfish," coral relatives, "worms," and what are likely crustaceans, some up to fifty centimetres long. They have been recognized on almost every continent, including Canada, where they are found in Newfoundland and the Mackenzie Mountains, but their most superb preservation is in south-central Australia. None of these biological events, however, is recorded in Ontario.

Beginning about 600 million years ago, at the end of the Precambrian Era, shell- and skeleton-bearing animals such as trilobites, molluscs, sponges, and sponge-like animals made their appearance all over the world. One has to wonder why, in a world with few, if any, predators, animals such as trilobites and molluscs developed with shells and skeletons at all.

The geologic record may provide a clue to the value of shells. At that time, the seas of the Earth appear to have contained high concentrations of calcium carbonate and calcium phosphate, minerals which can be built into shells and skeletons. Perhaps the animals got rid of excess minerals in their systems by turning them into shells and skeletons. Thus skeletons may have developed almost by accident, only later becoming an integral and necessary structural part of the organisms when they proved valuable as a defence against predators. Another, possibly more acceptable explanation, is that skeletons arose in conjunction with an increase in size and the need for muscle-attachment surfaces. It seems significant that all early skeleton-bearing creatures lived on top of the sea floor, rather than buried in the mud.

In the Ordovician Period, about 520 to 440 million years ago, much of the relief of the ancient Shield rocks which make up northern Ontario was very similar to that of today. There were, however, no creatures such as insects (not even mosquitoes), spiders, or any invertebrates. In fact, there were no trees, shrubs, or, in all likelihood, any plant life whatsoever.

South of the Shield, however, the land lay submerged under a shallow sea. The waters were warm because then their location was just south of the equator. This sea was vast, covering most of the interior of North America, and extending as far north as a line drawn from just north of Manitoulin Island eastward to just north of

Cephalopod.

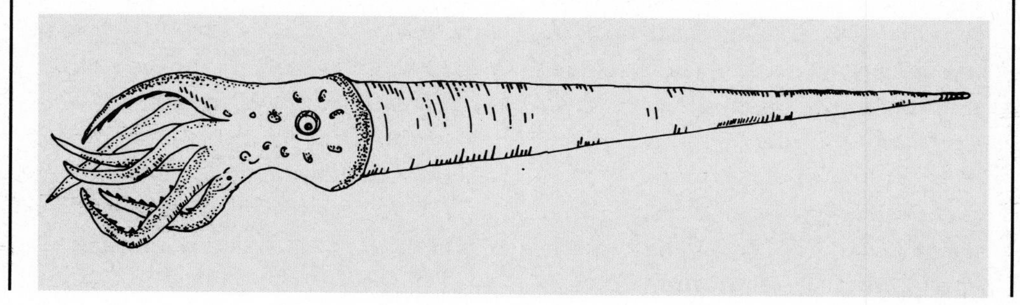

Ottawa. It may have extended even farther north in an arm connecting with James Bay and Hudson Bay, but any evidence would have been removed by erosion of the intervening rocks. In the sea, in contrast to the dry land, life was abundant. Living things included trilobites, brachiopods, bivalves, snails, corals, starfish, sea urchins, and cephalopods. Some cephalopods were giants; one found in Ontario was more than ten metres long.

The most intriguing animal of the Paleozoic seas was probably the trilobite, so named because of the three lobe-like divisions of the body. Trilobites appeared fairly abruptly near the beginning of the Cambrian Period, which preceded the Ordovician, and underwent rapid evolution until by the late Cambrian and early Ordovician they were more abundant than at any other point in their long history: more than three hundred genera and thousands of species are known.

Trilobites occupied many ecological niches: deep burrowers, shallow burrowers, crawlers on top of the mud. Some trilobites preferred swimming in deep, dark water, others stayed in water that was shallow, aerated, and well lit. Some species lived on the open sea floor, while more specialized forms frequented sheltered areas such as crevices in the reefs.

Trilobites, like other crustaceans such as crabs and lobsters, periodically were forced to shed their shells as they grew larger. The shells split in predetermined areas in the *cephalon* or head region, and the animal crawled out. In their lifetime they would do this many times, so that the vast majority of trilobite fossils represent moults rather than animals that died. This fact is particularly valuable for the paleontologist since it permits a better understanding of the life history of individual trilobite species.

Trilobites varied greatly in size. Some fully-grown species did not exceed five to ten millimetres in length, whereas a few, after numerous moults, attained the gigantic size of sixty centimetres. In fact, one of the largest trilobites ever found, a species appropriately named *Isotelus gigas* (*gigas* meaning giant), was found in mid-Ordovician limestones in the Kingston area many years ago.

Trilobite, *Pseudogygites latimarginatus*, of the Upper Ordovician, also common in the Collingwood area.
COURTESY OF R. LUDVIGSEN

Ordovician trilobite, *Triarthrus eatoni*, common in the Collingwood area.
COURTESY OF R. LUDVIGSEN

Trilobites, while common in most Ordovician, Silurian, and Devonian rocks of Ontario, are particularly abundant and often beautifully preserved in the Bruce Peninsula between Collingwood and Craigleith. The dark shales which occur near water level along the shores of Georgian Bay, referred to as the Collingwood Shales,

Phacops rana, a mid-Devonian species of trilobite found in Lambton County.
ROYAL ONTARIO MUSEUM, DEPT. OF INVERTEBRATE PALEONTOLOGY

sometimes contain myriads of whole as well as fragmented skeletons of the species *Triarthruseatoni* and *Pseudogygites latimarginatus*. Unbroken specimens are particularly fine treasures since details of the animal may be exquisite.

The presence of numerous whole specimens suggests that the animals died *en masse*. The even laminations of the rocks, their dark colour and high organic content tells us that the sea floor in which these trilobites and other organisms lived was hit periodically by *anoxic*, or poisonous, events due to the reduction or loss of oxygen. Similar conditions occur today in tropical areas or in areas of unusually high algal growth: the so-called algal blooms or red tides.

Trilobites attained their greatest diversity during the early part of the Ordovician, as already noted. Then they declined gradually, and by the succeeding Silurian Period were represented by fewer than one hundred genera. Following a modest resurgence during the Devonian, they again diminished in numbers until their extinction just before the end of the Permian, about 230 million years ago. Just before their extinction, they were represented by fewer than ten genera.

Silurian and Devonian trilobites were still very impressive, despite the reduction in the numbers of species. Unlike typical Ordovician trilobites, they generally possessed rounded bodies, higher in relief, and much more highly ornamented by nodes, bumps and spines of various sizes and shapes. They were capable of rolling themselves into tight balls, much like today's familiar sow or pill bugs. Most strikingly, they often possessed complex, diverse, and at times, bizarre eye structures. Like all crustaceans and insects, trilobites had multi-prismed eyes. Some species, such as the beautiful mid-Devonian *Phacops rana*, which may be found around Arkona and Thedford, possessed very large, elevated eyes with tens of prisms, assuring nearly 180-degree vision. Others possessed eyes with literally hundreds of prisms, similar to those of modern-day dragonflies, while still others bore their eyes on long stalks, which may have allowed the trilobite to lie buried in the mud with only its eyes showing.

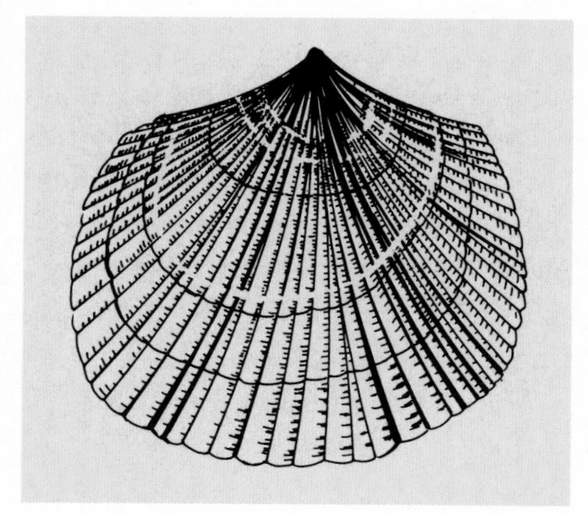

Brachiopod.

Why did the widely distributed and apparently superbly adapted trilobites become extinct? Perhaps they were unable to compete with the increasingly abundant carnivorous cephalopods (including squids and their modern-day relatives). One thing is certain: trilobites disappeared more with a whimper than with a bang; that is, they were in steady decline from the end of the Devonian until their demise near the end of the Permian, a period of more than 100 million years.

Trilobites were not the only creatures abounding in the Ordovician seas. Corals appeared about midway through the period and soon became so abundant and widespread that they contributed to the development of reefs. Bivalves, both surface dwellers and early burrowing types, as well as gastropods, or snails, were quite common, especially in shallow, nearshore waters. Brachiopods (the so-called lampshells) as well as their distant cousins the bryozoans, were especially abundant and ranged from very shallow inshore to deeper offshore waters. Members of the echinoderm, or starfish group, first became abundant during the Ordovician. Beautiful stalked crinoids (relatives of the modern "sea lilies") became abun-

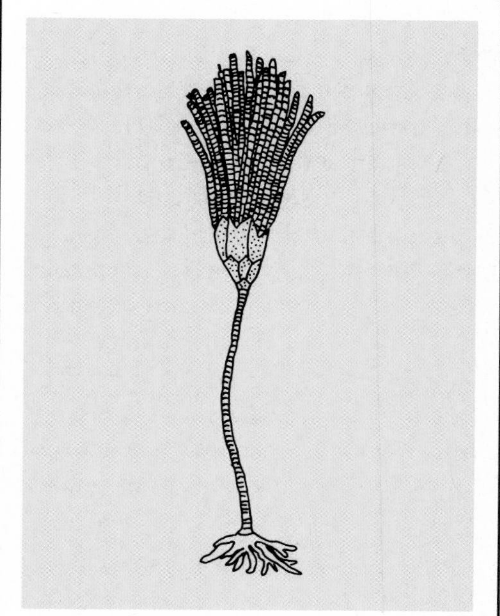

Stalked Crinoid.

dant. Ancient starfish and sea urchins, while not common, occur in fossil beds in many parts of the world, as well as moderate numbers of long-extinct members of the same group: carpoids, cystoids, and blastoids. The first known fish, called *ostracoderms*, made their appearance during the latter third of the period. They were heavily armoured, sluggish swimmers, living, most likely, near the sea floor.

The Ordovician seas also teemed with swimmers, notably the extremely abundant and widespread graptolites, the much larger nautiloids, and the enigmatic group called conodonts. *Conodonts* are known almost entirely by their tiny, toothlike, phosphate-rich remains. They were incredibly abundant at the time, so much so that a single kilogram of Ontario limestone from the mid Ordovician has yielded as many as fifty thousand individuals.

At the end of the Ordovician Period, many of the brachiopods, corals, bryozoans, and most graptolites became extinct. *Graptolites*, totally extinct today, were swimming or floating colonial organisms possessing a chitin-like skeleton. The extinction did not, like the later Permian event, wipe out entire groups, but instead was more selective. Destruction was more obvious at the family level. Significantly, however, those organisms that had inhabited shallow waters were particularly hard-hit, while those that lived in deeper and cooler waters fared better.

At that time, and continuing into the early Silurian, vast glaciers covered much of the northern part of the continent of Gondwanaland (the pre-continental drift continent comprising Africa, South America, Australia, India, and Antarctica) and extended as far as Saudi Arabia and possibly southern France and Spain. The South Pole was centred in what is now northern Africa. South America probably suffered some glaciation as well. Just as in the latest ice age, the large volumes of water tied up in glacier ice must have caused a considerable drop in sea level. As a result, more of the continents were exposed to air. The world's oceans cooled, causing severe temperature stress and reduced living space for marine organisms.

Following the extinction event, those creatures from the cooler and deeper waters moved in to fill the vacated niches, becoming ancestors of the succeeding Silurian organisms. We can see some evidence of these events especially on Manitoulin Island, where fossils of latest Ordovician faunas abruptly give way to younger Silurian species.

One of the strange and fascinating species that attained its heyday during the late Silurian, about 400 million years ago, was the *eurypterid* or sea scorpion, a distant relative of the trilobite and other crustaceans. Eurypterids were closely related, however, to the modern true scorpions and horseshoe crabs. Some of the most impressive and beautiful specimens in the world have been collected from platy dolostones, the so-called Bertie Waterlime, occurring from Cayuga and Dunnville near Port Colborne, eastward to the area around Buffalo, New York. These eurypterid-bearing rocks seem to have been the product of an unusual environment and suggest that the animals were tolerant of a wide range of salinities – up to 3.5 per cent salt. Eurypterids possessed a low, broad body, long forelimbs with strong "pincers," well-developed eyes, and a long tail with a paddle-like or *spinose* end. Some attained the remarkable length of nearly two metres. Their size, and their mouth and pincer morphology suggest they were carnivores. They appear to have eaten each other, because at times broken bits of smaller eurypterids have been found scattered around well-preserved bodies of larger specimens, and they may even have preyed on trilobites, cephalopods, and possibly primitive fish as well.

The low latitudinal position of Ontario during the Ordovician to Devonian, and the presence of warm shallow seas were ideal for other groups of marine organisms, chiefly corals. Corals appeared suddenly during the mid Ordovician. Corals found in southern Quebec and northern New York state are among the oldest known in the world. In a very short time, however, corals spread throughout warm regions worldwide.

Corals are simple, colonial animals. The skeletons of the earliest forms consisted of calcareous tubes with horizontal partitions (*tabulae*) and a few thin vertical walls (*septa*) used to support the soft tissue. By the end of the Ordovician, coral skeletons had become much more complex and contributed to the formation of modest-sized reef structures. During the ensuing Silurian and Devonian periods, however, corals, in concert with algae and extinct relatives of sponges called *stromatoporoids*, built massive mound-like and linear reef structures comparable in many ways to the reefs of today.

The most spectacular of these fossil reefs involved southwestern Ontario, adjacent areas of Ohio, Indiana, Michigan, eastern Wisconsin, and Manitoulin Island. During the latter half of the Silurian, this area was a massive circular depression, the Michigan Basin, around the margins of which grew thousands of reef mounds. The upward growth of these mounds more or less kept pace with the rate at which the basin floor was sinking. Consequently, individual reefs developed considerable vertical relief, sometimes as much as twenty to thirty metres. Relatively few of these basin-margin reefs are exposed at the surface in Ontario. Instead, they are found mostly in the subsurface where they have served as reservoirs for most of the oil and gas found in Ontario.

As these reefs grew, they eventually restricted the inflow of normal marine waters into the Michigan Basin. As a consequence of continuous evaporation in the tropical climate, the centre of the basin became highly saline, so much so that thick deposits of gypsum, anhydrite (calcium sulphate), and

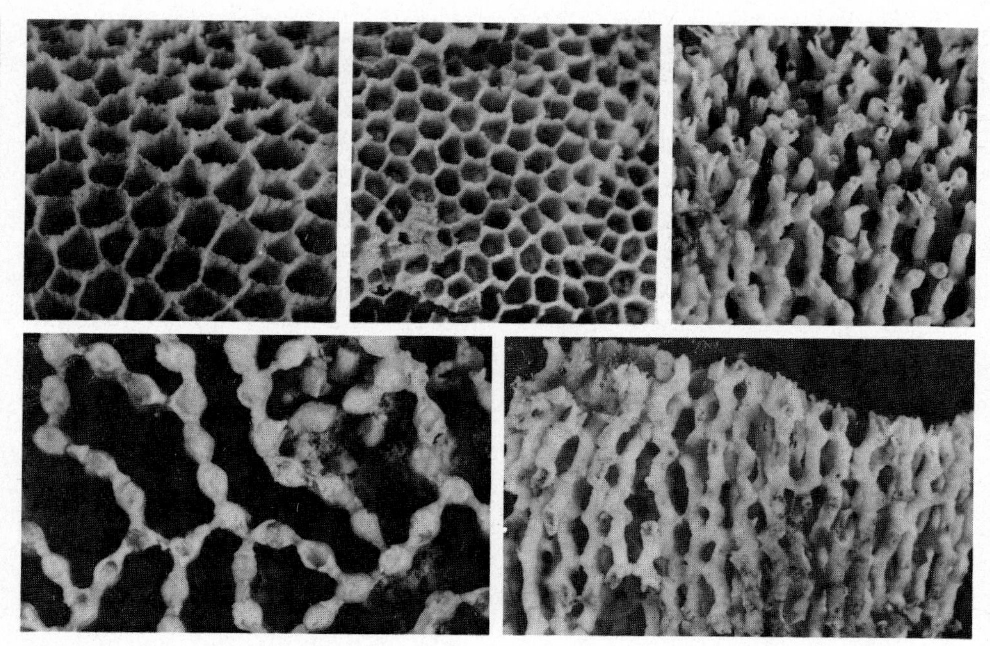

Common Silurian reef-building corals: "honeycomb" coral *Favosites* (two different species); top view of *Syringopora*; side view of *Syringopora*; "chain" coral *Halysites*. ALFRED LENZ

most importantly, salt, were formed. A comparable situation exists today in the Caspian Sea, where high summer temperatures and restricted inflow from the adjoining Aral Sea result in the deposition of vast quantities of salt. Some of the individual Michigan Basin salt beds, for example, the salt mined at Goderich, may exceed ten or more metres in thickness. When one considers that the complete evaporation of fifty metres of sea water is required to deposit only one metre of salt, the amount of water that had to be evaporated to form a ten-metre thick bed of salt is impressive.

To the east of the numerous reef mounds, a more or less continuous and

oped. The rocks, comprising mostly corals and stromatoporoids and probably algae, were once made entirely of limestone, but subsequently have been converted to a magnesium-rich dolomite through the action of sea water. These rocks attained a thickness well in excess of one hundred metres, and because of their resistance to erosion, stand out today as a prominent topographic ridge, the well known Niagara Escarpment. Corals and brachiopods are particularly abundant, and in some individual beds on Manitoulin Island for instance, brachiopods are so numerous that they make up a large volume of the rock. One can easily visualize rich coral gardens similar to those seen in the Caribbean today, with occasional large areas occupied by dense thickets of brachiopods, much like the oyster beds in modern-day coastal areas.

Following the close of the Silurian, virtually all of southern Ontario emerged from the sea. Whether this emergence was due to the land rising or the sea lowering is not clear. In any case, early Devonian marine deposits are relatively rare in southern On-

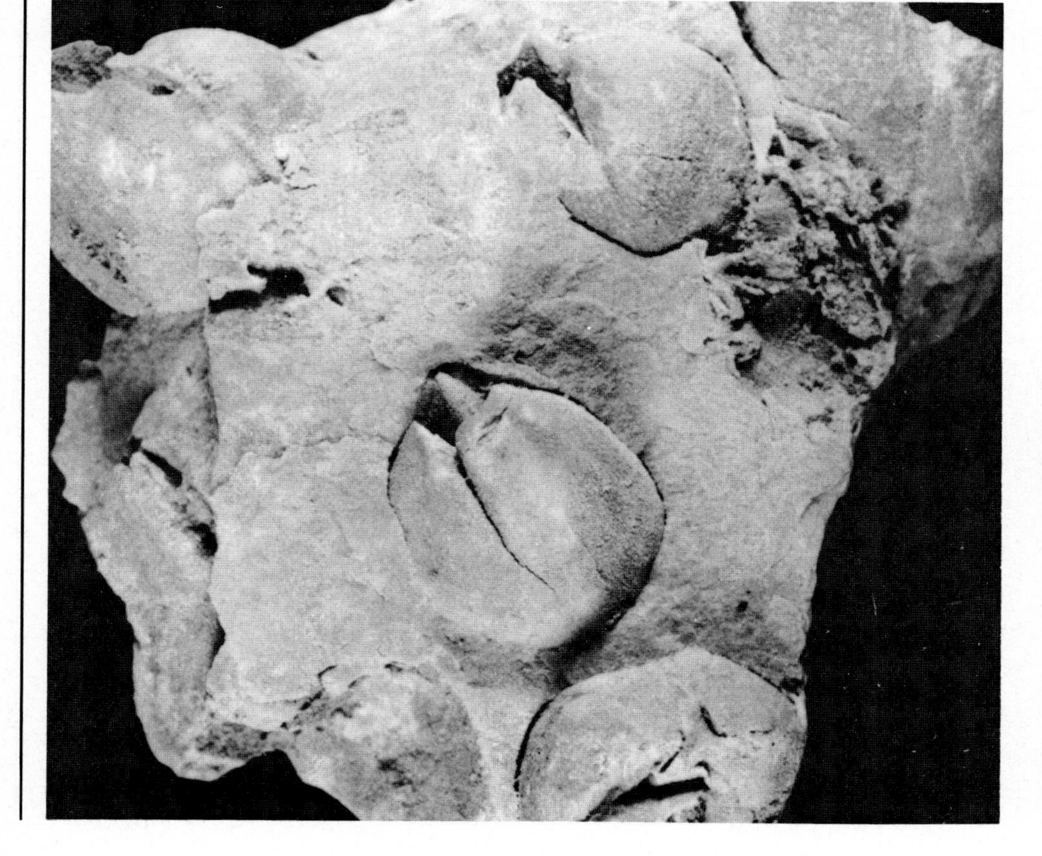

A cluster of the common Silurian brachiopod, *Pentamerus*, preserved in life-position. This brachiopod is common in rocks of the Niagara Escarpment. ALFRED LENZ

The Silurian eurypterid, *Eurypterus remipes lacustris*. COURTESY OF T.E. BOLTON AND THE GEOLOGICAL SURVEY OF CANADA

tario, although they are better represented in James Bay and Hudson Bay areas.

Beginning about the middle Devonian, about 375 million years ago, the seas returned to cover most of southern Ontario. Once again reefs developed, but this time in only a very small area. The most striking occurrence of these reefs today is in and around the village of Formosa, where dozens of isolated mounds grew in a few square kilometres. These reefs, like those of the Silurian, were built by corals and stromatoporoids, but trilobites, brachiopods, and snails are fairly common. Why reefs developed in such relatively localized areas of Ontario at this time is unclear.

Towards the end of the Devonian, about 350 million years ago, and continuing into the Mississippian Period, sedimentary conditions changed radically. Whereas older Devonian rocks are fossil-rich limestones and shales, the late Devonian and younger rocks, called Kettle Point Shale, are dark grey to black, very evenly and thinly bedded, and rich in pyrite. They contain few or no fossils. All these features point to deposition probably on a deep sea floor whose bottom waters were foul and mostly devoid of oxygen. Similar rocks and biologically barren environments occurred at that time in adjacent parts of the United States, western Canada, and elsewhere in the world.

Anoxic events such as this have taken place worldwide, as recorded periodically throughout the geologic record, particularly at times when the Earth's climate was generally much more uniformly warm than now. Conditions similar to those on the floor of the Black Sea today became widespread over large parts of the Earth. Bottom-dwelling organisms, other than special bacteria, were completely excluded from such inhospitable environments. On the other hand, organisms which swam or floated near the surface could survive quite easily.

Sometime following the Mississippian, probably most of Ontario, certainly southern Ontario, emerged from the sea again. After that, about 225 million years ago, little of Ontario appears to have been covered again by any deposits until the advent of the last glaciation, although important coal-bearing strata of early Cretaceous age, about 100 million years old, occur in the James Bay area. Neither the late Paleozoic ice age of what was then the southern hemisphere, nor the final uplifting and folding of the Appalachian Mountains had much influence on the rocks or terrain of Ontario, and did not create seas for marine organisms. So the Paleozoic fossil record in Ontario ends here.

Only a few million years after Ontario's final emergence from the sea, the living things of the world experienced one of the greatest extinction events of all time. A large majority of marine organisms, including cephalopods, brachiopods, bryozoa, many bivalves, all known corals, and the last of the trilobites were wiped out or their species drastically reduced. On the other hand, land dwellers such as the mammal-like reptiles which were found in great abundance in South Africa and the southern United States seem to have been much less affected. But, 80 to 90 per cent of all known living species disappeared. Once again at that time the world was experiencing low sea levels coupled with climatic deterioration and widespread desert conditions. Most likely, marine organisms died out because of changing environmental conditions. There is not yet evidence of meteoric impact or other extraterrestrial events, but research and speculation continues. Unfortunately, rocks – and therefore fossils – of that age do not exist in Ontario, and so we can contribute little to explaining this devastating event. Nor are there any rocks to help explain the great Cretaceous extinction, 65 million years ago, when again many marine invertebrates died off, along with the headline-grabbing dinosaurs and marine and flying reptiles.

The Earth and its inhabitants share a lengthy history. They have suffered together through many catastrophes. In Ontario, the confluence of geological change and biological evolution have given rise to a series of marvellous and continually varying living communities. The rocks still bear the evidence today of the rich life that flourished here when invertebrates ruled the Earth.

Fertile Waters
The Fresh-water Invertebrates
David Barr

A Well-watered Land

Ontario's air and land abound in lower life forms – creatures with many legs and no bony skeleton. They are multitudinous, and by their living and their dying they form an indispensable component of the natural system on which all other life depends.

So diverse and adaptable are these *invertebrates* (animals without backbones), that they have exploited every conceivable habitat for survival. Even the fresh waters which cover such a large percentage of the provincial map are home to dense populations of living invertebrates.

In the eastern corner of the province lies a land richly endowed with surface waters. Here lakes, bogs, marshes, rivers, and sluggish streams are supported by a varied geology. Especially productive is the chain of man-made lakes stretching over a hundred kilometres along the southern half of the winding Rideau waterway between Kingston and Ottawa. These lakes lie in the lowlands where they lap against the primeval Shield granites and long limestone ridges of the region.

Deadlock Bay is a quiet, one-hectare, nearly circular pocket of the south shore of Lake Opinicon, one of the man-made lakes about a hundred kilometres north of Kingston. Occupying a minor valley between the surrounding granitic eminences, Opinicon – and Deadlock Bay – are shallow-water bodies with extensive marshy shorelines and warm, nutrient-rich waters.

Vegetation grows rampant in Lake Opinicon, and Deadlock Bay is especially weedy. The bay is subject to reduced wave action, being separated from the open water by a narrow, rocky channel. The water is uniformly shallow, no more than two metres at the centre and with extensive areas only a metre deep.

As the canoe slices through the bay's dark water you can see a forest of potamogeton plants below; towards the shallows these give way to a wispy fairy garden of Chara, Elodea, and eelgrass. These dense groves, with their sun-driven protein and carbohydrate factories, make the food and are the sustaining life-support system of all aquatic animal life. The harvest is taken in by a host of different plant-feeding organisms, and these in turn serve as food for roaming predators, the highest feeding level in this seemingly peaceful bay. Invisible from the surface, vast multitudes of creatures live in these waters.

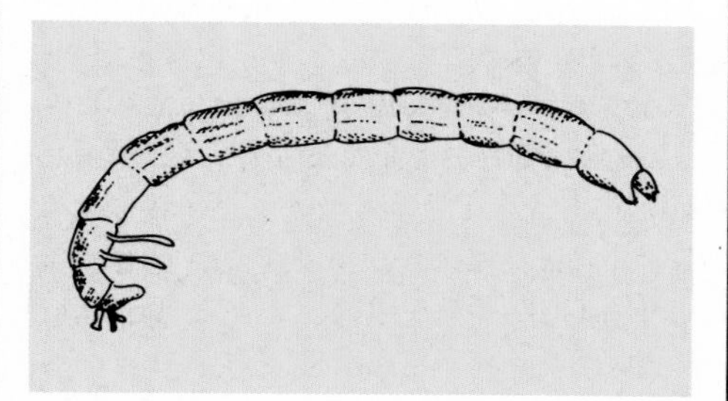

Midge larva.

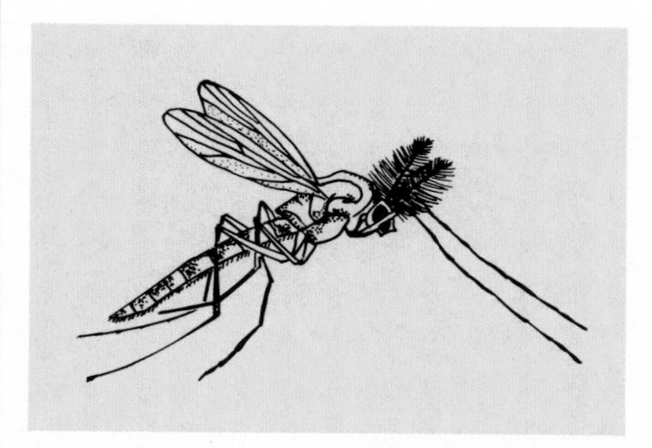

Adult midge, mosquito-like but without biting mouthparts.

A Fragment of the Web

Biologists have likened the feeding relationships of fresh-water animals to a tangled, multi-skeined web of interactions, sometimes called the food web – essentially a summary of who feeds on who. Beneath the surface in Deadlock Bay exists an extensive community of living creatures, mostly invertebrates, all involved in a complex series of biological interactions.

On a bit of submerged log, especially plentiful on the bed of this flooded former forest, lies a greenish mat of soft, fresh-water sponge. In the mud among the bases of the rooted plants live tiny, thread-like bristle worms and the equally worm-like larvae of countless millions of midges, a small, gnat-like fly. Sticking out of the soft mud is a sluggish animal, looking at first glance like a small, shiny rock which has miraculously avoided sinking into the ooze. It is a fresh-water mussel, a relative of marine clams and oysters, which flourishes in the lake and is intimately connected to the life-systems established there. A shell of two hard, mother-of-pearl valves protects its body from most predators. The mussel can poke a fleshy foot out of the slit-like opening between its two valves and use this organ to drag itself slowly across the bottom or even burrow down into the silty ooze.

But the mussel spends most of its time with one end of its shell tilted above the surface of the mud and the slit-like opening between the two valves open to the clear water above. In this position, oxygenated water is pumped steadily into its body, and microscopic, floating plants and animals suspended in the water are captured as the water crosses the mussel's gills. The de-oxygenated and filtered water then is pumped back out and the trapped food consumed.

When a mussel-loving aquatic mite in the water above detects the faintly clammy odour of water that has been used by the mussel, it immediately swims towards the source and the dark, inviting cavity within. Once inside the mussel, the tiny mite, which is an aquatic relative of the spiders and scorpions, settles down to complete its development to adult form, eventually laying its eggs in the gill tissues of its mussel host. The mite larvae have convenient access to the exterior simply by swimming into the continuous flow of outwardly bound water.

When the mussel is ready to reproduce, it too deposits its eggs in cavities of its own gill tissue where they are incubated in the flow of oxygenated water. When the eggs hatch, the tiny clamlets proceed to the outside world in the flow of used ventilating water. Once outside they can swim actively by snapping the two valves of their shell together. The thousands of clamlets soon settle to the bottom to wait until the surface on which they are lying is disturbed by the pectoral, pelvic, or caudal fins of any of a variety of species of small fishes that swim close to the bottom to feed or to escape enemies. The mussel offspring immediately clamp tightly to one of these fins with small hooks located on the two valves of their shell. They are now parasites of the fish and not only derive nutrients from its bloodstream, but also are transported far and wide to populate new areas of the lake where adult clams may be scarce. Upon completion of their parasitic phase they drop off, sink to the bottom, and begin the long, slow growth to adult size.

Swimming in the waters above the mussels is a small, active creature which makes its living in much the same way as they do. The mosquito larva lives in a world of creatures who spend much of their time swimming, and who live in the three-dimensional realm of the water column. Here are a host of tiny crustaceans, fresh-water relatives of crabs and lobsters – the so-called water fleas. With them are the floating larvae of predaceous midges, swift, actively swimming bugs and beetles with oar-shaped legs, tiny microscopic rotifers, and even single-celled protozoa. This is also the realm of microscopic floating plants, the phytoplankton, which form one of the important food bases of the system.

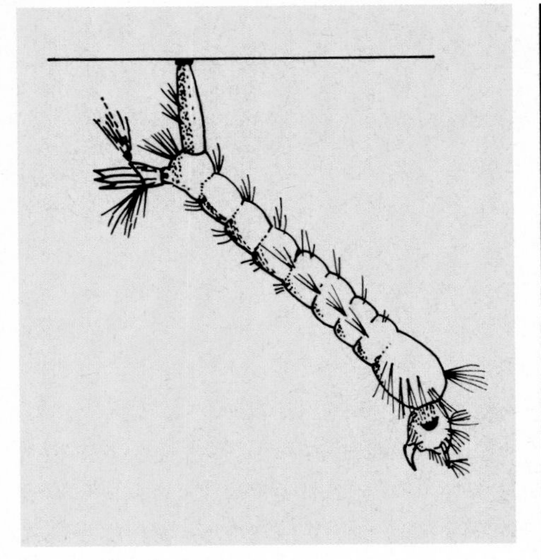
Mosquito larva.

The mosquito larva, or wriggler, makes a living with a fan of brush-like hairs in the region of its mouth. The hairs filter the surrounding water, collecting particles of food, algae, protozoa, and bacteria, which abound in this rich habitat. Feeding, growing, and shedding its skin to expand, the wriggler eventually reaches maturity, when it is transformed into a comma-shaped pupa. Like the chrysalis of a butterfly, the pupa represents a period of re-building; the worm-like larval tissues metamorphose into the long thin legs and filmy wings of an adult mosquito.

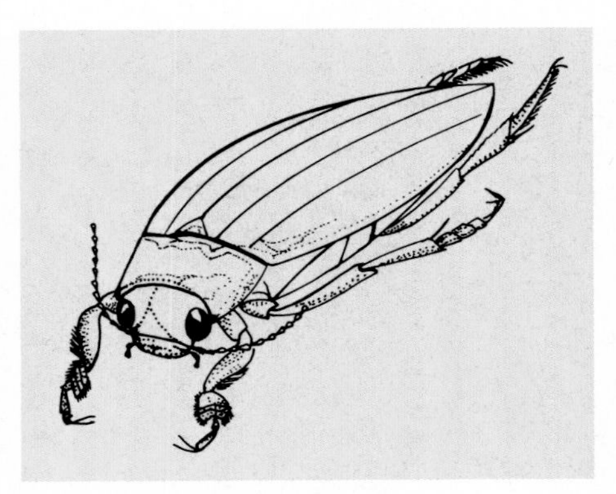
Predaceous diving beetle.

A mosquito wriggler seems as content hunting its food in open water as amidst the rooted plants, but the forest of underwater vegetation also supports a host of creatures which could never survive without plants. They munch on green leaves or scrape up the nutritious algal slime which soon coats all underwater surfaces. These flocks of herbivores in turn form an abundant source of prey for the lions, wolves, tigers, and jackals of the underwater world, the predators of the lake ecosystem. These meat-eaters include not only many fishes, but also a whole array of invertebrate predators including leeches, crayfish, dragonfly larvae, and predaceous bugs.

Perhaps the most ferocious carnivorous insect is the elongate creature sometimes called the water tiger. This is the larva of the predaceous diving beetle, and its long, sickle-shaped jaws mounted on a powerful, muscular head are among the most fearsome in the lake. The larva has multiple light-sensing cells grouped together as eyes on its head capsule and bears many sensitive body hairs, the better to detect its prey nearby. It can swim rapidly by throwing its body into snake-like curves while at the same time thrashing its long, oar-shaped legs to propel itself towards a source of food. It is capable of attacking and killing not only insect larvae but also small fishes and sluggish tadpoles. It reaches a full size of almost five centimetres in length. Following pupation the water tiger turns into a slim, torpedo-shaped aquatic beetle which streaks through the water, carrying on the predatory ways of its juvenile stage.

Virtually all of the lives in this underwater realm are tied together. For instance, a bright bluish-green, eight-legged, aquatic mite swimming by is only one of the six life-history stages of its species, one of which, the larva, is parasitic on dragonflies. The dragonfly, like the mosquito, spends its larval stage underwater, while in its adult stage, it flies above the waters of the lake where it feeds on mosquitoes, its former nursery mates. The mite larva swims until it finds a dragonfly larva almost ready to emerge from the water. When the dragonfly hatches into the aerial world, the mite larva nimbly transfers to the adult insect and begins its parasitic existence. After it has gorged on dragonfly blood, the mite larva drops off its host and returns to complete its life cycle in its parents' watery habitat.

In examining these few species, we have glimpsed but a fragment of the multi-stranded web of interactions in the shallows of Lake Opinicon. For each species described, a dozen others follow entirely different lifeways. And for each of these dissimilar lifeways there are several tens, even scores of related species living by only minor variations on these main themes.

Take the water mite and dragonfly just described. They share Deadlock Bay with at least thirty very closely related mite species which differ in their life-histories only by being parasitic upon different species of dragonflies or by feeding on different species of crustacean prey. These mites are joined by another fifty or so species of less closely related aquatic mites which, while maintaining a relatively similar life-history, may feed as adults on insect larvae and may parasitize such diverse aquatic animals as water-bugs, midges, water-beetles, and mussels.

Lake Opinicon is home to many hundreds of plant and animal species. They crowd together in the shallow waters, and by equal numbers of subtly differing adaptations to their environment, manage to persist and coexist.

Every Seepage, Pond and Puddle

Ontario's fresh waters are far more than Lake Opinicon. A close examination of the average marshy pond along the fairway of a golf course would reveal a whole host of related organisms – dragonflies, mosquitoes, aquatic snails, planktonic crustaceans, swimming beetles and bugs, mites, and burrowing worms similar to, but distinct from, the species found in Lake Opinicon. Wherever reliable surface water is found – in silent depths hundreds of feet below the whitecaps of the Great Lakes, along boulder-strewn shores of a northern Shield lake, in the brown waters of a southern swamp, or in the acidic pools of a northern bog – invertebrate animals find a home and a source of food and sustenance.

Remarkable adaptations make these lives possible. The creatures in an ice-cold spring or seepage area must carry out their whole life-cycle at temperatures so low that ordinary pond life would be torpid. But they reap the rewards of waters rich in life-sustaining oxygen. In contrast, the creatures which make their life in ephemeral vernal woodland pools must scramble through birth and maturation in a few short weeks and then find some way to survive when their aquatic birthplace dries up totally for several months of the year. The inhabitants of a wave-swept lakeshore must burrow or cling tenaciously to the undersides of large rocks to avoid being swept away or dashed to bits by the pounding breakers.

A World in Motion

Among the most captivating environments of all is the realm of running water: babbling brooks, deep swift channels, foaming rapids, and the rolling majesty of great rivers. For all life in Ontario's streams and rivers, the one great challenge is the incessant, demanding, bending, and shaping current, the constant rush of water that sweeps all before it and brings all things eventually to those who wait.

The Niagara Escarpment, with its ridges, cliffs, and magnificent gorges, spawns a multitude of running waters. Most streams everywhere have their origins in highlands; they start out as a tiny, sparkling brook, then pick up speed and momentum as they churn wildly down the slopes, and finally wind lazily across the flats until they empty into a lake or the sea. The Escarpment's streams fill the air with their mist and your ears with their gurgling and crashing. Their energy has carved the very face of the rock into strange and grotesque forms.

Midway in its course across the Bruce Peninsula, near the northern end of the Escarpment, Albemarle Brook is a narrow, tumbling and boiling spate of clear, cool, spring-fed water. Its bed is a deep layer of gravel, thickly embedded with limestone cobbles and boulders up to half a metre in diameter. Many stones are covered with a green, mossy growth, beneath which are shallow cavities – lairs for crayfishes, Ontario's largest inland invertebrate animals. A close look at one of these holes will reveal the claw tips and antennae of a lurking crayfish lying in wait for its invertebrate prey.

The crayfish, a fresh-water crustacean related to marine lobsters and crabs, has true aquatic gills hidden beneath flaps of its hard shell. It can survive for two or more years, longer than most aquatic invertebrates. Crayfish hatched from eggs held in protective clusters beneath their mother's tail will continue to grow all of their lives. That tail is also an organ of locomotion; if the rock is overturned or the animal otherwise disturbed, the crayfish snaps its tail forward, curling it beneath its body to rocket away backwards through the water.

Although it can subsist on many kinds of food, a crayfish normally finds an abundance of stream invertebrates to prey upon. Large populations of organisms are supported by the richness of organic food in the water. The surface of every underwater stone and submerged twig is coated with a slippery and nutritious golden-brown layer of algae, diatoms, and bacteria. And although it is hard to imagine how water so clear and pure could be laden with food, the problem is merely one of concentration. Actually each stream becomes a catchment basin and a fun-

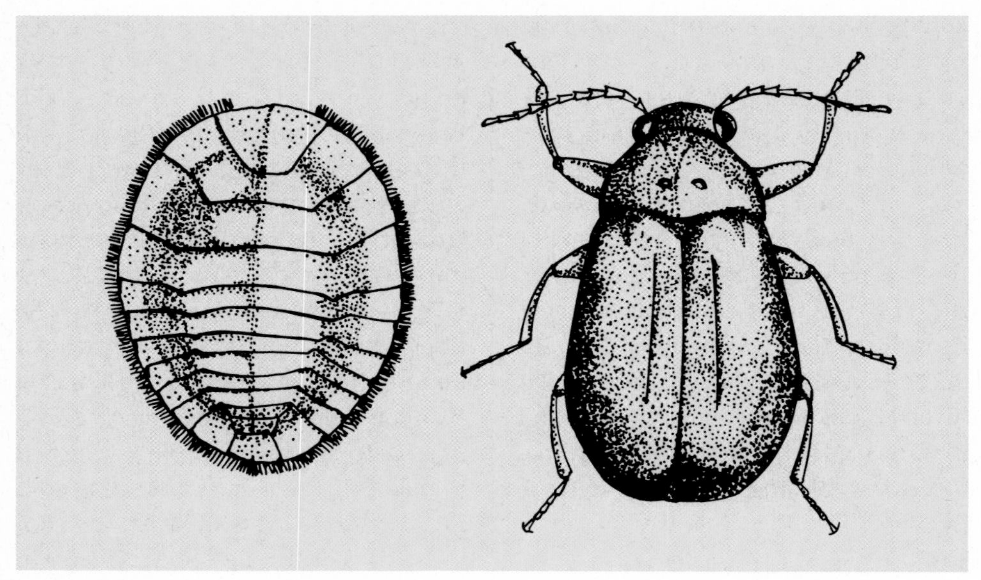

Water penny larva and adult.

nel for all the dying and fallen vegetation that blows, drifts, falls, or is washed into its course. As the stream flows through woodlands in particular, it is fed with tons of leaves, especially in autumn. Trapped in pockets and backwaters, this rich source of food remains to sustain underwater life all year long.

A prime example of a stream-dwelling insect that feeds on the underwater diatom gardens is the water penny. This larva of an aquatic beetle avoids the ripping force of the constant current by sticking its round, flat, limpet-like body tightly to the rock surface. The coppery colour of its upper surface completes its resemblance to a small penny. The larva grazes the rock surface to which it clings, and extracts oxygen from the rushing water with several tufts of white, thread-like gills protected beneath arching body plates. The adult water penny, quite a conventional-looking beetle, also lives in the rushing water of the stream. It clings tightly with large claws and breathes with a sort of "aqualung," a thin jacket of air held to its body by a layer of fine hairs.

The stream is home, in fact, to a full community of invertebrates, most of whom frequent the slick rock surfaces or the delicate mossy forests that cover so many underwater objects. Flatworms glide among colonies of bryozoan and sponge animalcules, while legions of stonefly and mayfly larvae feed either on plant materials or each other. Nimble crustaceans such as scuds and aquatic pill bugs navigate the still-water spaces beneath rocks, scavenging the remains of both plant and animal life.

Some caterpillar-like larvae of stream-dwelling caddisflies feed on those fallen terrestrial leaves that fuel the stream economy, while others prey on the community's animal life. One kind of caddisfly competes with sinuously waving larvae of blackflies for a special food resource, the tiny food particles, some algae, some bits and pieces of organic detritus, that are carried along by the current. The problem in tapping this rich source of food is the same one faced by the mussel and mosquito in Lake Opinicon – how to strain the relatively rare food particles out of the large volumes of water that carry them.

Blackfly larvae accomplish the task with a pair of mouth parts, each consisting of a basal stalk from which radiate thirty to sixty thin, curved rays. When these rays are spread wide, they form a fan-like filtering basket which strains food particles out of the water and transfers them to the mouth. The caddisfly has no such mouth parts but can spin a silken web a little like a hockey goalie's net, with its open mouth facing upstream. Water flows continuously over the upper surface of the caddisfly's rock and through the net, leaving behind microscopic food particles tangled in its silken skeins. All the larva has to do is emerge periodically from its retreat and scrape the net clean of another meal.

It is not surprising that this stream community has no swimmers. The bugs

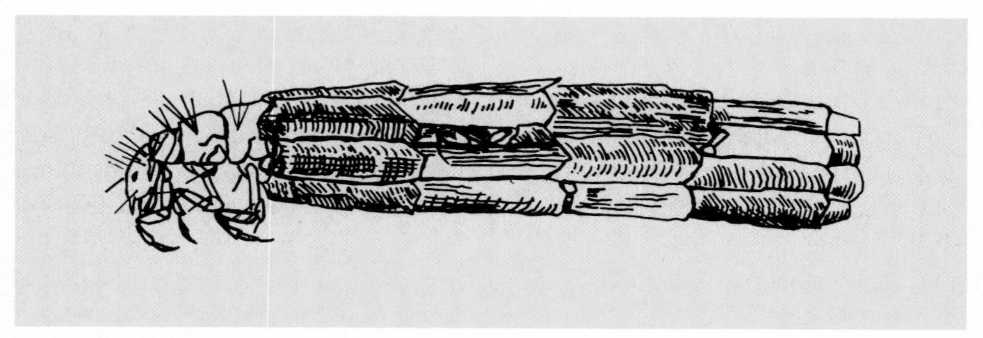

Caddisfly larva in a bark case.

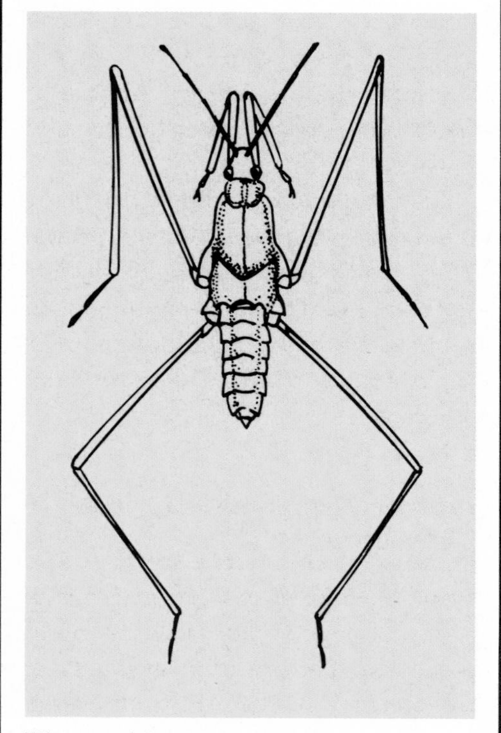

Water strider.

and beetles with paddle-shaped legs and cunning devices for hanging from the surface of still water to breath would be swept away in an instant, or they would expend all their energy simply swimming to stay in place. Surprisingly enough, however, the water strider, a type of true bug which "skates" on the surface-water film and which has many still-water relatives, manages to survive on the surface of some of Ontario's swiftest streams. Instead of allowing itself to be swept downstream, if caught in the current it simply skates madly for shore. It spends most of its life feeding on hapless terrestrial insects that fall into the water in the still backwaters always found along the edges of even the fastest streams.

The fauna below the floor of the stream form a community unique to flowing-water habitats. Beneath the beds of many streams lie deep layers of porous gravel, and the stream water commonly flows through this gravel to a depth of at least a metre. Down in the gravel, stream water percolates through tiny spaces between the grains of stone carrying life-giving oxygen. And living in the flow of this subterranean river is a community of very small, weakly swimming creatures that likely spend their whole lives without ever seeing sunlight. Some have spent so many generations in the darkness that they no longer have eyes.

Water fleas – minute crustacea related to some of the swimming plankton of Lake Opinicon – clam-like ostracod crustacea, and thread-like bristle worms all navigate the narrow waterways. Many thousands of the smallest larval stages of aquatic insects from the stream above burrow down in the gravel for shelter until they are large enough to brave life in the open water. Predatory aquatic mites stalk the lightless environment, finding each meal more by touch than by sight.

Wildlife Foundation

Ontario's plentiful and ever-changing fresh waters abound in invertebrate life. The underwater invertebrates are equally as diverse in kinds and lifeways as their terrestrial relatives, and their habitats are so rich in the nutrients of life that their populations are among the most abundant and most concentrated on Earth. So productive are the communities of freshwater invertebrates that they form the foundation of all fish and wildlife in Ontario's wetlands. Their biology is intimate to the processes of change and regeneration that keep the freshwater habitats vigorous.

The rules of these communities are much the same as for those on dry land. The species fall into the same familiar ecological groups – plant feeders, meat eaters, scavengers, and parasites. But in the water the pace is quickened, the tests more severe, the barriers to success more stringent. Each aquatic species is the product of a long evolutionary history that has fitted it to its challenging habitat. And each species displays one of a fascinating array of solutions to the problem faced by them all – how to survive and how to thrive. . . underwater.

Richest Estate
The Terrestrial Invertebrates
David Barr

A Community of the Small

There is yet another estate of the living world in Ontario, and this is the richest of all. The most obvious members of this community – butterflies and dragonflies – are readily seen at almost any time during the warm months, patrolling field and meadow, stalking the woodlands' edge and the bright sunlit flecks within, or soaring over city park and ravine. But these brightly coloured aerialists that seem to carry the heart of the beholder on their joyous flights of fancy over the countryside are only the most visible relatives of a mighty multitude of less-conspicuous cousins. Mosquitoes too and blackflies, just as noticeable in a different way through much of spring and early summer, are part of the ever-present and vital insect world. So are many thousands of species of backbone-less animals which abound in every part of the natural environment from Point Pelee to James Bay.

Flying, crawling, jumping, running, burrowing, swimming: invertebrates are mostly small, secretive creatures that seem to be everywhere. A treetop hosts millions of tiny living inhabitants, while even a square metre of soil hides a maëlstrom of subterranean activity. Beneath a meadow stone lurks a whole city of inhabitants avoiding the light of day. Even the summer evening sky above us is alive with almost invisible legions of insects.

The Grazers

Because insects are so small in comparison to vertebrate animals, an exceedingly thin slice of the environment can represent the entire territory of an individual. A leaf forms a whole pasture for a minute, mining caterpillar. A tree trunk is a universe for a wood-boring beetle grub. More than two-thirds of Ontario's tens of thousands of invertebrate animals are insects, and at least half of these, like the examples just mentioned, feast on

Despite their size and spectacular appearance, the giant silkworm moths are not well known because of their largely nocturnal activity and because they live only for a week or two. Cecropia moths are the largest moths in North America, with a wingspan of up to fifteen centimetres. Polyphemus moths are only slightly smaller; when alarmed, they expose their huge eyespots to frighten predators. Lunas, or moon moths, are perhaps the most beautiful of all. The somewhat smaller promethea moth is most commonly found in the southern-most part of Ontario where they often feed on sassafras and spicebush. CECROPIA, LARRY LAMB; POLYPHEMUS, JOHN THEBERGE; LUNA, DON GUNN; PROMETHEA, POINT PELEE NATIONAL PARK, B. FORD

plants. These plant feeders are the grazers of the insect world, the intimate associates of green life everywhere.

The most succulent plant parts are usually leaves. Accordingly, trees, bushes, grasses, and herbaceous plants support astonishingly large insect populations. Grasshoppers, crickets, caterpillars, beetles, and bugs busily munch up the nutritious leaf tissue, converting many hundreds of thousands of kilograms of plant tissue into animal life each year. Some species, like the spruce budworm and the forest tent caterpillar, are pests which endanger the forest harvest. Others, like the cecropia moth, are harmless and spectacular. The cecropia caterpillar is one of Ontario's largest insects, but its life-history as a leaf feeder is typical of many others.

The gorgeous reddish and tawny brown female moth, emerging from her over-wintering pupa in June, mates and flies on bat-sized wings in the dead of night to the favourite food plant of her offspring-to-be. Usually she selects a wild cherry or birch tree, although maple, beech, and a variety of other deciduous trees may be acceptable. In late June she lays a hundred or more disc-shaped eggs, each about a millimetre in diameter, and glues them carefully to the surface of a leaf. From two days to ten weeks later, tiny caterpillars, about two millimetres long, gnaw their way out of the tops of their egg shells and begin to spread out over their nursery leaf. Some are so weak they die before reaching the leaf's edge, but others make it and begin tentatively to crunch into the leaf cells with their sideways-moving jaws or *mandibles*.

From that point on, it's eat, eat, eat! The larvae are voracious, consuming several times their weight in leaf tissue each day. They grow rapidly, pausing every few days to shed the skin which does not grow with them and restricts their enlargement. After only a few weeks the caterpillars are nine centimetres long, two centimetres thick, a light pearly green, and bristling with strange orange knobs and blue spines dotted up and down the length of the body. Sometime in mid to late August the cecropia larva gives up its relentless attack on the leaves of its host and spins the spindle-shaped cocoon in which it will pupate and spend the winter.

Ontario is home to a glowing array of sun-loving butterflies. Even those that seek shaded woodland glades, like the mustard white and the little wood satyr, are only active when the sun sends slanting shafts of illumination to brighten the forest's golden carpet of leaves.

Our most familiar butterfly species, however, are creatures of sun-washed meadows and woodland edges. A patch of nettles along a stream bank is patrolled by the flashing, scarlet-banded wings of a red admiral. A milkweed blossom is host to the darting tawny flash of a Pocohontas skipper or the jewel-spotted underwings of an Acadian hairstreak. And glorious swarms of golden tiger swallowtails soar close to the boggy ground in a boreal forest clearing.

Even closer to the ground, the tortoise beetle must be one of the most bizarre and unusual of insect grazers, for both larva and adult live sedentary lives on the prickly leaves of the common thistle and its relatives. The tortoise beetle larva is spiny and prickly looking like its food plant, and it sports a long, forked and spiny tail which it carries arched over the back. Attached to this tail it carries its own cast-off skins and excrement, all bundled up in a large mass that acts like a kind of camouflage parasol. A hungry predator might be persuaded that this is no larva at all, but only a bit of debris, a bird dropping perhaps.

The adult tortoise beetle which develops from this somewhat inauspicious beginning, although only one-half a centimetre long, is a glory to behold. Its dorsal body plates on head, thorax, and wing covers are expanded and drawn down on all sides to form a broad, protective shield, very like the carapace of a tortoise. Protected under its bowl-shaped armour, the beetle crawls again over the thistle, feeding on the same luscious, green tissues that sustained it as a larva.

And as if tortoise-shell armour were not enough protection from enemies, the tortoise beetle is also an inver-

Swarm of tiger swallowtail butterflies on wet sand in Pukaskwa National Park. JOHN THEBERGE

Red admiral. POINT PELEE NATIONAL PARK, W. WYETT

Banded purple of the white admiral group. SHAN WALSHE

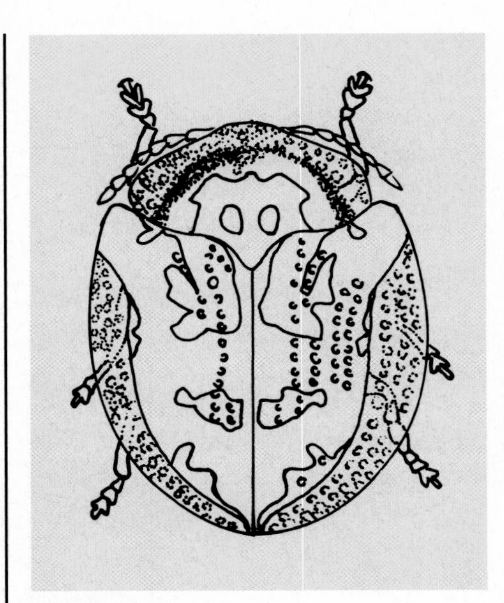

Tortoise beetle.

tebrate chameleon. Grazing on a green thistle leaf, it is a pale, yellowish-green. But when it rests on the lace-like portion of a leaf which has been skeletonized through feeding, it can become a breath-taking and brilliantly metallic gold. To the meek and retiring are awarded survival – and the opportunity to consume vast quantities of thistle.

Obviously, Ontario is green; our plant life seems to be holding its own, even flourishing. How can plants withstand the continual onslaught of these plant-eating invertebrates? The checks on unrestricted insect feeding are many and include invertebrate parasite and predators as well as many birds, and even a considerable variety of viral and bacterial diseases. Plants themselves have developed protective mechanisms to reduce the appetites of those who would consume them. The bitter and poisonous chemicals found in many plants probably evolved largely as a defence against insects, even the oil of poison ivy that is so irritating to humans. The fuzz or carpet of tiny hairs on so many plant leaves also is designed to confuse and inhibit a six-legged herbivore. Most amazing of all, carefully controlled laboratory and field experiments have shown that some plants even benefit from attacks by leaf feeders. Apparently plant growth is stimulated and vegetation increased when a plant has some of its leaves consumed by insects.

The Decomposers

On land, soil is the wellspring of all life. Rich, dark, and loamy, it is a fertile alloy of the biological and the inorganic. The ground beneath our feet could never be more than a coarse, hard cake of sandy gravel if it were not for the efforts of decomposer invertebrates. To maintain a steady supply of the nutrients necessary to sustain plant life, and thereby all other life as well, soil must continually be replenished by the decomposition of organisms that die. Bacterial and fungal action is very slow on large animal and plant bodies, and many of them would simply mummify on the surface of the ground and persist for decades without the work of invertebrate jaws. Armies of hungry

Larva of pandorus sphinx moth. LARRY LAMB

The eyed elater, one of the largest members of a family of click beetles. The two "eyes" are only spots to frighten predators. POINT PELEE NATIONAL PARK, J. R. GRAHAM

scavengers mince each carcass into finer and finer particles which can be dispersed into the soil and broken down again into their essential elements by micro-organisms.

Split open a rotting log on the forest floor. Within are beetles, grubs, ants, slugs, and wood lice, slowly reducing their own home and shelter to sawdust. Or stoop in the cool shade and sort through a spadeful of soil and leaf litter in the deciduous forest. The neatly arrayed layers of humus, twigs, leaf fragments, and whole leaves, rudely disturbed by our inspection, contain thousands of small, secretive creatures such as springtails and silverfish, earwigs and crickets, beetles, snails, mites and millipedes. Worms are there too and tiny single-celled protozoans invisible to the naked eye. Or – if you dare – gingerly use a fallen branch to turn over the moist, redolent carcass of a small mammal that has fallen prey to disease or natural accident. Observed at the right stage, both dissolving flesh and soil beneath will be seething with maggots, beetles, and grubs. The air over the feast hums with the buzz of flies and perhaps a wasp or two.

All of these creatures, the wholesome and the repulsive, are decomposers. Perhaps the most important of their number, certainly the most familiar, are earthworms – not only the bait of choice for a child's fishing expedition, but nominated even by Aristotle over two millennia ago as the "intestine of the Earth." In rich, arable soil, there are more than half a million earthworms in every hectare of land.

Every earthworm is a reproductive factory, for each carries both male and female organs and the ability to produce eggs. Although they must pair (usually at the soil surface) for mutual cross-insemination, each earthworm can produce a drought-resistant cocoon containing six or eight fertile eggs every week or two.

As soon as tiny earthworms hatch from the egg, they begin a voracious career. While growing to a mature length of up to thirty centimetres for some of our species, they are virtual garbage gobblers. They literally eat their way through the upper surface of the soil, ingesting any particle, whether twig, leaf fragment, or small portion of the body of some other animal. Everything is passed through a long and active digestive tract where organic materials are broken down, reduced to their simplest elements and mixed with assorted calcareous and nitrogenous compounds. When the material reaches the end of the digestive system, it is passed through the anus in the form of small, friable pellets. These *worm castings* are the very stuff of fertile soil.

Earthworms slowly and persistently blend organic waste into the organic soil and are major contributors to the rich susbstrate of life in the province. Estimates made over a hundred years ago by Charles Darwin are still valid today. The earthworms in a hectare of land can turn over as much as ten tons of soil per year, meaning that the top three centimetres of soil is totally replaced every ten years. This is probably the reason why so many fields, even those which are uncultivated, appear relatively flat. With time, earthworm activities alone will smooth out all minor bumps and irregularities.

The Hunters

Insect communities, although their inhabitants are smaller and therefore less visible, are no different in organization than the mammalian communities with which we are more familiar. It seems that if any conceivable source of food exists, some member of the community will be suited to feed on it. Judging by the size of the community of decomposers reducing dead animal and plant bodies to their basic elements and that of the community of herbivores feeding in their legions on plant tissues, it seems obvious that one of the most abundant food resources in the invertebrate world is other invertebrates.

And because their prey is everywhere, the predators are everywhere too. Dragonflies soar high over field and wetland, gathering small flying insects like mosquitoes and midges into a thorny basket of legs. Leaves of all kinds of green plants are patrolled by an irregular guerrilla force of praying mantids with forelegs modified into a wickedly clawed snap-trap; predaceous bugs with piercing, drilling mouth parts; and the stubby muscular larvae of lacewings, wielding sabre-like jaws to impale aphids and suck their body juices dry.

Even the soil of pastures and woodlands is full of predaceous creatures. Centipedes, carnivorous mites, and tiny pseudoscorpions exploit the many decomposer and fungus-eating invertebrates that are the base of the food system in these communities. Probably the most efficient predators of all are spiders, lurking patiently by the thousands in each hectare of field and forest. Many spin webs to catch unwary insect aerialists, while others course swiftly over forest floor to run down less fleet-footed inhabitants.

Few spiders are as conspicuous or as successful at the job as the silver-banded argiope whose elegant vertical webs are suspended between the stalks of taller weeds in field and roadside. The web is almost invisible, except when its threads are strung with beads of dew, so grasshoppers, flies, and small flying insects of all types become trapped in the sticky spiral threads and end up as a meal for the landlord. The web, however, could also be destroyed by a passing bird, and to avoid this, the spider itself is conspicuous, brightly banded with silver and cream stripes, and it spends most of its time hanging in full view in the centre of the web. To make the job even more effective, the argiope adorns its web with a shining vertical zig-zag band of dense white silk. The result is a trap that is invisible to flying insects with their limited senses, but completely obvious and avoidable to passing birds.

Not all carnivores trap their prey

Calosoma species, one of a large family of ground beetles. This species hunts caterpillars. LARRY LAMB

A praying mantis demonstrating protective coloration. LARRY LAMB

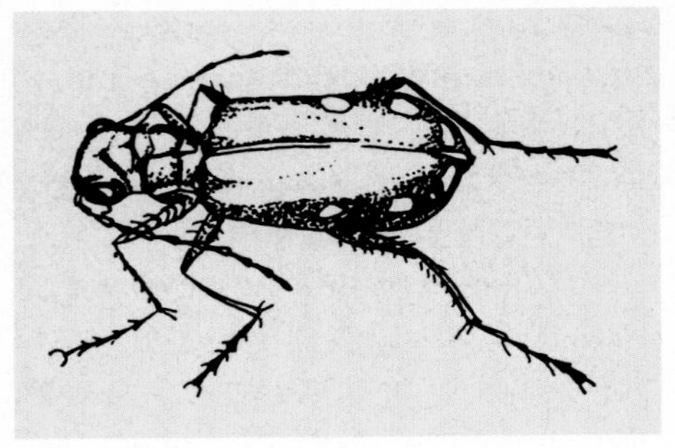

Six-spotted tiger beetle.

from ambush. Some, like the six-spotted tiger beetle, stalk their prey and overpower it with speed and ferocity. This handsome, gleaming metallic green beetle alights along a forest trail, waiting for unwary insect prey. When a fat blow-fly arrives to warm itself in the June sunlight, the tiger beetle darts forward on long, athletic legs and slices with its scimitar-shaped jaws. If startled in the process of consuming its newly slain meal, the beetle will spread its gleaming wing covers and, in an instant, unfurl the membranous wings beneath, launching itself into the air, as swift to escape on the wing as it is to attack on the ground.

An excellent example of the boundless energy of insect predators in pursuit of their food is the solitary Bembix wasp, which constructs a burrow in which to rear its young. In many areas of southern Ontario, careful observation of a small patch of sandy soil in early summer will often reveal a bustle of solitary wasp activity. Two or three greenish-yellow wasps usually hover in the air a few centimetres over the site, while others are continually arriving or departing. Each female has constructed her own burrow, sloping fif-

Bembix wasp.

teen to twenty centimetres down into the soil, with an expanded chamber, two to five centimetres in diameter, at the end. She may spend hours excavating the burrow, laboriously digging with front legs and casting sand behind her in much the same way as a dog digs holes.

When her burrow is complete, the wasp carefully covers the entrance with a little loose soil and takes off in search of flies. At a nearby carcass or some animal dung she will capture one fly after the other on the wing, giving each a sting to induce quick paralysis. As each fly is caught, it is taken quickly back to the burrow where it is secreted underground. A single egg is laid on the first fly placed in the underground chamber. Soon the chamber is packed with ten or fifteen flies which will remain alive and fresh, in a kind of suspended animation, for at least several days. The wasp egg hatches into a predaceous grub which feeds upon the provisions left by its mother. After consuming the entire store of flies, it pupates and transforms to the adult stage.

The female Bembix of course feeds on some of the flies she captures herself in order to maintain the energy required for continuous digging and hunting. She goes on to dig and provision one burrow after the other throughout the entire span of her active life. In this way each Bembix, like most other insect predators, destroys many, many times her own weight of herbivorous or decomposer insects during her short lifespan.

The Parasites

Once you start looking hard at things that are small, you soon become drawn into ever more minute levels of being. The hand lens gives way to the dissecting microscope, which in turn gives way to the compound microscope, and finally to the electron microscope. At each increase in magnification one discovers whole new orders of miniaturized complexity. Invertebrate life in Ontario is truly a succession of worlds within worlds.

The smallest and least conspicuous invertebrates of all are those whose lives depend totally on other animals. These are the parasites. Most of them feed on blood, body juices, hair, skin, or scales of living animals, and most of them are very much smaller than the host species which supports them. To many of us, the parasitic way of life seems repugnant, but it is just another example of the apparent rule in nature that for every exploitable source of food, there is an organism to exploit it.

Many of the simpler kinds of invertebrates exist only as parasites. Tapeworms, flukes and some roundworms are internal residents of the digestive and other systems of birds, fish, and mammals, and could not live in the adult stage anywhere outside their protective hosts. Some of these, moreover, have complex life cycles involving temporary hosts for their offspring in other organisms such as snails, and the planktonic microcrustacea of lakes and ponds.

There is also a whole range of external parasites, creatures which usually suck blood or feed on fur and feathers while attached to the outside of their host. These include fleas, lice, and mites – tiny *arthropods* (animals with jointed legs) – found among the feathers and fur or in the nests and dens of birds and mammals. Leeches, those worm-like, blood-sucking swimmers, are parasitic upon the bodies of fish, turtles, and frogs. In small numbers, most parasites cause negligible damage to their hosts.

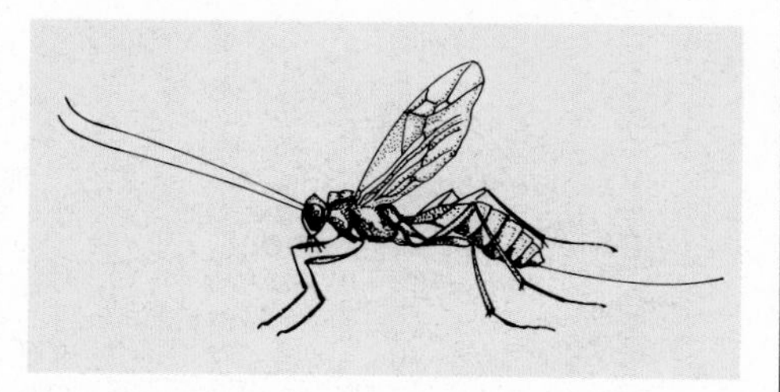

Braconid wasp.

One of the most important parasites of all is the Ichneumon wasp, which lays its eggs inside other living insects. Ichneumon wasps are usually called *parasitoids*, because the feeding activity of the parasitic wasp grubs inside the body of its host usually kills the host. But a well-adapted parasitoid will allow its host to survive just long enough for complete development of its fast-growing grub. One parasitoid wasp, called a Braconid, is so effective that it is able to lay a single egg in the body of a leaf-eating caterpillar. The Braconid grubs are small, and a single one will not kill the host. But soon after the egg is laid, it divides many times to produce scores of grub larvae which by their joint activities cause the caterpillar's death shortly after they have completed their own development. The tiny wasp larvae attach their pupating cocoons to the outside of the body of their doomed host.

If it is true of nature that any resource capable of sustaining life usually has organisms which exploit it, it is equally true in Ontario ecosystems that every living species depends on some other species for food or the essentials of life, and is itself in turn attacked or exploited by other organisms. Herbivorous insects which could become numerous enough to denude field and woodland are kept in check by a defensive team of predators and parasites. Decomposers return all life back to the soil and are themselves a source of food for others. In this complex network of biological interactions, invertebrate animals are the major players just because there are so many of them. Looked at in this way, the legions of tiny creatures without backbones can be seen as an ecological glue. Invertebrate lives hold the interacting parts of the system together; without them, all else would quickly fail.

Dutch Elm Disease: An Environmental Epidemic

David Barr

During the 1950s, Ontario residents began to notice that specimens of one of their most elegant and familiar trees were being converted to grey skeletons. They watched, horrified, as more and more dead silhouettes appeared against the horizon. With a sense of despair and helplessness, they saw an epidemic sweep over the land, felling a native species before it. After the skeletons came chainsaws, piles of logs, and angry fires leaving heaps of smoking ash.

The invader was a parasitic fungus carried by a bark beetle. Its victim was the tall and gracefully spreading white elm. The epidemic was Dutch elm disease (DED). Only after years of intensive research has the story of the disaster become clear.

Dutch elm disease was first recognized by modern science in Holland in 1919. In the years that followed, it swept across Europe and England, devastating the European elms. Where had it come from? Of the eighteen or so species of elms in the world, only two, the Siberian elm and the Chinese elm, are strongly resistant to DED. It is likely that Chinese labourers, brought by the Allies to Flanders to dig trenches during the First World War, imported the infestation in the wicker baskets they used to carry their belongings; these baskets were constructed of the tough, springy wood of Chinese elm.

The disease was detected in the United States as early as 1929, with a major focus in New York state. Apparently, veneer manufacturers had been importing diseased European elm logs, thus introducing the infection to North America. By 1959, Dutch elm disease had made the once-common white elm a rare sight all across the eastern United States, from Maine to Kansas, and throughout a broad swath across southern Quebec and Ontario.

Ontario's other two species of elms, rock elm and slippery elm, although equally susceptible to DED in the laboratory, seem to have escaped devastation. Their smaller populations and less dense distributions have helped protect them by slowing down the epidemic spread of the disease to them.

Dutch elm disease results from an intricate interaction between two organisms, insect and fungus, which together attack the elm tree. Either by itself is relatively benign. The elm bark beetle (*Scolytus multistriatus* is the most important of several species), feeds on twigs and crotches of elms, and tunnels into sickly or freshly damaged trees to lay its eggs under the bark. The fungus (*Ceratocystis ulmi*) grows microscopic, thread-like hyphae into the wood of either a healthy or a dying tree, clogging its internal water transport system and releasing toxic chemicals which kill the host's tissues. First symptoms of disease are wilted and yellow leaves in the crown of the tree. As the fungus spreads, more and more of the tree becomes defoliated.

On its own, the fungus can kill only one tree, or occasionally more than one where trees grow very close together. In combination, however, fungus and beetle are lethal. After feeding through late summer on elm wood as larvae, elm bark beetles pupate and emerge in spring – carrying on their bodies the infective spores of the DED fungus. An insect which carries another organism from one host to another is known as a *vector*, and the elm bark beetle is the vector for Dutch elm disease. After the beetles emerge, they can fly up to six kilometres on their own; they can be blown much farther.

Unfortunately, the adult beetles begin burrowing into damaged elms early in the growing season, when trees are most susceptible to fungal invasion. They carry the infective spores through the elm's protective bark layer and into the defenceless growing tissue. Just under the bark, each adult female forms a central burrow with long, radiating arms, at the ends of which, in mid summer, it lays its eggs. The fungus grows and produces its spores in the beetles' tunnels, and the beetles feed on these spores indiscriminately, along with the wood of the elm.

Tunnel system of an adult elm bark beetle under the bark.

Not surprisingly, decades of research have gone into finding a cure, or at least a control, for DED. One of the earliest methods tried, simple sanitation, is still moderately effective at combating the disease. This strategy consists of cutting and removing dying and recently dead trees, broken branches, and fresh stumps. The wood need only be debarked and the bark burned, because without bark to hide under, the beetles cannot breed nor the fungus proliferate.

Spraying elm trees in spring with an insecticide like methoxychlor is effective in reducing populations of bark beetles, but it is expensive and carries potential environmental hazards. A more recent measure focusing on control of the bark beetle makes use of advanced knowledge of insect *pheromones*, communication chemicals which affect insect behaviour. Multilure, an aggregation pheremone which attracts elm bark beetles, has been used to bait sticky traps which kill millions of the six-legged vectors. Unfortunately, this wholesale slaughter must still allow some beetles to survive, because it does not seem to slow down the advance of DED in heavily infested areas.

An even more cunning approach has shown better promise. If infected trees (which are likely to die anyway) are injected with an arboricide, a chemical which kills trees, they die faster and become extremely attractive to elm bark beetles. Fortunately, trees killed in this way are not favourable for the growth of beetle larvae, and only 10 to 20 per cent of the normal crop of beetles will emerge. Even though still experimental, this approach actually has succeeded in decreasing the incidence of DED in areas where it has been used.

The newest hope involves bacteria that produce toxins which kill the DED fungus. Inoculating experimental trees with the bacteria protected the majority of them from infection with DED, but it may take another five or ten years before the treatment becomes commercially available.

Most effective of all, but still too time-consuming and expensive for any but carefully selected shade trees, is high-pressure injection of a fungicidal chemical called benomyl into trunk or root of healthy trees. The procedure must be carried out repeatedly to ensure continued protection, but it appears to be highly effective. Even this method has its drawbacks, however, for when carelessly administered, the fungicide can cause greatly increased decay in treated elms.

Although DED appears recently to have reached a kind of equilibrium in Ontario, now that the most susceptible elms have been killed off and those that remain have some resistance, a potential new danger may be at hand. During the past fifteen years, a different and highly virulent strain of DED was discovered in England, and has since been identified in Canada as well. It is not yet clear whether this variant of the disease has been around for a long time and only recently been recognized, or if it is a new and more dangerous killer.

Clearly the battle is not yet over. More and better methods of control for Dutch elm disease are still required if Ontario's remaining white elms are to be protected from complete extermination.

◆ SCIENCE ◆ EXCURSION ◆

Biting Flies in Ontario

Steve M. Smith

One of the most predictable (and annoying) features of spring and summer in Ontario is the abundance of biting flies that harass and torment naturalist, hiker, picnicker, and gardener, as well as domestic and wild animals. Ontario, indeed all of Canada, is home to a fascinating diversity of blood-sucking insect pests, and their densities here are among the highest in the world. These insects are more than simply annoying; they also spread a number of viruses and parasites. While biting flies are relatively unimportant as vectors of human diseases in Ontario, they are important in the transmission of parasites among wildlife and birds. For example, ducks suffer large losses among the young of the year due to a malaria-like parasite transmitted by blackflies.

The insects that bother us are members of the order Diptera (*Di* meaning two and *pteron* being Greek for wing), and include: mosquitoes (family Culicidae), blackflies (Simuliidae), horse and deer flies (Tabanidae), no-see-ums (Ceratopogonidae, also called sand flies or punkies), and stable flies (Muscidae). These flies bite, or more correctly, suck blood. In all the biting flies except the Muscidae, blood-sucking is restricted to the female; she requires one or more blood meals as nourishment for the maturation of her eggs. Usually, after each blood meal, the female lays a single batch of eggs – sixty to three hundred in blackflies and mosquitoes, up to a thousand or more in horse flies. As a female often will feed more than once during her lifetime, she may lay several batches of eggs.

In most instances, the blood meal is not needed as food; both males and females feed extensively on nectar and honeydew, the sweet droplets excreted by plant-sucking insects such as aphids. In June, when blackflies are swarming about in large numbers and it is impossible to talk without ingesting a few, you may notice that they taste sweet, a reflection of the large quantities of nectar they sometimes contain.

Some of the biting flies in Ontario really do bite. Blackflies, horseflies, and no-see-ums, in particular, feed by macerating the superficial tissues of the skin with an ingenious set of cutting and snipping mouth parts that operate like scissors. The blades are equipped with backward-pointing teeth to help prevent accidental dislodgment during feeding. The scissor-like action of the mouth parts causes a local haemorrhage, and the fly sucks up the blood and tissue fluids that flow into the wound. Mosquitoes, by contrast, are elegant, refined feeders, using a narrow tube formed by the mouth parts. This tube is much narrower than the long proboscis – only the fine stylets held within the proboscis are inserted into the host. The proboscis itself bends progressively as the mouth parts are inserted. With some luck, and a bit of exploratory probing, the female can insert the tube into a branch of the circulatory system and imbibe the blood directly. The wound left behind by a feeding mosquito is much smaller than that left by a blackfly.

In the process of blood-feeding, the fly injects salivary secretions into the wound. The mouth parts actually form an intricate, double-channeled structure so that saliva can flow from the insect into the host at the same time that blood is being drawn from the host up the other channel. It is the salivary secretions that cause the allergic responses so familiar to the victims of biting flies. These allergic reactions differ among people and also within a person over time. With some persistence, many individuals are able to develop a marked immunity to the bites of some flies, but the number of bites required to develop immunity is larger than many people are willing to suffer, and there is always the possibility of becoming hypersensitive instead of immune! Unfortunately too, immunity to a mosquito, for example, will usually not confer immunity to a blackfly, although there may be some cross-immunity to other species of mosquitoes.

Biting flies locate their hosts through a sophisticated navigation system, relying on a variety of cues including odour, heat, and vision. For most groups of biting flies, long-distance detection of the host almost certainly involves odour. Having detected a host odour, or sometimes just respired carbon dioxide, the flies move upwind, using visual, ground-level cues to orient themselves. The extent to which various groups of flies rely on different cues explains their different attack behaviours, as well as the variable effectiveness of repellents. Mosquitoes and blackflies that rely extensively on odour and/or heat will often fly very close to your body before selecting a landing site. For such insects, repellents offer an effective means of interrupting the landing response. You may have noticed that a repellent does not really "repel" flies; it just keeps them from landing on you, or induces them, once they have landed, to take flight again immediately. Other biting flies, such as the horse, deer, and stable flies, make extensive use of vision. Typically, these flies approach rapidly, make swift exploratory circuits around the intended host, and land quickly. Repellents offer little protection from these flies.

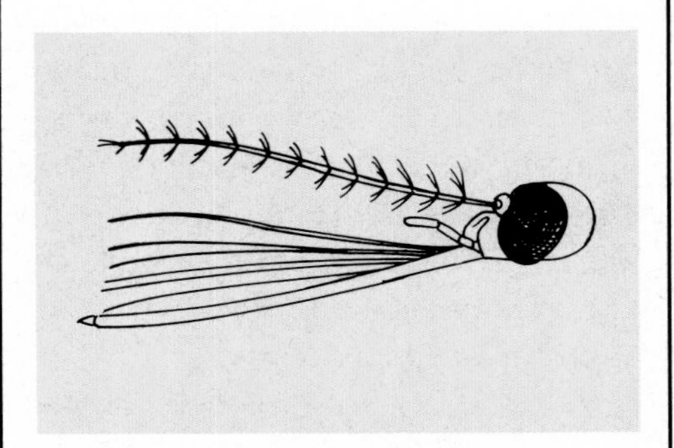
Mouthparts of a female *Aedes* mosquito.

Mosquitoes

Mosquitoes are found throughout Ontario, from Point Pelee to the Hudson Bay Lowlands. About sixty species, in ten genera, are found in the province. Among the most common are members of the genus *Aedes*. For the most part, these mosquitoes breed in temporary pools, especially of snow-melt origin. Eggs are laid in the soil at the margins of pools and will not hatch until they have been frozen. In the spring, submersion in cold, snow-melt water, especially if it is low in oxygen, will result in a nearly simultaneous hatch, within an hour or two. The larvae, called wrigglers, pass through four stages before pupation. After several days, the adult insects emerge from the comma-shaped pupae, using the pupal skin as a raft.

Aedes are among the first mosquitoes to emerge in the spring. Following emergence, their first activity is to find a nectar meal, and their emergence is closely timed to the availability of nectar. When the cherries bloom, expect to see blood-sucking mosquitoes within a couple of days. Flowering trees and shrubs, especially cherries, are important sugar sources. After nectar feeding, the females fly to species-specific assembly sites where males form mating swarms. The female mates only once in her life; sperm is stored for later use in fertilizing the eggs. After mating she sets off in search of a blood meal. Most species of *Aedes* have a single generation per year.

Mosquitoes of the genus *Culex* will be familiar to many southern Ontario residents as the mosquito that is so prone to enter our houses in September and October but is reluctant to bite. These mosquitoes overwinter as hibernating adults, not as eggs as in

Aedes. A final blood meal in autumn is not used for the development of eggs; instead, it is turned into a store of protein and fat for winter hibernation.

July visitors to marshes on the Great Lakes will often be persecuted by large, banded-legged mosquitoes – the appropriately named *Mansonia perturbans*. Unlike most mosquitoes in Ontario, this species breeds in marshes, breathing air from the underwater air tissues of aquatic plants.

An interesting subset of the Ontario mosquitoes breeds in tree holes and plant cavities, and one species, *Aedes triseriatus*, in small man-made water catchments: bird baths, undrained gutters, discarded tires, and tin cans. *A. triseriatus* is a common inhabitant of woodlots throughout Ontario south of the Canadian Shield. It is an important vector of human viruses in other parts of the world, but little is known of this aspect in Ontario. The mosquito *Wyeomyia smithii* breeds only in the leaves of the pitcher plant; both the plant and the mosquito are found throughout Ontario. Unlike most Ontario mosquitoes, this species does not suck blood. The adults feed only on nectar, the female maturing her eggs from nourishment stored up during the aquatic larval stages. *W. smithii* overwinters as larvae. If you remove the ice core from a Pitcher Plant leaf, you may be surprised to see the curled-up yellow mosquito larvae frozen in it. Thaw the ice and within an hour or two the larvae will resume swimming and feeding.

Blackflies

Blackflies are notorious pests, partly because of their persistent habit of flying about the face. About fifty species inhabit Ontario. Most species are highly host-specific, fortunately, and many feed only on big game, small mammals, or birds. One species in Ontario, for example, feeds only on loons and is the only blackfly species in Ontario to feed on these birds. A few species however, regrettably some of

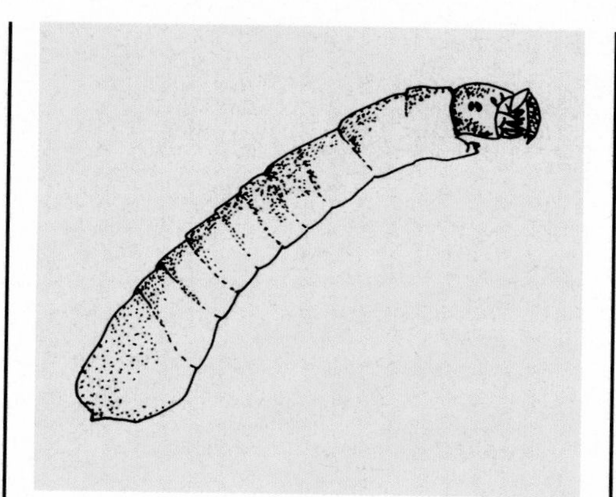

Blackfly larva.

the most common and abundant, will attack people readily.

Blackflies breed only in flowing water. The larvae are filter feeders or grazers, scraping material from submerged rocks, twigs, and leaves, or filtering suspended matter from the water with the aid of an elaborate set of fans. The larvae are very sensitive to degradation of water quality, especially to increased sediment loads. Partly for this reason, blackflies are no longer common in the agricultural areas of southern Ontario. However, wherever in the province there is an abundance of clean, flowing water, from roadside drainages with only a barely detectable flow to the most torrential rivers, blackflies will be found.

After the larvae have completed their development (there are usually six to eight larval stages), they spin cocoons on or under substrates in the water. A few days later, the cocoon splits, and the newly formed insect floats to the surface on a bubble of gas. On reaching the surface, the insect flies off immediately to begin a search for nectar, blood, and mates.

Some species of blackflies, those of the large river systems, hatch in late fall and spend the winter growing slowly, ready to emerge as soon as the river warms up in the spring. These fall-hatching larvae are the source of the early May plague of blackflies. Most blackflies in Ontario are different species that overwinter as eggs in the bottoms of rivers and streams and hatch in the spring, biting us in June and July.

Horse and Deer Flies

These pests of late spring and midsummer are well known throughout the province. The approximately sixty species fall largely into two main groups – the deer flies with their black-spotted wings, and the larger horse flies that come in various shades of grey and brown. The deer flies are aptly named; their ancestral hosts are believed to have been deer. Most species attack deer high on the body; they carry that behaviour over to their attacks on man, buzzing persistently around the head.

Horse flies might better be known as "moose flies"; they tend to prefer larger hosts, where they attack low, on the legs or flanks. Although occasionally they will bite people, they are not a serious human pest.

The larvae of horse and deer flies are found in a wide variety of habitats, ranging from the edges and bottoms of streams and marshes to wet woodland sites. The life cycle usually takes more than one year to complete. The adults feed extensively on nectar. Little is known of their mating behaviours, but at least some male horse flies are known to hover low over meadows early in the morning. They are easily detectable by their loud buzzing. During such bouts of hovering, which may persist for an hour or two, the flies reach and maintain body temperatures close to those of warm-blooded animals.

No-see-ums

These microscopic little pests are aptly named. They are members of a large group of flies, most of which feed on insects or pollen. A small group has taken up the blood-sucking habit, attacking birds and mammals throughout the province. They are best known for their habit of passing through window screening to annoy people on humid, warm July evenings. The biology of these insects in Ontario is poorly known, but the larvae are found in a variety of aquatic and semi-aquatic habitats.

Muscids

Stable flies are well known in Ontario as the house fly-like pest so common on our beaches. The larvae breed in decaying vegetation, often in the windrows that accumulate on lakeshores. Both male and female stable flies suck blood. They are aggressive, active flies, doubly annoying because their superb vision and rapid escape responses make them difficult to swat. Flies similar to stable flies harass moose and deer throughout the province. Huge clouds of female flies sometimes follow moose for days at a time.

Epilogue

It is easy to dwell on the negative aspects of the biting flies in Ontario, so unpleasant can they make an outing. Careful use of repellents and adequate dress will often go a long way to countering them. Wear beige or light yellow clothing to inhibit their landing. In blackfly season, keep your clothes, tucked in – these flies love to burrow. And wear a hat to fend off the deer flies attacking your head.

It may help your state of mind in fly season to remember that these insects are not all out there just to annoy you. The presence of many species of biting flies is indicative of healthy aquatic ecosystems where they play a vital role in a diversity of food webs. Adult mosquitoes are an important food for flycatchers, swallows, warblers, and other insect-eating birds, and they also help to satisfy the voracious appetites of dragonflies and damselflies that, in turn, become bird and frog food. Larval blackflies are important pollinators of blueberries, which feed grouse, raccoons, foxes, black bears, and people. Thus, however much they may annoy us, the biting flies are an integral part of a healthy Ontario environment.

Ice-Age Fossils and Vanished Vertebrates

C. R. Harington

The record of extinct vertebrate species in Ontario is virtually confined to the last few hundred thousand years. This period corresponds to the end of the most recent geological age, the Quaternary. But, despite its brevity, the record is fascinating, with highlights such as giant beaver from the last interglacial deposits at Toronto's Don Valley; abundant mastodon and mammoth remains, including some nearly complete skeletons in southern Ontario; and whale and seal bones deposited during the Champlain Sea episode some 12,000 to 10,000 years ago, when Atlantic waters flooded valleys far into eastern Ontario.

The Great Gap: Missing Pages in Ontario's Fossil Vertebrate History

Earlier parts of the vertebrate fossil record are preserved in other parts of Canada, but not in Ontario. For example, fossil fishes have been found at Escuminac Bay, Quebec, and in the Canadian Arctic, and extinct amphibians in Nova Scotia. Prehistoric reptiles abound at Dinosaur Provincial Park in southern Alberta, birds are known from western Canada, and early mammal remains have been recovered in Saskatchewan and Alberta.

Why this spotty record? Only a small percentage of living animals, primarily invertebrates, ever become fossils. To paraphrase Charles Darwin, the geological record is like a badly damaged history of life on Earth, written in a changing dialect. We have the last volume, covering only part of the world, preserving here and there a brief chapter, and on each page of that chapter only a few lines.

Consistent with Darwin's view, in southern Ontario, for example at Toronto and Ottawa, a great gap exists between Ordovician rocks, about 440 million years old, important in preserving animals without backbones, and ice-age deposits less than about 100,000 years old directly overlying them. Either sediments that preserved vertebrate life of the intervening periods were never laid down, or once deposited, they were eroded away. Because geologists have gone to great lengths to describe and map various kinds and ages of rock and unconsolidated sediment in the province, the likelihood of finding new formations bearing vertebrate fossils seems poor.

Although primitive fish probably occupied Ontario's Paleozoic seas, they were not common or did not preserve well. Nor have vertebrate fossils been found south of James Bay in Ontario's one patch of Mesozoic rock – Jurassic-aged, about 170 million years old, and Cretaceous-aged, about 100 million years old. Furthermore, no trace has been found in Ontario of Tertiary vertebrates from some 65 million to 2 million years ago, when mammals flourished following the extinction of dinosaurs.

Ontario was affected by several glacial episodes spreading south from the Labrador centre and melting back. In southern Ontario, which is the province's primary region of fossil vertebrates, the glacial advances are commonly marked by till deposits, and the intervening warmer periods, called interglacials or interstadials, by lake, stream, or sea deposits. The latter contain the best known fossil vertebrate localities.

Pikas in Ontario: The Penultimate (Illinoian) Glaciation

In Kelso Cave, west of Milton, the remains of animal species have been discovered that may have sought shelter there more than 200,000 years ago – toad, grouse, varying hare, cottontail rabbit, woodland deer mouse, muskrat, little brown bat, and striped skunk. The most remarkable discovery of all has been the lower part of a thigh bone of a large pika or rock rabbit (*Ochotona* sp.). The pika suggests an Illinoian age. This species, larger than pikas today, occupied the mountains in eastern North America during the Illinoian glaciation, but apparently died out before the onset of the next glaciation. However, this evidence for Illinoian age is tenuous. All other members of the related fauna are still found in southern Ontario, and pollen remains in the limey matrix surrounding the bones indicate a flora like that described from nearby Crawford Lake, which dates to only about 10,000 years ago.

Giant Beavers in Toronto: The Sangamonian Interglacial

Among geologists and paleontologists, Toronto is famous for the Don formation, and the classical fossil locale is the Don Valley Brickyard. Here, interglacial deposits are sandwiched between glacial tills of the Illinoian glaciation and the succeeding Wisconsinan glaciation. The seven-metre-thick layered clays and sands contain vertebrates such as whitefish, trout, either pike or muskellunge, shiner, channel catfish, burbot, yellow perch, and a fish like a fresh-water drum, as well as woodchuck and giant beaver. The lower part of the deposits include pollen of a flora that indicates a climate as much as 2.8°C warmer than today's.

The Don formation appears to have been deposited near a fresh-water estuary at the edge of a large lake at least eighteen metres higher than the present level of Lake Ontario. Evidence for this conclusion comes from the remains of fresh-water ostracodes, mollusc shells, wood, leaves, pollen, diatoms, and insects that became buried in the sediments. Several of the fishes present suggest relatively warm, turbid, slow-moving water with weedy areas, whereas the mammals indicate the presence of nearby open forests with patches of grassland and lakes or ponds. Analysis of amino acids in wood and fresh-water shells from the Don formation suggests that they date to the last Illinoian interglacial, the Sangamonian, which reached its warm peak about 120,000 years ago.

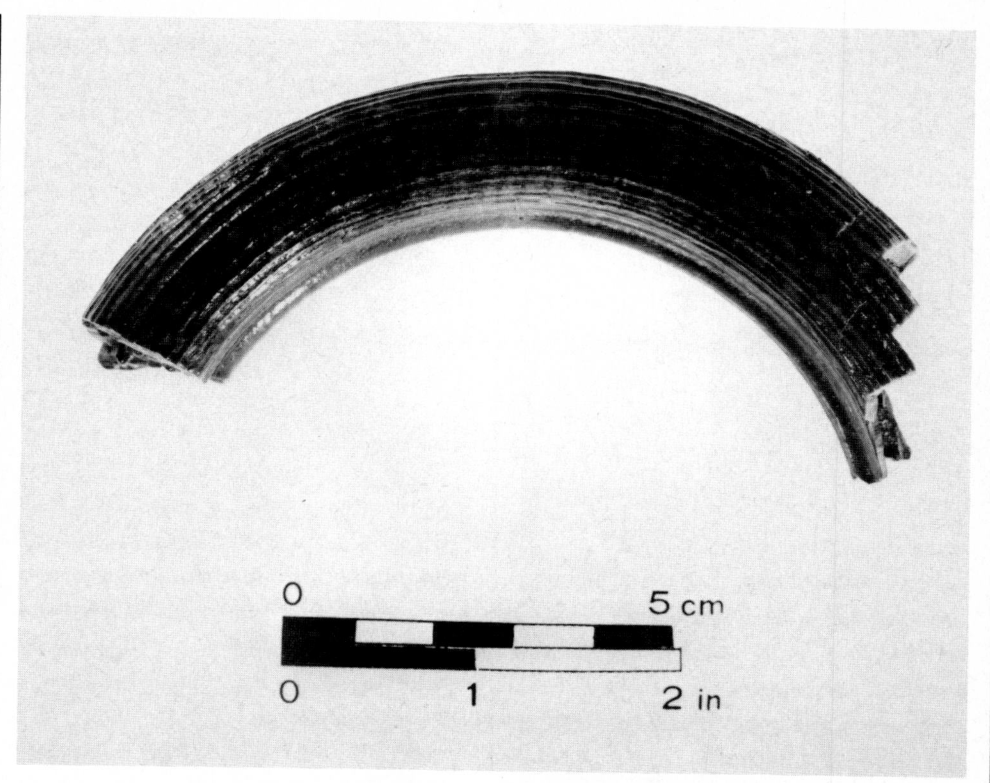

Outside (lateral) view of part of a giant beaver (*Castor ohioensis*) cutting tooth collected by A. P. Coleman in the Don Beds, Toronto, in 1925. The Don Beds are of an interglacial age about 130,000 years ago. NATIONAL MUSEUM OF NATURAL SCIENCES

The most interesting mammal from the Don formation is the giant beaver, represented by a cutting tooth. The giant beaver reached the size of a black bear – a skeleton in Chicago's Field Museum is nearly 2.5 metres long! An animal of this size may have weighed as much as two hundred kilograms. Modern beavers are best considered "distant cousins" of the giant beaver, as the two differed in more than size. Modern beavers have short, smooth-surfaced cutting teeth, whereas giant beavers had cutting teeth up to fifteen centimetres long, with ridged outer surfaces. Such teeth could have acted as both efficient wood-cutters and gougers. Giant beaver cheek teeth also differ from those of modern beavers in their larger size and different enamel patterns on the grinding surfaces. A comparison of the tail vertebrae of the two suggests that giant beaver had roundish, muskrat-like tails rather than flat, broad ones. Perhaps they didn't slap the water with their tails to give an alarm signal as today's beavers do; perhaps they didn't need to!

Giant beavers were confined to North America, ranging from Florida to the Yukon, and New York state to Nebraska. The most northerly records are from the Old Crow area in the Yukon Territory, which lies 150 kilometres north of the Arctic Circle. However, giant beavers seem to have flourished south of the Great Lakes toward the close of the last glaciation. Perhaps there was a rather sudden reduction of the lake and pond habitat they frequented. With their apparent inability to build dams and to disperse readily overland to new drainage systems when drought occurred, such a habitat change may have resulted in their extinction while the smaller, more adaptable modern beaver survived.

Giant beavers evidently died out near the close of the last glaciation about 10,000 years ago. Because they co-existed with early humans in North America, it seems unusual that there is no evidence that people hunted them. A single pelt would probably have made an excellent sleeping robe.

When they have been more thoroughly explored, Sangamonian interglacial deposits in the Moose River Basin of northern Ontario may also provide greater insight into the ice-age vertebrate faunas of that region. Cyprinid (minnow and carp family) fish remains and beaver-gnawed sticks have already been collected from sediments exposed near Moose River Crossing, and a mastodon jaw with tooth was reported in 1898 from the bed of Moose River in the same area.

Cooling Climate and the Enigmatic Stag-Moose: Early Wisconsinan

The last great advance of the ice is known as the Wisconsinan glaciation. The earliest deposits cover the transition from interglacial to glacial conditions as ice spread over the region. It was a period of cold climate and extensive glaciation. These deposits are well exposed near Toronto where several scattered but important ice-age mammal finds have been made.

Stream deposits of the Pottery Road formation at the Don Valley Brickyard have yielded the bones of white-tailed deer. But the big find came in 1933, when the renowned ice-age specialist A. P. Coleman reported bones from sandpits probably of this age between Shaw Street and Ossington Avenue in Toronto. Represented in the fauna are bison, bear, stag-moose (*Cervalces*), and mammoth or possibly mastodon. A possible tundra musk-ox footbone found in 1974 near the base of the Scarborough Bluffs, east of Toronto, could also be of this age.

Don Valley brickyard, one of the outstanding fossil sites in Canada.
R. J. DAVIDSON

Coleman's stag-moose antler beam was particularly interesting. It represents an animal slightly larger than the modern moose and differing from it in the character of the bones in the nasal region. It is distinctive, above all, in the unusually long antler beams with highly complex "shovels." Studies in New Jersey and Ohio of plant and invertebrate fossils found in sediments with nearly complete stag-moose skeletons indicate that these animals lived in marshy areas with lakes and ponds surrounded by open forest. Stag-moose were contemporaneous with giant beavers and American mastodons in eastern North America about 11,000 years ago. After that, stag-moose died out, perhaps due to rapid alterations in habitat and competition with modern moose.

Turtles and Brown Bears of a Warm Interval: Middle Wisconsinan

Turtles, rodents, and deer occupied a richly vegetated pond margin site near Innerkip more than 50,000 years ago. Insect and plant remains at this site indicate that the climate of southern Ontario was as warm then as it is now.

Mammoth and brown (grizzly) bear bone fragments came from 45,000-year-old gravels overlying Sunnybrook till (of early Wisconsinan age) at Woodbridge, near Toronto. This important discovery overturned a prevailing opinion that brown bears had not entered this part of North America until the retreat of the last ice sheets.

Tundra Mammals of the Last Ice Advance: Late Wisconsinan

Brown bears were present in Ontario toward the close of the last glaciation too, as shown by a well-preserved skull found in beach deposits near Orillia. Radio-carbon analysis of a limb-bone fragment associated with the skull indicated that the specimen is about 11,700 years old. It is intriguing to picture a fat grizzly waddling along the beach of Glacial Lake Algonquin – a giant prehistoric body of water that, with the retreat of the last ice sheet, covered most of the area of the present Upper Great Lakes and spread eastward beyond Lake Simcoe.

Tundra musk-oxen and caribou foraged near the shores of Glacial Lake Iroquois, a large lake that formed in the Ontario basin 12,000 years ago. This impoundment, with its outlet in New York state, lasted only a few hundred years.

Another unusual find, made while tunneling for the westerly extension

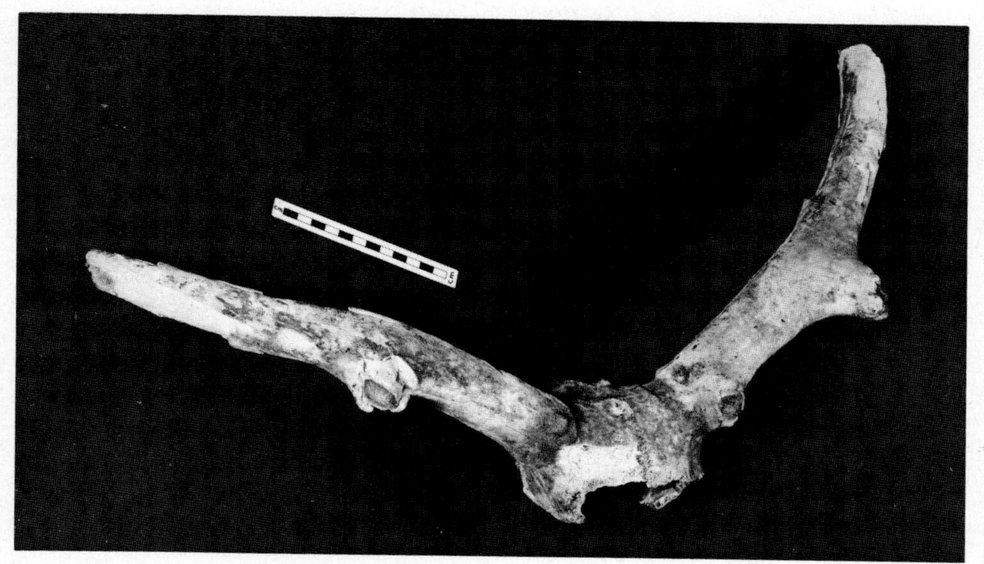

View from high on right side of a skull fragment with broken antlers from an unusual deer (*Torontoceras hypogaeus*). It was collected from 11,000-year old deposits west of the Islington subway station, Toronto.
COURTESY OF C. S. CHURCHER, UNIVERSITY OF TORONTO

of the Toronto Transit Commission subway near Islington Station, was a partial skull with broken antlers of a caribou-sized deer, aptly called *Torontoceras*. This robustly antlered deer lived about 11,300 years ago, near the margin of early Lake Ontario, where spruce, pine, and sedges were common. It is most unusual to have a new genus of deer pop up so recently, but the study of fossils holds many surprises.

Proboscideans, including mastodons, mammoths, and their relatives, were a dominant, widespread group during the last 50 million years. They were found on all continents except Australia and Antarctica, in environments ranging from tropical jungles to Arctic tundra. Only two species, African elephants and Asiatic elephants, survive. The latter are most closely related to the woolly mammoths.

Woolly mammoths (*Mammuthus primigenius*) and American mastodons (*Mammut americanum*) are known from Ontario. They are notable because they were among the largest land animals living during the ice age. They were widely distributed in North America and were relatively abundant, as indicated by well-preserved fossils – particularly the massive tusks and cheek teeth. Mastodon remains are much more common in Ontario than those of mammoths.

The earliest records of American mastodon are from Idaho and extend back about 3.5 million years. Toward the close of the last glaciation, the species ranged from Alaska and the Yukon to southern Mexico, and from the Pacific to the Atlantic coasts. In Canada, fossils are known from every province and territory except Newfoundland, Prince Edward Island, and Manitoba. Perhaps the best Ontario specimen is a partial skeleton collected near Welland in 1912 that has been restored, mounted, and is displayed in the Royal Ontario Museum.

Compared to living elephants, and to mammoths, American mastodons were squat (between two and three metres at the shoulder), long in the body, and often had straighter tusks. The upper tusks (enlarged second incisor teeth) extended two metres or more beyond the sockets. Some mastodons had vestigial tusks in their lower jaws, but often these were lost by maturity. Their cheek teeth usually had several low, paired cusps made of thick enamel – quite different in appearance from the series of enamel plates that characterize the cheek teeth of mammoths and modern elephants. American mastodons had coats of fine under-wool overlain by coarser guard hairs ranging in colour from amber to dark brown. A whelk-shell pendant found in peat deposits in Delaware may provide a glimpse of the American mastodon as it appeared to Paleo-Indians thousands of years ago. The figure incised on the surface seems to be that of a long, squat "elephant" with thick hair and rather short, straight tusks.

Nine well-preserved specimens of American mastodons have provided evidence on what this species ate. Two died with food in their mouths, now turned into resins and tars with a high percentage of spruce pollen, twigs of larch, and some pine, grass, and herbaceous composite species. Stomach contents of the remainder included hemlock and cedar wood, conifer twigs, swamp plants, and mosses. Nearly 250 litres of plant material comprised the stomach contents of a mastodon found at Hackettstown, New Jersey.

What caused the extinction of mastodons in Ontario? More than sixty mastodon occurrences are known from the province. They are mainly from southern Ontario and are of post-glacial age, between about 13,000 and 9,000 years old according to radiocarbon dates. There is much evidence to show that mastodons were especially adapted to open spruce woodlands or spruce forests with swampy areas or stream valleys nearby. A prominent glacial geologist, Aleksis Dreimanis, has suggested that their extinction in southern Ontario was initiated by rapidly increasing dryness 11,000 to 10,000 years ago, which first caused the spruce forests to retreat to moister lowlands and finally led to their disappearance. He believes that growth of an intervening belt of pine and hardwood forest on the better-drained moraine areas in central Ontario tended to prevent mastodons from migrating to the more northerly spruce forests. Cut off from the northern forests, they were left to die out among the shrinking southern spruce "islands."

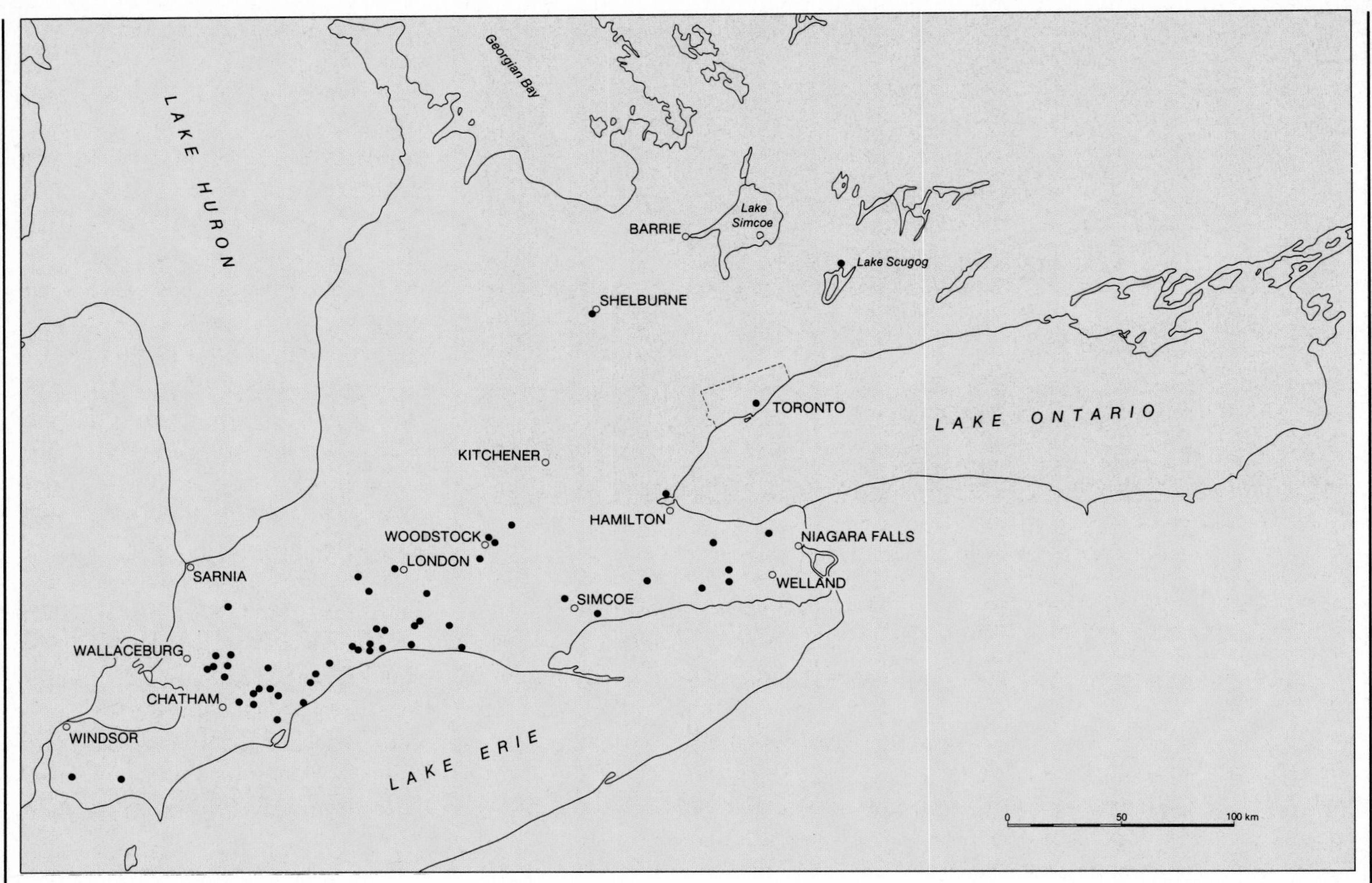

Mastodon locations in Ontario.

Two factors may temper the preceding interpretation. It has now been discovered that mastodons could have survived in the supposed barrier of pine parklands. And in 1978, a molar from an American mastodon was found as far north as the shore of Lac Saint-Jean, Quebec. Although Paleo-Indians may have contributed to mastodon extinction, the rapidly changing climate of about 9,000 years ago seems to have been more significant.

Woolly mammoths often are considered to be symbolic of the ice age. A great deal is known about the appearance of these hairy elephants because several well-preserved carcasses have been collected from frozen ground in Siberia. Other information has come from the study of many detailed carvings, engravings, and murals made between 10,000 and 30,000 years ago in Paleolithic caves in Europe.

Woolly mammoths grew to the size of Asiatic elephants, about three metres high at the shoulders, and had similar teeth. Their coats were like those of musk-oxen, with long, dark-brown guard hairs and fine underwool. Under the skin lay an insulating layer of fat up to nine centimetres thick. Their high, peaked heads sometimes appear knob-like in many cave pictures. They had large, elaborately-curved tusks, especially the adult males, sloping backs, and relatively small ears. Stomach contents found in frozen carcasses include abundant grasses, sedges, and other boreal meadow and tundra plants, along with a few twigs, conifer cones, and the pollen of boreal trees. Sixty plant species were identified in the fifteen kilograms of material found in the stomach of the Berezovka mammoth – one of the best-preserved woolly mammoths from Siberia.

Woolly mammoths stemmed from the Steppe mammoths (*Mammuthus armeniacus*) in Eurasia during the second-last glaciation, about 200,000 years ago. They entered North America over a broad, grassy, land connection, the Bering Isthmus (now the Bering Strait). As time progressed, they became better adapted to survival under increasingly cold conditions. As well as surviving the last glaciation in unglaciated refuge areas of northwestern North America, they lived in patches of tundra-like terrain south of the ice sheets from southern British Columbia to the Atlantic continental shelf.

Adult woolly mammoths would have been formidable adversaries, although extinct carnivores such as scimitar cats and American lions may have preyed on the young. Paleolithic hunters evidently killed mammoths in large numbers in Eurasia, particularly in the Ukraine. Bones found in the Old Crow Basin of the Yukon often show breakages by humans, who probably developed special methods for making and using tools of mammoth bone.

Woolly mammoths could not cope with the rapidly changing environment and increased human predation toward the close of the last glaciation, and became extinct about 11,000 years ago, or perhaps even later according to a radio-carbon date of about 8,300 years on a skeleton recovered near Muirkirk, Ontario.

The Muirkirk mammoth is the most complete skeleton of this species found in Ontario. It was discovered in 1895 three kilometres northeast of Muirkirk by a farmer who noticed bones in a burnt-over field that was being ploughed for the first time. The bones were excavated, and a study of fossil pollen preserved in the surrounding clay indicates that the animal died in periglacial surroundings. The last set of cheek teeth (the third molars) are well worn, indicating that the animal was fairly old. The skeleton seems quite small, even if it is that of an adult female, which may be indicative of stress caused by the rapidly changing postglacial environment.

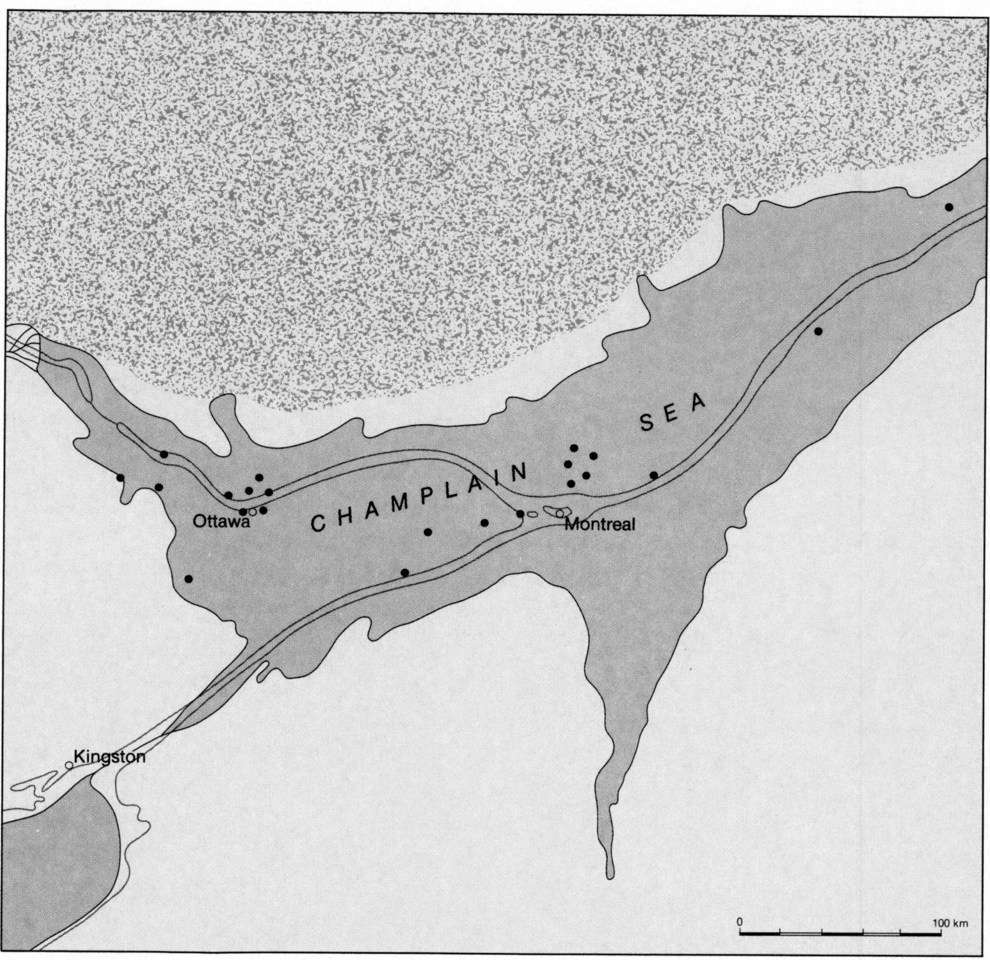

Locations of fossil whale bones (black dots) discovered in the former bed of the Champlain Sea.

Whales Over Ottawa: Close of the Last Glaciation

The quickly changing environment is well exemplified by the history of the Champlain Sea. This inland sea was a major feature of the landscape of eastern North America toward the close of the last glaciation. It formed about 12,000 years ago when the Laurentide ice sheet retreated north of the St. Lawrence Lowlands, leaving the depressed trough open to the Atlantic Ocean. At maximum extent, the sea stretched from Quebec City to Brockville, and included part of the lower Ottawa River Valley and the Lake Champlain Valley in New York and Vermont. With the invading seawater came shrimp-like crustaceans, molluscs, ostracodes, foraminifera, and seaweed. Then came the vertebrates: oceanic fishes, birds, seals, and whales.

Champlain Sea deposits have yielded many interesting fossils of marine mammals. Five species of whales have been reported, most specimens representing white whales or belugas. Harbour porpoises, humpback whales, common finback whales, and bowhead whales are also recorded. Radio-carbon dates indicate that the large bowhead whales and common finback whales lived in this inland sea about 11,500 years ago, whereas dates on white whales suggest an occupation of only about 10,500 years ago. A nearly complete skeleton of a white whale was found about 1870 near the railway station at Cornwall. It lay approximately five metres below the surface. The specimen is now mounted and displayed in the National Museum of Natural Sciences in Ottawa.

One of the most spectacular finds was that of a massive part of the skull and the partial skeleton of a bowhead whale from high Champlain Sea deposits near the town of White Lake, west of Ottawa. In life, bowhead whales average about sixteen metres long and weigh about fifty metric tonnes. They feed on multitudes of tiny krill or plankton. A radio-carbon date indicates that this Arctic-adapted whale either died and was washed ashore, or was stranded and died when the sea was near its maximum extent about 11,500 years ago.

Seals also occupied the Champlain Sea, especially those adapted to breeding on pack ice, such as harp and bearded seals, and those adapted to breeding on land-fast ice, such as ringed seals. A lower leg bone (tibia) from Plattsburgh, New York, indicates that harbour seals occupied water along the Champlain Sea's southern arm.

The best-preserved seal skeleton is that of a ringed seal that was collected about 1888 in a clay pit in Hull, Quebec, just across from Ottawa. Other ringed seal remains also have been found there. The skeleton was excavated from a sandy layer in the clay. Chalky shells of a marine clam associated with the seal suggest that it probably died and was deposited during an early cold phase of the Champlain Sea. Study of the growth rings in a tooth root show that the seal had reached an age of seven years. The specimen is important because it suggests that land-fast ice existed near the sea's northwestern margin during winter and spring.

The ringed seal from Hull, like the Muirkirk mammoth, seems to have been unusually small for its age, perhaps because of poor nourishment caused by early separation from its mother. Such situations are especially likely to occur along straight coasts with unstable fast ice, and these conditions may have prevailed along the northern edge of the Champlain Sea.

Already we can see that the presence of ringed and bearded seals and bowhead whales indicate a cold, Arctic climate for the sea. This observation is borne out as well by studies of invertebrates – ostracodes and foraminifera, showing that frigid, very salty conditions existed during the earliest phase of the Champlain Sea.

Of all fossil localities in Canada, none preserves a better record of life as it was about 10,000 years ago than at Green Creek, ten kilometres east of Ottawa. Calcareous nodules of Champlain Sea clay, about ten centimetres in diameter, when split, occasionally reveal remains of animals and plants. So far, at least fifteen species of vertebrates, twenty species of invertebrates, and twenty-seven species of plants have been identified from nodules collected near Green Creek. Shells of bivalve marine molluscs and bones of fishes such as capelin are particularly common. The delicacy of preservation is demonstrated by remains of tiny shrimp-like crustaceans, flying insects, and the feather impressions of birds. One of the latter was collected in 1881 by a former Governor General of Canada, the Marquis of Lorne. At the other end of the scale are large, spectacular specimens such as the skull and forelimbs of an American marten, and a complete twenty-four-centimetre-long skeleton of a longnose sucker in which bones and scales are preserved intact.

A study of the habitats of eleven species of fish from the Champlain Sea suggests a cool, marine, coastal situation fed by streams from nearby deep lakes. The fishes indicate four main ecological groupings. Those species that mainly inhabit cool lakes or sometimes streams throughout their lives include lake cisco, lake trout, longnose sucker, spoonhead sculpin, and deepwater sculpin. There are *anadromous* species that spend part of their lives in salt and part in fresh waters like the rainbow smelt and threespine stickleback. Others, such as the Atlantic tomcod, simply tolerate a wide range of salinities. The more strictly marine species include capelin, Atlantic cod, and lumpfish. The centre of these species' modern ranges is southern Labrador – more than eight degrees farther north than they lived in Champlain Sea times. This fact implies that the environment at the Champlain Sea was much cooler than these latitudes are today.

From this and other evidence, it is possible to build an entrancing picture of the prehistoric Champlain Sea: eleven thousand years ago, somewhere near the site of modern Ottawa, blue-green water with scattered pans of ice extends eastward in a broad sweep. To the north lies the dazzling Laurentide ice sheet, streaked and smudged along its edge by grey heaps of morainic debris. Several ringed seals bask by their holes in the land-fast ice still clinging to the northern shore. Two small flocks of common eiders whistle over the wavelets stirred up by cold winds draining off the edge of the ice. They curve towards a low rocky island where females are nesting. Other eiders in the colony dive for clams in shallow water nearby.

Side view of a sucker (*Catostomus catostomus*) skeleton from a Green Creek nodule. COLLECTED BY R. CHEEL AND PROVIDED BY NATIONAL MUSEUM OF NATURAL SCIENCES

In deeper water, several kilometres off the northern coast, a massive black shape cruises at the surface, periodically blowing a V-shaped mist skyward. The migrating bowhead whale swims steadily westward toward the broad, sloping sands of the Petawawa Delta, the sun making rainbows in the vapour of its moist breath. A pod of white whales is arriving from the eastern approaches to the sea. They slide smoothly through the cool, greenish water, their gleaming white backs leaving chevron-like wakes. A few newborn calves press close to the females like small shadows. More than five hundred white whales already loll in shallow, river-warmed waters near the southern shore.

On sandy southern beaches, small birds, pecking fitfully with sharp bills, scuttle back and forth in harmony with the advancing and retreating waves. Dead starfish and stray patches of kelp lie partly exposed on the beach. Just offshore, the sea is alive with spawning capelin. Hundreds of their decaying silvery bodies rise and fall in rows at the level of the last high tide, their stench overriding the salt tang of the onshore breeze. Through the glare of the sun on the water, silhouettes of a dozen harp seals can be seen leaping and cavorting. A solitary bearded seal, whiskers glistening white against its rotund dark body, hauls out on a nearby sandbar to rest.

The Champlain Sea became progressively shallower, warmer, and fresher until, by about 10,000 years ago it had largely receded from the St. Lawrence Valley. Despite the fact that the sea level rose as ice sheets continued to melt, the land rebounded faster, causing the sea to regress. So the Green Creek fauna and flora mark the sea's closing phase. Then the valley was partly covered by Lampsilis Lake, which rapidly drained, and the landscape assumed its present character.

About this same time, Glacial Lakes Agassiz and Barlow-Ojibway formed on the southern margins of the retreating Laurentide ice sheet, centred on Manitoba and northern Ontario respectively. Again we encounter the energetic A. P. Coleman; from Lake Agassiz beach deposits along Rainy River near Fort Frances, he excavated the large bony plate of a sturgeon, Ontario's largest fish, and parts of smaller fishes, along with shells of many species of fresh-water molluscs. In addition, the durable jaws with crushing teeth of a fresh-water drum were ploughed up on a farm north of New Liskeard, a part of the Clay Belt and former lakebed of Glacial Lake Barlow-Ojibway. Perhaps this species of fish entered that lake from Glacial Lake Agassiz about 8,000 years ago, when a connection between the two may have existed, for fresh-water drums still occur in Lakes Abitibi and Timiskaming, remnants of Barlow-Ojibway.

Many of North America's characteristic ice-age vertebrates, such as mammoths and mastodons, had died out by approximately 8,000 years ago. All vertebrate remains for the last 5,000 to 6,000 years have a distinctly modern character.

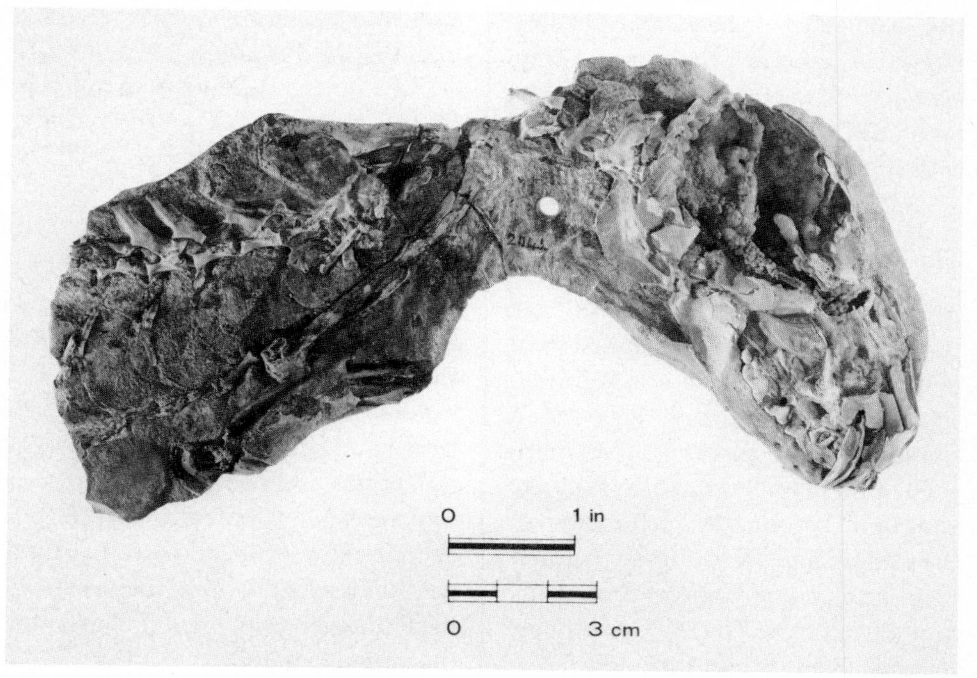

Right side of skull and part of body of an American marten (*Martes americana*) from a nodule found at Green Creek near Ottawa. About 10,000 years old. NATIONAL MUSEUM OF NATURAL SCIENCES

After the Great Extinction: Holocene Faunas from Toronto and Hamilton

Specimens from the Scarborough Bluffs in Toronto consist of eastern chipmunk, meadow vole, and gray fox. They lay near the surface in soil that has been radio-carbon-dated as between 5,200 and 5,600 years old. The presence of these mammals suggests a moist, mixed forest environment with grassy patches. White pine, maple, and probably American beech were prevalent according to species identified from charcoal in the soil. Snail shells in and below the organic soil add to the evidence for a mixed woodland and are consistent with a period of relatively warm climate, or "climatic optimum," known to have existed in the region about that time.

The Hamilton Bay vertebrate fauna, like that from the Scarborough Bluffs, may be 5,000 to 6,000 years old, and also suggest a moist, mixed forest habitat with grassy areas. The bones, from a sandy gravel layer, represent: fish (pickerel), frogs, snakes, birds (wood duck, barred owl, red-winged blackbird, common grackle), mammals (short-tailed shrew, gray squirrel, red squirrel, eastern chipmunk, flying squirrel, white-footed mouse, muskrat, meadow vole, pine vole, red fox, wolf or small bear, and possibly moose). The bone layer seems to be a lake-bottom deposit that became covered with beach sediments as the water level dropped.

The Spread of the Wapiti

Another feature of Ontario's late post-glacial vertebrate fauna is a period in which wapiti were widespread. Their remains have been found at such places as Northern Light Lake, Pickerel Lake, Sydenham, Kingston, Toronto, Waterford, and in the Lanark area. A specimen of antler from Lanark was radio-carbon-dated at about 300 years ago. These large, majestic deer occurred in the areas that were the first ones settled and cleared for agriculture. Evidently, growing human populations and intensified clearing quickly reduced wapiti numbers, and by 1850 the eastern form was completely extinct in Canada.

A Vertebrate Perspective

Although the Ontario fossil vertebrate record is not long, being virtually confined to the last part of the ice age, it is a most interesting one. It is fascinating to look back and think of beavers as large as black bears lurking in interglacial ponds where the largest city in Canada is now situated; and to consider that great bowhead whales cruised near the surface of an inland sea above the Parliament Buildings in what is now the nation's capital.

Why did animals such as giant beavers, mammoths, and mastodons, that had survived for such a long time in North America, become extinct some eight to ten thousand years ago? Why did such conspicuous extinctions of seemingly well-adapted and abundant mammals occur so late in the ice age? After all, many had survived earlier severe glacial phases and warmer interglacials.

Although no real answers have been found, it should be noted that the extinction of large ice-age mammals in North America coincided with rapid environmental warming and a rise in the number of people highly skilled in big-game hunting. Perhaps the alarming effects of human activities on today's Ontario environment are just the latest examples of a process that has been steadily gaining momentum for over ten thousand years.

On the Trail of the Tadpole Madtom

Ontario's Fish

Allan Wainio

Fish love Ontario. And so they should.

Ontario has oodles of what fish have to have – water. This province has more lakes (about 250,000) and more kilometres of rivers and streams (unmeasured) than any other political jurisdiction on the continent. Within this vast water supply is a diversity of habitat that harbours 144 fish species, the greatest variety of any province. If there is a fish paradise in Canada, Ontario is it.

This aquatic heaven was not always here. During the last ice age, all of Ontario lay beneath the glaciers. As the ice receded, fish surviving in the unglaciated areas repopulated the myriads of new lakes and streams. Most, if not all species, found their way into the province from the ice-free Atlantic coastal plains and Mississippi Valley. Just before the final retreat of the last ice sheet, an arm of the Atlantic Ocean, called the Champlain Sea, extended right into Lake Ontario. Later, this salt-water extension was cut off, but it left behind and isolated some marine fish species. Eventually they adapted to their strange fresh-water environment and lingered on into our times.

Recently, a greatly increased fascination with fish is giving rise to a new hobby – fish watching. While watching fish may never attain the popularity of watching birds, it can be equally or more intriguing, exciting, and challenging. First-hand experience with a face mask, snorkel, and fins in the underwater world of plants and animals is like a voyage of discovery – something one never forgets. It can easily become addictive. In searching for new nature studies, this unfolding aquatic world may be the last frontier for naturalists.

Countless opportunities exist in Ontario for fish watching, even without resorting to snorkelling, scuba diving, or glass-enclosed underwater walkways: rainbow trout jumping vainly against old mill dams, schools of dark walleye shifting with the racing current, longnose suckers splashing and scrambling by the thousands over rocky rapids, portly carp swirling about in muddy marsh waters, sleek pike cruising the narrow channels of a swamp, and powerful Pacific salmon leaping and twirling high in the air at an old hydro dam.

Learning the names of some of the more obscure fish can be a comic exercise. Ever hear of the killifish, a small robust species whose ancestors and present descendants hail from the tropics? And then there is the kiyi, a Great Lakes cisco that is not too common anymore. Chub fishermen of Lake Michigan nicknamed it kiyi, and the label stuck. What about the bigmouth buffalo? No, it is not a bison, but a tough-skinned member of the sucker family that can grow up to thirty-five kilograms. And let's not forget the tadpole madtom. Although it looks like a tadpole, it is actually a pygmy catfish. It is not mad, but it can cause madness of sorts; that story, however, comes later.

Geographically, Ontario is divided into two distinct zones in which the fish populations generally differ. In the south, rich soils continually release abundant nutrients which fertilize rivers and lakes. More nutrients result in greater abundance and variety of both aquatic plants and animals. But in northern Ontario, roughly from Algonquin Park northward, the soils are thin and less fertile. The waters that flow over and through these soils cannot pick up abundant nutrients, and so aquatic growth is much more impoverished. Fish grow slowly and mature late.

The Great Lakes can be viewed as providing another subdivision of Ontario's fish stocks. The Canadian portion of the Great Lakes extends more than 54,000 square kilometres. This vast, convoluted, inland sea harbours many fish species, some found only within its confines.

Many of Ontario's waters, especially in southern regions, are suffering from man's encroachments: silting dams, sewage, irrigation, acid rain, drainage, and diversions. Despite all this mismanagement, much of this water base is still in a fairly healthy state.

European man's early relationship with the fish of the Great Lakes is a fascinating chapter in our pioneering era. The early settlers were astounded by the bounteous fish supplies. And they were grateful too. For decades, many lumber camps in the upper Great Lakes depended upon fish for their chief supply of protein. On farmland near the lower Great Lakes, when crops failed or meat was scarce, fish were always available. Many of the small coastal communities present today around the Great Lakes had their origins as early fishing ports. In the nineteenth century, no one thought the fish would ever disappear.

What happened to the fish of the Great Lakes makes for sad reading. Before the turn of the century, the runs of Atlantic salmon in the tributaries of Lake Ontario literally clogged the streams. Homesteads were bought and sold on the basis of salmon runs in rivers flowing through the land. But then, hundreds of dams for sawmills and gristmills sprouted up and down all the tributaries. Within only a few decades, the Atlantic salmon, cut off from their spawning beds, began to decline. The flourishing commercial fishery depleted stocks even further. It was hopeless. The last salmon was recorded in 1896.

Other species nosedived, as well. In Lake Erie, the blue pickerel and lake trout disappeared. Other species, such as whitefish, held on, but only just.

Today, the saga of the Great Lakes fisheries continues, but the prospects are more promising. Commercial harvesting is under control, and water quality is showing signs of improvement. The native fish are slowly rebounding, but it will take time.

Despite all this harassment by man in the Great Lakes and elsewhere, most of our native fish have survived surprisingly well. Some have become "stars" in the aquatic world and are readily recognizable by almost everyone: the tasty perch, the pucker-lipped sucker, the barracuda-like pike, the flashy brook trout.

Then there is a host of species, strange and interesting, known only to *ichthyologists*, the experts who spend their lives studying fish and enjoying it. One such fish is the secretive and scarce tadpole madtom, active only at night and hiding in cavities or under debris during the day. In fact, it is the tadpole madtoms of our lakes and rivers that keep the ichthyologists nosing about and adding to their scientific lore.

But, you do not have to be chasing down the tadpole madtom to enjoy fish. The best time to see fish in action is during migration. For most species, migration is also spawning time. In spring or fall some fish may travel hundreds of kilometres, while others may only move a few hundred metres.

Fish ladders are ideal places to watch and photograph jumping, silvery rainbow trout. Rainbows were introduced into the Great Lakes watershed from the west coast in the late 1800s. Fish ladders, built at one end of impassable dams, allow rainbows to bypass such barriers and reach better spawning beds farther upriver. When the rainbows first encounter the dams, spectators are treated to some thrilling aerial acrobatics. The fish take turns rushing at the dam and jumping futilely before they locate the entrance to the fishway and leap into its dark swirling waters.

Most fish ladders are simple, slanting, concrete chutes subdivided by planks into a series of compartments, each one higher than the next. The chute becomes a series of aquatic steps up which the rainbows manoeuvre, jumping from one section to the next or swimming through small holes in the bottom planks. At some ladders, the fish are briefly trapped in cages and removed with long-handled dip nets. Conservation officers measure, weigh, and tag the big silvery trout, and scrape off a few scales to calculate age and rate of growth. Later recoveries by anglers help determine migration routes.

Several fish ladders are located on the Ganaraska River in Port Hope, on the Nottawasaga River just east of Alliston, on the Boyne River in Earl Rowe Park west of Alliston, and on the Beaver River in Thornbury.

After most of the trout have passed through the ladders and fought through the main rapids, they can be

Green sunfish, found in scattered locations throughout Ontario. POINT PELEE NATIONAL PARK, J. R. GRAHAM

followed farther upstream where the climax of this annual trek takes place. Streams to explore are the small tributaries or even the main branches of the Pine, Saugeen, Sydenham, Boyne, and Mad rivers, to name just a few. All of these flow into southern Georgian Bay. In the Lake Ontario watershed, the Ganaraska and Shelter Valley rivers can be investigated. If your timing is right, you may readily spot five-kilogram rainbows scooping out their spawning nests in just a few centimetres of water. Or you may be rewarded with the sight of a jostling pair of large rainbows in the midst of their spawning ritual. The nest-building and egg-laying never take long; spawning is over in a day or two. Then the trout quietly and quickly swim back to the protective, deep waters of the Great Lakes.

In April, just after the ice has gone, take a walk along some marshy shoreline; you may surprise a large, vicious-looking pike searching for suitable weed beds in which to scatter eggs or sperm. A nine-kilogram pike cruising like a miniature black submarine along a cattail edge or in a narrow channel between grassy hammocks is a menacing sight. Pike inhabit flooded marshes and shallow, weedy areas throughout the province, from the St. Lawrence River and all around the Great Lakes to Lake of the Woods. Even at the mouth of the Humber River, within Metropolitan Toronto, pike move in to spawn.

Pike are voracious feeders, lunging after small fish and gulping them down. They are by nature vicious aquatic carnivores, eating any living vertebrate of a size they can engulf. They consume a staggering amount of food.

Closely related to the pike and frequenting the edges of weedy beds or rocky shoals is the muskellunge, or muskie, as it is better known. Some people call these fierce-looking fish with their duck-billed snouts and rows of pointed teeth "water wolves." Native only to eastern North America, they are found close to the shores of the Great Lakes and in the inland waters of the Rideau Lakes, the Kawartha Lakes, Lake Nipissing, and Lake of the Woods.

Muskies grow much larger than pike. Some people swear that forty-five-kilogram muskies are hiding in the waters of the St. Lawrence River in the vicinity of the Thousand Islands. Like pike, muskies have voracious appetites, eating any fish, duckling, or small muskrat that will fit into their shark-like mouths. When food is scarce, young muskies will become cannibalistic and readily devour each other. Their voracity is legendary.

Later in the spring, marshes come alive again with the swirling and splashing of spawning carp. They wallow in shallow water while scattering their sticky eggs. Carp were introduced to this continent in 1880 from Europe and are now well established throughout the Great Lakes and in inland waters such as Lake Simcoe, Lake Scugog, and many of the Kawartha Lakes. They are bottom scavengers, grubbing about in the debris with their thick lips, in the process stirring up the mud and rotting plants. The silty waters caused by carp feeding soon drive other fish away. But, robust and hardy themselves, they tolerate man's presence and even our pollutants to a certain degree, surviving in waters unfit for anything but themselves.

Paddle quietly along the shores of a small picturesque trout lake in Algonquin Park and you may spot a large brook trout swimming ahead. The Park, with its hundreds of clear, cold lakes, is one of the last strongholds of our native wild brook trout. In November, colourful brookies spawn at spring seepages in about one metre of water. On a bright fall day, anyone who takes the time may be rewarded by seeing hundreds of brilliantly coloured brook trout milling around on their spawning beds.

In this spawning rite, the female digs a shallow depression in the clear gravel over or above a spring. The male hovers nearby. When the pit is ready, both fish swim over it and side by side they quiver and shake as the eggs and sperm are spread on the rocks below. Then the male swims off, leaving the female to scrape and push small rocks over the eggs with her underside, hiding them from predators. The female does all the work.

Neither brook trout nor the closely related lake trout are true trout. They are char. When the last glaciers retreated from Ontario, some char remained in headwater streams and evolved into brook trout. Other char chose the deep lakes and became lake trout. These two chars, and others farther north, have been successful in some of the coldest and most inhospitable of all fresh-water habitats. Inuit have a legend that chars came from the skies on a rainbow, and have remained colourful ever since.

The lake char or lake trout, found in about two thousand of Ontario's lakes, is the undisputed monarch of our northern waters. That number represents less than 1 per cent of our lakes, but even so, Ontario accommodates about one-quarter of the world's supply of this species. Drift over a rocky shoal in a canoe on an October day, and just maybe you might make out the big lakers winding and circling above the rubble during their simple spawning ritual.

An editorial in the *Ontario Fish and Wildlife Review* pointed out that "The lake trout is a fragile species, living in an inhospitable environment low in nutrients. It grows slowly, matures late and possesses a low reproductive potential. Genetically it is ill-equipped to withstand the stresses imposed by modern man."

One of the most controversial fish in Ontario is the splake, a cross between a brook (also called speckled) trout and a lake trout, a hybrid both genetically and linguistically. While splake have been produced periodically since the 1870s as a scientific curio, since about 1957 they have been propagated as an early-maturing, deep-swimming fish that could survive attacks by sea lampreys in the Great Lakes better than can lake trout. This breeding program is the first deliberate large-scale genetic manipulation of fish in history and an example of animal husbandry in the wild. Because splake is a stable hybrid which will not revert to the parental species, strains may be developed to fit specific environmental conditions.

While splake have spawned and established populations in several inland lakes, plantings in Lake Huron have not fared too well. To offset some of the problems of their initial hatchery life, additional lake trout genes have been bred into them, resulting in offspring called lake trout backcrosses. In the vast waters of Georgian Bay, however, the success of both the backcrosses and splake is still in question.

The best time to sneak up and watch smallmouth and largemouth bass is from late June to early July. That is when males of both species build their nests. Once the nest is completed, the males and females engage in pre-spawning rituals, rubbing and nipping each other. Finally, the two rest on the bottom of the gravelly nest, and the eggs and sperm are deposited. The female then leaves the pugnacious male to guard the nest, fan the eggs, and later protect the young.

These two fish species are common in Lake St. Clair, Long Point Bay, the Kawartha Lakes, the Rideau Lakes, the Thousand Islands, southern Georgian Bay, and Lake Nipissing. Their popularity among ardent fishermen is almost legendary. Once harvested commercially, both bass are now designated as sport fish.

Related to these large bass are the smaller but more colourful pumpkinseeds and bluegills. These laterally compressed fish are often referred to as sunfish. Like their larger brothers, they too build nests, but earlier in the spring. Both species are found close to shore in weedy areas and are often stocked in farm ponds. With quick, short bursts of speed, these fish dart among the weeds, eluding larger predators.

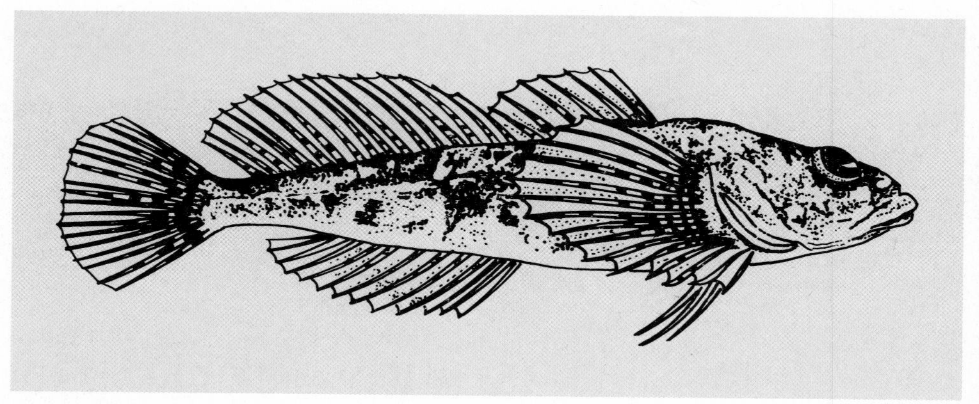

Mottled sculpin.

In our small headwater streams live numerous species of small fish that most people know very little about. They are rarely seen. Yet they are among the most colourful and strangest fish in the province. The tiny Johnny darter is one, with distinct M's, V's, and W's etched on its sides, as if by some calligrapher. It is a common inhabitant of swift waters. Its cousin, the rainbow darter, equally as small, is among the most brilliantly coloured of our native fishes. At spawning time it resembles a tropical fish, so beautiful is its attire, with rich hues of red, green, blue, and yellow. Just as the names of both these fish imply, they dart about from one spot to another, spending most of their time on the bottom. Both are spring spawners, and both feed with relish on small aquatic insects.

Sharing these fast waters with the darters is the grotesque-looking mottled sculpin, like something from the world of science fiction with its swollen head, stunted body, and immense fan-like front fins. When people first see it, they are often startled. It, and the slimy sculpin which it resembles, form an important part of the diet of the brook trout. Sculpins are bottom-dwelling fish and do not have typical scales.

The minnow family has more representatives in Ontario than does any other family of fish. Almost all are small. Their teeth are located not on their jaws but in their throats. These throat, or *pharyngeal*, teeth, grind food against a horny pad at the base of the

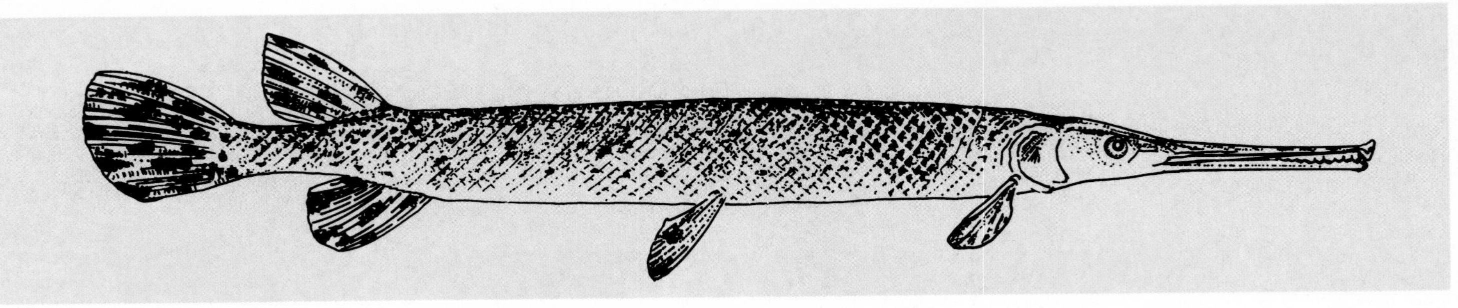

Gar pike.

skull. The redbelly dace, creek chub, fathead minnow, emerald shiner, hornyhead chub, and blacknose dace are just a sampling of the minnow varieties inhabiting our waters. They reside in all kinds of aquatic habitats – the swift-flowing headwater streams, the wide main rivers, the quiet lakeshores, the shallow marshes, and even the drainage ditches. Believe it or not, the piglet-sized carp is actually a minnow!

In aquatic food webs, the small minnows play an important role. They are the forage base that sustains the larger game and commercial fish species. They convert planktonic plants and animals into a form suitable as food for larger fish. But, like the tadpole madtom, because they are small and rarely seen, very little is known about their life histories. We know they are out there, but what are they doing?

Ontario's waters have their share of prehistoric leftovers from the last ice age. One is the gar pike. It is not a true pike. With its long beak-like jaw filled with many sharp teeth, it *looks* like something from the dinosaur era. This prehistoric denizen of shallow, weedy bays along the shorelines of the Great Lakes from the St. Lawrence River to Sault Ste. Marie is primarily a warm-water fish, found all the way south to Mexico. It is rarely seen, but an observant person may find it just below the surface in quiet bays, motionless, waiting to prey on any smaller fish. The gar's scales are hard, diamond-shaped bony plates covering its body like armour. It has an unusual ability to take a fresh supply of air into its air bladder at the water's surface, a trait which allows it to live in near-stagnant water.

Another link to prehistoric times is the bowfin, or dogfish. It occurs in the Great Lakes as well as in some inland marshes such as at Lake Simcoe and Lake Nipissing. This archaic, robust fish with its long dorsal fin is, like the famous coelacanth, the sole living representative of its primitive family. It resides only in eastern North America. It too can live in stagnant waters by gulping air at the surface.

The bottom-feeding lake sturgeon is another living fossil, not much different from its relatives in the Mesozoic Era. Even among fish, the sturgeon could not win a beauty contest. With its large eyes, a moustache of barbels, a retractable protruding tube for a mouth and its clumsy appearance, it belongs in a museum of the grotesque. And its awesome strength is not fictitious.

The largest recorded lake sturgeon in Ontario weighed 140 kilograms, was 2.41 metres long, and was caught in Lake Superior on June 29, 1922. Determining the age of large specimens can be difficult, but a 94.4-kilogram sturgeon caught in Lake of the Woods in 1953 was calculated to be 154 years old.

Sturgeon were once so plentiful in the Great Lakes that they were dried in stacks and burned as fuel in steamboats. Today, sturgeon exist in about a hundred lakes and rivers in Ontario, mostly in the north. Dams, pollution, and fluctuating water levels have destroyed sturgeon habitat. Their slow rate of reproduction has added to their misery. It takes fifteen, twenty, or even twenty-five years for them to mature, and then they do not spawn every year.

Hiding in the cold, deep waters of our lakes and larger rivers throughout Ontario is the province's only freshwater cod, the burbot or ling. It is one of our few fish that spawns in midwinter under the ice. It shares the depths with lake trout and lake whitefish. At first, one might be repelled by the burbot's appearance; rather snake-like in shape, with a slimy skin, long dorsal fin, and flattened snout, but it is a harmless enough fish.

In fact, there really are no dangerous or poisonous fish in Ontario. Large muskies have been known to have lunged at swimmers, but such incidents are rare and cause only bad gashes or cuts. Unbelievably, the diminutive tadpole madtom and its equally small cousin, the brindled madtom, are probably the two most "dangerous" fish in Ontario. Each can inflict a wound that smarts like a bee

Bowfin.

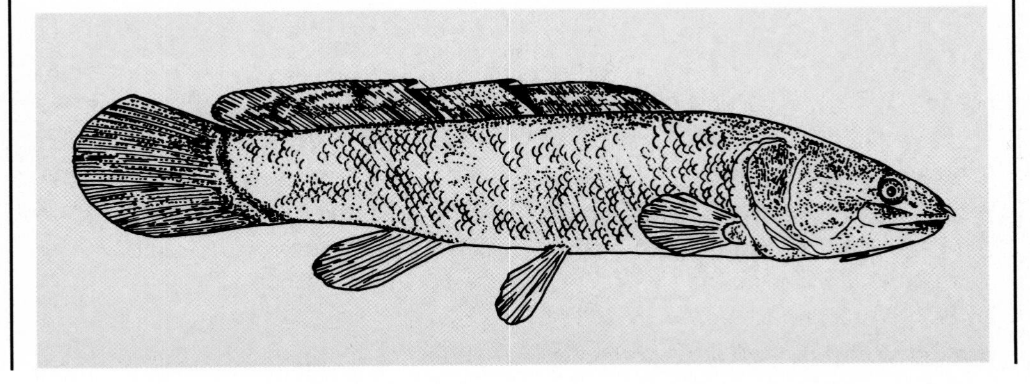

sting, but is actually worse. The sting is inflicted with sharp spines attached to each front fin. At the base of these spines is a poison gland. And this in an eight-centimetre fish!

Walking through silty flats along river edges you may disturb pencil-sized lamprey. These are not young of the infamous sea lamprey, but the adult forms of Ontario's two species of brook lamprey. Although classified with the fish, lampreys are not typical fish. They have no distinct jaws, no paired fins, no scales, and no gill covers. Sometimes mistakenly called eels, lampreys are not related to true eels, either.

Besides the sea lamprey, which is a marine intruder, and the two species of brook lampreys, the silver lamprey is also an Ontario resident. Unlike the brook lampreys, the silver lamprey is parasitic, but only slightly so. The brook lampreys do not eat at all in the adult stage.

The sea lamprey, however, is large and predaceous. With its circular, sucking mouth endowed with rows of sharp teeth, the sea lamprey is a blood-sucking machine. This aquatic vampire attaches itself to the side of a large lake trout or whitefish with a suction-like grip, scrapes away the scales, and with its rasping tongue pierces the flesh and slowly proceeds to suck out the blood.

The sea lamprey's destructive invasion of the upper Great Lakes after the opening of the Welland Canal now ranks with other biological disasters such as the introduction of the water hyacinth to the southern United States and the rabbit to Australia. In almost juggernaut fashion it wiped out the lake trout populations in Lake Huron and Lake Michigan. Effective chemical control saved the lakers of Lake Superior, but only just. The ongoing control makes use of a specific lampricide that kills the *ammocoetes*, lamprey larvae, in their stream burrows.

Complete elimination of the sea lamprey is impossible. Maintaining numbers at a low level, 10 per cent of their previous high, is the goal of the control program. This goal has been achieved in Lake Superior. The program is the largest of its kind and has attracted world-wide attention in biological circles. The idea of controlling a single species among the many in a convoluted sea the size of the Great Lakes boggles the mind even now.

True eels, migrating from the Atlantic Ocean, are common in Lake Ontario and have been known to penetrate the other Great Lakes as far as Georgian Bay. On the sloping face of the Moses-Saunders Dam in the St. Lawrence River near Cornwall, a long trough-like zig-zag ladder has been installed to allow thousands of eels to reach Lake Ontario, their natural destination. In the lake, they inhabit mud-bottomed bays and rivers, feeding mainly on other fish. In contrast to lamprey, for which they are often mistaken, eels have true jaws with small, sharp teeth. After years in fresh water, they mature, return to the mid Atlantic just off the West Indies, spawn, and die.

In early summer, windrows of small, silvery, dead fish float along many beaches around the Great Lakes. It is an annual phenomenon, and when the die-offs are unusually big, they make the headlines. The fish are alewives, small members of the herring family. They inhabit the deep open waters of the Great Lakes but spawn on sandy shores in spring and early summer. Apparently, slight rises in temperature critically affect them, and thousands die.

Theories conflict about how alewives gained access to Lake Ontario. They definitely have been present since the mid 1880s. They, like sea lampreys, reached the upper Great Lakes through the Welland Canal.

During the past one hundred years, many introductions of foreign fish have been made into our waters. Rainbow trout, brown trout, carp, and alewives are some. The Great Lakes alone have harboured thirty-four different aliens at one time or another. Fortunately, only half that number "took." Many fisheries biologists gnash their teeth at the disruptions to fish communities that some aliens have caused. In our lakes and rivers, an ecological balance exists that can be as fragile as the first film of ice along the water's edge in late October.

The alien fish that have received the most publicity in recent years are the Pacific salmon: pink, coho, and chinook. The latter two have been planted annually since the mid 1960s. They wander widely and may eventually become established in our inland sea. However, at present their numbers must be maintained annually by artificial stocking. Poor spawning beds and incomplete adaptation, as yet, to a wholly fresh-water existence have resulted in low reproduction.

The smaller pink salmon, after one planting in the late 1950s in Lake Superior near Thunder Bay, is now reproducing successfully on its own. In recent years it has spread as far "downstream" as Lake Ontario.

Alewife.

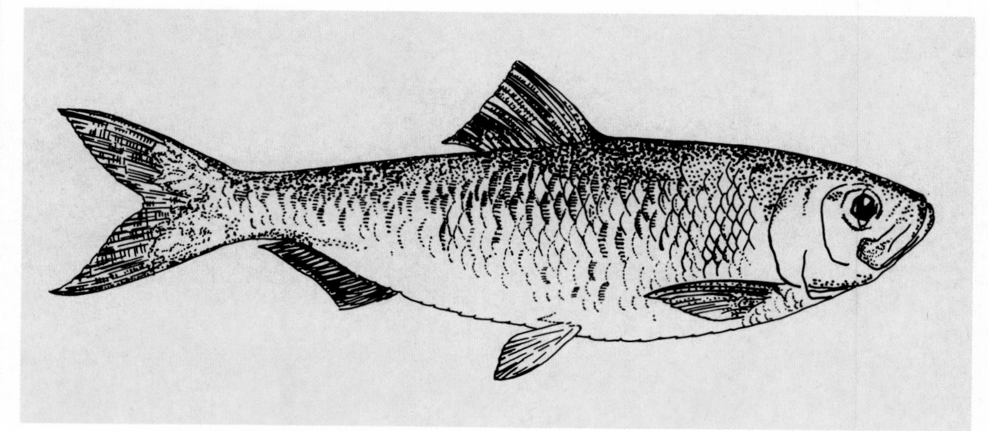

These western salmon bring back forgotten memories of pioneering days when Atlantic salmon flourished in Lake Ontario. A bit of the past has been resurrected.

The most popular game fish in Ontario is the pickerel, or walleye. The name *walleye* describes the appearance of its distinctive large, smokey and silvery eyes, similar to those of blinded – or "walleyed" – domestic animals. Their eyes possess a special layer extremely sensitive to bright light. This sensitive layer forces the walleye to feed at twilight or after dark. The walleye is a true perch and is found throughout the province. Its relatives are yellow perch, sauger, logperch, and the darters. All these fish have two well-separated dorsal fins.

What about rare or endangered species? In this category are some of the suckers: black redhorse, river redhorse, and spotted; some minnows: pugnose minnow, silver shiner, silver chub, redside dace, and central stoneroller; and a catfish, the brindled madtom, found in scattered sites in the Lake Erie watershed and the Sydenham River. Rare in Ontario too are species that are common farther south but live here at the extreme northern edge of their range. The blackstripe topminnow, common in the United States, is found in Canada only in the Sydenham River. Five deep-water species of ciscoes, at one time common in the Great Lakes, are now classified as rare or endangered.

And what about our leading character, the tadpole madtom, the smallest catfish in Canada? It has a reasonably strong foothold in Ontario, found in the St. Lawrence River, Lake Ontario, and Lake Erie. If you want to find one, look in open tin cans at the bottom of streams or lakes. Not only do they hide in cans but they spawn in them too.

But why is it labelled mad? No, not because its poison causes maddening pain. It is called mad because of its hyperactive, seemingly insane swimming behaviour. In other words, it swims like a madman – all over the place and going nowhere.

The tadpole madtom is a fascinating little creature, something right out of a Tolkien fantasy. It deserves recognition for being just that – fascinating. And there are a lot more like it, making our waters alive with a colourful finny assortment of brindles, stonerollers, pugnoses, and hornyheads.

Let's keep it that way.

Grass pickerel, found in Canada only in tributaries to the St. Lawrence River and Lakes Ontario, Erie, and Huron as well as the Severn River-Muskoka Lakes. POINT PELEE NATIONAL PARK

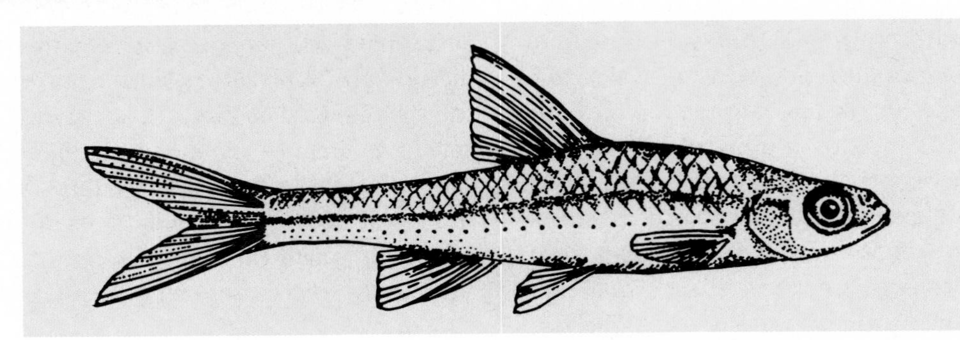

Pugnose minnow.

Tadpole madtom.

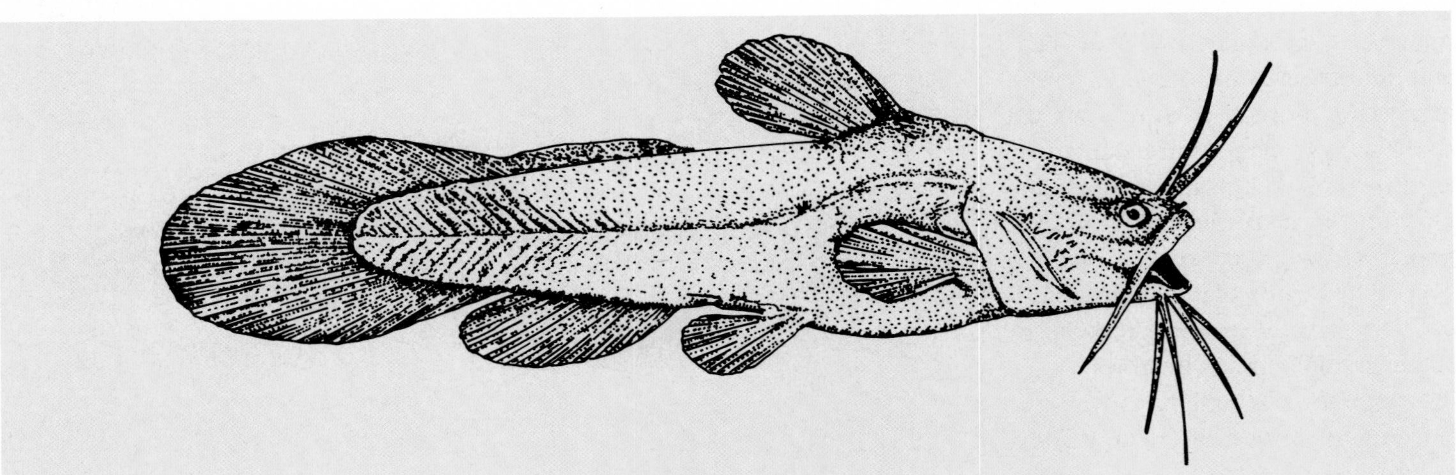

Ancient Rhythms on Annual Display
The Amphibians of Ontario
Francis R. Cook

Each year, from the shores of Lake Erie to the coastline of Hudson Bay, even before the last of winter's snows have melted, the renewal of spring is heralded by the urgent calls of frogs, filling the crisp air from ponds, ditches, swamps, and other low places. The few hardy amphibian species which sing this chorus produce some of the most characteristic of all Canadian sounds.

As the late spring temperatures begin their annual climb above freezing levels, one frog species after another joins the chorus, calling for a time, then yielding its vocal dominance to another. The stage gradually shifts from the shallowest, earliest-warming water to margins of the deeper, more permanent lakes, rivers, and bays. By midsummer, only a few species still call. But later, on warm days in autumn, after summer has faded, the faint voices of the spring frogs trill again from woods and low places. That late in the year they rarely call in large numbers, but those that do seem to be defying winter's inevitable approach.

Among amphibians, frogs are the reverse of the idealized "good child"; they are often heard but seldom seen. Salamanders, on the other hand, are neither heard nor readily seen. Some go about their spring reproductive rites at the same time as frogs, and often in the same ponds, but in silence.

Amphibians are the most abundant terrestrial vertebrates in Ontario, but the number of different species here is relatively low. Of the 3,260 amphibian species in the world, Canada has only 21 native frogs and 20 salamanders, and of these, Ontario has a combined total of only 24. None of Ontario's species are confined to this province, and most are in northern projections of their eastern or occasionally central North American ranges. Within Canada, many are found east to the Maritime provinces and west at least to eastern Manitoba. Five species reach the Rocky Mountains and one, the wood frog, extends its range beyond the Arctic Circle in the Mackenzie Valley.

The word *amphibian* is derived from Greek and means literally "both lives," a reference to the dual aquatic and terrestrial life cycle of these animals. The eggs, protected only by a jelly-like envelope, are laid in water. They hatch into gilled larvae which later metamorphose into air-breathing terrestrial animals. Thus, the dramatic invasion of land by vertebrates that occurred millions of years ago is re-enacted each summer.

This transformation is so common in north temperate regions of the world that we often consider it the norm for amphibian behaviour. However, many amphibians, particularly in tropical areas, lay their eggs in moist places on land, and their young pass the larval stage within the egg itself. In at least two species, a toad in Africa and a salamander in Europe, the female retains her eggs and bears fully-developed young.

Amphibians play important roles in their ecosystems. They are major predators of insects and other invertebrates and in turn are preyed upon by herons, mink, otters, raccoons, many snakes, turtles, fish, and even insects; the aquatic giants – predaceous diving beetles and giant water bugs readily take tadpoles and even adult frogs of the smaller species.

Amphibians depend upon their surroundings for their body temperature. Of all the vertebrates, amphibians form the only group with no protective feathers, fur, or scales. However, their skins are highly glandular, exuding profuse and often toxic secretions which protect them from both desiccation and predation.

Ontario's amphibians have evolved an assortment of different ways to survive the cold of winter. All species become dormant in response to cold, but wood frogs, chorus frogs, spring peepers, and gray treefrogs show some tolerance to temperatures below freezing. Glucose in the body fluids of wood frogs acts as an antifreeze that allows them to survive temperatures of −5°C. Toads, however, are not freeze-tolerant. When summer is over they use the cornified "spades" on their hind feet to dig down below the frost line. Or, they may spend the winter in the burrows of other animals. Consequently, their northern limit is reached at the southern edge of permafrost soils.

Many amphibians avoid freezing by spending the winter in deep or flowing water. Included among these are stream dwellers such as the two-lined, dusky, and spring salamanders, the pond and lake-dwelling eastern newt, the river- and Great Lakes-inhabiting mudpuppy, and the widespread leopard, pickerel, green, and mink frogs as well as the bullfrogs. If their overwintering sites freeze to the bottom, or if the oxygen supply is exhausted, they will die.

The paleontological record for frogs and salamanders is especially fragmentary because so many species are small and fossilize poorly. Despite this, many of the present-day species have been documented in North America back to the Pleistocene, and some to the Pliocene, 10 million years ago. After the retreat of the last glaciation, all the species now in Ontario reoccupied their ranges from the south. Stream salamanders probably re-invaded from a stronghold in the Appalachian Mountains. Mudpuppies moved back from the Mississippi River drainage. A number of southwestern Ontario species – the smallmouth salamander, tiger salamander, Fowler's toad, and cricket frog – may have survived the last glaciation as far south as Texas and Mexico. The two races of chorus frogs that are in Ontario undoubtedly re-invaded from glacial refugia south of the Great Lakes and in the west respectively. Both races prefer open fields and clearings: the Midland chorus frog of southern Ontario, and the boreal chorus frog north of Lake Superior to Hudson Bay. A wide band of thick forest east of Lake Superior still separates them today.

The present geographical limits for at least some species may not represent their northern-most distributions. Today, blue-spotted salamanders occur north to the Hudson Bay Lowlands while Jefferson salamanders, similar in appearance, live only in southwestern Ontario. However, Jefferson–blue-spotted hybrids occur to the southern edge of the Canadian Shield. Farther north, blue-spotted salamanders do not show any evidence of hybridization. Possibly Jefferson salamanders lived north to the edge of the Shield during warmer climates five thousand years ago, leaving some genes behind in their close relatives.

Salamanders lay fewer but larger eggs than frogs. Unlike frogs, salamanders (other than newts or the mole salamanders) often remain with their eggs until they hatch. Breeding male salamanders court females through elaborate "dances," which follow patterns characteristic of each species. The males of all Ontario salamanders produce *spermatophores*, a cap of sperm on a stalk, and entice a female to pick it up to fertilize her eggs as they are being laid.

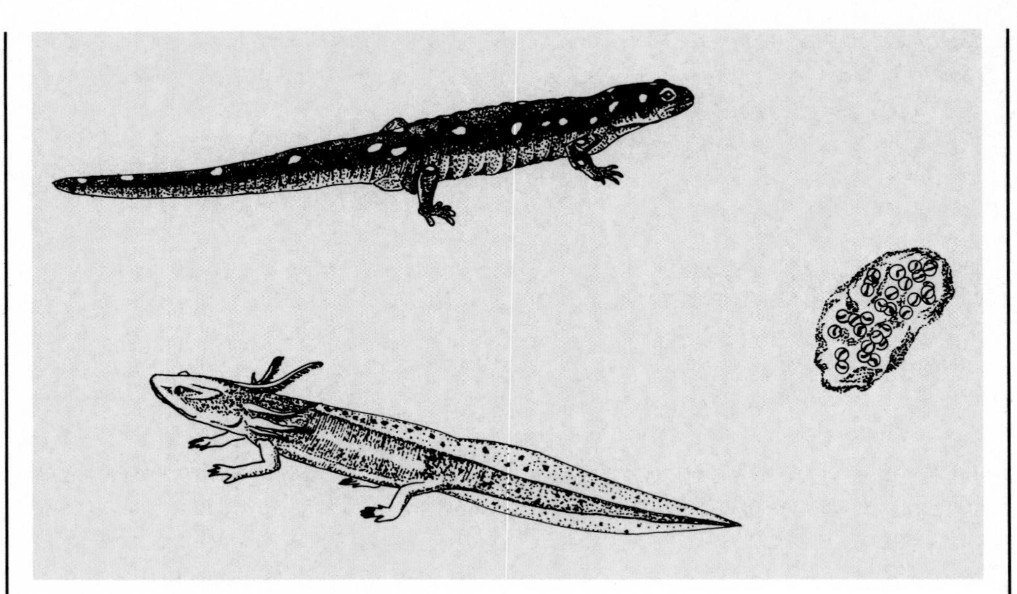

Life cycle of a spotted salamander.

The eggs of all Ontario salamanders, except those of the eastern redbacked, hatch into larvae with external gills. The eastern redbacked passes the entire larval stage within the egg. The large gills of pond-inhabiting mole salamanders and newts serve to improve oxygen uptake in warm water.

Salamanders are sometimes mistaken for lizards, but their scaleless skin characterizes them as true amphibians. Most have lungs in the adult stage, but individuals of one group are lungless, respiring through their skins and the roofs of their mouths. These lungless salamanders are the most diverse in their habitats and habits: two-lined, dusky, spring, four-toed, and eastern redbacked salamanders. The first three species are probably closest in habits to the ancestral stock which is thought to have evolved in cold mountain streams. Here, the absence of lungs results in lower buoyancy, an advantage in fast-flowing water. The high oxygen content of the water compensates for their lack of lungs. These species are found under rocks, both in and out of water, along fast-flowing streams or in spring seepages.

Another departure from the "typical" amphibian development is found in the mudpuppy, which retains its larval gills as an adult and never transforms into a terrestrial form. The black-and-yellow-striped larvae are strikingly different in colour from the muddy brown, smudgy-spotted adults. Both inhabit permanent water: large streams, rivers, and the Great Lakes. They are rarely seen unless actively searched for by turning over large flat stones underwater. Fishermen sometimes unintentionally catch them on baited hooks, particularly in winter, and often regard them with surprise as monsters – fish with "ears" (the fluffy external gills) and legs.

Of Canada's two newt species, one – the eastern newt, lives in Ontario. Each spring newts lay their eggs in ponds or shallow lakes. Following the aquatic larval stage, the animal is transformed into an *eft*. Efts are brick red, strikingly different in colour from the adult, and they may be terrestrial, spending the next one to three years on land. They then return to the water and transform into aquatic adults. If the adult newt is forced to live out of water, say, for instance, if a woodland pond dries up in the summer, it will become very dark brown, almost black, in marked contrast to the normal olive-green. Aquatic adults develop tail fins, and remain aquatic all year. In the dry forest areas of northwestern Ontario, the land stage may be omitted, the larvae transforming directly into adults and the larval gills being retained into maturity.

Mole salamanders are heavy-bodied

and rarely seen, due to the primarily subterranean habits from which the group derives its name. Five species have been recorded in Ontario: tiger salamander, collected only on Point Pelee and possibly Pelee Island; smallmouthed salamander, recorded only on Pelee Island; Jefferson salamander, restricted to a few localities in southwestern Ontario; and yellow-spotted and blue-spotted salamanders, which are widespread. All breed in ponds in the early spring soon after the snow has melted. Sometimes, during the first warm spring rains, large numbers of them migrate to breeding sites; at night a flashlight often will reveal them crawling on pond bottoms searching for and courting mates. After breeding, they retreat to the woodlands where they are only rarely found by turning over logs or stones. The larvae transform to adults in July and August before the ponds in which they develop dry up completely.

Blue-spotted salamanders hybridize with all Ontario species except the yellow-spotted. On Pelee Island some blue-spotted salamanders show the influence of tiger salamander genes. With the Jefferson and smallmouthed, blue-spotted salamanders interbreed readily, and *triploids*, usually female but occasionally male, are produced. Triploids receive two sets of chromosomes from one parent and one from the other, instead of the normal one set from each. These triploids are sometimes considered distinct species – Tremblay's and silvery salamanders: Tremblay's receive two sets from the blue-spotted parent; silvery receive two sets from the Jefferson.

Yellow-spotted salamander.
GARY ALLEN

Frogs, in contrast to salamanders, are so distinctive in structure that they are never confused with any other animals. Ontario's frogs fall into three distinct groups: treefrogs, toads, and typical frogs. All have elongated hind legs and none has a tail as an adult.

Of the three groups, toads are the best adapted to dry habitats. Two species of toads live in Ontario: Fowler's toad (a race of Woodhouse's toad), confined to extreme southwestern Ontario, and the common American toad. Fowler's toad prefers lighter, generally sandier soils, and consequently is lighter in colour than the American toad.

Ontario's four species of treefrogs are unequal in their climbing habits. The largest, the gray treefrog, ascends high into mature trees. Spring peepers usually do not climb above bushes. Both are woodland species. Chorus frogs climb primarily on grasses, and the cricket frog in the extreme southwest is mostly aquatic and found at permanent pond margins.

Habitat of the six species of typical frogs may be characterized as follows: damp woodland (wood frog), woodland streams and swamps (pickerel frog), marshes and fields (leopard frog), and permanent ponds, lakes, and rivers (green frog, bullfrog, and mink frog). All, however, may forage widely and be found away from their typical habitats.

All northern frogs lay large numbers of eggs; the larger the frog the more eggs it can lay. Frogs that breed earliest and in the coldest water tend to have the smallest eggs. Eggs of the more northern species develop faster, even in cool temperatures, than do those of southern species. The early-breeding wood, leopard, and pickerel frogs anchor their compact globular masses of eggs to stems or twigs well below the surface where they will not be killed by freezing during cold nights. Late breeders, however, such as green frogs and bullfrogs, lay mats of eggs on the surface.

All Ontario frogs fertilize their eggs externally as they are being laid. In a few weeks the eggs develop into tadpoles, or pollywogs, whose rotund bodies accommodate long, coiled intestines. The mouth is specialized with a cutting beak, several rows of small rasping teeth, and a border of papillae. Although the tadpoles are initially legless, their hind legs soon appear as small buds. Front legs develop beneath the skin and are not seen until they erupt just before transformation to frog form. Development to adult stage can be rapid, in response to warm conditions in shallow, spring ponds. However, the tadpoles of the large-pond species – the bullfrog, green, and mink frogs – must overwinter at least once, generally twice, and in the case of the bullfrog sometimes even three times.

The size of tadpoles at the time of transformation to adult frogs varies considerably depending on species.

Bullfrog. POINT PELEE NATIONAL PARK, D. WILKES

Size also influences the time required to mature after transformation. In some species, such as chorus frogs and spring peepers, the males may mature in the fall of the same year in which they leave the tadpole stage, at least in southern and central Ontario. However, bullfrogs may require at least three years after transformation to reach maturity. Thus, from the egg stage, a bullfrog may take as long as six years to become mature!

The males of all eastern Canadian frog species have distinctive calls. When temperatures are suitable, calling continues throughout the breeding season. Calling usually is most pronounced during the hours of darkness, although some species will continue throughout the day. The call of the American toad is a trill sometimes lasting half a minute. At low temperatures the pulse rate of the trill is slowest, the pauses between trills longest, and each trill most extended. The call of Fowler's toad differs by being distinctively higher pitched, more rapidly pulsed, much shorter, and more of a bleat than a trill. The chorus frog produces a rasping call best simulated by drawing one's fingernail slowly over the teeth of a pocket comb. The spring peeper utters a shrill "peep" which may be rapidly repeated on warm nights. The gray treefrog's call is a pulsed, flute-like short trill. The cricket frog's call resembles the sound of several small stones being grated together. The wood frog's "quack" call is often repeated rapidly. Leopard frogs and pickerel frogs snore. The pickerel frog's snore is more rapid and higher pitched. In both, the snore often is followed by a series of sharp grunts. Green frogs give a "chung," somewhat like a note on a banjo, mink frogs "tuk," and bullfrogs offer a deep bass "jug-o-rum," or, in French, "oua-ouaron," somewhat reminiscent of the distant mating bellow of a bull.

Most frog calls are made to attract females and/or defend territories. The clearest expression of purpose is the leopard frog's snore to attract females, and grunts in response to the calling of a nearby male. Bullfrogs and green frogs establish and defend territories against other males. Aggressive encounters are sometimes fought out by wrestling until one antagonist gives up and swims away. The eardrums of males of these two strongly territorial species are markedly enlarged, being much wider than the diameter of their

Leopard frog. NATIONAL MUSEUM OF CANADA, A. G. AUSTIN

Gray treefrog. GARY ALLEN

Spring peeper. NORM LIGHTFOOT

eye. In females and immature males the eardrums are about the same diameter as the eye. Males of both species have bright yellow throats and undersides. The largest and probably the most dominant males have the largest eardrums and the most extensive yellow colouring. Both of these characteristics presumably are important in recognizing rivals and assessing whether or not they can be displaced from the better breeding sites.

The often secretive habits of most amphibians throughout the year, their frequent occupation of habitats which are low and wet, and their peak conspicuous activity at night or in damp weather, all combine to make studying them difficult for many naturalists. Working against amphibians, too, is the perception that they are of little use to man. Nonetheless, bullfrogs, and occasionally the largest individuals of other frogs, are hunted by humans. Generally, only the legs are eaten, by people who have acquired a taste for them or who regard them as *haute cuisine*. Bullfrogs are now protected in Ontario by a law which governs numbers and sizes that can be taken. Many small frogs and some salamanders become fish bait. Quantities of bullfrogs, leopard frogs, and one particular salamander, the mudpuppy, are collected by biological supply firms for sale to high schools and universities to demonstrate the anatomy of lower vertebrates. Many also are used in the study of embryology and physiology.

While direct uses of amphibians by humans are limited, it is increasingly evident that amphibians may be important biological indicators of the effects of acid rain and other pollutants. Amphibian egg or larval deaths occur when water has low pH values or when concentrations of some metals in the water increase. Because many species breed in spring melt-water and rain-fed ponds, they are particularly vulnerable to yearly changes in the addition of these contaminants.

Thus, the future of amphibians in Ontario depends not only upon the obvious need for conservation of their wetland breeding sites, but upon the maintenance of uncontaminated ecosystems.

Checklist of Ontario Amphibians

SPECIES	SCIENTIFIC NAME	DISTRIBUTION
Salamanders		
mudpuppy	**Necturus maculosus**	S & C
eastern newt	**Notophthalmus viridescens**	S, C, & NW
blue-spotted	**Ambystoma laterale**	Widespread
Jefferson	**Ambystoma jeffersonianum**	SW
small-mouthed	**Ambystoma texanum**	Pelee Island
yellow-spotted	**Ambystoma maculatum**	S & C
tiger	**Ambystoma tigrinum**	Pelee[1]
dusky	**Desmognathus fuscus**	SW[1]
two-lined	**Eurycea bislineata**	C & NW
spring	**Gyrinophilus porphyriticus**	SW[1]
four-toed	**Hemidactylium scutatum**	S, C, & NE
eastern redbacked	**Plethodon cinereus**	S, C, & NE
red	**Pseudotriton ruber**	?[2]
Frogs		
American toad	**Bufo americanus**	Widespread
Woodhouse's (Fowler's) toad	**Bufo woodhousii**	Lake Erie
spring peeper	**Hyla crucifer**	Widespread
gray treefrog	**Hyla versicolor**	S, C, & NW
striped chorus frog	**Pseudacris triseriata**	S, NW
northern cricket frog	**Acris crepitans**	Pelee
bullfrog	**Rana catesbeiana**	S & C
green frog	**Rana clamitans**	S & C
pickerel frog	**Rana palustris**	S & C
leopard frog	**Rana pipiens**	Widespread
mink frog	**Rana septentrionalis**	C & N
wood frog	**Rana sylvatica**	Widespread

[1] Ontario population possibly extirpated.
[2] Probably introduced and not persistent in Ontario.

S – southern part of the province
C – central part of the province
N – northern part of the province
E – eastern part of the province
W – western part of the province

Once They Ruled
The Reptiles of Ontario
Francis R. Cook

The word *reptile* conjures many images from the past, none more vivid than that of the gigantic dinosaurs that vanished at the end of the Cretaceous, 65 million years ago. But the less spectacular reptile groups living today all have fossil records that run far back into Triassic antiquity, over 213 million years ago. Both turtles, now represented by 222 species, and crocodilians, today with only 22 species, were more diverse in the distant past.

In contrast, snakes and lizards – the Squamata – are comparatively modern, attaining their greatest diversity and success since the Cretaceous. Their combined total of over 5,700 living species is even greater than that of mammals. Although their greatest variation is in the tropics, many widespread and abundant species occur in the temperate zones as well.

Reptiles in Ontario are represented by sixteen species of snakes, eight species of turtles, and one lizard. Lizards are the most common reptiles on Earth today, with about three thousand species, but the single Ontario species is the only representative of its group in all of eastern Canada. All these twenty-five species of reptiles presently in Ontario spread into it from refugia south of the Great Lakes after the retreat of the glaciers. Some turtles moved north from the Mississippi drainage. Some snakes appear to be remnants of a prairie and marshland fauna that extended eastward in a warm, arid peninsula across southwestern Ontario some 5,000 years ago.

Evolutionary Adaptations

Reptiles, in common with amphibians, are unable to maintain their body temperature internally and so are dependent for heat on their surroundings. Reptiles tend to require higher temperatures than amphibians and commonly bask in the sunshine to warm themselves, particularly in the spring and fall. They often adjust their body temperature precisely by moving from sun to shade or back as they heat and cool. Like amphibians, reptiles in the north must hibernate in shelter below ground or in water underneath the ice. When their body temperatures fall below 10°C, they become increasingly inefficient at seeking and digesting food, or escaping from predators.

Externally, dry skins covered with scales or plates immediately distinguish reptiles from amphibians, which have moister, unprotected skin. Reptiles have few skin glands, and therefore lose little moisture. As a consequence they are quite active and successful in dry climates, although they thrive in moist ones as well.

Hearing is much less important to reptiles than are the other senses. Although they will sometimes hiss when threatened, none of our species uses sound to attract mates. Perhaps ancient lineages developed sound more fully, as is suggested by the resounding bellow of alligators. Sight and odour, however, play a role in recognition of both mates and prey.

The most spectacular evolutionary advance accomplished by reptiles was the development of the large-yolked, shelled egg. This advance, together with the development of organs for internal fertilization, permitted freedom from water or very moist environments for reproduction. A further advance in some lizards and snakes was a delay in egg-laying until the embryo was partly developed. This delay has been carried farthest in some lizards and snakes which give birth to fully developed young.

Turtles

Turtles, with their unique encasing shell (carapace above and plastron below), are universally recognizable. They had already accomplished the anatomical innovation of accommodating

Common snapping turtle. GARY ALLEN

their limbs and associated structures inside their modified rib cages before the first forms were preserved as fossils.

The reproductively conservative turtles all lay shelled eggs on land. In Ontario this activity occurs from May through to early July. All but the stinkpot, our smallest turtle, dig nests. These nests are usually as deep as the female's hind legs can reach, and afterward are carefully covered with soil or debris. Young turtles hatch in the late summer or fall after an incubation period of up to ninety days, and may dig out of the nest almost immediately if the weather is warm. If the weather is cool, however, they may overwinter, not emerging until the following spring. The northern distribution of turtles may be limited by a combination of summers too short for complete development or emergence of the young, followed by severely cold winters with deep frost that kills the eggs or hatchlings in the nest.

Summer temperatures dictate not only the length of the incubation, but in many species of turtles, temperature even determines their sex. High incubation temperatures produce all females, more moderate ones, all males.

The eggs of the large snapping and softshell turtles are round, like miniature ping-pong balls, but all the smaller species in Ontario lay oval eggs. Shape may be influenced by the need for a large yolk to assure adequate nourishment of the embryo as well as by the restraints of the turtles' inflexible construction which, in a small species, leaves a relatively small space for the passage of eggs. Snappers lay the most eggs, usually from twenty to forty. Stinkpots and spotted turtles lay only two to five eggs. In Ontario, most turtles deposit one clutch a year, but occasionally two clutches may be produced by some painted turtles.

Turtles seem to have a universal appeal – with one exception, the snapping turtle. This often-maligned species has three strikes against it: some people regard it as excellent eating; it is often perceived as a major predator on

Box turtle, an introduced species from the northern United States. POINT PELEE NATIONAL PARK, B. REYNOLDS

ducklings; and it has, to human eyes, a prehistorically ugly appearance and belligerent disposition when surprised on land. Consequently, it is persecuted; local populations have been reduced in some areas of southern Ontario.

Snapping turtles can grow shells of up to forty-seven centimetres in length and appear even larger because of their massive heads, muscular necks and limbs, and long tails which are vertically studded with prominent bony plates. Large snappers often weigh ten kilograms; an exceptional one weighed twenty-two and a half kilograms! They inhabit almost any standing water: marshes, ponds, ditches, lakes, creeks, rivers. A few of the northernmost records may represent hardy adults that have wandered beyond the limit of successful reproduction. They are most agile and secure in water, but every year females must trek overland to nest. On land, they will face prospective danger squarely and will lunge out at any provocation simply because they are at such a disadvantage, a trait that provokes people into killing them needlessly.

In contrast to those who torment or kill snappers, others will stop when they see one crossing a busy highway, remove it to the relative safety of the ditch, and ignore its savage attempts to prevent handling. If a snapper must be carried, it should be held by the wide rear margins of the shell. Its long neck can reach about one-third of the way back over its shell, and its razor-sharp beak must be avoided. The sturdy-looking tail is not a good handle; it cannot bear the weight of the turtle without the possibility of strain and injury to the vertebrae.

The future of the snapping turtle may be better assured than in the past because quotas and seasons are being formulated to control potentially devastating harvests. The extent of its predation on ducklings has been exaggerated and is offset anyway by the positive environmental benefits of the snapper's taste for a wide variety of coarse, non-game fish and dead animals.

All other turtles in Ontario are now completely protected by provincial regulations to assure they will not be overharvested for food or pets. None may be collected or kept without a permit.

The most inconspicuous and smallest turtle in Ontario is the relatively secretive stinkpot, or musk turtle,

Blanding's turtle. POINT PELEE NATIONAL PARK, DON ROSS

Spotted turtle. JOHN THEBERGE

named for the foul odour it may release when defending itself. This brownish, nondescript turtle has a large head but a maximum shell length of under fourteen centimetres. Its shell is distinctively narrow and high-domed. It is restricted to southern Ontario, where it frequents the shallows of creeks, rivers, and lakes.

Ontario has six species of pond and river turtles belonging to the family Emydidae, a group which is widely distributed over the northern continents of the world. The best known species, because of its abundance, wide distribution, and conspicuous behaviour is the painted turtle. Groups of these turtles often bask in the open on logs, rocks, or secluded banks, sometimes piled on top of one another. The turtle's name follows from its colourful appearance: head, limbs, and tail are streaked with yellow in the race occupying northwestern Ontario, with red and yellow in the one occurring in southern and central Ontario. The former race apparently spread east from the Prairie provinces.

The other five turtles in the family Emydidae are the map, Blanding's, spotted, wood, and box turtles. Map turtles, which frequent deep water, have low, flat shells. Their heads and limbs are striped with yellow, and their upper shell has a reticulated appearance like a detailed map. Blanding's and spotted turtles live in the quiet, shallow water of marshes and small ponds in southern and central Ontario. The Blanding's is the larger of the two, and has a vividly distinctive yellow throat. The orange-limbed wood turtles of central Ontario frequent sandy or gravelly rivers but spend much of the summer on land, where they are particularly fond of strawberries when available. The few records of the entirely terrestrial box turtle are all from extreme southern Ontario, but possibly they represent pets that have escaped from the adjacent United States. This turtle is com-

Spiny softshell turtle on a Rondeau beach. P. A. WOODLIFFE

mon south of the Great Lakes and is often picked up as it crosses roads.

Spiny softshell turtles are representatives of an old and worldwide family. They occur in some of the larger rivers and in the shallow, sandy waters of Lake Erie. Softshells resemble pancakes in outline, with flat, flexible shells that lack scutes (growth plates). They are exceedingly shy, spending much of their time resting on the bottom, partly covered with sand, their long necks elevated so that their projecting nostrils can just break the water surface. When cornered, they are at least as vicious as snapping turtles.

Lizards

The only lizard in Ontario is the five-lined skink. It has an incongruous bright blue tail which fades to grey with age, particularly in males. Being a reptile, it is encased in scales, which distinguishes it immediately from the soft-skinned salamanders. In contrast to the generally secretive habits of salamanders, skinks are most active on sunny days. When disturbed in the open, they instantly take cover. Their tails will readily break off if grabbed, but a replacement will regenerate. Skink distribution appears to be discontinuous in scattered populations. They lay eggs in rotting logs or under stones. Females apparently stay with the eggs until they hatch.

Snakes

Ontario's snakes belong to two families: typical snakes and pit-vipers. Our two species of vipers are both poisonous. Both have rattles: hard, thin, interlocked segments at the tip of the tails that buzz when vibrated. The large timber rattlesnake, a colourful black-and-yellow mottled species, can attain a length of 189 centimetres. It once occurred in southern Ontario, but its presence was last verified in the Niagara Gorge in 1941. Its loss leaves the much smaller Massasauga as Ontario's only dangerous snake. Massasaugas rarely exceed 76 centimetres, and the maximum length for one is 100 centimetres. They are grey snakes with dark brownish or black blotches, a rattle, and a prominent pit between the eye and the nostril. Their range has been greatly altered, and although they probably never did live farther east than the Muskoka Lakes, they are most often found today in the Georgian Bay area. In southwestern Ontario, only a few fragments of former populations remain between Lake Huron and Lake Erie and on the Niagara Peninsula. They are protected in Georgian Bay Islands National Park, where long-term study of their life-history and movements is an important park function.

Massasaugas are generally lowland snakes but will hunt frogs and rodents in uplands as well. Their potent poison is ideal for subduing small prey and is injected by a pair of hollow, hypodermic-like, curved fangs at the front of the mouth. These teeth are connected by ducts to modified salivary glands which manufacture the poison. The poison acts by breaking down red blood cells and other tissue. Effective antivenin is available in all regional hospitals within the snake's range; if one is bitten, medical attention should be sought as soon as possible. However, snakebite can be prevented by wearing stout hiking shoes and exercising caution in placing feet or hands. Massasaugas are not aggressive and generally will retreat from any disturbance, only striking when threatened, cornered, or surprised.

The fourteen harmless snakes in Ontario all may attempt to bite in defence, but most are too small to be successful. Many will vibrate their tails when agitated, and if they are lying on dry leaves, can produce a buzz easily mistaken for a rattlesnake. Most of these snakes simply grab and swallow their prey: fish, amphibians, or invertebrates. Three species, however, the rat, fox, and milk snakes feed mainly on small mammals. They wrap one or two coils of their body around their prey, constrict, and thus quickly suffocate it with little struggle.

Three species of garter snakes occur in Ontario. All have similar patterns: a black or brown background marked with three prominent light, longitudinal stripes. This pattern is ideal for active snakes which often bask or hunt by day in open habitats. Stripes are confusing to predators who hunt by sight, as they make it difficult for them to focus on one part of the body. Any hesitation by the attacker may allow the

Five-lined skinks. GARY ALLEN

The Massasauga rattlesnake, Ontario's only poisonous snake. NIAGARA ESCARPMENT COMMISSION

Smooth green snake. DON GUNN

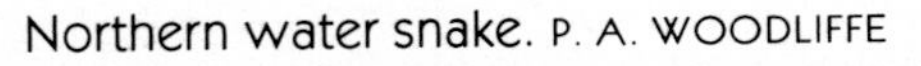

Northern water snake. P. A. WOODLIFFE

snake to flow out of sight, the converging stripes on the disappearing tip of the tail signalling that the intended prey has magically vanished.

The common garter snake is the most abundant snake in the province. The subspecies represented in Ontario is called the eastern garter snake, with minor differences from a maritime subspecies and four western subspecies. This snake has the largest litters, up to eighty-five though normally fewer. It also varies the most in appearance. Stripes may be bright or dull yellow, or sometimes bluish, tan, grey, or red on a variable checkered background. A stripeless jet black phase with a white chin is often present in populations occurring along Lake Erie at Long Point, Point Pelee, and Pelee Island and has been introduced on Toronto Island. Common garter snakes are generalists, frequenting both terrestrial and aquatic-edge habitat. They eat fish, amphibians, and some invertebrates, particularly earthworms.

The other two species of garter snakes, the ribbon snake and the Butler's garter snake, are both much smaller: a maximum of 96 and 69 centimetres respectively, in comparison with 124 for the eastern garter snake. The sharply striped ribbon snake occurs in southern and central Ontario along the margins of lakes, streams, and ponds where it feeds on amphibians. The brownish Butler's garter snake is confined to southwestern Ontario in relics of former prairie. This snake feeds largely on earthworms.

Two species of water snakes inhabit Ontario: the northern water snake and the queen snake. The northern water snake, marked with alternating bars of dark and light brown, grows to at least 135 centimetres. It ranges through southern and central Ontario. On Pelee and Middle islands in Lake Erie a distinctive race occurs that is totally grey or barred dorsally and on its sides. Like most garter snakes, northern water snakes feed primarily on amphibians and fish. Water snakes are particularly efficient aquatic hunters but often bring their prey out of the water to swallow it. When not hunting, they bask or find shelter on land.

The brown-striped queen snake is smaller, up to about 92 centimetres, and slimmer. It mainly frequents rivers where it feeds almost exclusively on crayfish, searching for soft-bodied individuals that have recently shed their exoskeletons. It is found along rivers in southwestern Ontario and also at Point Pelee and Long Point. Queen snakes are secretive, and when not hunting are usually found under stones near water.

Two water snake relatives are the descriptively named redbelly snake and the brown snake, attaining maximum lengths of 41 and 53 centimetres respectively – both relatively small snakes. The redbelly is the most widespread, ranging to central and northwestern Ontario. It lives in forests and clearings where it feeds mainly on slugs and, to some extent, on earthworms. The brown snake does not range as far north. Either species may be locally abundant but rarely in the same locality.

Most Ontario snakes quickly glide away from disturbance, but the eastern hognose snake will face danger with a fierce display, spreading its neck and raising the front half of its body. It may even strike out, but always with its mouth closed. If this display fails to frighten whatever is threatening it, the hognose snake rolls over, lolls out its tongue, and gives the appearance of having suddenly died. If left undisturbed, however, it will right itself and crawl away. The hognose has a thick body, and can attain a length of more than a metre. It lives in sandy areas in southwestern and central Ontario, where it feeds primarily on toads.

The two "giants" among Ontario snakes are the black rat snake and the fox snake, attaining maximum lengths of 256 and 174 centimetres respectively. The black rat snake is a woodland and forest-edge species, black as an adult with only a trace of the blotched

Eastern hognose snake. GARY ALLEN

pattern that is characteristic of its young. Its range in Ontario is fragmented into two portions: the Rideau Lakes region and the southwestern part of the province. Extensive clearing has reduced its numbers in the latter area, but thriving populations survive in the former. Black rat snakes are excellent climbers and occasionally raid bird nests for eggs and young, but they also hunt in clearings for mice. The brown, blotched fox snake occurs mainly in marshes around Lake Erie and Georgian Bay. The former extent of its habitat has been steadily reduced by marsh drainage for agriculture. Both of these large snakes are made vulnerable by their very size, which makes them conspicuous to most humans and terrifying to some. Actually they are inoffensive.

All of the snakes discussed have *keeled* body scales, that is, scales with a longitudinal raised ridge. These keeled scales are weakest in the black rat and fox snakes, totally lacking on their lower sides, but are very pronounced on the other species. The value of the keeled scales is not understood, though often they are most pronounced on aquatic species. The eastern hognose snake is an exception, however, and there are strongly keeled prairie species as well. In contrast, the remaining four snakes in Ontario all have smooth scales with no trace of keels.

The smooth green snake is bright green above and white or yellowish below, with no other markings. It is found mainly in fields and brushy areas where its colour matches its surroundings so well that it is rarely seen. It feeds primarily on spiders and soft-bodied insects.

The ringneck snake is a small, particularly secretive woodland species, dull grey above with a bright yellow neck ring and yellow belly with black dots. It feeds on salamanders and sometimes other snakes.

The eastern milk snake's name comes from its supposed habit of milking cows. This myth originated because the snake readily frequents barns; however, it is there to pursue rodents, not cows. In fact, no cow would stand the touch of its needle-sharp recurved teeth, but the human willingness to persecute snakes will allow some people to accept the flimsiest of pretexts. This species is similar in appearance to the fox snake, but smaller. It is more widespread, not tied to marshy or wetland habitats. It feeds mainly on small mammals, but it belongs to the widespread king snake group, whose members are not averse to eating other snakes.

The rarest Ontario snake is the fast-moving blue racer, a generally nervous, active snake, which takes a variety of prey from insects to small mammals and birds. The adults are bluish, but the young are blotched. It is a snake of fields, clearings, and similar open areas, and once occurred more widely than its last surviving Ontario population today on Pelee Island might indicate, though it was never widespread. Some of its mainland decline has been accelerated by its habit of rearing up to see over the top of surrounding grasses when disturbed. When the mowing machine came into general use, it declined.

Hognose, rat, fox, green, ringneck, milk snakes, and the blue racer all lay eggs, depositing them in rotting logs or under rocks in early summer to have them hatch later that same summer. All other Ontario snakes, including the Massasauga, bear living young. At hatching or birth, young snakes, like newly hatched lizards and turtles, fend for themselves and receive no maternal care or attention. The common garter snake's retention of eggs allows it to keep embryo temperature high by moving to the warmest area on cool days. This, along with its varied diet and habitat flexibility, contributes to its ability to range well north of other species.

Because of their prey preferences, snakes are either beneficial to man's economic interests, or largely of no consequence. This fact alone should justify a far more positive attitude toward them. Their uniqueness – unblinking, lidless eyes covered by a transparent scale; undulating movements, possibly caused by their 140 to over 400 vertebrae; and constantly flicking, forked tongues, which can pick particles from the air – place them in a world differently felt and perceived than ours, but, because of this, a world fascinating for us to try to understand.

Checklist of Ontario Reptiles

SPECIES	SCIENTIFIC NAME	DISTRIBUTION
Turtles		
common snapping turtle	**Chelydra serpentina**	S, C, & NW
stinkpot turtle	**Sternotherus odoratus**	S & C
painted turtle	**Chrysemys picta**	S, C, & NW
map turtle	**Graptemys geographica**	S & C
Blanding's turtle	**Emydoidea blandingii**	S & C
spotted turtle	**Clemmys guttata**	S & C
wood turtle	**Clemmys insculpta**	S & C
eastern box turtle	**Terrapene carolina**	S (introduced)
spiny shoftshell turtle	**Trionyx spiniferus**	S & C
Lizards		
five-lined skink	**Eumeces fasciatus**	S & C
Snakes		
timber rattlesnake	**Crotalus horridus**	S[1]
massasauga rattlesnake	**Sistrurus catenatus**	S
common garter snake	**Thamnophis sirtalis**	S, C, & N
eastern ribbon snake	**Thamnophis sauritus**	S & C
Butler's garter snake	**Thamnophis butleri**	S
northern water snake	**Nerodia sipedon**	S & C
queen snake	**Regina septemvittata**	S
redbelly snake	**Storeria occipitomaculata**	S, C, & NW
brown snake	**Storeria dekayi**	S & C
hognose Snake	**Heterodon platyrhinos**	S & C
rat snake	**Elaphe obsoleta**	S & C
fox snake	**Elaphe vulpina**	S
smooth green snake	**Opheodrys vernalis**	S, C, & NW
ringneck snake	**Diadophis punctatus**	S & C
milk snake	**Lampropeltis triangulum**	S & C
blue racer	**Coluber constrictor**	S

S – southern part of the province
C – central part of the province
N – northern part of the province
E – eastern part of the province

Wild Wings
The Birds of Ontario

Paul F. J. Eagles

As first light creeps over the eastern sky, the dawn chorus of the birds welcomes another day. The plaintive call of a white-throated sparrow – "Oh, sweet Canada, Canada, Canada" – drifts from the forested edge of the nearby lake. The flute-like notes of a hermit thrush flow out of the spruce forest, and two winter wrens weave through their intricate, tinkling songs in an attempt to drive each other away from a particularly big pine stump that will soon make an ideal nest site for one of them. The haunting call of a loon, far out in the lake, echoes through the mist, and a distant loon answers from a lake beyond.

Nothing is more enthralling but ephemeral, full of pulsing vitality but brief and fleeting, than the spring chorus of birds in the northern forest. It is a feature of the landscape that in some way every Canadian secretly treasures.

Wild birds inhabit all parts of Ontario. The cold ocean shores of Hudson Bay provide habitat for nesting red-throated loons, snow geese, whimbrels. The broad sweep of the conifer forests harbour boreal chickadees, red and white-winged crossbills, three-toed woodpeckers. The fields of southern Ontario are home to eastern meadowlarks, bobolinks, vesper sparrows, and many more. The trees of the cities and towns provide for mourning doves, northern orioles, rose-breasted grosbeaks, and an aggressive newcomer, the house finch. In every conceivable habitat, birds are there, nesting, singing, flying, and making a living.

Slightly more than three hundred species of birds are known to breed in Ontario. Another approximately one hundred species have been recorded as visitors at various times of the year. Many of these non-breeders stop over every year on their way through to some other part of the world, such as the high Arctic. Others arrive suddenly from far-away places, perhaps blown off course by a storm. They stay awhile and disappear.

Strategies for Survival

The time of year most influential to the welfare of birds in Ontario is winter. Birds either adapt successfully to cold and snow or they perish. There are only two basic strategies: to exploit the limited food sources (overwintering berries, seeds, or insects trapped in bark, carrion, or prey) or simply to leave. A very large number migrate to more favourable southern climates. Birds are unique as a group because of their physical ability to travel long distances in short times.

Ontario people take pride in the arrival of "their" warblers, orioles, tanagers, buntings, and other species that stream across the Great Lakes and into the province each April and May. But it is probably more correct to consider these summer species as truly tropical birds that leave their preferred habitat in steaming jungles only briefly to raise their young in relatively unoccupied environments. As early as July some of the tropical migrants quietly leave again and start their arduous journey back "home." Their leaving is much less obvious than their conspicuous arrival. With breeding over, song dwindles, and many moult into subdued winter plumage. On clear, calm, starry nights in August you can hear

Rose-breasted grosbeak. DON GUNN

Eastern bluebird. I. JELKIN

tiny "peeps" up in the sky from the passing multitudes.

The conditions to be met for successful long-distance migration seem impossible. Above all else, an individual bird must be in sufficiently good physical condition to carry it through a journey of thousands of kilometres. The supplies of fat must be adequate to provide flight energy, and the feathers must be capable of protecting against storm and temperature as well as sustaining hundreds of hours of flight. To lay down extra fat and grow a new crop of feathers, many migratory birds spend several months in their nesting grounds after the young have left the nest.

As well, birds face seemingly insurmountable problems of navigation. How is the destination learned? How does the bird know what route to fly? What height? What areas to avoid? When to move on? While the answers are not known, research indicates that a substantial amount of genetically inherited memory is involved. Perhaps the pattern of migration is linked all the way back to early drift of the continents.

We do know that different species use different environmental clues for navigation. Pigeons can detect and orient from the Earth's gravitational field. Warblers, migrating at night, use the stars as a map. Hawks appear to recognize the points of the compass and migrate by day, using their eyes to carefully avoid bodies of water that would be dangerous if a touch-down was required. Most remarkable of all is the recent discovery that some shorebirds have the ability to hear very low frequencies of sound – ultrasound. These sounds have extremely long wavelengths and travel for hundreds of kilometres. They are generated by phenomena such as thunder, or ocean waves crashing on beaches, or wind roaring through mountain passes. The ability to hear such sounds provides potentially valuable information for a migrating bird. Scientists now speculate that some birds migrating through the mid-continent may hear the Atlantic beaches and the resonant tones coming from Rocky Mountain passes – simultaneously!

The precision of migration is incredible. In September, the tiny indigo bunting that has sung all summer from the forest edges near my house in southern Ontario travels for a month to the very same opening in the rain forest in Central America where it spent the previous winter. Then, the following spring, it wings back to the exact same woods in Ontario to breed. This feat of navigation resides in a creature weighing about fifteen grams! And of course, the same skill is demonstrated by millions of individuals, of hundreds of species, each year.

Most Ontario residents do not realize that their province is also a winter home for many birds that nest farther north. These hardy creatures find the winters too harsh on the northern tundra and forests but are capable of finding food in Ontario's more moderate climate. Snow buntings and rough-legged hawks appear each year in southern Ontario, as they leave the more northerly winter behind.

Despite the adaptability of birds, the invasion of Ontario by Europeans has caused the largest ecological change since the last ice age and has affected birds dramatically. The first species to feel the effect were large and easy to kill. The trumpeter swan, a huge bird with a resonant voice, was hunted to extinction in the province. The whooping crane, always uncommon, also was killed off. Fortunately, a few individuals of these species survived in isolated spots elsewhere in northern Canada. The provincial wildlife agency is now attempting to reintroduce trumpeter swans and whooping cranes and their wild music back into the province after decades of silence.

Indigo bunting. DON GUNN

But the greatest loss of all was a total one. The earliest European settlers reported that in the late 1700s the sky would be darkened for several days when passenger pigeons were migrating. It took a little over one hundred years to annihilate the species. Now, to try to sense the drama that was once one of Ontario's most exciting wildlife spectacles, one has to view mounted passenger pigeons in a museum. As lifelike as they may appear, these few stuffed bags of feathers can never substitute for the real creatures that are gone forever.

Because Ontario is a large place, however, most species of birds were able to survive the initial onslaught. Some species have even benefited, taking advantage of new human-created niches. The shift in the south from forest to field provided tremendous opportunities for birds that nested in open country. Bobolinks, eastern meadowlarks, and upland sandpipers increased many-fold as their preferred breeding habitat inadvertently was created by man. In the south, too, forest hawks such as goshawks and broad-winged hawks were replaced by the kestrels and red-tailed hawks of open country.

Europeans also brought with them city birds from the old country. House sparrows, rock doves, and starlings especially became very successful transplants, and are now well – perhaps too well – established.

So, Ontario lost one species of bird permanently and several other species temporarily. But it has been fortunate in retaining the vast majority of species, and has gained field species from prairie grasslands and urban species from European towns.

A Sensitive Reflection of Quality

All wild creatures reflect the environment in which they live. Birds are particularly good environmental indicators because they exploit such a wide range of conditions. This fact is well known by scientists who use birds as "instruments" to detect environmental change. In fact, most people who watch birds soon get an intuitive feel for the relationship between wild birds and their environment.

One of the most famous examples of the ability of birds to signal changes in the environment took place in Ontario in the 1960s. For millennia the protected western bay of Lake Ontario contained extensive marshes, open water, and isolated beaches. As the city of Hamilton developed and grew, the amount of natural habitat was reduced by heavy industry which took over the shores. Most of the wetland bird species ultimately were limited to a handful of small, protected parks, but a few moved into man-made places. Small rocky islands had been created in Burlington Bay for the construction of hydro towers. These islands proved to be ideal nesting sites for certain species of gulls and terns which fished in the neighbouring harbour for food for their young. In the late 1960s, scientists discovered that the young of these fishing species had developed gross deformities – crossed bills, blindness, and bone defects. Their rate of death was high.

Extensive study, debate, and research showed that the birds of Hamilton harbour were showing the effects of chemical pollution in the surrounding waters. The older birds collected fish, each with a little bit of pollution. After being fed many such fish, the young birds built up sufficient levels of chemicals in their bodies to cause the damage.

The story of chemical pollution in these water birds is a dramatic example showing quite well that animals, including humans, ultimately reflect the quality of the environment in which they live.

Northern Outpost: The Tundra

Ontario still has many high-quality environments with intact avifauna. The top of the province is a thin strip, up to fifty kilometres wide, of tundra along an ocean shore. This area of Arctic climate contains the southernmost tundra ecosystem in the world. The short, cool summers provide a sudden pulse of growth which is exploited by some species of birds with specific adaptations. They must be hardy and capable of incubating eggs in below-freezing temperatures. They must be strong fliers to travel long distances for food and to withstand the omnipresent strong Arctic winds. They must be able to breed quickly in the short time available. Usually, the young are precocious and capable of considerable movement, such as walking, swimming, and foraging, within hours after they hatch.

Fewer species of birds breed on Ontario's tundra than in other more southern habitats. Shorebirds and waterfowl, both with precocial young, dominate among tundra birds. Relatively fewer *passerines* (perching birds), such as thrushes, warblers, finches, and sparrows with young that stay in the nest until fully fledged, live there, although a few of the latter species live in shrubby environments. The adaptations of a few species can illustrate the survival strategies of others.

The red-throated loon, for example, is a bird of far northern lakes. In the short summer along Ontario's Hudson Bay shore, this smallish loon attempts to raise a brood of young before winter freezes the lakes. To save time, the birds pair up before they arrive on the breeding grounds. The lakes are still frozen when the adults first visit their intended nesting sites. Messy nests of wet vegetation and mud are used for a month's incubation, which often begins before all the snow is melted. Food is found on long-distance trips to the open sea or to river mouths.

Young red-throated loons swim soon after hatching. Parents of all loon species often protect their chicks from water-borne predators by carrying them on their backs as they swim. The chicks grow quickly on a fish diet, reaching adult size by early September. By the time ice closes out their fishing grounds, most young loons are capable of the sustained flight necessary to carry them to wintering grounds along the Atlantic coast, from southern Newfoundland to Florida.

Red-throated loon. DON GUNN

In Ontario, red-throated loons are known only to the few hardy birders that visit the Hudson Bay Lowlands in summer, or brave spring and fall storms along the Great Lakes for a glimpse of them bobbing far out on the waves with a flock of horned grebes and other diving ducks. But another tundra-nester, the snowy owl, is seen more often, especially in periodic years when winter lemming populations on the tundra are low.

Often a crash in lemming populations takes place right after a period of high lemming numbers. The resultant food shortage sends snowy owls south looking for mousier pastures. The invasion of large white owls is awaited eagerly by naturalists, but it occurs only every six or seven years.

The snowy owl is a daytime, open-country species, unlike most other owl species which are creatures of the deep forest and the night. Snowy owls have evolved various means to survive on the tundra throughout the year. They are very heavily feathered, including a thick layer on legs and feet. They can hunt throughout both the brightness of the non-stop summer days and the dark, long, winter nights. And they demonstrate one of the most sophisticated means of birth control known.

The male snowy owl must go on a gift-giving spree before the female will mate with him. He must catch and present her with a large number of lemmings in a very short time. If he achieves this, she is suitably impressed. If not, she will not mate with him. Thus, no energy is wasted on producing young that might starve, or if they survived, might compete with the adults the following winter for scarce food supplies.

Another northern nester is the whimbrel, a large, robust shorebird with a grotesquely out-of-proportion, long, curved beak used to probe mudflats for invertebrate food. Whimbrels owe their tundra success to their ability to find food in partially submerged mudflats, and to their strong flight that carries them annually all the way from the beaches of South and Central America to the northern tundra. Adults vigorously defend their nest areas with aggressive attacks on any bird or mammal that poses a threat to the young.

Whimbrels and ruddy turnstones.
DON GUNN

Heartland: The Boreal Forest

South of the tundra, many more species of birds breed and live in the vast boreal forest that occupies most of Ontario. Among the spire-shaped spruces, the many ponds, marshes, rivers, bogs, and fens all provide an abundant diversity of habitat and summer supply of insects and other foods. Some species of birds stay all year; many others come for only the warmest months. The boreal forest is heavily utilized by the wood warblers – small, brightly coloured birds that breed in vast numbers. Because this forest contains only a few species of trees, insect outbreaks tend to be of immense proportions. When the spruce budworm finds thousands of hectares of suitable forage, it quickly takes advantage of the situation. And so do some birds. In areas of budworm outbreak, the warblers, vireos,

Bufflehead. DON GUNN

thrushes, and sparrows find plentiful larva to feed their voracious young.

Typical of the warblers is the bay-breasted warbler, a neotropical migrant that travels from Central and South America to the great green north to take advantage of the copious insect-life to be found there. This tiny warbler with white, black, and brown plumage, spends our fall, winter, and spring in company with scarlet macaws, resplendent quetzals, and tropical parula warblers of the rain forests. But in early spring the lengthening days signal the bird's pineal gland to release hormones that start the mental and physical transformation into a migrating bird. Some time in April it begins the long journey over ocean, forests, deserts, farmlands, cities, and lakes, ultimately arriving in the conifer forests of northern Ontario.

If the bay-breasted survives the storms, predators, tall buildings, and strange food along the way, it seeks a patch of forest with sufficient food to raise a nest of young. An ideal patch is one experiencing an outbreak of spruce budworm. While forest managers dislike the outbreaks because they kill large tracts of forests, the bay-breasted warbler is of a different opinion. In a good outbreak, it may successfully raise two broods!

The bufflehead is a small duck that uses the abundant ponds and lakes throughout the boreal forest. Small flocks arrive at the forest ponds as soon as the first leads appear in the ice. The early adult males vigorously defend their small territories against other males who arrive later. Small lakes will harbour one pair of buffleheads, while larger lakes will provide room for more.

Buffleheads are unusual for ducks in that they nest in tree-holes. Old woodpecker holes are ideal. Such a site provides good protection from both large predators and biting insects. Research has suggested that the ability to escape the majority of ground-flying mosquitoes and blackflies may be a considerable benefit of nesting in trees. When the young ducks are partially fledged they jump out of the nest and fall to the ground. They then form up in a platoon under mother's care and walk through the forest to the lake.

Because the amount of breeding habitat for buffleheads is immense, they are still abundant in Ontario. Hunting does not appear to have reduced their numbers. However, one can only speculate on the future impacts that acid rain will have on boreal lakes and all the species of wildlife dependent on them.

Phantom of the boreal forest is the great gray owl – large, secretive, mysterious, and seldom seen. Several obvious adaptations enable it to live permanently among the spruces and firs of the conifer forests. A very thick blanket of feathers provides winter insulation. Acute hearing, even more so than that of other owls, allows it to detect a mouse under snow up to a metre deep. Observers have been startled to see a great gray owl dive into fluffy snow so deeply that it disappears from sight, and emerge with a squirrel or mouse impaled in its talons. But one of the owl's most important adaptations is its wide individual range, ensuring that each bird has a greater chance to find sufficient prey during the long winter season.

Splendid Diversity:
The Northern Deciduous Forest

The northern deciduous forests that stretch across central and southern Ontario south of the boreal forest produce copious supplies of berries, fleshy seeds, nuts, and invertebrate life – all resulting in an even greater richness of birds. Among the many species of passerines here, the sight of a scarlet tanager flashing through the canopy of maples overhead seems a temporarily misplaced piece of tropical splendour. For some reason, this one species of magnificently coloured bird, among many tropical relatives has evolved a migratory habit. Tens of thousands of scarlet tanagers leave the tropics each April to arrive in the Great Lakes forests in May.

For breeding, scarlet tanagers need large tracts of mature, deciduous forests with a closed canopy and no clearings or openings. Forest clearance has left fewer and fewer sites that meet their exacting requirements; most woodlots now are too small. A pair of breeding scarlet tanagers in a southern Ontario woodlot today is a sign of quality, the red seal of a premium ecosystem. Such woodlots still occur, fortunately, in large parks, some private woods, places along the Niagara Escarpment, and some steep-walled river valleys, as well as more continuous forests on the southern parts of the Pre-cambrian Shield.

Other species have benefited from the scalping of the land south of the Shield. The rufous-sided towhee is a brush-loving species, more often heard – with its bell-like "chewink" – than seen among the tangle. Though the towhee normally migrates south to the southern United States or northern Central America at the first sign of snow, the recent increase in bird feeders has tempted more and more of them to remain in Ontario all winter.

Great gray owl. DON GUNN

Cardinals, too, are altering their traditional ranges. Unknown one hundred years ago in the province, now they are conspicuous and colourful additions to Ontario's avifauna. Mourning doves may be at an all-time high and more commonly overwinter in Norway spruce or Austrian pine plantations or native cedar thickets. Turkey vultures, rare only a few decades ago, are seen more often now, soaring with tilted wings over the farmlands.

Field sparrows, once restricted in Ontario to Indian clearings, beaver meadows, and fen-edges, are common today in old-field habitats. While suitable habitat still may limit the numbers of field sparrows, they often encounter other problems such as nest-parasitism by brown-headed cowbirds. Female cowbirds never build nests, but lay their eggs in those of other birds who then unwittingly raise the foreign young. The cowbird egg usually hatches earlier than those of its host, giving the young parasite a weight advantage over the host's chicks. Usually the host's chicks die from lack of food or as a result of being pushed out of the nest by the more aggressive cowbird chick. Warblers, thrushes, finches, sparrows, or almost any passerine bird may be a target. The field sparrow and some others have a means of fighting back against the cowbird. They may abandon their nests and build new ones, often right on top of the old one. This defence is energy-expensive, but it is better than raising some other species at the expense of your own.

Precarious Survival:
The Carolinian Zone

In extreme southern Ontario, the Carolinian life zone stretches along the north shore of Lakes Erie and Ontario between Windsor and Toronto. In it live almost one-third of Canada's people. The few pieces of wild nature left harbour many of the same species found in the hardwood forests immediately to the north, but also a group of unique, southern species.

The Carolina wren is one of these southern species, precariously holding on in forested valleys where it nests. This wren is very vocal, with a full resonant call that seems much too loud to come from such a small creature. The population grows slowly over several years of good nesting success, only to be savagely cut back by severe winters that occur every half a dozen years or so. Its survival is closely tied to the provision of food at winter feeding stations.

The Louisiana waterthrush is a rare little warbler which migrates from tropical forests each April. Less than forty pairs breed in Ontario, each one restricted to the pristine habitat of

Carolina wren. JIM FLYNN

Hooded warbler. POINT PELEE NATIONAL PARK, J. R. GRAHAM

deep, forested valleys. Representative of high-quality habitat, this species is threatened by logging, dams, and urbanization. Fortunately, several of its traditional breeding sites are protected by park status.

Rare, too, is the hooded warbler, a bright yellow tropical species with a jet black hood over the head of the males. Until very recently, only a couple of breeding sites were known in all of Canada. But between 1981 and 1985 a massive volunteer effort, involving over fifteen hundred birders, to produce a breeding bird atlas for Ontario turned up more than one hundred pairs of hooded warblers in the Carolinian life zone. The birds like to breed in small clearings surrounded by a good-sized deciduous woods. No other kind of habitat is utilized; neither logged woods, immature woods, or small woods. This specialization makes the hooded warbler very susceptible to change. In 1985, eleven pairs were found in a Norfolk County woods, by far the largest single population in Canada, but that fall and winter the woods was devastated by logging. In 1986 only one pair could be found.

The demise of a hooded warbler population is representative of the fate of many creatures in the Carolinian life zone. Little is left. The only chance for many of the birds unique to Canada in this zone is for conservationists to act quickly to save those remnant bits of natural lands.

A Hopeful Signal

Wild birds are a source of pleasure to most people. They provide us with strong symbols of freedom and renewal, and their liveliness, colour, and song attract feelings of empathy. Their study has become very popular, as shown by increasing visits to parks and nature reserves, memberships in naturalist clubs, sales of bird seed, bird feeders, and bird books. At the same time, more and more people are recognizing the links between the welfare of birds and the general health of the environment. Concern is growing over the threats of chemical insecticides, water and air pollution, seemingly uncontrolled urban growth resulting in habitat destruction in parts of the province, and even the rapid felling of the tropical forests that provide winter habitat for many migratory species.

Prothonotary warbler, a rare southern species in Ontario. Less than eighty pairs are know to nest in Canada. P. A. WOODLIFFE

As long as birds still splash their colours and fill Ontario's landscapes with song each spring, the world will be a habitable place. May wild birds always signal a livable world.

Bird Migration

John B. Theberge

On August 15, 1985, a tiny, immature (about two months old) semipalmated sandpiper flew from the hands of a bird bander at the tip of Long Point in Lake Erie. Twenty-one days later it was recovered at Berbice, Guyana, after flying a minimum straight-line distance of 4,667 kilometres, or 222 kilometres a day.

On September 18, 1982, an immature least flycatcher banded thirty-two days earlier at Long Point was found at Las Rosas, Mexico, having flown a minimum of 3,135 kilometres, or 98 kilometres a day.

In January 1986, a blue-winged teal was shot at El Gran Eneal, Venezuela, a distance of 3,577 kilometres from Long Point. Most remarkable about this bird, however, was that it had been banded twenty years and six months earlier.

A flock of snow geese (blue colour phase) migrated apparently non-stop from James Bay to Louisiana, a distance of 2,700 kilometres, in sixty hours, which required a constant rate of speed of 46 kilometres per hour.

Between 1970 and 1980 the same tree swallow returned from the south to nest ten times at Long Point. All of its nests were within 348 metres of one another.

Among the most puzzling and evasive questions in vertebrate biology are the origins and mechanisms of bird migration. Without migration, the northern one-third of the world could support little bird life. Gone would be all the species that feed on invertebrates except those that probe crevices in bark or wood in winter. Gone would be most of the waterfowl, especially those species that feed in shallow water. For lack of winter food, the summer forests, fields, and waters of Ontario would be largely silent.

A full understanding of the origins of migration will always remain, at best, an educated guess. Patterns of migratory behaviour must have arisen at different times for different species, as environmental conditions stressed them. Indeed, new migratory behaviour has been observed in expanding populations of some sedentary species even today. European starlings, recently expanding at the northern limits of their range to the southern tip of James Bay, have developed a new, annual north-south migration.

All migration likely originated from environmental stress of one kind or another. If individuals – or their offspring – that moved, ultimately survived better than those that stayed, then natural selection would have favoured the dispersal genotypes. Experiments on many species have demonstrated that today the urge to migrate is largely innate. Also innate is the recognition of environmental cues that trigger migration and an ability to home to an exact location, both obviously conferring an advantage on those individuals who "got it right." On the other hand, not all is programmed. The finches, siskins, redpolls, and various species of owls that periodically invade southern Ontario do so in response to food shortages on their more northern breeding range only in those winters when food is scarce.

A theory exists that Pleistocene or earlier glaciations were important to the origins of migration, causing withdrawal from the north. A contrary theory proposes that migration originated in the tropics where, during the breeding season, the food requirements of raising young magnified population pressures, triggering dispersal. Yet another theory links the origins of migrations to the breakup of the supercontinent Pangea, 135 million years ago. Over the millennia, the drifting apart of a breeding area and a wintering area was so imperceptibly slow that it could not have strained the flying ability of any one generation, or ten thousand generations of a species. Over time, however, long-distance migration developed. This explanation is not sufficient, because not all species, indeed a minority, migrate between continents. This continental drift theory and the one related to glaciations most commonly are viewed as influences, rather than fundamental origins of migration. The simplest and most accepted explanation for migration, both from breeding and wintering grounds, is dispersal that gradually may have become longer as required, due to shortages or competition for food or nesting sites or the need to escape predators.

However they originated, some extraordinary migrations do occur. Golden plovers nesting across the high Arctic and along Ontario's Hudson Bay coast migrate to the southern half of South America. Adults fly an elliptical rather than a straight course, southeast to the Maritime Provinces or New England and south out over the open Atlantic Ocean to South America. The young, which leave the nesting grounds later, fly, with no guidance or previous experience, a straight, inland course down the Mississippi region and on through South America, eventually joining the adults. The return migration for both young and adults follows the inland route.

Arctic terns, some of which nest along the Hudson Bay coast in Ontario, are long-distance champions, and as a result live in more summer conditions each year than any other bird. After flying across the Atlantic Ocean and down the European and African coasts, some birds fly back across the South Atlantic to winter below the Antarctic Circle on sub-Antarctic islands.

How birds navigate presents a perplexing question, studied since the days when Greeks domesticated pigeons and used them to speed news of Olympic victories back home. *Goal orienteering*, that is, returning to a specific location even if laterally displaced *en route*, is possible for many species, especially adults, as has been shown experimentally with purple martins, white-crowned sparrows, bobolinks, and bank swallows, among Ontario nesting species, as well as with birds which nest elsewhere. Many young on their first migration, however, tend only to keep a constant direction. After stopping and perhaps exploring laterally, they migrate again following the same bearing. In this case, the existence of an innate compass bearing is implied, and has considerable experimental support.

Controversy has developed over whether or not birds use a combination of memory maps of landscape features and compass clues to maintain direction, or if, after displacement, they truly navigate by being able to identify where they are and where their goal lies by latitude and longitude; in other words, can they "read" a grid and determine the direction to fly? This ability to determine exact location could be achieved by recognizing the change in sun or star angles over time, or by identifying differences in magnetism. Or, it could be achieved by some sort of internal gyroscope that records turns and speeds on the outward journey, as do jet airplanes and spacecraft. Despite much research, an ability to determine coordinates of locations has been demonstrated in only a few species, and even in these the results are still contested.

Memory maps of landscape clues may be seen as just extended perceptions of a local area. Familiar landmarks in a bird's immediate environment quite likely are known by direction and distance from one another, just as they are in humans. The size of an area around a nesting, wintering, or even migratory stopping place that may be explored, and thus become part of a memory map, may have been underestimated in the past. As well, the environmental information may be fed in not only by vision, but by sound, smell, and differences in the strength of gravity or magnetism, all of which have been shown experimentally to be detectable, and at great distances. For example, "ultrasound," with wavelengths of 1 to 100 Hertz, is generated by ocean waves, thunderstorms, magnetic storms, wind through mountain passes, and jet-streams. It fills almost all environments because it can travel several thousand kilometres. Experiments with pigeons show a remarkable ability to detect it. In different bird species, different senses may predominate the memory maps, although vision may be of greatest general importance. But in combination, memory maps of the characteristics of goals, such as nesting, wintering, migratory stop-over places, and even routes between them, may be extensive.

Compasses to maintain direction have been demonstrated based on recognition of sun and star locations, both of which must be used in combination with an internal clock to correct for changes over time. An internal clock is well known as the basis of *circadian* (twenty-four-hour) rhythms in animals. Ability to maintain direction also may be based on magnetism, again with experimental evidence. The search for magnetic receptor organs in birds and mammals has not been successful, although theories have been put forth of a sinus or olfactory position due to ferric compounds in the bones and the molecules of the retina of the eye.

In synopsis, the case rests today with most specialists in the field believing that the combined mechanisms of memory maps and compasses provide sufficient explanations for direction-finding and homing; other specialists are still on the trail of grid-mapping abilities. Research continues on ultrasound and magneto-receptors.

In the meantime, on a spring morning, when a warm front moves in from south of the Great Lakes with a mist or light drizzle, it is bound to bring with it a host of migrants, all reading *something* to reach their goal.

Territoriality

J. Bruce Falls

Territoriality – defence of an area – is widespread in the animal kingdom but especially obvious in birds. Most Ontario birds are territorial in one way or another. Some, like the ring-billed gull, live in colonies, defending their nest sites but gathering food elsewhere. Red-winged blackbirds are loosely colonial, but males defend areas in which one or more females may nest. Although they feed in their territories, they also travel farther afield to obtain food on common ground. Grouse defend display areas, while hummingbirds may defend a patch of flowers. However, the most familiar form of territoriality is found in songbirds such as warblers, sparrows, and meadowlarks. They defend territories ranging in size from a fraction of a hectare to several hectares, in which they nest and carry out most of their activities. The following description of territoriality includes the results of studies of ovenbirds, white-throated sparrows, and meadowlarks in Ontario by my students and myself.

Territoriality consists of defending a fixed area containing some resource(s) which include food, nest sites, and cover from predators. Even a mate may be guarded. Comparisons among species indicate that birds will only defend territories if the resources in question are reliable and if the benefits of territory ownership outweigh the costs of defence. Most Ontario birds are territorial only in the breeding season, and one obvious benefit is that only territory holders seem able to breed.

Typically, males defend territories against other males, while females choose to mate with males that have obtained adequate resources and can drive out other females. Since different species use different resources, their territories usually overlap, and defence is directed to members of the same species. An exception which proves the rule is that eastern and western meadowlarks, which are very similar in appearance and which undoubtedly use the same resources, defend territories against one another.

Although it is difficult to determine which resources are defended, circumstantial evidence often points to food. Territory size tends to increase with the size of the species; however, raptors, whose food is sparsely distributed, have larger territories than their size alone explains. Ovenbirds feed on invertebrates in the leaf litter. By screening the litter for food items and measuring territory size, our studies have shown that territories were smaller where food was most abundant. This trend could be a direct response to food. Alternatively, more ovenbirds trying to nest in rich habitats may increase the cost of defence and force birds to occupy smaller territories.

Male birds usually attempt to evict other males from their territories, but in dense vegetation it may be difficult to detect intruders. Ovenbirds do, in fact, wander quietly into each other's territories. Territorial male white-throated sparrows on which we placed tiny radio transmitters to reveal their movements, concentrated their activities within their own territories, but also visited considerably larger areas,

White-throated sparrow. DON GUNN

trespassing on their neighbours' grounds.

Song is typically associated with territorial behaviour. Males advertise their presence by singing in the areas that they defend. If we play recorded songs of its own species to a territorial male, it will only attack the source of the sound when it lies within its defended area. This provides us with a rapid method for mapping the boundaries of territories. In the course of such research, we discovered that birds respond more strongly to songs of strangers than to those of their territorial neighbours. Correspondingly, strife between neighbours diminishes during the breeding season. Apparently, birds learn to recognize each other's songs individually.

Is song a deterrent to intruders? To tackle this question, we temporarily removed male white-throated sparrows from their territories. We replaced some birds with recordings of their songs played from loudspeakers in their territories. In other cases we left the territories silent. Normally, when a resident male is present, we hardly ever hear another bird sing in its territory. However, when a male is removed, leaving the female in the territory, trespassing males begin to sing within a few hours, and soon one takes over the vacated territory. In our experiments, where we played the original owner's song, invading singers were delayed and made fewer attempts to sing than in silent territories. Thus, it seems that song may help a bird maintain its territory and at least keep the intruders quiet.

When a territory is vacated, where do the replacements come from? They are seldom neighbours; these already have territories. They may come from inferior habitats elsewhere, but the rapidity of takeovers suggests that they were hiding in the vicinity all the time. Transmitters put on several such "floaters" showed that these birds were indeed non-territorial males wandering quietly through the territories of residents. The finding of both wandering territorial birds and floaters in an area argues that territories are not always the exclusive domains that casual observation would suggest.

Evidence of floaters in a number of species has further implications. They may represent a surplus population excluded from breeding by territorial behaviour of residents. Especially where floaters of both sexes have been found it has been claimed that territoriality limits breeding populations. This is most likely to occur in densely populated, preferred habitats. Alternatively, where no floaters are present, territories may simply spread the residents out evenly.

Thus, at least under some circumstances, territoriality, and the bird song that accompanies it, is a very serious matter. They may determine which individuals are able to contribute their genes to successive generations.

◆ SCIENCE ◆ EXCURSION ◆

The Bald Eagle in Ontario

John B. Theberge

Steeped in symbolism as the national bird of the United States, the bald eagle, since about 1960, has also become symbolic of a threatened biosphere. Today, after its continent-wide decline, probably more bald eagles nest in Canada than in the United States, even though they are still numerous in Alaska. In 1983 the North American population was estimated at 70,000 birds, of which more than 52,000 were in Canada, although confidence limits on these estimates are wide. Healthy populations live in the southern Yukon, southern Northwest Territories, British Columbia, Nova Scotia, northern Saskatchewan, northern Manitoba, and even northern Ontario.

But across most of the United States, southern Ontario, southern Quebec, and New Brunswick, a precipitous decline that began in the 1950s indicated that something was seriously wrong. That something was DDT, whose breakdown product DDE was causing eggshell-thinning and failure of eggs to hatch. Bald eagles are primarily predators and scavengers of fish. While shooting and habitat destruction have had some negative impact upon their populations, it was pesticides, concentrated mainly in aquatic food chains, that threatened the species.

To maintain their populations, bald eagles must produce a minimum average of 0.7 young per nest per year. They do not breed until they are three or four years of age. Early mortality of nestlings is high, with the largest chick often commandeering most of the food. Mortality also is high in the first year. In northwestern Ontario, north of Lake of the Woods, Red Lake, and Lac Seul, that average of 0.7 has been achieved and bettered ever since 1966 when surveys began, although a dip in productivity occurred in the late 1960s and early 1970s coincident with the appearance of higher levels of DDT in eagle eggs. Over the approximately 23,300 square kilometres in this region under periodic survey, bald eagle numbers today are estimated at roughly 500 to 1,000 nesting pairs, or 1,000 to

2,000 adult birds, plus about as many non-breeders.

In northern Ontario, nest sites on Crown Land are protected through "Modified Management Agreements," which classify a radius of 400 to 800 metres around nests into two zones: an inner 200-metre "zone of minimal disturbance" in which logging, mining, road building, and cottage construction are not permitted, and an outer zone in which resource extraction is limited to the period between September 1 and March 1. Bald eagles are protected, as well, by the Ontario Endangered Species Act, with stiff fines or imprisonment for killing or injuring the birds or for destroying their nest sites or habitats.

In southern Ontario, the history and present status of bald eagles is different. Prior to 1950, bald eagles commonly nested from northern Georgian Bay to Pelee Island, Concentrations were found in Prince Edward County and the Kingston area, where famous eagle researcher Charles Broley once estimated fifteen nests within a thirty-two-kilometre radius of his cottage, and along the north shore of Lake Erie, where naturalist W. E. Saunders estimated an average of one eagle nest per eight kilometres. In 1951 the eagle decline began, with only one nest out of twelve producing any young near Delta, Ontario. The last successful nest in the Kingston area was reported in 1955. By 1969 only five active bald eagle nests could be found in southern Ontario, with a total of only one fledged young. From then until now, the number of active nests has varied between three and eight.

Bald eagle. NORM LIGHTFOOT

The use of DDT was banned in Ontario in 1970 and in the United States two years later. However, its toxic breakdown product, DDE, persisted and continued to have an effect through subsequent years. By 1980 some signs of recovery became evident. Since then, new nests have been showing up at a rate of one a year. Nesting success has risen, with most nests producing at least one fledged young.

In 1983, a recovery program was initiated by the Ontario government, with support from the Canadian Wildlife Service, the Elsa Wild Animal Appeal of Canada, and the World Wildlife Fund (Canada). Between 1983 and 1987, twenty-eight eaglets, ranging from five to eight weeks of age, were transferred from northern Ontario to the Long Point National Wildlife Area. This location was chosen for the recovery efforts because it is relatively undisturbed and has an abundance of fish and carrion. Eaglets were raised in "hack boxes" consisting of an enclosed platform raised above the sand dunes. There, the eaglets were fed fish until August when they became old enough to hunt for themselves.

About five of these eaglets have been sighted in the Long Point area in subsequent years, and one released in 1983 was still being seen in 1987. None of the released birds has yet nested. If and when that occurs, the program will have met with success.

◆ SCIENCE ◆ EXCURSION ◆

Black Duck: A Species in Trouble

Darrell Dennis

The black duck, probably Ontario's most common species of waterfowl a hundred years ago, is fast disappearing from the province. From the turn of the century until the 1950s the slide in numbers was slow, but since then numbers have dropped dramatically. In south-central Ontario, black ducks are down ten birds to one over the past thirty-five years, and 80 per cent of that decline has taken place since 1971. In central Ontario south of Lake Nipissing, numbers have fallen by 40 per cent since 1971.

This rapid decline has been documented by Canadian Wildlife Service surveys. Despite restrictive hunting regulations initiated in 1984 in both Canada and the United States, the decline has continued. Neither government nor university research has explained it, although some causes have been ruled out and one particular hypothesis has gained strength.

The possibility that acid rain has reduced the invertebrate food supplies of black duck broods seems unlikely, because the largest declines have occurred in southern Ontario where the natural buffering capacity of lakes, ponds, and other wetlands is greatest. The hypothesis that overhunting has caused the decline seems unreasonable, too, because the mallard duck, a species that is at least as vulnerable to hunting as black ducks, has not declined.

Mallards, in fact, have increased, especially in southern Ontario, even more than blacks have declined. Not only have mallards increased, but so have the relative numbers of mallard-black duck hybrids per black duck, as shown in annual wing collections of the Wildlife Service. Hybrids appear at a ratio of one for every ten blacks. Certain geographical blocks, notably those where black ducks are declining rapidly, have a ratio as high as one hybrid to three blacks!

Genetically, mallards and blacks are very similar. One study using protein analysis on mallards from various places such as California, Saskatchewan, Manitoba, and Ontario, and blacks from Newfoundland, Nova Scotia, and Ontario, found as much genetic variation within mallard populations as between mallards and blacks. These results are not surprising when one considers that the black duck probably evolved only during the Pleistocene glaciation as a colour phase of the mallard and simply has not had enough time to become genetically different.

Once hybridized, however, these ducks appear to be a transitional genetic stage in a transformation from black to mallard. Subsequent generations of hybrids tend to resemble mallards rather than blacks. Thus, even a small amount of hybridization represents an eventual loss of blacks from local populations.

Why would members of either species mate with other than their own kind? Captive studies have shown that mallards and blacks choose the type of mate with which they were reared. For example, black duck hens reared with black duck drakes chose black duck drakes as mates; if reared with mallard drakes they chose mallards as mates. But when black duck drakes were put on a pond with mallard drakes, where the natural dominance of the two species was allowed to occur, both black duck hens and mallard hens selected mallard drakes, regardless of the species with which they were reared. In encounters between drakes, mallards normally are more dominant.

Not only dominance, but availability may influence hybridization. Studies on wild populations of mallards and blacks near Ottawa indicate that male mallards pair with female mallards when possible. However, when no unpaired female mallards are available, the male mallards may court and eventually pair with previously paired female black ducks.

Black duck. DON GUNN

Curiously, observations of both nest ing black and mallards ducks living in the same area do not include enough mixed black-mallard pairs to adequately explain the high proportion of hybrids in fall flights. Much of the hybridization may occur during second, rather than initial nesting attempts. Surveys are most reliable early in the nesting season and so may miss these later cross-species nestings. When a black duck hen loses her original nest to predation or flooding, and the pair bond with her original black duck drake is diminished, it is possible that she will re-mate with a mallard drake.

The hybridization theory for the decline of the black duck fits the observation that blacks are declining fastest where mallards are becoming most numerous. Blacks appear to be holding on most successfully in Precambrian Shield country of central and northern Ontario. They may owe this success to a tiny blood parasite, Leucocytozoan, that is carried by blackflies. Blackflies are more numerous on the Shield because of their dependence on flowing water for egg-laying and the larval stage. Mallards exhibit low resistance to this parasite, while black ducks are much more immune.

Mallards, nevertheless, gradually have been invading blackfly country. Some biologists feel that this invasion may be enhanced by cross-breeding with black ducks. The resulting hybrid, that in later generations appears in mallard plumage, may still contain appropriate black duck genes for Leucocytozoan resistance.

If hybridization with mallards is the primary cause of the black duck decline, reversing the trend poses a severe problem for wildlife managers. Hunting regulations might be changed so that a higher percentage of mallard drakes is included in the hunter's bag. However, mallards are so well established in Ontario that their population will never drop far enough for black ducks to gain in abundance as a breeding species. In addition, Ontario hunting seasons open at a time when many waterfowl are not in breeding plumage and so are difficult to identify. For example, most mallard drakes resemble hens on the opening day of the hunting season. Thus, neither restricting hunting nor even re-introducing the species, techniques which worked with the wood duck and giant Canada goose, is likely to have much success.

We may be witnessing in Ontario a natural evolutionary phenomenon, a shuffling of genes between two species that blur the definition of species. The process is remarkably rapid compared with most genetic events in populations. Where they are relatively isolated from mallards – in the Maritime Provinces and Newfoundland and Labrador, for instance – blacks may continue to do well for some time. But in Ontario, with no opportunity for isolation from the dominant species, the black duck soon may cease to exist as a breeding bird.

◆ SCIENCE ◆ EXCURSION ◆

Gray Jay: A Unique Bird with a Unique Strategy

Dan Strickland

The great coniferous forests of northern Ontario are home to over a hundred species of breeding birds. Most are elusive and flit away at the approach of a human. Soon after the short breeding season, almost all of them vanish from Ontario altogether. One bird, however, breaks from the usual pattern, and in doing so becomes indelibly associated with the rocks, lakes, spruces, and balsam firs of the north country. This is the gray jay, sometimes called the whiskeyjack, a bird which not only spends all year in the boreal forest, but which fearlessly approaches campsites and with a bit of coaxing often can be induced to land on human hands and shoulders. Added to this confiding nature, the silent gliding flight, the dark inquisitive eyes, and the soft appealing plumage combine to win for the gray jay a special place in the hearts of everyone who lives or travels in the north.

How is it that gray jays can remain all year in the boreal forest when almost all other birds are forced to leave? The gray jay has evolved a remarkable strategy for survival in a hostile environment. The basic secret of the bird's success is that it stores food in summer and fall and draws upon these stores all winter, effectively smoothing out the natural yearly cycle of summer abundance and winter scarcity.

But far more is involved in an effective food storage system than merely hiding food – berries, insects, mushrooms, and meat – behind pieces of bark and under lichens. What guarantees that the food will stay where it is hidden or will last until winter? Even then, how can an individual jay ever find the food it has hidden?

Gray jays choose hiding places where the food cannot be seen by any competitors that pass by, and they often make doubly sure the food is hidden by jamming another piece of bark or lichen in on top. In addition, gray jays produce copious amounts of sticky saliva which they use to cover and impregnate pellets of food by working them back and forth in their mouths. Thus prepared, a morsel of food will remain firmly stuck in its hiding place and may benefit as well – though this is not proven – from possible food-preserving properties of the saliva.

Merely storing food is of no advantage unless the jay has a good prospect of recovering its investment later. For many years, most authorities guessed that gray jays probably found their hidden food stores by random searching, but recent studies of them, and of other food-hoarding birds, now indicate that they actually remember their individual hiding places. Not only that, they apparently can remember which kinds of food they have hidden in each place and which locations they already have emptied.

It seems preposterous that a seventy-gram bird could keep track of hundreds of storage locations in the incredibly complicated, three-dimensional space of even one large spruce tree, let alone the thousands contained in the square kilometre or so of a single gray jay's territory. Nevertheless, the evidence is that they do. This mental accomplishment, while surprising, really is no greater than that of successfully finding the way to South America and back each year in the dark, as many other birds do.

For a gray jay, the benefit of storing and recovering food is that they never have to leave their territory in the boreal forest and expose themselves to the dangers of migration. Adult, territory-holding gray jays have an annual survival rate of around 83 per cent, a figure usually matched only by birds in the tropics (which also forgo annual migrations). By comparison, over half the populations of many migratory boreal forest species die every year, and only the prolific nesting output of the survivors keeps them from becoming extinct.

The success of the gray jay's store-food-and-stay-at-home strategy is even more striking because most gray jay deaths do not occur in the long, cold winters. Most die in summer, presumably because their principal predators – migratory sharp-shinned hawks and merlins – are present only at that season.

The gray jay's food-storage way of life does more than merely confer a high survival rate. It both permits and encourages the evolution of extremely early nesting. Gray jays start building their bulky and well-insulated nests as early as late February and are incubating their eggs (usually three, sometimes four) by the third week of March. In the boreal forest, March is still winter, often with a metre or more of snow on the ground and temperatures still almost constantly below freezing. Even when the young hatch, twenty days later, little or no obvious food is around, the lakes are still frozen, and the ground is still snow-covered. Nevertheless, gray jay nestlings grow as quickly as any chicks, and it is remarkable that no case has ever been recorded of nestling gray jays starving to death or succumbing to the cold. It seems obvious that the food stores are the safety margin which permit gray jays to nest when at least one or two normally lethal snow or sleet storms are still bound to occur.

By nesting so early, gray jays produce young which begin storing food that much earlier and which become that much more proficient before cold weather sets in. Then too, bringing their young to independence early in the year allows the adults to begin to store food as early as June and to devote all summer and fall to the crucial task of building up their winter food supplies.

Despite these advantages, early nesting and food storage are accompanied by a bizarre behavioural twist that means life or death for particular fledglings. In June, just after fledglings have acquired the ability to find and store their own food, they start to fight among themselves. Within ten days the strongest youngster, a male in two-thirds of known cases, has driven off its one to three weaker sisters and brothers, and it alone continues to accompany its parents for the rest of the summer and through the next winter. Such dominant juveniles survive reasonably well because of parental guidance and familiarity with their natal territory, and they are in an ideal position to wait for a vacancy in the breeding population to open up on a nearby territory.

The ejected birds, about 60 per cent of them females, are forced to leave home when barely six weeks old. Al-

Gray jay. DON GUNN

though a few of them succeed in getting accepted by unattached gray jays with no young of their own, fully 80 per cent of all "ejectees" die by their first autumn. Many of the few survivors are females lucky enough to have found a widowed male at just the right time.

Thus the dominant chick consigns its siblings to a high probability of early death. What could account for such strange behaviour? The answer rests on the evidence that a gray jay territory appears unable to support a whole family over an entire winter. No observations have been made of five jays overwintering together on a natural territory (without a bird feeder), and only rarely have four jays been seen. Further evidence comes from the failure of ejectees to even stay in the territory and carve out their own space from the seemingly ample room, eventually breeding there themselves. Three gray jays per territory is the limit.

Why does the dominant juvenile expel its siblings in June, rather than allow them to store food all summer, expel them in October, and reap the benefits of their labour? Gray jays recover their stored food by remembering where they hid it, or by watching other birds. Given the enormous "unpoliceable" size of a gray jay territory, the expelled birds, if allowed to stay all summer, could always sneak back and raid the widely scattered summer caches. Early expulsion, therefore, serves the dominant chick best.

To people used to the fluffy, friendly, curious gray jay, the behaviour described here may seem rather harsh. But no creature can escape the brutal realities of the boreal forest environment. The remarkable thing about gray jays is that they survive with unparalleled ease in the face of those realities – much to the pleasure and interest of humans. A truly unique bird with a truly unique strategy.

• SCIENCE • EXCURSION •

Canada Geese Numbers of the Hudson Bay Lowlands

Harry G. Lumsden

Stretching south and west from Hudson Bay, the Hudson Bay Lowlands in Ontario, Manitoba, and the Northwest Territories provide breeding habitat for several stocks of large- to medium-sized Canada geese. These subspecies vary somewhat in weight and colour. They are separated from breeding giant Canada geese of southern Ontario by the rocky, infertile Precambrian country that probably never has provided nesting habitat for geese.

The Hudson Bay Lowlands, which remain today largely in a pristine state, have always had a great capacity to produce geese. However, the number of geese that nested there was probably always limited by the ability of the wintering grounds to support them, rather than by conditions on the nesting grounds.

These northern geese follow three migratory traditions: the birds nesting at the southeastern corner of James Bay winter in the Atlantic states; most of those breeding south of the Albany River now go to the Tennessee Valley west of the Appalachian Mountains; geese from north of the Albany west into Manitoba, which now outnumber the others three to one, winter in the Mississippi Valley. In the case of the Mississippi Valley stock, the birds historically must have been confined in winter to the islands and sandbars of the Mississippi River, where they fed on sedges and willow buds and visited the limited areas of Indian cultivation.

A vast change in the wintering areas took place with the clearing of the forests and the establishment of European-style farming. Pastures and corn fields provided highly preferred foods which the geese avidly accepted. The numbers of geese should have increased dramatically, and initially they probably did.

However, with trade and settlement came increased hunting, both on the northern breeding and southern wintering ranges. In the Hudson Bay Lowlands, the Cree Indians' efficiency in hunting geese increased with the sale of guns by the Hudson's Bay Company. After the establishment of the fur trade on James Bay, the Indians were hired to supply the Hudson's Bay Company posts with both blue and Canada geese. Each year many thousands of geese were salted in barrels and sent by boat from such places as the mouth of the Kapiskau River to the posts on the bay.

The Catholic Mission at Attawapiskat also bottled geese until the late 1940s for their own use and for sale. For many years geese were the main source of protein for those living near the coasts of James and Hudson bays.

This northern harvest by itself appears to have had little effect on numbers until the kill by sport hunters on the migration route and wintering grounds increased. No goose census data were collected prior to the 1930s to clarify what was happening. It seems likely, however, that the northern goose stocks of Ontario declined steadily in this century. The passage of the Migratory Bird Convention Act of 1918 did little to halt the trend. What was needed was more stringent hunting laws and intensive local management of individual stocks. As perception of progressively reduced numbers of geese increased, efforts were made to reduce the harvest. For example, in Illinois authorities took steps to conserve the geese wintering in the Mississippi Valley. In the late 1920s the limit of geese was eight per day; in the mid-1930s this was reduced to four, and in the early 1940s to only two.

Such restrictions were not enough to counteract the increased hunting resulting from wartime economics and greater mobility of hunters. Goose harvests increased to such an extent that from 1943 to 1945 the harvest in southern Illinois alone was about 40 per cent of the fall flight of birds – a rate well in excess of their reproductive. In 1945, the Mississippi Valley stock was reduced to about 26,000 birds, and the winter inventory suggested only 49,000 birds in all fourteen states of the Mississippi Flyway.

In 1946, local season closures and restrictive regulations for goose hunting throughout the Mississippi Flyway began to restore numbers. Since the early 1950s, the management of waterfowl in North America has been regulated by four Flyway Councils in concert with the two federal governments. Annually, each council and its staff review the available data and make decisions on research and management. The Mississippi Flyway Council, of which Ontario is a member, consists of fourteen states and three provinces.

Evidence was collected many years ago that a very large proportion of the annual goose mortality was caused by hunting. Therefore, harvests of geese are now strictly regulated by quota in parts of Wisconsin, Illinois, Kentucky, Tennessee, and Michigan in those areas where the bulk of the geese are shot. Hunters must register their bag with the State Conservation Commission within twenty-four hours of taking the birds. When the pre-determined quota is shot in any area, the hunting season is closed by proclamation of the governor. Elsewhere in the Mississippi Flyway, the harvest of geese is regulated by bag limits and the time and length of the hunting season.

Under this regime, while management mistakes have been made and the goose populations have had their ups and downs, the recovery of the stocks has been remarkable. In 1985 the winter inventory for the whole Mississippi Flyway was 1,127,500 Canada geese, and Mississippi Valley birds numbered 618,900.

If we can continue to regulate hunting properly, there seems to be no reason why both viewers and hunters cannot continue to enjoy this spectacular bird in perpetuity.

Tooth and Claw
The Mammals of Ontario
John B. Theberge

Seventy-six native species of mammals inhabit Ontario. One of them, by virtue of approximately eleven thousand years of occupancy, is man. Surrounding us are our closest evolutionary relatives, sharing biological features of unmistakable common origin: mammary glands, body hair, four-chambered heart, characteristic lower jaw with two successive sets of teeth, and other skeletal features. Man, now representing the largest biomass of all living mammals in Ontario, indeed the world, is the dominant mammalian species, but we are far from alone.

Our close relationship with the other species of mammals that inhabit Ontario has not led us to hold them in any especially high regard. The evolutionary connection dates back too long ago – 50 or 60 million years. So we treat mammals as we do any other "resource," that is, we exploit them. We eat them, wear their fur, and mount their heads on recreation room walls. In turn, but not in revenge, they eat our crops, become urban "pests," and transmit diseases to us. It is logical that we, and our man-made environments, should be exploited too as a resource. All living species are bound together in ecological relationships.

Yet a black squirrel performing high-limb acrobatics is a moment's diversion when seen out of an office or kitchen window, and a white-tailed deer standing on the highway-edge never fails to excite a vacationing family. The children come home from school with big news about a raccoon up a tree in the schoolyard, and for wilderness canoeists, the howl of a gray wolf is an unforgettable experience.

Mammals may have lived in Ontario for much of their 175- to 200-million-year evolutionary history. In the first 100 million years, however, they were few in species or abundance, and lived only in localized habitats. When mammals first evolved, the continents as we know them today were one huge landmass, and what is now Ontario was much closer to the equator. By 10 million years ago, when the number of species of mammals peaked, North America had assumed much of its current shape and latitude. Hoofed mammals were here: horses, deer, camels, and peccaries, as well as carnivores – ancestors of our wolves, foxes, coyotes, bears, raccoons, and cats. Most evidence of their existence, however, was wiped out in the glaciations and subsequent periods of erosion during the last 2 million years.

For any accurate picture of modern Ontario mammals, eleven thousand years ago forms the logical beginning, as the Pleistocene ice sheets retreated for the last time from the province. Tundra vegetation gradually took over the bare gravels and rock left behind by the glaciers. As the ice-edge retreated, species of typical northern mammals that had been pushed south by the ice, like caribou and muskoxen, recolonized southern Ontario. Man came too, the Paleo-Indian, whose dart heads have been dated at ten thousand years in southwestern Ontario. Here also were many species now extinct: woolly mammoths, whose bones have been found near Toronto, American mastodons, camels, giant bison, and giant beavers.

As the ice retreated out of northern Ontario between ninety-five and eighty-five hundred years ago, the assemblage of tundra species moved on north, followed in southern Ontario by boreal forest species such as moose, red squirrels, fishers, and martens. Climates continued to warm, and deciduous forests, with their white-tailed deer, gray squirrels, and Virginia opossums, pushed up into southern Ontario. About five to six thousand years ago the province was slightly warmer than today, especially in northern Ontario, and the broad belts of tundra, taiga, boreal, and hard-

Raccoon. NATIONAL MUSEUM OF CANADA, A. G. AUSTIN

Woodland caribou, Otter Island, Lake Superior. PUKASKWA NATIONAL PARK, W. WYETT

wood forest all lay slightly farther north.

The distribution of mammals today reflects our present climate. It also reflects the environmental impacts of man. In relatively few years we have had a profound effect, beginning in Upper Canada with the fur trade. Beaver hats for the British gentry frivolously motivated an era of wildlife exploitation. Early commercial logging in the mid 1800s to early 1900s featured huge clear-cuts and large burns. Fires were started, either on purpose to burn slash or by lightning striking the logging debris. The result of all this disturbance was a shift in the ranges of large mammal species. Champlain recorded caribou but not deer in his travels across the upper Ottawa and French-Nipissing waterways. But with logging, caribou disappeared and white-tailed deer moved in from the hardwood-dominated forests to the south. Moose moved in as well, from both south and west of Lake Superior. Elk, believed once to be abundant and widespread in central and southern Ontario, became extinct. Re-introductions of elk made in the mid 1930s have resulted in the establishment of a few small herds counted in the tens, not hundreds. The nearest substantial elk population today is in Riding Mountain National Park north of Winnipeg.

Black bear. J. DAVID TAYLOR

The caribou, fortunately, have not gone; the southern margin of their range has only retreated northward. Remnant bands still live on islands in Lake Superior and in scattered places, such as near Armstrong. Farther north, in the taiga forests closer to James Bay, caribou are still plentiful.

But southern Ontario has experienced a wholesale shift in mammals. Gone are the "wilderness species" such as gray wolf and black bear, replaced by "farm game": woodchucks and cottontail rabbits. The simulated prairie landscape of southern Ontario has encouraged the coyote to expand eastward across the whole province and into Quebec. White-tailed deer undoubtedly are more common in the field–forest-edge environments that exist in southern Ontario today than ever before. Their natural predator, the wolf, has been replaced by the rifle, the automobile, and sometimes by roaming packs of dogs – but still the deer thrive.

Mammals are not just "here," passive parts of the environment; they are woven into complex ecological webs that form the very underpinnings of life. They are part of systems that capture energy, cycle nutrients, and make our world different from the moonscape it would otherwise be. This ecological organization reflects global patterns or recovery times after glaciation. There may be unoccupied "niches" or functional roles in environments that have remained unfilled since the last ice age. A wild pig niche, and a large cat predator niche,

Moose. J. DAVID TAYLOR

Skull of a pigmy shrew.

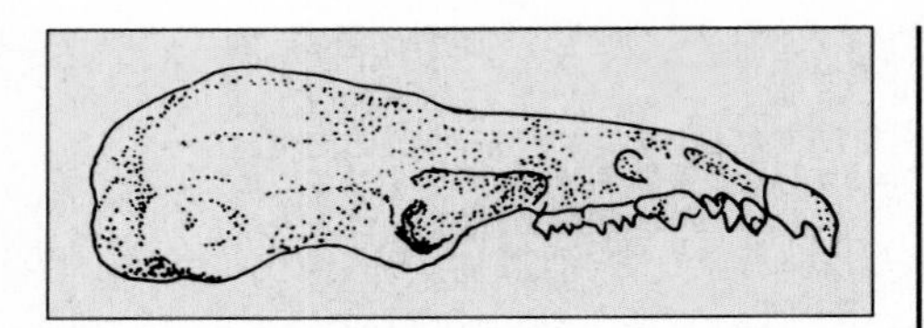

Skull of a polar bear (not to scale with the shrew).

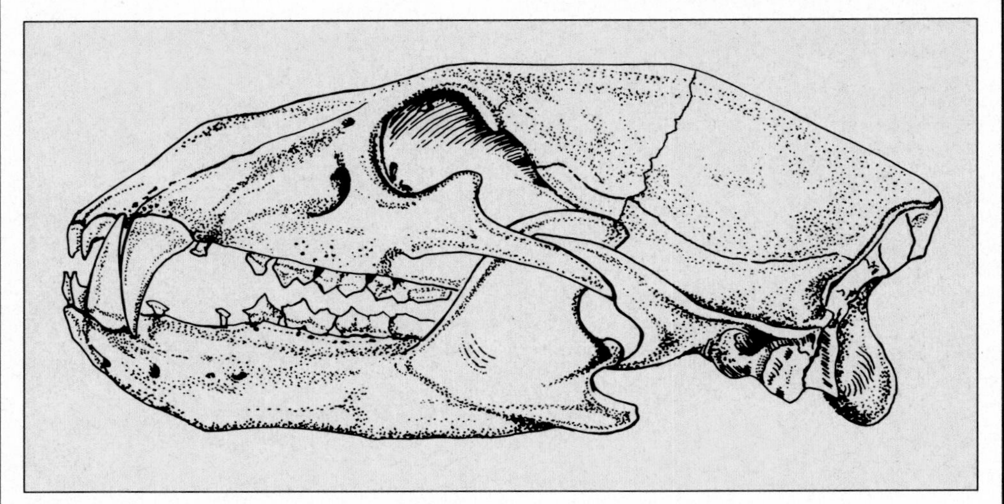

perhaps even a camel niche are available but unoccupied.

The smallest and the largest land mammals in Ontario are primarily carnivores, preferring only side-dishes of vegetables: the pigmy shrew, a tiny speck of mammalian life weighing less than a twenty-five-cent piece; and the polar bear, with an adult male weighing about 450 kilograms. Beluga whales in James Bay and Hudson Bay may exceed this weight, and a large eastern walrus bull can tip the scales at half again the polar bear's weight. Pigmy shrews are extremely rare, but with an extensive range across the entire province and much of Canada. Polar bears are the reverse – they are abundant only in a very restricted Ontario range along coastal James and Hudson bays. Their range is extensive in the circumpolar Arctic beyond Ontario.

These two drastically different mammals show other interesting extremes. The shrew is a member of the most "primitive" mammalian order, Insectivora, not because of its size but because of its lack of specialization. A key tenet of evolution used by taxonomists and proven over and over in the fossil record is that evolution has proceeded from generalist to specialist. Shrews have simple teeth, just a row of saw-tooth edges with each tooth quite similar to the next. Shrew origins fade back to the dawn of mammalian life.

Polar bears, in contrast, have highly specialized dentition: large canine teeth to pierce their prey, and massive pre-molars and molars to grind bone. The order to which they belong, Carnivora, includes dog, cat, and weasel families as well, and appeared much later in the evolutionary record.

Shrews are food generalists, eating any small insect they can find. Polar bears are food specialists, preying primarily upon ringed seals that poke up out of breathing holes or bask, unaware of danger, on the icepack.

Aside from the shrews, of which seven species are found in Ontario, the province's "small mammals" are all primarily herbivores. Most common are deer mice and white-footed mice of both boreal and hardwood forests, and meadow voles of the fields. These species fluctuate greatly in abundance. At high densities, one hectare of prime old-field or marsh habitat may support 375 meadow voles, or 7.5 kilograms of vole with an average weight of 20 grams. While the forest-dwelling mice may only reach one-tenth that density in prime early-succession habitat after fire or logging, that still represents more than 192 kilograms per square kilometre, or half the weight of a moose! The importance of all this small mammal meat is not overlooked by red foxes, coyotes, hawks, and owls. To small mammals these predators owe their existence.

Slightly larger, but also making an important contribution to the welfare of predators are the three species of native hares and rabbits that live in Ontario. Rabbits differ from hares by being born naked, blind, and helpless, often in underground burrows. Hares, in contrast, are born in surface nests and the young are precocious, that is, able to run and take care of themselves soon after birth. The snowshoe hare, common in the boreal forest, is a true hare. But the eastern cottontail, familiar in southern parts of the province where it is at the northern extent of its continental distribution, is a rabbit. Cottontails are immigrants, having expanded into Ontario in the mid 1800s and reaching the Toronto region by 1885. This expansion followed the "agriculturalization" of southern Ontario. But cottontail remains have been found in archaeological sites as well, indicating an earlier occupancy based perhaps upon forest openings created by Indian agriculture. Why they were absent in the period of European settlement is unknown. Possibly the extent of Indian agriculture had dropped off and forests had re-grown after the Iroquois conquest and subsequent abandonment of many Neutral and Tobacco Indian villages after 1650. But disease is another possibility. Rabbits and hares are susceptible to a number of species of tapeworms and other parasites.

The white-tailed jack-rabbit, despite its name, is a hare. It is also an immigrant, typically a species of the western short-grass prairie. Its range today extends east into what once was a continuous mix of tall-grass prairie and boreal forest from eastern Manitoba to the western end of Lake of the Woods. Hence it is rare in this province, but not rare in Canada, posing an intriguing conservation question. Should the white-tailed jack-rabbit have special protected status in Ontario? An affirmative answer rests on a concept of preservation that is accepted internationally, but is not widely known. Preservation can be directed not simply to species, but to genetic variety. Viewed in that light, it is distinctly possible that the range-edge pioneers differ genetically from those individuals selecting, and selected for, optimum range conditions. These pioneers may be the very individuals that, in expressing adaptations to new environments, have been an integral part of evolutionary success.

No species of mammal besides *Homo sapiens* has the capacity to modify its environment as much as the beaver. Without the consideration of a pre-construction environmental impact assessment, beaver dams sometimes get in the way of human developments. But their ecological effect on Ontario's landscape is profound. The wetlands either created or expanded by beaver dams punctuate life into the lowlands that otherwise would be unbroken tangles of alders. Fish, amphibians, aquatic birds, mink, and otters all benefit. But beavers do not build dams for other species. Beaver dams confer two advantages upon beavers – growth of aquatic plants such as yellow arum whose roots they eat, and, most importantly, an expanded range to forage for their staple woody food within close proximity to water which serves as escape terrain. A beaver discovered away from water by a gray wolf becomes wolf food.

Ontario's predators include the wild cats: the rare or possibly extinct eastern cougar, the rare eastern bobcat, and the more abundant lynx. Lynx are food specialists living primarily on snowshoe hares. Fur-return records of the Hudson Bay Company from 1845 to 1930 show a dramatic ten-year cycle of abundance in lynx pelts, with peak numbers being thirty times greater than lows. In that long span of years, lynx numbers repeatedly increased for five successive years, then decreased for five years. The explanation for the lynx cycle was a "predator-prey" relationship with the cyclic snowshoe hares. But in the fine-tuning of this relationship, an interpretive error was made that stayed in scientific literature until recently. It had been concluded that as hare numbers rose, so did lynx numbers until predation overtopped prey abundance, causing the hares to decline. Then the lynx would decline as well. This relationship could hardly be viewed as representing a wise adaptive strategy for the lynx. Why decimate its prey when it too must bear the consequence? The standard interpretation was questioned when a snowshoe hare population being studied in Alberta underwent the typical ten-year cycle with no lynx in that particular ecosystem to cause the decline. The lynx now appear to be just pawns in the system, simply responding to hare abundance caused by vegetation – the hares eat up most of their high-quality browse and crash until it recovers.

The eastern cougar is protected under Ontario's Endangered Species Act, but its status is uncertain. Taxo-

Beaver. NORM LIGHTFOOT

Lynx. MIKE JONES

Gray wolf. NORM LIGHTFOOT

Traditional white-tailed deer winter yard regions. Deer move into these regions in early winter in response to deepening snow.

nomically there is little justification to consider eastern and western cougars to be different subspecies. Western cougar populations are not endangered. While numerous reports of cougar sightings from all across the southern half of the province have accumulated in files of the Ontario Ministry of Natural Resources, no live or dead animal, or track, or scat has ever been obtained or photographed. A confirmed wild cougar, regardless of subspecies, would be an exciting discovery in Ontario. The nearest record is one shot in Manitoba in 1970, less than one hundred kilometers from the Ontario border.

Better known in Ontario than the members of the cat family are the "wild dogs" – wolf, fox, and coyote. Gray wolves once inhabited the entire province and were, indeed, the only mammal whose range covered all of North America, high Arctic tundra to desert. Wolves are undoubtedly the most interesting and controversial four-legged mammal in Ontario. A bounty was placed on them in 1793, only the tenth piece of legislation passed in Upper Canada, and it lasted

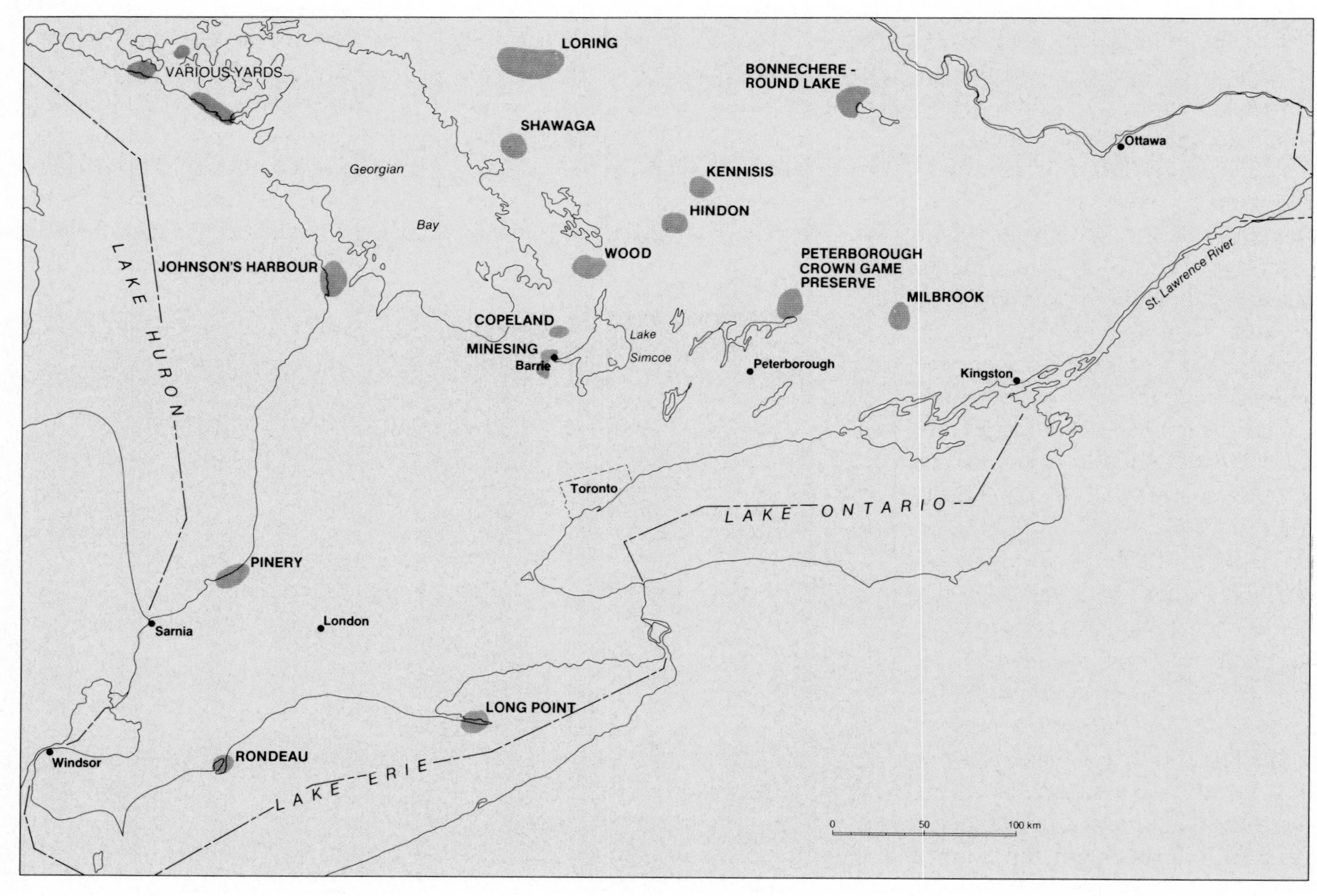

until 1972 – 179 years! During that time, farms hacked out of wilderness in the south coalesced in a wholesale transformation to agricultural land, and the wolf disappeared south of the Canadian Shield. In central Ontario, logging resulted in increased deer numbers, and wolves too. Attitudes towards wolves shifted over the years from fear and hate in pioneer communities, to indifference in growing cities, to a deep respect by the many who today enjoy the forest and lake country and who consider the wolf to be a symbol of wild Ontario.

The difference between dog and wolf is not great. The highly evolved social behaviour of wolves and their open displays of emotions, which we recognize in dogs and ourselves, have translated into considerable concern for the welfare of the species. And many people respect complete, naturally functioning ecosystems, with their predator populations intact. A proposal to virtually eliminate wolves from Ontario, made by a legislative advisory committee in the early 1970s, generated more protest mail to the government than any issue during the long premiership of John Robarts. The wolf bounty was repealed in 1972 as a result of a massive public outcry against it.

Attitudes towards wolves are not all favourable, mostly because of their predation on white-tailed deer and moose. But just what is the role of wolf predation? Studies in Ontario and elsewhere indicate that predation may contribute to what is only a very general "balance-of-nature." Natural populations of prey and predator commonly fluctuate broadly. The numbers of deer and moose in an environment are set ultimately by the amount of available forage and the weather conditions that influence its availability. For example, when snow exceeds about fifty centimetres, deer tend to "yard-up" or congregate in lowland cedar swamps where they may be forced to spend the winter. White-tailed deer in Ontario are at the northern edge of their range, set by winter severity and food availability. Populations of all species on the edges of their range typically show greater fluctuations in size than in optimal, more central locations.

Wolves may prevent a prey population from achieving a density it might otherwise be able to reach, based upon food availability. An intensive study of Ontario wolves in Algonquin Provincial Park in the mid 1960s concluded that wolves were a "major limiting factor" on deer. However, a prey population at another time or place may be depressed in size very little or not at all by wolf predation, especially when it is facing starvation close to its maximum possible size, as dictated by food availability.

A prey population may escape the influence of predators, as happened in Algonquin Park with moose in the 1970s and early 1980s and deer in the

White-tailed deer. *J.D. Taylor*

mid 1980s. Such escapes have happened elsewhere in recent years as well – a spectacular eruption of woodland caribou in northern Labrador, and an increase in barren-ground caribou in western Alaska. These escapes may have been facilitated in part by wolf behaviour. Wolves exhibit strong social hierarchies within packs, which normally restrict breeding to only the dominant pair. Clearly if a prey population is near or at the food-carrying capacity of its range, starvation will kill any surplus that wolves don't. Wolf predation under these circumstances is not important in changing the number of their prey.

Wolves tend statistically to select old, young, and sub-normal prey, as shown in many studies, including the one in Algonquin Park. A hunting human often goes after the best, unless he is having hard luck. In the long run, the pressure exerted by the two different species of predators, man and wolf, may be substantially different. The only reason why deer, moose, and other hoofed mammals exist today is that they have become skilled at avoiding predation. And that skill has evolved solely because of selection pressure put on them by their predators.

Gray wolf, timber wolf, and tundra wolf are all really the same species, *Canis lupus*. Coyotes, *Canis latrans*, are sometimes confused with gray wolves because occasionally they are referred to as "brush wolves." Coyotes occupy an ecological niche much closer to red foxes than to gray wolves. Coyotes, like red foxes, prey almost exclusively on small mammals rather than large ones. An ecological principle states that no two species can occupy the same niche in an ecosystem. One or the other species will become extinct. How coyotes and red foxes manage to co-exist in abandoned or marginal farmland-forest habitats is unclear. Perhaps neither species reaches densities sufficient to cause any severe food competition because of man-caused mortality. Both species are shot at on sight by many rural people, trapped, or hit by automobiles. Newspapers even tell of organized snowmobile drives across townships that culminate in coyotes being run down and crushed. We sometimes carry our dominance over nature to extremes of ruthlessness.

Furbearer is an illogical term given to the species of mammals exploited by humans for their fur. In fact, all mammals in Ontario except humans bear fur. One particular trait that has helped the commercially exploited furbearers to survive is their tendency to exhibit "compensatory reproduction" – they can increase the number of young produced per female in response to low population numbers. Increased reproduction is not a result of any conscious understanding of the situation, but is primarily the result of a physiological response to improved food supply. Muskrats, for example, in some heavily trapped southern Ontario marshes, may produce three litters instead of one per year. This compensatory reproduction is not a fool-proof way to avoid overexploitation, however, and care must be exercised in setting quotas to prevent overkilling. In places, furbearer populations have been damaged severely. Only recently, for instance, attempts have been made to re-introduce fisher to the Bruce Peninsula, where they had been extirpated by trapping.

Probably the least well-known family of Ontario mammals is the mustelids (although they contribute to the inclination of a rapidly declining number of people to themselves become "furbearers" on formal or festive occasions): mink, wolverine, otter, American marten, fisher, long-tailed and short-tailed weasels. Like the canids, the mustelids share some similarities but come in different sizes. And, like the canids, the species keep out of each other's way, for the most part, by exploiting different sizes of prey, the reason for their successful co-existence with one another.

Most familiar of the mustelids is the mink, inhabiting the shores of Ontario waterways throughout the entire province. Mink are predators, catching prey almost as large as themselves – muskrats and cottontail rabbits, as well as fish, frogs, voles, and shrews. Mink are important furbearers, although the bulk of the commercial market consists of genetically selected, ranch-raised animals.

The largest mustelid, with a reputation for ferocity, is the wolverine. They are exceedingly rare in Ontario, where only a few wolverines are trapped each year. Once more abun-

Muskrat. SHAN WALSHE

Short-tailed weasel. MINISTRY OF NATURAL RESOURCES, ALGONQUIN MUSEUM

dant in boreal forests across Canada, their scarcity must be attributed to over-trapping and hunting. Wolverines have a reputation for following traplines and destroying trapped animals before the trapper does. They also exploit food caches and break into cabins. Their strength is legendary; they reputably are able to roll over heavy stones and even defend themselves against grizzlies. Wolverines fear man, although, like their small relative the American marten, when cornered they will display a vicious-appearing open mouth with long, piercing canine teeth. Less is known about wolverines than any other Canadian furbearer, because they travel widely and are exceedingly elusive. These traits, and the animal's scarcity, make a wolverine sighting a fortunate event.

Otters are somewhat better known, at least among canoeists and cottagers. Otter slides are sometimes found along river banks, and winter "toboggan-like" trails in the snow can be seen by cross-country skiers. Otters are fish-eaters, catching fish by virtue of their remarkable underwater speed and manoeuvrability.

Species such as the otter owe their success to finely tuned physical adaptations to their environment. The key to these adaptations is the genetic variability inherent in all living populations. Natural selection has moulded this natural variation to create the tapered body of the otter, its webbed feet, its ears that can be closed under water, and its powerful leg musculature, giving mechanical advantage through shortened bones. The otters that first expressed these traits simply caught more fish, lived to produce more young, and thus shaped the species.

An array of adaptations is recognizable in some anatomical features in different mammals. Variation from the "typical" mammalian hand or foot is fundamental to success for many species. The fast runners – deer, moose, and caribou – are up on fused toes shaped into hooves. Moles, two species of which live in Ontario, have enlarged shovel-like hands to push earth laterally out of the way as they burrow through the upper soil. Lynx have big feet, which keep them up on the snow and help them run down snowshoe hares, which also have big feet to help them escape. Bats have greatly elongated fingers that act as a skeleton for their wings.

Eight species of bats live in Ontario, from the common little brown bat, familiar as it swoops and dives across the evening sky, to the provincially rare eastern pipistrelle. All bats exhibit the remarkable high-frequency eco-location adaptation for finding their aerial prey. But the species differ in other ways besides appearance. The silver-haired bat, for example, migrates, whereas most others hibernate.

Man has added six species to

Ontario's mammal fauna, other than himself. Both the house mouse and Norway rat spread from western Europe after immigrating on the ships of early explorers. Pre-adapted to urban environments, they had an obvious advantage over any native rodents in filling these new North American niches. European hares escaped from a farm near Cambridge in 1912 and were abundant in southern Ontario only a decade later. Fox squirrels were given a slight boost from their wide range in the United States up to the south shore of Lake Erie with an introduction on Pelee Island where they continue to survive. Nutria periodically escape from fur farms and form feral populations. They are potential competitors for native muskrats. For the past few years, raccoon dogs from Asia have posed a threat, but their introduction into Ontario fur farms has now been banned. When invading species find a competition-free niche, their populations are likely to explode.

There is little evidence that Ontario is decked out with its array of mammalian species just for our benefit. Black bears did not evolve just to support the present illegal commercial trade in their gall bladders, in the Orient a supposed aphrodisiac. Raccoons hardly emerged from evolutionary eons just to donate a hundred thousand pelts annually in Ontario to the former fad for long-haired fur coats. Nor do red foxes transmit rabies and beavers transmit tularemia and groundhogs dig holes in our pastures and coyotes kill domestic sheep just because Adam ate an apple. We are the only mammal species that has a capacity to assign values – "good" and "bad" – to other species, and to do something about it. As a consequence, the most remarkable fact about mammals in Ontario and worldwide is that the fate of all the species is dependent upon just one.

◆ SCIENCE ◆ EXCURSION ◆

Rabies in Ontario's Wildlife

John B. Theberge

Ontario holds the dubious honour of the North American record for the highest incidence of rabies in wildlife. Every year in this province about eighteen hundred cases are diagnosed, with the red fox accounting for the largest proportion, about 40 per cent. The striped skunk follows at about 25 per cent.

Not only wildlife species are susceptible, but so are domestic and agricultural animals: a ten-year average of 250 cows per year, 85 cats, 80 dogs, 33 horses, and 28 sheep. One exposure to rabies is normally lethal.

Yet rabies was rare in Canada prior to 1945, breaking out only periodically among sled dogs and arctic foxes. Then in the late 1940s, it spread rapidly south through the boreal forest, mainly carried by red foxes. Ontario's first case of rabies was reported in 1954, near Moosonee; by 1958 it had become widespread throughout even the southern sections of the province. Today, the greatest incidence is in the farmlands of southern Ontario which provide ideal habitat for the highly susceptible foxes and skunks, and which are rich in livestock and pets.

Rabies is a virus that thrives and multiplies best in the nervous tissue of mammals. Other vertebrates are not susceptible. The virus is bullet-shaped, rounded at one end, flattened at the other, and surrounded by an envelope of projecting spikes. It consists of RNA, a natural molecule essential for protein synthesis in cells, but not when coded inappropriately in an invading virus. In a mammal, besides concentrating in the central nervous system, the rabies virus infects saliva, urine, lymph, milk, blood, and faeces depending on the host species. Identification of rabies infection is accomplished by searching for tiny, oval or spherical inclusions called Negri bodies in the cytoplasm of nerve cells. These bodies contain rabies virus antigen produced by the virus itself.

Differences in physiology or behaviour mean that not all mammals are equally susceptible to rabies. Among Ontario's wildlife, after foxes and skunks the incidence is highest in bats, with a total of twenty-eight cases recorded on average per year. Rabies has been identified in seven different bat species among which the big brown bat is most susceptible. Rabid bats soon die, so do not present any danger to humans. Next is the raccoon with about ten cases recorded each year, considerably lower than one might expect for this abundant species. Why the incidence of rabies in Ontario raccoons is so low is puzzling, especially since rabid raccoons are a serious problem in the southeastern United States. Rodents are rarely diagnosed with rabies: two cases in groundhogs per year, and only one recorded in over ten years in a mouse. The weasel family, rabbit family, and deer family seem to be almost immune. Surprisingly, rabies is rare in both the gray wolf and coyote, close relatives of the number-one carrier, the red fox.

Humans are susceptible, but public education and an effective vaccine

Red fox. JOHN THEBERGE

have reduced mortality to zero since 1967 when a child died near Ottawa. Nevertheless, over a thousand people are treated each year in Ontario for rabies, and the combined costs of vaccination, compensation, and medical expenses exceed $13 million annually.

Infections in Ontario peak each year in the fall due to juvenile dispersal, which results in more contacts. A smaller peak occurs in April to June, especially in skunks, and is associated with increased contacts during the breeding season. Infections in red foxes show a pronounced three- or four-year cycle of severity for unknown reasons. Red fox populations in Ontario thrive despite their high mortality from rabies because vixens raise very large litters with an average of eight pups per female in some areas. The age structure of the population, consequently, is younger on average than it is in most other fox populations.

Research during the last decade holds promise that rabies can be reduced in Ontario. Earlier ineffective wildlife killing programs have been supplanted by efforts to vaccinate wildlife. Over a century ago Louis Pasteur developed the first vaccine for rabies. Since then, many other vaccines have been developed, primarily by passing the infection forty or fifty times through duck embryos or chicks, until the virus loses its attraction to the nervous system. It then provides a safe means of generating rabies antibodies (proteins produced in the host's blood in response to foreign antigens to combat the disease). Most vaccines used in Ontario do not include the live virus as just described because of the possibility that it will revert to the deadly form. Instead, the virus is killed chemically, but it can still stimulate the production of rabies antibodies.

Vaccinating free-ranging populations of foxes and skunks requires intimate knowledge of their ecology. Delivery has been accomplished in various ways. The Wildlife Research Branch of the Ontario Ministry of Natural Resources has perfected a method of dropping meatball baits from the air into fox habitat in October, with small plastic bags as parachutes. In tests, at a density of thirty-five parachuted baits per square kilometre, this technique has resulted in delivering vaccine to 74 per cent of resident foxes and 60 per cent of the skunks. These percentages exceed the percentage of dogs and cats in Ontario vaccinated by veterinarians for rabies – less than half.

Rabies research is ongoing, with a government Rabies Unit, a Rabies Advisory Committee, and activity at a number of universities.

◆ SCIENCE ◆ EXCURSION ◆

Predation

John B. Theberge

No phenomenon of nature is so poorly understood as predation. No phenomenon is so complex. On the surface it is deceptively obvious that if a fox kills a rabbit, or a wolf kills a deer, the prey population is that much smaller. It is, for the time being, but not necessarily so the next spring, when biologists again measure its breeding size.

Despite a seeming contradiction, four situations may occur where a predator may kill but not reduce the size of the prey population except very immediately. First, the prey may counteract losses from predation by increasing its birth rate. Such a situation may occur in a prey population so dense that it is reducing the quantity of food on its range. Because of poor nutrition, it has a lower than maximum birth rate. If predation then lowers the size of that prey population, individual prey animals that remain may experience better nutrition. Their birth rate may increase, offsetting losses. Examples of this "compensatory reproduction" have been observed in moose and deer. On high-quality ranges these species may breed at a younger age and produce twins more often, whereas on poor ranges, where they are up against nutritional stress, breeding commonly is delayed and twinning is rare. Contributing as well to lower numbers of calves on poor ranges is lower survival of calves if the females, while pregnant, have suffered nutritionally. On Isle Royale in Lake Superior, a series of harsh winters with deep snow confined moose and caused reduced food intake. Their calves were weak, died sooner, and were easier prey for wolves.

Another situation where losses due to predation may be offset is when other causes of mortality, such as disease, decrease as a result of increased predation. Called "compensatory mortality," any increase in one cause of death may be offset by a decrease in another. Compensatory mortality may occur because most mortality factors become more severe in proportion to the density of the population. Predators find prey more easily if prey is plentiful. Disease of almost any kind spreads more rapidly through dense populations.

Upon the idea of compensatory mortality rests much of the justification in wildlife management that animals can be killed by humans without causing corresponding population declines. But, mortality factors are not compensatory in all cases. After humans take their kill, if wolves, by hunting more persistently, kill just as many as they did before, then these mortality factors are additive. Then human hunting causes a reduction in the size of the prey population.

There are no set rules for predicting whether mortality factors are compensatory or additive. To complicate matters, there even may be degrees of difference that vary with absolute densities of prey and predators, and their closeness to starving, and the presence of alternative prey.

The "bottleneck" situation provides another example where predation may be relatively unimportant to the size of the subsequent breeding population of prey. In this case, some environmental factor other than predation sets the size of the breeding population at a near-constant level each year. Hole-nesting birds provide an example. If a woodlot contains 50 holes in trees in which chickadees may nest, then no more than 50 pairs of chickadees can breed, regardless of whether the late-winter population is 50 pairs or 500 pairs. If 500 pairs are present, Cooper's hawks and northern shrikes could kill 450 pairs without altering the size of the subsequent breeding population.

Finally, a deflating example for males. In many polygamous species, often it takes only a relatively small percentage of males in a population to assure that all the adult females breed. Caribou, moose, and deer can achieve full breeding with less than 20 per cent males in the population. If the non-breeding males are taken by predation, the subsequent breeding population will indeed be lower by that number, but there will be no difference in the number of young born into the population. This fact is the basis for "buck laws," or "male only" hunting regulations. Such laws are only valid, however, if the species is not monogamous. In most monogamous species, the help of the male is needed in raising young.

If none of these four situations occurs, then predation will decrease the size, or the productivity of the subsequent breeding population of prey. Even then, however, the effect of predation may result in more prey over a period of years, as contradictory as that seems. The reduction in a prey population caused by predation may prevent that prey population from increasing to the point where it consumes all its available food. If it consumes everything, it may crash and end up with lower numbers than if predators had been stabilizing them.

In attempts to predict future population sizes, these complexities in predator-prey relationships are sometimes estimated and related to one another in complex mathematical models. Taken into account must be the responses of predators to increasing prey numbers, both a *functional response*, being an increase in prey killed per predator, and a *numerical response*, an increase in the number of predators. Affecting these responses are variables such as the ability of predators to alter their specific hunting image and tactics to those appropriate for another species of prey if it should become more abundant. Or, a predator population may not reflect the size of its food supply at all, and cease to grow at some point because something other than the size of the prey population limits it. That something else may be a disease or a social restraint on breeding such as is found in wolf packs.

Despite the complexities of predator-prey relationships, however, one over-riding reality shines out. If humans do not upset the system too much, predators will go on killing prey and prey will go on escaping, and the two will co-exist indefinitely, as they have in the past. It is a fact that by killing, predators continuously select and thereby strengthen the ability of the prey to escape, and by escaping, prey continually select and thereby improve the ability of predators to kill.

◆ SCIENCE ◆ EXCURSION ◆

Parasites Welcome Moose to Ontario

Edward M. Addison

Moose evolved in Eurasia and extended their range to North America by crossing Beringia, the land bridge between continents. They crossed at least once but probably on more occasions. Being a relatively recent arrival to Ontario, they encountered new diseases which had evolved in native North American cervids, such as white-tailed deer and wapiti (elk).

The ideal relationship between a parasite and its host is accommodation. A parasite, by definition, requires a living host. If it kills its host, it normally kills itself. Therefore, evolutionary success depends upon finding ways to live off a host species without killing it.

The nematode *Parelaphostrongylus tenuis*, common name meningeal or brain worm, is a parasite of white-tailed deer, with which it evolved in North America. White-tailed deer host the worm with no pathogenic effect. Adult worms are found in the spaces and sinuses of the head. They pass eggs into blood vessels leading to the lungs. There the eggs complete their development and hatch. The larvae penetrate from the capillaries into the air passages of the lungs, then move up the trachea out of the lungs, are swallowed and pass from the deer on the surface of faecal pellets.

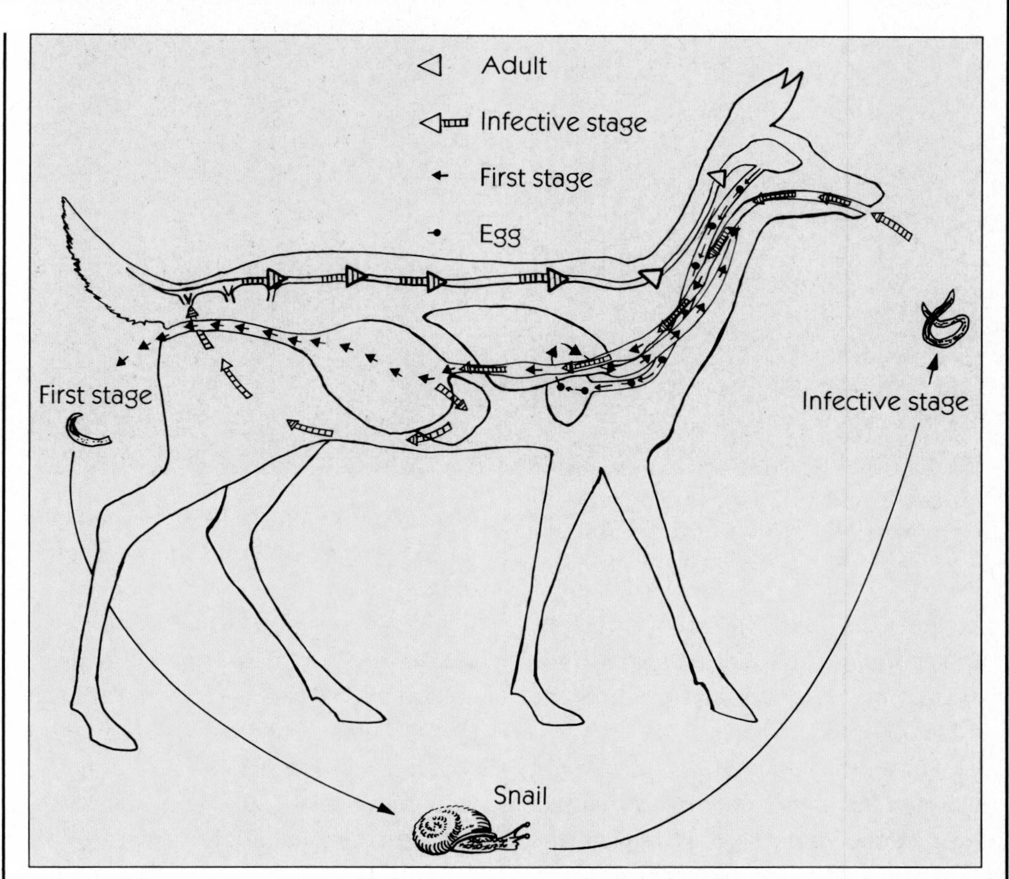

Cycle of brainworm (*Parelaphostrongylus tenuis*) in white-tailed deer.

From the pellets, the larvae penetrate the muscular feet of some species of snails and slugs which crawl over them. Following a period of development within the gastropod, the larvae are infectious to deer. Deer likely acquire an infection by accidentally ingesting snails and slugs, which in warm, moist weather are up on plants and shrubs.

Within the stomach of the deer, the larvae are released from the gastropod, penetrate through the stomach wall to the body cavity and continue on to the spinal cord. Some development occurs within the cord, but then the larvae move to the subdural space, which is a cavity between two outer

Moose in early spring showing hair loss caused by winter ticks, Algonquin Provincial Park. JOHN THEBERGE

membranes lining the spinal cord. The larvae follow the subdural space to the cranium where they mature, and the cycle is complete.

Moose, sharing the same range with white-tailed deer, acquire the infection in the same way. However, the migration of larvae to the cranial case, achieved without significant damage in white-tailed deer, is not duplicated so successfully in moose. The destruction of nervous tissue within the spinal column by worms causes reduced mobility of the hind legs and even lumbar paralysis. In addition, worms which reach the brain case without causing damage within the spinal cord may wander into the brain or eyes, destroying tissue as they move. Moose so afflicted have been noted to circle repeatedly, or stagger, prompting the popular name of "moose staggers disease." Moose may hold their head and neck abnormally, and may become blind.

The end result for the moose is death, but so it is for the worms. Moose probably are killed before the worms are able to produce eggs which exit in the faeces. Theoretically, with more time, an accommodation between parasite and host may evolve, but in the meantime the effect of the pathogenicity in moose is that moose and white-tailed deer cannot inhabit the same ranges in any great numbers. During the 1800s in Ontario, as white-tailed deer increased in numbers in response to increasing agriculture and lumbering, moose were extirpated from the southern limits of their ranges. Meningial worm undoubtedly was one of the reasons.

The winter tick, *Dermacentor albipictus*, is known only in North America, where it likely evolved as a parasite on wapiti, or possibly deer. As with meningeal worm, this parasite and moose had no opportunity to evolve a balanced host-parasite relationship. Winter tick differs from meningeal worm in that many moose successfully tolerate some ticks. However, when present on moose in large numbers, it is a serious pathogen.

Young larval ticks climb onto grasses, ferns, and shrubs in the autumn and await moose. If a moose brushes the vegetation with the ticks, the larvae attach to the moose, and unless disturbed, remain on their host until March, April, or May. The ticks grow a bit and moult to a nymphal stage shortly after attachment. The nymphs feed or develop very little until late January or February when they begin to engorge blood, moult to the adult stage, mate, and then females engorge again. In March and April the engorged female ticks are 1,000 to 1,500 times larger than the larvae which attached in the autumn. Engorged females may be the size of small grapes.

The rapid feeding by the winter ticks from February through April irritates moose so that they scratch, lick, and rub themselves. This grooming leads to extensive hair loss, particularly in the neck, shoulder, and perianal regions. Moose expend a lot of energy trying to maintain their body heat when their coat is interspersed with bare patches. They may survive with considerable loss of hair, particularly if the March and April weather is warm and dry, however, extreme cold or rainy weather at near-freezing temperatures are particular problems. Some moose die of hypothermia while others die from lack of sufficient energy reserves to help them through the winter. Ticks on moose which die before the snow is gone will die themselves.

As with meningeal worm, the winter tick-moose relationship has yet to reach a balance which is not detrimental to both parasite and host. Many moose have paid a high price to be residents of Ontario.

Native Man

Bill Fox

They were "ecosphere people," dependent upon the resources of the land they occupied and beneficiaries of little trade. Known today as the Paleo-Indians, they were the descendants of hunters who crossed the Bering land bridge millenia before. Over ten thousand years ago they came from the south into a pocket of land bounded by a huge ice sheet to the north and extensive lakes to the west and east.

When Ontario's native people first arrived, the western part of this pocket had been ice-free for close to three thousand years, yet ice still entombed three-quarters of the province, including the basin that would become Lake Superior and all land to the north. Enormous Lake Algonquin filled the Huron-Michigan basin, connecting to the northwest with Glacial Lake Agassiz and draining south through what today is the Trent Waterway. Lake Erie was much lower then, but Lake Ontario extended down to include Lakes Champlain and George in New York state.

The ice-free pocket of land was slightly higher than the surrounding terrain, which extended from today's Niagara Escarpment west to Lake Huron, but it was inaccessible, an island locked between the ice to the north and an even earlier fore-runner of the Great Lakes to the south. Humans may not have invaded Ontario until openings developed at either end of shrinking Lake Erie.

What they found was open spruce parkland, not greatly different than the taiga landscape bordering the Arctic tundra today. Temperatures were slightly cooler then, and many of the mammals, birds, and fish living there can be found today in central and northern Ontario. In addition, there were Pleistocene mammals such as woolly mammoths and American mastodons. Somewhat later, in southeastern Ontario, marine mammals and fish inhabited the Champlain Sea, which extended eastward to the Gulf of St. Lawrence.

Living in small, mobile bands, these hunters and gatherers travelled hundreds of kilometres in north-south seasonal migrations. Evidence suggests that caribou was a major source of food. One group of southern Ontario hunters apparently followed migrating caribou herds from their winter range at the southern end of present-day Lake Huron to their summer range around the Blue Mountains, then possibly a tundra plateau. Later, a similar migration may have been traced by northwestern native bands who spent the summer along the north shore of Lake Superior near present-day Thunder Bay and moved south to Minnesota in the winter.

An intimate understanding of their new environment was critical to the survival of these first pioneers. They quickly found their way through the maze of waterways on the ice-free southern edge of the Canadian Shield, locating strategic points for hunting and fishing, as well as important new sources of toolstone. Evidence at archaeological sites suggests that Ontario Paleo-Indian bands preferred one or two specific chert (flint) sources which became virtually their signature, allowing identification today of communication between groups based hundreds of kilometres apart. Their choice of particular high-quality snow-white and blood-red cherts for lanceheads and other tools reflected not only their consummate skill as flintknappers, but also their appreciation of colour. Rarely in the many millennia to follow did flintknappers express such a high level of technical skill.

Over the next one thousand years, the continental glacier continued its northward retreat, opening new outlets for the Great Lakes and causing the Superior and Huron basins to

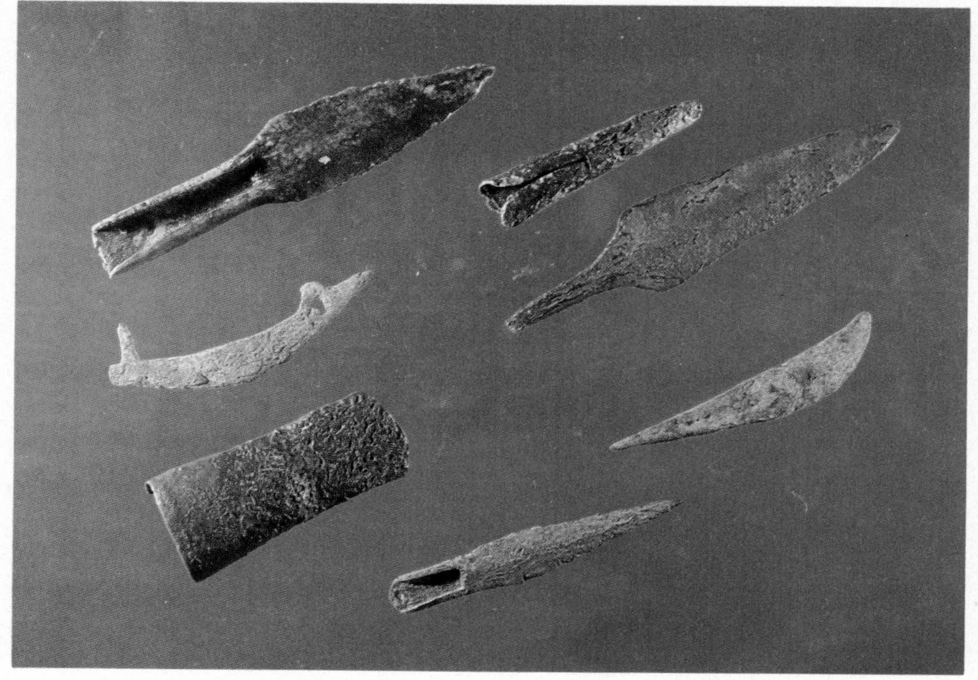

Prehistoric tools from northwestern Ontario archaeological sites, manufactured through hammering and annealing native copper obtained from float deposits or mined from bedrock exposures. D. ARTHURS, MINISTRY OF CULTURE AND COMMUNICATIONS

recede to their lowest levels, more than one hundred metres below present. A land bridge connected the Bruce Peninsula with Manitoulin Island and the north Huron shore. Spruce-dominated parkland gave way to spruce forest, and then pine. Mammoths disappeared, and mastodons were soon to follow. The vast herds of caribou dispersed in the new closed forest which they shared with other large mammals such as black bear and moose. In the south, new species such as white-tailed deer and elk arrived and settled in attractive mixed forest niches. All these changes in fauna influenced the native people. By nine thousand years ago, man was reducing his range of seasonal travel to match the more sedentary resident game populations. As well, the human landscape was filling up.

The web of Canadian Shield waterways emerging from the ice demanded some means of marine transportation. Even the earliest human occupants of northwestern Ontario appear to have used water craft. Certainly by Archaic times, seven thousand years ago, some sort of bark or skin craft must have been in use to allow exploration and settlement over all of Ontario's boreal forest zone. In winter, these people travelled the same complex water routes substituting snowshoe and sled for canoe.

Temperatures in the north reached modern levels some sixty-five hundred years ago and then increased further during the next thousand years. At this time prairie parkland vegetation extended into northwestern Ontario, supporting prairie animals such as bison. The discovery of prairie Archaic-style chert tools dating to between fifty-five and thirty-five hundred years ago as far east as Quetico Provincial Park provides some support for the theory of an eastward expansion of prairie environment at this time. However, no such warming has been documented for southern Ontario, where modern forest cover was established between eight and seven thousand years ago. By this time, most species of mammals, birds, and fish had established ranges that were documented in the early records of European inhabitants.

The period from seven thousand to three thousand years ago, which archaeologists term *Archaic*, was a time of slow change following man's initial adaptation to life in Ontario. The Great Lakes rose again to above-modern levels in the Superior, Huron, and Erie basins about fifty-five hundred years ago, receding after that. These changes in levels, as well as the slow disappearance of Glacial Lake Agassiz and the Champlain Sea, must have created many marshy embayments that seasonally teemed with waterfowl and spawning fish. Wild rice was available, as were numerous edible reptile species and shellfish.

During the Archaic period, bands of several hundred hunters and gatherers became established within specific river basins or portions of larger water systems. A seasonal cycle of subsistence became established which optimized the available plant and animal foods of Ontario's diverse biotic zones. Little deviation from the food procurement norm was possible, especially in the harsher Canadian Shield environment, where adaptations to life in the boreal forest developed early and continued with little change for millennia, with starvation as a constant winter spectre. Living through a winter in small bark- or skin- covered lodges or spruce-bough shelters was a demanding lifestyle, especially when food was not assured. Only the strong and fit survived, and the average life expectancy was probably around forty years.

A wide variety of plants provided food. Strawberries, raspberries, elderberries, and blueberries were important in the diet, often as seasonings for otherwise bland staples. To the south, hickory and butternuts were particularly favoured, although black walnuts also were harvested. Carbonized seeds and shell fragments recovered by archaeologists from prehistoric campsites suggest that nuts were boiled to extract their highly nutritious oil. As well as providing food, hundreds of plants were used by medical practitioners for conditions ranging from wounds to upset stomachs, tooth aches to pregnancy.

Autumn would bring an abundance of game, including flocks of migratory waterfowl, spawning lake trout and lake whitefish, and concentrations of deer, turkeys, and raccoons which gathered to exploit the nuts produced by a number of southern deciduous trees. It was a time of abundance before winter's hardships. However, as the water froze, the spawning fish dispersed to deeper water, and the game left the nut-bearing groves; so too the native people would scatter in small family groups to traditional hunting areas. Most people abandoned the shores of the Great Lakes and large river mouths, and moved inland in search of game. While there was some ice-fishing, most food was acquired by hunting. Beaver and rabbit were important in the north, especially if moose and caribou were scarce. Deer, and the occasional elk or moose were hunted in the south. Southern Ontario hunting groups travelled to extensive lowland black ash and cedar swamps, camping on the perimeter while hunting deer that had yarded there for winter cover and forage. On occasion, a hibernating bear might be discovered and killed. Naturally, large mammal kills were a time for rejoicing, especially on the Canadian Shield, and early Jesuit missionaries who lived among the northern Algonkian people recorded feasts where entire animals were devoured by hungry family groups over a period of only a few days.

Life for people in the Archaic period was undoubtedly rich in legend and lore, spiritualism and animism, although archaeological evidence for this facet of their existence is rare and circumstantial. Their whole landscape was alive and their natural environment interwoven with themselves in a spiritual sense. For example, the dangers of Great Lakes water travel were interpreted as due to great underwater monsters capable of lashing the lakes into terrible storms unless offerings were left at shoreline "power" sites. Particular species of birds and mammals played important roles in legends about the origins of life and natural phenomena, so that their skins symbolized or conferred specific powers. Hunting magic played an important role in native life, and a lore about cannibalistic winter spirits (Windigos) developed in the north.

Only during the later portion of the Archaic period are archaeologists provided with a glimpse of this rich symbolic system. During the Late Archaic, forty-five hundred to three thousand years ago, artifacts from campsites provide evidence for the widespread communication of technical ideas and religious concepts. Cemeteries often contain burials sprinkled with red ochre (iron oxide) paint and are accompanied by ornaments of marine shells from the Atlantic coast or native copper from the Superior basin. Ethnographic evidence suggests that the red paint may have generally symbolized bodily life, the white shells symbolized spiritual goodness, and the copper, spiritual power.

Little remains of the material belongings of these people to allow us to interpret their daily activities. Wood, cloth, feather, and animal skin have all decayed over time. Consequently, archaeologists must study Archaic stone projectile points – their sizes and shapes – to answer questions as basic as when the bow and arrow became a part of these peoples' hunting equipment. Similarly clouded is the significance of large-stemmed projectile points introduced thirty-seven hundred years ago that look like lanceheads or knife blades. These "Christmas-tree"-shaped weapons probably were developed in, and introduced from, the southeastern United States. Was it simply theirnovel size and shape that caused their spread in popularity, or did they contribute to improved hunting success? Possibly they were used in a revolutionary system of deer hunting involving communal drives using fences and corrals.

Daily life continued much as it had for millennia, until three thousand years ago when a new technology – clay cooking and storage vessels – was introduced from the south. The beginning of this ceramic technology in Ontario ushers in the Woodland period. Ceramic food containers provided another medium for artistic expression. However, this new class of implement appears to have had little economic effect on native life.

During the Early and Middle Woodland periods, until about twelve hundred years ago, a great volume of exotic goods was being traded into Ontario, especially chert from neighbouring states to the south as far away as North Dakota, and even some obsidian from Wyoming. The chert was identifiable to specific rock outcrops by physical characteristics and microfossils, and the obsidian identifiable by trace elements. In return, copper and silver from Ontario were traded as far away as the southeastern United States.

During this period, too, mortuary rituals reached their zenith. Large mounds of earth were erected as cemeteries by native groups from Rainy River in northwestern Ontario to the St. Lawrence in the east. In their form, contents, and use these mounds are very similar to the often larger ones raised in the more populous drainage regions of the upper Mississippi and Ohio rivers. These larger southern tribes had developed more elaborate, stratified societies, probably involving full-time religious specialists, or priests, and possibly also hereditary leaders, or chiefs. In Ontario, however, the closest known analogues to these southern societies developed along the Rainy River, as well as in the vicinity of the Rice Lake/Trent River waterway. At Serpent Mound Provincial Park is an example of a sinuous mound which may have been modelled after the much larger and slightly earlier Ohio Serpent Mound.

Over this period, new technical ideas were introduced to Ontario natives from the south – the bow and arrow, ceramic technology, and undoubtedly many concepts not registered in the archaeological record. However, none of these ideas resulted in any evident revolution in native lifestyle. Twelve hundred years ago that changed with the introduction of maize, or Indian corn.

Gourds and perhaps squash were known to southern Ontario peoples as early as twenty-five hundred years ago, but it was the introduction of maize that ushered a totally new way of life into the south of the province. A suitably lengthy growing season allowed its growth, and native people began to exploit the potential of this relatively dependable and storeable food resource. While all through the Woodland period wild plant foods and meat had been cached for winter use, quantities had never been sufficient to allow large bands to winter together. With corn, communal living in winter became feasible.

Availing themselves of this new opportunity, the Iroquoian-speaking peoples constructed villages of oblong bark lodges surrounded by palisades or walls of poles, perhaps modelled after more southerly villages. Here they lived in winter, normally dispersing to nearby lodges to tend the corn crop, and to smaller, more distant summer camps to hunt, fish, and collect wild plants. The corn was planted in partially cleared fields among stumps and trees killed by girdling.

Algonkian-speaking peoples to the west of the Iroquoian groups in southern Ontario, in the region of Lake St. Clair, also experimented with corn horticulture. Modifying their seasonal cycle only slightly, they grew corn around their summer villages and dispersed in winter to smaller settlements of isolated bark lodges. Throughout northern Ontario, however, the native lifestyle of most Algonkians changed relatively little until the arrival of European traders and adventurers. Small mobile bands continued their hunting and gathering existence, coming together at fishing sites in summer and dispersing more widely in winter – a pattern of land use most suitable to the low density and mobility of their food resources.

During this Late Woodland period some of the most vivid expressions of native spiritual belief, sometimes including astronomical knowledge, are recorded in *pictographs*, or rock paintings, and to a lesser extent as *petroglyphs*, or rock outcrop carvings. Recent research suggests that most pictographic art in Ontario represents the statements of Algonkian-speaking shamanic societies, such as the Wabeno, or star specialists, and the Djiski, or shaking-tent practitioners, each group taking its power from different sources.

Segment or panel at a northwestern Ontario rock-art site, possibly depicting Nenebush and his wolf brother Maheegun (central figures) standing above water symbols (large manned canoe and serpent). Note the zig-zag power line from the head of the Nenebush figure who holds aloft an animal-skin medicine bag in his left hand – both symbols of spiritual power. Powdered hematite was mixed with fish glue and grease to paint these figures. The mixture has invaded and stained the bedrock itself, thus contributing to the longevity of the images. G. RAJNOVICH

A bark lodge or longhouse reconstructed at the Longwoods Conservation Area near London. It typifies Ontario Iroquoian structures some 800 years ago. BILL FOX

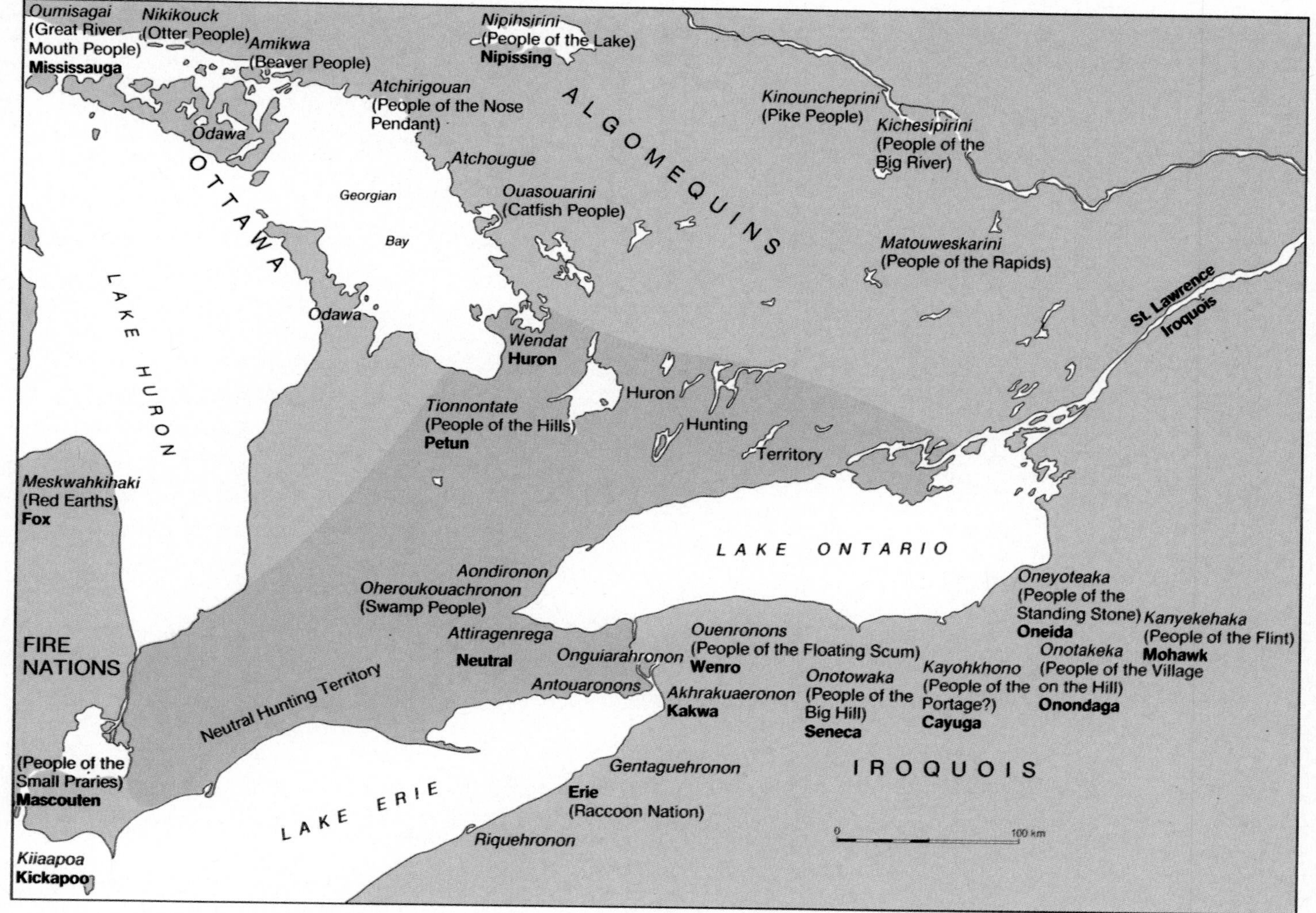

The locations of native tribes and bands in and around what is now southern Ontario at about 1600 AD. An attempt has been made to provide each group's name for itself, a translation of that name (in brackets), and the name by which they are now known. The coloured zone delineates the "island" of Iroquoian-speaking peoples in Ontario as depicted on the c. 1641 map of Nouvelle France. Information sources used to construct this map include seventeenth-century maps and accounts of European

Over the eight centuries between the arrival of maize and the arrival of Europeans in southern Ontario, Iroquoian groups established ever larger and more stable villages. Tobacco, which was a ritual item, may have been introduced prior to maize; however, sunflowers, beans, and edible squash did not appear in Ontario until about nine hundred years ago. With the cultivation of beans, the traditional Iroquoian triad of corn, beans, and squash was established, creating a truly agricultural economy.

The Iroquoian populations expanded north, west, and east to the climatic limits of corn growth, and reached their widest distribution of village settlements by the close of the sixteenth century. By then the earliest European trade goods were entering Ontario. In the early seventeenth century, when the first Europeans visited Ontario, Iroquoian peoples were living in palisaded villages of up to several thousand people, organized into tribal confederacies which became known to us as Huron, Petun, and Neutral.

Normally, soil fertility around these large villages gave out after about ten or fifteen years, causing them to be abandoned and new ones built. Because of this short period of land tenure at any one site, land clearance by humans was a major ecological influence in southern Ontario, possibly increasing abundances of "edge" species such as white-tailed deer and wild turkey. A misconception is that southern Ontario was always a vast, unbroken, mature forest before European settlers arrived. While, indeed, much of it was unbroken back from Lakes Erie and Ontario, it was that way because the agricultural societies came to an abrupt end in the mid-seventeenth century when the Five Nations Iroquois from south of Lake Ontario dispersed the Huron, Petun, and Neutral Indians. After that, the land had time to revert primarily to mature forests once again, broken only by windstorm, flood, and sometimes fire.

Thus it was that for ten thousand years a human subsistence economy was supported by Ontario's natural landscape. All that ended with the fur trade and the era of European settlement. It remains to be determined if the natural landscape can support a human industrial economy that long.

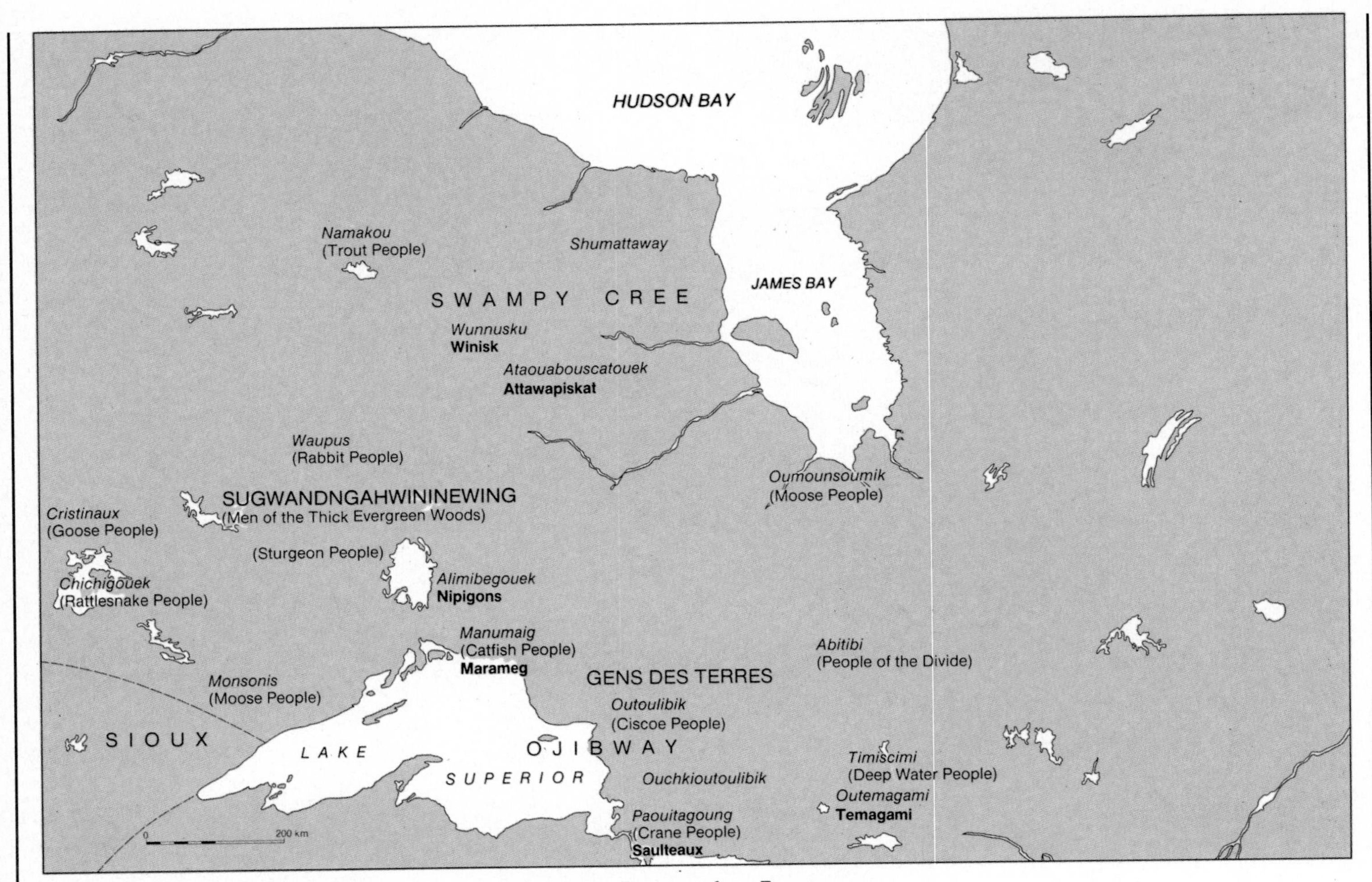

The locations of native tribes and bands in and around what is now northern Ontario. The same system of group identification has been attempted as on the map of southern Ontario. Large type refers to linguistic or multiband generic groupings of peoples. Because few Europeans visited the area prior to the major dislocations of native people around the Great Lakes in the mid-seventeenth century, the information is less complete and more conjectural than for the south.

Part Three

SPECIAL ENVIRONMENTS

The Erie Sand Spits
Long Point, Rondeau and Point Pelee
Gerald McKeating

Lake Erie's three famous sand spits – Long Point, Rondeau, and Point Pelee – like living things, have moved and changed through time. Water, current, and wind have slowly shifted enormous volumes of sand and silt from distant eroding shorelines and gathered it where currents converged. Over time, long, curved peninsulas extended like fingers into the lake. These were protected in many places by shifting barrier beaches facing in the direction of formidable natural forces. Continued erosion, movement, and deposition gave each sand spit a characteristic shape, size, and life of its own.

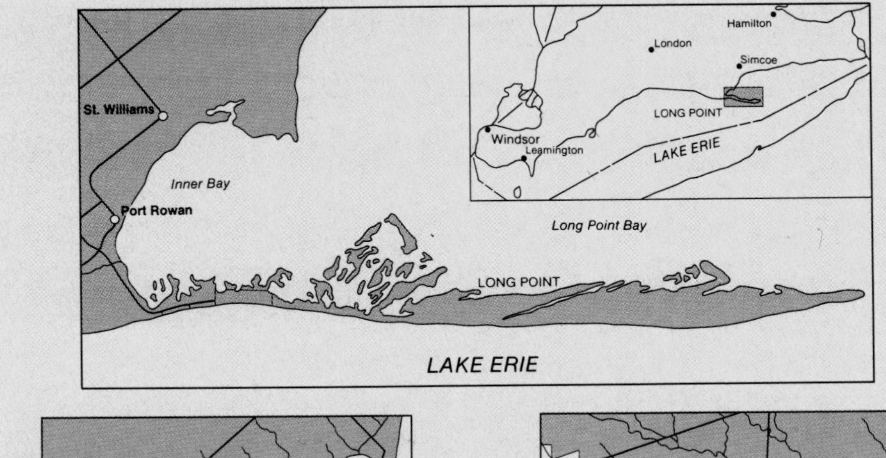

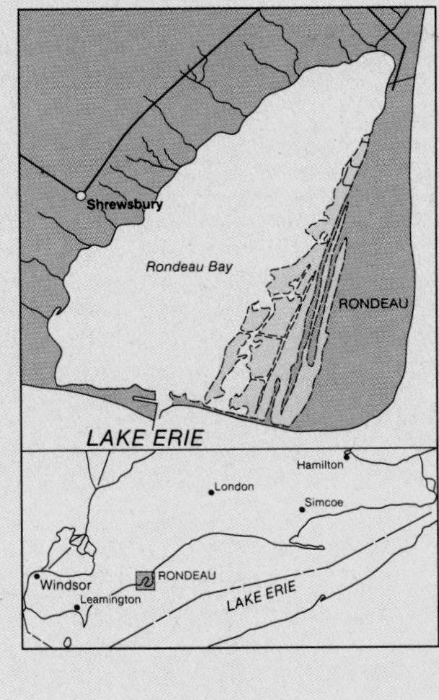

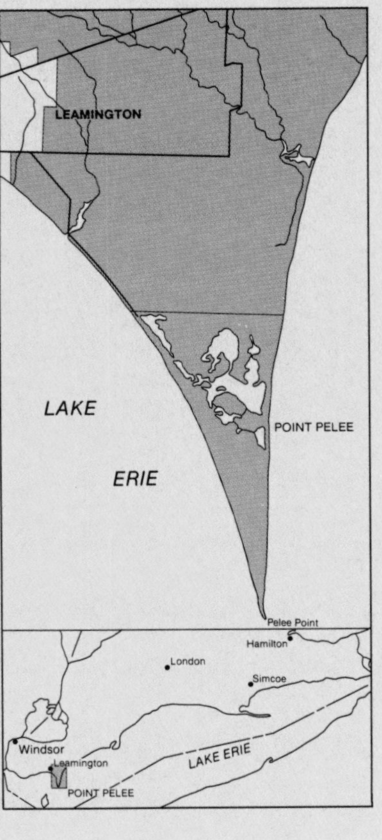

Gradually, all sand spits develop beaches, dunes, sloughs, and ponds. Pioneer dune plants begin to invade, followed in time by forest trees whose roots bind the soil and protect the surface from the wind. But in fifty or a hundred years along comes the inevitable powerful storm with giant waves and shifts in currents; the sand, and with it the vegetation, move on. After the storm, the process begins anew.

Adjacent to each of the Erie spits is an enormous shoreline scallop. High, eroding cliffs mark the centres of these scallops. Soil from these cliffs is washed into the lake, then moved by shoreline currents, and finally deposited on the sand spits. Until recent decades, the spits became ever larger, growing ever farther out into the deeper parts of the lake.

The three spits share a peculiar "ridge-and-trough" physiography which provides the most important clue to the manner in which wave and wind built them up over the centuries. This physiography is closely linked to gradually rising lake levels over many thousands of years. The highest ridges are the most recent; the lowest, now submerged, are the oldest, formed some three to five thousand years ago when Lake Erie was much smaller. Then the average water level in the western basin was at least six to ten metres below its present level. The nature of isostatic rebound (slow rising of the land ever since the weight of the glaciers was removed) in the Lake Erie region has been causing the land at the east end of the lake, its exit, to rise more rapidly than that around the western basin. Because of that, the farther west we go along the lake, the more the shorelines have submerged. On the Ohio side, in places where the shoreline was low, large areas which were forested only two hundred years ago are now part of the open lake.

Long Point. GERALD MCKEATING

The trend of rising average water levels is continuing to this day at the rate of about one-half metre per century. Water levels in the mid 1980s were the highest in all recorded history, and the sand spits were assaulted, eroded, and reshaped as never before.

The longest and the most easterly of the spits is Long Point. Long Point's shoreline sands move eastward, the offshore current bringing material from the scallop west of the point. Long Point, possibly the Great Lakes' most complex and unusual sand spit, reaches thirty-two kilometres into the deepest part of Lake Erie.

At the other end of the scallop from which Long Point receives its soil is Rondeau Point. In contrast to Long Point, Rondeau was built mainly from the east. This deposition along its eastern shoreline is the major factor shaping Rondeau today. Rondeau's unusual shape and the position of its barrier beaches is the result of a complex interaction of various wave forces and water currents which erode sand from both its east and its west shores. The parallel north-south ridges of Rondeau thus were built up starting in the west where, due to long-term rising water levels, the lowest ridges and troughs are now completely submerged in Rondeau Bay. This ridge-and-trough phenomenon can be easily witnessed by walking across the peninsula from east to west and seeing the interesting series of swamps and dry ridges. In sharp contrast to the deposition on the eastern shore, forces operating today at the southern tip of the peninsula are dramatically different. Here, powerful wave action is removing the shoreline altogether, and great trees of an old forest are being washed into the lake.

The third great sand spit of Lake Erie is Point Pelee, the southernmost point of mainland Canada. Its tip is at the same latitude as northern California. Unlike the curves of Long Point or Rondeau, Pelee's tip points straight out from shore, some sixteen kilometres into the lake. The shape of Point Pelee indicates that sand is being brought to the spit from both the east and the west. However, only the southwest shoreline has seen the development of a ridge-and-trough physiography as this shore was slowly extended by deposition beginning about twelve hundred years ago. As at Rondeau, the oldest, but in this case the easternmost ridges and troughs, are now submerged in the marsh below lake level.

All three spits have a unique local climate with the lake exerting a pronounced moderating influence. The water warms and cools more slowly than does the adjacent land, so the spits have markedly cooler springs and warmer falls. Snowfall is low, but summer rainfall is slightly higher than on the mainland. Overall, winter temperatures are slightly higher, but summer temperatures are distinctly lower.

The sand spits contain unique combinations of habitat including beaches, dunes, upland forests, grasslands, wet meadows, wet or flooded woods, marshes, ponds, and fields. Because of this variety, and the lake-modified local climate, varied and unusual ecosystems have developed. Many species found on the spits are considered rare or threatened elsewhere in Ontario, for that matter in Canada. For example, 15 per cent of Pelee's flora is unique in Canada, while at Rondeau 12 per cent is rare in Ontario. Unique, too, are total plant communities. Together, these unusual species and communities represent the greatest natural value of all three points.

Pelee and Rondeau particularly are rich in plants of southern affinity. Tulip-tree, pawpaw, Kentucky coffee tree, chinquapin oak, black gum, black walnut, red mulberry, sassafras, and blue ash are conspicuous. Two conifers – white pine and red cedar – are found on sandier, drier soils. Rondeau's thick understorey of shrubs like spice bush, mulberry, and flowering dogwood combines with vine-covered trees to provide an impression of vegetative richness not often seen elsewhere in eastern Canada. Eighteen species of orchids have been found, including the rare nodding pogonia. Swamp rose mallow grows throughout the marsh. Despite heavy lumbering in the nineteenth century, Rondeau Park now contains some of the best examples of climax (mature) or near-climax forest on the three spits. Once, such splendid canopied forests stretched across the entire southwestern peninsula of Ontario from the tip of Lake Huron to Niagara.

Long Point, too, has plants more common farther south, such as sassafras or a tulip-tree here and there, but it does not have the impressive variety of the more western spits. What it does have that the other two lack completely, however, is a mixture of plants of more northern affinity. We can descend a dune and suddenly find ourselves in a rich, low forest of white cedar and tamarack with such boreal forest herbs as early coralroot, starflower, twinflower, and green pyrola at our feet.

This more northern vegetation appears to have developed in response to Long Point's more maritime climate. Long Point extends out into the deepest part of the lake where the waters function as a heat sink. Consequently, in the spring, the cold lake water surrounding it retards plant growth. As well, lake depth, coupled with westerly winds, push ice floes into great stacks at the eastern end, lowering the air temperatures and prolonging the spring melt. Sometimes as late as May, the scene from Long Point's south beach out over the lake is one of ice packed in as far as the eye can see. A few ponds and open leads are filled with cackling old squaw ducks, restless to be on their way north.

The shallow-rooted wetland forests of the three points recently have been under siege from rising lake levels. Even in periods of low water, the groundwater is relatively close to the surface, and with the high water levels in recent years, the soil around the roots of these forest giants became soft and unstable. Many trees fell as the winds of autumn swept down the lake. The great wetland forests of Point Pelee are much altered now that most of the American elms are down. Once, bald eagles nested in the Post Woods. Today that woodland area is only a shadow of its former self, the trees toppled by the ravages of nature. Marshland is replacing forest.

The forests of both Long Point and Rondeau also are being radically altered by large herds of white-tailed deer. These abundant animals browse intensively upon the vegetation, and thus new saplings are unable to survive. Indeed, the impact of the deer on the forest is so severe that large areas, particularly on Long Point, look like intensively overgrazed cow pastures. Studies have shown that removal of many animals may be necessary if the forests and many rare plant species are to survive.

Not only are the points a national treasure for their spectacular forests, but migratory birds put on a display here as spectacular as can be seen anywhere in North America. Spring migration begins with waterfowl. After the ice begins to rot, cracks appear with open water. As if by magic, these leads immediately fill with ducks and swans. The haunting calls of tundra swans echo across the marshes, their white forms silhouetted against the brilliant blue sky. Wave after wave of swans land from the southeast, calling and greeting each other, fresh and excitable, seemingly oblivious to the hundreds of kilometres still to travel on their long, northward migration.

The arrival of the tundra swans heralds spring. With the swans come thousands of ducks – redheads, canvasbacks, blue-winged teal, and most of the other species which inhabit eastern Canada. Their stay is short; by early April most of them have moved on toward the prairies, northern forest, or Arctic tundra. But migration is far from over. April brings swarms of brown creepers, kinglets, white-throated sparrows, thrushes, and all the early migrants with their familiar calls of spring. At Long Point the birds move up the funnel towards the mainland. They often mass at the base of the last ridge adjacent to the famous Long Point marsh, undecided whether to try reaching the mainland over the treeless beach or across the marsh. At the outflows through the beach, many shorebirds congregate; with luck, a little gull might be seen.

Pelee acts as a funnel for migrants too, the islands to the southwest serving as stepping stones for the birds traversing the lake from Ohio. After they cross the open water, Point Pelee is the first landfall. This stepping-stone effect is important, but Pelee is also located at the juxtaposition of eastern and western flyways and hence rarities abound.

As the days grow longer and the sun warmer, the points become increasingly splashed with colour and filled with song. New species arrive daily: blue jays, rose-breasted grosbeaks, northern orioles, and scarlet tanagers. Birds of brilliant, tropical hues flit through the leaves, hotly pursued by throngs of birdwatchers on an annual pilgrimage.

Point Pelee, of course, is renowned as one of the best places on the continent to observe the spring migration of warblers. Pelee is a tiny park, about fifteen square kilometres, yet within its boundaries are diverse habitats and associated wildlife all demanding closer examination. Rarities are commonplace; excitement lies in anticipating what the dawn will bring. It may be a Franklin's gull from the west, or a willet, or some obscure sparrow more at home in Kansas, here merely to provoke intense debate. It might be a summer tanager high in a hackberry tree, or a Kentucky warbler maddeningly hidden under the mayapple.

The experienced birdwatcher starts the day at the tip of the point, searching the turbulent waters for terns, ducks, or an unusual gull. Shorebirds may arrive, but they sometimes remain only for an instant. The scrubby vegetation could hold other new arrivals. Moving northward up the point, migrants can be found almost anywhere – in woods, fields, hedgerows, sloughs, marshes, even in the agricultural fields north of the park boundary. By searching the many habitats, an active birdwatcher has little difficulty in seeing over one hundred species each day. At Pelee, Rondeau, or Long Point, there seems to be an environment for every bird.

After a light rain, swarms of white-throated sparrows, white-crowned sparrows, and other common species appear in such abundance that they create an illusion of moving ground. Should the weather co-operate with a warm front and a gentle rain at night, waves of sparrows and warblers can be brought down to flit from shrub to shrub and tree to tree. The excited birdwatcher soon forgets about the ache in the neck from constantly searching the tree-tops for those elusive warblers.

Rondeau Park is as important as the other two spits during migration, but it is also a special place to observe species that have remained to breed. The tall trees, dense shrubbery, and the inter-dunal sloughs give an impression of wildness and tranquility not possible at Point Pelee. While Rondeau does not seem to funnel the birds northward as much as Long Point or Pelee, a rich variety passes through. About 80 per cent of all bird species recorded in the province have been seen at Rondeau. This special place has the largest known breeding population of prothonotary warblers in Canada, although a swamp at the base of Long Point is not far behind. Acadian flycatchers nest here, and bald eagles occupy one of their last remaining nests in southwestern Ontario. A total of 124 breeding species have been listed, including many rarities such as Forster's terns and little gulls. In all, 323 species have been observed, but with each passing year the list grows.

Like Rondeau, Pelee provides breeding habitat for species that just manage to maintain a foothold in Canada. Breeding at the northern limits of

Point Pelee. POINT PELEE NATIONAL PARK, C. LEMIEUX

Rondeau marsh. P. A. WOODLIFFE

their ranges, these species may occur elsewhere in southern Ontario but usually are most abundant at Pelee. Among them are orchard orioles, white-eyed vireos, blue-gray gnatcatchers, yellow-breasted chats, and Carolina wrens.

Autumn too is extraordinary. For instance, the north shore of Lake Erie is renowned as one of the best places in North America to view flights of hawks. The birds become concentrated through a combination of wind and geography. Birds of prey try to avoid crossing large bodies of open water; hence, at Lake Erie they follow the shoreline and move down the spits. At the tips, they swirl around and head back up the peninsulas, reluctant to cross the open lake. Point Pelee is especially good for spotting sharp-shinned hawks. These bird-eating raptors fly at tree-top level, suddenly darting into the bushes in pursuit of prey.

In autumn at Long Point, widgeon, wood ducks, and other dabbling species of waterfowl pack the ponds, feeding in the extensive stands of wild rice. By late autumn the bay is alive with redheads and canvasbacks that spend their days in huge rafts on Lake Erie. In early evenings, black lines of ducks rise from the lake, and soon flock after flock fill the sky. They land in the sheltered bays to feed on submerged plants. Although invisible in the dark, the sounds of their purposeful feeding carry on the cool night air.

The points are extremely rich in amphibians and reptiles too. Many common species live there plus at least five rare or threatened species. As human pressures increase on other critical habitats in southern Ontario, these spits are increasingly important as last refuges for survival. The eastern fox snake, most of whose world range is in southwestern Ontario, can be found easily, and eastern spiny softshell turtle, Blanding's turtle, spotted turtle, Fowler's toad, and the eastern hognose snake are among the other rare reptiles that find suitable habitat here. Rondeau is especially rich, with seventeen species of reptiles and fifteen species of amphibians.

The mammals of the spits, on the other hand, are not extraordinary. White-tailed deer are abundant, particularly at Long Point and Rondeau. Raccoons, skunks, and muskrats are common, and coyotes, bats, meadow voles, and deer mice are there too. Bobcat tracks have been reported at Long Point, and otter slides and tracks were photographed there during the winter of 1979–80. Opossum, more typical of the southern United States, occasionally can be found.

Associated with each of the points and protected by them are large marshes. Besides providing habitat for breeding birds such as Forster's terns, Virginia rails, and other wetland-dependent bird species, these biologically productive ecosystems are extremely valuable as spawning, nursery, and foraging grounds for many fish of Lake Erie. With ice breakup, pike use the marshes extensively for spawning. As the water warms, the muddy bottoms are churned up by spawning carp. It is difficult to determine the true value of the marshes to the fresh-water fishery of Lake Erie. Without them, however, the fishery would soon be diminished. The marshes and quiet ponds also harbour many rare fish such as the yellow bullhead, green sunfish, lake chubsucker, brindled madtom, and pugnose shiner.

A real appreciation of the biological diversity of the Erie sand spits can only be obtained by spending time on them observing nature in its varied forms and moods throughout the seasons – a howling November storm, a horizon dark with ducks, the majesty of a gliding eagle, a flock of sanderlings dodging the waves in their seemingly incessant search for food. Even the summer deer flies, stable flies, and ticks add to the spectacular diversity, if not to the enjoyment. In an environment of small woodlots, factories, row housing, shopping centres, and all the trappings of modern urbanization, that these places still cackle with geese, swirl with ducks, flash with colourful migrants, harbour rare orchids, and provide a bastion for reptiles and amphibians is an enduring tribute to those before us who fought for their protection. These places are old – products of the ice age – yet as new as last night's storm.

Niagara Escarpment
The Spine of Southern Ontario
Mike Singleton

Images leap to the mind of anyone who has visited the Niagara Escarpment. Little streams cascading, like broadly ruffled sheets of silk, dozens of metres over luxuriant, moss-mantled ledges of rock; bogs woven from finest threads of life, cradled incongruously by towering, massive, stark, grey cliffs; sea-caves pummelled long ago into the scarp's surface, mysteriously perched today far up on its face, providing microhabitat for rare ferns, roosting bats, and hibernating bears; ice-beards in winter, gigantic in proportions, coloured blue, brown, and green by mineral-laced seepage; flowerpots – twenty-metre-high rock pillars standing like monstrous vases at the water's edge. All these things become etched indelibly in the visitor's mind, evoking a sense of drama and of personal minuscularity beside this stately heritage adorned with jewels of every biological description.

A majestic rock spine, 2,300 kilometres long and up to 250 metres high, the Niagara Escarpment technically is a feature rather than a region, but it generates such a wealth of microhabitats that it forms a broad regional belt of its own. This belt, snaking across the landscape like an overlay, infinitely enriches the tapestry of Ontario's countryside.

Southern Ontario holds but a section, albeit the richest, of the Niagara Escarpment. At its southern end, the scarp rises just south of Rochester, New York. Crossing the border at Niagara Falls, it winds west along Lake Ontario's southern shore to Hamilton. Then it snakes north to Collingwood, west inland from Georgian Bay's south shore to Owen Sound, and north again to form the backbone of the Bruce Peninsula. The Escarpment disappears beneath the water between Georgian Bay and Lake Huron, resurfacing as the spine of Manitoulin, Cockburn, Drummond, and St. Joseph's islands, the latter near Sault Ste. Marie. From there, the Escarpment swings southwesterly along Lake Michigan's western shore, becomes the backbone of the peninsula which creates Green Bay, then tapers out southwesterly in Wisconsin.

This giant horseshoe shape is no

Niagara Escarpment, Halton-Wentworth Region. NIAGARA ESCARPMENT COMMISSION

Bruce Peninsula, eastern shoreline.
NIAGARA ESCARPMENT COMMISSION

coincidence; it is the product of a 600-million-year history. And the geological events which created the Escarpment are responsible not only for the dramatic scenery, but also for the myriad of specialized habitats in which plants and animals thrive.

To understand that history, one must take a trip through time. Picture yourself in a boat, 600 million years ago, anchored where Chicago will eventually stand. You are floating near the edge of a vast inland sea, vaguely reminiscent of the Caribbean. Almost all of what will become the central United States lies covered by salt water, two to twenty-five metres deep, with islands projecting here and there. You are in a huge bay, ringed to the northwest, north, and east by a rugged, slowly-eroding land mass – the Canadian Shield. Drainage off the Shield carries phenomenal volumes of muds and nutrients, and forms a giant, shallow delta which projects into the bay from the east.

Time goes on – 100 million years or so – and far beneath your boat a downward vortex begins to form in the Earth's mantle. It pulls with it a giant depression in the Earth's crust. (Picture a large piece of Saran Wrap floating above the vortex of a draining bathtub.) Downward the crust sinks, ever so slowly, for more than 300 million years, creating an 800-kilometre-wide dish.

As the dish deepened, sediments settled to its bottom. Like modern-day seas, this one was highly structured. Areas near shore were inundated with great volumes of silt and sand, borne in and buried so rapidly that they were only sparsely colonized by animals; these sediments would become today's shales and sandstones respectively. Farther from shore, the muddy, shallow waters were colonized by marine creatures, while the nutrient-rich surface waters contributed a constant rain of plankton; these sediments would become limestones. Here and there, in clear-water areas, reefs flourished.

For over 300 million years, with water levels and shoreline positions constantly changing, these sediments built up in successive layers. The layers eventually hardened into rock, like a stack of giant, bowl-shaped pancakes within the crust's dish. At its fullest, this stack may have been 9,000 to 12,000 metres thick in the centre of the bowl, extending in a huge arc through the present-day locations of Sault Ste. Marie, Madoc, and Port Hope.

Then, about 300 million years ago, triggered by little-understood pyrogenic forces in the Earth's mantle, the whole process reversed. The entire basin began to lift, and continued to do so for about 200 million years, displacing the tropical seas and exposing the huge stack of bowl-shaped rock pancakes.

Had the sedimentary layers flattened back out, and been composed of uniformly soft rock, the whole basin would have eroded level once again. But the basin did not rise all the way back up. The rock layers retained their

Origin of the Niagara Escarpment in the context of the sedimentary layers of rock that first were laid down in a bowl-shaped depression then uplifted and eroded at the edges. This diagram helps explain why the sequence of bedrock on the surface of southern Ontario today becomes progressively younger from east to west (shown in the map "Paleozoic Rocks of Southern Ontario" in the previous chapter "Foundations of the Land").

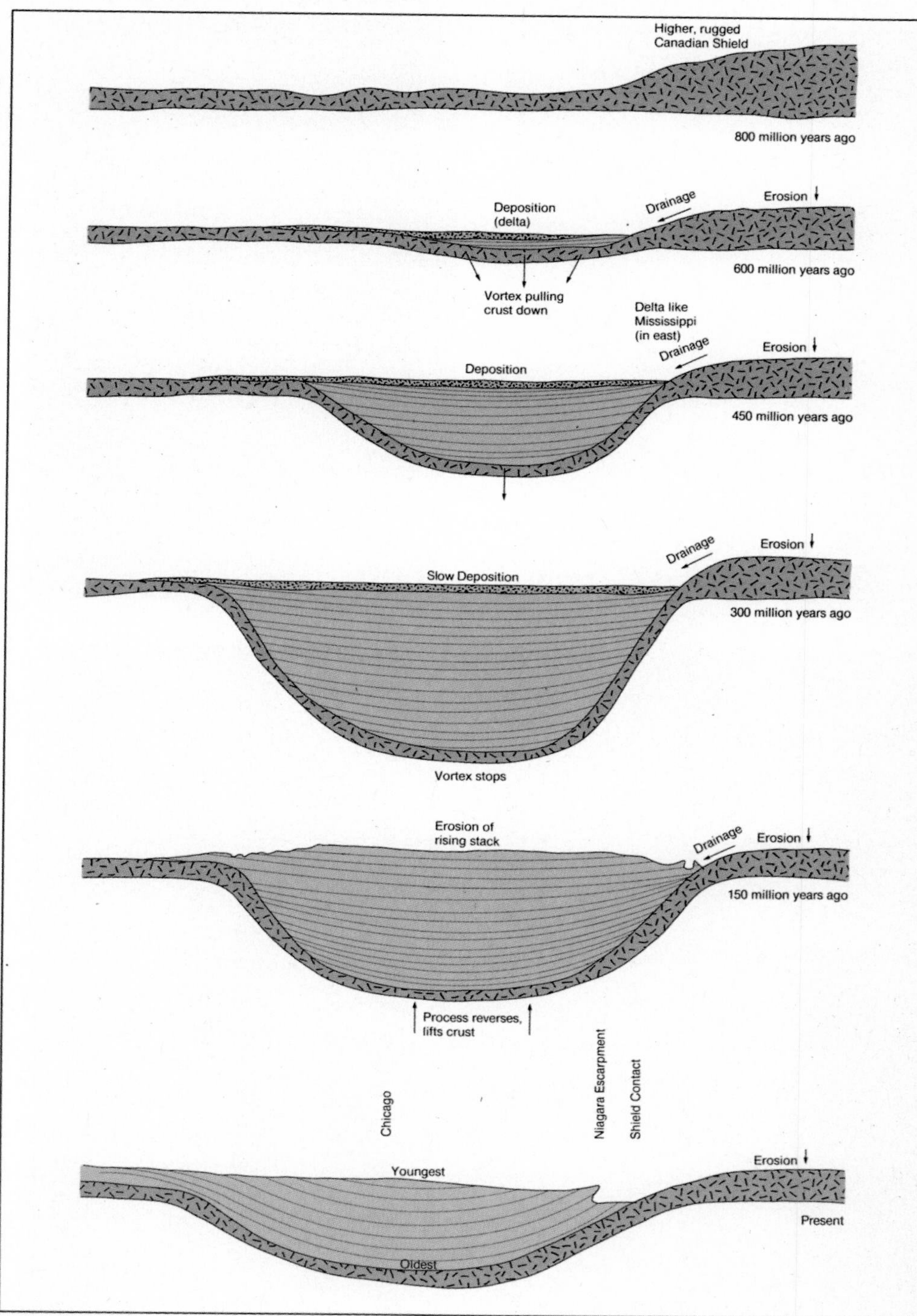

Cross-section of the Michigan Basin through the Bruce Peninsula. 1 is Guelph Formation, 2 is Amabel (Lockport) Formation, 3 is Clinton and Cataract groups, and 4 is Queenston Shales.

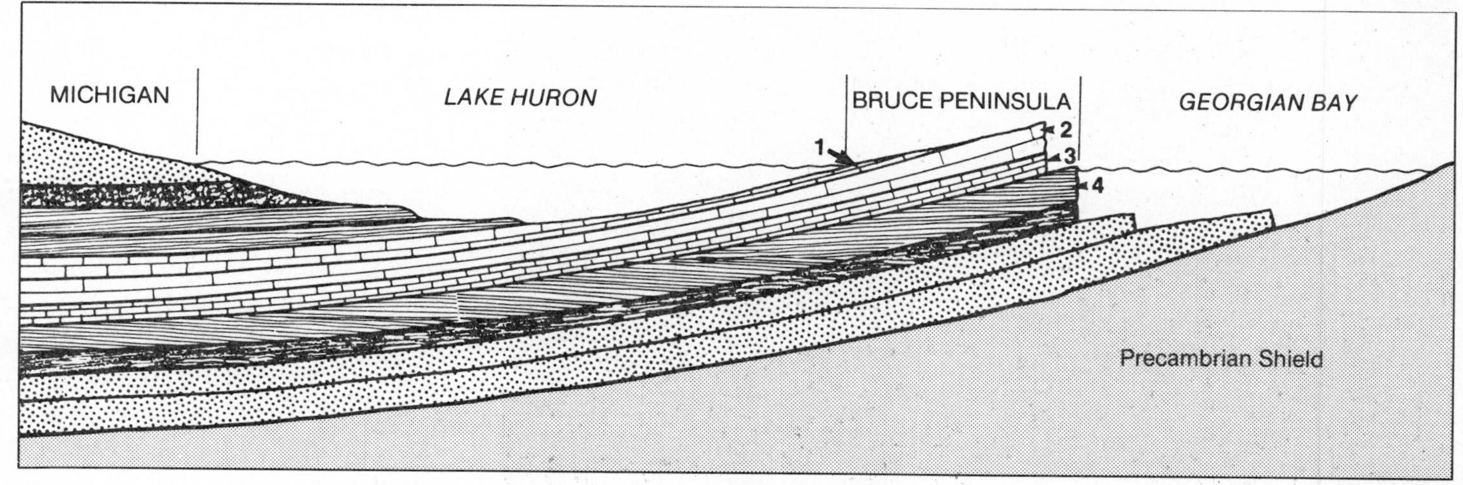

Not to Scale

Kalpore Uplands, Bruce Peninsula. NIAGARA ESCARPMENT COMMISSION

Flowerpot, Georgian Bay Islands National Park. LARRY LAMB

dished shape. Erosion sheared the raised margins of the dish, resulting in the sequence of surface sedimentary rock in southern Ontario – oldest to youngest, east to west.

As the stack rose, two things happened which eventually formed the Escarpment. Erosion proceeded easily through the soft layers of limestone and shale, until stopped by a great, sloping outer rim of highly resistant Lockport dolomite laid down about 430 million years ago in the early Silurian period. This dolomite acted as a huge cap, protecting the soft layers below. This rock draws its hardness from massively thick layering and from the incorporation of magnesium into the calcium carbonate structure of normal limestone. The magnesium was derived from salt water and marine organisms. The difference created by the addition of magnesium is like the difference between charcoal and diamond, both made of carbon, but one very soft, one very hard.

The other event was a fracturing and crumbling of the thin and weak outer edge as the basin rose. This created a small escarpment along that earlier-mentioned arc, located over eighty kilometres east of the Escarpment's present-day location. It also exposed the edge of this pancake stack to erosion which would "move" the Escarpment southwestward and make it "grow."

The profiles of many modern cliffs show how erosion has eaten away at the face of the softer rocks below the dolomite. The cliffs curve inward from top to bottom, and large amphitheatres have been eroded out all along the Bruce Peninsula's eastern shore.

Frost was clearly a major actor in the erosion of the Escarpment and can still be seen at work today. Water, seeping through fissures and crevices, froze, thawed, and refroze through countless years with astonishing hydraulic force. Every freeze jacked out small pieces of rock, especially the softer shales and limestones. Undermined, the larger plates of dolomite caprock collapsed from above and came tumbling down. A short walk along the Escarpment today will reveal the whiteness of fresh rock falls.

To the casual observer, it scarcely seems possible that this massive ridge could have "moved" over eighty kilometres. Yet, we have to bear in mind the immense time period involved. If the Escarpment eroded, or receded, merely two millimetres per year, it could "march" eighty kilometres in just thirty million years. In reality, it took much longer, and the process was erratic rather than steady.

Most of the fallen rock is gone now. Some of it simply dissolved or crumbled and washed away. The balance was ploughed away by repeated glaciations.

In addition to this continuous nibbling, rivers had their effect. Because the basin was shaped like a giant dish, it tended to trap water which accumulated in large lakes until deep enough to spill outward, over the Escarpment's edge. Across the span of millions of years, numerous falls, like today's Niagara, carved gorges into the stack. Such monumental gorges, long since abandoned as the surface tilted and eroded, form the Beaver Valley and the bays at Wiarton and Owen Sound.

A curious jog in the Escarpment to the west, below which Hamilton now sits, is the product of one gargantuan waterfall. Its gorge would have dwarfed Niagara Falls, being five times as deep and extending 300 metres down from the lip. Its bottom is now seventy metres below current sea level, and today the lower 125 metres lie below Lake Ontario's surface, extending as a trench filled with glacial debris under Hamilton Harbour and the Burlington Skyway. Yet another glacially filled trench, known as the Eregon Channel, nearly parallels the present-day Niagara River, and runs beneath Fonthill.

The penultimate stage in the Escarpment's development took place during the last ice age. Between 1 million and 10,000 years ago, four successive waves of glaciers ploughed across the Escarpment. Monumental scouring pads three and a half kilometres thick, these glaciers bore at their base a grit of boulders, house-sized rocks, sand, and other debris. They bulldozed away all life, soils, rivers, and other "soft" features. They scoured away loose rock and ground deeply into the bedrock, reshaping the basins in which today's Great Lakes sit.

Pausing in their retreat, as advance briefly matched melt, the glacier fronts dumped enormous ridges of debris in *moraines* that straddled, and in some places buried the Escarpment. On these sites would eventually develop towering forests – Carolinian in the south, northern hardwoods farther north.

The glaciers plastered down *drumlins* on their undersides – great mounds of clay that look like kilometre-long, longitudinally split eggs. On such high, drained sites, stately groves of pine, hemlock, and yellow birch eventually would flourish.

The glaciers deposited great jumbled mounds of rock in the lee of resistant ridges and fossil reefs. Upland sites would eventually become hibernacula for reptiles and warrens for myriad small mammals. Submerged sites would become shoals, essential as spawning grounds to the survival of lake whitefish and as feeding grounds to small-mouthed bass, yellow perch, and an array of other fish. Where shoals project, superb colonies of birds reproduce: terns; herring, ring-billed, and great black-backed gulls; black-crowned night herons, great blue herons, and double-crested cormorants.

Acting like a dam, the Escarpment trapped and re-directed phenomenal volumes of melt-water. The rivers carried fine sediments away while sorting heavier sands and gravels into thick deposits, many of them up against the Escarpment. Other rivers, winding beneath the melting glaciers, laid down narrow *eskers* – ten- to fifty-metre-thick deposits which today wind like giant snakes across the countryside. Such sites would eventually support belts of black cherry, white pine, and both red and white oak.

Stranded chunks of ice, some the size of football stadiums or larger, broke off and were buried in the glacial debris. These land-locked "icebergs" slowly melted, collapsing the till above to produce a myriad of isolated lakes. Some would remain as dramatic, steep-shored, miniature lakes, replete with beaver, American marten, and alder-loving warblers.

Other lakes would become ringed by white cedars and other wet-loving plants whose leaves would acidify the water, and, over thousands of years, they would develop a floating mat of vegetation. This mat would form into successive plant rings: water-edge reeds and cotton grass, open sphagnum, specialized shrubs like sweet gale and the laurels, and trees such as tamarack and black spruce. Steadily these rings would march toward the centre, one after the other, closing the open eye of the bog.

Loosely jumbled caprock, left near the edge of primordial lakes, was piled by the action of ice and wave into storm beaches. Some of these beaches later were stranded up against the wall of the Escarpment or farther inland by changing lake levels. Others were piled high, over time, into habitat for water snakes, dock and wolf spiders, and an array of sculpins and darters.

After being depressed into the mantle by the glaciers' weight, the Earth's crust sprang skyward, tilting as it rose. Upward it came, over thousands of years, in a process called *isostatic rebound* that continues even today. Indeed, the rebound has at least forty metres more to raise southwestern Ontario before it will be complete. Great stretches of the bowl's edge, rising like a chipped dish from a filled sink, reached and rose above the surface of the ever-changing Great Lakes.

Caves, pummelled into the scarp's face by the actions of ice and wave,

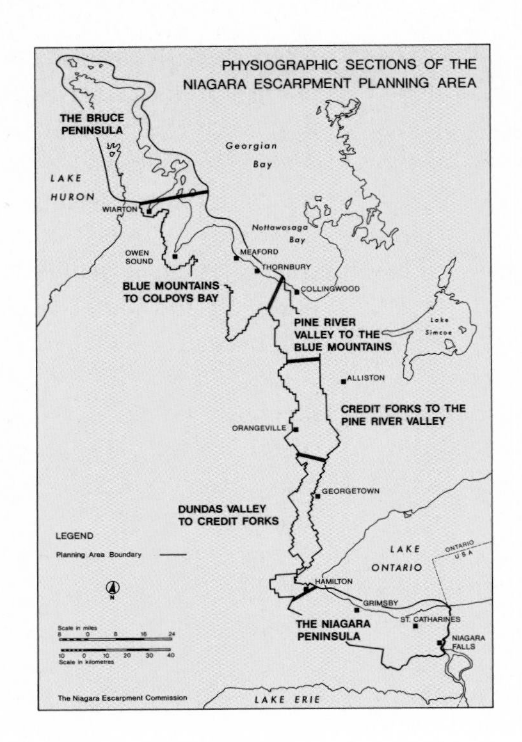
PHYSIOGRAPHIC SECTIONS OF THE NIAGARA ESCARPMENT PLANNING AREA
THE BRUCE PENINSULA
Georgian Bay
LAKE HURON
WIARTON
OWEN SOUND
MEAFORD
THORNBURY
Nottawasaga Bay
BLUE MOUNTAINS TO COLPOYS BAY
COLLINGWOOD
PINE RIVER VALLEY TO THE BLUE MOUNTAINS
Lake Simcoe
ALLISTON
CREDIT FORKS TO THE PINE RIVER VALLEY
ORANGEVILLE
GEORGETOWN
DUNDAS VALLEY TO CREDIT FORKS
LEGEND
Planning Area Boundary
LAKE ONTARIO
ONTARIO U.S.A.
HAMILTON
GRIMSBY
ST. CATHARINES
THE NIAGARA PENINSULA
NIAGARA FALLS
LAKE ERIE
The Niagara Escarpment Commission

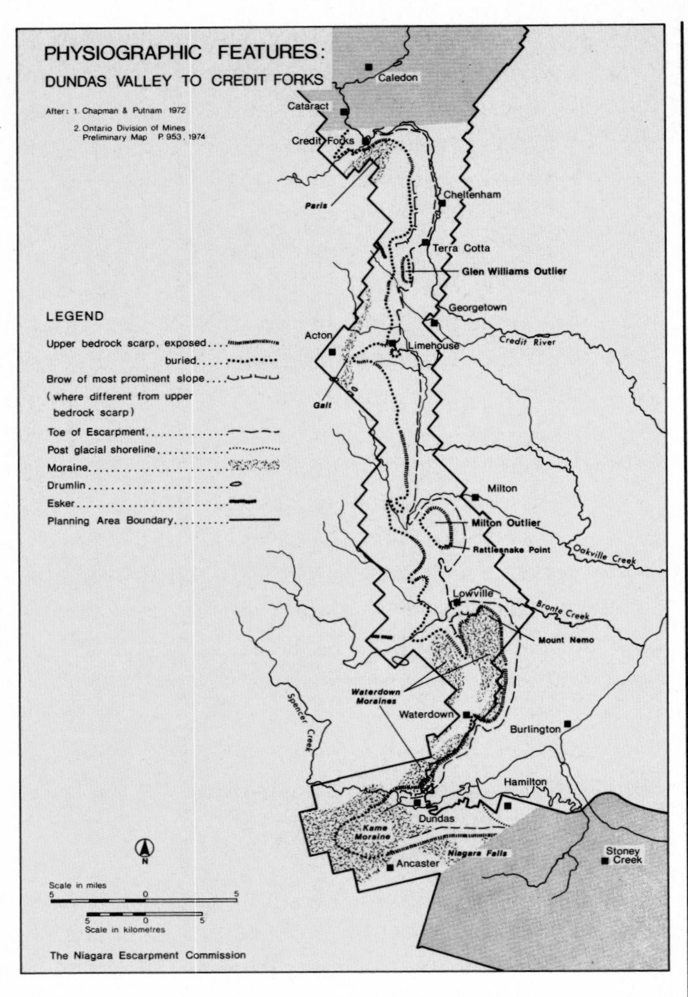
PHYSIOGRAPHIC FEATURES: DUNDAS VALLEY TO CREDIT FORKS
After: 1. Chapman & Putnam 1972
2. Ontario Division of Mines Preliminary Map P. 953, 1974
Caledon
Cataract
Credit Forks
Paris
Cheltenham
Terra Cotta
Glen Williams Outlier
Georgetown
Acton
Limehouse
Credit River
Galt
LEGEND
Upper bedrock scarp, exposed
buried
Brow of most prominent slope (where different from upper bedrock scarp)
Toe of Escarpment
Post glacial shoreline
Moraine
Drumlin
Esker
Planning Area Boundary
Milton
Milton Outlier
Rattlesnake Point
Oakville Creek
Lowville
Bronte Creek
Mount Nemo
Waterdown Moraines
Waterdown
Spencer Creek
Burlington
Hamilton
Dundas
Kame Moraine
Niagara Falls
Ancaster
Stoney Creek
Scale in miles
Scale in kilometres
The Niagara Escarpment Commission

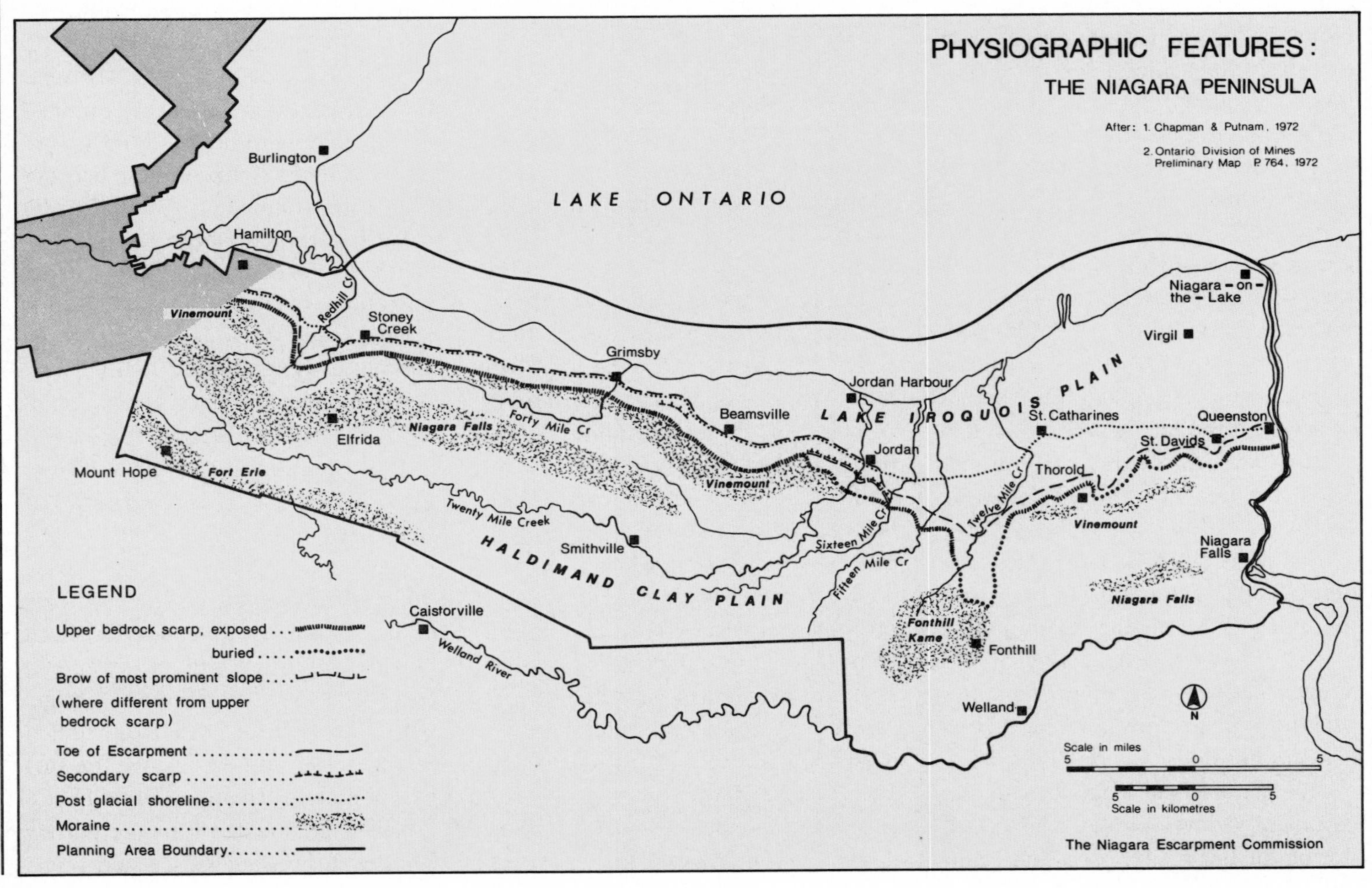
PHYSIOGRAPHIC FEATURES: THE NIAGARA PENINSULA
After: 1. Chapman & Putnam, 1972
2. Ontario Division of Mines Preliminary Map P. 764, 1972
Burlington
LAKE ONTARIO
Hamilton
Redhill Cr
Vinemount
Stoney Creek
Grimsby
Niagara-on-the-Lake
Virgil
Jordan Harbour
LAKE IROQUOIS PLAIN
Beamsville
St. Catharines
Queenston
Elfrida
Niagara Falls
Forty Mile Cr
Jordan
St. Davids
Mount Hope
Fort Erie
Thorold
Twelve Mile Cr
Twenty Mile Creek
Vinemount
Smithville
Sixteen Mile Cr
Fifteen Mile Cr
Niagara Falls
HALDIMAND CLAY PLAIN
LEGEND
Upper bedrock scarp, exposed
buried
Brow of most prominent slope (where different from upper bedrock scarp)
Toe of Escarpment
Secondary scarp
Post glacial shoreline
Moraine
Planning Area Boundary
Caistorville
Welland River
Fonthill Kame
Fonthill
Welland
Scale in miles
Scale in kilometres
The Niagara Escarpment Commission

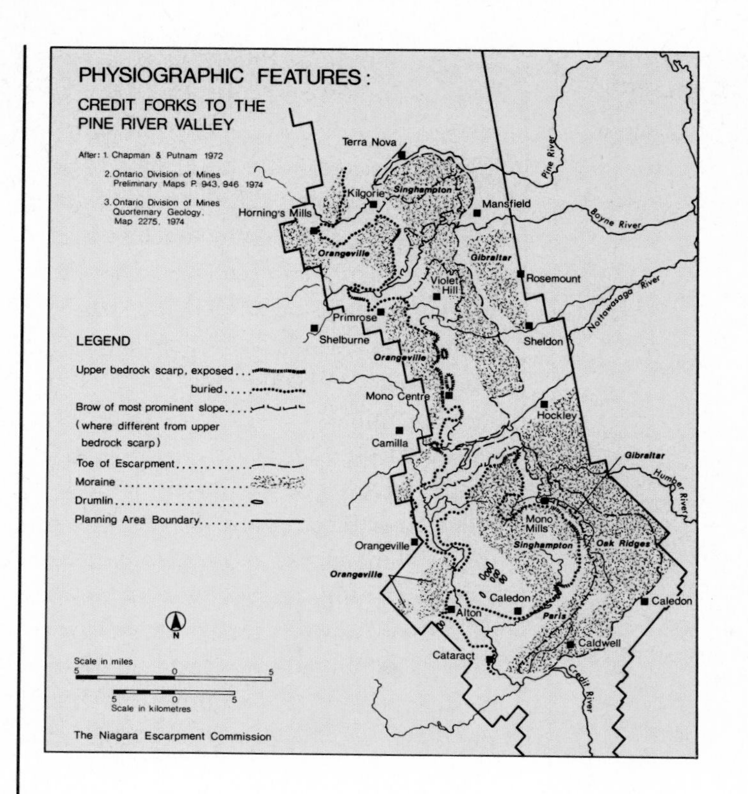
PHYSIOGRAPHIC FEATURES:
CREDIT FORKS TO THE PINE RIVER VALLEY
After: 1. Chapman & Putnam 1972
2. Ontario Division of Mines Preliminary Maps P. 943, 946 1974
3. Ontario Division of Mines Quaternary Geology. Map 2275, 1974
LEGEND
Upper bedrock scarp, exposed
buried
Brow of most prominent slope (where different from upper bedrock scarp)
Toe of Escarpment
Moraine
Drumlin
Planning Area Boundary
Scale in miles
Scale in kilometres
The Niagara Escarpment Commission
Terra Nova
Kilgorie
Singhampton
Horning's Mills
Mansfield
Boyne River
Pine River
Orangeville
Gibraltar
Violet Hill
Rosemount
Nottawasaga River
Primrose
Shelburne
Sheldon
Mono Centre
Hockley
Camilla
Humber River
Mono Mills
Oak Ridges
Paris
Caledon
Alton
Caldwell
Cataract
Credit River

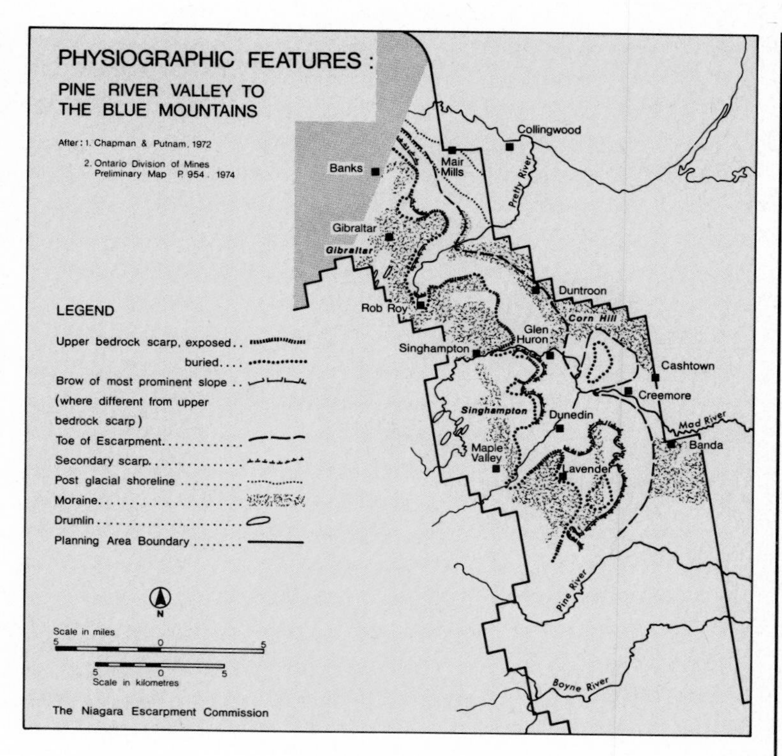
PHYSIOGRAPHIC FEATURES:
PINE RIVER VALLEY TO THE BLUE MOUNTAINS
After: 1. Chapman & Putnam, 1972
2. Ontario Division of Mines Preliminary Map P. 954, 1974
LEGEND
Upper bedrock scarp, exposed
buried
Brow of most prominent slope (where different from upper bedrock scarp)
Toe of Escarpment
Secondary scarp
Post glacial shoreline
Moraine
Drumlin
Planning Area Boundary
Scale in miles
Scale in kilometres
The Niagara Escarpment Commission
Collingwood
Banks
Mair Mills
Pretty River
Gibraltar
Duntroon
Rob Roy
Corn Hill
Glen Huron
Singhampton
Cashtown
Creemore
Mad River
Dunedin
Banda
Maple Valley
Lavender
Pine River
Boyne River

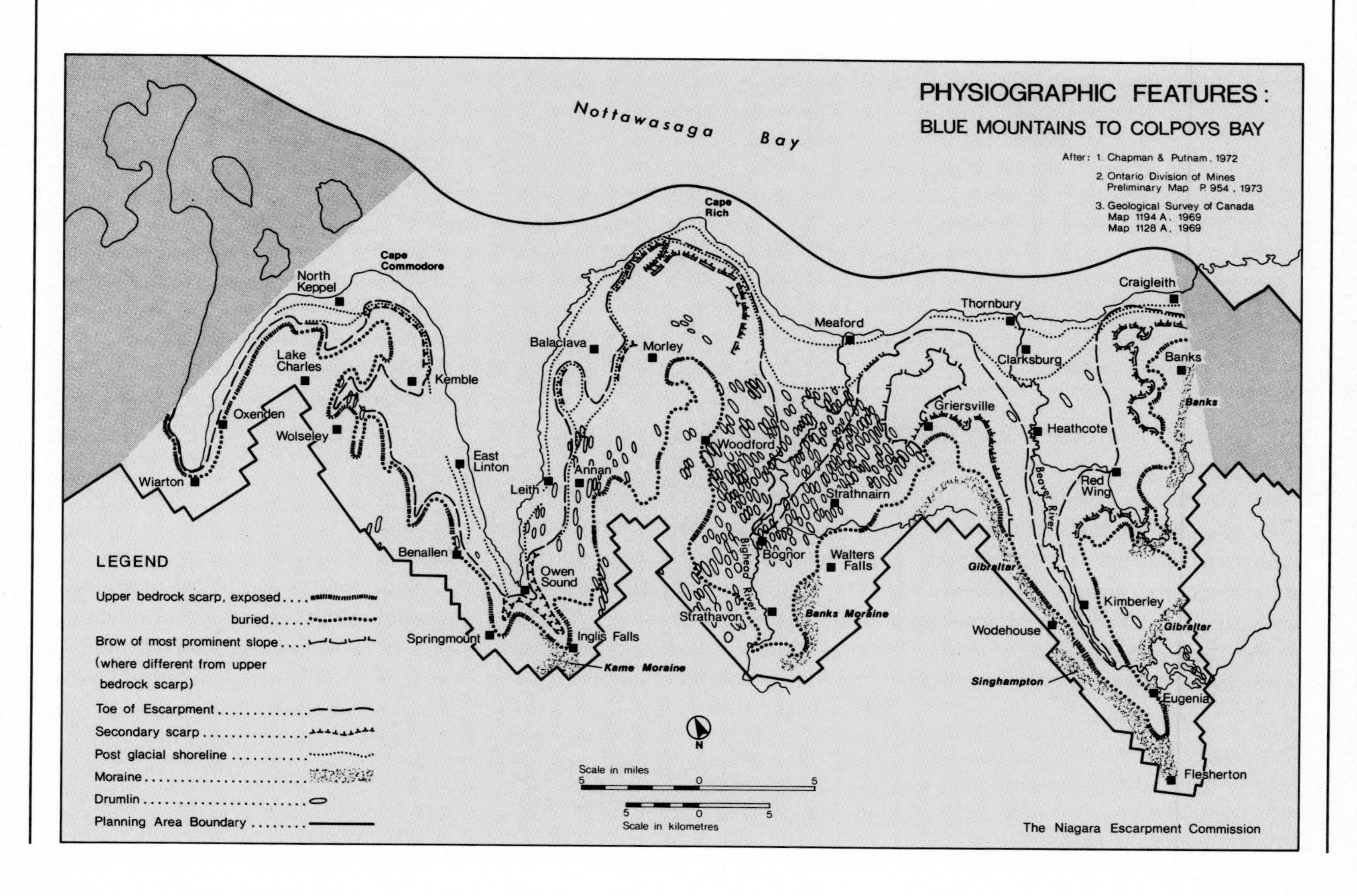
PHYSIOGRAPHIC FEATURES:
BLUE MOUNTAINS TO COLPOYS BAY
After: 1. Chapman & Putnam, 1972
2. Ontario Division of Mines Preliminary Map P. 954, 1973
3. Geological Survey of Canada Map 1194 A, 1969 Map 1128 A, 1969
Nottawasaga Bay
Cape Rich
Cape Commodore
North Keppel
Lake Charles
Kemble
Oxenden
Wolseley
Wiarton
East Linton
Balaclava
Morley
Meaford
Thornbury
Craigleith
Clarksburg
Banks
Griersville
Heathcote
Woodford
Leith
Annan
Strathnairn
Red Wing
Beaver River
Benallen
Owen Sound
Bognor
Bighead River
Walters Falls
Gibraltar
Strathavon
Banks Moraine
Springmount
Inglis Falls
Kame Moraine
Wodehouse
Kimberley
Singhampton
Eugenia
Flesherton
LEGEND
Upper bedrock scarp, exposed
buried
Brow of most prominent slope (where different from upper bedrock scarp)
Toe of Escarpment
Secondary scarp
Post glacial shoreline
Moraine
Drumlin
Planning Area Boundary
Scale in miles
Scale in kilometres
The Niagara Escarpment Commission

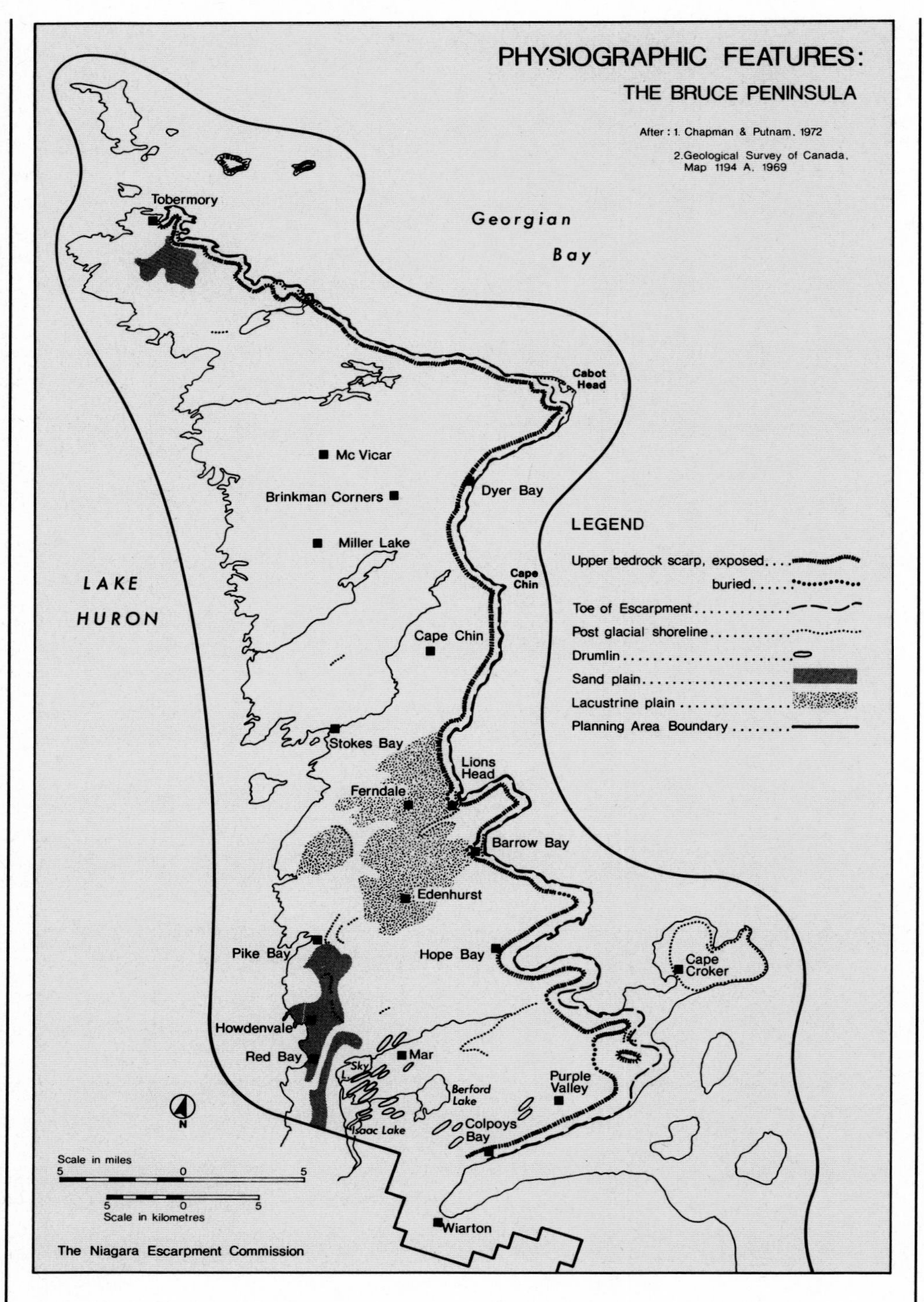

rose upward. Great swaths of barren limestone pavement "moved" inland. Some pavements, dissected by fissures, would provide a lattice for maidenhair spleenwort, chipmunks, and ring-necked snakes. Over centuries, a thin skin of soil would develop on the bare rock, creating environments called *alvars*, despite extreme diurnal temperature fluctuations of 15°C or more, and alternating flood and drought. On the alvars, wedging into crumble-filled fissures, would sprout some of the rarest plants: rubberweed, limestone polypody, and various orchids.

New areas of sloping pavement rose to become shoreline, scoured by wave and ice day after day, year after year, century after century. Devoid of shade or the protection of snow, the surface temperatures of this rock could rise in summer to over 50°C and plummet in winter to −40°C. Ground surfaces in forests, in contrast, rarely rise above 20°C or fall much below −2°C. Almost nothing could live on these pavements except in fissures, each of which acted like an island. In the smallest, harebells would survive. In the largest, cedars would grow, their roots binding and holding the thin soil, their canopies shading the rock, their trunks acting like a snow fence to trap winter's insulating blanket. The fissures gradually expanded, becoming hummocks and supporting an array of wildflowers, nesting warblers, and small mammals.

Glacial sand, exposed at the shore by the steady rise of limestone pavement, was blown into dunes. These dunes, knit by sand reed and marram grass and hosting a procession of other species, marched inland. Traversing them today from the shore to five kilometres inland is a trip through time and a succession of ecosystems, from the most juvenile grasses to mature forests.

Cedars, remarkable in their ability to tolerate drought and nutrient deficiency, grew from the most minuscule fissures near the Escarpment's edge. They have endured, gnarled by deprivation into grotesque shapes, through countless generations. In pockets where a little soil had accumulated, white pines eventually took hold. Their western faces have been repeatedly killed off by wintry blasts and wind-borne ice, causing them to grow eastward into Tom Thomson statements.

The Escarpment's faces themselves display an astonishing array of sites. High, unshaded surfaces stay bone-dry and baked. In partially shaded spots, these same dolomite surfaces sprout lichens – broad splashes of yellow, green, and brown. Cores of many lichens, from which growth radiates, may be up to two hundred years old.

Stark shelves and pillars in summer provide secluded sites for nesting turkey vultures and, in winter, shelter for ravens. High above, migrating hawks soar along the rising paths of air heated by the sun-baked rock.

Farther down, fed by the constant seepage of mineral-rich water through shattered shales and limestones, long, luxuriant shelves of mosses thrive. Vibrant green in colour, each bed is bedecked with myriad invertebrates. Where seepage is steady as a tap, growth continues far into the winter, warmed and fed by the near-constant temperature of 12°C provided by rock-percolated groundwater. Where the flow is slow, these seeps freeze into mammoth, colourful, mineral-rich ice-beards.

Lower still, these mineral-rich waters feed lush growths of summer wildflowers. In glades at the Escarpment's base, hosts of both common and rare species thrive together.

The frigid seepages amalgamate, like twigs to branches, branches to trunk, into life-packed, cold-water streams. Algae and microscopic invertebrates in the streams are devoured by stoneflies, mayflies, caddisflies, and the like, which, in turn, feed minnows and darters and enrich many of Ontario's finest trout streams.

Eugenia Falls north of Flesherton. NIAGARA ESCARPMENT COMMISSION, B. ARMSTRONG

Many of these cold, crystal streams cascade over the scarp. Some, like Bronte Creek, follow ancient riverways; others find new routes. They spread into thin films as they fall over the dish-like edge. Their constant spray feeds mounds of green and yellow mosses and plates of snake-skin-like liverworts. Many of these streams support their own assortment of creatures – aquatic invertebrates evolved in this unique habitat and found nowhere else.

Ancient waterfalls, long dried up, give rise to other habitats. Near Milton, a beautiful little acid bog woven of spruce and sphagnum, larch and lichens, grows within the plunge pool excavated by turbulence below an ancient falls. Incongruously, it sits framed on one side by a jumble of water-piled boulders and on the other by a horseshoe of towering rock.

Nearby, ancient caverns leave their mark. Fractures in the soft shales and limestones allowed water to seep through, eventually eating large caverns out of the soft rock below. Under geologic stress, perhaps the

Jones Falls west of Owen Sound. LARRY LAMB

Tews Falls north of Dundas. LARRY LAMB

weight of the glaciers, these caverns collapsed. In at least one spot, the cavern's debris, like a clogged sieve, slowed the water, creating a unique lake. Crawford Lake near Milton is so deep, relative to its small surface area, that wave action cannot turn over and mix the water to the bottom. The stagnant bottom waters, devoid of oxygen, have embalmed and perfectly preserved each year's layer of sediment. By analysing the pollen in these layers, scientists have reconstructed the history of ever-changing climate and forests.

In other places, the collapse of caverns has created *karst* – a wild jumble of broken caprock plates, some lying flat, others on end, and many on slopes in confusing array. Beautiful, cathedral-like forests have developed in such places. Beneath their leafy canopies, the tilted rock surfaces have shed the annual leaf fall, providing for luxuriant growth of rare plants like the walking and hart's-tongue ferns and the showy orchis.

Particularly at places along the Bruce Peninsula, the inclined rock has directed rainwater back from the scarp face into southwesterly-flowing streams. Percolating and tumbling along the cold rock surfaces, or flowing slowly through sand dunes, these waters emerge enriched into *fens*. Striking wetlands with shallow, decomposed soils, fens support a *Who's Who* of exotic plants – at least eleven orchids including yellow and showy lady's-slippers, calopogons, grass-pinks, and bog candles, as well as pitcher plants, three species of sundews, and a huge list of other interesting species.

Farther back from the Escarpment, some of these streams have been trapped in a remarkable chain of rich, shallow lakes. Sky, Isaac, and Boat lakes literally teem with life: a dozen species of frogs, toads, turtles, water and ribbon snakes, minnows, pike, and bass to name just a few. On land, wave after wave of migrant birds arrive to breed and raise their young. American and least bitterns, geese, mallards, and wood ducks all thrive.

It would be impossible to really describe the Niagara Escarpment in one chapter, or even in one whole book. Its many faces are simply too rich, varied, and ever-changing. Perhaps a sense of the Escarpment provided here, an understanding of what makes it function and a glimpse into a few of its habitats, will tempt the reader to explore and discover more.

Algonquin Provincial Park

Dan Strickland

Algonquin. The word conjures up an unparalleled wealth of natural images: a white-tailed deer browsing quietly in leafy summer hardwoods; a broad-winged hawk atop a dry snag surveying a sun-flooded beaver meadow for prey; a bull moose breaking the frosty silence of a golden September dawn with thrashing antlers and deep resonant grunts; the laughter of a loon echoing from a rocky lakeshore; wolf packs travelling tirelessly through long winter nights; exquisite orchids blooming unseen year after year beside thousands of secret ponds. Ravens execute barrel rolls high over ridges, and lake trout lurk in the unperturbed depths. All these and more are part of Algonquin.

It is a special place. Larger than some countries, the huge, wild tract of woods and lakes, hills, bogs, and beaver ponds stretches across 7,600 square kilometres of the rugged height of land between Georgian Bay and the Ottawa River. Established in 1893 on about half its present area, Algonquin is Ontario's oldest and most famous provincial park.

Because Algonquin lies in the transition zone between the southern deciduous and northern coniferous forests, it provides an outstanding showcase of nature. One instant you can be looking at an olive-sided flycatcher perched atop a black spruce beside a cool sphagnum bog, just as you could hundreds of kilometres to the north, and the next, as you turn around, you might spot a wood pewee in a maple, typical of the hardwood forests of extreme southern Ontario.

The Rocks

The key to understanding the park's living things and their distribution is a knowledge of the underlying rocks and landforms. Algonquin's rocks are of two basic kinds: metamorphic gneisses, and grey or pink igneous granites. The gneisses originated as sea-bottom sediments over 1.5 billion years ago, but their present layered structure dates from a more recent event. Just 1.05 billion years ago, the rocks we see today were twenty to thirty kilometres below the surface, where, during a mountain-building episode, they were subject to intense heat and pressure that "plasticized" them and squeezed and extruded them into their present alignments. Since then, they have cooled down and been exposed at the surface thanks to a billion years of erosion. Park granites had a similar origin except that they were once in a truly molten state and so do not show the layered structure of the gneisses. Perhaps the most important features of both rocks are their extreme hardness and their low amounts of potassium, phosphorus, and calcium, all vital nutrients for plants and animals.

Beyond their chemistry, however, the rocks of Algonquin influence life above them in another important way. Although the mountains that thrust up more than a billion years ago are eroded away now, Algonquin's west side is still significantly higher than surrounding areas. For example, many hilltops in the Highway 60 area reach well over 500 metres above sea level, whereas on the eastern boundary the land dips to a mere 200 metres. This simple fact has had far-reaching effects on Algonquin's soils and climate.

The park's soils all were left by the last glacier, which melted back just 10,000 years ago. Soils on the high, west side are generally glacial tills – unassorted "gravelly" material which had been carried along in the ice. They were deposited in a thin layer over the bedrock. Large parts of the lower east side of the park, however, were occupied for a time by a mighty river that drained glacial Lake Algonquin (the forerunner of Lakes Huron and Michigan) eastward to the Champlain Sea. This sea was an arm of the Atlantic occupying the St. Lawrence and Ottawa valleys. Staggering quantities of sand and other fine particles were carried along in these torrents and

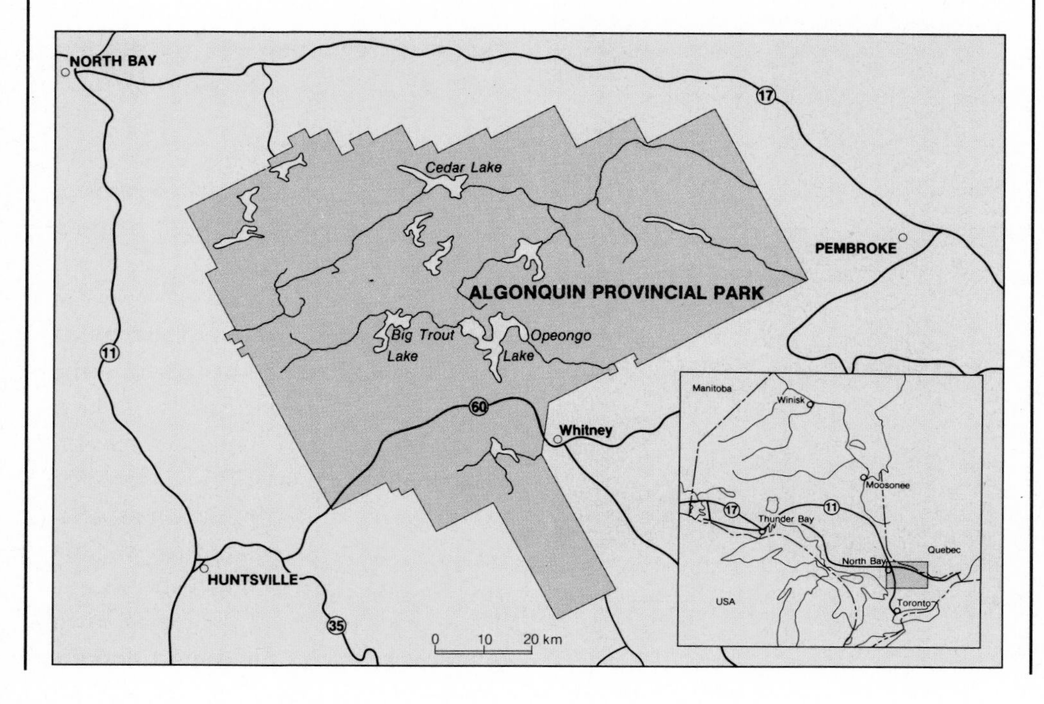

Fall colours, Algonquin Park. DON GUNN

deposited in broad areas which, now that they are high and dry, are called *outwash plains*.

The western uplands have influenced more than the park's soil types. The higher elevations cause west-side temperatures to be cooler on average. As well, they force air masses moving east from Georgian Bay to rise and lose most of their moisture on the west side of the park. Normally this sort of "rain shadow" phenomenon is associated with truly mountainous areas, but even the relatively slight elevational rise of the "Algonquin dome" has measurable effects. On the west side of the park, the frost-free period is about 84 days, and the annual precipitation is a hundred centimetres (33 per cent as snow), whereas on the east side the frost-free period is 105 days, and the annual precipitation is ninety centimetres (26 per cent as snow).

Lakes and Aquatic Life

Nowhere are the influences of rock chemistry and topography more apparent than in Algonquin's lakes. Because the bedrock they lie on is so hard and nutrient-poor, park waters contain correspondingly small amounts of dissolved nutrients. Algae and plankton growth is thus limited, which in turn, limits the number of dependent higher organisms. Accordingly, insect larvae, minnows, and large game fish are all much less numerous in Algonquin lakes than they are in nutrient-rich lakes on limestone, such as those in southern Ontario. Nevertheless, being cold and having little in the way of decaying vegetation, Algonquin lakes tend to be rich in oxygen and very suitable for trout. Both lake trout and brook trout are widely distributed in the over fifteen hundred park lakes, along with other cold-water fish such as burbot and lake whitefish. These species probably entered the park behind the retreating glaciers. Most warm-water fish, on the other hand, were excluded in post-glacial times because by the time summer temperatures were high enough to support them, the streams draining the highlands had diminished to the point of becoming impassable. To this day, sturgeon, walleye, and muskellunge are found only in the lower reaches of the Petawawa River on the east side of Algonquin, and the

Opeongo Lake, Algonquin Park.
JOHN THEBERGE

only reason smallmouth bass are more widely distributed is that humans introduced them to many of the west-side lakes around the turn of the century.

Vegetation

Many first-time visitors to Algonquin, impressed by the park's conifers, imagine they have arrived in the "north woods." Indeed, the park does have a northern element – balsam fir, tamarack, and spruce flourish, particularly around lakeshores and in spruce bogs. Nevertheless, on the park's west side, the forests consist mostly of broad-leaved hardwood trees – sugar maple, yellow birch, American beech – with groves of eastern hemlock and a few black cherries and ironwoods mixed in. But this southern-flavoured forest is pushing against the northern limits of some tree species. Basswood, white ash, and white elm, for instance, are very unusual in the slightly colder and wetter climate of the Algonquin dome although they are reasonably common just forty kilometres to the west. The same effect can be seen, interestingly enough, with Ontario's floral emblem, the white trillium. This flower is almost entirely absent from the spring hardwoods of Algonquin although it is abundant in many places just outside the park boundaries.

While climatic features exclude some species, they are favourable for others. Red spruce, for example, finds one of its very few Ontario strongholds in Algonquin, although it is generally restricted to widely scattered, small, isolated stands.

The west-side forests of Algonquin have been altered by man in a major way. Originally, scattered among the hardwoods were giant white pines, many of them over 120 centimetres in diameter and reaching heights of thirty-five metres – far higher than the maples and hemlocks below. But these pines attracted the pioneer loggers to the area, and by the time the park was established in 1893, the pines had all but vanished. Today, only two stands of Algonquin's original hardwood-pine association remain: the Crow River stand in the centre of the park, and the Dividing Lake stand just outside the park's southwest boundary.

Although almost all the giant pines are gone, much younger white pines are still common along lakeshores and rocky ridges. Indeed, on the east side of Algonquin, where conditions are warmer, drier, and more sandy, white pine is still the dominant species over large areas. In addition to white pine, the east-side outwash plains support extensive stands of red pine and jack pine, the latter species being almost unknown on the park's west side. The east side also features almost pure stands of red oak occurring along the many rocky ridges that parallel rivers and fault lines.

The park's east side harbours a far greater wealth of wildflowers than does the west side. Warmer climate contributes to this richness, but as well, the east-side rivers, notably the Petawawa and to a lesser extent the Barron and Bonnechere, serve as botanical "highways" running up from the Ottawa Valley. Along these rivers one can find dazzling displays of cardinal flowers and such less well-known southerners as ground peanut

Pinetree Lake, Algonquin Park.
JOHN THEBERGE

and the tubercled orchid. On the Petawawa there is even a silver maple swamp worthy of any to be found off the Shield in southern Ontario, and even more extraordinary are two stands of blue beech, an almost Carolinian tree that seems totally out of place in Algonquin. These stands may actually be remnants from a slightly warmer period 5,000 years ago.

A second major cause of the east side's floral diversity is the presence of rocks enriched in calcium carbonate (lime) along major fault lines. A hike along the Barron River Canyon, a spectacular gorge 100 metres deep which cradles the river for about two kilometres, will disclose such lime-loving plants as maidenhair spleenwort, purple-stemmed cliff brake, and the fascinating encrusted saxifrage. This saxifrage actually secretes lime around the edges of its leaves. It is a cold-climate plant whose nearest other localities are on the shores of Lake Superior and Hudson Bay. The small Algonquin population living on the cool, north-facing canyon wall may have descended from ancestors dating back to the days of the great and cold Fossmill River during the last glacial retreat. The Fossmill River ran east across the northern part of the park, draining huge Lake Algonquin, forerunner of Lake Huron, into the Champlain Sea.

Reptiles and Amphibians

Algonquin Park, with its long winters and relatively short, cool summers, is understandably rather poor in reptiles and amphibians: only fourteen species of reptiles and sixteen species of amphibians have been recorded, and several of these are very rare.

Some of these species contribute a great deal, however, to Algonquin's atmosphere. The first May choruses of quacking wood frogs and shrill, deafening spring peepers; the sonorous early-summer rumbles of bellicose bull-frogs; the banjo-plunking green frogs and stone-clacking mink frogs of July are all indelible parts of Algonquin spring and summer evenings. And, by day, the sight of painted turtles and snapping turtles basking on logs is familiar to every park canoeist.

Because of the warmer climate on the east side of the park, at least three species – the milk snake, smooth green snake, and pickerel frog – are much more common there, and two others – the common water snake and the wood turtle – are found exclusively there. The wood turtle and pickerel frog populations seem to be among the most significant remaining in the province. Chances are they will increase in importance as these two species continue to yield outside Algonquin.

Mammals

The park owes its creation, in part, to the widespread concern felt in the last century for the future of Ontario's game and fur-bearing mammals. Unrestricted shooting and trapping had decimated mammal populations even in the then very remote Algonquin area.

Beaver, for example, were very rare when the park was established. The protection afforded by park rangers turned the situation around in a very few years, however, and by 1908 beavers were so numerous that the Park Superintendent actually instituted a live-trapping program to re-stock beaver-depleted areas in Ontario and to supply zoos all around the world. Beavers in Algonquin have continued to prosper ever since, and the total park population is now believed to be approximately 20,000.

The park achieved a similar but less well-known success with marten and fisher, both easily trapped and quickly extirpated in many parts of Ontario. As recently as the 1930s and 1940s Algonquin was one of very few places in the province where any significant populations of these two furbearers existed. Today, the situation outside Algonquin is much better, thanks to the Ontario government's system of registered traplines. Nevertheless, Algonquin's marten and fisher populations continue to be important, and even quite recently the park has supplied animals to several northern American states to re-introduce populations within their borders.

Most people's imaginations are captured by the park's large ungulates – moose and white-tailed deer – along with their predator, the gray, or timber wolf. Surprisingly, white-tailed deer, for which Algonquin became famous, were not native to the park. The white-tail is a southern animal, ranging all the way down to South America, and is not really suited to deep snow or cold. When snow exceeds forty-five centimetres, as it often does in Algonquin, deer start to flounder, and they may very well be forced to expend more energy merely getting to their food than they obtain by eating it.

Deer moved northwards, however, when logging began on the Canadian Shield. Cleared areas were quickly taken over by new growth – shrubs and young trees which constituted ideal deer food in unprecedented quantities. Subsequently, estimates of Algonquin's deer population ran as high as sixty to a hundred thousand animals, and nobody thought twice when a few hundred deer were shot in 1917 to alleviate a war-time meat shortage in Toronto.

Moose, at the same time, were exceedingly rare, a fact which was taken for granted but never really understood until research conducted in Algonquin during the 1950s disclosed the reason. White-tailed deer carry a parasite, a nematode worm called *Parelaphostrongylus tenuis*, which causes no serious harmful effects to the deer, but which, in the moose, causes blindness, loss of co-ordination, paralysis, and, very quickly, death. In the days when deer were so abundant, then, they heavily infected their range with the nematode, which spends the intermediate

Sasajewun Lake, Algonquin Park.
JOHN THEBERGE

stages of its life cycle in snails. Almost every moose sooner or later ate an infected snail and died as a result. Deer were unknowingly but effectively killing off the moose.

All this was destined to change, however, after 1922, when airplanes were introduced to fight forest fires. Planes proved to be so efficient that the area burned each year in Algonquin Park dropped very quickly from sixty-five square kilometres to less than five. At the time nobody realized the implications for the deer. Nor did anyone realize that cutting hemlocks and other conifers in the park would someday mean a critical loss of winter cover for deer. But eventually both these factors caught up with the park deer herd, and, beginning with severe winters in the late 1950s and again in the early 1970s, deer numbers declined tremendously – from between twenty-five and forty per square kilometre to only about two and a half by the early 1980s.

Less deer, of course, meant less infected snails, and in the late 1970s and early 1980s, the park moose population exploded. The average density is now approximately one moose for every two square kilometres, with many locally higher concentrations.

Wolves, present in Algonquin throughout these ups and downs of white-tailed deer and moose, were affected by the fortunes of their prey. When deer were abundant, wolves were quite obviously "common." While they were infrequently seen, they were often heard howling or their tracks were found. A research program in the 1960s revealed that the park wolf population consisted of about thirty packs totalling at each winters' end about 150 animals. This figure doubled each spring after the pups were born, at one litter per pack, but dropped again to 150 by the end of the next winter. There seemed to be heavy mortality among pups. The summer diet of park wolves in those days consisted of about 20 per cent beaver and moose, and 80 per cent deer, mostly fawns.

As the park deer population began to decline drastically in the early 1970s, the identification of hair remains in wolf scats showed that wolves were turning more and more to beaver during the summer. In winter, however, beaver are secure under the ice of their ponds, and the wolves were forced to subsist on the dwindling numbers of deer. At first there was no sign that wolf numbers were declining, but by the late 1970s it seemed obvious that there were fewer wolves. From the wolf's perspective, the obvious solution to the scarcity of deer would have been to turn to moose. But, although wolves are well known as predators of moose elsewhere, and although there is no doubt that Algonquin wolves eat moose if they have a chance, there is little evidence at present that wolves in Algonquin very often actually kill moose. One possible explanation for this is that Algonquin wolves are so small (males average only twenty-five kilograms and females about twenty kilograms) that, unlike larger wolves elsewhere, they cannot make the switch. The suggestion has been made that Algonquin wolves are actually a hitherto undescribed subspecies that is adapted to preying on deer. Whatever the case, deer populations crept up in the mid 1980s and park wolves appear to have made an even more spectacular comeback. Nobody knows for sure if the increase in deer was responsible for the recovery of wolves.

One of the facts learned in the wolf research program was that wolves will answer human imitations of their howls. Indeed, this technique was a major breakthrough permitting biologists to find and study wolves during the summer, and it is now used by park naturalists to introduce campers to the wolf. Whenever an accessible pack is found, usually in August when wolves howl most readily, the park staff organizes an expedition – often with hundreds of cars and over a thousand people – to hear the incomparable music of wolves howling under a starry sky. Such "public wolf howls" have been remarkably successful, and their popularity has spread in North America and overseas. Thanks to them it can be safely said that more people have experienced first-hand contact with wolves in Algonquin Park than in any other place in the world.

Birds

Algonquin is rich in birds. The total park list includes 246 species, of which 128 have been known to breed, and 89 are considered common summer or permanent residents. Each of Algonquin's many habitats supports its own bird community, and a skilled observer can see or hear over a hundred species in a single May or June day.

On such a birding expedition, one might first visit a lake. Few species may be seen here, but one is the park's most exciting, the common loon. Wild, ringing loon-laughter has made these birds the very symbol of the north country.

Beaver ponds are the home of black ducks, ring-necked ducks, hooded mergansers, eastern kingbirds, and great blue herons. In beaver meadows and open bog mats one can find swamp sparrows and yellow-throats, and in extensive sedge meadows, small colonies of bobolinks and savannah sparrows living the way these species must have done before we humans provided the fields they so much favour nowadays.

Hardwood forests are the preferred habitat of red-eyed vireos, least flycatchers, wood pewees, ovenbirds, ruffed grouse, and barred owls.

Algonquin's most interesting birds, however, are to be found in the coniferous forests – northern species near the southern limits of their ranges: boreal chickadees, black-backed three-toed woodpeckers, spruce grouse, and gray jays. Coniferous forests are also the home of kinglets, winter wrens, white-throated sparrows, and over half the park's twenty species of breeding warblers such as Blackburnian, magnolia, northern parula, Nashville, and Canada.

Although the northern species are most sought after by amateur ornithologists, southern species are found as well. Warbling vireos and northern orioles are present in small numbers. Golden-winged warblers are increasingly prominent on the east side, and mockingbirds, of all things, visit the park almost every year.

Other equally prominent elements of Algonquin's bird life have not yet even been mentioned: there are the park's six species of breeding thrushes, flocks of colourful crossbills and grosbeaks that brighten the snowy landscape, ravens soaring high overhead looking for the remains of wolf-killed deer – the list goes on and on.

A Park Inviolate?

Even in an overview of Algonquin Park as brief as this, one cannot fail to be impressed by the park's extraordinary natural wealth. Algonquin is indeed a very special place.

It would be a mistake, however, to believe that the park is a pristine wilderness, or that it can continue as it is now regardless of events elsewhere in the world. As recently as the 1960s, for example, Algonquin lost its most magnificent bird of prey, the peregrine falcon, because of DDT contamination. It did not matter that very little DDT had ever been used in Algonquin Park itself; the falcons migrated every winter to areas where DDT was used extensively. In addition, while in the park they ate small birds that had also wintered in DDT environments. As large and wild as it is, Algonquin offered no refuge at all for the falcons. The last known peregrine nested in Algonquin in 1962, just about the last year that the birds nested anywhere in eastern North America until recent recovery efforts.

At present, the problem of DDT is abating because of stringent controls on its use, but other threats are emerging which, like DDT, are not in any way impeded by a park boundary. The most serious of these is acid rain and acid snow. Originating far away with the sulphur and nitrogen dioxides emitted by our highly industrialized society, acid precipitation is particularly serious in a place like Algonquin because its soils have an especially low capacity to neutralize, or "buffer," acids.

If acid rain continues, some lakes may be acidified outright, and others, classed as extremely sensitive, may suffer serious damage in the spring when highly acidic snow melts and flows into the lake. For a few days, or weeks, the poorly buffered lake is overwhelmed, and the top metre or two may be occupied by a lethal acidic "slug" of meltwater which bathes the most important and productive areas of the lake – including trout spawning beds.

About 23 per cent of Algonquin's lakes fall into this extremely sensitive category although it is too early to say how much long-term damage is being done. The really important point is that in this case, as with DDT, the existence of a park boundary means nothing. We must never forget that special places like Algonquin are still a part of our world and are very much affected by what we humans do elsewhere.

Mew Lake, Algonquin Park. MARY THEBERGE

Pukaskwa National Park

Michael Jones

Those who have never seen Superior get an inadequate, even inaccurate idea, by hearing it spoken of as a lake.... It breeds storms and rains and fogs like a sea. It is cold in mid-summer as the Atlantic. It is wild, masterful and dreaded....

The Reverend George Grant, 1872

Archaic rock, tea-brown water, and boreal hinterland form the core ingredients of the land. Meld with them moods of tranquility and the wild rage of a Superior storm, and one has the essence and spirit of Pukaskwa National Park, "the wild shore of an inland sea."

The name *Pukaskwa* (pronounced "Puck-a-saw") comes from the Ojibway tongue; however, its meaning has as many twists as the river that bears its name. Maps drawn in the 1800s give the name *Pukoso* to a river and high promontory along the northeast shore of Lake Superior. Legend has it that into this hinterland a marauder retreated with a young maiden, abducted from her family's lodge in Michipicoten. The culprit was caught and quickly dispatched, but not before he had killed his hostage. Her family name was *puck-us-wau*, or something that sounded similar to the first white mens' ears. Her spirit is said to live as a white doe that haunts the river bearing her name. In 1983, 1,880 square kilometres of the Pukoso wilderness were officially declared Canada's twenty-ninth national park.

The grey rocks of the Canadian Shield form the bulwark of the park's rough and broken terrain. Granites and basalts, now cold and still, log in their crystals an account of catastrophic birth. In the depth and darkness of nights long past, magma flowed in the cauldron beneath the Earth. As the surface cooled and cracked, the magma bubbled up into fissures and crevices and held fast. Volcanoes at times spewed and spat forth lava that hissed, scorched, gelled, and was stilled. Enormous pressures and violent earthquakes warped and folded the rocks, ruptured the land, and turned volcanic ash into hardened stone.

Today, the northwest corner of the park near the Hattie Cove Campground is surrounded by faults, dykes, and volcanic floes of rock rich in magnesium and iron. These floes indicate seeping volcanoes which oozed lava up onto the surface and created large pillow-shaped rocks. Found in the cove area too are pyroclastic rocks (*pyro* = fire; *clastic* = broken in pieces), attesting to the explosive forces of eruptions that radically altered the shape of the land. Colours, patterns, and textures forged in these fires remain clearly etched in stone, mute testimony to the three-billion-year antiquity of the Canadian Shield.

Time has buried, exhumed, and eroded this ancient land. Glaciers scoured it during their southern advances and flooded it in polar retreats. Fine parallel grooves in the rock – glacial striations – tell the direction of movement of these huge ice mountains. Smooth-sided potholes show where waterfalls cascaded, abraded, and drilled vertically into rock beneath the ice.

The post-glacial history of the park is recorded by abandoned cobble beaches and inland deltas of silt and clay. During glacial retreats, the ancestral waters of Superior formed massive catch basins, with levels at times up to 130 metres higher than today's. Most of what is now the park, including the Cascade Hills and the inland flats of the Pukaskwa River, once were washed by the waters of a massive inland sea. As the prodigious sea shrank, the denuded mountains and rocky hills of the Pukaskwa hinterland emerged.

Water still shapes and reshapes the land. In the annual baptism of spring, the White, Swallow, and Cascade rivers, and hosts of other named and nameless creeks rise, dance, and soar in the surge of a wild run. Buoyed by the force of snow-melt – a mini-glacial retreat – spring waters breach and cut their cedar-lined banks, unearth boulders and stones buried thousands of years past, and explore new paths to the Superior sea.

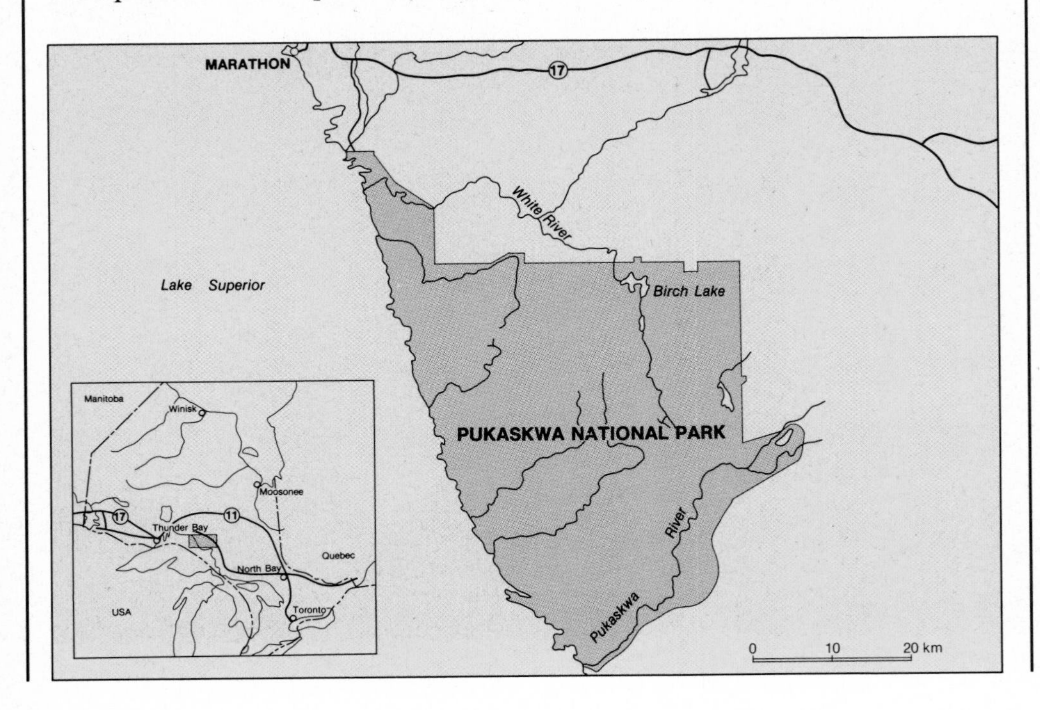

Wild Lake Superior shore near Oiseau Bay, Pukaskwa National Park.
JOHN THEBERGE

The Pukaskwa River best captures the spirit and challenge of the spring renewal. From the Trans-Canada Highway to Lake Superior, a canoeist experiences a nine-day wilderness sojourn; over eighty kilometres of water with three kilometres of portages; a 260-metre drop from the headwaters at Gibson Lake to the river mouth through pools, rapids, and eddies replete with speckled trout. Praises of the Pukaskwa have bordered on idolatry.

The river neither knows nor serves any master. It meanders through jack pine flats, ripples over gravel beds, then curls white, foams, and races through a bedrock fault or thunders down the kilometre-long Ringham's Gorge. Canoeists and kayakers have but four precious weeks to catch the water just right. Those who begin the trip too soon in May can be trapped in the torrent of canoe-crushing waves in rapids that cannot be run. Those who leave too late in June may be forced to portage around boulder beds exposed by low flow.

Rapid changes in character are not unique to the Pukaskwa watershed. Few changes can match the sudden power unleashed by tiny Oiseau Creek. Swollen by the torrential summer rain of June 1985, it burst forth in a wild rage that wrought havoc to the land. Generally less than five metres wide and a fraction as deep, it devastated a swath a hundred metres wide and five metres deep. Thousands of spruce, fir, and cedar trees were uprooted, broken, and tossed about or disgorged into Oiseau Bay on Lake Superior. The ruins of a lumber camp dating back to the 1940s virtually disappeared. A rare colony of Pitcher's thistles, the only one on the north Superior shore, was decimated. Remnants of the Oiseau Creek bridge, part of the sixty-kilometre-long coastal hiking trail, were scattered up to a kilometre from the site.

The forests of Pukaskwa are not quite so dynamic and unpredictable as the waterways. For five white months they lie cold and silent save for the weird sonics of cracking ice and the chatter or scurry of wildlife. The needles and limbs of spruce, balsam fir, poplar, and birch interlace in an expanse of greys, greens, and browns. The complement of animal life is typically boreal. Moose and snowshoe hares browse, fishers and red foxes hunt, and shrews, mice, and moles rummage though mazes of subnivean tunnels. Snowfleas – tiny black insects – crawl through the snow, often surfacing in the thousands to bask in the warmth of the sun.

Overhead, ravens soar and dance on the wind. Forever opportunists, they feast and squabble over whatever morsels nature avails. Woodpeckers, from the tiny downy to the crested pileated, pry and sound trees for the hidden treats beneath the bark.

Woodland caribou, near the southern limit of their range, trek the rocky knolls and coastal hills. Tracks, beds, and feeding craters trace the constant wanderings of the thirty or so caribou in the park. Their preference for the coastal area is not by chance. In the winter, as in all seasons, the omnipotent Superior exerts its unique modifying influence. With few exceptions, the lake waters are chilled but not frozen by polar winds. Even in the −30°C to −40°C grip of a cold front, vagrant puffs of white mist rise up from the grey waters to warm the coastal lands.

The bond between the caribou, the lake, and the land takes on a new dimension as spring approaches. Gravid cows migrate from the mainland to the shelter and protection of small islands along the coast. There, in the absence of predators – wolf and lynx – and in the abundance of new growth, they calve. This traditional migration is profound, not for the distance travelled, but for its simplicity and effectiveness in enhancing survival. It is, however, an accord man can easily upset. Coastal travellers, boaters, or canoeists who beach on the islands may, by their presence, alarm the cows and force the caribou to abandon their refuge.

Dwarfed and twisted spruce rooted in clefts upon stark rock headlands tell of Superior's storms, fogs, and winds. Arctic-alpine plants, normally found near Hudson and James bays, blossom in a delicate and colourful testimony to the short, cool, coastal summer. Encrusted saxifrage, butterwort, and bird's-eye primrose are three of over a dozen Arctic species in the park, possible relics of a northward floral migration following glacial retreat. They continue to survive in the quasi-Arctic summers of Superior.

Inland, in the coniferous forest, the naked and gnarled trunks of spruce, tamarack, and fir stand in closed rank, shaded by a canopy of needles overhead. Lichens, liverworts, and mosses, thick, moist, and fragrant, exploit a myriad of niches on the forest floor. Flowers of twinflower, bunchberry, and wild lily-of-the-valley mask the cryptic greens of northern orchids and the intricate tiny features of mitrewort. Warblers, wrens, and thrushes celebrate in song and colour the bounty of the northern summer.

Man has repeatedly been drawn to the Pukaskwa wilderness. Circular stone pits built on the boulder beaches of Superior are cultural relics of human prehistory. Excavations of these pits have uncovered bits of pottery, copper, and projectile points but few clues as to why the boulders were so carefully arranged. Some pits may have served as blinds, or possibly meat-caches built by nomadic hunters. Other structures may have been places of pantheistic worship, perhaps the nest sites of the great Thunderbird from whose eyes lightning flashed and thunder roared. The Thunderbirds are the guardians of the Ojibway, and their stone nests, shrouded in mist and fog, are sacred.

Explorers of the mid 1800s spoke of *Les Petits Ecrits* ("Little Written Rocks") and described images of men, monsters, and snakes with wings etched out of the rock lichens in the vicinity of Oiseau Bay. These images have gone, lost under the lichens that once gave them form.

Vintage cabins, tote roads, and grave sites are all that remain of the logging era at Pukaskwa Depot. During the 1920s and early 1930s the Depot supplied a network of camps on the north and east branches of the Pukaskwa River. Scandinavians, French Canadians, and other nationalities, over three hundred people in all, worked as jobbers, scalers, haulers, and cutters in a grand scheme to harvest the woods.

The Pukaskwa hinterland no longer answers to axes, saws, or implements of mercantile schemes. As a national park its purpose is to remain untrammelled, owned by no one, yet dedicated to all. The rockscapes, forests, and the brutal power of the Superior coast will forever frighten and fascinate man. Modern travellers will be drawn by the challenge and a need to touch and be touched by the "wild shore of an inland sea."

A sheltered cove, Pukaskwa National Park. JOHN THEBERGE

Quetico Provincial Park

Shan Walshe

Imagine a roadless wilderness, ninety-six by sixty-four kilometres, an area so vast that a person could spend a lifetime canoeing its lakes and rivers, climbing its cliffs, and tramping its forests and bogs. In this wilderness, nestled among virgin forests of pine and spruce, are more than 350 sparkling lakes interconnected by portages averaging only 400 metres long. Quetico is famous as an inviolate wilderness, where civilization seems very far away and age-old natural processes go on unhampered by man. Roads, logging, mining, hunting, mechanized travel, and commercial exploitation (other than trapping) are prohibited throughout the park.

Small wonder that Quetico is renowned for wilderness canoeing! Even the voyageurs thought so; two major fur trade routes to the prairies passed through the park. Although Quetico is not for white-water enthusiasts, its tranquil waters and short portages are ideally suited to families, youth groups, and senior citizens. It attracts people of all ages and from all over the world.

Biologically, Quetico is fascinating because elements of four life zones occur in the park: boreal forest, mixed forest, prairie, and sub-Arctic. The boreal forest covers about 60 per cent of Quetico, with jack pine and black spruce the dominant trees, often underlain by carpets of beautiful feather moss. Under the jack pines, Quetico's largest orchid, the stemless lady's slipper or moccasin-flower, blooms in June by the thousands. In June, too, the majority of boreal wildflowers bloom, creating patches of colour in the dark forest: white bunchberry, yellow bell-like bluebead-lily, delicate pink twinflower.

The boreal birds are here, too. Mixed in small numbers with the common black-capped chickadees are boreal, or brown-capped chickadees, distinguishable by their nasal call. Ladder-backed and black-backed woodpeckers of the dense, mature northern forest scale bark off black spruce and jack pine in search of insect larvae. And the northern forest owls, the boreal and the great gray, are here too. The whistle-like trill of the tiny boreal owl closely resembles the winnowing of a snipe. It is heard occasionally in Quetico, especially in early spring. Great gray owls are sometimes observed perched along rivers that wind through black spruce bogs.

The cry of the common loon is heard day and night on every lake in Quetico, and above hovers the greatest symbol of the wilderness, the bald eagle. Scarce in most of eastern North America, bald eagles are common in Quetico. Anyone spotting the white head and tail and two-metre wingspan of one of these majestic birds experiences a tremendous thrill, and a canoeist can expect to see four or five on an average trip through the park.

Sometimes mistaken for a bald eagle is the almost equally large osprey, or fish hawk. Its head, too, is mostly white, but a conspicuous dark band runs through its eye. Ospreys are common in the Quetico wilds, frequenting shallow, marshy rivers and lakes. What a dramatic sight it is to see an osprey, hovering motionless in the air, suddenly fold its wings, drop like a stone into the water, and come up with a fish clutched in its talons!

The earliest nesting bird in Quetico is the gray jay, common throughout the park. Sometimes these jays become tame enough to take food from the hand. Experts at winter survival in a bleak, cold land, they live on food cached in trees during the summer and preserved by a coating of saliva.

Among boreal forest mammals, one of the most abundant is the American marten. It eats primarily red-backed voles and the occasional red squirrel. Black bears are common too, particularly in areas of early forest succession with grasses and shrubs. Because large numbers of people do not frequent the park, most bears have not become spoiled through dependence on human food and garbage, and flee quickly at the sight of humans.

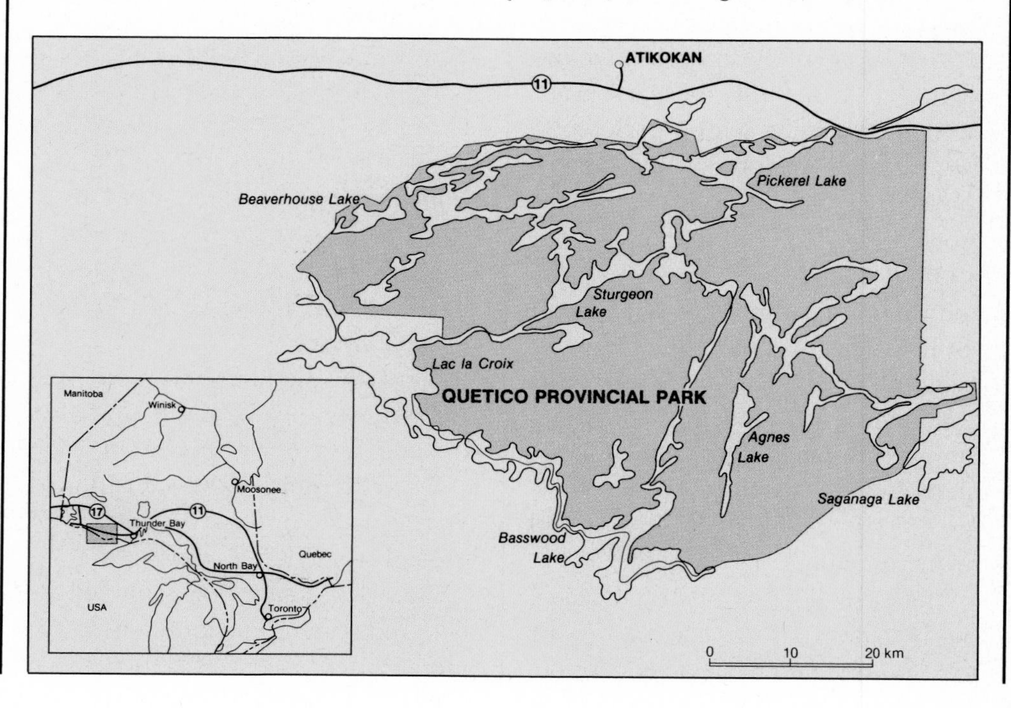

Narrows in Ottertrack Lake, Quetico Provincial Park. SHAN WALSHE

Close encounters with moose are frequent. In 1985 an aerial census in the northeastern section of the park resulted in an estimate of two and a half moose per square kilometre, one of the highest densities in Ontario. From mid June to August, canoeists can paddle close to moose feeding on aquatic vegetation in rich marshes scattered throughout the park. And, during the rutting season in September, bulls may be lured within camera range by imitating the call of the cow moose.

Otters range over the whole park, and canoeists stand a good chance of seeing some of these agile animals, especially when the water is calm early in the morning or late in the evening. Otter droppings, containing large quantities of crayfish exoskeletons, are plentiful along creeks, rivers, and on beaver dams.

The Canada lynx inhabits Quetico but is seldom seen. Sometimes crows will find one and make a commotion, but if you should be fortunate enough to see this ghostly cat, it will be only a glimpse, for it will see you too, and fade into the forest.

Quetico's rarest mammals are the heather vole and the rock vole. The heather vole was recorded first in the late 1970s. It is so similar in appearance to the much more common meadow vole that it has been given the scientific name *Phenacomys*, which means "cheater" or "deceiver." This species is found on open bedrock ridges where blueberry bushes are abundant. Telltale signs of its presence are large piles of twigs, often blueberry, with the bark removed. These twigs are the remains of its winter food caches.

The rock vole, a boreal forest species, is one of the rarest voles in North America. It was collected first in Quetico in 1978. Bouldery talus slopes seem to be the preferred habitat, thus its name.

The black spruce bog is one of the most interesting communities in the boreal forest. In May, Quetico's bogs are all pink and white with flowers of leatherleaf, bog laurel, Labrador tea, and bog rosemary. A little later, in early July, other flowers take over, especially the bog orchids: rose pogonia and grass-pink. Around the edges of the bog, spruce grouse, or "fool's hen" may be found. So reliant are these birds on camouflage that sometimes they actually can be touched before they fly away. Here, too, is the Connecticut warbler, bright yellow with a blue-grey hood. Although breeding has been confirmed by observations of fledged young, no nest of this bird has yet been discovered in Ontario.

In northwestern Ontario, as one proceeds westward, the climate becomes warmer and drier. Consequently, western and southern species of flora and fauna appear. In Quetico, this phenomenon is most evident in the southwestern section of the park near Lac la Croix, Iron Lake, and the Namakan River. Here are red oak, basswood, red-bellied snake, and white-tailed deer. As well, one of the very distinct shoreline plant communities in this area features big bluestem, a dominant species of the tall grass prairie years ago when bison roamed the plains.

Bedrock in Quetico consists largely of granite and metamorphosed sediments. No true sediments occur in the park. The rocks form towering cliffs, sparkling rapids, and picturesque waterfalls. On the cliffs, in cold microclimates where the sun never shines, a few sub-Arctic plants grow, such as encrusted saxifrage. As a bonus, pictographs, or Indian rock paintings, occur on granite cliffs at thirty locations in the park.

Quetico contains an ancient greenstone belt in its southeastern section, with rocks more than 2.5 billion years old. Characteristic of greenstone country is a series of northeast-southwest oriented ridges interspersed by deep valleys. A hiker travelling north or south over this terrain encounters a seemingly endless number of enor-

"Painted Rock" pictograph site on Lac Lacroix, Quetico Provincial Park.
SHAN WALSHE

mous hills separated by deep valleys. What seems like a kilometre on a map is, in reality, two or even three kilometres of up, down, and around.

Mineralization is common throughout the greenstone belt, with occurrences of iron, copper, asbestos, and gold. A vein of copper eight centimetres wide and bright green from oxidation is exposed on the shore of Cache Bay near beautiful Silver Falls. Outcroppings of brightly-coloured iron formation, or "ribbon-rock," occur in places. The "ribbons" consist of alternating bands of jasper, quartz, and magnetite. Legend has it that an Ojibway chief named Blackstone knew of a fabulously rich vein of native gold in the Bell Lake area, and went there to obtain a packsack full whenever he needed money.

Lime, absent or very scarce in much of Ontario's Precambrian Shield, is found in the greenstone belt, and makes a remarkable difference to the flora and even the fauna. The occurrence of lime can be detected on a rock cliff, even at a great distance, by the presence of the beautiful orange lichen *Caloplaca elegans* which grows only on rock containing lime. The sheets of orange lichen are stained white here and there by lime leaching out of the bedrock, giving the cliff a colourful, mottled appearance.

At first glance, the most conspicuous difference in the flora of the greenstone country is the unusual abundance and noteworthy size of white cedar. Elsewhere in Quetico, cedar is an uncommon, shrubby little tree no more than eight or ten centimetres in diameter. On greenstone it is often the dominant forest species, sometimes reaching a diameter of more than a metre. On the ground one discovers the presence of lime-loving ferns: maidenhair spleenwort, smooth cliff-brake, oak fern, and woodsia. The cedar forests attract white-tailed deer to "yard up" in winter, and black-throated green warblers, scarce elsewhere in Quetico, to nest in summer.

As rich as Quetico's biota and scenery are, the park's irresistible charm lies, too, in the soul-satisfying feelings evoked by wilderness canoeing. Battling metre-high waves on a wind-buffeted lake far from the nearest road; witnessing a double rainbow after the storm; watching dawn break as you paddle through the mist: this is Quetico, a special wilderness.

Hudson Bay Lowlands and Polar Bear Provincial Park

J. P. Prevett

The last angular granitic outcrops of the Precambrian Shield slip quietly beneath a vast sea of sodden peat approximately two hundred kilometres northeast of Cochrane. On a sunny day in June, one can fly northwest from this point for nearly a thousand kilometres in a straight line, never leaving the province of Ontario, and never escaping the bright glare of water-reflected sunlight. Beneath you, stretching ever farther than even the air-borne eye can see, a subtly beautiful mosaic of peatlands, lakes, and rivers captures the imagination. Repetitive yet never boring, intricate patterns of bogs and fens are interwoven in infinitely varying detail.

These are the Hudson Bay Lowlands, or, less prosaically, the Great Muskeg. In Ontario alone they occupy over a quarter of a million square kilometres. Although almost uninhabited, indeed scarcely known to most residents of Ontario, the muskeg covers more than a quarter of the province's surface area. Extending into Quebec and Manitoba, the Hudson Bay Lowlands are reputed to be the largest continuous peatland in the world.

The Lowlands are still actively rising following their release from the overpowering weight of 1,500-metre-thick ice sheets which melted only some 6,000 to 8,000 years ago. At the height of Pleistocene glaciation, the Earth's crust under the ice was depressed more than 160 metres. The resulting extensive melt-waters formed the Tyrrell Sea, whose maximum dimensions correspond closely to the present-day boundaries of the Lowlands. Hudson and James bays are its remnants. Today, glacio-isostatic uplift still proceeds at the extremely rapid rate of approximately 1.2 metres per century. By one estimate, every year about 7.5 square kilometres of "new" land reappears from under the two bays. The land is flat, on average sloping only about three-quarters of a metre in a kilometre. Except when engorged by spring melt-waters into briefly maddened elemental forces of nature, the great rivers of the Ontario Lowlands – the Severn, Winisk, Attawapiskat, Albany, and Moose – flow serenely north or east into Hudson and James bays.

The post-glacial Tyrrell Sea deposited impervious layers of marine clay, averaging about three metres in depth. The impermeability of this substrate, combined with the extreme flatness of the landscape, results in abysmally poor drainage. Moreover, the maritime climate in summer is both cool and damp. Taken together, these conditions severely retard decomposition of dead plant material. Thus, each year's production of leaves, needles, stems, and roots only partially decays. What remains is slowly but inexorably transformed into peat. Peat formation is the most fundamental and pervasive ecological process in the Hudson Bay Lowlands.

Over the centuries, immeasurable quantities of this organic residue have built up. Most of the Lowlands have been exposed above sea level less than four thousand years, yet in many places, peat depths now reach three or more metres. Gradually, as it continues to accumulate, the peat itself becomes the medium in which plants must grow. In time, roots completely lose contact with the underlying mineral soil. Conditions become progressively more acidic. Eventually, the only source of moisture and nutrients is rainwater, and bogs form with their characteristic set of acid-adapted plants: dwarf black spruce trees, sphagnum mosses, heath shrubs such as Labrador tea and bog laurel, carnivorous pitcher plants and the sundews.

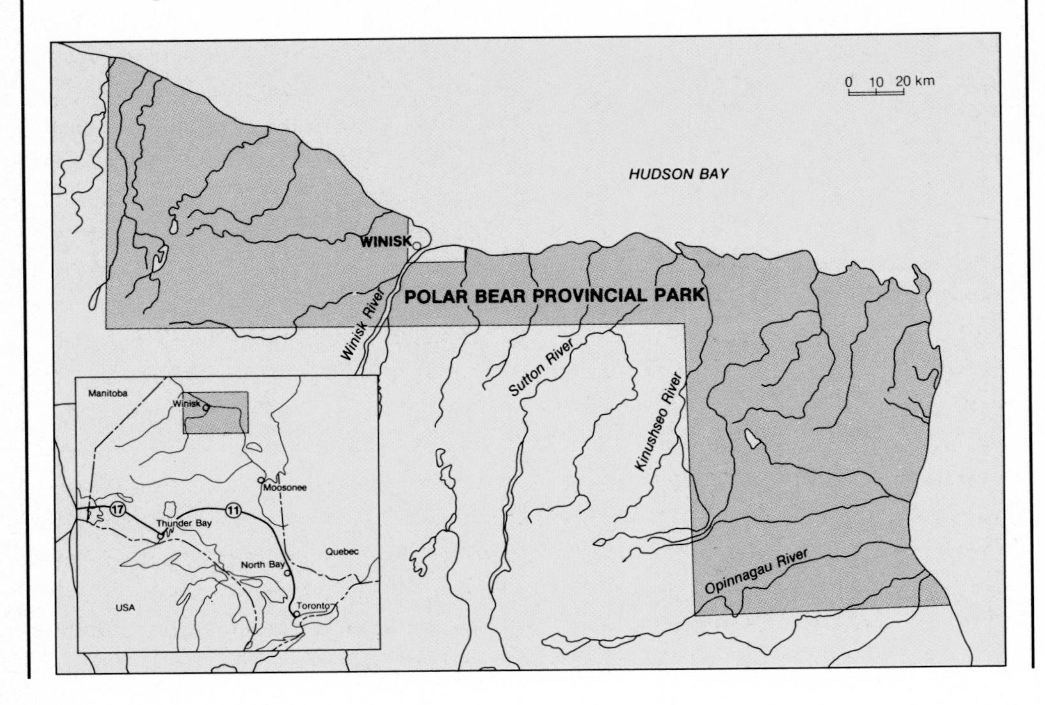

Arctic tundra of Polar Bear Provincial Park. HARRY LUMSDEN

North of the Attawapiskat River, frigid winter temperatures and brutal winds cause the peat and ice cores in many of the bogs to be permanently frozen. The vegetation covering the peat insulates this permafrost during the summer. The ice core slightly raises the surface of the bog, creating extensive low "peat plateaus" or round "islands" called *palsas*. Should the protective sphagnum mat somehow be disturbed, the insulation is destroyed and a prolonged melting sequence is initiated. Pools are formed which, assisted by the eroding force of wind-driven waves, gradually evolve into coalescing groups of shallow lakes. A system of such *thermokarst lakes* west of the Winisk River is the largest example in North America. Typical of the Lowlands, it has yet to be described and documented for science. In fact, probably only a handful of living humans have ever set foot on those strange peat shores.

Fens occupy earlier stages in peatland succession, when plants are still able to derive some nutrients from water in contact with the clay soil. These somewhat more nutrient-rich conditions support a different and dramatically more diverse array of plant life: numerous species of grasses and sedges, the so-called brown mosses, dwarf birch, and stunted tamaracks.

It follows that fens, being younger, tend to occur nearer the coast, and bogs, being older, are farther inland. In practice, these two basic types of peatland are often intermixed. They grade into each other through time as well as space, depending upon slight differences in ground level and water flow under the peat. The resulting mosaic is called *muskeg*.

Conditions during the brief summer on the Lowlands are by no means conducive to vigorous growth. In a treed fen near Moosonee, at the southern tip of James Bay, I once cut a "full-sized" tamarack that was only 3 metres high and 6.5 centimetres in diameter; under the microscope it showed 127 annual rings! In a fen near the Hudson Bay coast a similar-sized tamarack was found to be at least 450 years old.

Although the major rivers can be travelled by canoe, the Lowlands are virtually impassable by foot or ground vehicle in summer. However, during winter's deep freeze it is possible to venture at will into the muskeg country. Those who do will find a vast enchanted forest of crooked, gnarled tamaracks draped in shaggy grey lichens.

The only really practical way to get an overview of the Lowlands in summer is by small aircraft. Even flying low, one is not much aware of the ubiquitous small tamaracks and black spruces so characteristic of the muskeg. But looming ahead, dark green ribbons of larger spruce trees trace the path of rivers and their tributaries. Their banks are elevated somewhat and better drained than the adjacent muskeg, thanks largely to silt accumulated after the annual spring floods. It is mainly here that the "real" trees – spruce and balsam poplars – get their chance, attaining heights of fifteen to twenty metres. Elsewhere, ever-so-slightly raised areas – perhaps a former beach ridge, sometimes a round, ice-cored palsa or spruce "island" – protruding above the surrounding muskeg creates conditions for modest tree growth.

To complete the picture, a variety of pools, ponds, and small lakes is always evident. They tend to be more abundant and larger in areas farther from the coasts and dominated by bogs. Even though the larger lakes may cover several square kilometres, they are remarkably shallow, seldom deeper than about three metres.

As we continue north towards the Hudson Bay coast, the landscape gradually but perceptibly changes. Even stunted trees become less and less noticeable and more patchy in distribution. Then they disappear altogether as we fly out over the tundra of Polar Bear Provincial Park. Here, near the junction of James and Hudson bays, at Cape Henrietta Maria, the climate is so severe that trees are unable to survive at all. Reflecting the change in vegetation, the underlying permafrost now becomes nearly continuous. This region is the most southerly expanse of low Arctic tundra in the world. A variety of ground-hugging heaths such as the bearberries, crowberry, and the striking magenta-flowered Arctic rhododendron, Arctic saxifrages, and willows are characteristic of drier areas, while in the extensive wetlands other dwarf willows, birches, and several sedges, including cotton grasses, predominate.

As Hudson Bay comes into view, our attention is suddenly riveted by spectacular rows of low ridges, arranged parallel to the coast. They are former beaches, now "stranded" above sea level. Those nearest the coast consist mostly of raw gravel. Looking a few kilometres inland, we can traverse several hundred years of plant succession at a glance. From a few hardy beach grasses and other aggressive colonizers on the outermost ridge, we note progressively more complete and complex vegetation communities. The second ridge is ablaze with the flaming pink flowers of a vetch – the Mackenzie hedysarum. By the fifth ridge, there is a white spruce forest whose clearings startle the viewer with their dazzling snow-white ground cover of *Cladonia* lichens.

Any account of the Hudson Bay Lowlands must highlight the extensive, and biologically vital coastal marshes. They form a nearly continuous fringe around Hudson and James bays. Due to the very gradual slope of the land, boulder-strewn mud flats extend seaward for five or more kilometres at low tide. Near the upper reaches of the intertidal flats, the hardy and salt-tolerant "goose grass" takes hold on the mud, in places looking just like well-manicured golf greens. Moving inland up the slight gradient, progressively more species and denser growths of spike-rushes, arrow-grasses, sedges, bulrushes, true grasses, nut rushes, and such herbs as the brilliant, yellow-flowered marsh fleabane take over. An irregular patchwork of distinct plant communities forms where shallow pools, low ridges, and varying substrate alter moisture, salt concentrations, and nutrients.

The marshes average one to two kilometres in width, extending up to five kilometres in places. Their inland border is often marked by a dense, impenetrable jungle of willows and alders. Only in severe storm tides does the salt water penetrate this far inland. The thickets, in turn, meld into fens that form the vanguard of the Great Muskeg.

Polar Bear Provincial Park was established in 1970 when just over 24,000 square kilometres were demarcated from the rest of the Lowland wilderness. The park area was inhabited sparsely by Cree hunters for a thousand years or more, and today is still home to just over a hundred Indians. Their traditional hunting, fishing, and trapping activities have been largely unaffected by creation of the park.

Not surprisingly, this, the most remote and inhospitable territory in Ontario, received relatively scant attention from European colonists. Captains Thomas James and Luke Foxe explored the coastlines of the park in 1651, and by 1685 a few Hudson's Bay Company trading posts had been built along the Ontario coasts of

Hudson and James bays. Some of the posts gradually evolved into permanent Indian villages – today's Moose Factory, Moosonee, Fort Albany, Kashechewan, Attawapiskat, Fort Severn, and Peawanuck (which, until 1986, when it was moved thirty kilometres inland following a disastrous spring flood, was called Winisk). More recently, a brief flurry of activity took place in the mid 1950s when seven Mid-Canada Line radar stations were erected within the present park boundaries. The activity ended almost as soon as it had started; by 1965 all the stations had been abandoned. Their stark skeletons and deteriorating air strips are all that remain. Today the seven coastal communities have the basic federal and provincial government services, but commerce does not flourish. Perhaps fortunately, the Lowlands largely remain a charming and exotic wilderness backwater.

A place with such a singular physical and botanical setting is bound to be home to some special animals too. This surely is the case. Almost devoid of bird life throughout the prolonged and frigid winter, the tundra and coastal marshes swarm with a diverse array of migratory birds during the snow-free seasons. The presence of nesting red-throated loons, tundra swans, king eiders, rough-legged hawks, willow ptarmigan, stilt and pectoral sandpipers, whimbrels, golden plovers, parasitic jaegers, white-crowned sparrows, and Lapland longspurs attest to the low Arctic environment. Inland from the tundra, the muskeg peatlands support generally lower biological productivity. Birds are scarcer, but hardly less interesting.

Tiaga forest in the peatlands of the Hudson Bay Lowlands. HARRY LUMSDEN

Lesser snow geese (both "blue" and "snow" colour phases) on the tundra of Polar Bear Provincial Park.
HARRY LUMSDEN

The fens and bogs are breeding grounds for greater and lesser yellowlegs, Hudsonian godwits, short-billed dowitchers, sandhill cranes, and, associated with the many clusters of ponds and small lakes, a large proportion of the Canada geese from the Mississippi Flyway. Adjacent treed ridges favour such Lowlands' specialities as the hawk owl, merlin, gray-cheeked thrush, blackpoll warbler, and white-winged crossbill. If you are fortunate, you may have a never-to-be-forgotten encounter with the tame but ghostly great gray owl.

Without a doubt the surpassing ornithological spectacle of the Lowlands is one of the world's southernmost colonies of lesser snow geese. The colony resembles a monstrous, sprawling, noisy barnyard, and smells like one too. Early in the nesting cycle total disorder seems to reign as donnybrooks break out on all sides between ganders protecting adjacent nests.

When the colony was discovered in 1944, approximately 100 pairs were nesting there. By 1973 there were an estimated 30,000 pairs, and only six years later the total had nearly doubled to 55,000. The snow goose comes in two colours – the white "snow" goose and the slatey-coloured "blue" goose. At Cape Henrietta Maria, blues outnumber snows by three to one.

The geese are in peak physical condition when they arrive, usually just as snow-melt begins in earnest. A third of their body weight is fat accumulated on the northern prairies during spring migration. These fat reserves, and extra protein added to breast and leg muscles, must tide the geese through the lean period before grasses and sedges begin to sprout, and provide virtually all the nutrients required for egg formation. The more body reserves needed to maintain the geese before nesting, the less are then available for reproduction. Hence, a significantly delayed spring melt triggers a chain reaction that results in noticeably smaller clutches and fewer young. And females have only one chance. If a nest is destroyed by floodwaters or raided by a predator, insufficient time remains to accumulate nutrients for another set of eggs, or to raise young to flying stage before the end of the short, cool summer.

Historically the first geese to appear in early April often broke a period of late-winter hardship, even starvation, for the Cree. Today the spring migration is still anticipated with great eagerness by a substantial number of Cree living largely off the land. Whole families camp for a month or more at traditional coastal hunting grounds. Each year the Indians take large numbers of both Canada and snow geese along the coastal marshes. Just as soon as rising temperatures initiate the spring melt, the Canada geese disperse inland to nest, and many of the snow geese push on to more northerly breeding grounds. When spring comes late, these geese are forced to linger longer, and more are claimed by the Cree hunters. Consequently, delayed springs are a form of double jeopardy to the geese.

The fundamental importance of the Hudson Bay Lowlands to both breeding geese and uncounted hordes of ducks and shorebirds that migrate farther north can scarcely be overstated. The Lowlands provide a strategic link in the yearly cycle of some 2 to 3 million lesser snow geese, 750,000 large Canada geese and 200,000 of its smaller-bodied races, and 50,000 Atlantic brant. Indeed, the Lowlands are an indispensable spring and fall resting and feeding area of international significance.

The mammals of the Hudson Bay Lowlands also reflect an Arctic background. Many visitors to the Ontario portion of the Lowlands are astounded to see a herd of Atlantic walrus loafing on a shoal off the northern shore of the park, or a pod of beluga whales milling in the estuary of one of the large rivers, or perhaps a massive bearded seal hauled up on a gravel bar. More typical mammals of the muskeg and forest include beaver, otter, gray wolf, red fox (with a noteworthy incidence of the attractive "cross" colour phase), and especially marten. Arctic foxes prowl the tundra zone along the Hudson Bay coast. Lynx and wolverine, although present, are not so frequently encountered.

Perhaps the woodland caribou best typifies the Lowlands. Now increasingly scarce south to Lake Superior, substantial herds still roam the muskeg. Gregarious for much of the year, females seek isolation in spring just before giving birth to calves. Within a few weeks, however, small herds begin to re-assemble. Later in the summer there is a tendency to visit the Hudson Bay coastal area. It is not uncommon to encounter concentrated tracks of what appears to have been whole armies of caribou on manoeuvres considerable distances out on the mud flats at low tide. Evidently they are attempting to avoid the omnipresent plagues of insect pests. Such herds sometimes number over twenty-five hundred animals. In late autumn they migrate inland to traditional wintering areas in the muskeg. Here they feed on arboreal lichens and excavate characteristic oval craters in the snow with their rounded, widely splayed hooves to reach the underlying freeze-dried vegetation.

Canada geese are important in spring to native people living a hunting-fishing-trapping economy in coastal regions of the Hudson Bay Lowlands.
H. LUMSDEN

Polar Bear Park's name is not apocryphal. As our plane lumbers over the most shoreward beach ridge, we notice two large white objects below. They could be boulders or perhaps sun-bleached chunks of driftwood. But they're not. The polar bears are stretched out in adjacent pits excavated in the gravel. Now, in late July, they have just swum ashore after being forced off the rapidly fragmenting ice pack in Hudson Bay where they have spent the entire winter. Except for shifting pressure leads, and a few perpetually ice-free areas of upwelling warm currents called *polynia*, Hudson Bay completely freezes over. Temperatures of −40°C and almost constant strong winds make Hudson Bay one of the coldest places in North America on the basis of wind chill. Polar bears, however, are admirably adapted for these conditions and are completely at home on the bleak ice pack. Their diet of seals captured along open leads between the floes is extremely rich, and so the bears accumulate enormous layers of fat, stopping just short of total obesity.

This fat stands them in good stead, for it is their major source of sustenance from the time they come ashore in July until the sea ice can again support their weight in late November or early December. A few bears may try to catch flightless moulting geese or ducks, and they are known to consume quantities of beach grass and algae. A lucky polar bear might even find a seal or whale carcass washed up on the beach. Nonetheless, the total nourishment from the summer's diet is probably minimal. For the most part the bears take life easy. They lie quietly along the beach ridges, taking occasional leisurely strolls along the shore. Their biggest problem seems to be avoiding overheating. Presumably the bottoms of pits dug into the ridges are in contact with somewhat cooler moist gravel, and the deeper summer dens may also offer relief from insects.

Polar bears in Hudson Bay.
HARRY LUMSDEN

Pregnant females roam inland during the summer, eventually choosing a suitable denning site. Dens may be dug into peat hummocks or gravel banks, but sometimes a female may simply lie down in the lee of a ridge and let blowing snow drift over her, later hollowing out a chamber. Dens have been found as little as 10 and as far as 150 kilometres inland from the coast.

Usually two extremely tiny cubs, each weighing less than one kilogram, are born around Christmas. They grow very rapidly on their mother's nutritious milk and by February are ready to exercise in the vicinity of the den. In late February or early March the family departs for the sea ice. Normally their tracks follow a direct bearing to the coast, punctuated by occasional round hollows in the snow where the sow stopped to warm, rest, and feed her cubs. The female bear's anxiety to get back on the frozen bay is understandable – presumably she has had very little food since the previous July. Perhaps fortunately, female polar bears breed only once every three or four years. The family group is virtually inseparable for at least two years. It is estimated that approximately eight hundred polar bears call Ontario home.

Our aircraft finally turns back southward. As we retrace our journey, the puzzling, endlessly changing yet repetitive peatland landscapes continue to evoke an indefinable aura of intrigue. From bleak Arctic shorelines and treeless tundra to rich coastal marshes and mysterious sub-Arctic muskeg; from imperious polar bears and elusive Connecticut warblers to the delicately translucent calypso orchid, the Hudson Bay Lowlands' surprising contrasts and subtle beauties work a peculiar, lingering magic on the human observer. The Lowlands are fitting ecological bookends and a stark counterpoint to the remaining fragments of the lush Carolinian forest of Ontario's "deep south." They add just the right balance of biological diversity and natural beauty to a richly endowed province. And happily, unlike more vulnerable natural habitats to the south, their forbidding isolation and inhospitable terrain give us hope that the great muskeg wilderness will persist to captivate and inspire us for many generations to come.

Part Four

VIGNETTES OF NATURE

Spotlighted in the following vignettes is an array of natural features and events – some of the most exciting and spectacular aspects of Ontario's natural environments, at least to a human perspective. The vignettes are arranged roughly in geographical order from south to north: the Carolinian zone, the farmlands, urban nature, the Great Lakes, the hardwood-boreal forest, and finally the boreal forest that dominates much of the province. Each of these regions is introduced descriptively, to help break down the artificiality caused by dividing ecosystems into bedrock, landforms, mammals, birds, and other categories as was done in *Provincial Perspectives* for the sake of comprehension and convenience. Nature functions in regions, not in topics; each region expresses its characteristic moods and stages its own outstanding events.

The Carolinian Zone

John B. Theberge

You get a different feeling when you walk through southern hardwoods, the Carolinian life zone that touches Canada lightly along the Erie shoreline and Niagara Peninsula. It is a lacy, lazy feeling, with overtones of Appalachia and Alleghenia, the Ohio Valley, and the Mississippi. It conjures up visions of hill farms and hill people, of Ol' Blue and coon-hunting and corn pone – romantic folklore of the south.

Most of the Carolinian forests are gone from Ontario now, the result of an unfortunate coincidence of their location on some of Canada's richest agricultural land and most benign climate. But what is left is some of the best of what there was, a fortunate coincidence of their location on floodplains and in swamps that could not be easily converted to farmlands. They are found in patches: Pelee, Rondeau, Backus Woods, Springwater Woods, Catfish Creek – places of great significance to the birder and botanist – the richest lands in species in the province and possibly in Canada. With many characteristics of forests farther south, these places abound in national rarities.

Besides these famous remnants of Carolinian forest, isolated patches can be found here and there among the tobacco fields of Haldimand-Norfolk, Kent, and Essex, or down in the steep-sided stream gullies that plunge off the sand plain into Lake Erie, or tucked away in pockets on the clay plains that never dry. While scattered now, the Carolinian in Ontario may have been a patch forest even before white men entered its ecosystems. Indian agriculture introduced fields of maize, squash, and beans across the landscape. Indian longhouses were heated and cooking fires fueled from the forests. The Indian pattern of clearing the land, farming it for ten or fifteen years, and moving on must have created a mixture of both old and young forest. But, regardless of how extensive the Indian impact may have been, European settlement in the southwest corner of Upper Canada, and indeed all down the eastern seaboard of the United States east of the Mississippi, quickly built its own set of images into the Carolinian zone – split-rail fences snaking along the field edges, wagon roads to haul out timber, white-painted churches on the hill with neatly-trimmed cemeteries behind.

Carolinian forests are high-crowned, their tall trees arching into cathedral-like domes, their canopy leaves creating mosaics of tangled beauty and infinite detail. On a spring morning, the orioles, warblers, and grosbeaks saturate the cathedral with praise. On a spring evening, wood thrushes flute their benedictions to the day.

Characteristic of Carolinian forests is laciness – the delicate leaflets of black walnut, butternut, locust, hickory, and ash that fine-filter the light through their canopies and soften the

Carolinian zone (grey).

shadows below. Characteristic too is its luxuriance of wide-spreading oaks and sycamores, the lawn trees of southern plantations. Even the understorey witch hazel spreads broad, two-metre high umbrellas of green across the trail. In sunlit groves, sassafras and tulip-trees reach mittened hands towards the light.

Carolinian forests are energy-rich, and they spend that energy lavishly. Five-centimetre-wide yellow flowers of tulip-trees hang high in the forest crown; white robes of flowering dogwood, state tree of Virginia, garland the forest edge; orange-red flames of redbud burn in a sunlit clearing. The brilliance of the flowers is matched by brilliant birds: bright yellow prothonotary warblers, yellow and black hooded warblers, blue cerulean warblers.

But mostly, there is a pastel quality about the Carolinian. Its greens are not harsh, its high-canopy forests are sunlit, not sombre, its spring shades are delicate – the muted reds and yellows of slowly unfurling silver maple, mulberry, and the oaks. In autumn, the brilliance of its sugar maples is softened by the subtle yellow-browns and buffs of white ash, red oak, basswood, and black walnut.

There is some debate among botanists and naturalists over whether or not to call what we have in southwestern Ontario true Carolinian forest. The wild rhododendrons that characterize whole mountainsides in Appalachia are not in Ontario, nor is mountain laurel, or silverberry, or other important and widespread trees that grow farther south. What we have, however, is the northern fringe of the southern hardwoods, where some southern species have gained a toe-hold, straining against the limitations of insufficient frost-free days, low mean summer temperatures, and the like. What Ontario has is an ecotone, or transition, to the more typical northern hardwoods.

So you have to look carefully for the Carolinian in Ontario. It does not hit

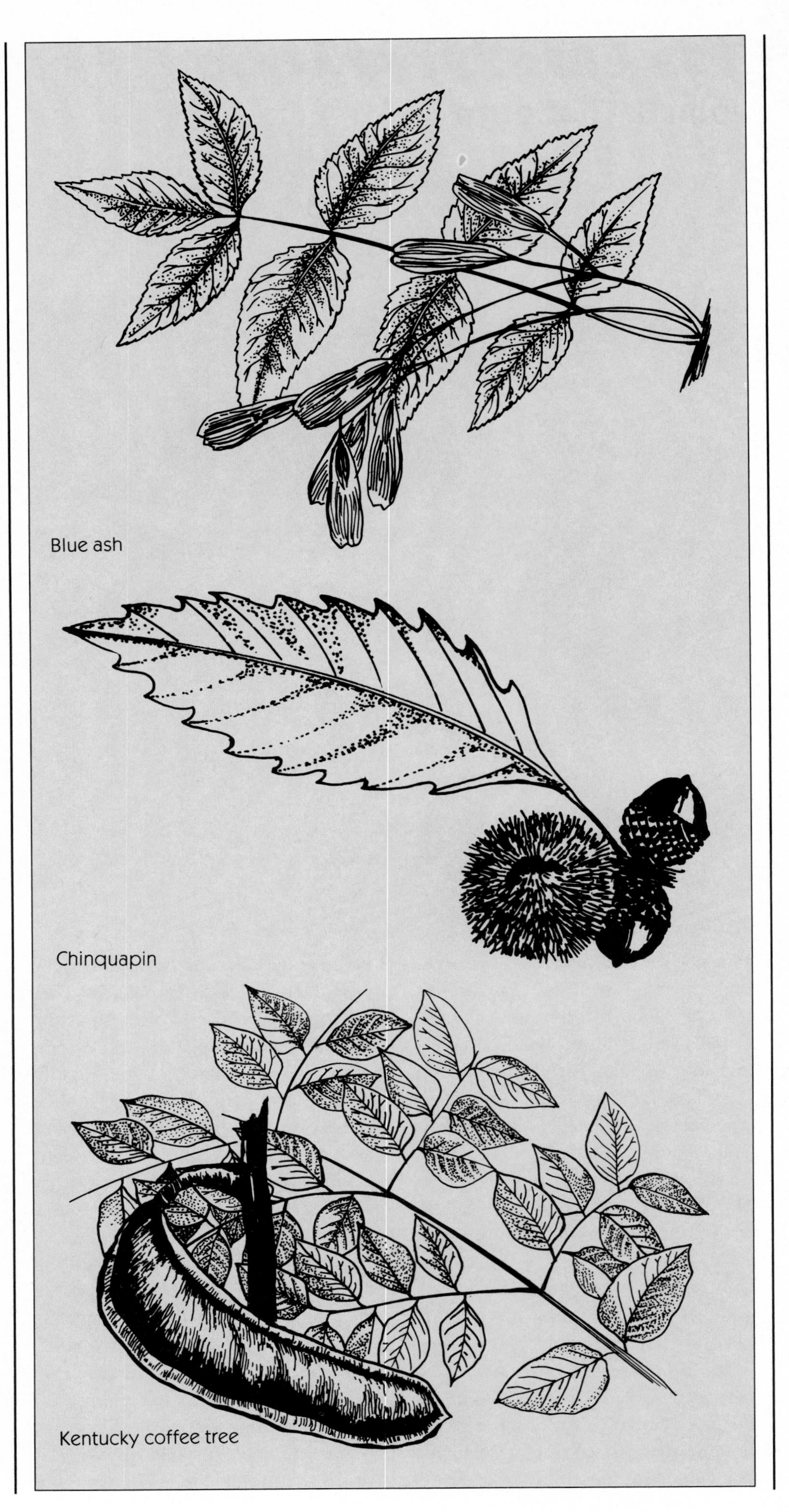
Blue ash

Chinquapin

Kentucky coffee tree

Flowering dogwood. JOHN THEBERGE

Redbud tree in Point Pelee National Park. GARY ALLEN

you all at once. Sugar maple and American beech still dominate. Incongruously, you find yellow birch, more characteristic of northern transitional and maritime forests, growing within fifty metres of huge tulip-trees. Only when you look closer do you recognize the subtle shift to more oaks near Lake Erie, and to more hickories. And only after even closer inspection do you discover the rare oaks – chestnut oak and dwarf chinquapin. Only when you extend your gaze up a massive trunk in the forest and search the crown with binoculars do you realize that you are standing beneath a tulip-tree, or when you study leaf shape and consult a botany book do you identify black gum. Only when you wade to the edge of a silver maple swamp do you recognize that what you may have thought was alder or willow growing out in the water was buttonbush. But even then, the notes of a northern water thrush, another more northern species, may ring out from the far side of the swamp, and on a clump of wet ground at your feet blooms the same wild lily-of-the-valley that carpets the ground under cool hemlocks along ridges and beside bogs in Algonquin Park.

The animal life of the Carolinian, like its forests, is dominated by many species of the northern hardwoods, but is enriched by southerners. The bulk of the wood warblers migrate farther north to breed, leaving yellow warblers and yellowthroats behind to nest in stream-side shrubbery or draping willows. But with them is a sprinkling of rarities such as golden-winged and blue-winged warblers, cerulean warblers, parula warblers. Singing all day with the red-eyed vireos of the northern hardwoods may be a yellow-throated vireo. A mockingbird may pour out its jumble of notes from a hawthorn thicket, or a Carolina wren, which provides more volume of song per gram of bird than almost any other species, may sing from a tangled ravine.

Once, wild turkeys searched for acorns in southern Ontario, and gray foxes stalked the turkeys. Wild turkeys are coming back, the result of introduction programs. The gray fox is now exceedingly rare. Now and then a bobcat is sighted in the Carolinian zone, or a Virginia opossum testing out survival on the northern edge of its range. An American egret may wade at the marsh edge. Occasionally someone will report a black rat snake or a spotted turtle.

It is the rarities that excite, and the green cathedrals that inspire in what is left of Ontario's Carolinian forests. Only public support for conservation efforts will assure their future on the fringe of agri-urban southwestern Ontario.

Wild Islands of Western Lake Erie

Gerald McKeating

Among the swirling gulls and crashing waves of Lake Erie are a group of limestone islands scattered northward from Ohio to within sight of the Ontario mainland at Point Pelee. Some are little more than gravel shoals. Others are buffered from the waves by great slabs of limestone. The Lake Erie islands are unique, possessing a type of biological richness not found elsewhere in Canada.

These islets comprise the southernmost land mass in Canada, comparable in latitude to northern California. Although they appear today as a series of stepping stones to the American shore, geologists believe that about 12,000 years ago, when the lake was considerably lower, they formed a continuous peninsula. The rock outcrops of today are the remains of hills on the peninsula prior to the last glaciation.

The biota on the islands is similar to that found much farther south in the Ohio Valley; indeed, it contains outstanding examples of plant and animal communities more typical of the southern mid-western states. The land connection of old probably served as a "migration corridor" for many species.

The islands experience a humid, continental climate. Polar and tropical air masses frequently conflict causing rapid changes in weather. Their low relief eliminates any topographical effect on wind or rain, leaving the lake itself as the most important moderating influence. Plant growth begins early and extends into November, a growing season similar to that of West Virginia. The islands have the highest July mean temperature in Ontario – 20°C (74°F) – and the least days of measurable precipitation – seventy-five.

Aided by a mild climate, geography helps create the rich variety of plants and animals. Like other areas of extreme southwestern Ontario, some species are at the northern perimeter of their range, while others are at their southern edge. A western flavour is contributed by species from the tall-grass prairie. Influencing most plants that live here, however, are calcareous growing conditions, the result of a thin soil barely covering the limestone.

Among the more spectacular features of the islands are their reptiles and amphibians. Fox snake, blue racer, and Lake Erie water snake, all with restricted ranges in Canada, exist in suitable habitats. The Lake Erie water snake on the islands represents the entire world population of that subspecies of the more common northern water snake. The blue racer's total range in Canada is on Pelee Island. Among amphibians are typical southern species such as

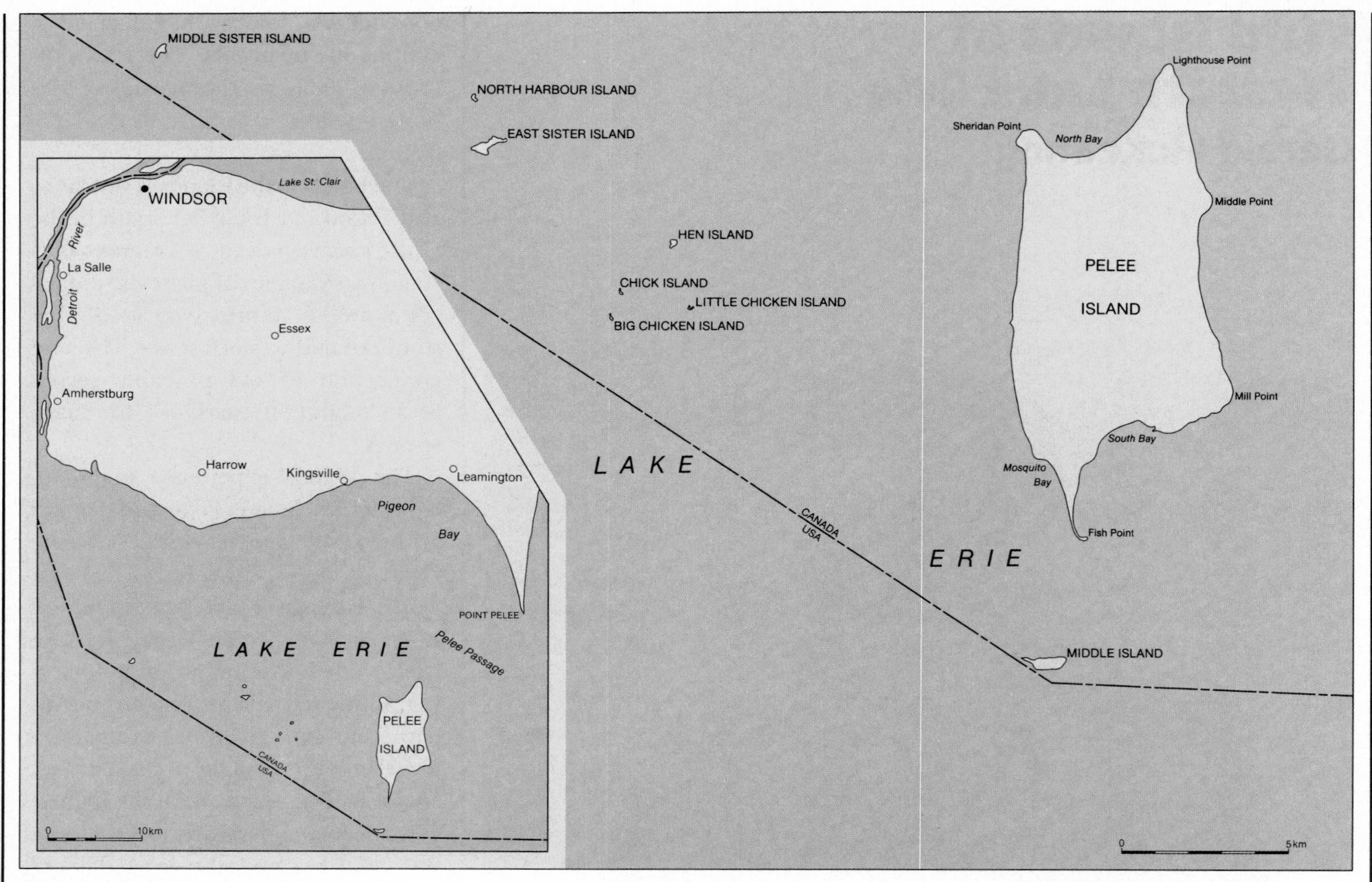

Islands of western Lake Erie.

cricket frogs and small-mouthed salamanders.

Even among butterflies are unusual species. The records of the Royal Ontario Museum include southerners such as the giant swallowtail, little sulphur, and tawny emperor. One can commonly locate the hickory hairstreak and the hackberry butterfly in areas where the food plants after which they are named occur.

The islands provide biological isolation for many species, especially mammals. Isolation, compounded by the effects of human settlement on Pelee Island, have resulted in an impoverished mammalian fauna. The inability of many mammals to swim to the islands has prevented colonization. Occasionally mammals may cross in winter if an ice bridge forms, or man may introduce them. Fox squirrels were brought to Pelee Island from Ohio over a hundred years ago, and flourish there today.

Pelee Island is the largest within the archipelago. More or less rectangular in shape, its twenty-seven square kilometres have little relief, in fact much lies below lake levels. The vast marshes were drained years ago, and now dykes hold back the lake from flooding the fields. For such a small area, Pelee Island possesses remarkable diversity, especially when the influence of man is so highly evident. Corn and soybeans appear to grow everywhere, but the concentration of rare plants in the remaining natural habitats make the island of national biological importance.

Forest cover on Pelee Island is sparse, as there was extensive logging during the 1880s. Only about 100 of the original 1,840 hectares of forest remain. Communities include a black oak-red cedar association, inter-dunal flats with dwarf chestnut oak, and swamp hardwoods. Rare plants include black locust, hackberry, red mulberry, yellow puccoon, tall bellflower, and American lotus. Pelee Island is one of few areas where blue ash can be found in Ontario, and the stand of shellbark hickory at Middle Point is one of the finest in Canada.

During migration periods, Pelee Island swarms with birds. An unusual number of cattle egrets may be spotted together in one small pasture, or hundreds of eastern meadowlarks. Some birds more common to the south remain to breed, including the blue-gray gnatcatcher, red-bellied woodpecker, and Carolina wren. At times the whole environment seems to be alive with colourful migrants.

The two prominent physiographic features of the island are Fish Point at the southwest tip and Lighthouse Point at the northeastern corner. Lake-caused erosion and high water levels cause the two dynamic points to shrink or grow with each wave.

Fish Point is the largest wooded area remaining on Pelee Island. Few sites in Ontario support such a diversity of rare species – 14 birds, 8 reptiles, 3 amphibians, 1 invertebrate,

Mill Point, Pelee Islands. P. A. WOODLIFFE

and 102 vascular plants. Living here is an exceptional diversity of trees: hackberry, blue ash, hop tree, black maple, eastern cottonwood, and red ash. Characteristic of the Point's drier parts are black ash woods and red cedar woods, underlain by great Solomon's-seal, and in damper areas, masses of Dutchman's breeches. The dune areas grow wild grape and prickly pear cactus. Until recently, one could often look across the buttonbush-fringed lagoon and see hundreds of black-crowned night herons nesting in the vine-festooned woods, a picture reminiscent of some lush, tropical forest. Although the herons have moved to another island in recent years, Fish Point remains a treasure.

Middle Point, on the east side of the island, contains an outstanding woodlot of 90 per cent hickory. The rich herbaceous ground layer here provides the best floral display on the island and includes spring cress, yellow corydalis, and false mermaid. Unfortunately, development for the site was being promoted at the time of writing. If allowed to proceed, a place unique in all of Canada will be lost.

The limestone plains, or *alvar*, in the southeast section of the island may look like a dull wasteland, yet this park-like savannah provides a habitat for many plants of prairie affinities typical of the mid-western United States. The Federation of Ontario Naturalists has acquired much of this area, a botanical treasure, thus ensuring its protection.

Lighthouse Point at the northeastern corner of Pelee Island is yet another location of special interest. Although the vegetation here is not as dense as it is at Fish Point, there are similarities. A number of sloughs and beach ridges exist, but much of the diversity has been lost owing to Lake Erie's recent high water levels. The site exhibits many special features; among its rare plants is the American lotus, which covers a large pond. Marshes are developing in the flooded land, and within the past several years, double-crested cormorants have begun to nest, no doubt a spill-over from the greatly expanded colony on Big Chicken Island. At Big Chicken the cormorants nest on the ground, but here the birds construct their nests in dead trees adjacent to the lake.

Big Chicken Island is hardly big, despite its name. It is a gravel shoal little more than half a hectare in size, rising scarcely more than three metres above the lake. Exposed to wind, rain, and storms from all directions, little vegetation can grow here, but these seemingly adverse conditions do not prevent a flourishing breeding colony of herring gulls and double-crested cormorants. The gulls use the lower levels of the shoal for their simple nests; the cormorants construct elaborate stick nests along the stone ridges, sometimes incorporating fishing tackle into their construction.

Cormorants, large black birds with an orange throat patch, flourish on a

Pelee Island. GARY ALLEN

fish diet. During the 1960s, their numbers on the Great Lakes declined significantly, likely from contamination of their food supply. Reduced in size, the Big Chicken colony hung on, and fortunately, since limitations have been placed on the use of DDT, the birds have made a spectacular comeback throughout the Great Lakes-St. Lawrence region. From banding returns it is evident that these cormorants winter on the Gulf coast.

The most southerly land mass in Canada is Middle Island, located within sight of the international boundary. Weathered limestone slabs ring the shoreline. Within the limestone is the richest collection of fossils in the area, including a colonial coral fossil almost three metres in diameter. Much of the island is wooded, dominated by hackberry. Fifty-two significant botanical species have been reported. Years ago, a small airplane runway bisected the island to serve a sportsman's club, but shrubs have invaded the runway, and now it is overgrown. An old bald eagle nest still stands, reminiscent of a once healthy population, and symbolic of the hope that they will once again nest on the islands. One of the largest herring gull colonies in Lake Erie, 992 nests in 1981, is located here, and the large black-crowned night heron colony that formerly nested on Fish Point has relocated to this island.

East Sister, a fifty-five-hectare flat dolomite and limestone island, is covered with dense woodland and understorey shrubs of elderberry and chokecherry draped with vines: grape, bur cucumber, and poison ivy. The island is owned by the Ontario Ministry of Natural Resources and is officially designated a Nature Reserve. A thin soil layer becomes thicker towards the island's south end, supporting hackberry, yellow (chinquapin) oak, and black maple among other trees, and a variety of ground plants such as wild licorice and Short's aster. The highlight of this island is a large stand of Kentucky coffee trees some as tall as twenty metres. This site is one of only four where the tree grows wild in Ontario, although it is found in about eight other landscaped sites.

Herons on East Sister nest within the swamp forest in large numbers, along with a few common egrets. The two dominant species – great blue and black-crowned night herons – sort themselves out in stratified layers: the former in the upper tree canopy, a location highly advantageous for takeoff and landing of such a large bird; the latter in the dense stands of chokecherry within seven metres of the ground. Around the shoreline and inland are numerous herring gull nests.

The other important island in the group is Middle Sister. Because it is seldom visited, owing to the large and treacherous expanse of water that must be crossed, not a great deal is known about its biology. It has lush vegetation, and both great blue herons and common egrets nest there. Its stone beach, as usual, has its share of nesting herring gulls. Both this island and East Sister provide habitat for rare reptiles, especially Lake Erie water snakes and fox snakes.

Part of the island chain is located in the State of Ohio. Because access to the American islands is far easier, they have been heavily developed for recreation. Other than Pelee Island, the Canadian islands are relatively undisturbed; thus the wild islands of western Lake Erie remain one of the most biologically unique areas in Canada.

East Sister Island. GARY ALLEN

Ontario's Marathon Butterfly: The Monarch

Gary M. Allen and Natalie E. Zalkind

For years, local woodcutters in one of the remotest sections of the Sierra Madre Mountains of central Mexico witnessed a most incredible sight. As they climbed the mountainsides, the dense evergreen trees glistened and shimmered before their eyes. Millions upon millions of colourful monarch butterflies covered the trees and ground, and more flitted and danced through the air.

For generations these woodsmen witnessed this spectacular phenomenon of nature. But as familiar as it was to them, it was not until 1975 that the rest of the world came to share their knowledge. The Mexican over-wintering site eventually was discovered for science by Dr. Fred Urquhart of the University of Toronto and his wife Norah.

The Urquharts spent forty years unravelling the mystery of monarch butterflies and finally found the site by tracking the movements of monarchs that carried tiny labels affixed to their wings. Years of experimentation with different labels took place before they found that the kind used to stick prices on glassware was successful. And the butterflies have caught public interest; since the 1950s, volunteers from throughout North America eagerly have recovered monarchs and sent valuable tag data and notes on observations back to Toronto. By the 1970s, enough information had been amassed through the collection of 300,000 returned tags that the Urquharts were able to plot trends in the insects' annual flights from Ontario and the northeastern United States through Texas to Mexico. With the help of two Mexican volunteers, the over-wintering grounds south of Mexico City finally were discovered and brought to the world's attention. Similar sites in Pacific Grove, California, used by monarchs west of the Continental Divide, had long been known due to their proximity to Los Angeles.

In common with many insects, monarchs have a "life-or-death" dependency on one group of plants. Their survival depends on the availability of milkweeds, the only food suitable for their larvae. The three subspecies of monarchs that range from southern Canada to the tip of South America are known to feed on several of the more than a hundred species of milkweed found in North America and the twelve species in South America. Of the eleven milkweed species found in Ontario, seven are at their range limits and are rare, while the other four are widespread in the southern part of the province. The monarch, however, owes its preponderance mainly to one species – the aptly named common milkweed, the most abundant species around the Great Lakes and the one that most of the eastern population of monarchs feeds upon. This is also the milkweed that grows the farthest north in Ontario, permitting, in turn, the extension of the monarch's breeding range well into the Canadian Shield to approximately forty-eight degrees latitude.

The monarch butterfly's range throughout the world expanded greatly in the 1800s as trade and oceanic voyages became commonplace. Presumably by accident, monarchs were transported over vast distances. They reached the Hawaiian Islands in 1845, spread rapidly through the South Pacific, and first were recorded in Australia, where they are now firmly established, in 1870. The monarch's reputation as an international traveller is well deserved.

Monarchs arrive in Ontario from the south in late May through early June. The female lays approximately three hundred cream-coloured eggs, each about one millimetre in diameter. Eggs are deposited singly on the undersides of healthy milkweed leaves. Open fields and woodland edges are preferred egg-laying sites, where warmer temperatures permit more rapid larval growth.

Under optimal conditions, a monarch egg will hatch in four to six days, revealing a two-millimetre-long caterpillar with a shiny black head and greyish-white body. From this humble beginning, the larva develops through a series of five growth stages, shedding its skin each time. The mature caterpillar sports the familiar tiger-striped

Mass of migrating monarch butterflies, Point Pelee National Park. POINT PELEE NATIONAL PARK, W. WYETT

pattern of alternating dark brown, cream, and yellow bands. On its steady diet of milkweed leaves, the larva increases its weight in this fifteen-day period to about 1.5 grams – 2,700 times its original weight!

In preparation for shedding its fifth and final skin, the caterpillar attaches itself to a small silk pad and hangs upside down, suspended in a J position. After the skin splits and falls off, a beautiful aquamarine chrysalis is revealed. The mature chrysalis is adorned with small gold spots that look hand-painted. These spots are thought to control colour in the developing wings. In the chrysalis, the amazing metamorphosis to an adult butterfly takes place.

After about nine to fifteen days, the developing wings of the adult monarch are visible through the skin of the chrysalis. The metamorphosis is complete when the pupa splits open, freeing the fully formed adult. The entire process from egg to adult takes about five weeks.

A monarch butterfly leaving Ontario faces an unbelievable 3,000-kilometre journey to Mexico. How such a frail insect can make its way over vast expanses of prairie, desert, mountains, and water is still not fully understood. And why does the monarch make this 6,000-kilometre annual round trip while most other North American butterflies remain within a few kilometres of where they were born? Is there a selective advantage to migration? If so, then why haven't other butterflies evolved this habit?

Better understood are some of the environmental conditions that trigger the annual flight to Mexico. Cool, blustery days and decreasing daylight stimulate the monarchs' southward migration. A characteristic of this flight is the establishment of overnight roosting sites. As insects are cold-blooded, monarchs are unable to fly when temperatures dip below 12°C, hence the practice of overnight roosting. A branch heavy with the weight of hundreds of monarchs will swing less in the breeze, therefore reducing the chance of butterflies being knocked to the ground. The roosting sites chosen often consist of a group of trees near a large body of water, particularly on peninsulas pointing in a southerly direction. Monarchs shy away from flying over large bodies of water, preferring to follow land as much as possible. That is why the Erie spits – Rondeau, Long Point, and Point Pelee – are ideal viewing places. Point Pelee National Park, with its southward orientation and triangular shape, is one of the best places in North America to witness this colourful migration.

The fall migration to Mexico is much less hurried than the northern flight in spring. The butterflies take time along the way to feed on nectar. They must accumulate much fat before reaching the over-wintering forests in Mexico. It takes a butterfly about six weeks, travelling an average of fifteen kilometres per hour, to reach its destination.

The Mexican mountain forests at 2,700 metres are ideal over-wintering spots for the monarchs. Brisk temperatures at this altitude are severe enough to numb the butterflies into dormancy without being lethal, as temperatures in Ontario would be. The tall evergreen roost trees provide shelter and protection for their fragile occupants.

In February or March, when temperatures rise above 21°C, the butterflies become active. They mate, and the eggs developing in the females' bodies spur them northward. Very few males will complete this journey. Many females lay their eggs along the way, and the resulting offspring continue the trek, some reaching as far north as Hudson Bay.

In a field in Ontario on a summer's day there may be three or possibly even four generations of monarchs. These generations might include the butterflies that migrated north from Mexico, offspring they produced along the way, and one or two generations from eggs laid in Ontario. The first generation produced by the migrant monarchs in Ontario will appear from mid July through August; the second from mid August through September. The first generation survives only about four weeks, its sole purpose being to produce the fall brood.

Prior to 1980, the forested Mexican over-wintering sites of the butterflies were threatened. Subsistence farming and lumbering, the main livelihoods of the surrounding rural population, were encroaching quickly on the roosting areas. Fred Urquhart worked with the Mexican people and in 1980, after careful negotiation, the government established a 16,000-hectare "Monarch Butterfly Ecological Reserve." Logging and agricultural development were halted immediately. Lost jobs eventually were replaced by a developing tourist industry. In 1985, 50,000 tourists paid to be guided through the roosting sites. Souvenir shops sprang up, costs of hotel accommodation increased, and wardens were hired.

As with migratory birds, however, protection at only one end is not enough. Dr. Urquhart has campaigned to conserve habitat for monarchs in both the United States and Canada. Expansion of cities and highways plus the liberal use of herbicides along roadways, railway lines, and marginal farm lands has resulted in a sharp decline of milkweed plants. Ontario citizens can help by planting milkweed to attract butterflies. A milkweed planting program has been established successfully in some elementary school biology curricula. While the survival of large populations of monarchs is still not guaranteed, conservation efforts have improved the chances that they will continue to grace meadow and field, and mass in spectacular fall flights on migration to a now-safe wintering ground.

The Prairies of Southwestern Ontario

Paul D. Pratt

No living man will see again the long-grass prairie, where a sea of prairie flowers lapped at the stirrups of the pioneer...

Aldo Leopold, 1949

The poignant sense of loss reflected in Aldo Leopold's words underscores the value of Ontario's rarest plant community – one whose very existence has only in recent years become widely known and understood.

Many accounts of early Ontario stressed the heavily forested nature of the land, and created the image of vast, unbroken forest. Yet the early French explorers and first settlers of southwestern Ontario also discovered extensive, open landscapes. They encountered the outlying remnants of oak savannah and tall-grass prairie which once dominated a large portion of mid-western North America along the eastern edge of the Great Plains.

About 8,300 years ago, when the

Ohio spiderwort, Walpole Island in Lake St. Clair. LARRY LAMB

climate was slightly warmer and drier than today's, Leopold's "sea of prairie flowers" extended much farther east than it did in the days of the pioneer, more so in the United States than in Canada. A "prairie peninsula" extended from the Great Plains through Iowa, Illinois, Indiana, to Michigan, Ohio, and into southwestern Ontario. Gradually, the climate became slightly cooler and wetter, allowing some re-invasion of forest and creating the mosaic of prairie and savannah that was encountered by the first European explorers.

Prairie persisted where a combination of soil type, microclimate, and fire continued to favour grasslands over forest. In southwestern Ontario, prairies are found on sandy soils with their limited capacity to store moisture. During the spring these soils can be completely saturated, yet by mid summer they invariably become extremely dry. The forests of eastern North America in general are less well adapted to such moisture stress than are prairie plants such as big bluestem, Indian grass, and prairie cord grass.

Fire caused by lightning or set deliberately by Indians undoubtedly was important in maintaining the prairies in southwestern Ontario. In prairie remnants today, fire is necessary to prevent shrubs and trees from closing them in. The significance of Indian-set fires is uncertain. Essex and Kent counties traditionally were the lands of the Central Algonkian people. Archaeological evidence shows this area was inhabited with villages until about 1500 AD. After that date, undoubtedly the Lake St. Clair–Detroit River corridor and the shore of Lake Erie were important travel routes. Interestingly, the Huron name told to the first French explorers for the inhabitants of this southwest corner of the province was the "Fire Nation."

Then the settlers arrived. A description of the Detroit River area in 1701 reads: "The banks are so many vast meadows where the freshness of these beautiful streams keep the grass always green...the teeming turtle dove, swarm in the woods and cover the open country intersected and broken by groves of full-grown forest trees which form a charming aspect." Even as late as 1791 the prairies of southwestern Ontario were largely intact. At that time, Patrick McNiff, describing Kent County, bordering Lake St. Clair and the Thames River, wrote: "Extensive natural meadows and dry in most places with a thin black soil....These meadows are from four to six miles in depth...and to the north of the river, the meadows are much wider."

Prairie coneflower, Walpole Island. LARRY LAMB

Tall-grass prairie scene in early August, Walpole Island. The tall magenta flower is blazing star. LARRY LAMB

More than 390 square kilometres of prairie still thrived in portions of Essex, Kent, and Lambton counties until the mid 1800s, but then it began to disappear fast. How much easier to plough the prairie, where mature trees average less than one per acre, or to clear the savannah with its widely scattered oaks, than to cut down the heavy forest. Throughout its range, the tall-grass prairie was rapidly, inexorably destroyed. Today, there remains less than one-tenth of 1 per cent of the original 1 million square kilometres.

The vestiges of the magnificent Kent County prairies exist today as odd clumps of gray-headed coneflowers or place names on maps, such as "Prairie Siding" and "Raleigh Plains." Dover Township, northwest of Chatham, presents endless vistas of corn, wheat, soybeans, and thin, widely separated patches of trees. The scattered trees are sadly ironic, for in many places (except on flood plains, in river valleys, and other natural forest sites) they are not remnants of a once great forest as is often imagined, but are recent conversions to trees of what was once prairie. The beautiful prairies that once extended "as far as the eye could see" have all but disappeared under the plough. Only recently, with increasing concern in Ontario about nature and the environ-

Michigan lily, Walpole Island.
LARRY LAMB

ment have there been many people to mourn the loss and marshal an effort to save what is left.

Among the remnants that make Leopold's prediction not entirely true are considerable stands of both oak savannah and prairie on the Walpole Island Indian Reservation near Wallaceburg. There, and at Windsor's Ojibway Prairie, one can still stand in fields of prairie wildflowers. The Ojibway Prairie is 175 hectares of oak forest, savannah, and prairie protected in four parks within the former townsite of Ojibway, now part of Windsor.

On warm, windy days in early spring, spectacular fires sweep through the thick mats of dry grasses every few years on these prairies and savannahs. Deliberately set, these fires remove the accumulation of ground litter and allow the soil to warm up sooner. Fire is essential to a naturally functioning prairie. Prairie plants are not damaged, being mostly warm-season perennials which are dormant in April. The large, scattered oaks are sometimes scarred but are seldom killed.

A visit to a prairie site on Walpole Island in mid May is breathtaking. By then, the black landscape of an April burn has been replaced by a carpet of small white lady's-slipper orchids, golden alexanders, blue-eyed grass, yellow stargrass, arrow-leaved violet, wood-betony, and hoary puccoon. In hardwood forests the wildflower display is most extensive in the spring, but prairies undergo a slow build-up of colourful blooms which reach their peak in late July. Mid-summer brilliance is displayed by the tall culms of Culver's-root, butterfly milkweed, flowering spurge, ironweed, dense blazing star, tall sunflower, prairie dock, and tall coreopsis. These waist-high wildflowers flow with the ever-present breeze. By August the flowering heads of prairie cord grass, big bluestem, and Indian grass reach three and four metres high!

At Ojibway, because of controlled burns, prairie is now reclaiming forest that had grown in since settlement times. More than a hundred of the rare plant species of Ontario and a variety of wildlife, including Butler's garter snake and Massasauga rattlesnake, contribute to a rich diversity.

Ontario's remnant tall-grass prairies and associated oak savannahs are up against the pressures of continued industrialization and expanding human populations. Fortunately, the Ojibway sites in Windsor are protected both as city parkland and as provincial nature reserve. These areas will be restored and managed as native prairie and savannah. The future of the Walpole Island sites and a few other tiny prairie remnants in the Carolinian zone is less certain. Every year, pieces of precious virgin prairie in these places go under the plough.

Small white lady's-slipper orchid, officially an endangered species in Canada, growing on Walpole Island.
LARRY LAMB

Fire, a natural restorative process at the Ojibway Prairie, Windsor, Ontario.
P. A. WOODLIFFE

Swans by the Thousands

John B. Theberge

March 31, 1935, was a raw day. A biting wind gusted across Hamilton Bay. From shore, four naturalists scanned the water with binoculars: Jim Baillie and Terence Shortt, well-known ornithologist and artist respectively of the Royal Ontario Museum; Thomas McIlwraithe, whose father had written the pioneering bird book of Ontario in 1894; and Richard Saunders, who later described the events of that day in his nature classic *Flashing Wings*:

> Far out over the glittering water I saw my first wild swans, great white birds, their wings flashing in the brilliant sun as they beat their way steadily across the Bay straight into the stiff cold wind, seemingly unconcerned, their long ramrod necks and black faces stretched out before them like an indication of unswerving purpose. Great brave birds, headed for the barren lands of the north where man's hand is weak against them. . . . At the edge of the reeds, not more than 125 yards 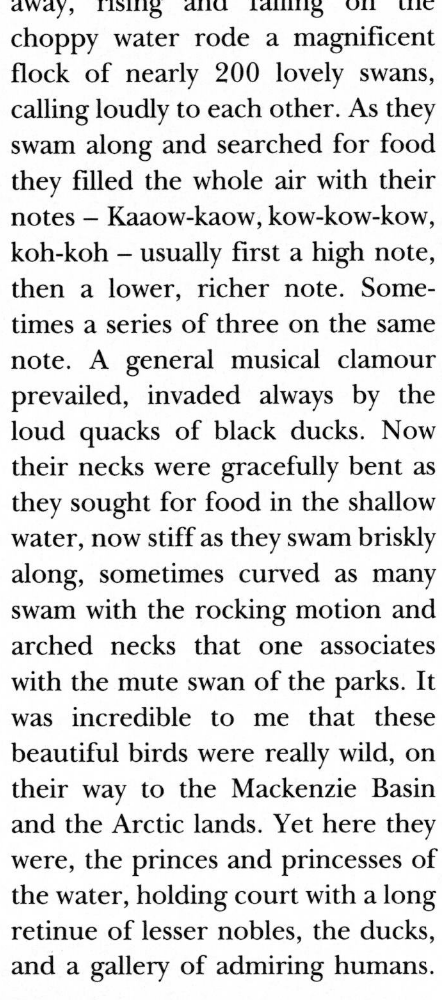 away, rising and falling on the choppy water rode a magnificent flock of nearly 200 lovely swans, calling loudly to each other. As they swam along and searched for food they filled the whole air with their notes – Kaaow-kaow, kow-kow-kow, koh-koh – usually first a high note, then a lower, richer note. Sometimes a series of three on the same note. A general musical clamour prevailed, invaded always by the loud quacks of black ducks. Now their necks were gracefully bent as they sought for food in the shallow water, now stiff as they swam briskly along, sometimes curved as many swam with the rocking motion and arched necks that one associates with the mute swan of the parks. It was incredible to me that these beautiful birds were really wild, on their way to the Mackenzie Basin and the Arctic lands. Yet here they were, the princes and princesses of the water, holding court with a long retinue of lesser nobles, the ducks, and a gallery of admiring humans.

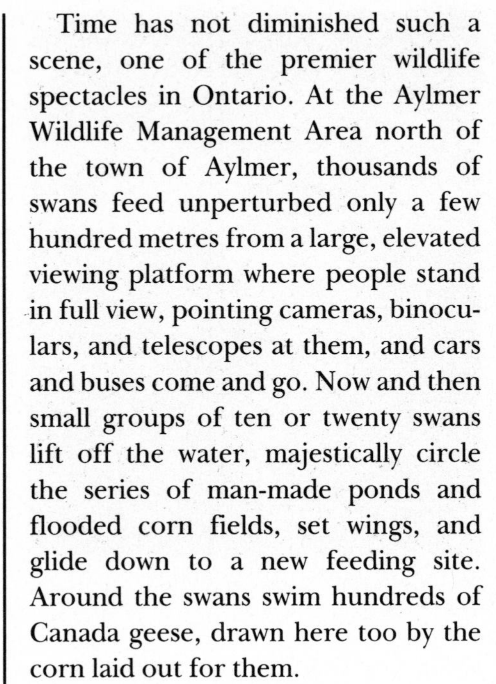

Time has not diminished such a scene, one of the premier wildlife spectacles in Ontario. At the Aylmer Wildlife Management Area north of the town of Aylmer, thousands of swans feed unperturbed only a few hundred metres from a large, elevated viewing platform where people stand in full view, pointing cameras, binoculars, and telescopes at them, and cars and buses come and go. Now and then small groups of ten or twenty swans lift off the water, majestically circle the series of man-made ponds and flooded corn fields, set wings, and glide down to a new feeding site. Around the swans swim hundreds of Canada geese, drawn here too by the corn laid out for them.

The Ministry of Natural Resources supervises, handing out a pamphlet that reads:

> Before its creation, the Aylmer Wildlife Management area site was used only occasionally by these birds. With the development of waterfowl habitat on the property and the adoption of farm management practices conducive to waterfowl use, swan use of the Area increased dramatically. In 1973, approximately 300 birds were seen. In 1977, in excess of 7,500 were estimated to have visited the area. The first swans arrive in late February. Gradually, their numbers increase throughout March, climbing sharply in the last week, and declining even more sharply in the first days of April.

These tundra swans are part of the 94,400 birds comprising the eastern population. An additional 68,000 winter from British Columbia to California near or at the coast.

A hundred years ago reports of swans were uncommon in Ontario. In Canada's first bird book published in 1872, Dr. A. M. Ross wrote: "this magnificent bird is rare in eastern Canada. . .it is occasionally met with in the vicinity of Lake St. Clair." In 1894, Thomas McIlwraithe wrote in *Birds of*

Tundra swans on spring migration near Aylmer, Ontario. JOHN THEBERGE

Ontario: "These beautiful birds, never at any point abundant, are seldom seen in Ontario, because they breed in the far north, and generally make their migratory journey along the sea coast, east or west, where they spend the winter."

By 1922, however, reports of swans had become more common. Ornithologist P. A. Taverner recorded that, "flocks of hundreds appear annually on Lake St. Clair," and, "this species also occurs in large numbers on the Niagara River where on misty or foggy nights in the spring, they often drift down with the current into the swift rough waters of the rapids and are carried hopelessly over the falls."

Swans migrating north through Ontario each spring are on their way from wintering grounds on the Atlantic coast from Chesapeake Bay south to northern Virginia. Many tidal marshes have been destroyed, and today most swans winter at Chesapeake Bay itself. When they leave there on their northward migration, they have only a short, 600-kilometre flight to the north shore of Lake Erie.

Until the early 1970s, the marshes at Long Point provided the major resting and feeding area for the swans. Busloads of naturalists came from all across the province to see the swans and attendant rafts of canvasback, redhead, and ring-necked ducks. Other flocks of swans alighted in other north-shore marshes from the Niagara River to Oshawa's Second Marsh and Presqu'ile Point.

In recent years, deterioration of these marshes as well as increases in corn and winter wheat as major field crops have resulted in the swans moving inland to the fields. Now, travellers anywhere in southwestern Ontario may see a flock of field-feeding swans.

After the tundra swans leave southern Ontario, they fan out to fly over Wisconsin, the Dakotas, and Manitoba. Devil's Lake, North Dakota, provides another major migration stopover. Most swans continue northwest across the Athabaska Delta to nest in the Mackenzie Delta close to the Arctic coast, or the Old Crow Flats in the northern Yukon. Some fly northeast to nest on Baffin Island or islands in Hudson Bay. On their return migration they fly high over Ontario nonstop from the Dakotas to the eastern United States.

The swans have survived habitat loss, hunting, and poisoning from lead shot that gets caught in their gizzards where it slowly breaks down and eventually kills them. Nevertheless, they have accepted man, spending more than half of each year in close quarters with cities, automobiles, airplanes, dogs, polluted air and water. Prior to 1916 their numbers were greatly reduced by hunting. However, their adaptability and more protective hunting laws have saved them. Their numbers have increased from an estimated 30,000 wintering on the Atlantic coast in 1950 to about 94,400 today.

Increasing crop damage in the Atlantic states has resulted in an open hunting season on them in North Carolina, Virginia, and New Jersey. In the west, Montana, Utah, and Nevada also have open seasons. The kill is limited by licence. Because tundra swans are no longer considered in danger, management plans call for a considerable reduction by the year 2000 to 80,000 swans in the east and 60,000 in the west! Thus, these magnificent white birds will continue to pay a price for their acceptance of man. Their ultimate fate as a species depends upon sufficient corn left unploughed in fields surrounding their wintering grounds. In southern Ontario and elsewhere along their migration route, it depends upon marsh restoration and the protection of reserves, on hunters refraining from shooting them illegally, and a reduction in the amount of lead shot lining the bottoms of marshes where they feed.

Hawk Cliff

Bruce Duncan

"The kestrels will soon be gathering along the wires," writes a veteran hawk bander to me almost every year, and once again, my thoughts turn to Hawk Cliff. It is mid August, and in two weeks the hawk banders will sweep the cobwebs from their blinds and set out their nets.

The first few eager watchers will park at the end of the Hawk Cliff Road on the north shore of Lake Erie near Port Bruce. To reward them a few ospreys, northern harriers, and perhaps a young sharp-shinned hawk will drift by to the west, and the kestrels will drop leisurely into the yellowing fields to catch grasshopper after grasshopper. To pass the time, visitors stroll up and down the road, glancing skyward frequently, and look down the forty-metre-high cliffs of eroding sand and clay to Lake Erie. Or they scan the grassy verges to find the beautiful fall flowers: grass-of-Parnassus, ladies'-tresses, great blue lobelia, fringed gentian, asters, and goldenrods.

By the second weekend of September, the people have increased and so have the hawks. Then, sometime after September 10, when rainy weather passes through followed by a northerly high-pressure system, cool, clearing air pushes the first big flight of raptors to the Lake Erie shoreline. Early morning watchers get not just a parking spot close to the cliff but also glances from sharp-shins and kestrels passing by at eyeball height just as the sun shows above the horizon. By ten o'clock hundreds of falcons already will have gone by to the west with a few dozen immature harriers and one or two ospreys. Late birdwatchers swell the crowd, a few puffy cumulus clouds begin forming, and soon someone spots a group of thirty or forty or fifty hawks – the broad-wings are coming!

At first, broad-winged hawks in small flights, called *kettles*, flap and circle on outspread wings, rising from the tree-tops to a hundred metres or so, and glide west into the breeze. By noon, the kettles contain hundreds of swirling hawks, adults and immatures, rising until they are only dots in the sky. The broad-wings pass over by the thousand. On special days, such as September 19, 1931, September 22, 1942, September 23, 1954, and September 18, 1982, thirty thousand or more hawks float by like autumn leaves on an easy breeze. And float they do, for the broad-wing, like so many migrant raptors, tries to use as little energy as possible in its long flight to South America. The sun is its workmate, heating the ground and the air next to it, causing the warm air to expand and rise as a huge bubble or *thermal* through the surrounding cooler air. At about 800 metres, moisture condenses to droplets and small cumulus clouds appear, sapping the warmth of the thermal. On the way up, however, the heat is found by gliding hawks who at once spread their wings and tails and let the shimmering air lift them as they soar in circles. Near the top, they tuck their wings and glide to the west, watching the birds ahead who have found the next thermal.

The air begins to cool in the late afternoon, and by evening, when the lift is gone, the hawks drop like bombs from the sky to roost in whatever woodlots they find along the lake. Next day, with the weather holding, thousands more move on, and later, smaller and smaller flights are seen until, by October 1, only a few hundred broad-wing hawks are left in the province.

One of the most intriguing aspects of the broad-winged hawk migration is that these birds may eat very little or nothing at all during their long journey to South America. They almost certainly fatten up in the late summer before beginning the flight, but they try to use as little energy as possible when flying. In the morning, they wait for thermals, give a few flaps to get started from their perches, and then soar up and up. Throughout each good flying day, they may flap their wings fewer than a dozen times.

Two habits work to their advantage. Broad-wings migrate early in the fall when the sun is still quite high in the sky, producing strong thermals from early morning to late afternoon – eight or nine hours of "free rides." In spring, they are late migrants, waiting for the long, warm flying days at the end of April before arriving in southern Ontario. And, because they do not eat during the autumn flight, they slowly lose weight, making them able to soar more efficiently.

That broad-wings go for many days, perhaps weeks, without food seems hardly believable considering that most of the other hawk species do feed during migration. Sharp-shins, who migrate at the same time as broad-wings, eat as regularly as they can. They have to, as they depend for long periods on energy-consuming flapping flight. Red-tails, who soar on the weaker thermals of October and November and do not fly nearly as far as broad-wings, also feed in passage. But, we know that broad-wings fast; a biologist who has examined areas in Central America where big flocks of broad-wings have roosted for the night, has never found excreta below the trees, a certain sign that none of the birds had eaten recently.

Most of the watchers at Hawk Cliff leave with the broad-wing hordes, even though other hawks continue to pass by, each in its time. Now, the adult sharp-shins and young Cooper's hawks are scattered across the sky, red-tails and red-shoulders begin their migration, and the few merlins and peregrines that use the Great Lakes shorelines instead of the Atlantic coast in the fall pass by. Even later, goshawks, rough-legged hawks, and golden eagles come south just ahead of the Arctic winds. By November 30, only a few straggling red-tails and rough-legs can be seen. The flight is over.

Since 1969, the keenest of the hawk enthusiasts have gathered at the cliff to capture, band, and release a total of 37,500 hawks. Only 500 of these hawks have been encountered again, but the banded birds have told many stories.

Cooper's hawk. POINT PELEE NATIONAL PARK

Kestrel. NATIONAL MUSEUM OF CANADA, A. G. AUSTIN

We now know that there is a sequence during the migration not just of species, but also of males and females, adults and immatures within each species. For example, immature female sharp-shinned hawks precede immature males by an average of five days, and adult females by eleven days, the adult females passing through a week before the adult males. The same pattern holds for the later-migrating Cooper's hawk.

With six banding stations stretching from the lakeshore to a hayfield two kilometres inland, banders have noticed also that more adult sharp-shins migrate inland, while immatures, making their first trip south, concentrate near the shore of the lake, a strong leading line for these inexperienced birds. The inland station is also a busy place when southerly breezes push the hawks away from the cliff face to follow woodlots and brushy ravines between the concession roads.

Once past the cliff, kestrels may move as far south as Florida, Cooper's hawk's as far as Louisiana, although most usually stay farther north, while the red-tails often double back, staying in southern Ontario, or they move south of Lake Erie, then east into Pennsylvania and New York. Sharp-shins have been recovered in Costa Rica, Guatemala, and Mexico. But the broad-winged hawks, so rarely caught and banded, drift constantly south and are seen by the hundreds of thousands passing over Panama on their way to South America.

So many questions about the hawk flight remain unanswered or not completely answered. Why do they leave? For many of them, their prey is disappearing: large insects die, snakes and frogs hibernate, small birds migrate. To find food, they must seek a warmer winter. Yet some stay; a few red-tails, American kestrels, sharp-shins, Cooper's hawks, harriers, rough-legs, red-shoulders, and goshawks manage to tough it out. Many of these birds winter where they have nested, while the migrants who travel farthest south have come from farthest north.

And why Hawk Cliff? The shoreline at this point bends in a gentle arc to the east and west. Hawks that have been following the Lake Erie north shore pass by here, and those that have been flying inland east of the cliff are forced to the edge by the geography. Northerly winds mass the birds more emphatically at the lakeside.

Whether it is the excitement of watching a sky full of milling broad-wings or of catching sight of an extreme rarity – a Swainson's hawk in September or a young gyrfalcon in November – the watchers and banders who so enjoy the spectacle will be back to share in it and to ponder the partly solved mysteries, autumn after autumn, year after year.

Herons and Heronries

John B. Theberge

Scattered in wild, wet places across the Canadian Shield and the larger woodlots, swamps, and marshes of southern Ontario are the bizarre nesting places of the great blue heron. This bird is familiar, standing motionless in shallow water, poised to jab at its prey with its long, dagger-like beak, or flying in slow motion across a marsh against an evening sky. Its unhurried wing beats and long, trailing legs bestow upon it elegance and grace.

Great blue herons are common; a recent provincial survey estimated more than thirteen thousand pairs. Their nesting places, however, are much less well known. Long-legged birds like great blue herons might be expected to nest on the ground, concealed among the cattails near their feeding sites. But, with few exceptions, these largest of herons nest high in trees, usually well out from the trunk where the birds are not only conspicuous, but appear ungainly and awkward. A bird with a 1.75-metre wingspan must nest where it can land easily; a ground nesting site in the open presents an invitation to predators.

Even in trees, predation is a problem. Raccoons may climb to the nests, or hawks and owls may descend upon them. The evolutionary "choice" of nesting singly, presumably with more secrecy, or in large, clearly visible

Great blue heron colony on East Sister Island in Lake Erie. GERALD MCKEATING

colonies must have been faced by some ancestral great blue herons, and they evolved nesting in colonies. Although a colony of great blue herons is certainly obvious, especially when located in dead trees, the advantage of more heron eyes and ears to recognize danger, and heron voices to sound an alarm, and the greater capacity to ward off a predator, must have taken precedence.

Great blue herons are not particular about the types of trees in which they nest. Trees may be deciduous or coniferous, live or dead, so long as they have horizontal limbs for nest support. Dead trees standing in water may be difficult for raccoons to reach, but nests located in them are certainly conspicuous to raptors. Colonies may even be located in dry, upland hardwood some distance from water. The trees of a colony are festooned with large, bulky stick nests, with as many as eighteen recorded for a single tree. In spring, these nest clumps located well out on branches may give the trees a cypress-like appearance. Later, when the canopy closes in, the flapping wings of the large adult birds as they come and go, or their neck-bending displays on the edge of the nest, make heronries impossible to miss. Noticeable, too, is the white guano on lower limbs and covering the ground. Droppings from the young herons may acidify the soil, eventually stressing and killing the nest trees.

One of the earliest descriptions of a heronry in Ontario is found in a report of The Ottawa Field-Naturalists' Club in 1883. It captures the feeling of such a place:

> After proceeding about half a mile into the swamp, our attention was arrested by a peculiar sound which we at first thought proceeded from some distant saw-mill or steamer on the river. As we advanced, however, the sound resolved itself into the most extraordinary noises, some of which resembled the yelping of dogs or foxes. On penetrating still deeper into the swamp, we discovered that the noises proceeded from immense numbers of herons, some perched on branches of trees, some sitting on the nests, and others flying overhead. The uproar was almost deafening, and the odor arising from the filth with which the trees and ground were covered was extremely disagreeable. We tramped all through the heronry, and calculated that it must extend about half a mile in each direction....The birds were very tame, making no attempt to fly until we began to climb the trees on which they were; and even then moved lazily off and manifested little or no alarm at our near approach to their young.

The results of an Ontario Heron Inventory, published in 1985, estimated 376 colonies in the province, with an average occupancy of 35 nests per colony. The largest colonies contained more than 250 nests, with a record of 292 nests established by a colony near Nanticoke in the Regional Municipality of Haldimand-Norfolk. The density of colonies appeared to be greatest on the southern parts of the Canadian Shield. However, average colony size – 35 nests – was smaller there than in southern Ontario – 66 nests – although it exceeded the estimate for the central and northern parts of the Shield – 28 nests. A few colonies, most notably at Luther Marsh near Orangeville, have now been bolstered by artificial nest platforms on poles, in this case constructed to replace dead trees standing in water, that had fallen down over time. More than half of that colony of about 160 pairs nests on these platforms.

Black-crowned night heron, Rondeau Provincial Park. P. A. WOODLIFFE

Sharing the heronries with great blue herons are other species: black-crowned night heron, green-backed heron, common egrets, and cattle egrets, especially in the large colonies on the Lake Erie islands. These other species nest with great blues only where colonies are located adjacent to marshes or swamps and only in the southernmost colonies. The two egrets only recently appeared in Ontario colonies; the first nesting common egret was found in 1953, and the first nesting cattle egret in 1962.

Even though great blue herons nest in colonies, they fly between nesting and feeding sites either singly or in small groups, and feed well spread out or alone. Hunting at the edges of ponds, they seem to pose for paddling canoeists or passing motorists. Letting their prey – small fish or amphibians – come to them, they poise like drawn bowstrings ready for release. The tendons of their necks are stretched with the neck's curve, owing to a peculiar anatomy of unequal-length vertebrae, and so they are ready to shoot head and beak forward at unsuspecting prey.

While the great blue heron is more widely distributed than any other North American heron, it still needs habitat protection. Wetland drainage and shrinking woodlots have undoubtedly reduced heron numbers south of the Canadian Shield, and logging has destroyed traditional sites farther north. Still, these herons are tolerant, and they persist. They remain a picturesque symbol of wetlands and the need for wetland conservation.

Niagara Falls

John B. Theberge

Called one of the seven wonders of the world, Niagara Falls and the Niagara Gorge, as natural features, are dramatic, compelling, powerful – the single greatest tourist attraction in North America. Sadly, however, they are much diminished. At night and in winter, three-quarters of the river's flow is diverted through penstocks rather than crashing over the falls. The river is probably the most filthy and contaminated in North America. And the naturalness of the scene has largely disappeared under urban, industrial, tourist, and power developments.

Still, Niagara Falls is a semi-natural feature of immense proportions, and the form and force of the scene is enthralling. Much of the bedrock history of the lower Great Lakes basin is laid out here on superlative display. The parkway landscaping and historic monuments soften the glaring commercialism to a pleasing degree.

It takes a vivid imagination to see the picture described by the first Jesuit missionaries of a large encampment of Neutral Indians at the mouth of the Niagara River, and the footpath through the forest along the rim of the gorge to the falls. In its natural setting of dense woodlands and flat relief, the sight of the gorge slashing across the land, and of the falls itself, was overwhelming to early explorers. They recorded their impressions in notebooks, later gathered together and published in 1921 by Charles M. Dow, former Commissioner of State Preservation at Niagara.

The earliest written description of Niagara Falls is accorded to the Récollet missionary Father Louis Hennepin, whose original description in French soon was translated into other languages:

> On the 6th [December 1678], St. Nicholas day, we entered the beautiful river Niagara, which no bark ever yet entered. . . .Four leagues from Lake Frontenac (Lake Ontario) there is an incredible Cataract or Waterfall, which has no equal. The Niagara river near this place is only an eighth of a league wide, but it is very deep in places, and so rapid above the great fall, that it hurries down all the animals which try to cross it, without a single one being able to withstand its current. They plunge down a height of more than five hundred feet, and its fall is composed of two sheets of water and a cascade, with an island sloping down. In the middle these waters foam and boil in a fearful manner.
>
> They thunder continually, and when the wind blows in a southerly direction, the noise which they make is heard from more than fifteen leagues. Four leagues from this cataract or fall, the Niagara river rushes with extraordinary rapidity especially for two leagues into Lake Frontenac.

Hennepin's misjudgement of the height of the falls attests to the impression it made on him. Rather than being "more than five hundred feet," the American, or Rainbow Falls, is 167 feet, or 50.9 metres high, and the Canadian, or Horseshoe Falls, is 158 feet, or 48.2 metres high.

The earliest description in English was written seventy-two years later by the famous Swedish botanist Peter Kalm who travelled widely in North America. Kalm had read Hennepin's description, both the original and later more embellished versions, and set out to be what he considered more accurate:

> Before the waters come to this island, it runs but slowly, compar'd with its motion when it approaches the island, where it grows the most rapid water in the World, running with a surprising swiftness before it comes to the Fall; it is quite white, and in many places is thrown high up into the air! The greatest and strongest battoes would here in a moment be turn'd over and over. The water that goes down on the west side of the island, is more rapid, in greater abundance, whiter, and seems almost to outdo an arrow in swiftness. When you are at the Fall, and look up the river, you may see, that the river above the Fall is every where exceedingly steep, almost as the side of a hill. When all this water comes to the very Fall, there it throws itself down perpendicular! It is beyond all belief the surprize when you see this! I cannot see it without being quite terrified; to behold so vast a quantity of water falling headlong from a surprising height!

One of the most dramatic accounts of the falls was written by the famous English author Charles Dickens, who travelled from Buffalo to Niagara by train in 1842:

> When we were seated in the little ferry-boat, and were crossing the swoln river immediately before both cataracts, I began to feel what it was: but I was in a manner stunned, and unable to comprehend the vastness of the scene. It was not until I came on Table Rock, and looked – Great Heavens, on what a fall of bright-green water! – that it came upon me in its full might and majesty.
>
> Then, when I felt how near to my Creator I was standing, the first

effect, and the enduring one – instant and lasting – of the tremendous spectacle, was Peace. Peace of Mind: Tranquillity: Calm recollections of the Dead: Great Thoughts of Eternal Rest and Happiness: nothing of Gloom or Terror. Niagara was at once stamped upon my heart, an Image of Beauty; to remain there, changeless and indelible, until its pulses ceased to beat, for ever....

To wander to and fro all day, and see the cataracts from all points of view; to stand upon the edge of the Great Horse Shoe Fall, marking the hurried water gathering strength as it approached the verge, yet seeming, too, to pause before it shot into the gulf below; to gaze from the river's level up at the torrent as it came streaming down; to climb the neighbouring heights and watch it through the trees, and see the wreathing water in the rapids hurrying on to take its fearful plunge, to linger in the shadow of the solemn rocks three miles below; watching the river as, stirred by no visible cause, it heaved and eddied and awoke the echoes, being troubled yet, far down beneath the surface, by its giant leap; to have Niagara before me, lighted by the sun and by the moon, red in the day's decline, and grey as evening slowly fell upon it; to look upon it every day, and wake up in the night and hear its ceaseless voice: this was enough.

In the late 1700s Niagara Falls became a focal point of discussion about the age of the Earth. Could the falls have cut its way back from its original location, eleven kilometres downriver on the Niagara Escarpment above Queenstown, since October 23, 4004 BC, when, claimed James Usher, an Irish archbishop, the world began? (The established estimate now of the time the falls has been cutting its way back is 12,000 years.)

Next the falls entered into the heated controversy about whether or not glaciers once covered northern North America. In 1841, Charles Lyell, the famous British geologist, identified the buried St. David's Gorge and correctly interpreted it as evidence of glaciation. He discovered this gorge by noting the absence of bedrock on the northwest wall of the Whirlpool Basin. The only explanation possible for the gravels that filled the St. David's Gorge was that they represented glacial deposits. It is now known that the St. David's Gorge was the forerunner of the lower Niagara Gorge before the last glacial advance, and that it was buried in glacial till by the re-advance of the ice, dated now at about 22,000 years ago.

The particular geology that led to the creation of the falls is none other than the geology of the Niagara Escarpment. The caprock of both is hard Lockport dolostone, below which is softer Rochester shale. The falls and escarpment both recede due to undermining collapse of the shale from flowing water, or in the case of the escarpment, due to rain water and snow melt working their way through joints and cracks. The only difference between falls and escarpment is that river water erodes the rock faster. Whole pieces may break off both falls and escarpment, such as the spectacular fall of Prospect Point into the Niagara Gorge on July 28, 1954. Today, construction work has shored up both the Canadian and American falls, slowing their retreat. Without it, the American Falls threatened to become no more than a series of rapids.

The falls at Niagara will continue to attract people, so long as policy makers do not turn all its water into the powerhouses and its mist does not become toxic to the skin. Neither event is beyond possibility. But, as one of the major North American attractions, public concern hopefully will stem any further aesthetic desecration.

Gull City

Michael D. Cadman

November and December are quiet months along the Niagara River. The throngs of tourists are gone, and the air is not yet cold enough for the famous ice-bridge to have formed in the gorge beneath the falls. But there are days in this period when it is difficult to find a space along the railing overlooking the Horseshoe Falls. Many of the people crowding the rail are armed with tripods and telescopes,

Gulls on an island at the brink of Niagara Falls. LARRY LAMB

binoculars and field guides. Oblivious to the spectacular torrent of water only metres away, they have been drawn here by a phenomenon known to few who are not avid naturalists. Every autumn the Niagara River is home to an enormous number of gulls. In fact, on a good day, an experienced naturalist can identify as many as thirteen species of gulls – a feat that cannot be matched anywhere else in the world.

This assemblage is a surprisingly cosmopolitan mixture. Of the thirteen species, only four are local nesting birds. Herring, ring-billed, great black-backed, and little gulls are known to nest on the Great Lakes, although many of those seen at Niagara may have come from farther afield. The little gull, a recent colonist from Eurasia, now nests in small numbers on this continent. Two other Eurasian species are visitors to Niagara: the common black-headed gull, which also now nests uncommonly in North America, and the lesser black-backed gull, which has never been found nesting here. The small and dainty Bonaparte's gull comes down from the boreal forest, where, unlike other gulls, it nests in trees. Iceland, glaucous, Thayer's, and Sabine's gulls are all Arctic-nesting birds. From the marshy sloughs of the prairies comes the Franklin's gull, while the black-legged kittiwake makes the trip from the rocky cliffs of the North Atlantic coast.

Despite their varied origins, to the casual observer many of the gulls look quite similar. But even the most uninterested bypasser cannot fail to be impressed by the numbers and vitality of the wheeling flocks of birds. Some days, the air over the river seems alive with the energetic, buoyant throngs of Bonaparte's gulls, patrolling, turning, and dipping to the water to pick up edible morsels. Roosting aggregations of gulls are less impressive, at least until some disturbance – a hawk, but more often a low-flying airplane – puts the flock to flight. On a calm day, as many thousands of large, white birds burst from the rocks, the rush of wind from their wings can be heard half-way across the river.

The reasons for their congregation here are not fully known. Some of the species will winter in the area, taking advantage of the year-round open water of the river and nearby Lakes Erie and Ontario. Others are only stopping by on their fall migration to the Gulf or Atlantic coasts. Some, especially the species which occur here less frequently, are probably off-course, having "taken a wrong turn" at Newfoundland, or perhaps North Dakota, on the way to their wintering grounds.

Once on the river, though, there appears to be plenty of food. Gulls are opportunistic feeders, and often scavengers. The giant turbines through which much of the river water is diverted shred fish, and the falls themselves undoubtedly kill or stun large numbers, providing a good supply of easily available gull food. Not surprisingly, the gulls often are concentrated at the outflow from the generating stations and at the foot of the falls itself. A sort of pecking order is apparent in these places. The large gulls are often closest to the overflow, where they gain first chance at claiming the bigger chunks of fish. The small gulls, more adept at hawking over the water, wheel further down stream where they pick up whatever small items their larger relatives have missed.

Birdwatchers come to Niagara from across the continent and even from abroad to witness the river's autumn spectacle, but few leave the river without reflection on the irony of the situation. The Niagara River is well known to be severely polluted with toxic chemicals. The gulls are at or near the top of their food chain, eating fish and other organisms that have already concentrated these chemicals. There can be little doubt that the gulls spending time on the river ingest these pollutants, but how much, which chemicals, and what effects they have on the birds are little known. The eggs of gulls on Lake Ontario, downstream from the Niagara River, have been shown to contain the deadly chemical dioxin. Studies of these gulls are providing us with an early warning system to alert us to dangerous levels of these toxins in Lake Ontario, from which more than six million people draw their drinking water. But these studies also alert us to the fact that the many thousands of gulls on the river are ingesting the chemicals. For species such as the Bonaparte's gull, a significant proportion of whose entire population spends time on the river, the unknown long-term effects of this intake are particularly menacing.

The clean-up of this vital waterway is essential, not only for the health of people, but of the many thousands of gulls that wheel over Niagara Falls and the Gorge, veiling the natural beauty of the scene with swirls of white and forming a glittering cloud above the dark waters.

Flying Pebbles: The Shorebirds

John B. Theberge

They come out of the night. As first daylight filters through the mist, phantom-like they pebble the beaches. Running on almost invisible legs, flying from one place to another beyond the retreating wave and between the strand lines, they create motion where there should be none. They flow over the boulders, race helter-skelter over the mudflats, glide across the sand. They are the shorebirds – sandpipers and plovers – that make a birdwatching spectacle out of May and September days on the still-wild beaches of the southern Great Lakes.

Ontario owes these concentrations of bird life to the Great Lakes themselves. These water bodies create a reason for the shorebirds to rest and feed, both after over-flying them in the spring, and again before over-flying them in the fall. Among the most-favoured places for shorebirds are the three peninsulas of Lake Erie – Pelee, Rondeau, and Long Point – the Lake Ontario peninsulas of Presqu'ile and Prince Edward County, the Lake Ontario marsh-mouths such as Willow Beach, Whitby Marsh, and Oshawa's Second Marsh, and the Inverhuron-Grand Bend beaches of southern Lake Huron. While shorebird concentrations sometimes can be found on inland lakes and marsh edges, the big flocks are on the Great Lakes.

At these places, where mudflat, beach, and water meet, where pools ripple and waves pound, the shorebirds madly feed, darting this way and that, tiny legs a blur, probing, running, probing some more, anxious to be off on the next stage of migration.

The sandpipers probe with their thin bills; the plovers run and look and feed from the surface. Both groups of shorebirds frantically work over the tiny crustaceans and invertebrates lying half concealed or partially buried in mud or wet sand. Each species has its own specialized searching technique. Sanderlings often follow the advancing and retreating wave-edges,

Sanderling. DON GUNN

scurrying to avoid water above leg height. The large dowitchers use their long beaks to probe rapidly, like the needle of a sewing machine. Ruddy turnstones do just that; turn over stones with their short beaks. The tiny look-alike "peeps" – least, semipalmated, white-rumped, Baird's sandpipers – pick and dab and suddenly fly off in a group, skimming the waves to land again farther along the beach.

With the morning sun the shorebirds seem to evaporate from the beaches. Small groups of birds stand motionless on the ends of sandy points, or on sandy islands out in the water, and doze, often on one leg and with head tucked into shoulder feathers. There, no predator can approach without being in full view. If one bird sounds an alarm, the whole point or island may erupt in flight.

Observing shorebirds is like collecting old books. Somewhere among them may be a rarity. In Ontario, the rare species may be one of the large prairie-nesters such as a marbled godwit or a black-necked stilt, aptly named for its unrealistically long legs. Or, it may be the largest eastern shorebird, the whimbrel, formerly called the Hudsonian curlew, with its very long, downcurved sabre of a beak. A purple sandpiper might show up, normally an Atlantic coastal migrant, or a red phalarope.

Shorebirds as a group are champion long-distance migrants. Most of the species scattered on a May morning across the mudflats of a Great Lakes beach will fly on to nest somewhere on the Arctic tundra. Ontario's one piece of tundra, on the James Bay and southern Hudson Bay shorelines, provides nesting habitat for some species, such as golden and semipalmated plovers, whimbrel, least, pectoral, and semipalmated sandpipers. On fall migration, most shorebirds stopping at the Great Lakes are heading for South America to spend the winter.

There are exceptions, including two of the best known shorebirds in Ontario: the killdeer and the spotted sandpiper, both of which nest throughout the province. Killdeers, one of spring's first returning migrants, announce the new season in the open farmland country of southern Ontario; spotted sandpipers typify stream and lake margins where they fly up and skim the water with impossibly short wing strokes and repeated cries of alarm.

Another exception is the piping plover, formerly a Great Lakes nester, but now an endangered species. This pale, sand-coloured bird has lost out to beach disturbances and now is found only rarely on protected beaches such as at Long Point.

The shorebirds play the survival game with their own particular twists. Their eggs, large in proportion to their bodies, hatch more slowly than those of comparable size in other birds, but chicks emerge more fully developed. In a week they can swim; in ten or twelve days they can fly. Food is their own responsibility, and time is short for both parents and chicks before migration.

The plovers show another adaptation, shared with the grouse family although not with the more closely related sandpipers – the "broken-wing display." A disturbed killdeer will flop across the ground, tail and one wing fanned and dragging. Female killdeers will come far out from the nest to attract attention this way. Specialists in animal behaviour describe

Dunlin. DON GUNN

the act as a conflict between two drives: defence of the nest and fear. Regardless of how it is motivated, the resulting behaviour has been effective in helping assure survival of young, or the display would not have become a genetically selected trait.

It is evening now, and the wind that whipped up the surf in the afternoon is dying down. The shorebirds fan out once again to feed. Again they run helter-skelter across the mudflats. Platoons of ruddy turnstones work their way up the beach; squadrons of sanderlings wing low to the water to find a more promising patch of shore; fleets of pectoral sandpipers gather on a point. At the edge of its own patch of mud a whimbrel wades out into deeper water.

Under cover of darkness the shorebirds leave. The beach is deserted again in the moonlight, waiting for the next wave of flying pebbles near dawn, or in a few days, or next fall on their return, or the next spring. As long as their winter habitat survives, and as long as relatively undisturbed beaches remain along the lower Great Lakes, they will return.

Mammals of Canada's Deep South

Mark Stabb

Ranging just far enough north to be included on Canadian checklists is a handful of wildlife species that depend upon the subtle but distinct Carolinian vegetation and climate in southern Ontario. The natural history of these southern specialists includes tales of immigrations, adaptations, and ecological unknowns.

The term *Carolinian* is bestowed on this "deep south" region of Canada because the flora and fauna resemble that of the Carolinas, as well as of the Ohio Valley, Virginia, Tennessee, and non-mountainous regions of east-central United States. More accurately, Canada's portion of the Carolinian zone is transitional, with many elements of northern hardwood mixed in.

Our most indicative Carolinian mammal, if there is one, is the small, unpretentious, chestnut-coloured woodland vole, often referred to by the misnomer "pine vole." While not as exciting a symbol of the Carolinian zone as other species, the distribution of this fairly sedentary mammal closely follows the range of the Carolinian forest. Woodland voles are smaller forest counterparts of the much more common meadow vole that inhabits open country throughout Ontario and much of Canada. Woodland voles are more *fossorial* (soil-dwelling) than meadow voles, however, with more shrunken eyes, ears, and tail that attest to a life underground.

Biologists were unaware of the woodland vole's local abundance until recently when a wildlife survey discovered them all over the Regional Municipality of Haldimand-Norfolk, a region centred by Simcoe, Ontario. Mature, deciduous forest with a thick leaf litter is prime woodland vole habitat, where tubers of wildflowers and nuts of hickories and oaks abound. The woodland vole population was most evident in Backus Woods near Long Point, a tract with nearest-to-natural conditions of any Carolinian forest stand in Canada.

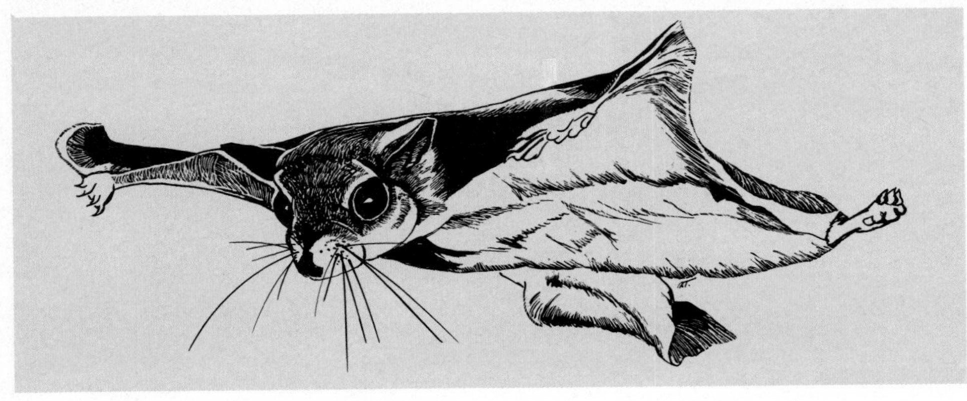

Denigrated south of the Great Lakes for their tendency to invade orchards and feed on the roots of fruit trees, woodland voles showed no evidence of this habit in the Haldimand-Norfolk survey. Perhaps on the northern fringe of their range the voles are too few in number to be an identifiable problem.

A better known but more exotic species of southern mammal in Ontario is the Virginia opossum, which has now taken up more-or-less permanent residence in the province. "Possum" populations have been edging their way north since the turn of the century, invading southern Ontario in migration waves from New York state. Historically they had to either swim the Niagara River, walk across the river ice, or raft over on ice floes. More recently, people have seen them waddling across bridges and hitching rides on trains.

Immigration to Canada is likely a consequence of dispersal activity common to all mammals. Individuals, especially juveniles or young adults, often range widely although not always successfully, to seek out unoccupied territory. Female opossums are prone to long-distance migrations that take them to new habitat and, consequently, it is females that are most commonly found as roadkills along southern Ontario highways.

Opossum. MARY GARTSHORE

Opossums are marsupial mammals – they bear "premature" young which crawl blindly to their mother's abdominal pouch. Adult females found dead along roadsides often have pouched young still alive and feeding. Opossums, like most animals, have not yet evolved a way to deal with highway projectiles moving at 100 kilometres per hour.

Ironically, opossums do not appear to be particularly well adapted to our climate either. For a southern species, it seems unusual that opossums possess no sweat glands and must wet their feet with saliva and put them up in the wind to dissipate heat on hot days. At the other extreme, the furless ears, feet, and tail are highly susceptible to frostbite. Many opossums in the Carolinian zone now bear the scars of having struggled through a Canadian winter. Opossums have adapted by denning up in very cold weather.

Southern flying squirrels are longtime residents of Carolinian Canada and are better prepared for winter conditions. Nocturnal and non-hibernating, these night gliders of deciduous woods are geared for energy conservation. In northern latitudes they occasionally exhibit torpor (reduced body activity) during spells of extreme cold, and rely on winter aggregations to maintain body temperatures. Research using chambers that measured gas, heat, and energy exchanges showed that, at normal winter temperatures, southern flying squirrels needed the company of at least one other individual to maintain constant body temperature and avoid burning up too much of their own energy. In the wild, groupings of more than two squirrels increase the prospects of winter survival.

In 1910, a naturalist reported finding a heap of at least fifty flying squirrels in a winter aggregation, but such phenomena have not been observed lately. In recent years, a typical clan of eleven was discovered in a dead yellow birch trunk near Simcoe. A rap on the trunk caused five of these dazed squirrels to glide away in slow aerial formation and retreat into an adjacent cavity.

Common havens for winter aggregations are the much-maligned "wolf trees" – large, hollow stems of dead or dying trees. Left in the forest, these trees take up space that healthier trees could use, so they are regularly culled from managed forests. As den trees, however, they contribute to the workings of the forest community in unseen but important ways.

Southern flying squirrels, although locally common, may be rare in Ontario. Because of their nocturnal activity they are certainly rarely seen. They probably reach their highest population levels in Canada in the Carolinian zone, although they range as far north as the Ottawa region, reflecting the distribution of several nut-producing trees. Hickories and oaks are favourite winter foods, and their nuts often are stored in large quantities near nest sites.

Eastern moles are as unfamiliar as are flying squirrels, because they keep out of sight beneath the ground. A near-blind mole with a pig-like snout, the eastern mole prefers the moist soils and humus of open woods, pastures, and grassy areas. More than one hundred years ago, Linnaeus, the zealous taxonomist, received a specimen of this animal and labelled it "*aquaticus*" because of its broad, paddle-like forefeet and partially webbed toes which implied an affinity to water. The stoutly clawed feet, rather than being paddles, are, of course, powerful digging tools used to excavate characteristic networks of tunnels just beneath the soil surface. The moles rarely emerge from these underground passageways but reveal their presence in the form of small, mucky furrows or pushed-up dirt piles, alias molehills.

The twenty-centimetre eastern mole has a hearty appetite for earthworms, insect larvae, and other soil animals, and its quest for these prey knows few bounds. Explorations of the subterranean world of flower gardens, lawns, nurseries, and golf courses are not uncommon and are not treated lightly by horticulturally inclined humans. At least one Canadian mammal guide accommodates mole-control interests by describing in detail how to kill the species when it causes trouble.

It would be unfortunate if our encounters with the eastern mole reduce its numbers further. Rare not only in Ontario, but in Canada, the mole exists in numbers only around Essex County and the protected habitat of Point Pelee National Park.

Moles and woodland voles are fossorial animals that burrow and live primarily underground. Southern Ontario soil is criss-crossed with their tunnels, but their digging cannot match that of the powerful and reclusive badger. Badgers prefer sandy soil for their excavations and find suitable habitat in the region's mosaic of woodlots and farm fields. The clearing of the Carolinian forest for agriculture provided prime sites for badgers, and recent reports indicate that badgers and their diggings, while uncommon, are widespread in the region.

Badgers south of the border prefer to dine upon ground squirrels, prairie dogs, and other fossorial rodents that do not range into this part of Canada. Trappers say that southern Ontario badgers feed on the ubiquitous eastern woodchuck, as well as on cottontail rabbits and other smaller mammals that populate the Carolinian region. A nocturnal but anomalous member of the weasel family, the badger relies primarily on luck and brute strength to make a living. It may pounce on a mouse or vole that blunders into sight, or it may bulldoze into a mammal den in hopes of cornering a meal in a dead-end tunnel. Occasionally it uses ambush. One population of badgers studied on the American prairies was reputed to have entered and enlarged existing ground squirrel dens, and then partially closed the entrances to conceal their presence. A deadly surprise awaited the first ground squirrels to return home.

Badger behaviour is not well known in Canada (they also inhabit Ontario's

Rainy River District, the prairie provinces, and interior British Columbia) and the animals will not likely divulge their secretive ways very easily. Besides residing underground, the wide-ranging badger is inactive in winter, lives at low population densities, and has a reputation for being a scrapper. Unlike many other elusive mammals, even its scats are not easily studied. The badger commonly deposits them in burrows or buries them in piles of dirt. Perhaps this mysterious nature is an ideal strategy for a pugnacious mammal living in a region populated by millions of humans. The less that people know about the attractive but scrappy badger, the less likely it is to be tormented or disturbed.

Even more unfamiliar in Canada is the gray fox. This carnivore is slightly smaller than the more common red fox and has obviously shorter ears and legs. The fur is a salt-and-pepper grey with a prominent black band reaching along the back to the tip of the tail. Identifying this species occasionally confounds both trapper and wildlife biologist. The confusion is caused because only one-third of red foxes are actually the familiar orange-red. The rest are comprised of two distinctly dark colour phases: the "cross" fox which is greyish-brown, and the less common "silver" fox, which is almost pure black. Luckily for field biologists, however, almost all red foxes have white-tipped tails.

Gray foxes are woodland predators, sticking far more to forested habitats than does the less selective red fox. In fact, gray foxes take to the trees in a big way. Numerous accounts of gray foxes lounging in trees or retreating from dogs up tree trunks and along branches mark this fox as one of the few tree-climbing canines. Their sharp, hooked claws, reminiscent of those of cats, suggest that arboreal activity is not a mere recreational pursuit but is, in fact, an evolved adaptation.

The history of the gray fox in Ontario is an enigma. Archaeologists have found gray fox remains to be as common as those of red fox amid the bones of Indian settlements. But for a three-hundred-year period, dating from about the mid-1600s, no substantiated record had been found for the species in the province. Then in 1946, an account in the *Canadian Field-Naturalist* announced their return. Records came first from eastern Ontario and the semi-open forests of the Rainy River District. Soon afterwards the gray fox reappeared in the Carolinian zone, following closely on the heels of the eastern cottontail, a preferred prey item.

Why did the gray fox disappear for three hundred years? The *extirpation* (local extinction) seemed to precede the widespread removal of forests that precipitated the decline of so many other southern Ontario mammals. The bobcat, elk, gray wolf, American marten, fisher, and subspecies of other animals have never returned. Early historians do not report any intensive extermination program carried out by pioneering settlers that would have wiped out the gray fox, although this is still a possibility. Perhaps the decline in this instance was not totally caused by people.

Today the gray fox is classified as rare in Canada by COSEWIC (Committee on the Status of Endangered Wildlife in Canada), and survives in Ontario primarily where extensive forests still stand.

The least shrew, so much tinier than the gray fox, also provides a historical challenge. These miniature insectivores join the fox squirrel and the evening bat in maintaining the smallest of toeholds on southern Canadian soil. In 1929, biologists on a collecting expedition to Long Point caught a large milk snake amid the grassy dunes and brought it back to their cabin. With the collectors looking on, the snake proceeded to regurgitate three juvenile stubby-tailed shrews, so recently eaten that one actually revived soon afterwards. They also caught two cinnamon-coloured adult shrews, presumably of the same species, nearby. These shrews resembled miniature short-tailed shrews (*Blarina brevicauda*), a mammal common throughout southern Ontario. But further examination verified the biologists' initial hunch: these were least shrews, *Cryptoptis parva*, a new species for Canada. Subsequent trapping revealed that a healthy population existed on a portion of the north beach of Long Point and nowhere else in the vicinity. Because least shrews inhabit the American shores to the south, mammalogists have since suggested that the Long Point population originated from individuals that "rafted" across Lake Erie, perhaps on flotsam from the United States shore. This would have been a truly incredible journey for the least shrew. Like other shrews, least shrews have a very high metabolic rate and must devour more than their weight in food every day. The Long Point progenitors would have required a plentiful stash of insects, worms, or other food to survive a Lake Erie passage, especially considering winds, waves, and the vagaries of lake currents.

An alternative hypothesis might be that the shrews were stowaways on one of the many boats ferrying between the secluded marshes of Long Point and the states to the south for hunting, fishing, and rum-running in earlier years. Or, the shrews could have been remnants of widespread populations reduced today by habitat change.

Diverse as they may be in habit and habitat preference, the mammals of Canada's deep south have one thing in common. They are relatively rare in the region while much more abundant in the United States. Why be concerned about such marginal populations? Along with the rest of the biota of Carolinian Canada, these southern mammals represent a unique aspect of the natural history of the province and the nation. As such they deserve our interest and concern. While this justification may seem like nationalistic conservation, if we treated all of our wildlife populations as if they were the last survivors of their species, the animals could only benefit.

The Farmlands

John B. Theberge

Spread like a patchwork quilt across a flat or gently rolling landscape are the farmlands of southern Ontario. From the air the dominant impression is one of order, precision, and regularity. The multi-shaded rectangles of greens and browns demonstrate the human imperative for organization and control, and the constraint of straight-line land surveying. Here and there, dark patches of green stand out, the straight-sided woodlots, the remnant pockets of wild. In places, long thin forest belts run midway between, and parallel to, the concession roads – historic artifacts of the settlers' "back forty" woodlots joined one to another at the far ends of the farms. In other places, dark green ribbons meander aimlessly across the land, out of place, with no regard for regularity – woodlands lining rivers or streams, or tracing the outline of steep-sided eskers. Farm ponds break the regularity, too, glinting in the sun. An occasional sprawling wetland defies total human dominance, and serves as a reminder that there was a different past for this land.

From the ground, the impression is different, the imposed order less apparent. There are indeed hills and valleys, vistas and pleasing scenery. The 10 to 20 per cent of the original forest cover that remains in many counties adds vertical dimension to the landscape, green depth to the horizon, and, in winter, sketches dark shadows over the predominant whitescapes.

Southern Ontario is a pastoral environment. Black and white cows dot the fields. Red-sided or grey barns anchor long, maple-lined farm lanes. White clapboard or red brick farmhouses nestle behind windbreaks of Norway spruce. Somewhere nearby a red or green tractor is always crawling over the fields, combing the land or the crops, and spewing out a different colour behind it. At night, specks of light – yard lights and farm windows – twinkle all across the land, clumped together at towns and hamlets. Only at

The farmlands (grey).

night do you realize that the land is crowded.

The entire character of the countryside, and about 90 per cent of its productivity and biomass, depends upon a prodigious application of human labour and big machines and fossil-fuel-driven energy. Without these, eager plant succession – goldenrod, milkweed, ragweed, wild mustard – would quickly crowd back into the fence corners and edge out into the fields. Woody shrubs would follow – hawthorn, buckthorn, raspberry, sumac – and behind them would march the pioneer tree seedlings – black cherry, ironwood, and finally the maples, all eager to reclaim the farmlands. But plough, rake, disc, cultivator, mower, sprayer, fertilizer, and harvester all keep wildness at bay.

Ecosystem "health" in such an ecologically unstable environment cannot be measured by the degree to which all native species are present, or the completeness of food webs, as it can in wildlands. We have chosen to reduce these things to produce crops and feed livestock. Yet the pockets and strips of wild all add diversity to the landscape, break the wind, form barriers to the spread of agricultural pests, hold up the water table, reduce spring flooding, and allow the songs of indigo buntings and rose-breasted grosbeaks to intermingle with those of the field species: bobolink, horned lark, eastern meadowlark, and savannah, field, and vesper sparrows.

All this human-dominated landscape, stretching across the Paleozoic Lowlands south of the Canadian Shield, has been this way for only two hundred years or less. Before that, Indian agriculture was here, but it represented only irregular patches of human domination in a sea of wild. Most of the land grew Canada's most productive hardwoods – tall maples, beech, elm, basswood, and black cherry. Descriptions of these seemingly endless ranks of forests were given by the surveyors as they dragged their chain along compass bearings where straight concession roads now run.

Aerial photo showing the patterned agricultural land that typifies much of southern Ontario. Remnant woodlots are scattered across the landscape, especially in mid-concessions and in ribbons following streams and rivers. Bottom right in the photo is the north end of Waterloo, north of which is the town of St. Jacobs and the Conestogo River.

The surveyors were in the vanguard of the forces to transform the land. Driving them were pioneer settlement policies to "open up" the land, the political shenanigans of land-holding companies, and Governor John Graves Simcoe's edict of 1792, modified as the years went by, that land was to be set out into 200-acre parcels. The image of Canada in the minds of politicians, surveyors, and settlers alike was that of pastoral England and northern Europe.

With rare exceptions, the pioneer literature of southern Ontario is not known for its descriptions of natural beauty. The forest was a formidable adversary to very survival. Cut it down, pile it up, burn it, pull out the stumps, break the soil, and get the crops in. Most of the forest vanished into ashes, smoke, and stump fences well before the beginning of the twentieth century.

With the extensive forest vanquished, so too were elk, gray wolf, bobcat, fisher, and some other creatures – the wilderness wildlife. But everything did not disappear. Indeed, conditions for some species improved dramatically. Cottontail rabbits, coyotes, red foxes, and even white-tailed deer thrived in the more open countryside. Many species of birds and mammals prefer the forest edge, surviving best where sunlight strikes the ground and results in abundant herbaceous and shrub growth – food within reach rather than high in the forest canopy.

Ecological processes, while altered, still kept functioning after the transformation, as they do today. Green leaves – of wheat, corn, oats, clover –

NIAGARA ESCARPMENT COMMISSION

still capture sunlight. Insects – too often corn borer beetles and other agricultural pests – still convert plant matter to animal matter. The hydrological cycle – while carrying more soil off the land and into the streams – still functions. Populations of animals – now groundhog and farm dog – replace former species as predators and prey. Other scavengers, competitors, parasites, and hosts are there, and red-tailed hawks still toss on the wind, now above rippling grain fields.

And deep in a summer woodlot, you can still get lost in yesterday. The trees may be smaller, and red elder and raspberry vines may crowd the clearings where too many sawlogs were taken at one time. But red-eyed vireos still sing all day, as they probably did before the forest was broken. On the edge of the corn field are deer tracks in the mud. Down at the margin of the creek lies a broken clamshell left by a foraging coon.

In early spring, when the farmers are first ploughing the wet fields, the woodlots are strewn with trilliums, bloodroots, and yellow trout lilies, and the eastern pheobe is back exploring roof eaves and bridge abutments for a place to nest.

By the time the scent of new-mown hay hangs over the fields, and the corn is hand-high, and the winter wheat has headed up, the robins and cardinals are bringing off their first broods. In the hardwoods, the songs of wood thrushes and wood pewees greet and end each day.

By midsummer, the winter wheat is ready for harvesting, and crickets are chirping in the second-growth hay. Cicadas are droning in the woods. Orioles flit in the maples along the farm lane, bringing food to their second broods, now about ready to leave their hanging baskets.

When the oat crops are ripe and the harvesters slowly circle the fields, then the swallows are flocked on the telephone wires, and the blackberry vines bend with their loads of fruit.

The first fall frosts turn the corn plants from green to brown, and the sumac flames, the sugar maples yellow, and the goldenrod touches up the roadsides and abandoned field corners. Blue jays stream through the trees and across the open land in tens, twenties, hundreds.

After the cows have cleaned up the corn stubble and been stabled in the barns, the winter's first snows homogenize the farmlands. The bare-limbed maples sway under winter blasts, and the deer seek shelter in the stream-side cedars. Along the road edges, wintering horned larks pick at the gravel and try to find grass heads exposed by the snowplough. A few wintering mourning doves and the occasional kestrel sway on the telephone wires. Flocks of black-capped chickadees, dark-eyed juncoes, and tree sparrows forage in the woods.

The farmlands are rich in nature. What is lost to the corn fields is gained on the field-forest edges. The danger to the ecological integrity of this landscape is not what was done when the forests were cut, but what is slowly being done now to lower soil fertility, silt the streams, sterilize the land, dry up or eutrophy the wetlands, and annihilate with urban sprawl. These things threaten ecological functions that survived even the near-wholesale transformation of forest to field in an earlier day.

The all-too-common perception that wild patches of land are "waste space" in this transformed foodland is the greatest threat to its future. The challenge is to manage field and remnant forest, livestock and wildlife, as an integrated ecological system. As long as the farmlands grow deer and red-eyed vireos as well as corn and wheat and cows, this man-dominated landscape will continue to contribute to, not lessen, the stability and diversity of nature in Ontario.

Wetlands of the Agricultural South

Ron Reid

Glance at a map of southern Ontario, and at first the land and water seem all neatly parcelled out, all clearly defined. The pale blue uniformity of the lakes is bounded cleanly by the green and brown of the countryside; the thin blue lines of rivers run crisply across the square grid pattern of civilization.

But look more closely, and in places the mapmaker's definition seems less certain. Broken lines of blue mix with the tawny brown of the land; curious little symbols like clumps of reeds are added to the chart's vocabulary. Destined to defy the orderliness of mapmakers, these little pockets of part-water, part-land are the wetlands of the agricultural south.

On the ground, wetlands may look every bit as untidy as on the map. Streams divide and divide again among a tangled maze of vegetation. Shrubbery struggles for space below a diverse mix of trees. Clusters of marsh marigolds crowd along the stream; pockets of orchids thrive in the shadows.

But the first impressions of disorder are deceiving. Like the streets of a busy city, wetlands appear chaotic simply because they are bursting with life. That life, from the smallest water flea to the tallest maple, coexists in a network of producers and consumers, predators and prey, all interwoven in a resilient web. Unlike the monocultures of farm crops or urban lawns, wetlands are marked by a wealth of species.

Wetlands are among Ontario's most productive and diverse habitats, in large part because of the irregular mosaic of "edge" created where land and water meet. The edges of wetlands are ever-constant and ever-moving frontiers between water and dry land. The nature of these frontiers determines the nature of the wetland. Marshes, for example, develop in sheltered coves and estuaries along the edges of lakes, where water levels fluctuate slowly and mineral-rich sediments are carried in abundance by the waves. Cattails, bulrushes, pickerelweed, and water lilies combine nutrients and sunlight at an amazing rate to produce plant growth, but the constant presence of water keeps the marshlands from becoming overgrown with trees. The marshes of the Great Lakes shore and along inland lakes are critical feeding areas not just for migratory waterfowl, but also for marsh wrens and bitterns, frogs and salamanders, and a whole array of fishes that approach the frontier from the watery side.

Along streams and rivers, nutrient-rich sediments are also abundant. Flooding may occur only during the spring, creating a temporary wooded swamp. For a time in late summer, the frontier retreats and disappears, and the rooting zone is free of water, allowing the survival of trees. Near the headwaters, these swamps may be dominated by cedar and spruce, often creating a layer of spongy organic soils among their roots. Farther down-

Silver maple swamp, Backus Woods, southwestern Ontario. JOHN THEBERGE

stream, where the flooding is greater, the swamplands are usually populated by hardwoods with colourful names – black ash and white elm, red and silver maple.

In a few places, specialized wetlands such as bogs and fens add to the diversity of southern Ontario's roster of wetlands. Both of these communities are more typical of the north, but their organic soils can develop also in areas of restricted drainage and low nutrient levels in the south. Typical sites for these distinctive environments are the "kettles" left by blocks of ice in the moraines as the glaciers retreated. Most of these specialized wetlands are well-known, since there are so few of them. The rich fens of the Bruce Peninsula, and the core of the Minesing Swamp near Barrie are well studied, as are such bogs as Alfred, Byron, and Spongy Lake. Wooded swamps, on the other hand, are too often ignored because they seem so commonplace.

Besides that, swamps have image problems. The story goes that an early surveyor in the swampy townships of the Dundalk plateau could only be persuaded to finish his arduous task by being allowed to name the new municipalities. A staunch Irish Catholic, the surveyor chose names signifying his repugnance – the reformists Luther and Melancthon!

For many of the farmers of southern Ontario, that image of swamps as useless wastelands has led to energetic attempts to convert them to more "useful" purposes. Drainage was viewed not just as an economic decision, but as a progressive, public-spirited endeavour leading to general improvements for all. This attitude was strengthened by government agencies, who assisted with generous grants.

The result over the past century is an impressive testament to man's determination to subdue his environment. Of the 2 million to 2.4 million hectares of wetland which originally existed in southern Ontario, approximately 70 to 80 per cent has been severely altered or destroyed. That process continues; the swamps grow less commonplace at a rate of 1 to 2 per cent per year.

But as the growing scarcity of wetlands is recognized, so is their value. Conservation authorities increasingly base their water management programs on the ability of wetlands to slow floodwaters and to release cool waters in summer. Researchers document the ability of wetlands to absorb nutrients and pollutants from the waters that flow through their tangled vegetation, dramatically improving water quality. Planners identify and recommend protection for wetlands as valuable patches of green in an urbanized landscape. Slowly, the pendulum swings, and wetland drainage is regarded more as an act of environmental vandalism than as a public service.

Still, it is the wildlife value of wetlands that commands most public sympathy. Years ago, the Nature Conservancy of Canada put out a small poster which posed the question, "Who loves a swamp?" The answer was poignant – "Frogs do. And turtles. And little silvery fishes that flash in the dark waters. . . ." By implication, those who love wildlife and want to see it survive love wetlands too. And if we want to teach our children to appreciate the value of wetland habitats, how better than to begin with the wildlife?

Wetlands are natural treasures, as much a part of the inheritance of humanity as any artistic treasure. Only strong public support and an attitude of caring will safeguard the treasure.

The Maple Sugar Bush

John B. Theberge

It's the sugaring season. The sap is running, "sweet good-bye to winter, sweet welcome to spring." The forest floor, snow-blanketed when the spiles are set in, is transformed to bare, brown leaves by the time the ritual is over. From hundreds of patches of wild across southern Ontario, steam is rising out of the corner woods. On the sunny south slopes in Muskoka, Haliburton, and Parry Sound, too, where maples march more expansively across the landscape, the annual ritual has begun.

The sugar bush is a feature of both wild and not-so-wild Ontario. It is not exclusively ours. *Acer saccharum*, the sugar maple, extends across southern Quebec and New England as well. But Canadians have adopted the sugar maple leaf (slightly stylized) as the emblem on our national flag. In southern parts of Ontario's sugar bushes, maple trees and our provincial flower, the white trillium, live together.

In southern Ontario, sugar bushes survive as historic remnants, often in linear corridors mid-way between concession roads, the "back forty" of pioneer farms. When wood fueled farmhouses, every farm valued its bush. But many woodlots were felled when oil, natural gas, and electricity took over, and farmers felt an economic urge to put more land into "production." Other sugar bushes declined to disuse or misuse; junked cars, old threshing machines, and mounds of tin cans found a final resting place there – future archaeological middens of an industrial society. Ironically, a good-quality woodlot would yield more money per hectare per year today in veneer-quality logs than in field crops, at the same time as it held up the water table, reduced spring flooding downstream, yielded more beauty – and maple syrup.

Throughout the northern hardwoods biome, sugar maples are ecologically dominant trees. They outnumber other species, capture the most energy, and their seedlings and saplings dominate the understorey. Called "shade tolerant," the young generations of seedlings await the death of a maple giant and the resulting increase in sunlight to spring upward, making a dash for the light ahead of other species that lag behind because they are unable to germinate in advance on the dark forest floor.

For their dominance alone, sugar maples are significant. However, there is more. Sugar maples offer man a chance to participate in a ritual that is rooted in antiquity, in a holy communion with nature, where the products of sun and soil, autumn rains and spring frosts, and human labour are forged to yield much more than a sweet syrup. To those fortunate enough to participate, the ritual offers an opportunity to get close to the Earth, to strengthen the man-land relationship, to leave behind for a while the artificial and man-made. Much of the act of sugaring-off is elemental: fire driving steam back into the sky where it originated – cycle complete; condensation of sucrose manufactured by photosynthesis from the sun's energy; recovery of last year's autumn rains which soaked the soil, were sucked up by rootlets, and stored frozen all winter in living cells.

And, while slinging buckets, even for only an hour a day in a small hobby operation, a person can watch spring come in. As you go from snowshoes to running shoes, parka to shirt sleeves, the early migrant birds return: the first tinkling horned larks in a nearby field, the first eastern bluebirds splashing sapphire on the edge of the woodlot, the first vibrant notes of a song sparrow from a thicket of cedars, an evening flight of Canada geese or even tundra swans just clearing the tree-tops, the "beep" of a woodcock or the "whinny" of snipe-wings. From the first chipmunk to emerge from hibernation to the first wild leeks poking up at the edge of a late patch of snow. From ice in the pails to night-flying Noctuidae moths who come for a drink of sap and cannot get out, to ladybird beetles and flies in the pails – and then it is time to stop for the year.

Most people, of course, do not own their own sugar bush. For them the experience is different: perhaps a Sunday afternoon at a local sugaring operation run by a conservation authority or provincial park. Dominant images may be of people: kids running gaily from bucket to bucket, or mobs on a horse-drawn sleigh. But even here one can garner the special feeling of being out among the maples, with chickadees poking around and blue jays calling. Even here you can hear the plink, plink of sap-music as sap drips into freshly emptied pails. And the geese may fly overhead.

The science of sap flow is complex and poorly understood. A good theory must take into account the observations of old-timers. For sap to flow you need temperatures below freezing at night and warm during the day; sap flow ends by the time trees bud out and leaves open, just when you would think that leaf transpiration would drive more flow, not less, up from the roots; even a tree that has snapped off in a winter storm will yield sap moderately well in its first "dead" spring; sap begins the season with less than half the sugar concentration (sixty litres of sap for one litre of syrup) than it has at the end of the season; sap flow does not seem to correlate with the severity of winter, or the amount of snow on the ground, or spring rains or wind; most other tree species do not produce sap flow in spring, and none so sweet. Even among the more than one hundred species in the genus *Acer* scattered around the northern hemisphere, our sugar maples yield the most sugar per litre of sap, about twice the concentration of silver or red maple.

The best theory goes like this: soluble carbohydrates, the products of photosynthesis, move from leaves to sites where sugars are needed for energy to grow flowers, fruits, buds, leaves, rootlets, and cambium cells in the tree trunk. The movement down to the cambium cells takes place through elongated cells called *sieve cells* within the *phloem*, just inside the bark. During late summer and autumn, maple trees shunt large amounts of starch from phloem to *vascular rays*, which are ribbon-like arrangements of cells running horizontally from phloem in towards the centre of the trunk. With the arrival of cold weather, a large proportion of the starch is converted by enzymatic action into sucrose. During the winter this sucrose diffuses into dead *xylem* cells, which make up most of the wood in a tree trunk.

Fluctuating pressure within the xylem is responsible for sap flow. Pressure increases during warm days to as much as 1.4 kilograms per square centimetre. If there is any nearby source of release from this pressure, such as a tap hole, sap will run to it from all directions. Then, with cooler temperatures at night, the pressure decreases. Water molecules apparently cling to vessel walls within the xylem and are

Cross-section of wood.

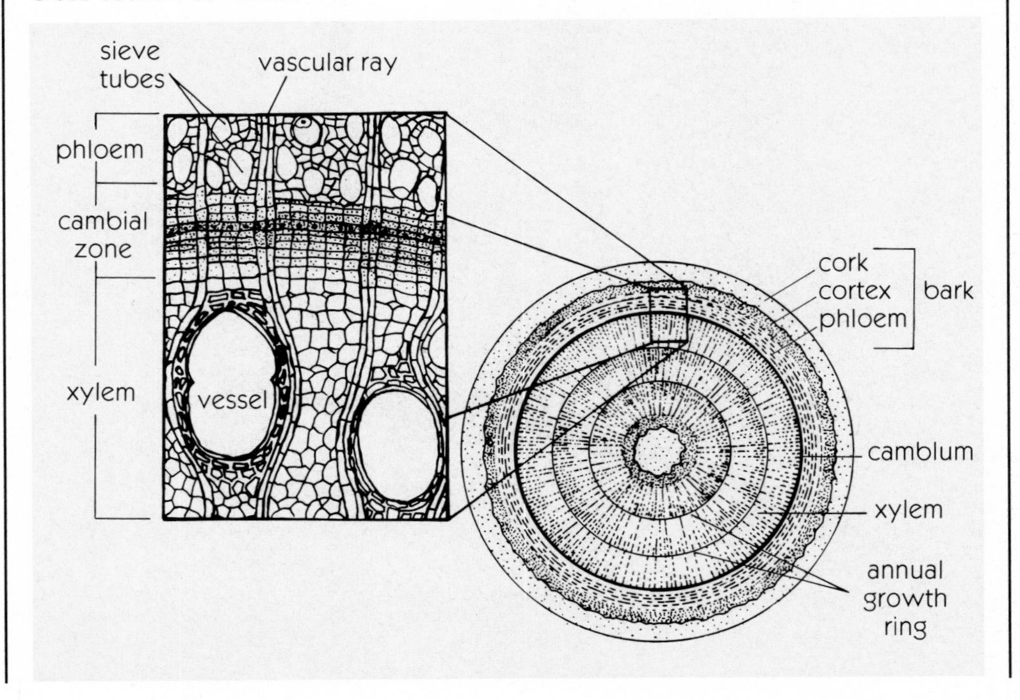

Sugar shanty. JOHN THEBERGE

drawn inward. Careful measurements actually have shown that tree trunks swell and shrink minutely with the different pressures.

The mechanisms of pressure increase are not well understood. In an uninjured tree, or one with no tap hole, the pressure does not create sap flow. Contrary to popular belief, there is no unidirectional flow within a maple or any other tree until leaves are produced, causing an upward pressure on water columns in the vessel cells. By then, however, the sugar has been transported to growing cells and concentrations have dropped.

All tree species contain sap, but the amount varies with species, season, and even the time of day. Why sugar maples, among the most prolific sap producers in spring, also concentrate more sugar than other species is still a mystery.

The exceptional sweetness of sugar maple sap has long been recognized and exploited. Native people in Ontario had their own words for maple sugar: *sinzibuckwud* (Algonquin); *ninuutik* (Ojibway); *sisibaskwat* (Cree). They made spiles, or taps, from reeds or concave pieces of bark. Sap buckets were fashioned from birch bark sewed with thongs of elm. Clay evaporating vessels were heated by throwing in red-hot stones.

Today, highly mechanized sap producers string plastic tubing between trees and use pumps to draw out more sap. Stainless steel holding drums have replaced clay pots; hygrometers indicate when the concentration meets provincially set standards. Oil and natural gas replace wood and strenuous hours of chopping. More efficiency, greater yield – but maple sap and maple sugar taste just the same, no matter how they are produced.

The future of the maple sugar bush, however, is far from assured. County or regional "Trees Acts" offer some protection, and the provincial government offers a "Woodlot Improvement Program" to manage for forestry, recreation, wildlife, or sugaring. But new hydro lines and highways still tend to seek out the linear wooded corridors. Over-harvesting, including the common practice of removing other tree species, lowers woodlot diversity and hence resistance to disease. And acid rain threatens to defoliate limbends and lower the germination rate of seedlings, especially where maples grow on non-calcareous soil such as on the Canadian Shield.

The popularity of commercial maple products may help to raise public concern over woodlot management. But the real value of the maple sugar bush is not commercial. It anchors a lifeline to the past, when maple-dominated forests clothed southern Ontario. It provides wildness in a man-altered land.

Spring Ephemerals

John B. Theberge

In a few places, where conditions of temperature, sunlight, and soil moisture are just right, nature unveils its most dazzling and profuse wildflower displays. Such wild gardens are subalpine mountain meadows in summer, the tall-grass prairie in June, the Arctic tundra after snow-melt, and the hardwood forests in spring.

Beginning just as the last patches of snow melt, and lasting until the trees leaf out, Ontario's hardwood forests exhibit a magnificent annual wildflower show featuring the *spring ephemerals*. Called "spring ephemerals" because they flower early and disappear soon, for a short time these blooms are strewn across the forest floor in wild abandon.

That they exist at all is only because of an ingenious solution to a severe, almost restrictive ecological condition; low light intensity. The vast majority of wildflowers require considerable sunlight to produce flowers and set seed. Each year, annuals must grow new leaves, flower-stalks, flowers, and roots. Even perennials, growing from over-wintering rootstocks, must develop all their aboveground structures again. Growth requires light. But the hardwood forest floor, after the leaves emerge, is a dark place.

The solution? Store energy over winter in bulb or tuber. Use that energy to quickly throw up leaves and flower stalks. Bloom as soon as possible, and produce seed while there is plenty of light. A race against the advancing season.

Hepaticas often are the first to bloom, doing so even before they produce any leaves. Their strategy is to put almost all their stored energy into raising flower heads, expending little on leaves. The previous year's leaves persist over winter and may capture a small amount of sunlight after they poke up through the dead leaves of the forest floor, but new leaves appear only later, when the plants are setting seed. Snow-white, pink, lavender, mauve, blue – hepaticas are among the most variable of all Ontario's wildflowers. Often colours differ in adjacent clumps of hepaticas growing so close together that blooms are intertwined. This colour variability appears to have a genetic base.

Bloodroot. LARRY LAMB

Flowering at the same time or almost as early are bloodroot, spring beauty, and blue cohosh. Bloodroots display large, showy clumps of white flowers which open wide in the warm April sunshine to attract the insect pollinators. The name "bloodroot" comes from the orange-red plant juices that ooze out of flower stalk, roots, or petiole if it is picked. Spring beauty's pink, candy-cane striped flowers appear in low mats. Ladybird beetles that have over-wintered in colonies under the leaves can often be seen crawling among the blossoms, spreading pollen from one plant to another. Blue cohosh is the strangest of all the ephemerals. It first appears as a dark blue bulge among brown leaves. Then blue, withered and folded hand-like leaves appear, among which are tiny maroon flowers with sulphur-yellow stamens. You have to get down on hands and knees to see them. Later, the blue hands unfold as compound leaves and become green. The plant grows rapidly into a shrub-like form.

In the following days, the brown of the forest floor rapidly transforms to green. The leaves of dogtooth violet (more prosaically yellow trout lily) are primarily responsible. Here and there, other shades of green provide variety: patches of wild onion leaves, clumps of emerging trillium leaves, Dutch-

Marsh marigold. JOHN THEBERGE

Hepatica. NATIONAL MUSEUM OF CANADA, A. G. AUSTIN

Spring beauty. JOHN THEBERGE

Yellow trout lily. JOHN THEBERGE

man's breeches, squirrel corn. On perfectly calm nights, especially after rain has moistened the soil, you can actually hear all these leaves growing – rustling like small animals scurrying about. What you hear is not growth itself, but the sound of dead leaves being moved by the growth. Cell division at peak rate!

With warmer spring days, these later ephemerals rush into bloom. Now the flower display is at its peak. White is the predominant colour: mats of white trilliums, white Dutchman's breeches, white squirrel corn. Colour is added by patches of red trilliums, painted trilliums, and blue and yellow violets. Flowers of yellow trout lilies hang between enfolding green leaves. Down in the moist bottomlands, the rare white trout lily may bloom.

Only a small percentage of trout lilies of either species actually flowers, just where soil moisture and temperature are optimum. Only there do bulbs become large enough to store enough energy. Often, yellow trout lilies bloom at the base of trees, on the south side, where reflected light and protection may create a slightly warmer and brighter micro-habitat.

Trout lily leaves are small and die very soon after the trees leaf out. So do those of Dutchman's breeches and the very similar squirrel corn. The leaves of bloodroot, however, grow very large and persist until late summer, gathering what light they can. Trillium leaves persist too.

Wild onion, or leeks, employ the reverse strategy to that of hepatica. Their leaves are among the first green things in the woods, poking up often only a few centimetres away from patches of snow and ice. They grow rapidly and soon are large, harvesting all the light they can. When the trees leaf out, the leaves die. Only later, in the shady summer forest, do they produce showy heads of small, white flowers.

The spring ephemerals are not the only plants to win out by flowering early. So do many trees. Red maples and silver maples brandish showy wands of clustered red flowers, and sugar maples wave yellow-green against deep blue spring skies. The catkin-producers – willows, poplars, alders – flower early too, providing abundant pollen for bees and other insect pollinators. Among shrubs, across central Ontario the abundant beaked hazel produces tiny red hair-brush blooms at the same time as the red maples are in flower.

Gradually, the trees leaf out. The cold-adapted species are first: the dominant sugar maples and American beeches. Trees with more southern affinities follow: the hickories and oaks. Petals fall off the hepaticas and bloodroots. White trillium blossoms turn pink, fooling some people into thinking that they are a different species, before withering and dying. The wildflower show in the hardwoods is over for another year.

Owls of the Kingston Area

Ron D. Weir

The vast majority of people have never seen an owl in the wild, yet the birds hold a fascination for them. Perhaps this fascination arises from their secretiveness – their mainly nocturnal habits and silent, ghostlike flight. An owl discovered by day intrigues us with its large eyes and stoic expression suggesting great wisdom.

These birds of prey are magnificently adapted to the extremes of the Canadian climate. Their soft and fluffy plumage provides insulation. Their flight feathers, those long quills growing from the outer ends of the wings, contain toothed edges and a velvet pile permitting that silent flight so advantageous in capturing prey. Their excellent hearing and night vision make them efficient predators. Owls have good vision during daylight too, but the extraordinarily high density of light-gathering cells in their eyes allows them to see accurately at night, as long as it is not pitch black. To aid depth perception, however, owls commonly bob their heads up and down as they gaze at an intruder from close range. They may swivel their heads 270 degrees or even turn them completely upside down. All these antics are necessary for owls to judge distance of approach, since their eyes, unlike ours, are fixed in their sockets.

Twelve species of owls normally occur in Ontario; eleven of them breed in the province. Rodents, especially rats, voles, and mice, are their staple food. Fluctuations in their prey populations in the boreal forest or tundra cause regular migration of some owl species and the sporadic eruption southward of several others from their breeding ranges.

One of the few areas in North America to provide an opportunity for closely observing the cryptic world of owls is the Kingston region. When owls migrating from the tundra or boreal forest meet the north shore of Lake Ontario, they turn and follow the shoreline in search of suitable wintering areas rather than cross the open water. Kingston's offshore islands, Wolfe and Amherst, situated at the northeastern end of Lake Ontario, are especially attractive to migrating owls. These islands, with a sparse human population, provide extensive habitat to sustain large numbers of owls. The combination of agricultural land and woodlots results in abundant food. Whenever the peak in the islands' three- to five-year rodent cycle coincides with owl eruptions into southern Ontario, the consequence is dramatic – the difference between only a few owls and dozens.

Amherst and Wolfe islands perhaps are best known for their snowy owls. These large white birds migrate more than 2,700 kilometres from north of the Arctic Circle to the Kingston region. They leave the north in greatest numbers in years when populations of lemmings, their staple food, are low. Every winter, Amherst and Wolfe islands host at least a few snowies, but some winters they shelter many – eighty-seven on one island alone one year! By mid-December, the first individuals arrive, and numbers may peak in either January or February. Each bird stakes out a winter territory of flat farmland and defends it against any intruder that might pirate its supply of meadow voles. Clashes are common whenever a hawk or another owl ventures into the territory for food. To see the snowies at this time is easy since they survey their domain from atop telephone poles, fence posts, haystacks, and, on occasion, even barn roofs.

The snowy owl is active by day, an adaptation brought about by the

Snowy owl. DON GUNN

twenty-four-hour daylight north of the Arctic Circle. Birds on Amherst and Wolfe islands often are seen capturing voles from beneath the snow during daylight hours. As the voles travel beneath the snow, they disturb the smooth upper surface, leaving a trail like that of a mole beneath a lawn. On occasion, to the surprise of novice owl watchers waiting patiently for hours to witness a successful catch, a resting snowy will straighten up, pluck a dead vole from between its feet like some wizard, swallow it whole in a single gulp, and resume its stoic pose. Presumably this strategy of sitting on its prey for several hours keeps the catch from freezing until mealtime.

Swallowing voles whole requires a special digestive system. Necessary nutrients must be extracted and processed, and the undigested parts – bone and fur – must be eliminated. These indigestibles are formed into the shape of small sausages within the owl's stomach and regurgitated at regular intervals as pellets, which litter the ground below favourite perches. Analysis of the skulls and bones contained in these pellets tells what and how much the owls are eating.

Each wintering snowy on these islands consumes from 7 to 12 voles per day. As with most raptors, females are heavier than males and therefore must consume more food. Assuming an average of 10 voles eaten per day per owl, one owl will consume 300 voles per month. During invasion years when eighty-seven snowies lived on Wolfe Island, some 26,100 voles (10 per hectare) were consumed per month! Farmers recognize the great benefits wrought by these owls and are their great friends.

When the southward movement of several species of owls is synchronous, the outcome may be phenomenal. The winter of 1978–79 was such a time; ten owl species over-wintered on Amherst Island. Among the ten species were eastern screech owl and great horned owl, both breeding species and both nocturnal hunters. The first of two great horned owl nests that winter was found on February 22. Thirty snowy owls and twenty short-eared owls over-wintered, the latter species staying to nest. The short-eared, like the snowy, is a diurnal hunter, most active around dusk when it hunts over the fields. Its floppy wingbeats suggest a mothlike flight. Most numerous species, however, was the long-eared owl; there were fifty of them. This phantom-like species is dif-

Boreal owl. POINT PELEE NATIONAL PARK, W. WYETT

Saw-whet owl. NATIONAL MUSEUM OF CANADA, A. G. AUSTIN

ficult to locate as it remains inactive and well hidden in dense cover by day and hunts exclusively by night.

But probably the species that brought birdwatchers from the greatest distance to Amherst Island that winter was the great gray owl. This magnificent owl is rarely seen in its breeding areas among the northern forests and is even rarer in the south during its irregular irruptions. The thirty-four on Amherst Island were therefore an unprecedented number. The first one appeared on January 20, but the major influx occurred during February when fifteen were seen in one woodlot alone. Birds were arriving from farther north, finding an abundant food supply, and setting up territories.

A single hawk owl accompanied the great grays, yet another rare find in southern Ontario. This species is aptly named because its appearance, habits, and daytime activity mimic those of a small hawk. It perches atop trees with its body inclined forward and long tail flicking, and during the day hunts by hovering on the wind like a kestrel.

One other rare species that over-wintered was the dove-sized boreal owl, another bird of the northern forests. This owl can be easily over-looked, huddling against a tree trunk in the thick foliage of a conifer. No fewer than eight boreals were present that year. They were joined by nine saw-whet owls, a photogenic bird even smaller and more inconspicuous than the boreal owl, although not rare. At Prince Edward Point just southwest of Kingston, banders netted, ringed, and released more than 4,200 migrating saw-whets during Octobers between 1975 and 1986.

The tenth species spotted during that winter was a single barn owl, seen only twice. Unlike the other nine, the barn owl's range extends through most of the United States, reaching only the extreme southerly portions of Ontario. This wandering individual may have just happened to stray northwards.

To witness a great many owls, as was possible during that famous winter, is a rare event, perhaps occurring no more than three times a century. Low rodent numbers in the north must occur synchronously with high rodent numbers on Amherst and Wolfe islands. But naturalists, knowing it *can* happen, await its recurrence. Even in other years, however, some snowy owls come down from the north, and resident great horned, screech, short-eared, and saw-whet owls can be found. No great burst of colour or song is part of this natural event. Rather, the owls of the Kingston area represent a silent, secretive, ethereal phenomenon, on a par with the best.

Canada Goose: A Success Story

Harry G. Lumsden

More Canada geese may be living in Ontario now than ever before. Their recovery from previously depleted numbers is a success story in conservation and a model of what can be accomplished with public concern.

Several stocks of Canada geese, distinguished by their size, colour, and migratory traditions, have bred in Ontario since the glaciers retreated. The giant Canada goose nested primarily in southern Ontario between the Precambrian Shield and the Great Lakes. Some of these large geese stayed in winter but most probably moved to the adjacent states. Besides Ontario, giant Canada geese bred throughout the Great Lakes region and across the prairies to the Rockies.

Before Europeans arrived, much of southern Ontario consisted of vast, largely mature forest, unattractive to geese. Exceptions may have been the extensive prairies lying between narrow belts of forest bordering rivers and lakes in the extreme southwest, now Essex and Kent counties, and

Canada goose on nest. NATIONAL MUSEUM OF CANADA, A. G. AUSTIN

Huron Indian or Neutral Indian corn fields in the Midland and Niagara regions respectively. The fields at Midland are known to have attracted Canada and blue goose migrants. Breeding geese in southern Ontario, however, while probably widespread, were confined to the larger marshes with extensive sedge areas that offered abundant food for goslings. The smaller marshes and lakes were less attractive, especially if fringed with trees and willow or spirea shrubs which limited opportunities for geese to graze.

If Indians had any effect on goose numbers, likely it was slight and confined to marshes near their settlements. Killing geese with bows and arrows was not easy, and many of the goose bones found in Indian sites may represent locally breeding birds that were rounded up while flightless during the moult.

In the mid 1640s, the Indians obtained guns through trade. The effect, if any, of this advance in hunting technology on geese in southern Ontario was short lived. In 1649 the Iroquois attacked the Hurons and the following year turned on the Neutrals, driving both tribes from their lands. The forests once again closed in on the corn fields, and migrant geese overflew the Midland and Niagara regions on their way south. Local breeding geese, exterminated near the villages, probably recolonized the marshes near the deserted settlements.

For the past three hundred years, however, the manner in which European settlers have used the land and hunted geese has had a much more pronounced effect on goose numbers. Wars, economic booms and busts, and changes in technology all have had their impact, directly or indirectly.

Life was hard on the frontier, and wildlife played a major part in the subsistence of the settlers. A frequent practice was to drive moulting pairs of geese with their broods from the local marsh to the barn, to be penned and fattened for consumption in fall or winter. This practice, common throughout the Great Lakes region, destroyed both breeding stock and progeny. The geese were not spared even in the winter and were hunted wherever they migrated.

It seems likely that geese disappeared from southern Ontario everywhere except for Lake St. Clair by the 1920s. A few remained as captives at duck-hunting clubs and in the possession of aviculturists. Paradoxically, at this time of decline and disappearance, clearing of the forests for farming created infinitely better habitat for geese than had ever existed earlier.

This lowest point in goose fortunes in southern Ontario caused public-spirited citizens to intervene. In the late 1920s and early 1930s people with captive flocks of geese allowed some of the birds they bred to fly free and colonize the local area. In this way the Calder brothers at Holstein, Horace Mack at Guelph, and Dr. King at

Amherstburg, established local wild flocks.

In 1961, Dr. Norman Scollard, Curator of the Riverdale Zoo, released geese on Toronto Island. These birds bred and increased rapidly. They also acted as decoys for geese that had been nesting elsewhere in southern Ontario. By 1968, about a thousand feral geese were established in southern Ontario from all releases combined. To further increase goose numbers and distribute them more widely, the Department of Lands and Forests contracted with Kortright Waterfowl Park at Guelph to have geese released in the Hockley Valley and on Long Point, Norfolk County. From numerous releases of goslings to many locations across the province, a rapid increase and spread took place.

The success of the giant Canada in southern Ontario is due to a combination of factors. In certain townships where releases were made, goose-hunting seasons were closed. Most important of all was commendable restraint among hunters and the protective attitude of farmers who posted their land. The birds also tended to migrate to the United States so late that hunting seasons were generally over when they arrived.

By 1985 the Canada goose population of southern Ontario had increased to about sixty thousand birds. Today many urban and near-urban residents can look up to the evening sky when they hear the haunting calls of the geese and see a wedge of them flying low over the trees or apartment buildings. Urban park visitors can enjoy these magnificent birds as they graze on lawns and golf courses. The geese come to these places in early summer not just for the plentiful food supply represented by the extensive lawns, but to spend the vulnerable flightless moult period in safety. There are those who complain about their droppings, but the geese can be relatively easily driven away from places where they are not welcome to other places where they are.

Through the all-out efforts of dedicated people, the giant Canada geese of southern Ontario have gone from a species on the brink of local extinction to a species requiring management to reduce human-goose conflicts.

Passenger Pigeons: They Darkened the Sky

John B. Theberge

The passenger pigeon is today only a second-hand memory. There is possibly nobody now alive who ever actually saw one. Yet, because once it may have been the most abundant bird in Ontario, perhaps in all of North America, the memory is worth recalling.

Pigeon Facts

All of forested Ontario was included in the passenger pigeon's breeding range. The majority of documented breeding sites, however, were crowded into southwestern Ontario: the Bruce Peninsula, from Orillia south to Toronto, and along the north shore of Lake Ontario. This distribution may have reflected greater opportunities for observations in the south than in less settled parts of the province. Nesting in the north appears to have been less common and more irregular, especially north of the height of land, but even there, scattered records exist at places such as Rainy River, Moose Factory, and the Abitibi and Mattagami rivers. Attesting to the bird's once wide distribution in Ontario is a scattering of place names that must have been assigned

Location of known passenger pigeon colonies in Ontario.

on the basis of an abundance of pigeons: four Pigeon Lakes (in Haliburton and Peterborough counties, Sudbury and Thunder Bay districts), one river (Victoria County), one island (St. Lawrence River), a bay (Essex County), and one rapid (Mattagami River).

Outside Ontario, the passenger pigeon's breeding range extended from the middle of the Mackenzie District in the Northwest Territories, through central Keewatin, across to central Quebec and Nova Scotia, and south to Kansas, Mississippi, and Kentucky. It wintered from Arkansas and North Carolina south to central Texas, Louisiana, and Florida. Rarely was it seen west of the Rocky Mountains.

Passenger pigeons remained in large flocks year-round and often nested in enormous colonies. One colony, in Dufferin County, Mulmur Township, between 1852–55 was reported to have covered four square miles; one of five square miles was reported at Durham County, Darlington Township, in 1827; one covered a ten-mile radius of marsh at Elgin County, between Dutton and West Lorne, from 1868–70; one of thirteen miles by eleven miles at Huron County, Ashfield Township, in 1870; one was ten miles square at Oxford County, Blandford and Blenheim townships, in 1846 or 1847; and one stretched eight miles from Guelph to Rockwood along the Speed River in Wellington County in 1835.

The largest nesting colonies recorded in Ontario were described as containing "millions" of birds. These were reported on the Abitibi River in 1876–78; on the Mattagami River between 1869 and 1872; along the banks of the Grand River in Amaranth and Luther townships; in a variety of places in Grey County such as Artemesia and Keple townships; along the shore of Georgian Bay between Meaford and Collingwood between 1856 and 1873; and in Whitchurch Township of York County in 1850.

"Thousands" were described in nesting colonies in Bruce County (1869, 1878), Dufferin County (about 1884), Durham County (1856–63), Grey, Halton, Middlesex, Perth, and Prince Edward counties (about 1870), Rainy River in the Kenora District, Simcoe County near Wasaga Beach, and in the vicinity of the Holland Marsh, York County (1869), and Welland County (1874).

Nesting habitat for colonies was extremely varied. Upland deciduous forests, cedar swamps, spruce and tamarack forests, mixed forests, second-growth thickets, pine stands, and swamps all seem to have been suitable. Daily flights took place from the nesting sites for food and water. Both males and females incubated the eggs, and those birds not on the nest usually left and returned in large bodies at definite times of the day.

Passenger pigeons in the hardwood forests ate nuts, especially beech nuts and acorns; berries such as cherries, elderberries, and raspberries; buds; and seeds such as those of maple and especially American elm. In the boreal forest, American elm was still important to the northern extent of its range, and other seed species included white birch and pin cherry. In the north, there were also blueberries, cranberries, and crowberries. Thus, the passenger pigeon could be considered a cosmopolitan feeder inhabiting a wide variety of habitats. After European settlement, they broadened their food habits to exploit grain crops, especially wheat, buckwheat, and peas. These seeds often were eaten right after they were sown, because hand sowing left the seeds on top of the soil. After harvesting, they also exploited the grain in stooks. Their destructiveness to crops was undoubtedly one motivation for much of the killing. However, in a questionnaire distributed by the Royal Ontario Museum in 1926, a significant number of respondents from Grey, Bruce, and Huron counties, where many of Ontario's largest colonies had been, stated that the pigeons had *not* been destructive to crops. In fact, pigeons here apparently could not even be baited by the netters with grain. This could be because in these areas American beech was especially abundant, and pigeons preferred the nuts.

Passenger pigeons did not follow any annual migration routes in Ontario, although the frequent observations of large flocks in the Niagara region and at the west end of Lake Ontario indicate some migratory concentration there. Many, but not all flocks appear to have skirted Lakes Erie and Ontario. Fall migration was much more dispersed and unorganized than was spring migration.

Historic Quotes

While quartered at Fort Mississauga...near Niagara, I had one year (probably about 1860) in the month of May, the gratification of witnessing a spectacle I had frequently heard of – namely, a grand migration of the Passenger Pigeon....Early in the morning I was appraised by my servant that an extraordinary flock of birds was passing over, such as he had never seen before. Hurrying out and ascending the grassy ramparts, I was perfectly amazed to behold the air filled, and the sun obscured by millions of pigeons, not hovering about but darting onwards in a straight line with arrowy flight, in a vast mass a mile or more in breadth, and stretching before and behind as far as the eye could reach.

Swiftly and steadily the column passed over with a rushing sound, and for hours continued in undiminished myriads advancing over the American forests in the eastern horizon, as the myriads that had passed were lost in the western sky.

It was late in the afternoon before any decrease in the mass was perceptible, but they became gradually less dense as the day drew to a close. At sunset the detached flocks bringing up the rear began to settle in the forest on the Lake-road, and in such numbers as to break down branches from the trees.

The duration of this flight being about fourteen hours...could not have been less than three hundred miles in length, with an average breadth, as before stated of one mile.

(R. W. King, 1866. *The sportsman and naturalist in Canada*. London).

I once accompanied the Doctor [Dr. Dunlop] on an exploring expedition through the tract [Huron]. We encamped close to a breeding-place of these birds, when we were kept awake all night by the noise they made.... Towards morning, the sound of their departure to their feeding-grounds resembled thunder. For nearly two hours there was one incessant roar, as flock after flock took its departure eastward. The ground under the trees was whitened with their excrement, and strewn with broken branches of the trees.

Major S. Strickland, 1853.
Twenty-seven years in Canada West,
Volume I. London.

In the neighbourhood five or six miles east of Yonge Street straight from Mulock's Corners is a place called Pine Orchard properly called, as there is, or was, a grove of pines of from ten to a hundred feet high with close branches and very dense, suitable in every way for nest building and the natural instinct of the pigeons preempted this place for a Rookery and to say that there were millions of nests there would be a mere assertion. But no matter how many there were the facts would not account for the myriads of birds found in the country about....

In the season Pine Orchard was inundated with people from the country. Waggon loads of Farmers with their sons from miles about came during the daytime and at night with lanterns and torches and slaughtered with wholesale vigor. Caught the old birds and wrung their necks and carried the squabs in bags by the waggon load.

N. Pearson of Aurora,
in response to a 1926 questionnaire
of the Royal Ontario Museum.

I have seen them move in one unbroken column for hours across the sky, like some great river, ever varying in hue; and as the mighty stream sweeping on at sixty miles an hour, reached some deep valley, it would pour its living mass headlong down hundreds of feet, sounding as though a whirlwind was abroad in the land. I have stood by the grandest waterfall of America and regarded the descending torrents in wonder and astonishment, yet never have my astonishment, wonder and admiration been so stirred as when I have witnessed these birds drop from their course like meteors from heaven.

S. Pokagon, Pottawattomie Chief,
1895. "The wild pigeon in
North America." *The Chautauquan*
Volume 22, Number 20.

...we got bushels of them [in Middlesex County] in summer and early fall, both by shooting and netting. Early in September and sometimes in late August people used to go to the roosting places in "second-growth" pines with torches and long poles, and kill hundreds of fat young birds. Buffalo (New York) was our market, and shot pigeons were worth five cents each, and netted ones brought five-and-a-half or six cents a piece. We usually hung the birds in small lots of two or three over night, to cool off, and packed them in layers of straw in apple-barrels, and sent them, I think by express, consignee to pay all charges. My father's net sometimes furnished three or four barrels in a single day. If I remember correctly a barrel held about 100 or 120 birds. Sometimes the netting season lasted two or three weeks. When the visible supply diminished it would not pay to have two persons attending a net. We never heard it was illegal to net. The birds were a nuisance to the farmers, a menace to the next year's crop of wheat, and in some instances destructive to spring wheat then standing in stook.

M. W. Althouse of Toronto,
in response to a 1926 questionnaire
of the Royal Ontario Museum.

Eulogy

In 1887, and for a decade after that, despite the great decline in passenger pigeons that had occurred already, the Ontario Small Birds Act stated: "No bird, except game birds, eagles, falcons, hawks, owls, wild pigeons, black birds, crows, English sparrows and ravens to be killed at any time or molested." In 1897, this clause was altered to protect all "wild native birds (other than game birds, English sparrow, hawk, crow and blackbirds)." Thus, protection for the passenger pigeon in Ontario came in 1897. It was too late.

1874 – Toronto Island, York County: "Last large flock over Toronto."
1876 or 1877 – Middlesex County: "There went...the great flocks to the east or northeast and never returned."
1882 – Hastings County: "Last one seen or heard of was shot by me in the fall, in October, about 1882, at Coe Hill."
1882–84 – Northumberland County: "Still scattered flocks during these years."
1884 – Lennox and Addington County: "In 1884 killed my last two. But a year or so later noticed a wounded one around part of the summer. Quite tame."
1885 – Lake Scugog, Ontario County: "One seen."
1885 – Simcoe County: "I was out hunting ruffed grouse with an uncle. I saw a pair of pigeons alight on a hemlock tree about 60 yards distant. He took my gun and aimed between them and both fell. These were the last shot in our section."
1886 – Myrtle, Ontario County: "...July 4th, 1886, when I saw the last male wild pigeon alive near Myrtle Station on the CPR north of Whitby. When the train stopped to take water a male pigeon came to quench his thirst and, after doing so flew up to a fence and started to preen his feathers. Then the engine started, and I had my last look at a live wild pigeon."
1891 – Toronto, York County: "April 13, saw a male specimen in University Park ravine, which I pursued for half an hour but failed to collect."
1891 – Belleville, Hastings County: "One male shot" (This is the last record of a killing in Ontario.)
1893 – St. Vincent Township, Grey County: "There were three that summer that visited Deer Lake spring on high clay banks on east side. Were seen often at spring and grain fields, but they failed to come again."
1902 – Penetanguishene, Simcoe County: "May 18. One pair seen." (This is the last known sighting of the passenger pigeon in Ontario).

The source of much of the material and quotes used here is M. H. Mitchell's 1931 work, *The Passenger Pigeon in Ontario*, from the University of Toronto Press.

Urban Nature

John B. Theberge

Ravines fingering through the subdivisions, city parks plastering green Band-Aids on an ash-coloured landscape, maple-lined boulevards, shady subdivisions, abandoned lots, clouds, sunrises and sunsets glimpsed from between tall buildings: these are all part of urban nature. Admittedly stretched thin in many places, especially in downtown cores and sprawling shopping centres, trees, shrubs, and grasses in the city still capture solar energy and pass it on to urban-adapted herbivores: squirrels, rabbits, house sparrows, and meadow voles, that in turn pass it on to chickadees, woodpeckers, and skunks. A red-tailed hawk will ignore the sight and sound of freeway traffic and nest in a city park as long as voles are down in the grass. Chimney swifts, known to some as "flying cigars," will skitter across the sky, and common nighthawks will flap, moth-like, over the crowded downtown, so long as there are insects over the city to hunt. Chimney swifts nest in old factory chimneys and nighthawks nest on flat factory roofs, neither of which represent ancestral homes.

The majority of Ontario's residents spend the majority of their time in cities, so there is reason to look for nature there. There is reason, as well, to be able to manage the vestiges of nature in the city. "Urban forestry" is a new field directed at evaluating and saving specific woodlots and specific shade trees. It involves calculations of their economic value in property appraisals, even calculations of their aesthetic value where they break the heat of the pavement with shade and the noise of traffic with cicada and oriole song. Development of a forestry strategy is now an accepted part of urban planning.

"Urban hydrology," another accepted new field, involves the management of water, both its quantity and quality, through the city. It is functionally connected to urban forestry, or should be, even more than to urban engineering. Forests and marshes mete out water over the year much more effectively than do cement dams.

Ecology is on the curriculum in many university programs leading to urban planning degrees, and enlightened urban planners appreciate that one-species (human) environments are inherently unstable, nonfunctional, and unattractive.

Our efforts to keep vestiges of nature around us, such as the planted birches in the mall and the flowerpots on the windowsill, argue that we trail our own evolutionary roots wherever we live. That should be no surprise. A city is a new environment for *Homo sapien*, one we have experienced for less than one-three-hundredths of our history, if you date the first members of our species to a conservative 2 million years ago, and the first cities, in Mesopotamia, to 6,000 years ago. Our broad cultural adaptability does not make us non-biological or non-ecological beings. So, fortunately, you can still list a lot of birds in an older subdivision, even in a new subdivision if it has been planned with environmental sensitivity. In fact, a hardwood forest with about 40 per cent crown opening from housing will support more species of birds than a closed climax forest, by virtue of the shrubs and berries and vines that can grow there.

Most cities that have waterfronts are rich in waterfowl and gulls. Cities with river ravines leading into them (even Toronto) have white-tailed deer, raccoons, and mink among their inhabitants. Cities with concerned people have urban parks with blue jays (the birds, not the baseball players), squirrels, wood frogs, and trees full of warblers in the spring.

The lichens may be gone – victims of too much sulphur dioxide in the air; the streetside trees may be trimmed back for telephone lines; the space-demanding wildlife species will have moved elsewhere, but ecosystems are cunningly adaptive at the same time as they are vulnerable. Dandelions come up through cracks in the asphalt, and abandoned lots soon are full of grasses, wildflowers (albeit mostly aliens), and shrubs.

"Green," however, does not necessarily mean "natural," and natural is worth saving, even in the city. Natural implies time-tested. It is fully functional ecosystems, not just green ones, that will persist, helping to cleanse the air and purify the water, and surrounding us with environmentally sensitive wildlife species that may warn us when we have gone too far. Keeping ecological functions going is a comparatively new challenge in urban environmental management, as urban sprawl claims more and more land, especially in southern Ontario. It is a challenge that home owners can contribute to in their own backyards, and one that every taxpayer can insist upon. The benefits lie in a cleaner and more liveable environment, a cardinal at the feeder, or a wide-eyed cottontail rabbit looking out from under the hedge.

Birds of the Cities

Gerry McKeating

Ever since a homesick European introduced the starling to New York City in the last century, birds, for better or worse, have been the form of wildlife most visible to urban residents. Time has shown that exotic introductions have been a bane rather than a boon, yet even these exotics – common pigeons, European starlings, house sparrows – living in the canyon cliffs of centretown, add colour, diversity, and song to our often monotonous cityscapes.

But there is much more birdlife in cities than these introduced species. In fact, the city is bird habitat from one side to the other, with a great diversity of species reflecting local habitat conditions.

Imagine the city as one large environment for birds, then divide it into numerous different habitats: backyard gardens, formal parks, cemeteries, sewage ponds, ravines or woodlots, tree-lined streets, river valleys, shorelines, vacant lots, and back lanes. Even the gravelled, flat-roofed factories, building ledges, and city light standards provide habitat components for birds. Birds can live in cities and towns wherever habitat, or a niche comparable to a non-urban situation, is available to them.

Habitat constitutes a complex set of interacting biological conditions and limiting factors such as food, water, escape cover, nesting sites, foraging areas, predators, human disturbance, and singing posts that, when combined, determine the survival of a species. Great differences in bird diversity exist in cities depending upon the complexity of vegetation. Habitats in older, well-maintained neighbourhoods often have a mixture of tall, deciduous trees, conifers, smaller trees, fruit-bearing shrubs, and herbaceous ground cover. In such places, habitat nooks and crannies are everywhere and consequently bird diversity is greatest. Red-eyed vireos sing their monotonous song from the tree-tops while song sparrows forage in the dense patches of shrubbery. Northern orioles add artistic splashes of colour as they flit to their bag-like nest structures well up in tall trees. Yellow warblers, common in well-established gardens or thickets, often can be found nesting in ornamental shrubbery less than a metre from the ground. The main food of yellow warblers consists of insects, and as every gardener knows, insects are not usually in short supply.

The urbanization process in the cores of cities reduces the variety of birds but it can result in great numbers of some species. Because vegetation is usually sparse, these core areas are more simple in structure and unable to support the variety of birds found in older neighbourhoods. Pigeons thrive, as we all know. The ledges of bridges, window sills, or roof eaves replicate their old-world cliff habitat, while garbage provides an abundant supply of food. This aggressive introduced species dominates a biologically simplified habitat.

However, the tumultuous brick and glass canyons of downtown streets can provide habitat for more "desirable" species as well. A summer's night draws hordes of insects, attracted to the city lights. Common nighthawks, often visible in the reflected glow of street lamps, swoop down with impunity upon their aerial prey, their wings producing a booming sound as the birds pull out from a steep dive. The nighthawk's eggs will be nearby, on the flat, gravelled roofs of city buildings. These level places resemble the pastures or clearings favoured by the bird in a country setting. During the day, the bird roosts on the gravelled roofs, safe from disturbance by man or other predators.

Kestrels utilize the urban environments too, though less commonly than do nighthawks. In wilder habitats, these small hawks nest in natural tree cavities or woodpecker holes, but in cities they readily use bird boxes or recesses of buildings. They perch on TV aerials or the rooftop edges of buildings. Kestrels often prey on house sparrows, an abundant city food.

Evening grosbeaks are a common bird at backyard feeders. DON GUNN

Gaze skyward from a city street on any hot summer day. Chimney swifts dart back and forth across the sky, foraging like nighthawks, on the wing after flying insects. These highly gregarious birds have adapted well to town and city life, clinging to the sooty, interior walls of chimneys and using them both as nesting and roosting sites.

Sewage ponds provide another example of a new urban environment for birds. Sewage effluent is warm and normally ice-free all winter, conditions which attract waterfowl that otherwise would have to migrate. The nutrient-rich water generates a rich variety of aquatic invertebrates that supply an important source of protein, especially to female ducks at egg-laying time in the early spring.

Canada geese have been enormously successful in cities, to the extent of being considered a nuisance by some residents. The geese are quite at home among people, houses, factories, and automobiles. The closely manicured lawns of urban parks and golf courses provide an abundant food supply. In Toronto, nest sites are plentiful within the city's ravines and along the waterfront. The legendary sagacity and wariness of the Canada goose come somewhat into doubt, however, as it gobbles down your popcorn at Ontario Place.

Bird distribution varies from city to city. Cardinals, common in such southwestern Ontario cities as London, are uncommon in others, such as Ottawa. But in Ottawa, and not London, winter incursions of Bohemian waxwings are to be expected, gorging themselves on the berry-bearing shrubs and trees at the Central Experimental Farm.

Most cities contain relatively unmodified natural patches within them – oases of green. These places are not really urban habitats like the manicured parks and sewage ponds but rather remnant rural or natural environments. Ravines, wetlands, woodlots, and other urban green spaces become important stop-over sites for migrating birds. The trees in May come alive with warblers, tanagers, and a multitude of other species, some remaining to breed. Even great horned owls and pileated woodpeckers can occupy these urban "wildernesses," often all year. These places provide important refuges for species in cities, interspersed as they are with man-modified environments.

As urbanization spreads out into the countryside, the original variety of birdlife decreases. Farmland and open-country species, such as eastern kingbirds, decline, and veeries and other species that require the solitude of undisturbed woods for nesting move elsewhere. As the woods are cut down, wood thrushes and indigo buntings, residents of the woodland edge, disappear. Some birds may appear to adapt, yet studies have shown that even the familiar robin, exposed to the activities of humans and their pets, can suffer reduced breeding success.

The quality of habitat for birds can be improved, while the monotony of most suburban landscapes is reduced, by appropriate landscaping and the retention of existing natural vegetation. The cardinal, a southern bird, has extended its range greatly in Ontario over the past fifty years. The gradual maturity of our suburban neighbourhoods has created the niche requirements for this species. Cardinals nest two to three metres up in tall shrubbery, an ideal spot for concealment, insect food, and cover from the neighbour's cat.

Many birds will use new growth while tolerating moderate human activity. Plantings around houses of fruit-bearing shrubs of different heights, and of various coniferous and deciduous trees will result in more species. Mountain ash trees are especially favoured by robins and cedar waxwings. Evening grosbeaks feed upon Manitoba maple keys, and common redpolls and pine siskins enjoy white birch seeds. Black-capped chickadees prefer some conifer cover. The fruit of autumn olive is eaten by many species.

Many excellent publications provide advice on what to plant in your backyard. By providing a variety of trees, foliage, food, water, and cover, you not only help ensure the survival of migratory birds in urban environments, but you also make cities more interesting places to live.

The Leslie Street Spit

John A. Livingston

March. Icy lake water laps murkily at the lower end of a cedar six-by-six, storm-tossed onto a jumbled beach of broken bricks and stones. From its upper end, the yellow unblinking stare of a snowy owl swivels over the bleak and endless flat grey cityscape...

May. An abandoned barge alongside a derelict mooring precariously supports on its sunny rotting foredeck the nest of a pair of mallards...

June. A red fox glides airily, daintily, through grasses and ox-eye daisies...

September. A shimmering squadron of monarch butterflies clusters on a bobbing clump of Canada goldenrod. A great blue heron solemnly, effortlessly flaps across the Toronto skyline, past the condominiums and the commercial towers, past vomiting black industrial smoke, over the freeways and the sailboats and the oily shipping, and through the deafening cacophony of a white whirling turmoil of gulls.

When the ring-billed gulls are in full throat at Leslie Street Spit you are not

Ring-billed gulls on Leslie Street Spit. HANS BLOKPOEL

likely to hear much else. Over two dozen species of bird are known to nest here, but most prominent are the thousands upon thousands of strident, raucous, screaming, cackling ring-bills. It is one of their two largest colonies in the world. So overwhelming is the sound, especially at the appearance of an intruder, that when biologists were working here they wore ear-protectors like those used by airport employees while parking jet aircraft on the tarmac. For obvious reasons the biologists also wore slickers with hoods, and kept delicate equipment under wraps. Such inconveniences are minor, however, because for biologists and naturalists this natural spectacle is unique.

Paradoxically, the spectacle is only partly natural. The Spit is a human-made structure which has been recovered by natural processes. Ecologists speak of the phenomenon of *succession*. Primary succession is the development of plant life on the primal bare rock, usually beginning with lichens. Secondary succession is the retrieval by plant communities of areas temporarily denuded or drastically changed by flood, fire, hurricane, or some human-caused disturbance. Strictly speaking, what has happened at the Leslie Spit is neither. It may better be described as an outstanding example of *colonization*, with vegetation and wildlife from surrounding areas taking advantage of an opportunity to expand. The wonder of the Spit is in the extraordinary speed with which an extraordinary variety of plants and animals have been able to move in, settle, and prosper – smack in the effluent-and-asphalt heart of a giant metropolitan-industrial natural wasteland.

The Spit is an artificial headland or breakwater jutting south into Lake Ontario just to the east of the Toronto Islands, its base at the foot of Leslie Street. There was once a great cattail marsh here, but that is another story. The Spit was conceived out of great expectations arising from the St. Lawrence Seaway, which would deliver much new shipping to the city. The harbour would need extension and protection. Land-fill began in 1959, but the period of greatest construction activity was between 1965 and 1976. A building boom was altering downtown Toronto, and enormous excavations meant enormous quantities of debris – subsoil, stones, sand, and gravel, together with miscellaneous brick and concrete rubble from demolition. Muck, with its dubious contents, was added from dredging. Eventually the new headland arched more than five kilometres into the lake, its inner (landward) side having a series of "fingers" and lagoons.

Nature's abhorrence of vacuums is well known; the phobia extends itself to naked ground. Plants arrived almost immediately, and kept arriving as fast as the dump trucks extended the land. Ground-binding species appeared as soon as wave action had begun to grind and pulverize the rubble and flatten the sands and muds. Perhaps the most important plants in the early stages were the willows and silverweeds, whose root structures function like chickenwire over rip-rap.

As the "soil" was secured, colonization continued with speed rivalling the illusion of "time-lapse" film. The most visible plants, apart from grasses, became the poplars, especially eastern cottonwoods. One cottonwood reached a height of over twelve metres as early as 1982, by which time an astonishing 275 plant species had been identified. Some seeds arrived on the wind, some in floating masses of vegetation, others in the guts of passing birds. Still others, dormant in the soil, were dump-truck stowaways awaiting their moment in the sun. None, so far as anyone knows, was actually planted. All were "happenstance" arrivals.

Birds disperse somewhat less passively than plants. Apparently they liked what they saw. Ring-billed gulls first nested in 1973 when twenty-one pairs were a pleasant surprise for local naturalists. Only three years later, the colony had increased to *ten thousand* pairs! Five years after that, in 1981, the total was seventy thousand pairs – and counting. Presumably other ring-bill populations around the Great Lakes subsidized the colonizing population until its own reproductive momentum took over.

The first ring-bills of the season arrive in early March, and by late April nesting is well advanced. The gulls normally nest in flat, open places, but once these were fully occupied, the fringes of the expanding colony were forced into newly treed areas. Now you can see gulls nesting in total shade in dense groves of thriving poplars. Other gulls – California, herring, and great black-backed – joined the ring-bills to nest.

Two months after the gulls arrive, the Caspian terns appear. Their presence has been one of the more noteworthy events since the Spit's construction. The Caspian tern has a peculiarly scattered world distribution, and for naturalists this urban colony must be the most accessible anywhere. These birds need exposed sites, and because they arrive well after the gulls have settled in, they may encounter some difficulty in finding unoccupied places.

The first Caspian tern nesting was in 1975 when seven nests were found. By 1981, more than ninety pairs were breeding. The colony has continued to grow, but its expansionist days may be numbered by the pressing encirclement of the gulls. For a time, biologists of the Canadian Wildlife Service kept the Caspian area clear of gull nests. That work has now been suspended, however, and only time will tell whether the Caspian terns will be able to persist. Events move swiftly at the Leslie Street Spit.

There is also a large colony of common terns, the nucleus of which no doubt came from the Toronto Islands across the harbour. By 1981, at twelve hundred pairs it had become the largest concentration of this species on the

Great Lakes. These terns nest on sandy dunes and beaches, some of which emerged on the inland arm of the Spit. There, however, the nests may eventually be overtaken by silverweeds, thistles, willows, and whatever plant cover succeeds them as vegetation continues to swarm over the bare places. Or the terns may well be forced out by the gulls.

Other breeding waterbirds include black-crowned night heron (in the poplars), Canada goose, black duck, mallard, blue-winged teal, gadwall, and redhead, but in the off-season there are many more species. Wintering ducks and other waterbirds have always used the several sheltered areas along the Toronto waterfront, but the Leslie Spit has added significantly to feeding and resting space for pintail, American widgeon, scaups, oldsquaw, common goldeneye, all three mergansers, and others. At least thirty-three species of swans, geese, and ducks have been observed at various times, including Eurasian widgeon, king eider, and all three scoters. Common and red-throated loons both occur, four grebes, and even gannet and great cormorant have made the list. Southern wanderers include snowy and cattle egrets, and glossy ibis.

Even with all this birdlife, it may be that the most important residual contribution of the Spit has been the creation of mudflats. Dredging and construction have grievously reduced the availability of migrant shorebird habitat around the Great Lakes. The Spit had provided replacement to the extent that by 1982 thirty-four species of plovers, sandpipers, and their kin had been recorded. And there are lots of them. It used to be that one could spend a lifetime birding around Toronto and never clap eyes on a Hudsonian godwit; now individuals and small groups are seen regularly, and marbled godwits turn up as well. Even the American avocet has visited.

Migration is also the best time for birds of prey, of which only the American kestrel has been known to nest. Northern harriers, however, should by this time have found the attractive meadows to their taste. Both peregrine and gyrfalcon have been recorded in this remarkable place, as well as osprey and both eagles. As elsewhere in southern Ontario, migration is streamed along the north shores of Lakes Ontario and Erie; every birder (and every saw-whet owl) knows the strategic importance of precious natural stop-over sites along the way.

Few songbirds actually nest at Leslie Spit, but a splendid variety passes through on migration, and the usual winter finches forage for snow-scattered "weed" seeds. As always, the key is habitat, and the Spit has become sufficiently rich and diverse that the 1982 official list of birds totalled 258.

There are many unanswered, perhaps unanswerable, questions about the Leslie Spit, and one that much intrigues naturalists is the success of the bird colonies in such apparently unhealthy and inhospitable surroundings. After all, the Spit is a part of a very large city, with all its distasteful – even dangerous – byproducts. Having in mind the torrents of abuse and refuse that are heaped onto and into the unresisting waters and bottom sludge of Toronto harbour, it is difficult to comprehend how fish-eaters such as the two species of terns have been so successful in bringing off young – and in adult survival, for that matter. So far, at least, there appears to have been no ill-effect, either upon the terns or upon the wintering loons and mergansers, or, indeed the migrating shorebirds – so far as anyone knows. The ring-billed gull's more catholic diet presents no problem. Two and one-quarter million human inhabitants of the Toronto area generate stupendous volumes of garbage; this is readily available in a ring of repositories around the periphery of the city to which the gulls fan out in the early morning hours each day. But the undeniable success of the water-dependent feeders remains a fascinating puzzle.

Also problematical is the future of the entire Spit as a natural area. It falls under the responsibility of the Metropolitan Toronto and Region Conservation Authority, whose major priority after watershed protection is public recreation. It can be expected that at least portions of the area will be dedicated to boating and related support facilities. Parts of the swiftly developing natural community will no doubt remain, but just as in the case of the Caspian terns, the shape of tomorrow is never clear.

At present, the Leslie Street Spit offers a rich, varied, and delightful menu for the naturalist at every season. Above all, the Spit provides a stunning and unforgettable experience of the ineffable dynamism and creativity of natural process – against what would seem to be overwhelming odds.

Skyscrapers and Peregrines

John B. Theberge

The peregrine falcon, reputed to be the fastest bird alive, is also the most paradoxical. It epitomizes wilderness, yet for most people the most likely place to see one is in the city. In some ways it is among the most sensitive creatures alive to the environmental insults of humans, yet in other ways it is among the most tolerant. The subject of vigorous conservation programs at the local level, its ultimate success or demise as a species is linked to the health of the biosphere.

In the contrasting environments of a far northern Arctic island or at Queen's Park in downtown Toronto, the peregrine may stage a performance of speed and agility of unequalled proportions anywhere in the natural world. Hunting from above, it spots its prey – one out of a flock of golden plovers lifting off a mudflat which stretches out from the edge of a tundra pond, or one out of a flock of domestic pigeons flapping awkwardly into the air from a dropping-stained, tenth-storey window ledge. Instantly the peregrine transforms itself into a projectile, its wings folded tightly to its body, its feathers sleeked. It aims its momentum downward at a spot about three metres behind a perceived contact point with its victim. The plover or the pigeon, unaware that it is living its last seconds, beats on, gaining altitude. With lightning speed and unbelievable precision the falcon stoops, checks its descent just behind its prey, then lifts slightly, and, with extended talons, rips its victim up the back and neck. A bundle of feathers explodes, and the plover or the pigeon, spirals downward. The falcon drops to the ground beside its prey, grasps it in its talons, and carries it to a tundra tussock or to a high steel strut of a building under construction to consume its meal.

That the forces of evolution could ever perfect a high-speed aerial predator such as the peregrine is wonder enough, but we humans have another reason to respect this species. The peregrine recently has done us a favour of inestimable value, despite the fact that in earlier times we totally eliminated what must have been two of its most important prey species: the Carolina paroquet and the passenger pigeon. Together with a few other bird species, peregrines have warned us with their unhatched eggs and the deaths of their chicks, that excessive amounts of man-made chemical insecticides and herbicides have been released into the environment. Peregrine populations declined due to egg-shell thinning and breakage to the point that eastern North American populations became – still are – nearly extinct.

Only a fluke of nature dictated that

peregrines and a few other "summit predators" would be the ones to suffer first, and not humans. We can be thankful that, unlike birds, we mammals do not wrap our ovum in a calcium shell. Had pesticides affected protein metabolism in animals, and not calcium metabolism, the effects on us could have been disastrous. No biological tests preceded the broadcasting of DDT or other chlorinated hydrocarbons into the environment. Peregrines ceased nesting in eastern North America by the early 1960s.

It was this unfortunate decline of the peregrines that preceded their move to the city. Peregrine nesting sites are typically, although not always, on steep cliff faces. The sides of skyscraper buildings are structurally similar. Equally or more important than cliff faces, however, peregrine success depends upon conditions suitable to its particular aerial hunting technique. It must encounter potential prey – flocks of birds smaller than itself – flying below it in an open environment. Only then may the falcon pursue them at high speed from behind, or stoop on them from above. Wherever such conditions exist, wilderness area or city centre, anywhere in its worldwide range, peregrines may survive, although rarely in large numbers. Thus, part of recovery team efforts, begun in the mid 1970s in the United States and the early 1980s in Canada, have included peregrine releases in Montreal, Boston, New York City, Toronto, Hull, Calgary, Edmonton, and Winnipeg.

The Canadian recovery program uses chicks hatched at captive breeding facilities run by the Canadian Wildlife Service at Wainwright, Alberta. From there, four-week-old peregrine chicks are shipped to release cities. At the release sites they are put into artificial nest cages called *hack boxes*, slung against the sides of buildings. Chicks are confined in the hack boxes and fed ranch-raised quail until they can fly and hunt on their own.

In a wilderness recovery part of the

program, hack boxes with chicks are lowered along cliff faces in places such as Algonquin Park. As well, single peregrine chicks are placed in the nests of wild peregrines along the cliffs of the Yukon River. There, adult birds raise an extra chick in addition to their own.

Since 1981, Ontario releases have been made in Algonquin Park, Brockville, Arnprior, Waterloo, and Toronto. The Toronto releases appropriately have been made on the side of the Whitney Block offices of the Ministry of Natural Resources at Queen's Park, the agency in charge of the program. Releases also have been made at Upper Canada College, and on the Canada Life Assurance Company head office building. This company, along with the World Wildlife Fund, has helped fund the recovery efforts.

The birds have thrived, for the most part, in the sites selected for them. Abundant pigeons, starlings, and house sparrows provide urban prey. The released birds have migrated from all three of the Toronto release sites and returned briefly the following spring. In 1983, a pair of peregrines released at Hull, Quebec, nested at Arnprior, the first Ontario nesting of the species in twenty years. This nest was unsuccessful, however. The female was shot and the fledglings disappeared.

In the United States, prior to 1987, a total of almost two thousand young falcons had been released. The first natural reproduction of artificially raised peregrines took place in 1980. In 1986, thirty-three pairs laid eggs. In the wild, the greatest loss is to great horned owls, a primary reason for continuing with the urban release sites.

The peregrine falcon is still one of Ontario's official endangered species, as it is throughout Canada and the United States. Only healthy populations in Iceland keep it off the world list of endangered species. Although reasonably healthy populations live in the Yukon and Alaska, the species is not out of trouble. DDT is still used in Central and South America for malaria control. Even in Canada, governments continue to sanction the manufacture and release of other potentially persistent chemicals without adequate testing, a threat to more than the peregrine. The birds are poached in Canada by international rings for sale in Arab countries where they are worth thousands of dollars each as symbols of wealth and power and for falconry. And ill-informed people still kill peregrines and other hawks because they consider such predators "bad" – the fate of the Arnprior peregrine.

Immature peregrine falcon. DON GUNN

Whether present recovery efforts will represent the last chapter in the story of the peregrine's North American extinction, or whether peregrines will again grace Ontario's wilderness and cities with displays of speed and power, is not certain. Thin egg shells are still noted, although presently not so thin that broken eggs result. If the peregrine's struggles to recover are successful, if eventually it can be removed from the endangered species lists, then undoubtedly it will become a premier symbol of conservation, representing successful human coexistence with nature, depicting cities that are fit for fragments of the wild, and announcing a healthier biosphere.

Pembroke Swallows

John B. Theberge

The scene is like an over-washed water colour. The grey-blue Ottawa River sweeping from horizon to horizon, white church spires away off on the Quebec shore, soft yellow-green grasses and sedges. A stand of silvery willows drapes a sandbar where the dark Muskrat River loses itself in the Ottawa. For a while, a gentle floodlighting is cast by a setting sun, but it soon fades in a bank of horizon-cloud and is replaced by a shadowless light.

Here, in the gathering dusk, an aerial dance of fluttering wings and swirling feathered bodies is performed every evening in late July and early August. It is a dance of unbelievably dramatic proportion.

But this tribute to flight, this wild mingling of sky and wings does not flash across a wilderness setting. Just beyond the trees and sweeping around 160 degrees, are brick factories, the backs of stores, hydro poles, and paved streets. To witness the swallow display you stand on a jetty beside the muddy Muskrat River, a marina of brightly coloured boats immediately at your back. A high-speed freight train may bellow by just behind the parking lot, only a few metres from the willow roost trees. When you scan the estuary to identify the blue-winged teal and mallards swimming there, your binoculars are likely to pick out a rusty oil can or a white plastic coffee cup deposited in the shallows. The swallow display in downtown Pembroke is indeed an urban phenomenon, a demonstration of tolerance.

Swallows are among the most adaptive passerine species. Barn swallows nest in barns; tree swallows nest in boxes set out along roadsides; purple martins nest in mini-condominiums centred on spacious lawns; cliff swallows nest under eaves and bridges. If aerial insects are present, swallows are there, determined in some avian resolve to exploit human habitats while totally ignoring human beings.

As the sun sets over the Ottawa River, the swallows fly to Pembroke – people, cars, and trains notwithstanding. A few swallows dipping overhead build into myriads at a measured rate of as high as five thousand arrivals per minute! The air fills with feathered life. The birds come in swirls low over the Ottawa River and in clouds dropping down from the sky. With soft twittering they flutter and dance in thickening numbers, each bird independent of the others but the whole co-ordinated into legions flying in one direction against a backdrop of counter-flying legions, and more behind that in a kaleidoscope of breaking and forming symmetry.

Suddenly, into the midst of the swirling eddies of birds darts a merlin. Larger than the swallows, it flies faster, more purposefully. Prey and predator together. The eddies of swallows separate. More swallows seem to form a swirling wake behind the hawk, the safest place to be. But the merlin puts on more speed. Only a split second separates selection of a victim and the act of predation. The hawk is momentarily positioned just over its prey, then drops very slightly onto its back before the swallow can swerve. Scarcely missing a wingbeat the merlin flies on, now with the swallow clutched in its talons. It lands in a willow on the far side of the parking lot to consume its catch.

Between two and five merlins centre their activities on the Pembroke swallows. A secretive and somewhat uncommon falcon, merlins too ignore the cityscape. They could want no more than the Pembroke swallows offer them – a certain meal every evening, and again in the morning as the swallows leave. Why the swallows continue to provide for the predators in this way is unclear. Merlins would have a more difficult time if the swallows roosted in a dispersed fashion all along the Ottawa River rather than concentrating as they do. But communal roosting must confer some benefits, such as an early alarm against tree-hunting predators like raccoons, martens, owls, and other hawks. The odds of an individual swallow being caught by a merlin in such a large roost are perhaps 3 to 100,000 or more – the average number of merlin strikes each evening compared to the number of swallows. The larger the flock, the better an individual bird's chances of survival. For obscure reasons only avery few merlins hunt at the swallow roost.

Pembroke's swallow roost, to which all six species of swallows come, is relatively new. The small cluster of willows they roost in has only been in existence for about fifty years, growing on an accumulating sandbar. Numbers of swallows have increased since about 1960, but only in the late 1970s did numbers become spectacularly large. In 1984 and 1985, counts estimated roughly 150,000 birds, dropping below 75,000 in 1986 possibly due to poor nesting success in the cold, wet spring weather that year, but increasing to over 100,000 in 1987. The species appear to be represented in about the same proportion as their relative abundance in southeastern Ontario: tree swallow most common, followed by bank and barn swallows and purple martins. Cliff and rough-winged swallows are relatively rare. Identifying species in the swirling masses of birds is difficult, except for the fork-tailed barn swallows, and the larger purple martins which soar more than the others.

The Pembroke roost is a migratory staging area. While the swallows fly out some unknown distance to feed each day, up and down and across the Ottawa River and inland, it is the migration urge that brings them together to roost. Successive cold fronts passing through Pembroke in late August carry with them thousands of swallows on their way to Central and South America, until by early September the roost is empty.

The merlin in the willow by the parking lot has eaten its prey and made another aerial foray, this time flying downriver out of sight. The fading light has darkened the willows across the Muskrat River to a black silhouette. At peak numbers, the swirling ranks of swallows fill the air in all directions of the sky. Then, suddenly, comes the dramatic climax of the air show. Over the willows, great eddies of swallows plunge from the sky into the blackness of the limbs. Thousands upon thousands of plunging birds, falling at breakneck speed, drawn like iron filings to a magnet. Behind the first ranks come others darting down with half-folded wings, flipping to avoid collision with one another in a perceptual field more instantaneous than humans can imagine. Some birds level off just at tree-top height to spot a roosting place for themselves; others seem to crash straight into the trees. More and more suction-driven birds, swirling vortexes of birds falling from the sky. And still the air all around is full of swallows, as if none had left.

It takes about twenty minutes for the sky to empty. By then the streetlights of Pembroke and those along the Ottawa River shore have transformed the scene to urban night. Near the end of the show, another merlin flies along the crest of the willows and daintily picks off a luckless swallow an instant before the swallow would have hit its roosting spot. From the roost comes a waterfall of swallow-twitters, gradually subsiding. In fifteen minutes the roost is quiet.

How long will the swallows roost at Pembroke? Will they find a different clump of willows somewhere else along the Ottawa River? Will the colony grow as the tradition becomes even more established? Do different species roost together? Do some species plunge in sooner than others? In time, the phenomenon may become better understood, but even without answers to these questions, it is marvel enough to witness the high-speed coordination exhibited by masses of dancing swallows in the twilight.

The Great Lakes

John B. Theberge

Vast, fresh-water seas. Endless, rolling breakers. A wilderness of waves. As wild today as when shorelines were dominated by uncut forests. The Great Lakes anchor Ontario's natural environment. They moderate the climate, funnel migratory birds, provide vast marshlands, and create unique habitats offshore for living things by virtue of their very scale.

High human population density and what has turned out to be lower than expected ecological resilience have affected the Great Lakes profoundly. Yet their essential physical character has endured. Statistics on water budgets, lake levels, size of water surface and drainage basin are about the same as when Étienne Brûlé first gazed over Lake Huron in 1610.

But, when you look at water chemistry, or aquatic biology, or shoreline processes, the lakes bear little resemblance to what they once were. New statistics on these things appear year after year. Fish species take their leave; others appear. Under the surface, few, if any, unaltered "pockets of wild" are left. "Pristine" has vanished. It all has changed.

Great Lakes as a Physical Environment

John B. Theberge

The Great Lakes make up the largest fresh-water lake system in the world, although the term *fresh* is no longer applicable. The drainage basin itself covers 755,200 square kilometres, with 538,000 and 216,000 square kilometres of land and water surface respectively. Included in the Great Lakes themselves is approximately 20 per cent of the world's total fresh-water surface.

Lake Superior holds the greatest volume of water, twenty-five times as much as Lake Erie. Partly accounting for this difference is Lake Erie's surface area, which is only one-third the size of Lake Superior's, but the major difference is that Lake Erie's maximum depth is only 65 metres, whereas Lake Superior reaches 410 metres – six times as deep.

The drop in elevation from Lake Superior to Lake Ontario is approxi-

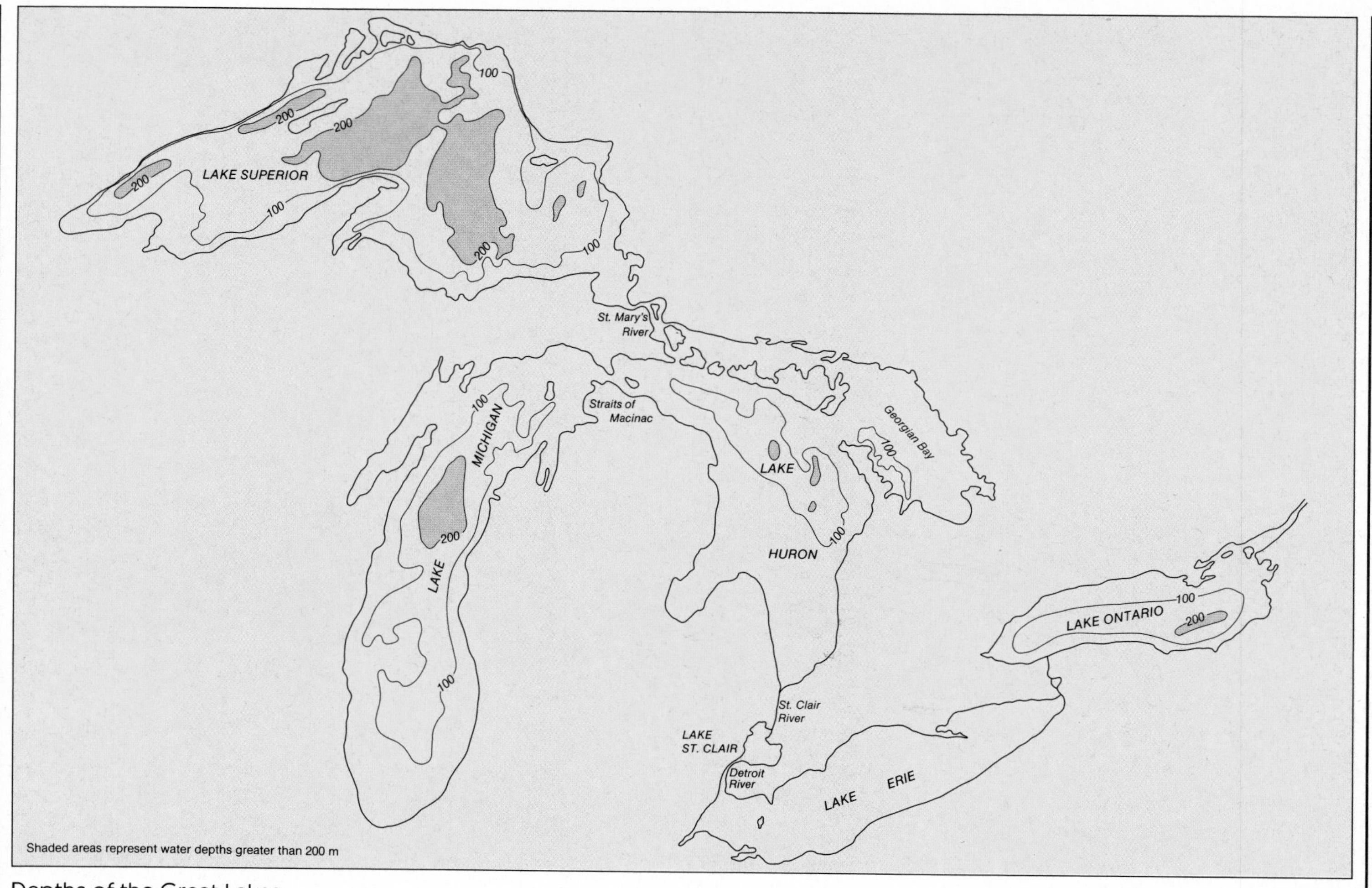

Depths of the Great Lakes.

Elevations of the Great Lakes.

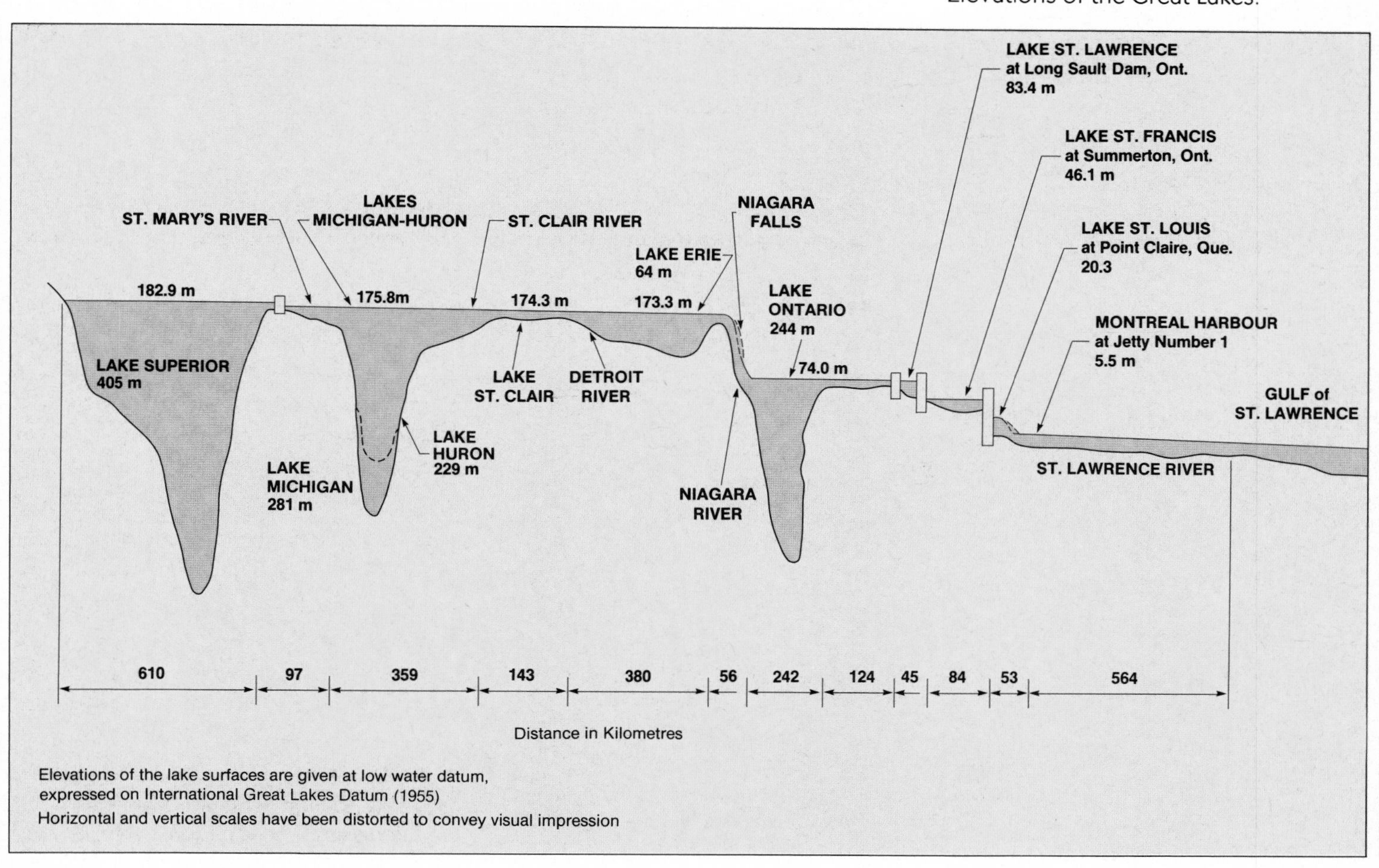

Physical Dimensions of the Great Lakes Basin

Waterbody	*Drainage Area* (sq. km.)*	*Water Area (sq. km.)*	*Shoreline** Length (km.)*	*Water Volume (cu. km.)*
Lake Superior	127,700	82,100	4,380	12,100
St. Mary's River	2,600	230	397	
Lake Michigan	118,000	57,800	2,630	4,920
Lake Huron	131,300	59,600	6,160	3,540
St. Clair River	3,290	60	101	
Lake St. Clair	12,430	1,110	413	
Detroit River	2,230	100	212	
Lake Erie	58,800	25,700	1,400	484
Niagara River	3,370	60	171	
Lake Ontario	60,600	18,960	1,150	1,640
St. Lawrence†	7,190	610	1,050	
Total	527,510	246,330	18,064	22,684

**Drainage Area* includes small lakes and rivers in the basin.
***Shoreline Length* includes islands.
†St. Lawrence measured from the outlet of Lake Ontario to Cornwall, Ontario.

Shoreline Uses and Ownership of the Great Lakes

Use	*Total km. (Canada)*
Residential	2,032
Commercial	529
Agricultural & undeveloped	1,118
Forest	5,464
Recreation	574
Public buildings & related lands	159
Wetlands	238
Total	10,114
Ownership	
Federal	602
Prov. & Municipal	3,825
Private	5,687
Total	10,114

mately 110 metres, almost half of which (52 metres) occurs at Niagara Falls. Outflows vary from an average of 2,440 cubic metres per second for Lake Superior to more than twice that amount for Lake Ontario. These figures indicate that almost half of the water flowing into the St. Lawrence River once was in Lake Superior.

Three water diversions affect the Great Lakes. Lake Nipigon, which drains into Lake Superior near Thunder Bay, is bolstered by the Ogoki Diversion which redirects water from the upper Ogoki River that normally would flow into the Albany River and on to James Bay. This water contributes to hydro-electric production on the Nipigon River. The Long Lac Diversion brings about 4,377 square kilometres of Hudson Bay drainage basin water into Lake Superior near Terrace Bay. Together, these two diversions carry about 140 cubic metres of water per second, approximately equal to the portion of the consumptive use by humans that is taken from but not returned to the Great Lakes (about 95 per cent is returned). The third diversion is at Chicago, where 90 cubic metres per second are withdrawn for urban use and discharged into the Mississippi River system. These three diversions have little impact on water levels in the Great Lakes.

Two other diversions represent water taken out and put back in again: the Welland Canal takes and puts back up to 250 cubic metres per second, and the New York State Barge Canal takes and puts back about 30 cubic metres per second.

Dams regulate the outflows of Lake Superior at Sault Ste. Marie, and of Lake Ontario in the upper St. Lawrence River. The effect of these dams on water levels is minor because of the constraints imposed by the capacity of downstream river channels and downstream water uses.

Water levels are influenced, however, by changes in precipitation in the Great Lakes basin. Fluctuations are the norm, but a hundred years of data have turned up no cycles. Variations in water levels within years normally range about .3 metres for Lakes Superior, Michigan, and Huron, and .5 for Lakes Erie and Ontario. These within-year changes range from winter low levels to summer highs, and are caused primarily by differences in runoff. Runoff is greatest in the spring and early summer, and least in winter. Evaporation also has some effect, being least in spring when lakes are cold relative to air temperatures, and

Outflows from the Great Lakes

	Outflows (cubic metres per second)		*Outflows (cubic metres per second)*
Lake Superior		Lake Erie	
Average	2,120	Average	5,800
Maximum	3,600	Maximum	7,760
Minimum	1,160	Minimum	3,340
Range	2,440	Range	4,420
Lakes Michigan/Huron		Lake Ontario	
Average	5,150	Average	6,800
Maximum	6,570	Maximum	9,910
Minimum	3,000	Minimum	4,360
Range	3,570	Range	5,550

most in fall and early winter when water is warm relative to the air. In one month up to ten centimetres can be lost from lake surfaces through evaporation.

The most rapid influence on water levels is diurnal variation caused by wind. Blowing strongly and steadily from the same direction for a few hours, wind can pile water up at one end of the lake. Periodically, wind effects on Lake Erie are recorded that raise water over two metres in less than a day.

At the other extreme, *isostatic rebound*, the continuing vertical uplift of the Earth's surface that has been taking place ever since the removal of the tremendous weight of the glaciers, is very slow to have an effect on water levels. In the Great Lakes region, the land to the north and east is rising faster than the land to the south and west. Consequently, Lake Ontario's outlet is rising seventeen centimetres per century faster than the west end of the lake, tipping the water back and causing a slow increase in level at the west end.

Water currents in the Great Lakes are weak in comparison with those in oceans. Over most of the lakes they are less than 1.6 kilometres per hour. Average speeds near the surface are only about .3 kilometres per hour. Currents are generally weaker at depth than they are at the surface. Stronger currents develop where flow is constricted between bodies of water, such as in the Little Current channel separating the North Channel and Georgian Bay, in the Straits of Mackinac between Lakes Huron and Michigan, and at the mouth of the Niagara River.

With few exceptions, currents in the open lakes do not persist for long, but change direction with the wind, a force considerably more influential than that of flow-through in all the lakes except for Erie and Ontario. In those lakes, the forces are about equal. Shore currents particularly flow in the direction of the wind. Mid-lake flow in deep water is less influenced by wind and frequently meanders under the influence of the rotation of the Earth. Temperature differences also have an effect, both near shore and distant.

A water molecule entering upper Lake Superior as runoff in a stream or

Lake Huron coastline at Pinery Provincial Park. JOHN THEBERGE

river, or directly as rain or snow, may, someday, flow over the first dam on the St. Lawrence River, but there are many perils along the way. It may be lost from the Great Lakes by evaporation, or by seepage into ground water, or through the Chicago diversion. It may make short forays away into urban or industrial water supplies and be spewed back some days later. It may be held over many winters as ice. But barring any of these obstructions, the journey, end-to-end, through the Great Lakes will take approximately 329 years: 186 in Lake Superior, 111 in Lake Michigan, 22 in Lake Huron, 2½ in Lake Erie, and 7½ in Lake Ontario, based on the length of time that inflow must proceed to fill each water body.

If you can forget what is dissolved in the water, or how the native aquatic biota has been altered or destroyed; if you just watch three-metre-high waves come crashing into shore on a windy day, or run before them in a sailboat or cruiser, the Great Lakes are a still-superb natural wonder. Blue water meets blue sky. Whitecaps march across the seascape. Clouds build dimension to the watery horizon. Sunrises reflect brilliance across the waves, and the moon paints a strip of wrinkled light out from the marsh edge to open water. Gulls wheel, terns scold, and these inland seas still look good. Better, in fact, than they are.

Changes in Water Characteristics and Aquatic Life

John B. Theberge

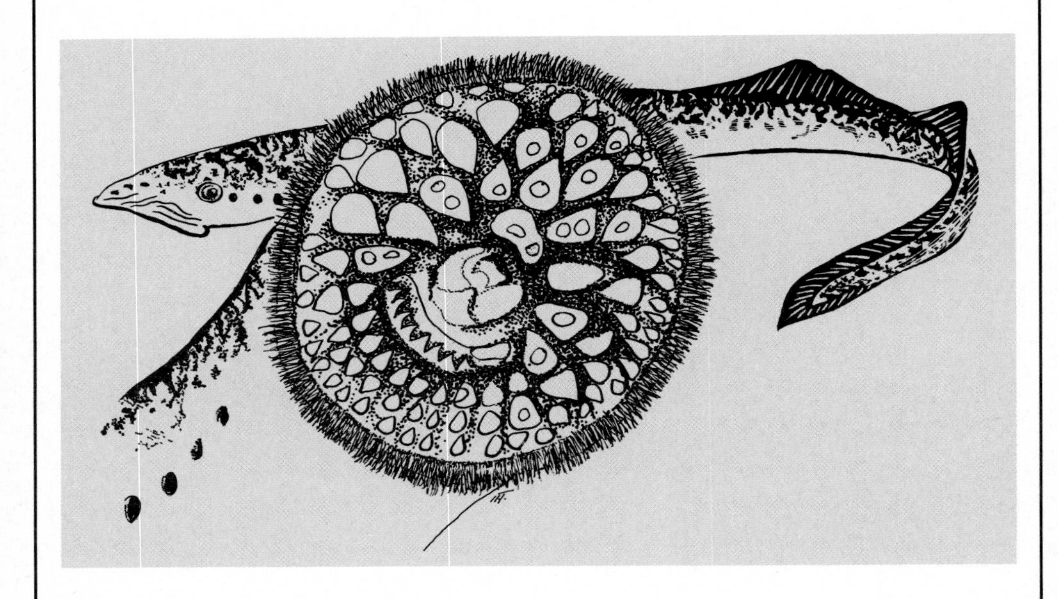

The Great Lakes have been called dying. Lake Erie has been pronounced dead. A magazine article recently referred to Lake Superior as "Lake Inferior." Government brochures advocate that we "Fish for the Fun of It," but warn against consuming our catch. Signs on beaches read "Polluted – Closed."

There is no doubt that the Great Lakes, as a naturally functioning aquatic ecological system, are in great trouble. Increasing concern is being expressed by people who drink water from them, especially downstream from the Niagara River. However, the journalistic terms *dying* and *dead* cannot accurately be applied to a lake such as Erie that may be more productive in biomass of living things today than ever before. While threatened by toxic chemicals that can extinguish life, the lakes have not died, and there is still hope that they never will. What has happened to them, however, over the last three hundred years of being surrounded by an increasingly industrial society, is great change – in water quality and in living things.

The complexity of a lake system as large as the Great Lakes guarantees that it will never be fully understood. While a scientific understanding of the lakes is paramount to detecting and interpreting environmental threats, perhaps the fact that we can never learn all has an important side benefit. A little mystery may breed humility, and humility may breed respect.

In water, a constant interplay goes on among temperature, dissolved salts, suspended solids, penetrating light, oxygen, nutrients, and living things. Temperature regimes in the Great Lakes have been influenced by increasing warmth from inflowing streams. Lake Erie has warmed by about 1°C in the last sixty years, an equivalent to being situated almost a hundred kilometres farther south.

Seasonal temperature patterns, however, remain much the same. Water temperature in winter is relatively uniform throughout the lakes at a few degrees above freezing. As the lakes slowly warm up in early spring, temperature layers form. This layering begins when shallow, near-shore water warms to 4°C, the temperature at which water reaches its maximum density (or weight) and sinks to form the bottom near-shore layer. As time passes and the lakes continue to warm, progressively warmer and less dense layers form above this first layer. Meanwhile, off-shore water, still below the temperature of maximum density, remains mixed. At the convergence of the mixed off-shore and layered near-shore water masses, a thin, vertical zone of maximum density, called a *thermal bar*, develops and separates them. This thermal bar migrates out into the lake as off-shore water gradually warms up too.

By June, the Great Lakes, with two exceptions, have warmed sufficiently to become stratified from shore to shore. The exceptions are deep parts of Lake Superior and all of Lake Erie, which is so shallow that wind action causes thorough mixing. The other lakes develop a wind-mixed, warm surface layer, and a deeper zone of rapid temperature drop called a *thermocline*. Below that a deep, cold, stable zone extends to the bottom. By September, cooling of the surface layer progressively destroys the summer temperature stratification down to the bottom, and complete mixing occurs once again. This annual thermal regime is very important to aquatic life; every organism must stay in environments that fall within its range of temperature tolerance.

Influencing the distribution of organisms, too, is the distribution of nutrients – the dissolved and suspended solids. These nutrients vary with both the geologic and the land-use characteristics around each lake. Basin geology differs from hard, igneous-metamorphic bedrock around the upper lakes to deep glacial till over a limestone-dominated bedrock around the lower lakes; land-use varies from largely forestry to agriculture and urban. As a result, Lake Superior contains only about thirty-five parts per million (ppm) salts whereas Lake Ontario contains five times that amount. Light sufficient for photosynthesis penetrates thirty-seven metres in off-shore Lake Superior, but only sixteen metres in Lake Ontario.

Few places in the world better illustrate a far-reaching chain of ecological effects on an environment caused by human activity than the Great Lakes. The interconnections between the physical features and living things are such that in the Great Lakes, when any one characteristic of water quality is altered, then change reverberates throughout the ecological system. At the base of the Great Lakes' food webs is *phytoplankton*. Once, the most abundant forms of phytoplankton in the Great Lakes were diatoms, tiny one-celled organisms with blobs of chlorophyl making them photosynthetic. Their welfare depended largely upon adequate supplies of phosphorus (often a limiting factor to plant growth in aquatic systems), usable forms of nitrogen, and a supply of silicon dioxide for cell walls. This high demand for silicon dioxide is unusual among phytoplankton, but it is what makes diatoms different.

Despite the abundance of diatoms, their populations were being limited by the availability of nutrients, especially phosphorus. Nutrients that enter the Great Lakes from inflowing streams do not circulate completely freely because of the vertical thermal bar which holds them in the near-shore environment in the spring, and thermal temperature stratification which prevents vertical mixing in summer.

Even with these natural constraints on nutrient distribution, however, the greatly increased phosphorus loading from inadequately treated sewage and runoff from fertilized fields eventually allowed diatom abundance to spiral upwards. But, the proliferating diatoms depleted the available silicon dioxide, as well as the available nitrogen, and further increase in their numbers was prevented. But then another algal group, the blue-green algae, found conditions just right. Blue-green algae are familiar to most people as the "seaweed" that washes up on beaches. The blue-green algae neither need large amounts of silicon dioxide nor suffer from low levels of nitrogen in water. They have the unique ability of being able to utilize (or fix) atmospheric nitrogen at the surface.

As the water surface of especially the lower Great Lakes became more densely covered with blue-green algae and the incidence of suspended solids from soil erosion and pollution increased, light penetration decreased, further reducing the numbers of diatoms. These changes also reduced the numbers of *zooplankton* that feed upon diatoms, while favouring other species of zooplankton that could feed in the surface layer on blue-green algae. This shift in zooplankton populations worked against deep-feeding species of fish: indigenous chubs, ciscoes, lake herring, and lake trout. It favoured the widely tolerant yellow perch and the exotic alewife, a marine species.

Alewives, like blue-green algae, are a nuisance; large, periodic die-offs leave them rotting on the beaches, often tangled in mats of algae, dual evidence of environmental mismanagement. At high population densities, alewives suffer mass mortality from cumulative stress.

The alewife always had a potential to populate the Great Lakes from the St. Lawrence River, but speculation is that the abundant and predatory Atlantic salmon kept it out. Atlantic salmon became extinct in Lake Ontario apparently because of increased water temperatures and dams across spawning streams.

The warming of tributary streams occurred because of forest removal too close to the banks. While this warming contributed to the demise of Atlantic salmon, it also helped a population explosion of invading sea lam-

Smelt washed ashore on a Lake Erie beach. POINT PELEE NATIONAL PARK

preys, whose larva are exacting in their requirements for warm stream conditions. This invasion, even more than that of the alewife, was aided by the building of the Erie Canal which unfortunately connected the lower lakes with a region of historic abundance for sea lampreys off the Atlantic coast. The sea lamprey was largely responsible for the destruction of lake trout populations first in Lake Ontario and later in all the other Great Lakes after the Welland Canal provided access above Niagara Falls.

And so, as a consequence of human impact, gone or almost gone are many species of fish from the Great Lakes. Replacing them are others. Gone with the original fish are the characteristics of water quality that supported them. Gone, too, is the original balance among different forms of phytoplankton and zooplankton. All this cannot soon – or likely ever – be restored.

More sobering than the knowledge of the ecological links and the losses, is the trajectory of events on the Great Lakes – the evidence of "just one problem after another." The first problems were relatively easy to combat. In the late 1950s, when the sea lamprey was levying its greatest impact on lake trout and lake whitefish, chemical treatment to control the larval stages in spawning streams helped reduce (but not eliminate) the threat.

Then followed a crisis of persistent pesticides such as DDT, which may have peaked in the mid 1960s with the near-decimation of fish-eating bald eagles and ospreys around the lower Great Lakes and mass mortality in many colonies of gulls and terns. Today, some, but not all, of the potentially dangerous pesticides have been banned.

Next came phosphate enrichment, which peaked in the early 1970s. That was truly frightening, because the consequence of phosphate enrichment was oxygen depletion, holding out the real spectre of death for all aquatic life and the terrestrial species that depended upon it. Parts of the western basin of Lake Erie really were dying. Regulations have since reduced phosphate use and improved its treatment at sewage plants, and the algal problem has begun to reverse. It certainly is not eliminated.

Now we are in a new era of concern over atmospheric acids and other contaminants such as toxic metals, PCB's, dioxin. . . .Several hundred different chemicals have been detected in the waters of the Great Lakes. Many are known mutagens; some are recognized human carcinogens; the majority have not been tested adequately to know what their effect may be, either singly or in combination synergistically.

Forty million people live in the Great Lakes basin, eight million of them in Canada. Thirty-seven million people drink Great Lakes water; others depend upon Great Lakes commerce, fisheries, shoreline management, recreation, and waterfowl. Degraded lake ecosystems do not support healthy biotic communities around them. It may be too late to bring back the diatoms and Atlantic salmon, but when the alewife and the blue-green algae go, then some future description of the ecological chain of events and devastating population changes in and around the Great Lakes could well include us.

Distintive Natural Habitats of the Great Lakes

Paul G. R. Smith

Life in and along the Great Lakes is rich in species, with representatives from far-away places: Carolinian, boreal, Arctic, Atlantic coast, and western montane. As well, a surprising number of unique species and subspecies have evolved along their shores and in their depths, considering the relatively short time since the last glaciation for speciation to occur. Most regions with such an assemblage of endemic species are geologically much older. For example, the Queen Charlotte Islands, touted as "Canada's Galapagos," escaped most of the great continental glaciers. Yet the unique Great Lakes habitats apparently created conditions of isolation which were conducive to the evolution of new biota.

Most mysterious of Great Lake habitats are their deep waters. Only in 1986 did humans, housed in a research submarine, first venture into the greatest depths of Lake Superior to study fish that dwell almost exclusively near the bottom: deepwater cisco, kiyi, bloater, and the now-extinct longjaw cisco. These unique Great Lakes species have remained virtually unknown except to some commercial fishermen and a handful of scientists. They, and other fish of the depths, exhibit adaptations similar to fish that live deep in oceans. For example, the bodies of siscowet, a variety of lake trout living below the 100-metre mark, may be up to 80 per cent fat!

Many "almost islands" lurk beneath the surface of the Great Lakes. For example, Superior Shoal, rising in the middle of the deepest one, is a series of steep underwater pinnacles and plateaux jutting up from the depths. These and other shoals provide vital spawning and nursery habitats for the predators, such as lake trout and lake whitefish, at the top of the lakes' food web.

There are 2,414 "real" islands on the Canadian side of the Great Lakes. Lake Huron has the most with 1,720, followed by Lake Superior with 615, Lake Ontario with 50, and Lake Erie with 29. (Lake Michigan is completely within the United States.) These islands owe their origins to a multitude of forces, but all bear the mark of the glaciers. The western Lake Erie archipelago is formed from two parallel limestone and dolomite ridges that peak barely above the surface of the lake. Gouges as deep as two metres, inflicted by the passage of the ice, are incised in this bedrock. In contrast, the igneous and metamorphic rocks of the Slate Islands of Lake Superior may represent the remnants of the central rebound cone of a meteorite crater. Yet these too bear the signature of glacier ice. Another consequence of glaciation is the relative youth of some of the Slate Islands. Because of slow isostatic rebound, some of them rose above the surface of the lake only about three thousand years ago.

Isolation tends to simplify island ecosystems by selectively eliminating certain species. This simplicity is a boon for some wildlife. The absence of predators attracts great multitudes of nesting herons, egrets, cormorants, gulls, and terns to islands, sometimes even when the islands are quite distant from prime feeding areas. With no wolves to check populations of caribou and beaver on the Slate Islands, their numbers vary widely and populations often become quite dense. Along the shores and shoals of the western Lake Erie islands, the Lake Erie water snake swims and hunts along the shallow bedrock shelves to which it is specifically adapted.

Some of the most diverse and productive biological communities of the Great Lakes thrive in protected warm-water bays, estuaries, and lagoons. Often such bays are soft-bottomed and fringed with wetlands. Warm-water fish – yellow perch, walleye, and pumpkinseed – abound. While coastal wetlands escape the full fury of the waves in protected locations, they do experience *seiches*, wind-driven fluctuations in water levels of up to one metre within one hour that are somewhat analogous to ocean tides. Also causing disturbance are the now infamous long-term cycles of high- and low-water levels. Because of these disturbances, coastal wetlands are in constant flux and undergo perpetual rejuvenation. Consequently marshes predominate, with few closed-in swamps or bogs. Wetlands along the Great Lakes shore often display a gradual zonation of vegetation which is seldom encountered in inland lakes. The drop in Great Lake levels from prehistoric highs has exposed coastal barriers, deltas, and natural levees as an unusual testament to the higher waters of the past.

Relentless erosion and subsequent redeposition of sand and sediment elsewhere has fashioned the numerous dunes, strands, and bars of the Great Lakes. Thousands of years ago, along what is now the southeast Lake Huron shore, glacial Lakes Algonquin and Nipissing gave rise to the topography of what is now Pinery Provincial Park. Today the Pinery's foredunes, its youngest dunes, rise only one metre high, while the dunes most distant from shore stand thirty metres. From the foredunes sprout sand cherry, little bluestem grass, puccoon, ground juniper, and balsam poplar. In places, the song of the prairie warbler creeps chromatically up the musical scale. The older dunes are blanketed with forests of oak and pine. Wedged between the dunes, wet meadows protect their own distinctive flora including blue hearts, one of Ontario's threatened plants, as well as grass pink and ladies'-tresses orchids.

The same forces that feed the spits, strands, and dunes have cut and sculptured many spectacular shorecliffs along the Great Lakes, like the Scarborough Bluffs near Toronto and the twenty-nine kilometres of cliffs north of Grand Bend. Other cliffs are made of rock, such as the dramatic Agawa Rock and the towering cliffs at Old Woman Bay on Lake Superior. These cliffs originated in volcanic upheavals followed by millions of years of erosion. A hard, igneous diabase cap on softer, more erodable rocks created the Sleeping Giant mesa towering 300 metres above the waters of Thunder Bay.

The harsh environments of Superior's cliff faces and barren shores harbour Arctic and alpine plants like encrusted saxifrage and the alpine woodsia fern. Ironically, on these cliffs, cold temperatures, fog, ice, and thin acid soils create an "oasis" for plants that are as much as eight hundred kilometres south of their normal range.

Probably few other natural habitats for fish and wildlife have been so transformed by human actions as have those of the Great Lakes. Prior to European contact, close to a million hectares of coastal wetlands lined the shores and teemed with wildlife: bitterns and rails, snakes and turtles, molluscs and crustaceans. The lake waters were free of pesticide residues, and lake trout, lake whitefish, and Atlantic salmon were the dominant fish, rather than alien alewives and smelt. Such pristine conditions can now only be remembered as part of the past. Yet many Great Lakes habitats remain of high ecological value; they must be staunchly defended by those who appreciate their importance.

Ice along Presqu'ile shoreline, Lake Ontario. LARRY LAMB

The Hardwood-Boreal Forest

John B. Theberge

North of Orillia, Peterborough, and Ottawa the southern fringe of the Canadian Shield stretches like a crumpled blanket over the land. It folds to the St. Lawrence and even across it at the Thousand Islands, but to lie so far south seems like a mistake. The Shield is Canada's northern reality.

Here, the forests, the bedrock, the whole mood of the country expresses the antithesis of the farmlands to the south. Here is the demarcation between foodlands and forest lands, between pastoral and wild, between perceived "south" and "north." Instead of patches of wild in a sea of farm fields, the scene shifts to patches of field in a sea of forest. And it happens suddenly. Where the Shield rocks finally slide under the Paleozoic sediments, the land immediately flattens, and soils are deep enough to cultivate. The ragged Shield country puts an end to the rectangular grid of straight concession roads and replaces them with narrow gravel trails which wind and dip and climb through the forest, exposing secret lakes nestled among the hills along the way, and pines, rocks, and water.

The Hardwood-Boreal Forest (grey).

The land is marginally higher up on the Canadian Shield, just enough to lower average temperatures and increase precipitation, especially on the Haliburton and Algonquin highlands. The deciduous trees of the northern hardwoods – silver maple, American beech, red oak, white ash, basswood, black cherry, yellow birch, red and sugar maple – feel the temperature difference and they drop out of the forest in about that sequence, south to north, from the north shore of Lake Huron to half-way up the east side of Lake Superior. Other species, such as striped and mountain maple, and white birch, push farther north, into the more typically boreal forest.

In this broad transitional belt, micro-climate sorts the tree species out. Cool air draining to the lowlands works against the hardwoods, and permits conifers to finger their way south from the boreal forest and grasp the land by the lake-edges, river-sides, and the bogs. So, on the lower slopes boreal-dwelling wildflowers such as tiny twinflower and shade-loving wood sorrel can meet hardwood-dwelling species such as starflower and foam flower.

Muskoka, Haliburton, and Parry Sound districts are full of holiday images for southern city dwellers: a white-throated sparrow's song drifting through an open cottage window at daybreak; loons yodelling back and forth in the darkness; an osprey quartering on the wind as it eagerly scans the water for a surface-feeding bass; a ruffed grouse bursting from a birch thicket in a swirl of newly fallen leaves; or a moose belly-deep in white pond lilies. Lazy summer days – deer flies buzzing and circling and looking for a place to land; a broadwing hawk screaming as it orbits a hardwood ridge; thunderheads building down the lake and lightning flashing, and

Paudash Lake, south of Bancroft.
LARRY LAMB

the next moment rain is lashing the forest. When it is over, in the evening calm, the pines drip, and a nighthawk flops across the sky. The campfire holds back the darkness, its smoke rising straight up, and the veeries pipe out the day.

These characteristic sights and sounds carry the melody and set the mood of the hardwood-boreal forests. But twice during the year-long performance, the harmony builds to a dazzling crescendo. The first of these occurs in late spring, as the migrant birds filter back to this prime nesting habitat. By early June the forest erupts in song. The habitat diversity: deciduous and coniferous, upland and lowland, lake and bog, is the reason these forests are preferred by so many species. Wood warblers, thrushes, sparrows, finches: the bird chorus here at dawn is unexcelled anywhere else in Canada.

The second crescendo is one of colour, not song. It, too, builds slowly. The maples under stress from disease or water shortage solo in early August, the hardwoods with more southern affinities strike up next, and then, as the first frosts rake the hills, the whole landscape crashes to a climax of colour.

Reds are more dominant here than in the farmlands to the south, primarily because red maples are more common. Even the sugar maples seem more orange, less yellow. But yellow is not forgotten; the trembling aspens and white birches splash it boldly about. Deep green is stroked in by hemlock ridges, scattered pines, and the spruce-dominated lowlands. Later in the season, when the brilliance fades from the hardwoods, then the tamaracks prolong autumn, shining in the bogs with a "smoky-gold."

Giving this land a sense of permanence and strength are the rocky cliffs rising from the water's edge, the rock cuts along the highways, and the smooth granite ridges etched with 9,000-year-old glacial scars. Shield rocks have endured for over a billion years. Grey granites, dark diabase, colourful banded gneisses – products of molten ages before life advanced beyond a single cell. Smoky quartz, rose quartz, ruby-coloured garnets, red jaspers: minerals concentrated in the fractures of ancient rocks, lying exposed now where they boldly criss-cross a rock face by the water, or hiding under a scattering of fallen leaves and bracken ferns.

Even in winter, stripped to a skeleton of life by dormancy, hibernation, and migration, and faded to monochromes of contrasting shadows, the beauty of the hardwood-boreal forests cannot be subdued. Although lashed by wind and snow, this is not a land of white-outs like the farmlands to the south, nor a land of austere, dark conifers like the boreal forests to the north. These mixed forests hold deep snows on the hardwood hills, where marten and fisher race on top of the crust, and hide in snow hollows in the coniferous lowlands, where snowshoe hares dance in the moonlight and red foxes embroider the edge of lakes with their tracks.

Seed, bud, egg, larva, and den carry life through winter's lock-up, and the first spring rains release the land. Icicles hanging from rock cliffs start to drip. Melt-water trickles in the depressions, gushes from the hillsides, and roars in the rivers. Dark patches blotch the lakes, then open water appears, and finally the ice goes out. Then the white-throats come back to the hill behind the cottage, and their song again drifts through the open window.

Acid rain and atmospheric pollutants, over-harvest and over-development can cheat nature of its riches and slowly undermine the wildness, abundance, and beauty of the hardwood-boreal forests. The rocks may be hard and enduring, but the living things on these thin soils are not. We can wipe the colour of autumn maples from the hills and silence the spring chorus of the amphibians and the music of the loons . . . unless we value them and manage this resource-rich land, this recreation land, with great care.

Manitoulin Island

Stewart Hilts

Manitoulin – home of the Great Spirit Manitou, island of rich natural beauty and diversity, land of forests and farms. Bordered on the north by the popular yachting waters of the North Channel, and on the south by the treacherous shoals and storms of Lake Huron, Manitoulin is an island of contrasts.

The heavily glaciated landscape leaps out at the perceptive eye. Scattered rocky outcroppings of limestone support mixed forests; rich soil deposits left by retreating ice and melt-waters support farmland. Hiding in the corners of this varied land are wildlife and plant treasures and quiet places where visitor and islander can experience a solitude with nature.

Today, visitors approach Manitoulin from both the south and the north, via the ferry from Tobermory past numerous islands, or via the highway from Espanola through the white quartzite of the LaCloche Mountains near Whitefish Falls. Too many tourists see little more than that, speeding on their way to other destinations, but islanders know the beauty and resources of the land, and botanists and geologists have been exploring Manitoulin for years.

The island consists of a giant slab of rock slanting upwards towards the northeast and downwards to the southwest where it disappears into the waters of Lake Huron. The rugged outcrops of rock which make up Manitoulin's north shore represent a continuation of the Niagara Escarpment, so well known on the mainland. From Manitoulin this scarp of Silurian and Ordovician limestones and shales arcs westward into Michigan, forming the northern edge of a giant geological bowl known as the Michigan Basin.

The glacial ice which scraped across this rocky land gouged a pattern of southwest-trending ridges and swales. Later, as the waters in the post-glacial Great Lakes slowly lowered, sediments were deposited in the valleys between rocky outcrops, leaving today's landscape as an alternating series of flat farming areas and rocky forested uplands.

The sinking levels of the glacial lakes preceding Lake Huron (known to geologists as Lakes Algoma, Stanley, Nipissing, and others), occasionally stabilized for periods of time, building up beaches of rock or sand. These ancient beaches are still plainly visible in places, for instance, on the slopes of McLean's Mountain, just south of the town of Little Current. The Nipissing shoreline, approximately four thousand years old, forms a distinct line about 1.6 kilometres inland from the present south shore and can be traced easily on air photos or followed by driving from Providence Bay west almost to Evansville.

Manitoulin once was connected to the Bruce Peninsula by dry land. Later, high water actually severed the island in three or four places; just west

View north from High Hill, Manitoulin Island. STEWART HILTS

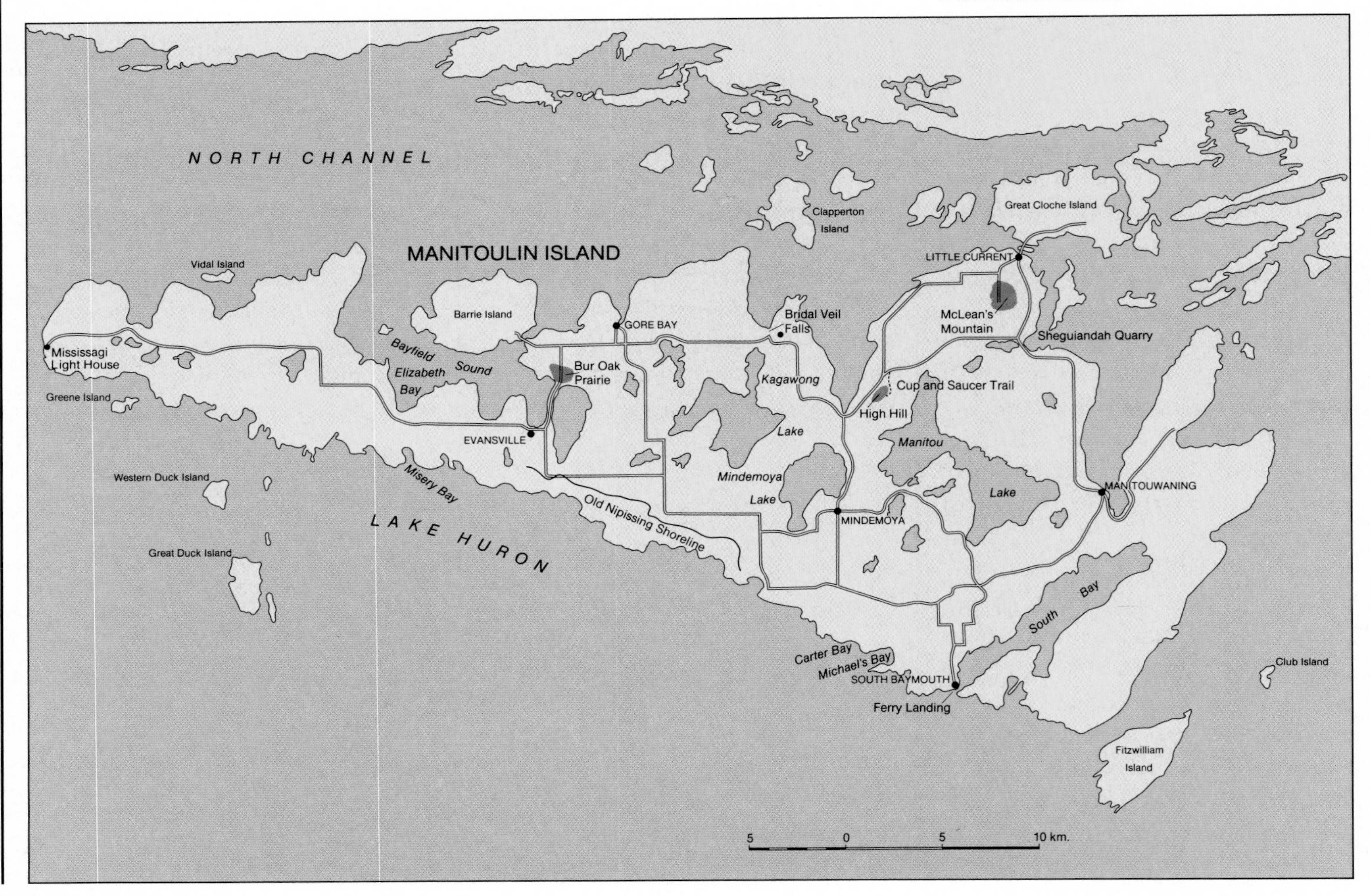

Manitoulin Island.

of Evansville through the Burpee Flats, for one, and at the narrowest point of Manitoulin from Elizabeth Bay through to Misery Bay for another.

More recent geological features also can be seen on today's shorelines. One of the most spectacular series of former storm beach ridges in Ontario south of Hudson Bay extends inland from Michael's Bay near the southeast corner of Manitoulin. Here, a prehistoric, deep, narrow bay was gradually filled in by a parallel series of sandbars built by storms. The bars rise only a metre or so above lake level, but trapped between them are wet sloughs of various depths. Starting from the lake shore one walks up over the wet sand beach and down into the ankle-deep water of the first slough, up a slightly inclined, cedar-covered ridge and down into a wide marsh, up again across another cedar ridge and down into a band of cattails, up over a dry sand ridge of white spruce and bracken fern and down into another slough, and so on. Even then the formation is difficult to picture from the ground and is best understood from the air.

Two of the oldest, least-disturbed sand dune complexes in North America are to be found on Great Duck Island, in the middle of Lake Huron south of the west end of Manitoulin. There a sand spit called Desert Point extends from the present water level back into forested dunes at the former Nipissing Lake level, and another set of dunes wraps around Horseshoe Bay. Back on Manitoulin itself, other dunes, now considerably disturbed by development, are found at Carter Bay just west of the town of South Bay Mouth.

Rock outcroppings, from gentle protrusions in the fields to massive cliffs, add great diversity to the landscape. Beautiful Bridal Veil Falls in the village of Kagawong is created by a ledge of limestone known as the Georgian Bay Formation. This fall is almost identical in form to another waterfall, Indian Falls, farther south on the mainland near Owen Sound. Manitoulin Island's most prominent outcrop of scarp-face, High Hill, can be reached along the Cup and Saucer Trail, a popular walk. From the top is a wide vista, encompassing most of the northeast quarter of the island. Little Current and Lake Manitou are close at hand, and on a clear day the white quartzite hills of Killarney Park, sixty kilometres away, can be picked out. If the wind is right one can also smell the distant pulp mill in Espanola!

Aerial photo of Michael's Bay on Manitoulin Island showing a remarkable series of storm beach ridges that have filled in much of the bay over time.

The Sheguiandah Quarry, a quartzite outcrop among the limestone, was quarried by native North Americans at least nine thousand years ago. Controversy has arisen among archaeologists over the antiquity of human activity here, since a number of artifacts appear to be mixed with or below the glacial till at the bottom of the quarry. Such a deep location could mean that the site was used prior to the last glaciation. If that is so, it would provide the oldest evidence of human occupation in Ontario.

Botanically, Manitoulin probably has been explored more thoroughly than any other equal-sized area in Ontario. Manitoulin's flora is remarkably varied, with Arctic, western, prairie, and maritime elements, as well as typical Great Lakes species. This variety has led in turn to a remarkable diversity of plant communities, from rich deciduous forests to sand dunes, from bog and fen to limestone alvar. Bur oak-prairie is one unique example, best seen along the main highway north of Lake Wolsey. Here, acres of extremely thin soils over limestone are covered with grass and scattered with oak trees. The sand-dune habitats have their own characteristic species, from sea-rocket on the exposed beaches to Kalm's lobelia, grass-of-Parnassus, and fringed gentian in the wet slack behind the dunes. One rarity found in these places is the Pitcher's thistle; it grows only on sand dunes around the Great Lakes and is nearly extinct farther south in Ontario.

Rocky shores provide colourful but extreme and relatively cold micro-habitats for plants. Arctic species grow here, such as the grasses *Poa alpina* and *Poa glauca*. The small quartzite outcrops on the island near Sheguiandah support their own flora. So do the rocky cliffs of the Niagara Escarpment, where ferns, such as both smooth and slender cliff-brake, are most notable. Growing on the boulders in shaded woods below the cliffs

Carter Bay dunes, Manitoulin Island.
STEWART HILTS

are common polypody and the rare walking fern.

Perhaps the island's most outstanding complex of plant communities is found on the south shore at Misery Bay. A large part of this bay area has been partly donated and partly sold to the provincial government for a nature reserve park. At the head of the bay is a fascinating wetland complex grading inland from shoreline marsh through fen to bog. Behind these wetlands extend dry sand ridges formed as concentric sand beaches by various higher lake levels. Flanking both sides of the bay are extensive limestone pavements consisting of flat expanses of calcareous rocks covered in places with prairie flora such as the vivid pink blazing star, the wispy prairie smoke, and the island's special rarity, the Manitoulin daisy or Manitoulin gold – a yellow, daisy-like flower that carpets the limestone in early spring.

Once, woodland caribou inhabited Manitoulin's forests. They disappeared – with the extensive forest cover – by the late nineteenth century. Replacing them were white-tailed deer, which are now plentiful and owe their abundance to the varied rural landscape of mixed and coniferous forests, especially on the west end of the island, and to the clearings and second growth provided by both farming and lumbering. In the early years of settlement, black bears and gray wolves lived on the island; bears are still found, but today the wolf has been replaced by the eastward-expanding coyote.

Manitoulin's bird populations are well known thanks to the efforts of a dedicated group of amateur ornithologists. Great Duck Island off the west end of Manitoulin acts as a major funnel for migration, similar to Point Pelee on Lake Erie. Thousands of birds have been sighted on this small island as they make their way north across the vastness of Lake Huron. However, the lighthouse and a 120-metre microwave tower on Great Duck have sometimes proved to be very hazardous obstructions for migrants.

The greater prairie chicken, like the woodland caribou, is gone from Manitoulin. Its tenure there was brief; it arrived as the result of range expansion in the late 1930s, and disappeared due to hybridization with resident sharp-tailed grouse in the early 1960s. Muted hybrid varieties survived until approximately 1970. Sharp-tailed grouse still can be seen occasionally on their spring dancing grounds, especially in the Billings Township area.

Today, the island's landscape tells of the struggles of the early settlers to wrest a living from the land, sometimes with success but often without. The good timber on the island all has been cut; all the land with agricultural potential has been cleared; rocks have been quarried wherever economically possible. What is left wild today is set in the context of attractive rural scenery and a strong cultural heritage. Historic sites such as the Mississagi Lighthouse and native sites such as the Ojibway Cultural Centre at West Bay broaden the attractiveness of the island. Even the place names reflect the mixed cultures of past and present, and portray a beauty and fascination all their own – Manitowaning, Mindemoya, Sheguiandah, Wikwemikong, Silver Water, Misery Bay.

Manitoulin, called in song "Ojibway paradise," is a mecca for botanists, geologists, ornithologists, and anyone attracted to the semi-wild, semi-tame, rugged yet pastoral beauty of farmland, rocky headland, sand dune, prairie, and forest.

The Brent Crater

Dan Strickland

Just inside the northern boundary of Algonquin Park, along the rough road leading to the tiny town of Brent on Cedar Lake, stands a wooden observation tower looking out over what appears to be a typical rolling Algonquin landscape. No one recognized anything special about this area until 1951 when a high-altitude aerial photograph revealed an astonishingly circular depression. The circle was some four kilometres wide, contained two lakes, and was surrounded by a ring of irregular, eroded hills.

The Brent Crater had been discovered. Because of its relative accessibility, it soon became one of the best known and most studied craters – holes blasted out of the Earth's surface by meteorites – in the world.

The crater was formed some 450 million years ago, and time has blurred many of its original sharp features. Nevertheless, scientists have managed to probe its hidden structure with twelve diamond-drill holes sunk at various places in and around its floor. The hole drilled at the crater's very centre was the most revealing. At the bottom, 1,065 metres below the present surface, the rock is quite similar to that found in surrounding parts of Algonquin Park. Above 930 metres, however, the rock is cracked and shattered. The cracking becomes more pronounced up to the 850-metre level where a 40-metre-deep "pool" of once-melted rock is found. The composition of this pool suggests that it was formed by the vaporization of the meteorite and much surrounding rock at the instant of impact. Above the melt zone and continuing up to the 260-metre-level is a layer of jumbled, broken rock believed to have originated from blasted fragments of local rock that fell back into the crater or slid in from the sides. Many of these fragments were badly deformed or even melted from the intense shock of the collision.

Most of the remaining rock that now fills the crater is sedimentary, laid down on the bottoms of seas that filled the crater at various later times. Ten different kinds of sedimentary rock have been found, including, at the deepest level, thin pans of gypsum. Similar layers of gypsum are created today in areas like the Persian Gulf where shallow salt lakes periodically dry up. Above the gypsum are layers of sandstone, suggesting that the crater wall was breached by a larger sea, or that the entire crater was submerged. Limestone beds higher up are interpreted as representing other shallow seas which periodically covered the crater floor. Because these rocks contain fossils of marine animals, scientists have concluded that the crater must be at least 450 million years old.

Today, the limestones and sandstones in the Brent Crater represent the only extensive area of sedimentary bedrock in Algonquin Park. Sedimentary rock undoubtedly was found elsewhere in the park area at one time, but it has almost entirely disappeared during millions of years of erosion and glaciation. The Brent Crater rocks have persisted, however, for two reasons. As the sedimentary layers accumulated in the depression, their weight compressed the thick layer of rock rubble below. Consequently the bottom of the shallow lake or sea occupying the crater gradually sank. The water occupied the crater for a long time, so that new sedimentary deposits were laid down on top of the earlier ones. As a result, the final accumulation of sedimentary rock inside the Brent Crater probably ended up being

Aerial photo of the Brent Crater, showing Gilmour and Tecumseh lakes (left and right centre) forming a horseshoe in the crater. At the bottom of the picture is Cedar Lake with a road running to the peninsula village of Brent. ALGONQUIN PARK MUSEUM

much thicker than that accumulated outside. A second reason for the persistence of the sandstone and limestone layers is that they were at the bottom of a deep, saucer-shaped basin of rock. There, "down in the hole," they were protected from the eroding effects of running water and ice.

Today, if you follow the interpretive trail from the observation tower near Brent down the now-gentle slopes of the crater wall to the present crater floor, you will see rocks and soil that are common in Algonquin Park – the usual assortment of sand, gravel, and boulders of granite. Nevertheless, evidence of limestone can be found on or just below the thin mantle of material left by the last glacier. And here and there, at the floor's circular edge, are rock outcrops consisting of rounded pieces of granite embedded in a matrix of softer rock – limestone formed when salt water lapped at the rounded rocks which had accumulated at the foot of the then-steep crater walls. On these rock outcrops grow little clusters of bulblet bladder fern, a lime-loving species found nowhere else in Algonquin Park.

Even more dramatic (though less visible) evidence of the limestone is found in the waters of Gilmour and Tecumseh lakes which lie on the crater floor. Of all the lakes in Algonquin, these two contain by far the highest concentration of bicarbonate, a substance derived from limestone which has a strong ability to neutralize acid. Most lakes in Algonquin, with their low amounts of bicarbonate, cope poorly with acid rain, but not Gilmour and Tecumseh. In fact, Gilmour Lake has such a high bicarbonate concentration that it is considered to be "totally insensitive" to acid rain.

This acid insensitivity and the presence of lime-loving ferns are present-day signs of the original meteorite impact. In contrast, the immediate effects of the collision, 450 million years ago, were less subtle. In less than one second, more than a billion tonnes of rock were vaporized, melted, or crushed and blasted into the atmosphere. A gaping hole was torn in the Earth – 4 kilometres wide, 600 metres deep, with a rim raised 100 metres above the original surface and sloping outwards from there. The force of the explosion is estimated at 250 megatons (equivalent to 250 million tons of TNT). The largest thermonuclear device ever detonated by man is about 60 megatons, and a 5-megaton bomb is quite sufficient to utterly obliterate any city on Earth. If the Brent Crater impact were to be repeated today, every tree in Algonquin Park and well beyond into Quebec would be flattened and buried by material ejected from the crater. Windows would be blown out in Ottawa, 225 kilometres away, and the buildings would sway and crack as an earthquake more powerful than any yet recorded rolled under the city.

Notwithstanding the extraordinary devastation unleashed in the creation of the Brent Crater, the meteorite that caused it was a rock perhaps only 150 metres in diameter. But it was travelling fast – possibly twenty kilometres or more per second. Even if it had merely overtaken the Earth in its orbit and fallen to the surface, rather than colliding with it head-on, it still would have been travelling at eleven kilometres per second upon impact. Marine trilobites, the most advanced creatures present on Earth at that time, would have had no inkling of what had hit them. Even an alert human, had one existed, would have heard nothing before the impact, and would have missed it by blinking.

Such catastrophic events are by no means unique in the history of the Earth. Over a hundred fossil meteorite craters have been found around the world, with fully twenty-four on the relatively small Canadian Shield. The rest of the world undoubtedly was hit just as often, but the hard, granitic bedrock of the Shield has preserved the evidence better than elsewhere. Evidence from the Moon, where erosion acts far more slowly to obliterate craters, also indicates that it and the Earth were subject to heavy bombardment by asteroids and other space "junk" early in their histories. Even today, with most of the hazards already removed in earlier collisions, the Earth may be hit by a meteorite large enough to form a crater roughly once in every ten thousand years.

The Brent Crater collision was not particularly large compared to others that have befallen the Earth. For years scientists have puzzled over the several sudden mass-extinctions of life that have taken place, including the most famous of all, the disappearance 65 million years ago of the dinosaurs and many other animals living then. Many theories have been proposed, but one now gathering particular support is that an enormous meteorite, possibly ten kilometres in diameter, was responsible. It may have been a stray asteroid orbitting the sun from the asteroid belt between Mars and Jupiter. Ten kilometres is more than the distance from sea level to the top of Mount Everest. If a "rock" that large hit the Earth at the minimum gravitationally generated speed of eleven kilometres per second, it would instantaneously blast out not just a little pothole like the Brent Crater but a cavity 30 kilometres deep and 100 kilometres wide.

If such an apocalyptic collision took place, it would have blown hundreds of billions of tonnes of dust into the upper atmosphere. From there, the choking pall would have spread around the globe, remaining airborne and blotting out the sun for months or even years. The Earth's temperatures, even in summer, would have plunged below freezing, just as modern computer simulations predict they would after an all-out nuclear war. Plants, except for some of their seeds or spores, would have died in the cold, dark world. Dinosaurs and other animals would have frozen or starved.

While no 65-million-year-old crater has been found to back up this theory, the impact could have occurred in an area now covered by water. The asteroid theory is supported by the presence of a thin layer of iridium-rich clay distributed in sedimentary rocks world-wide and aged at about 65 million years. Iridium is a rare element on Earth, but it has been found in high concentrations in meteorites.

Mammals filled the biological voids left after many large reptiles left the stage. If the dinosaurs had not been destroyed, it is doubtful that we or other modern mammals would have evolved as we have.

Likely the Earth will be struck again by an asteroid. More than a thousand asteroids over one thousand metres in diameter are now calculated to possess orbits intersecting that of the Earth. With enough time, one of them almost inevitably will hit the Earth. Will the damage be serious, like that thought to have been caused by the hypothetical meteorite 65 million years ago? Or will it be a mere "local" phenomenon, like the creation of the Brent Crater?

The Loring Deer Yard

John B. Theberge

Called the "Golden Valley" on the tourist brochures, a narrow swath of picturesque farmland runs back from Highway 522 at Trout Creek west 100 kilometres to the Parry Sound Highway. On air photos, the Golden Valley farmlands create a ragged strip of pastureland through rolling, forested hills of maple and birch on the uplands, spruce, tamarack, and balsam fir down low. The hills arch gently to form a landscape of rounded domes. Many of these domes to the south and west are either bald or sport brush-cuts of sapling forests, the combined results of glacial scouring and extensive logging. Scattered small lakes and beaver ponds dot the valley and lie cradled in the surrounding land.

In spring, the valley flushes a pastel yellow-green and pink as trees flower and buds open and the hayfields come to life; in summer, its greens deepen with hardwoods in full foliage; in fall, its forests flame with vibrant colour. Then the highway provides as colourful a drive as any in the province. In winter, deep snow buries the fence posts along the fields, blankets the spruces, and etches detail into the tapestry of limbs that seem thrown across the hardwood hills.

It is not its scenery, however, as beautiful as it is, that attracts attention to the valley. Nor is it the small towns of Golden Valley, Loring, Port Loring, or Arnstein. Its significance, from the standpoint of nature, is that here is Ontario's largest concentration of wintering white-tailed deer.

The Loring Valley deer yard is a region of about five hundred square kilometres centred on the villages of Golden Valley, Arnstein, and Loring. Throughout this region, the deer concentrate in winter in discontinuous pockets that shift somewhat from year to year. They come from great distances to this winter "yard," from as far as ninety, but on average about forty kilometres, as shown by a government study which involved radio collaring and tracking the deer. The migration in the direction of the yard starts as early as November, if snows begin to accumulate, or as late as January in late winters. On average, the deer are in the yard for sixteen weeks. They come from all directions, from a

summer range of about five thousand square kilometres, and they come in numbers. The lastest estimate – in 1986–87 – was between 12,000 and 15,000 deer!

Winter concentrations of deer are part of the species' response to the deep snow they encounter throughout Ontario, situated as it is on the northern edge of its range in eastern North America. When soft, uncrusted snow exceeds about fifty centimetres in depth, deer are forced to expend great energy to move. Partially crusted snow creates difficulties for them even if it is not as deep. Forced to live with a *negative energy balance* (less energy is obtained in food than is expended in staying alive), especially in mid to late winter, the deer must take measures to survive or face possible starvation. They begin to move in the direction of the traditional yards. Among the lowland conifers, snow is shallower and less wind-packed. Stands of eastern hemlock and white cedar provide the predominant cover in most of Ontario's winter deer yards. Both of these tree species hold snow off the ground, especially hemlock with its stretching, horizontal limbs and flat needles. In the Loring deer yard, spruce and balsam fir also provide important cover components. Food is packaged as twigs of red and sugar maple, basswood, aspen, cedar, dogwoods, yellow birch, and other preferred browse species. To reach the food, the deer make an extensive network of trails, each animal minimizing its energy expenditure. Here, with a combination of cover and food, they make their stand against winter.

The outcome of deer versus snow, even in the yards, is uncertain. A fawn of the previous spring weighing twenty-five to thirty-five kilograms requires about a bushel basket or more of browse each day. Browse can run out, and deer may be trapped in the yard by deep snow. Under these conditions, fawns and bucks that went into the winter with low fat reserves after the rut are the first to suffer. Deer are forced to browse less palatable and less nutritious tree species such as balsam fir, which is digested too slowly to be of much use. If the deer survive, nutritional stress may show in poor physical condition and, most importantly, in lower natality or weak and underweight fawns.

Winter deer yards are scattered across Ontario. In the agricultural south, deer may yard in remnant bogs or on the forested flood plains of river valleys or conifer woodlots. Farther north, the yards are more diffuse, spreading over lowland-dominated regions rather than specific sites. Some of the better known mid-Ontario yards are: Bonnechere-Round Lake on the southeast side of Algonquin Park, Cannoto Lake in eastern Ontario, the Peterborough Crown Game Preserve, the Minesing Swamp near Barrie, and Johnson's Harbour near the tip of the Bruce Peninsula. The latter yard, although relatively small (less than ten square kilometres) has been supporting about four thousand deer each winter – a high concentration.

But the sprawling Loring yard has the most deer. In the area of the yard, snowfall depths and winter severity tend to be low in contrast with the surrounding region. An abundance of south-facing slopes receive warmth from the winter sun. Active and abandoned farmland creates favourable field-forest edge conditions.

The annual migration of deer into the Loring deer yard, as dramatic as it

White-tailed deer in early winter. J. DAVID TAYLOR

is, cannot be classed as a wildlife spectacle. Some deer remain in the yard year-round. The rest take part in a subtle, seasonal shift over a large, forest-dominated environment. The summer deer concentration in this part of Ontario is not unusually high, especially compared with that in some southern townships and the southern edge of the Canadian Shield; the yard owes its importance to the large area it "drains." In some years, the areas of concentration shift, enlarge, or contract. The only evidence that the concentration takes place at all is occasional sightings of deer standing along the field edges, plenty of deer tracks on the trails, pawed-over windblown feeding sites in fast-frozen fields of alfalfa or clover, and chewed stems of favoured browse species.

In places, however, deer trails, browse, and droppings are so dense they create a forest "barnyard" effect. These places are at artificial feeding sites – hoppers placed in strategic places and filled with mixed grain, predominantly corn and oats. "Supplementary feeding" such as this may be part of the reason that the Loring deer yard has supported a high winter deer population, but mild winters and food plots where browse has been cut for deer also are important. Each winter, many tons of grain go into the hoppers. The practice is somewhat controversial; one study in the Loring yard showed that optimal diets were not being met as well with supplemental feeding as they were with natural browse, possibly because of competition at the food hoppers.

Deer were reported using the Loring area before artificial feeding or deliberate habitat improvement began, ever since the 1880s when logging and settlement inadvertently improved range conditions. A decline in numbers took place in the early 1930s, possibly due to severe weather, and again in the late 1950s. Habitat management began to bring deer numbers back up in the early 1960s. This work was initiated to counter the negative effects of forests which were maturing beyond the stage that provides good habitat for deer. Both fire control and reduced logging were contributing to the maturation of these forests. Much of this management has involved the co-operation of landowners, because 70 per cent of the yard is privately owned. Trees were cut and their tops left to provide food. Snowmobile and tractor trails were driven through the bush to facilitate deer movements. Restrictions were put on the cutting of hemlock, and thousands of hemlock seedlings were planted. Selective hunting to limit the human kill of antlerless deer has promoted a greater proportion of females and young in the population. And – in the most controversial measure of all – wolves have been killed annually since 1972 in a program initiated because of estimates that wolf predation killed a mere 2 or 3 per cent of the deer herd each winter. Between twelve and twenty-four wolves have been trapped, snared, or shot annually through a government-funded program. As a combined result of some or all of these measures, deer numbers have increased by at least five thousand animals over the last decade.

Because of these management interventions, the deer yard at Loring is not a true natural phenomenon. But neither are the ducks in a managed marsh, or the "farm game" exploiting much of southern Ontario, or the giant Canada geese and gulls congregating in a city, or birds around a backyard feeder. Ontario has the stamp of man all over it. The deer migrating to the Loring yard now represent a provincially significant wildlife event. Whether the management practices involved are socially acceptable or objectionable is a fair question, just as it is fair to periodically question and review all land management practices that influence wildlife. For now, however, the deer yard at Loring represents the largest concentration of white-tailed deer in the province.

The Slate Islands

Barry Snider

Away out in the midst of the roughest, open stretch of Lake Superior, eleven kilometres from the mainland, lie the incongruous Slate Islands – rugged beauty, splendid isolation, but incongruous because they emerge so abruptly from the depths, and because their ecosystems are so different from the mainland Superior shore.

The islands, eight in all, are small, totalling only thirty-six square kilometres. Most of that land is invested in only two of them, named Paterson and Mortimer, that form what looks almost like two halves of a clam, open at both ends, cupping a large, interior waterway perfectly protected from the wild Superior storms.

Cataclysm surrounded the birth of the Slates, regardless of which of two competing theories you accept. The large array of metamorphic rocks provides evidence of ancient pressures and violence. One theory proposes a volcanic origin; what we see today is the eroded stump of a volcanic cone. The occurrence of the island on a major fault line tends to support this theory. However, the possibility that the Slates were formed by a meteorite impact is even more widely accepted. In this case, what we see is the central rebound cone of the crater, formed in the instant of impact. The presence of shattercones provides evidence for this theory.

Forests of balsam fir and white birch cover most of the Slate Islands, typical in some ways of many stands growing on the mainland. However, most of the forests on the Slates are relatively young; those on the western half of the two large islands, for instance, are the result of wildfire at the end of the nineteenth century. And in these forests, unlike those on the mainland, shrub undergrowth is conspicuously lacking. As well, much of the replacement forest of saplings and seedlings is balsam fir, indicating a future shift away from the birch component. The reasons for this blend of typical and unusual reflects both natural and human influence.

Man has been on the Slates since the turn of the century, when prospectors searched for gold there. They found nothing, but left behind two adits still visible on the shore. Perhaps they lit the forest fires to better expose the bedrock. Lighthouse keepers have lived there, too. A story survives from the early days of lighthouse-keeping, of a Mrs. King and her two sons who capitalized on the extensive raspberries that grow in profusion on burnt-over land. They would row the eleven treacherous kilometres to the mainland and five more along the shore to the village of Jackfish, now long gone, to sell their raspberries to passengers on the CPR mainline trains.

Loggers too have visited the Slates. The history of logging along the north shore of Lake Superior has been relatively short, beginning only in the 1930s. The first forests to be cut were those growing along rivers flowing into Lake Superior or on the shoreline and islands of the lake itself. The eastern half of the Slates – the portion that had escaped fire at the end of the nineteenth century – was logged in

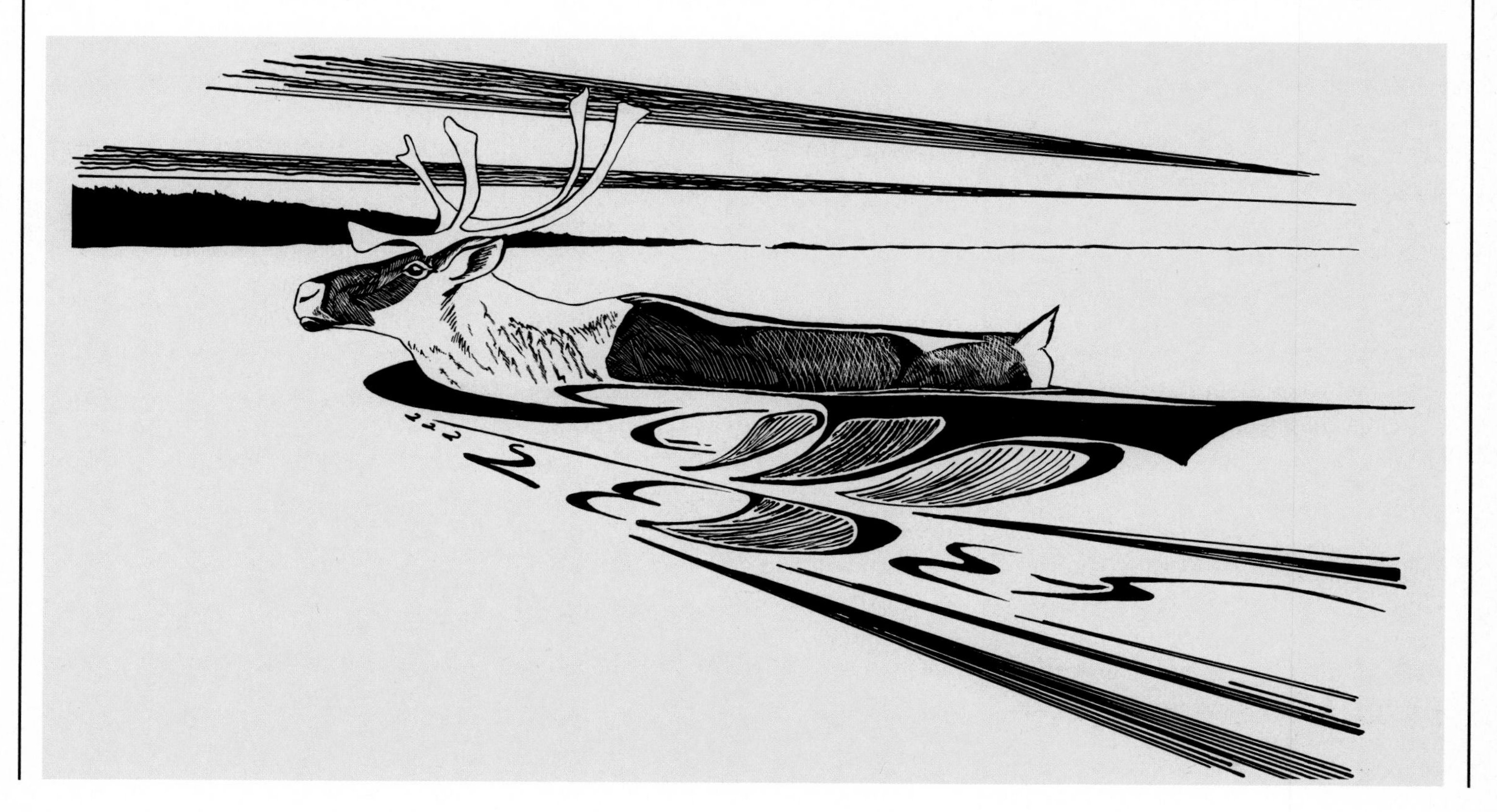

the thirties. Horses and men were barged over from the mainland, bunkhouses and barns were built, and the spruce and fir forests fell. Today, caribou crop the spring grasses in the clearings where the buildings once stood. Perhaps nutrients concentrated by horse dung still enrich the grasses, making these areas attractive for feeding.

When the saleable wood was all cut, the resident loggers left, but the bays of the islands were used to store pulp wood for years thereafter. The pulp logs were eventually picked up by ship and transported to the United States. This export of raw wood was stopped by the Ontario government in the late 1940s. All that is left of the log-storing days are the boom logs that enclosed the bays, and rusty logging chains lying along the shore. But on some nights a north breeze will carry a reminder that logging has not gone from the Superior country. A faint sulphurous odour is carried from the Terrace Bay pulp mill across the lake from the Slate Islands. The pulp mills along the north Superior shore were built as a result of the ban on wood export.

Even with these human impacts, the eleven kilometres of open water have had a greater effect on the wildlife of the Slates than has man. The water has served as a barrier to colonization by many species that live on the adjacent mainland. Conspicuously missing from the Slate Islands are moose and white-tailed deer, leaving woodland caribou, beaver, and snowshoe hare as the islands' three principal herbivores. Both deer and moose are found along portions of the Superior shoreline opposite the Slates, and moose, good swimmers, might be expected on the Slates, especially since they live in great numbers on a sister island in Lake Superior – Isle Royale – that lies about twenty-seven kilometres off the Sibley Peninsula. Missing, too, are most of the large predators: gray wolf, Canada lynx, black bear, marten, fisher, and striped skunk. However, red foxes are numerous and particularly friendly. Anyone who has travelled the edges of frozen lakes has probably seen fox tracks running delicately across the thinnest ice, a high-risk characteristic of foxes that undoubtedly allowed them to reach the Slate Islands. Beaver are plentiful, as are otters, but for aquatic mammals such as these the islands are not so isolated.

The caribou of the Slates have done exceedingly well in this predator-free environment. Caribou are relative newcomers; Dolf King, wintering at the Slate Island lighthouse with his family in 1907, saw caribou crossing on an ice bridge from the mainland. He is quite sure there were no caribou on the islands prior to this crossing. No earlier reports about the Slates mention caribou, but they frequently do after 1907. Caribou numbers rose to remain very high from at least the 1940s onward. On two occasions since 1974 they have exceeded six hundred animals to represent the densest population of caribou in North America!

Although free from predators, the caribou must meet the challenge of finding enough food. Because their winter diet of tree lichens is widely scattered, they travel mostly alone or in cow-calf pairs. Most of the slow-growing tree lichens within reach have been eaten, so now their main source of winter food consists of lichens blown off trees by winter storms. The fiercer the winter, the more food available for the caribou.

In spring and summer the caribou turn to the shoots of seedling shrubs and trees, and in so doing, have greatly modified the vegetation of the Slates. They have created an open understorey, considerably different from the usual thick undergrowth of the boreal forest. This open-forest feature and the abundant caribou trails makes walking for humans on the islands comparatively easy.

The size of this caribou population appears to be limited by periodic starvation. Poor nutrition also results in animals with small antlers; some of the males do not grow antlers at all. When winter nutrition is poor, fewer calves are born the next spring.

Beaver, like caribou, benefit from the absence of predators. Most of the inland waterways have been re-structured by their dams. Without predators, the beavers venture farther from the protection of their ponds and lakes while searching for their preferred foods – aspen and mountain maple. The beaver and caribou, together with a lack of recent fire, are altering the forest composition on the Slates. Because of beaver, the proportion of aspen and white birch is declining, especially near the waterways, and caribou reduce all deciduous seedling and sapling growth. With less competition than normal, balsam fir is increasing.

The Slate Islands attract many birds migrating out over the waters of Lake Superior, especially warblers and sparrows. Many warblers nest on the islands. In October, bald eagles migrate through; up to twenty of these birds have been observed at one time.

The protected waters around the Slates provide the last stronghold for original, native-stock lake trout in Lake Superior. Lower incidence of sea lampreys in this isolated location, and protection from commercial fishing since 1969, have helped the trout survive while stocks all around them have declined.

The Slate Islands became a provincial park in 1985 and are classed as a "natural environment park." When the lighthouse becomes fully automated, the last full-time human inhabitants of the islands will leave. Uncertainty exists, however, about the exclusion of future mineral exploration and mining, despite park status. As a one-of-a-kind natural treasure, the Slate Islands deserves to remain undisturbed – for the caribou to seek their tree lichens and the beaver to build their dams, and the forest systems to evolve under their unique, isolated conditions.

Ontario's Cape Cod: Misplaced Flora of the Atlantic Coast

Paul Keddy and Anita Payne

Many residents of southern Ontario think of the Muskoka-Parry Sound region as being typical of northern Ontario. While this perception is generally true – most of the flora and fauna are representative of the southern part of the Canadian Shield – there is a dramatic exception. Some lakeshores support a rich flora of species hundreds of kilometres away from their expected ranges along the Atlantic Coastal Plain.

The Atlantic Coastal Plain is a narrow band of relatively flat land sandwiched between the Appalachian Mountains and the Atlantic Ocean, and extending from Cape Cod to Georgia. Much of the plain is covered with extensive wetlands.

The first clue to the occurrence of these species in Ontario was the discovery of the showy, pink-flowered Virginia meadow beauty in Muskoka. Recent botanical exploration has since added nearly a dozen species with similar geographical distributions. The list includes Carolina yellow-eyed grass, screwstem, ridged yellow flax, and many other less obvious species such as the grasses *Panicum spretum* and *Panicum longifolium*, and sedges *Rhynchospora capitellata* and *Carex folliculata*. Undoubtedly, exciting new additions to this list still remain to be found.

Why do these southern plants occur within the northern hardwood and boreal transition region of Ontario, so far from other populations of their species? An explanation appears in the glacial history of eastern North America. During the melting of the last ice sheet approximately ten thousand years ago, the lower Great Lakes drained through the Mohawk Valley in what is now New York state, and out onto the Atlantic Coastal Plain. This drainage system provided a direct route for the gradual migration of plant species upstream from the coastal plain into the Great Lakes Basin. Later, when the area east of present-day Georgian Bay was covered by glacial Lake Algonquin, the larger forerunner of Lake Huron, its shores provided a series of sandy beaches and lagoons stretching north from Lake Simcoe almost to Lake Nipissing.

As the water levels of Lake Algonquin receded to those of present-day Lake Huron, they left behind them an extensive sand plain, stranded beaches, lagoons, and scattered lakes. Around these lakes the Atlantic Coastal Plain species have persisted right up to today. Thus, a map of an Atlantic Coastal Plain disjunct species such as Virginia meadow beauty shows a present-day distribution in Ontario largely restricted to the region between the old shores of Lake Algonquin and the present shores of Lake Huron. Similarly, other coastal plain species grow in other former shoreline areas: near southern Lake Michigan and in northwestern Wisconsin.

Although the receding waters of Lake Algonquin may have spread coastal plain species across this entire area, these plants have persisted only under specific sets of conditions, as discovered in studies of this unique flora conducted by the University of Ottawa. Coastal plain species are largely restricted to wave-washed sand and gravel shores of lakes with low alkalinity. Waves reduce both the nutrient content of the soil and competition from shrubs such as sweet gale that dominate the shoreline in sheltered bays, often growing right out into the water when the soil is nutrient-rich and physical disturbance from waves and ice is minimal. The herbaceous coastal plain species have little chance of competing for space under these conditions.

These species flourish, however, on lakeshores where water levels fluctu-

Lakeshore vegetation typical of sites where Atlantic Coastal Plain species survive in Ontario. Axe Lake, northwest of Huntsville. P. KEDDY

ate over a period of several years. During years when the water level is high, the encroaching shrubs are killed because they cannot tolerate prolonged flooding. A few coastal plain species are capable of growing while flooded, but a majority persist as buried seeds. Seeds may occur at densities approaching 30,000 per square metre – exceptionally high densities relative to many other natural plant communities. In years when water levels remain low, these seeds germinate, flower, produce seeds, and thus replenish the population of buried seeds to maintain the species when conditions are less favourable.

Under natural conditions, beaver often contribute to such a cycle of year-to-year fluctuations in small lakes. Their dams may maintain high water levels for several years until they break. The most outstanding example of beaver-controlled water-level fluctuations producing a rich coastal plain flora once occurred in Matchedash Lake (Long Lake) near Orillia. However, a dam was built to stabilize lake levels in the belief that this would improve fishing. This dam has reduced the numbers of rare plants and threatens those that still remain.

As this example shows, the principal threat to these species is indeed human alteration of shorelines. Although the Atlantic Coastal Plain disjuncts survived thousands of years of changing shoreline configurations, fluctuating water levels, and the combined effects of ice and waves, they are threatened today by dams, cottages, marina construction, trampling of shorelines, and clearance of "weeds." Such problems are exacerbated by the fact that both people and coastal plain plants prefer sandy shores.

Several of the best examples of coastal plain vegetation are informally designated as Areas of Natural and Scientific Interest (ANSI's) by the Ontario government, but at present, no examples of this unique flora in Ontario are fully protected.

Distribution of Virginia meadow beauty in Ontario. Solid dots are records since 1964; open dots are records between 1925 and 1949. The dashed line encloses the ancient shorelines of glacial Lake Algonquin. The solid line depicts the approximate southern limit of Precambrian Shield.

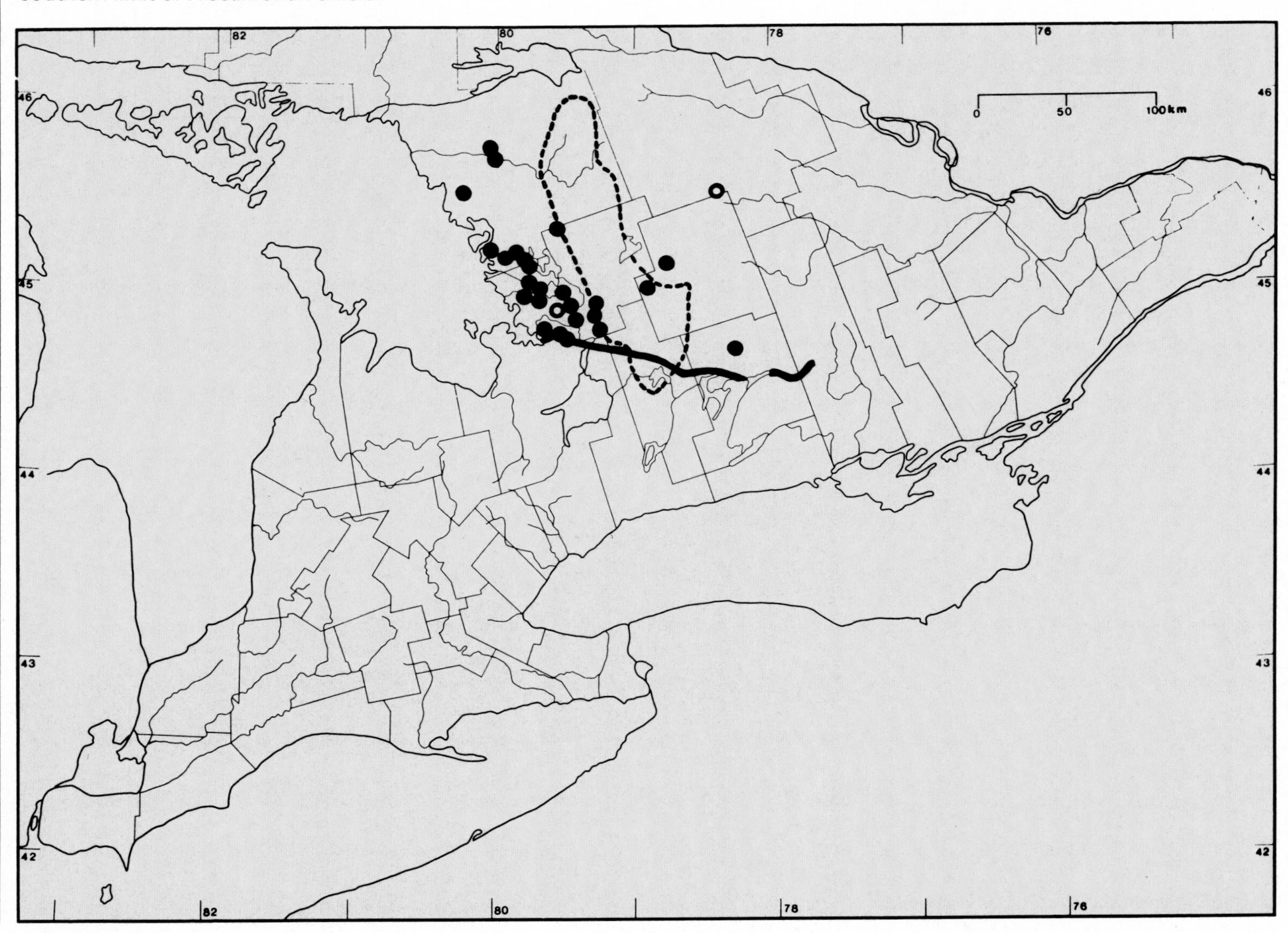

OPPOSITE
Virginia meadow beauty, an Atlantic coastal species in Ontario. M. J. SHARP

Night Sounds

John B. Theberge

It begins low and distant, barely audible over the gentle rustling of leaves. Then it lifts, clear and pure, rising in pitch, vibrating through the dark spruces, echoing off the black rocks across the lake. The howl of a wolf. No sound in nature evokes such immediate attention, from man and from all other forest creatures. Does our attention root itself in the distant past, the late Pliocene, when human and wolf competed for dominance on the savannahs of East Africa?

The pitch of the howl drops suddenly, mournfully, and holds a lower note. Then it drops again, gathering rich harmonic overtones from deep chest, thick neck, and wide muzzle. Slowly sliding down-scale, the attenuating sound doesn't end; it simply fades away into the leaf rustle where it began. Silence again grips the forest. But the mood of the night has changed from one of calm to one of expectancy. The wolf, master predator, is abroad.

Now, as the first traces of light etch the eastern horizon, in the distance an entire wolf pack raises its voice in chorus. The pups are there, yipping and yapping. High-voiced animals, low-voiced animals, howls weaving and braiding into one another, ravelling and unravelling, rising and falling, chord and discord. It sounds like a celebration, and quite often it is. Wolves often group-howl when hunters return to the pack. Their greeting ceremony is an expression of wild exuberance – animals jumping and milling around one another, tails flicking high in the air. They sniff each other's muzzles for the scent of food, to learn if the returning wolf has made a kill during the night. A group howl is spontaneous emotion for wolves, and for human listeners.

Wolf howls may be heard anywhere in Ontario's Canadian Shield country. Densities of wolves appear to be highest in the northern hardwood-boreal forest ecotone, where the major prey is both white-tailed deer and moose, and where prey numbers at times have been unusually high due to the effects of both logging and fire.

Individual wolf voices differ in resonance or harmonic overtones from one another, just as different human singing voices, or musical instruments do when playing the same note. Research has shown, too, that pack members have an uncanny ability to recognize individuals through very subtle differences in howl harmonics. Also encoded by a higher pitch of howl appears to be emotional excitement.

While the "language" of wolves is poorly understood, research has shown the benefits of howling. Single howls help mark pack territories, help pack members keep track of one other while out hunting, and appear to be an emotional response to separation that may express loneliness. Group howls seem to express pure merriment while at the same time strengthening social ties.

Wolves howl most frequently from mid summer to late fall, and whatever the howls mean to wolves, they mean excitement to many canoeists or backpackers who come out of the bush bursting with an account of the event. Few people who hear wolves would deny that the forest seems wilder because they are there. Wolves are symbols of retreating wilderness. But they are still persecuted in places in Ontario. If persecution is taken too far, if ever their howls no longer ring through the night forests, then the irreplaceable essence of wild will be gone, because wolf howls are a distillate of wilderness.

A distillate too is the cry of the common loon, its long drawn-out notes sometimes mistaken for those of wolves from a distance. But even this "wolf-imitation" loon call is distinctly different – more of a wail, a complaint. It is cold out there, and wet, and lonely. And then the loon entirely gives itself away with its bold, characteristic "laugh."

The calls of common loons have rebounded across Ontario's lakes, in non-glacial periods, ever since the Miocene, for the loon is a "primitive" bird. Loons wail, yodel, hoot, laugh, in all possible combinations, but the emotional connotations of these words are human, not loon. The "laughter" warns of danger; the yodel is territorial defence. Yodels differ among individuals and allow adjacent birds to recognize each other from visiting intruders.

Common loons, like wolves, are broadly scattered across the Canadian Shield. It seems that every lake supports its breeding loons, more than one pair on the sizeable ones. Ontario's Breeding Bird Atlas shows no really vacant regions in the species' distribution. But, ironically, just like wolves, their wide distribution does not assure that in future their calls will always carry across northern lakes. The fish eaten by loons, especially as they migrate, may be loaded with deadly chlorinated hydrocarbons. These chemical compounds are fat-soluble, and loons, more than most other birds, store large amounts of subcutaneous fat. Threatening too are the effects of dams that change water

Common loon in Quetico Provincial Park. SHAN WALSHE

levels and flood nests, and motorboats that create swells. Ontario lakes catering to intensive recreational boating have been correlated with low loon productivity. Loons normally lay only two eggs, so the margin for accidental mortality is slim.

But perhaps even more threatening to loons are the effects of acid rain. Studies in this province in 1982 showed that lakes classed as acidic produced only one-quarter the number of loon chicks as did those classed as non-acidic. Adult loons may return year after year to the same lake, breed, and lay eggs, only to watch their chicks die of apparent starvation. Lack of fish, however, is not the only danger caused by acidification of lakes. Acids can free metals from the soils of lake bottoms, and these metals in the water may either kill fish or be passed on to fish-eating birds. Aluminium and mercury are two metals with high toxicity at low concentrations. The loons lose either way.

But for now, and, we can only hope for always, the calls of loons are characteristic of cottage country and beyond in Ontario, part of the feeling of "getting away," part of the purity of the wild.

No night sounds really compete in volume or emotion with those of wolves and loons, but the spring frogs try. They do it not singly but *en masse*, and indeed for a time they make all of Ontario's forests ring. Some, like the spring peepers and wood frogs, announce spring; others, like the green and mink frogs, announce summer. All Ontario species announce their tie to water for egg-laying, and so proclaim their evolutionary antiquity, and proudly declare that "primitive" does not mean "unsuccessful." They were calling long before man took form, even before mammals arrived, and they just might outlive us.

Once again the leaves rustle from a gentle night breeze. A current of warm air slips up the ridge and sets the white pines to whispering. The stars are bright overhead: Big Dipper, North Star, Cassiopeia, the Summer Triangle. And again, a single wolf howl floats on the air. This time it disturbs a white-throated sparrow. The white-throat pipes its crystal notes in full voice – but it cuts them short near the end. The middle of the night is the wrong time to sing. An ovenbird might awaken and give a weak imitation of its daytime song. Why wolf howls, and sometimes loon calls, occasionally stimulate white-throats and, less often, ovenbirds to sing is entirely unknown.

From the pines on the ridge, a barred owl calls, repeating its fast, hollow "song" twice. Barred owls and great horned owls also often respond to wolves. After calling a few more times, and stimulating no other owls, the barred owl falls silent again. Midsummer is long past the breeding season. There is no purpose to calling now.

There is purpose for owls to call in very early spring. Owls are among the first birds to nest. In late February and early March, great horned owls construct their nests high in the limbs of bare maples, or take over a squirrel's nest which has survived from the previous summer. Great horned owls stake their large territories by calling back and forth at one another. Individual birds usually differ in the pitch of their hoots.

Screech owls nest early, too, and repeat their rising and falling tremulous whinny over and over in the darkness. They intermingle this call with a series of soft "tuks." Other owls are heard less commonly – a long series of low whistles from a saw-whet owl, or the soft hoots of a long-eared owl.

These are the dominant night sounds in the northern hardwoods. In spring, American woodcocks add their nasal "beeps," and sometimes on warm nights ruffed grouse drum periodically all through the night. A flock of Canada geese may call in the moonlight, first from a distance, then overhead, and finally from a distance again, their music fading as they fly on to the Hudson Bay Lowlands to nest. A whip-poor-will lashes out its song over and over again, oblivious that such loud, prolonged vocalization is out of character with other, softer night sounds – the hum of mosquitoes or the splash of trout jumping at a hatch of insects on the lake. In fall, on crisp, clear, starlit nights, the tiny "peeps" of hundreds of migrant songbirds passing overhead speak of the winter silence soon to be left behind. The only night sounds in that season's gripping cold will be the occasional rifle-shot crack of trees as their trunks split from the frost.

The night sounds tell of territorial defence, of hunting and hiding, and of intense activity going on throughout the forests each night – all invisible to the human eye. The soft sounds whisper in the dark; the loud ones destroy, defy, render apart, and punctuate the silence. Together they add an auditory dimension to darkness.

Forest Jewels

John B. Theberge

Each spring they star in a pageantry of colour. They dangle like bright ornaments from the limbs of the trees. They flit through the greening canopy in such abundance that the forest seems to move. They evoke exclamations of wonder as they flash through cottage or campground clearing. They fill the northern forest with song.

These are the forest jewels – bright, singing fragments of life collected from tropical wintering grounds, filtered up the Mississippi and Atlantic flyways, and scattered across central and northern Ontario in multitudinous abundance. Many spill out along the way onto the southern forests: some yellow warblers, black-throated greens, ovenbirds. Most species, however, fly on to nest eventually across the Canadian Shield, especially in the northeastern forests where hardwoods and conifers intermingle. These mixed forests are the most richly bejeweled of all.

Fifty-three species nest in North America (with some disagreement over the validity of hybrid "species"), and of these, thirty-four nest in Ontario. North American warblers were classified as a distinct family of birds until 1983 when a revision in taxonomy moved them to sub-family status. However, they have no completely similar European counterpart. In North America, where they apparently evolved, they present a triumph of speciation and a marvel of evolutionary divergence from a common theme. The species differ only slightly from one another in the size or shape of either body or bill. These characteristics often distinguish between species in other families, such as woodpeckers and finches. However, while warbler sizes are similar, their breeding plumage and song represent lavish variety.

The majority of Ontario's nesting warbler species, about two-thirds, co-inhabit and breed in the same geographical area, from the southern edge of the Canadian Shield to mid-way up the east side of Lake Superior. Some, blackpoll and orange-crowned for instance, fly on to the pure boreal forest, but most live together among the trees in these mixed forests. They dip and dive, searching for foliage-eating invertebrates, picking off insects on the wing, hunting down larva, cocoon, and caterpillar. Each species has its own habitat, for the most part, and plays its own role within it. While some overlap occurs among niches, differences are sufficient to prevent undue competition among species.

Some species, such as the bay-breasted warbler, the brown-faced Cape May warbler, and the fiery-orange-throated Blackburnian warbler, are conifer specialists. Among the conifers the Cape Mays and Blackburnians nest high, while the bay-breasteds nest only about five metres from the ground. Blackburnians stay high to feed as well as nest, but Cape Mays will descend to within about seven metres of the ground. Thus, the habitat is roughly partitioned.

Two other species, the yellow-rumped and the black-throated green warblers, are common in the conifers as well, but they are habitat generalists that also nest in the hardwood forests. While they feed at variable heights, they prefer the outer, sunny branches. Competition between them is partly reduced because they reach peak numbers in different forest types: the yellow-rumped in the boreal, and the black-throated green in the hardwoods. Similar habitat separation typifies warblers in each of hardwood, shrub, and wetland environments.

Black-throated green warbler. POINT PELEE NATIONAL PARK, J. R. GRAHAM

American redstart. POINT PELEE NATIONAL PARK, J. R. GRAHAM

Blackburnian warbler. POINT PELEE NATIONAL PARK, J. R. GRAHAM

Cape May warbler. POINT PELEE NATIONAL PARK, J. R. GRAHAM

Brewster's warbler, a rare hybrid of two southern species: golden-winged and blue-winged warblers. ROBERT MCCAW

How they all managed to evolve, to "speciate," is fodder for scientific speculation. At one time, only a decade ago, textbooks explained that geographical isolation was necessary to split a parent stock. However, many species now are suspected to have evolved without geographical isolation, on the periphery of their ranges or even in the midst of prime range. This speciation may take place if social relationships cause a tendency for more inbreeding than outbreeding. The warblers, however, demonstrate no social organization or even kin-grouping on their nesting grounds. They are territorial and aggressive to all members of their species except their own mates.

We in Ontario have a biased view of warbler ecology based on their three or four months of residency here. The warblers are really birds of the tropics, where they spend the six or seven months of the year between fall and spring migrations. Only recently has research begun to unravel their relationships "at home" in the tropics.

At home, warblers must crowd into the southern United States, Mexico, Central America, and very northern South America, an area less than half the size of their breeding range. How they accomplish this involves an even greater triumph of niche-specialization than their behaviour on the nesting grounds, especially because they must fit in with a rich variety of other non-migratory, resident species of warblers. The potential for competition is severe. But, just as on the nesting grounds, various species occupy different geographical areas. For example, Cape May warblers winter mainly in the West Indies, while chestnut-sided warblers winter in Panama and Central America. As well, in mountainous regions some species occupy different altitudes: in southern Mexico, for example, black-throated greens are a highland species, Wilson's, magnolia, and yellow-rumped warblers are found somewhat lower down, and lower still are the yellow warblers and American redstarts. Then, there is habitat specificity: pine-inhabiting black-throated greens, broadleaf-inhabiting Wilson's, thicket-dwelling hoodeds, scattered-forest-dwelling northern parulas. As a final means of separation, some feed high in the trees – black-throated greens; some feed in outer foliage of trees and saplings – Nashvilles; some feed in undergrowth – Wilson's; and some forage in valley-floor shrubbery – yellows. Habitat preferences on the wintering ranges bear little similarity to those on the breeding ranges.

In the tropical summer, few of the resident, non-migratory species of warblers widen their niches after the migratory species have left, which reduces competition when the migrants return. However, the fact that competition between residents and migrants has influenced the evolution of habitat specificity is evident from the distribution of these two groups across the total winter range. More individuals and species of migrant warblers winter in the northern than the southern part of warbler winter range. Farther south, there are more resident species. Thus, competition between these two groups is reduced.

Unfortunately, all is not well for the jewels of the forest on their winter range. The rate at which the tropical forests are being felled poses a serious threat, especially in highland areas being converted to agriculture. If present rates continue, specialists in tropical ornithology predict major reductions in many species by the end of this century. These specialists make the point, too, that displaced birds cannot just go elsewhere because other winter ranges are saturated. Every spring now, birdwatchers, sensing fewer warblers migrating through southern Ontario, have to ask each other, "Have the warblers just overflown this area because of good weather for migration, or is a decline really beginning to occur?"

The threat to the warblers lies not only in the tropics but in Ontario as well. In the past, chemical insecticides sprayed over vast forested regions to control spruce budworm and other forest pests have certainly not benefited the warblers, nor are we considering them today as we attempt biological control by spraying a Bacillus bacteria. The Bacillus is not host-specific. It kills all foliage-eating invertebrates, the total diet of all warblers as well as of many other birds.

Warbler song is so much a part of spring in Ontario that it is impossible to imagine a June day in the hardwood-boreal forests without it. None of the forest jewels are melodious like the thrushes. None really warble, like some finches. Yet warbler song is distinctively warbler. Closely related species of warblers sing songs of similar quality. The black-throated blue and black-throated green, very different looking birds except for their black throats, both have a similar lispy, seedy, rapid "zee-zee-zee" call that includes a faint echo, as if the bird needs to clear its throat. Tennessee warblers sing a staccato "tizip-tizip," often in a three-part rendition, while Nashville warblers give a two-part and softer variation on the same theme. Catchy phrases in the bird books help us to remember similar songs – "I wish to see Miss Beecher," of the chestnut-sided warbler, and "Sweet, sweet, sweet, I'm so sweet," of the yellow warbler.

From daybreak until the breeze begins to rustle the leaves about nine A.M., the dawn symphony is a celebration of song unequalled in any other Canadian biome. The melody is carried by the violin-like hermit thrushes, the veeries, and the flute-like white-throats. Winter wrens, song sparrows, orioles, and grosbeaks alternate with virtuoso performances, and flickers and pileated woodpeckers beat out the percussion. But through it all, tying it all together, giving it emphasis, harmony, richness, and depth, weaves the chorus of the forest jewels.

Singing Wings

John B. Theberge

It is dusk, down where the wet meadow grasses flattened from last winter's snow meet the alder thicket. The evening is calm, but expectant. Winter is over; it is that time of year just before the release of bud, shoot, leaf, and bird song. The cool air settling over the wet fields smells like spring – wet earth, wet grasses, moulding leaves. In the distance the redwings call among last year's brown cattails, and the spring peepers tune up for their night's chorus. A pair of wood ducks comes dodging down into a net of bare silver maple limbs to splash-land in the swamp.

Then, when the setting has achieved just the right backlighting from the western sky, and the peepers lull for a moment, the time is right for the American woodcock to begin the warm-up exercises that precede its dazzling courtship flight. From the edge of the alder thicket where it has spent the day, it gives its first nasal "beep." For a shorebird like a woodcock, this call is unusual; while the shorebirds do give a variety of raucous calls, none are so bold and unmusical as this "beep."

As the light fades still further, accentuating the difference between eastern and western sky, the "beeps" come more frequently, with intervals between them of only a few seconds. The bird may be visible to a discerning eye – larger than a robin, predominantly brown, with black and white striping over the back of the head, and with overly large and slightly bulging eyes. Now it is out in the short grasses, turning this way and that between "beeps." Each "beep" is preceded by a barely audible "hiccup," whose function is unknown.

By this time, Venus is visible in the western sky, but the stars have not yet emerged that form Orion's Belt and

Taurus the Bull with its "red giant" for an eye. A few wood frogs have joined the spring peepers, quacking more like ducks than frogs. The honking of Canada geese drifts in from the distance. At last, the woodcock is ready. Its "beeps" speed up. Suddenly it bursts into the air. On about a forty-five-degree trajectory, it quickly gains altitude. The wind whistles through its wings in a pulsing tremolo of sound. Up and up the woodcock flies, visible at first against the western sky, but then fading into the east, its singing wings the only evidence that it is up there.

Now the singing loses its pulsing constancy and comes in volleys as the bird flies with short burst of wing movement. The woodcock is visible for a moment, high up in the sky, flying in tighter and tighter circles, spiralling on up to almost ninety metres. Anticipation that something more is about to happen builds as the volleys become more rapid. Then, from on high, the woodcock sprinkles a musical jumble of twittering notes down on its listeners, including a female woodcock somewhere on the edge of the thicket.

The American woodcock, at the peak of its performance and the summit of its upward spiral, is doing what relatively few birds do – singing in flight. Bobolinks do it while flying over a hayfield, just before landing on a fence wire. Rose-breasted grosbeaks and northern orioles sometimes get half their song out before they land. Some other shorebird songs, such as the wheezy call of the upland sandpiper and the wild notes of the golden plover, are given on the wing. Many birds utter alarm notes while flying. But the woodcock, using its song only at the climax of its courtship flight, outperforms them all.

Abruptly the song ends, right in the middle of a phrase. At the same instant, the wings stop singing. Now the woodcock is plummeting almost straight down from the sky. As it crosses the western horizon it is visible again, coming in with last-second flopping from side to side to check its speed. With a final flutter it lands, often in almost the same spot of damp meadow where it took off about sixty seconds earlier. In a few more seconds, a "hiccup-beep" reveals its exact location near the alders. Another long series of "beeps" builds again until the bird's excitement seems to spill over into another flight.

Other woodcocks are displaying, too, their singing wings and twittering songs flavouring the approaching night with woodcock music. More stars are lit now, and the night air is a few degrees cooler. A rising moon might silhouette a spiraling bird for an instant. Somewhere, off in the deeper woods, a bittern begins to pump.

The woodcock is able to "sing" with its wings because its three outer wing feathers are remarkably stiffened and narrowed to pencil-thinness. When these feathers are spread apart during flight, the air rushing through them causes them to vibrate with a high, whistling sound. This sound, combined with the woodcock's song at the height of its spiral helps to advertise the bird's presence. Some ducks, especially common bufflehead, and doves such as the mourning dove, have similar modifications on their wings to produce a whistling sound, but no other bird uses this adaptation in such a spectacular flight display.

A woodcock's "beep" is individually recognizable, each bird having its own distinctive frequency at the beginning, middle, and end of each "beep," and its own total number of pulses and duration, but only a sound spectrogram – or a woodcock's ear – can identify these characteristics. The birds call from the ground, most commonly near the centre of their territory. Territories may range from less than one to more than forty hectares, although the area actually defended is normally less than three hectares. The rate of calling may be as rapid as every two seconds just before flight.

Woodcocks are specialist-feeders on earthworms, which they pursue with their long, flexible beaks. Remarkably, the distal portion of the upper mandible can be lifted to grasp a worm or other prey without opening the entire beak. They are specialists, too, in requiring open habitats surrounded by scrub or second growth forests. When trees grow over three metres high and cover more than about 60 per cent of an area, the land grows woodcocks no more.

Closely related to the woodcock is the common snipe. Often on soft, spring evenings, when the woodcocks are performing, snipes may be as well. Snipe feathers whistle too, as the bird swoops through the sky, but it is their outer tail feathers that create the sound. The snipe's courtship flight is more horizontal than the woodcock's, attaining only about fifty metres. The bird circles, generally around its territory, and then begins a forty-five-degree-angle dive with its tail fanned. During the dive, the outer tail feathers vibrate, but this soft whistle is repeatedly broken by the wings interrupting the wind flow, modulating the sound into a hollow tremolo.

The similarities in display of snipe and woodcock may reflect the common origins of these closely related species in the distant past. But the woodcock wins the contest for artistic design. Its "sky dance" is an annual spring ritual across southern Ontario and less commonly across the central part of the province. One outstanding place to watch it is at Algonquin Park's airfield beside the Mew Lake campground along Highway 60. But nobody need travel far. In countless wet thickets, from late April until mid May, the woodcocks, with their singing wings and spray of aerial song, weave together winter and spring, day and night, wet field and forest, land and sky.

Bat Roosts

M. Brock Fenton

Everyone knows that bats live in caves or old buildings. This is an example of a widely accepted but only partially accurate "truth," as only a minority of the world's eight hundred and fifty or so species of bats, and only two of Ontario's nine species, commonly roost in such places. In Ontario, red bats and hoary bats roost in trees, usually hanging alone in the foliage. Silver-haired bats also are called "tree bats," but they take refuge under pieces of bark or in abandoned woodpecker holes. Small-footed bats, northern long-eared bats, and eastern pipistrelles rarely roost in buildings, and we know little about their "normal" hang-outs. The two species which commonly roost in buildings are the little brown bat and the big brown bat, the most abundant species in the province. The ninth species, the evening bat, has been recorded only once in Ontario, probably an accidental occurrence. Farther south, however, evening bats also roost in houses.

Understanding why bats roost where they do requires knowing something about the roles roosts serve in their lives, as well as something about bat physiology. Some bats, including the ones which occur in Ontario (all members of the family Vespertilionidae) have variable thermostats. They may choose to maintain their body temperatures at high levels, around 40°C, or they may let them follow the ambient temperature down to freezing and become torpid. This approach to temperature control has an important ecological side-effect, because it influences their seasonal choice of roosts to allow bats to save fuel.

Five of Ontario's species of bats

Big brown bat. DON GUNN

solve the winter shortage of food that faces any insectivorous animal by allowing their temperatures to drop and hibernating locally. Only red bats, hoary bats, and silver-haired bats avoid the problem by migrating to warmer climates. Most bats that hibernate in Ontario appear to use caves and old mines, underground sites that provide stable, above-freezing temperatures throughout the winter. Periodically, hibernating bats rouse and move about. Arousal is the most expensive part of hibernation, for the bat must internally generate enough heat to raise its body temperature from the ambient (say 3°C) to about 40°C. Because hibernating bats will arouse in response to changes in external conditions, such as warmth or cold, the sites they select for hibernation must have a relatively steady temperature all winter. Hibernating bats also arouse in response to internal stimuli about which we know virtually nothing. Big brown bats may hibernate inside buildings as well as underground, apparently using sites within the walls, reflecting a greater tolerance to lower temperatures and drier conditions than the other species.

The problems facing bats in summer are different from those they face in winter. The summer bat's problem is heat, either too much of it when flying, or not enough, when roosting. The variable thermostat and appropriate roosts help bats to deal with the problem. During the summer in Ontario, bats do not roost by day in caves and old mines because the stable, cool temperatures there make these sites too energetically expensive. A bat trying to roost in such places would either spend a huge amount of energy keeping warm, or need a completely dependable alarm system to trigger arousal when it was time to go out and feed.

Using tiny radio transmitters with pulse rates determined by temperature, we have found that in attic roosts some big brown bats keep their body temperatures above the ambient. Others allowed their body temperatures to cool down to ambient and become torpid. The strategy an individual uses depends, in part, upon the prevailing air temperature; on May evenings when air is around 10 °C, many bats do not bother to leave their roosts. Bats and entomologists know that at 10°C there are few flying insects about.

Even on warmer nights in June, with temperatures up to around 15°C, some bats still were in torpor, apparently because still relatively few insects were flying. However, other bats maintained body temperatures of about 25°C. Active animals were usually lactating females; the torpid ones were males or females that were nonreproductive, pregnant, or post-lactating. Clearly, it is more important for a lactating female to feed her young than it is to enter torpor and save energy.

Radio transmitters have greatly helped those who study bats to progress beyond the elementary questions. Now it is easier to find roosts by following individuals, and to study the bats while they are feeding. But, the answers to some questions only pose others. For example, radio-tracking has shown that colonies of big brown bats are more than mere aggregations formed because of limited roosting opportunities. A study of a population near Ottawa showed that the individuals forming the colony behaved as a social unit. When colonies of big brown bats were evicted from buildings, they moved *en masse* to alternative sites. Furthermore, groups of bats that roosted in one building rarely mixed with individuals from other colony sites. The challenge now is to find out the nature and basis of the units.

Furthermore, although big brown bats roosting in buildings predictably returned to the same roosts day after day, those roosting in trees unpredictably switched from site to site. Some biologists traditionally have interpreted roost-switching as a mechanism to thwart predators. While this explanation is appealing, we have found no evidence of predation, and only further study will clarify the reasons.

Thus, roosts are vital resources for bats, providing appropriate microclimates that reflect current energetic needs and security. With such variability in roost sites, bats can be described as opportunists. Not only do they quickly locate and exploit new roosting opportunities, but they dependably return to the same sites year after year. For instance, in August 1985 I found some little brown bats roosting under rocks along a lakeshore in Quetico Provincial Park. The bats revealed themselves by squawking at my approach. Accumulations of droppings under the rocks suggested regular use. In other parts of the world some species with flattened skulls and wart-like protuberances on their wings roost only under rocks.

Because any roost with suitable conditions may be used by bats such as big browns and little browns, people often find bats sharing their houses with them. The resulting conflict often leads to persecution of the bats. Although many people find bats frightening, myths about them being dangerous or acting as carriers for rabies have no basis in fact. When you remember that each bat eats half its body weight in insects each night it is active, their potential as agents for biological control may exceed the nuisance they represent as opportunistic tenants. The erratic and graceful flight of a bat across the evening sky always draws exclamations and is a characteristic delight of city, farmland, and cottage country.

The Boreal Forest

John B. Theberge

Sprawled across two million square miles, the boreal forest is the dominant forest reality of North America. Rooted in the boreal forest is the "up north" mystique of wilderness. Its vastness – from Labrador to the western mountains – and its sense of permanence help to moderate our anxiety over man's destruction of wildlands. Green forests in summer, green forests in winter, none of the ephemeral pastels of the hardwood forests in spring or their brief flaming autumnal reds and oranges. While agriculture and urbanization have transformed the south, the boreal forest has survived.

It conjures up images: moose wading belly-deep in yellow pond lilies, iron-coloured water foaming over rocks, and shadowy bogs where the heaths bloom – bog laurel, leatherleaf, and scented sweet gale. We think of blackflies, campfires, a canoe drawn up at the head of a portage, wolf tracks on wet sand, a lake trout breaking a calm surface to snap at a mayfly, the whir of a spruce grouse...more blackflies.

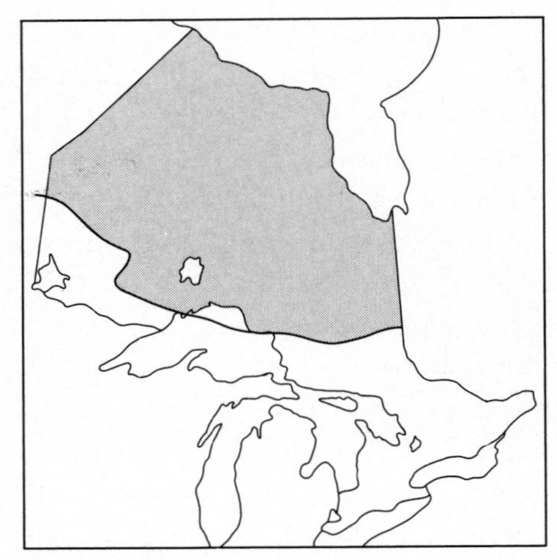

Boreal Forest (grey).

The boreal forest has stripped away the superfluous, the weak, the animals and plants adapted to softer southern climates. Rid of the sugar maples, beeches, oaks, and yellow birches, its simplified communities march north across a subdued topography – the butts of ancient mountains. At its northern edge it hands on to the tundra only the hardiest of species: a few widely adapted willows, bog laurel, bearberry, Labrador tea. Scattered, slanted tamaracks, spruces, and trembling aspens pick their way northward up sheltered valleys, searching for the deep soils where lower permafrost may permit tree growth. But eventually even they can grow no farther. Woodland caribou wander here, their minds focused on sedges and lichens, always alert for wolves. At the edge of the tundra, hundreds of willow ptarmigan flock each winter.

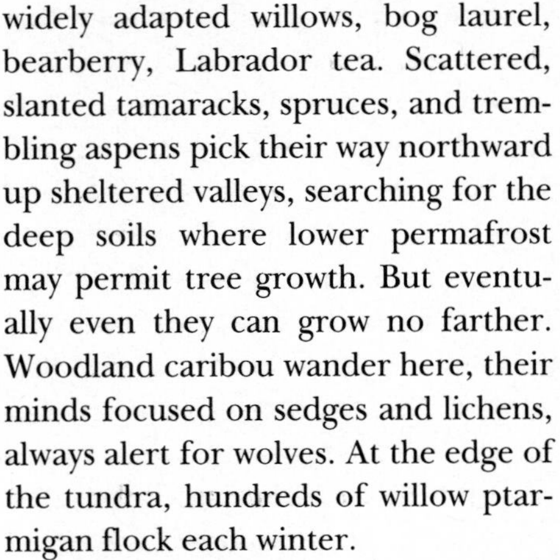

The boreal forest is the post-glacial progenitor of three-dimensional ecosystems, with crown and canopy and the feeble upward reach of biomass towards photosynthesis-driving sunlight. The consequent rich variability in microclimate and microhabitat provides niches for more species than does the tundra. Spruce cones feed crossbills, siskins, red squirrels; tree cavities provide nest sites for great gray, boreal, and hawk owls.

Life is snow-adapted in the boreal forests. The down-sloping spruce limbs shed snow, unlike the uplifted ones of white or red pines farther south. Young aspens and birches bend with the weight of their winter burden. Mammals are either subnivean, adapted like white-footed mice to live under the snow, or have big feet to stay on top, or they hibernate. Moose seek out the denser coniferous stands, preferably close to burns where they can forage for the twigs of young poplar or beaked hazel. The only birds left are seed- or bud-eaters, or predators on dormant insects in tree bark or crevices, or species uniquely adapted to live from food stored in caches. Gray jays spend all summer storing food within their territories to exploit later.

As the sun gains heat and the days lengthen, the snow crusts by night and melts by day. This is the critical time for those many species that have lived all winter in a negative energy-balance and whose fat reserves are now near depletion. "Late winter mortality" often levels any potential population gains of moose, ptarmigan, grouse, and hare. But the increasing heat eventually unlocks the land. Photosynthesis renews, and the energy pathways swell. Woodland caribou and moose seek island calving sites where they gain some protection from wolves. The waterfowl and the migrant songbirds return. The great ecological machine of the boreal forest swings into high gear.

Tested throughout the Pleistocene when it was pushed farther south by the glaciers, tested circumpolar, the boreal forest *seems* permanent. Like all ecosystems, however, it has its vulnerabilities. Its lichens are susceptible to sulphur borne by air pollution; its lakes, low in buffering calcium or magnesium carbonates, fall victim easily to acid rain. Forests many not regenerate for two hundred years after cutting. Chlorinated hydrocarbons concentrated in fat deposits may silence the echo of loons on northern lakes. Prejudice may kill the wolves.

The rewards for the boreal forest naturalist are to discover tiny twinflower growing among the mosses under the spruce trees, or a showy lady's-slipper orchid. These are not rare plants, but typical and beautiful. There are few real concentrations of wildlife in the boreal forest to draw tourists from afar, yet a mass of ten or twenty tiger swallowtail butterflies quivering on the wet sand can be observed on the shore at any northern lake. So can a flock of teal, flashing their powder-blue wings in unison. A lone osprey or a loon needs no magnification of its beauty by numbers, and both are found throughout the boreal zone.

JENNY THEBERGE

Few of the vignettes to follow have specific locations. They describe features of boreal forest ecology. You may experience, or see the evidence of these features on any trail, beside any lake, or down in any bog.

JOHN THEBERGE

Avian Seedeaters

John B. Theberge

Were it not for seeds, few birds could survive winter in the boreal forest. No bright white-winged crossbills hanging upside down like parakeets from hemlock limbs. No wild gangs of pine siskins or redpolls dipping in undulating flight over the spruce-spires. No chattering pine grosbeaks to break the stillness or defy the wind.

Seeds are concentrated energy, carbohydrate packages that make the energy gained in consuming them worth more than the energy spent in finding them and breaking them open. Only buds, berries, and seeds manage to package up the carbohydrates. The rest of the vegetation that sticks above the snow – branches, twigs, needles – is too energy-poor to support the high metabolic demands of the passerine birds.

Why the seedeaters of the boreal forest are among our most brightly coloured birds is unknown. Curiously, all of them display either reds or yellows. Evening grosbeaks combine bright yellow bodies with sharply-contrasting black and white on their wings and tail. And pine siskins, dullest of all the winter finches, nonetheless display flashes of yellow when they fly. Red clothes both species of crossbills, purple finches, most of the bodies of male pine grosbeaks, and the caps of both species of redpolls. Taken in aggregate, the flashes of finch colour amid a monochromatic winter landscape, their conspicuous flight, their call notes, and their chatter are an important part of the wildness of winter in the boreal forest.

To live there, these species have had to adapt both to exploiting seeds and to reducing competition among each other. In the boreal forest, few seeds of deciduous trees are available in winter. The small, persistent cones of yellow birch shed their trident-shaped seeds throughout the winter. Speckled alders that etch the river banks with tints of grey clutch their tiny seeds in cones that do not open until the following spring. In the swamps, the keys of black ash hang on all summer, but fall to the ground early in the winter.

A richer fare is laid out by the cones of the conifers, though not as rich as one would expect. Balsam fir casts off seeds and scales from cones in the autumn, leaving nothing for the winter finches. Jack pine cones are too tough to open. White spruce cones ripen in early winter, as do white and red pine, but when their downward-pointing cones open, many seeds fall to the ground to be buried in the snow. Hemlock cones open throughout fall and winter but their cones point downward too, so seeds immediately fall to the ground. Besides, eastern hemlocks barely reach north into the boreal forest. Most tamarack cones open in the autumn, and while the seeds may lie cupped between the scales, wind soon disperses them. Thus, the winter finches must rely to a large extent upon the immature seeds from white pines, whose cones do not ripen for two years, or from black spruce, whose cones do not open until spring.

The cone specialists are crossbills, whose lower and upper mandible tips cross each other, forcing an opening wedge between cone scales as the bill closes. A modified tongue procures the seed from beneath the cone scales. Although a clever evolutionary contrivance, the bill and tongue of the crossbill are not essential for the full exploitation of cones. Pine siskins, with their more standard bills, apparently do just as well. And the crossbills have paid a price for their unique bill; they cannot feed easily on seeds of grasses or weeds because their bills cannot grasp. They have become specialists, able to extract alder seeds as well as the conifers, but little else. When the unpredictable cone crops fail in the boreal forest, as they sometimes do, crossbills must move south to exploit seeds of hemlocks, exotic Norway spruces, and a few species of deciduous trees and shrubs.

The bills of both pine and evening grosbeaks substitute mass for dexterity. Pine grosbeaks use their broad, thick bills to break up conifer cones, but strangely, evening grosbeaks, with nearly identical bills, do not. Both grosbeaks supplement the seeds of conifers with the berries of mountain ash, a resource that often remains on the tree all winter. Evening grosbeaks also heavily exploit the seeds of Manitoba maple in southern Ontario and sunflower seeds at bird feeders. Evening grosbeaks are recent migrants into Ontario, expanding their range from western coniferous forests and first found nesting in the province at Lake of the Woods in 1920.

The smaller finches, often found together in mixed flocks, adorn the forest openings where grasses and goldenrods stick above the snow, or they flutter in waves from alder thicket to alder thicket, or hang from the lacy crowns of yellow birches. Among these species, purple finches search more diligently than the others for mountain ash berries. Pine siskins periodically flock from the alders to the spruces, whose cones they also know how to open. Redpolls with scarlet caps pulled down over their foreheads flit to the cedars to pull apart the small cones, then back to the alders to join the siskins.

When spring comes, the avian seedeaters of the boreal forest will be swamped numerically by the migrants from the south. The flood of crossbill notes will be submerged under the crescendo of song from white-throats and winter wrens. But winter will come again; the land will once more be stripped to its survival-core, and the seedeaters will re-emerge, far-flung sparks of intense life scattered across a dormant snow-filled land.

Bogs and Beaver Ponds

John B. Theberge

Bogs, fens, beaver ponds, and beaver meadows punctuate the uniformity of the boreal forest with exclamation marks of life. They are the showpieces, scattered gems set in a vast forest crown. They are the pulsing, throbbing, precious distillate of diversity.

Life settles out into the lowlands because water is more permanent here and microclimate and vegetation more variable. More species of animals find more of their life requirements, and so the commerce of nature is most intense: birth, death, growth, decay, graze, browse, hide, stalk, kill. Species that live in these special places are not much different in Ontario's portion of the boreal forest than elsewhere, but Ontario's share is an important central portion of this biome that stretches clear across Canada, and typifies, more than any other, the Canadian wilderness.

In some places, bogs and fens are small, discrete, and easily recognizeable from the surrounding terrain. In other places they form a vast semi-dry landscape popularly known by the Indian term *muskeg*. Huge fens extend over much of the Hudson Bay Lowlands. Both types of wetlands result from impeded drainage which creates waterlogged soils and accumulations of peat. Peat consists of undecomposed or partially decomposed vegetation. It forms because decomposition is very slow under standing or slow-moving, oxygen-deficient water.

Most remarkable about these lowland places is the far-reaching influence of pH levels, or levels of acidity. A bog is acid, the result of completely blocked drainage. A bog may form in a depression in either bedrock or hard-pan clay soil where the only input of water is from precipitation, and the only output is evaporation from the surface or evapotranspiration by aquatic plants. As a consequence of the blocked drainage, peat accumulates. Acid-loving sphagnum mosses invade and not only flourish, but increase the acidity. Both sphagnum and peat produce humic acids by absorbing bases; these acids do not flush away.

In contrast, a fen is more alkaline. Water seeps slowly through fens, either from surface flow or from ground-water movement. Consequently, acids are flushed out.

The difference in pH level between a bog and a fen has a profound effect on vegetation. The acid-adapted heath family thrives in bogs: Labrador tea with its sprays of white flowers, pale and sheep laurels with their showy cup-shaped pink blooms, and shy bog cranberry creeping across the sphagnum mat. Certain species of sedges, rushes, and other plants such as swamp loosestrife and buckbean flourish in these acid conditions, too. However, fens are invaded by base-loving willows, dwarf birches that grow to about head height, grasses, cattails, and different species of sedges.

Whole books have been written about the ecology of bogs and fens, and relationships are complex enough to assure that more books will be written. Not only does pH level affect plants in these wetlands, but nutrients do too, especially nitrogen, phosphorus, and potassium. Despite the relatively high productivity of bogs and fens compared with that of the surrounding boreal forest, plant growth in them is actually limited by low nutrient availability. Nutrient cycles are in low gear because most of the nutrients are tied up in the peat. Bogs are most affected due to the relatively small amounts of nutrients brought in by rain or snow compared with the greater inputs into fens from surface or ground-water.

Both bogs and fens, like other wetlands, are cool environments, especially on calm nights. Cold air drains into the lowlands. That is why bogs located south into the hardwood forests are typically surrounded by boreal species of trees such as black and white spruce and tamarack.

Time works a slow, magical transformation in the peatlands. It moulds and shapes them as it can no other environment. It inexorably transforms some of them from open lake to dry land. Others, it is content to build and destroy by permitting plant succession for a while, then flooding them back to an earlier stage, as if discontent with what it has made. Still others it converts to "floating bogs," or "raised bogs," or "string bogs" – the variations with water, pH levels, and nutrients are almost unlimited. In all its experiments, Time works with shallow, impounded water where no wave action will disrupt its creativity, and with seed and rootstock of submerged aquatic plants, emergent plants which root themselves underwater, floating plants, a variety of different water-logged or wet-soil adapted shrubs and trees, and with the patience of millennia.

Cross-section showing cellular structure of a leaf strand of sphagnum moss.

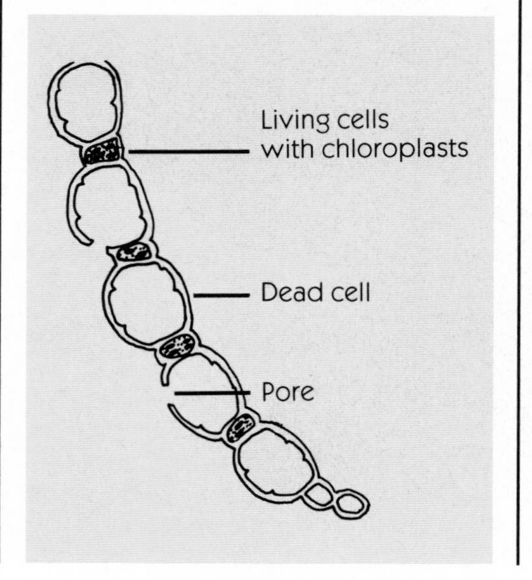

Across a physical spectrum, from shore to open water, Time plants the various species, each according to its needs, with the care of a backyard gardener: speckled alder, balsam fir, black spruce, and red maple where the edges of the peatland rise to "dry" land; leatherleaf to scent the air with its white, bell-like flowers, Labrador tea, stunted spruces, and tamarack out a little farther; sphagnum to creep from under the shrubs and dominate still farther from shore; and pioneering buckbean and sedges to grow to the edge of the open water, to float on the surface, and to reach with long rhizoids down into the organic soup on the bottom, or back shoreward to find a toe-hold on the sphagnum.

Decade after decade this plant succession – trees to sedges – slips outward, like a shutter closing over a stopped-down lens aperture of open water. All these plants, when they die, bequeath their remains to the organic soup – the slow accumulation of peat – and hence to the filling of the wetland. Eventually, if not set back by flood or drainage, the shutter will draw completely closed.

After that, Time may build a "raised bog," like a giant, inverted saucer. Sphagnum mosses are largely responsible for raised bog formation, as indeed they are for much of bog succession. The sphagnum family differs from other mosses by being greatly absorbent. A spongy leaf structure results from many large, perforated, water-absorbing, dead cells which are interwoven among live epitheleal cells. As a result, generations of sphagnums can grow on top of previous ones, watered from below by an upward-drawn, elevated water table. When older sphagnum, buried by new generations of sphagnum, dies to become peat, it retains this water-absorbing characteristic. Because the closed-over lake is deepest at the centre, sphagnum peat accumulation, and hence potential height, is greatest there. Thus the raised bog phenomenon.

Also contributing to the inverted saucer shape of raised bogs may be the curious development of a moat of open water around the very edges of the bog, especially if the bog is deep-set in hills. This moat – called the *lagg zone* – forms because conditions at the edges of the bog are less stable than they are towards the centre. Water may drain into the lagg zone from the raised centre of the bog or from the surrounding hills. This drainage may vary in volume seasonally from snow-melt or rainstorms. The level of pH may vary, too, especially if the water draining from surrounding hills is filtered through limestone-derived glacial till, as it may be south of the Canadian Shield. Sphagnum is less successful in this less stable environment, and thus the process that raised the bog in the centre fails at the edges.

A raised bog stops rising when water can be lifted by capillary action no higher, and when evaporation from the surface of the sphagnum equals rainfall. Then the peat dries, causing the rate of decomposition, now in air, to speed up. Eventually decomposition comes to equal the rate of growth. For a while, Time will leave this bog alone.

Typical bog filling in a former lake.
SHAN WALSHE

"String bogs" characterize much of the Hudson Bay Lowlands as well as other northern areas throughout the boreal forest. Vast, unbroken string bog landscapes may be visible from the air. The term *string bog* is a misnomer; most of them are actually huge fens with slow, shallow water movement. They form not only on thin soils over

String bog. JOHN THEBERGE

bedrock, but on permafrost soils as well.

Time follows a different sequence of steps to build a string peatland. First, shallow depressions are punched in the mat of vegetation, accomplished by planting patches of weak peat-producers, such as buckbean, in with the sphagnums. Water accumulates in these hollows, further slowing peat production in them, while on the humps, strong peat-producing sphagnums, sedges, and rushes grow more abundantly. The humps continue to grow, accentuating the contrast between humps and water-filled hollows. Then, as if through sleight of hand, the humps become linear. A very gentle slope is necessary, and in the process of upward surface-building, the humps and hollows align. If you raise a crumpled bedsheet from one side, the random humps and hollows align themselves into linear wrinkles. This is a process perhaps defying understanding or description. Time must keep some secrets.

More understandable, however, are processes of peatland formation initiated not by slow vegetative creep, but by beavers. These landscape architects almost instantly can create either bog or fen out of ground-water seepages or slow-moving streams, depending upon the extent to which they restrict water flow. Full formation to a closed-over peatland is unusual, however, because of the the tenuous nature of beaver dams. When beaver cut all their preferred food species – aspen and alder – faster than they can regrow, they may abandon their pond. Eventually ice or a floating log may poke a hole in the dam, and the pond will drain in a flash. The exposed organic soil dries out and decomposes. The old bottom of the pond is transformed into a meadow of grasses. Meadow voles tunnel and deer come to graze. After a while, black spruce begin to colonize from the edges, aspens and white birches regrow. Until, one day a wandering beaver recognizes the potential of the area. . .

So the sequence of bog or fen, beaver pond, beaver meadow, bog or fen, repeats – generations of communities following each other, just as generations of individuals follow one another in a stream of endless renewal.

An olive-sided flycatcher whips out its song from the top of a dead tamarack. A family of ring-necked ducks skitters away from your canoe. A beaver slaps its tail at a real or imaginary intrusion.

A damselfly lands on a yellow arum leaf. A tiny fritillary butterfly opens and closes its wings on a pink pondweed.

Brilliant yellow bladderworts, magenta-coloured rose pogonias, mottled red-green-and-brown pitcher plants scatter the green carpet with colour.

These specialized environments exclude some animals, for example most fish, because of a lack of oxygen, and snails and other molluscs because of low calcium. Zooplankton in the water is less abundant than might be expected when phytoplankton does so well. But the absence of a few is made up by an abundance of others. Aquatic insects abound. Leopard frogs find abundant food. Warblers nest in the bog-fringe trees. Beaver and moose browse the alders. Many species which live in bogs, fens, and beaver ponds have evolved special adaptations to do so. The plant carnivores – pitcher plant and the sundews – trap and "digest" insects, thus supplementing the little nitrogen available from the soil. The heath family depends upon an association with mycorrhiza fungi to help glean sufficient nitrogen and phosphorus from the soil.

Guarded by mosquitoes and alder tangles, and lacking exploitable resources, the peatlands and beaver ponds may remain less affected by humans than most other environments in Ontario. Some of them, already acid-adapted, may even hold out against atmospheric acidification longer than the upland forests. Their ultimate value may be as ecological anchors against the over-cutting, over-spraying, over-developing, and over-acidifying of the boreal forest.

Beaver dam. MINISTRY OF NATURAL RESOURCES, ALGONQUIN MUSEUM

Boreal Mammals Adapted to Snow

John B. Theberge

Upsik: wind-blown pellets of snow lashing the spruces, assaulting the forest, blotting out the trees, hissing against the ground, and consolidating into a frozen pack. That any living creature can endure such a blizzard is a tribute to evolutionary tolerance.

Api: piled in deep drifts across hillside and bog, softly shadowed by moonlight on a deadly calm, frozen night when trees crack like rifle shots from bursting ice crystals in their trunks. How fellow mammals in the boreal forest can withstand such cold is a marvel of adaptability.

Many northern native languages are much richer in their vocabulary for snow than is English, perhaps none more so than the language of the forest Inuit in northern Alaska. This richness reflects an ecological awareness. Snow is not just snow: it can robe the spruces in white – *qali*; it can blow over the surface – *siqoq*; it can form overhanging drifts – *mapsuk*.

Snow, in one form or another, is a dominant reality for more than half of each year in the boreal forest. To deal with it, living things have three options: leave, perish, or adapt. Every species of plant and animal living today in the boreal forest exhibits adaptations to snow, or else, long ago, it followed some other option. Migration, dormancy, hibernation, pupation: all are part of the winter shutdown. Leaf fall, energy storage in bud, bulb, tuber, seed, root, or in kidney fat, back fat, or winter food piles are adaptations, too. Trees such as black spruce adapt to shed snow with downward-sloping limbs. Other species, like poplars, birches, and alders, flex and bend with the weight of *qali*; their limbs often bow to the ground. Then they feed snowshoe hares that congregate to eat the tender buds and bark, and to dance in the moonlight.

Migration out of the boreal forest in winter is an option no mammals (other than a few bats and humans) have chosen. Perhaps the risks of long-distance travel on land or water are too high, or the energy costs too great. Only a few species hibernate: non-migratory bats, woodchucks, chipmunks, jumping mice, skunks, and bears. The rest, those that stay and are active, have chosen one of two fundamental strategies: to live in the *supranivean* (above-snow), or *subnivean* (below-snow) environments.

Adaptations to the supranivean environment typify mammals from the size of red squirrels on up, and range from walking through the snow on stilts (moose) to wearing permanent snowshoes (snowshoe hares and their predator the lynx). Larger animals can live above the snow because the ratio of their body surface to their internal volume is small, that is, they have a relatively small amount of surface area from which to lose heat relative to their body core. Even within one species, in fact, a general "rule" is that individuals living in the northern part of the range are larger than those living farther south. There is an exception; the boreal-dwelling subspecies, woodland caribou, is much larger than the high-Arctic-dwelling Peary's caribou, but caribou have exceptionally well-insulated bodies because their coats have hollow hairs.

Another general "rule" related to heat conservation is that northern species have shorter extremities than southern ones. Arctic foxes, which range along the boreal-tundra fringe and on to the north have considerably shorter ears, muzzle, legs, and tail than do red foxes, even though red foxes invade the tundra as well. Tundra-dwelling wolves, too, have shorter extremities than do more southern subspecies.

Wolves have neither stilts nor snowshoes to help them travel through snow. The reason they are not long-legged like the moose they chase is undoubtedly due to some evolutionary balance reached between the advantages of long legs in snow and their disadvantages in manoeuvring at high speed and in digging dens. Feet large enough to support body weights of twenty-two to forty-five kilograms on soft snow would have to be enormous. Snowshoes are ideal for lynx that hunt prey by stealth, with only a short chase at the end. In contrast, small feet are good adaptations for heavy wolves preying on large animals and relying primarily on speed, stamina, and group strategy. Both predators have made their evolutionary adjustments to snow.

Moose, deer, and caribou know innately how to use snow to their best advantage. They remain dispersed through the forest singly or in small groups as long as the snow is shallow enough not to hinder mobility. On good footing, they can outrun a wolf.

As well, scattered, they are more difficult for wolves to find. As a consequence, in winters of shallow snow, wolf predation normally is less severe. However, when snow lies deep, these ungulates head for the lowland conifers or the hemlock ridges where they will not have to expend so much energy getting around. There they are easier prey. As long as the snow is not excessively soft, wolves have the advantage.

Aquatic mammals are adapted to live in water temperatures right down to freezing while remaining active. All of them – beaver, muskrat, mink, and otter – construct lodges or use bank burrows for protection from cold and from predators while out of water. Otters travel extensively over the snow, benefiting from the coincidence that streamlined body, short legs, and webbed feet for swimming are also adaptations for tobogganing, and their body-prints across the snow are common features along or between stream courses.

Arboreal mammals reduce the problems of floundering through deep snow by spending much of their time in trees. Both red squirrels and their predators, American martens, play out much of their hunter-and-hunted dramas among the limbs of spruce and fir.

Piercing winter cold works a greater disadvantage on smaller mammals, with their less favourable surface-to-body ratios. Snowshoe hares, on very cold, clear nights, crouch in the shelter of low, overhanging conifer limbs, thus escaping the "heat sink" effect. Without cloud cover, heat and infrared radiation reflect from the ground back into the sky. Cloud cover reduces that effect and generally results in warmer nights. So can overhanging, snow-laden limbs, on a microclimatic scale. Red squirrels avoid temperatures below -30°C. by retreating under the snow and becoming creatures of the subnivean environment.

The subnivean environment is exploited not only by red squirrels on occasion but by all smaller mammals – voles, mice, and shrews – most of the time. The insulating properties of soft snow are so great that when air temperatures are well below freezing, under twenty centimetres or so of snow the temperature may just approach freezing. Without this significantly insulating blanket of snow, small mammals would be unable to live in the northern part of the boreal forest; they are physiologically incapable of producing sufficient heat to offset the losses. Without them, the boreal forest would be greatly reduced in its capacity to provide for hawks, owls, foxes, martens, fishers, and weasels.

When snow reaches fifteen to twenty centimetres in depth, the small mammals largely retreat from the surface. They remain active the rest of the winter at the ground-snow interface, tunnelling at that level. Down under the snow, however, their lives are not problem-free. Foxes can smell them and dig them out. Or they may be forced to the surface by stagnant air. With such relatively warm temperatures, bacterial action may take place, causing a build-up of carbon dioxide. Because of the carbon dioxide, the small mammals build ventilation shafts to the surface. As a result, they feed more hawks and owls than they would otherwise, but they have no alternative. Sometimes, ice storms trap small mammals underground and prevent them from building ventilator shafts. Adaptations to winter have their limits. The boreal forest is a harsh place.

Under the spruce trees are depressions in the snow known as *qamaniq*. These depressions result from overhanging limbs intercepting the snow and protecting the ground below. Small mammals recognize that these places represent cold spots in their subnivean environment, and avoid them. Cold places are created, too, by compacted snow which is less insulating than light, fluffy snow. Snowmobile trails or even heavily-used ski or snowshoe trails form temperature, and sometimes physical, barriers that may sever subnivean territories and constrict movements.

Because of these and other successful time-tested adaptations, mammals are able to survive wind-driven *upsik* and frigid *api* in the boreal forest. Thus, there are snowshoe hare tracks down in the alders, and red squirrels jumping among the spruces, and the paired prints of martens loping off to find a better squirrel-hunting range. There are moose bedding places among the hemlocks, and drops of blood on the snow where a red fox pounced on a white-footed mouse. And the tracks of a pack of wolves weave and braid and decorate the snow-blanket on the lake, tying together at the shore where the wolves, in single file, turned in to the spruces in search of their prey.

OPPOSITE
Snowshoe hare. PUKASKWA NATIONAL PARK, W. WYETT

White Pelicans of Lake of the Woods

John B. Theberge

The word *pelican* raises images of coastal Florida or the Caribbean where these ungainly, pot-bellied birds perch awkwardly on a pier, surrounded by fishing boats and palm trees. Or it may recall the sight of these big white birds formation-flying high over the prairie landscape in Saskatchewan or Manitoba, their wings stationary, each pelican holding its position relative to the rest, like precision-flying military aircraft in a slow-motion air show. But pelicans in Ontario?

They were not always here. Early ornithological books either make no mention of breeding records or, as late as 1909, comment that none have been found nesting in this province. Occasionally, groups of up to five birds were observed on migration in places like Hamilton Bay or along the north shore of Lake Erie.

In 1938, eight pairs of white pelicans were discovered, or first began nesting, on Dream Island in Lake of the Woods, becoming the easternmost colony in North America. To Ontario's avifauna was added a bird that is unique in many ways. Its three-metre wing span is equal to that of golden and bald eagles, placing it in the "big three" for Ontario nesting species. Its body measures more than a metre and a half from the tip of the bill to tip of the tail, making it the longest bird in Ontario, longer than either the great blue heron or the tundra swan. The white pelican undoubtedly holds the record for soaring the greatest length of time in V or other formations without any wing beat. And, white pelicans exhibit a degree of co-operative fishing that sets them apart from even the closely related brown pelican.

White pelicans are largely prairie breeders, nesting on islands in large lakes from desert regions in California north into the boreal forest. The most northerly colony is at the Slave River rapids near the town of Fort Smith on the Alberta-Northwest Territories border. An almost identical species lives in Europe, nesting on the Black and Caspian seas.

Typically, a flock of white pelicans will locate a school of fish from the air. The birds alight, and, heads submerged, attempt to scoop up the fish. They do not store fish in their gular pouch but swallow them almost immediately. A flock will stay together to feed, and, in doing so, will inadvertently co-operate to trap the fish and increase each other's chances of success. But, even more obvious co-operation has been described. The flock typically will land in a line or a crescent shape with the fish between them and shallow water. Then they splash their way forward, apparently driving the fish in front of them. Group fishing tactics, such as this, are exceedingly rare among birds.

Pelican flight is a marvel of beauty. It includes group-soaring, spectacular in birds with such huge wing spans and colour contrast – snow-white bodies and fore-wings, and jet-black primary and secondary flight feathers. It also includes slow, in-unison flapping, or flapping staged as a rhythmic ripple down a long line of birds, followed by a long group glide. Every motion is stately and unhurried. At times the birds soar high, lifted as if riding an elevator by thermal updrafts against their broad underwings. At times they fold up in the air and plummet down from a great height, wind vibrating through set wings. At times they flap slowly, so low that their wing-tips seem to touch the water.

Ontario's pelicans have done well, but so have other North American populations, at least in recent years. In the 1970s the North American population was down to an estimated sixteen thousand breeding pairs, due to habitat loss and chemical poisoning. However, successful recovery efforts, funded largely by the World Wildlife Fund (Canada) and Canada Life Assurance Company, were directed at the larger colonies on prairie lakes in Manitoba and Saskatchewan. These lakes provide more than half of the North American nesting habitat. In 1987 the white pelican was removed from Canada's list of endangered species. An estimated fifty thousand pairs now breed in Canada.

The Lake of the Woods colony has increased, although not steadily, since it was first discovered, and today consists of about four thousand pairs. In the 1940s the birds were shot by commercial fishermen who blamed them for the decline in fish. White pelicans disappeared from the lake, becoming re-established again about 1958 on a new island. By 1960, about fifty adults were found, and numbers have increased since then.

Since 1968, the pelicans have nested on two tiny remote islands in the south part of the lake – two of the "Three Sisters." Non-nesting subadults occupy the third Sister, and a new island, Burton, was added in 1982. All these islands lie very near the United States border which crosses the southwest corner of the lake. Sharing the islands with the pelicans are nesting herring gulls and some double-crested cormorants. Wave-washed granites fringe the islands; patches of grasses and low shrubs grow sporadically on the rocks. The pelicans populate the exposed rocks away from the shore, each nest about pecking distance from the next one. Orange, grotesque beaks and big orange feet add the only bright colour to the scene. Aesthetically unpleasant as waves spit against the shore and the rank smell of guano reaches the nostrils, the beauty of the pelican colony lies in the soaring flight above and the set-wing landings. The take-offs, in contrast, consist of ungainly kangaroo-like hops with wings wildly flailing.

The chicks are far from beautiful; rubbery and gawking and very unlike the majestic soaring birds they will soon become. The adults feed them regurgitated, not live, fish from their gular pouches. Recent studies have shown that fish eaten by pelicans at Lake of the Woods are primarily noncommercial or non-sport species such as bullhead, ling, yellow perch, and sunfish. Crustaceans make up about one-tenth of the diet, and only 13 per cent is walleye and bass.

White pelican, Lake of the Woods.
P. KOR

Usually, individual birds of a species will all nest simultaneously, but the white pelicans at Lake of the Woods stagger their single annual nesting over about two months. They make no apparent attempt to time hatching to possible maximum food availability for young, or maximum time for young to gain weight before migration, or to allow enough time to nest more than once. Staggering the nesting this way makes the colony less vulnerable to a single storm that could kill all the very young chicks. That explanation assumes that individuals are cooperating for the good of the colony. Co-operative behaviour, however, must confer advantages to the individual in order to be a worthwhile activity for individuals to engage in, and to become a genetically selected trait. Perhaps the value of co-operative feeding, combined with other forms of co-operative behaviour, assures the welfare of the group, which in turn assures the welfare of each member. But how the colony achieves this staged nesting is puzzling. Timing of egg-laying in birds is largely determined by the environment, not genetics. How can each female pelican gain a perception of, and time her own egglaying to, the proportion of other females that have already laid eggs?

Colonial birds such as the white pelican offer room for speculation and further study. That opportunity is only one reason to protect this colony. Another is its range-edge position; the colony at Lake of the Woods is made up of pelican pioneers with the adaptability to push against environmental limitations. And important too is simply the knowledge that the white pelicans are there to grace northern Ontario with their stately presence.

Part Five

PERSPECTIVES ON NATURE

A Celebration of Nature

John A. Livingston

This morning, on the carpet in my library there was a stricken bumblebee. After a careful touch prompted no response, I gingerly picked her up. Even under a magnifying glass, she appeared to be perfect in every detail – except that she was without life. I have no idea what befell her. May is not the time for any worker bee to die. She was carrying no pollen; her hind legs were clean and smooth. Her wings were fresh, shiny, and crisp, not tattered and frayed as they would have been had she survived until fall. There are no chemical insecticides hereabouts. Cause of death – unknown.

Bumblebees are fairly common here, because the ground has never been savaged into domestic servitude, and there is an abundance of nest holes bequeathed by small mammals. One individual worker bee, one unit in the greater social organization (one cell in the greater single organism?) will not be missed. Presumably not by her peers, who are single-mindedly doing the task they must continue until autumn frost kills them. And certainly from the ecological point of view the demise of one bumblebee is not an event of statistical significance. For those who measure energy flows in ecosystems, this death is, quite literally, without meaning.

This is vexing. Ecology tells us that every event has ripple effects, and that no happening in nature is without consequence. Obviously, the subtraction of one bee from the local community would have no measurable effect simply because of the scale factor. However, were our theoretical models and our techniques more sophisticated, we *should* be able to cope with it. Does this mean that the death of a worker bumblebee has significance only in relation to our ability to measure it?

Further, ecology would suggest that the effect of the disappearance of the entire population of this species of bumblebee should *in theory* be demonstrable, but *in practice* might not. Although fairly numerous, the bumblebee is not a major player in this community, and in any case, honeybees are much more efficient pollinators. Thus, the effect on the community of the removal of an entire species might not be evident either. Does this mean that the loss of a species has significance to us only in relation to our ability to measure it?

This is the point at which we naturalists (conservationists, preservationists – call us what you will) all too easily can get ourselves into a double-bind. We live in a society dominated by the "resource" mentality, whose unfailing bottom line is "What good is it?" The desired good is to the human enterprise. In those cases where the direct human benefit cannot be shown, the fall-back position is usually "benefit to the environment" – by extension, in the human interest. In the case of the bumblebee, we struggle to show either its contribution to us as a pollinator, or its mechanistic value as a "component" of the hypothesized ecosystem.

Of course we can prove neither. But under unrelenting pressure from the dominant forces in our society, too often we feel that in order to be credible, and even to be able to communicate, we must adopt the language and idiom of the utilitarian majority. In doing so, we inadvertently embrace the burden of proving the unprovable. This is a towering irony. In our enthusiasm to be "respectable," we co-opt ourselves while at the same time reinforcing the relegation of nature to a supporting role in the greater human endeavour.

Unmoving on my hand, the bumblebee is an object for my curious scrutiny. Were she alive, she would not be on my hand – not if either of us could help it. Alive, she would be not an object but a subject. The bumblebee and I, as individuals, would regard each other with total subjectivity – with the apprehensions, perceptions, and responses peculiar to each of us. I cannot be stung by an object – only by an independent subject with an individual will. Were she alive, our relationship would be entirely personal.

Unhappily, the majority view of nature held by high civilization is overwhelmingly *im*personal. Nature is viewed as a stockpile of objects, an emporium of commodities ("resources"), an inventory of inanimate stuff the ultimate meaning, purpose, and destiny of which lies in whatever human utility may be devised for it. If it has no human utility, it has no meaning, and therefore it simply does not exist.

Even we naturalists have our own ways of "objectifying" nature. Our plant presses, our herbaria, our checking cards, and our "life lists" are collections of objects, or – at yet another remove – arcane symbols *representing* objects. Such dry accounting does little for nature or for us. Also, too often some naturalists tend to be proprietary about nature, as though it were a private preserve for their exclusive edification, delectation, and delight. At its extreme, this sense of proprietorship can seem little different from that of the resource extractor; in both cases nature exists for the human purpose. Whether our use of it is consumptive or nonconsumptive becomes irrelevant, because the perception of the relationship between ourselves and nature is the same. There is something in it for *us*.

This attitude, which is the dominant one in our society, shows up in the language of too many of our argu-

Bumblebee on milkweed. DON GUNN

ments on behalf of nature protection (our scenic resources, our wildlife resources, our inalienable natural heritage, use and enjoyment of future generations, etc.). Except in the case of endangered species and habitats (and regrettably often even there) too few of us argue for nature in nature's own interest. We are inhibited from doing that by our expectation that such an approach will take us – and nature – nowhere, the utilitarian bias of our culture being what it is. It is this inhibition that forces us to express ourselves in the "resource" idiom. We must be "credible," we must be pragmatists, we tell ourselves.

I turn to the body of the worker bumblebee. As I look at her, I ask myself what demonstrable benefit her brief career could possibly have had for me. I do not know. Outside the window, two other bumblebees are assiduously working on the geraniums. Clearly there is nothing in their activity of tangible benefit to me, nor, indeed, to the geraniums. There is only something in it for a dark, subterranean cluster of bees somewhere nearby. How my interest is served by this is beyond rational understanding. I simply could not make a compelling pragmatic case for the bumblebee.

Yet the individual bumblebee is utterly compelling in herself. Magnetic. The extraordinary delicacy and intricacy of her structure, the perfection of her form. And the inexplicable miracle of her mere presence. Why in the world this diminutive event? Why, after thousands of millions of years of evolutionary manifestations, why *this*? And why should this be so beautiful?

The only honest answer is "Why not?" I think a child might say that. I think most of the honest answers come from children. Certainly the uninhibited answers are those of children. So we ask ourselves what it is that allows children to be honest and uninhibited. No doubt it is that children of a certain age have not yet been conditioned into the cultural mainstream. Their perceptions are still their own. They have not yet been instructed that all things are knowable, predictable, and controllable through the systematic and methodical application of human reason, and that magic is a hoax. On the contrary, children accept things wondrous and miraculous at face value – as wonders and miracles. Things like bumblebees.

A child does not "observe" the bumblebee; a child *experiences* the bumblebee. The little fuzzily buzzing surprise is taken into the child's very being; it literally becomes part of that developing human entity. Indeed, it is said, this act of "ingesting" the bumblebee may also be the act of *imprinting* upon bumblebees – imprinting upon nonhuman existence. Each such act is an experience of the child's own biological being. Young children seem to be insatiable for these experiences.

So are some adults. The insatiability of the bird-lister and the rock-hound are well known. But this should not

necessarily be construed as greed – it can be *need*. And the need is not always for trophies or checkmarks on a scoreboard; it can be the need for personal experience – intimate contact – with phenomena that are not human. Every naturalist knows the irrepressible joy, not so much of discovery as of *re*-discovery of the childlike capacity to experience and accept things wondrous and miraculous. It may be a "new" species or community, or it may not be, but the spirit itself is of electrifying poignancy. It is the rekindling of the formative event, the celebration of the primal bond.

My wife and I have put a little park bench by a pond near our house. The pond is home for many individuals of several species of frogs and toads. One warm spring evening after dark I went to sit there and take in the choral concert. I brought with me a steaming mug of coffee almost too hot to hold, and put it beside me on the bench. Having taken a minute or two to let the singers forget about my presence, and then, as I thought, another minute to make a brief mental note of the relative abundance of the specific trills, clacks, peeps, growls and clungs in the tumult rising from the pond, I stealthily reached for my coffee. It was stone cold.

What had taken place I cannot say. It would appear that I had had a journey deep into the elemental non-self-conscious awareness. The medium for the journey seems to have been some mysterious synergism created by the sound of the amphibians and my recollective responsiveness to it. Naturally I was astonished by my "lapse," but at the same time felt unaccountably, profoundly content and serene. Quietly celebratory.

Celebration of nature is essentially celebration of our own naturalness – our innate ability to relinquish human ego for the reawakening of the relationship that transcends inter-species barriers and revitalizes inter-species bonds. To be "one with nature" is to participate in events at once wondrous, miraculous, timeless. It is the rediscovery of the ancient experience of authentic belonging. You *can* go home again. And marvelous to relate, you don't have to be a child to do it. That is worth celebrating too.

OPPOSITE
Red Pines, Algonquin Park.
JOHN THEBERGE

The Wholeness of Nature

John B. Theberge

The time is ten P.M. The August night is cool and perfectly calm. The scene is Algonquin Park. The moon is rising, silhouetting the spruces across the bog. Its soft light reveals traces of mist over open water. Overhead are legions of stars, reminders of galactic space and universal order.

The stars, the moonlight, the mist over the bog portray an ancient scene. It could be any evening in the past 8,000 years, any time since trees recolonized the land following the retreat of the glaciers. But the darkness is deceptive. A logging road runs beside the bog, and on it stand fifteen hundred people! A line of some four hundred cars glints in the moonlight. They project the date forward to recent years, sometime in the last decade or so since the park's interpreters realized that the opportunity to hear the howls of wild wolves was a magnetic event for people that somehow exceeded all other experiences in appeal, up there in the "north woods."

Why should wolf howls be so special? Is it just the excitement of something unusual, or the desire to be near an animal that many people still want to fear? Is it a subconscious memory of the ancient and greatest contest in mammalian evolution when man, with newly acquired bipedal stance and primitive weapons, exempted himself from being wolf prey? Is it a touchstone to a more stable past, without high-tech or high-speed living?

All those people made a disturbance getting there, to be sure – car lights, slamming doors, chatter, and laughter. But now they are silent. As instructed, not even a foot rasps on the gravel. A lone wolf, less than half a kilometre away, is filling the night with its wild sound. Its howls transfix, even shock the audience on the logging road. Perfectly adapted large mammals like us actually do exist out there in the cold moonlight among the spruces – fellow creatures, with speed and stamina and night vision that exceed ours, poignant evidence of another order, a natural order that we have not yet completely struck down.

Another wolf, with alto overtones, joins in from the ridge beyond. Their unfettered voices duet and chorus, rise and fall, braid and unbraid, at one instant in harmony, at another in discord. Over and over the wolves pour their wild music into the night. Crystal sound, the distillate of the wild, the essence of wilderness, the reassurance that here, at least, is a wholeness of nature.

It has been said that a land that can grow a wolf is a whole land, a healthy land. Much of central and all of northern Ontario still can. A wolf needs a wild environment that is not laced with traps, snares, guns, or hatred. It needs healthy populations of white-tailed deer, moose, or, in the far north, caribou. For the ungulates to survive, the forest or tundra must be, at least to some degree, intact. For the vegetation communities to be intact, the soil must still be fertile, the hydrological cycle must still run, the nutrients must still move in their ancient pathways – living to non-living and back again. The wolf is a "summit predator," on the top of all terrestrial food chains not dominated by man, but its existence requires that all the links be there.

The wolf is also a "functional ecological dominant." Its predatory impacts reverberate through the lands it occupies. It illustrates the connections that forge individual species into communities. By its choice of prey and the mortality it inflicts, it often (but not always) influences ungulate densities and the ratio of species. The ungulates, by selectively browsing preferred species of trees and shrubs, influence the species and age composition of the whole forest. Forest composition, in turn, influences almost everything else – the composition of breeding bird populations, insects, other mammals, even characteristics of the soil such as pH. Pine seedlings selectively and repeatedly browsed by deer, for example, will not mature into pine trees that contribute acid needle-drop to the soil. Instead, red maple and poplars may grow. Bacteria will replace the more acid-adapted fungi as principal decomposers. High in the forest canopy, the larvae of the maple leafcutter will consume foliage, instead of white pine weevils, and red-eyed vireos, specialists in the hardwoods, will replace pine warblers.

In the ecology textbooks are charts depicting food webs, species related to species by culinary habits. Such charts, for any particular habitat, may be further embellished with two-way arrows that illustrate relationships at a population level, where food limits the size of predator populations or vice versa. Symbols show how the relationships are expressed – on birth rates or mortality rates, or both. Other symbols may depict non-food relationships, where species create microhabitats for one another, or provide transportation, or a substrate for growth, and may include symbiosis, commensalism, mutualism, parasitism.

If these food webs are used to depict energy flow, then caloric values and percentages show up beside the arrows. If the webs are used to indicate cycling of various nutrients, then another set of symbols appears. At this point, the charts become unreadable – beyond comprehension. Persistent scientists feed all the data into computers to see what electronic storage, sorting, and plotting can do. But the wholeness is just too great. Here, science gives way to wonder.

In an effort to deal with this complexity, we categorize nature into convenient "disciplines": geology, ornithology, mammalogy, vertebrate paleontology, invertebrate paleontology, botany. In doing so we lose perspective. Ours is no longer the outlook of, say, an oriole busy feeding its young that are about to emerge from its nest slung high in a basswood tree. The oriole is an expert in ornithology: bird territoriality, niche partitioning, avian migration, and navigation. It is proficient as an entomologist in identifying potential prey, and as a forest ecologist in picking a suitable habitat, and as a mammalogist in knowing enough to hang its nest beyond the reach of skunk or raccoon. Orioles integrate all the relevant aspects of their environment into some cognitive ecological mosaic. All this knowledge is encoded in oriole genes, or recognized and acted upon within the bounds of behavioural plasticity. For the oriole there are sun and wind, deciduous forests and insect food, stimuli and response, biological drives to be satisfied and accepted oriole ways of achieving satisfaction. The oriole represents a wholeness of non-partitioned nature.

So, too, does a red-backed salamander lying in the moist coolness between bark and wood of a black cherry log. The salamander reflects a historical continuity, a flow of events. It owes its hiding place to a heavy wind a few months earlier, a cyclone storm that moved up from the Gulf of Mexico and blew over the cherry tree. But the cherry was doomed anyway, being crowded by forest succession and dominated by more shade-tolerant sugar maples. The cherry tree, in turn, owed its sixty years in the forest to a swath cleared by a more severe windstorm than the one that toppled it, and a cedar waxwing that inadvertently transported a cherry seed, via its faeces, into the clearing.

The salamander chooses such a concealed place not only for its protection against predators and for its humid conditions, conducive to skin-respiration, but because of its unconscious understanding, its blind instinct that here will be sow bugs, millipedes, and a variety of invertebrates that also choose to spend their lives under bark, for a variety of adaptive reasons. Its instinct is built up from a genetic continuity, from millennia of selective culling of salamanders, and their genes, that chose less successful and more dangerous places to live. Nature's wholeness reaches back in historic and genetic continuity too, to events we know nothing about or only dimly perceive. Such events shaped each living individual and species.

Wood duck. NATIONAL MUSEUM OF CANADA, A. G. AUSTIN

Under the black cherry bark, the rich assortment of living things hunt and kill each other and live their short but fiercely competitive lives. Ground beetles prey on soil nematodes; predatory mites eat herbaceous mites; spiders, centipedes, and pseudoscorpions kill a host of small arthropods. At a microscopic level, in the film of water around soil particles, protozoa, nematodes, and rotifers feed on bacteria and algae, and are trapped and digested in turn by various parasitic fungi. Soil bacteria and fungi attack dead leaves and other detritus on the forest floor to unlock nutrients that are used again by living things. The wholeness of nature builds from the unicellular too.

But it builds from even a more fundamental and profound level than the unicellular, in a way that if totally comprehended would radically alter the outlook of society. All objects in this world, living and non-living, share the same basic make-up. All consist of molecules, atoms, electrons, neutrons, protons, quarks, and possibly even sub-quarks, in roughly descending order of size. One set of only four physical principles drives the behaviour of matter, according to the physicists in their ultimate of reductionism: strong and weak nuclear forces, electromagnetic force, and gravity. And, remarkably, all ninety-six naturally occurring elements – nickel,

JOHN SHAW

copper, oxygen, arsenic, and so on – come from the explosive reactions of only one, the hydrogen atom. Every atom of every element on Earth was "made" in hydrogen-to-helium fusion reactions in other suns that blew apart long ago, dispersing these atoms into the void of space, eventually to coalesce in a primordial nebula from which our planet, sun, and solar system came.

We share this common origin, and these reactions of matter, with every sand grain, rock, tree, frog, fish, bird, and mammal on Earth. Against this similarity, when viewed from a universe-wide perspective, our differences, even between living and non-living things, are minor. Rocks and humans are all part of the same design and part of the same unique celestial experience, at least as far as we know or as far as is discernible from our corner of space. Among living things, the structure and behaviour of cells is essentially the same whether they be packaged in earthworm or human. When you slap a mosquito you destroy a nervous, circulatory, excretory, and reproductive system that is more similar to ours than different – the same essential blueprint for life. This fact, while not enough to spare every mosquito, is profound enough to compel a much elevated level of environmental respect.

So here we are, locked together in a common fate, all in the same spaceship, and in Ontario, all in one stateroom. Atoms and molecules flow from rock, soil, plants, and other animals to us, and from us to them, so that "we-they" is only a short-term condition. That makes all living things kindred, one no "better" than the other. All around us are species of greater antiquity with better records of longevity on Earth than ours.

A sense of kinship, and wholeness, if truly understood and accepted, invariably must breed a sense of caring. Caring leads to a need to know more, and vice versa. Humans may be unique in being able to care beyond their own species, but we are unique also in our ability to destroy.

MINISTRY OF NATURAL RESOURCES / Courtesy of *Algonquin Park Museum*.

This wholeness of nature that encompasses the very structure of every living thing dictates that all forms of life, from frog's eggs to maple trees to humans, are linked in our requirements for life. We, the living entities of this planet, all ask the same things of the biosphere, that thin shell of air, water, and soil that surrounds our globe and supports life. If we alter conditions of the biosphere too far, we, and other species, will all fail together. This way of proving wholeness we must manage to avoid. But, many of the authors in this book are apprehensive about the future. Whether they wrote of atmospheric warming, wetland drainage, massive loss of soil fertility through erosion, air pollution killing lichens, acid rain killing amphibians and forests and sterilizing Algonquin's lakes, pesticides concentrating in food chains, concentrations of heavy metals in wetland ecosystems, loss of rare flora such as the Atlantic coastal disjuncts, over-cutting of forests, toxification of the lower Great Lakes, or threats to such endangered or rare species as the hooded warbler, a glance back through this book shows that scientists who study many aspects of Ontario's natural and semi-natural environments are concerned. Clearly, human pressure is exerting a sudden and cataclysmic impact on much of this province, if viewed in the time-frame of evolution and geology to which the rhythms of ecosystems are tuned.

The precious natural features of Ontario described in this book will endure only if the groundswell of environmental concern taking shape among us, its citizens, results in public pressure for new and stronger strictures on human exploitation and desecration, implemented both voluntarily and through legislation. Such action is needed as the embodiment of an ethical responsibility to the land and living things, for our own well-being as well as for that of all other species. Nature in Ontario will not retain its richness and natural beauty by default.

References

In broad overviews of subjects such as this book contains, authors lean heavily on the work of other experts in scientific, technical, and popular publications. Some authors felt that specific acknowledgement was necessary; others felt that their treatments of the subjects did not require references.

Ontario in the Sweep of Continent

Bjorek, S. 1985. Deglaciation chronology and revegetation in northwestern Ontario. *Canadian Journal of Earth Sciences* 22: 850-87.

Hare, F. K., and M. K. Thomas. 1974 *Climate Ontario.* 2nd edition. Toronto: John Wiley and Sons.

Liu, K. B. and Lam, N. S. 1985. Paleovegetational reconstructions based on modern and fossil pollen data: an application of discriminant analysis. *Annals of the American Association of Geographers* 75: 115-30.

Schwart, D. P., T. W. Anderson, A. Morgan, A. V. Morgan, and P. F. Karrow. 1985. Changes in late Quaternary vegetation and insect communities in southwestern Ontario. *Quaternary Research* 23: 205-26.

Webb, T., E. J. Cushing, and E. J. Wright Jr. 1983. Holocene changes in the vegetation of the midwest in *Late Quaternary Environments of the United States*, H. E. Wright Jr. (ed.). University of Minnesota Press, Vol. II, 142-65.

Dating Earth Processes and Features

Table of important natural radioisotopes, after Mason, B. 1966. *Principles of Geochemistry*. 3rd edition. New York: John Wiley and Sons.

Ontario's Biota in Space and Time

Map of bird species diversity in North America, after MacArthur, R. H. and E. O. Wilson. 1967. *The Theory of Island Biogeography*. Princeton, New Jersey: Princeton University Press.

Foundations of the Land

Baer, A. J. 1974. Grenville geology and plate tectonics. *Geoscience Canada* 1: 54-61.

Bolton, T. E. 1957. Silurian stratigraphy and palaeontology of the Niagara Escarpment in Ontario. Geological Survey of Canada, Memoir 289.

Dimroth, E., W. R. A. Baragar, R. Bergeron, and G. D. Jackson. 1970. The filling of the Circum-Ungava geosyncline, Symposium on basins and geosynclines of the Canadian Shield, A. J. Baer (ed.). Geological Survey of Canada, Paper 70-40, 45-142.

Dott, R. H. Jr., and R. L. Batten. 1971. *Evolution of the Earth*. New York: McGraw-Hill.

Douglas, R. J. W. (ed.). 1970. Geology and Economic Minerals of Canada. Geological Survey of Canada, Economic Geology Report 1.

______. 1980. Proposal for time classification and correlation of Precambrian rocks and events in Canada and adjacent areas of the Canadian Shield. Part 2: A provisional for correlating Precambrian rocks. Geological Survey of Canada, Paper 80-24.

Liberty, B. A. 1969. Palaeozoic geology of the Lake Simcoe area, Ontario. Geological Survey of Canada, Memoir 355.

______ and T. E. Bolton. 1971. Paleozoic geology of the Bruce Peninsula area, Ontario. Geological Survey of Canada, Memoir 360.

Price, R. A., and R. J. W. Douglas (ed.). 1972. Variations in tectonic styles in Canada. Geological Association of Canada, Special Paper Number 11.

Pye, E. G., A. J. Naldrett, and P. E. Giblin (ed.). 1984. The geology and ore deposits of the Sudbury structure. Ontario Geological Survey, Special Volume 1.

Ricketts, B. D., and J. A. Donaldson. 1981. Sedimentary history of the Belcher Island Group of Hudson Bay, in Proterozoic Basins of Canada, F. H. A. Campbell (ed.). Geological Survey of Canada, Paper 81-10, 235-54.

Sanford, B. V., and A. W. Norris. 1975. Devonian stratigraphy of the Hudson Platform. Part I: Stratigraphy and economic geology. Part II: Outcrop and subsurface sections. Geological Survey of Canada, Memoir 379.

______, A. W. Norris, and H. H. Bostock. 1968. Geology of the Hudson Bay Lowlands (Operation Winisk). Geological Survey of Canada, Paper 67-60.

Sims, P. K., K. D. Card, and S. B. Lumbers. 1981. Evolution of Early Proterozoic Basins of the Great Lakes Region, in Proterozoic Basins of Canada. F. H. A. Campbell (ed.). Geological Survey of Canada, Paper 81-10.

Stauffer, C. R. 1913. The Devonian of southwestern Ontario. Geological Survey of Canada, Memoir 34.

Wallace, H. 1981. Keweenawan Geology of the Lake Superior Basin, in Proterozoic Basins of Canada. F. H. A. Campbell (ed.). Geological Survey of Canada, Paper 81-10.

Wilson, A. E. 1946. Geology of the Ottawa-St. Lawrence Lowland, Ontario and Quebec. Geological Survey of Canada, Memoir 241.

Winder, C. G. and Sanford, B. V. 1972. Stratigraphy and paleontology of the Paleozoic rocks of southern Ontario. XXIV International Geological Congress, Excursion A45–C45.

Map of Paleozoic rocks of southern Ontario, after Hewitt, D. F., and E. B. Freeman. Rocks and Minerals of Ontario. Ontario Department of Mines and Northern Affairs, Geological Circular 13.

The Wrinkled Surface

Barnett, P. J. 1978. Quaternary geology of the Simcoe area, southern Ontario. Ontario Division of Mines, Geological Report 162.

Boissoneau, A. N. 1966. Glacial history of northeastern Ontario 1. The Cochrane-Hearst area. *Canadian Journal of Earth Sciences* 3: 559-78.

______. 1968. Glacial history of northeastern Ontario 2. The Timiskaming-Algoma area. *Canadian Journal of Earth Sciences* 5: 97-109.

Bostock, H. S. 1970. Physiographic subdivisions of Canada, in Geology and Economic Minerals of Canada.

R. J. W. Douglas (ed.). Geological Survey of Canada, Economic Geology Report 1.
Coleman, A. P. 1933. The Pleistocene of the Toronto Region. Ontario Department of Mines, Annual Report 44: 1-55.
______. 1941. *The Last Million Years: A History of the Pleistocene in North America*. Toronto: University of Toronto Press.
Cooper, A. J. 1975. Pre-Catfish Creek tills in the Waterloo area. Geological Society of America, Geological Association of Canada, and Mineralogical Association of Canada, Abstracts with program 7: 739-40.
Cowan, W. R. 1976. Quaternary geology of the Orangeville area, southern Ontario. Ontario Division of Mines, Geological Report 141.
______, P. F. Karrow, A. J. Cooper, and A. V. Morgan. 1975. Late Quaternary stratigraphy of the Waterloo-Lake Huron area, southwestern Ontario. Geological Society of America, Geological Association of Canada, and Mineralogical Association of Canada. Field Trips Guidebook. P. G. Telford (ed.). 119-60.
Dreimanis, A. 1957. Stratigraphy of the Wisconsinan glacial stage along the northwestern shore of Lake Erie. *Science* 126: 166-68.
______. 1958. Wisconsin stratigraphy at Port Talbot on the north shore of Lake Erie, Ontario. *Ohio Journal of Science* 58: 65-84.
______. 1960. Pre-Classical Wisconsin in the eastern portion of the Great Lakes region, North America. XXI International Geological Congress, Section 21. 108-109.
______. 1969. Late Pleistocene lakes in the Ontario and Erie basins. XII Conference on Great Lakes Research Proceedings. 170-80.
______. 1971. The last ice age in the eastern Great Lakes region of North America. VII International Quaternary Congress 1: 69-75.
______ and P. F. Karrow. 1972. Glacial history of the Great Lakes-St. Lawrence region: the classification of the Wisconsin(an) stage and its correlatives. XXIV International Geological Congress, Section 12. 5-12.
______ J. Terasmae, and G. D. McKenzie. 1966. The Port Talbot interstade of the Wisconsin glaciation. *Canadian Journal of Earth Sciences* 3: 305-25.
Flint, R. F. 1971. Glacial and Pleistocene geology. New York: John Wiley and Sons.
Goldthwaite, R. P., A. Dreimanis, J. L. Forsyth, P. F. Karrow, and G. W. White. 1965. Pleistocene deposits of the Erie lobe, in *The Quaternary Geology of the United States*. Princeton, New Jersey: Princeton University Press. 89-97.
Karrow, P. F. 1963. Pleistocene geology of the Hamilton-Galt area. Ontario Department of Mines, Geological Report 16.
______. 1967. Pleistocene geology of the Scarborough area. Ontario Department of Mines, Geological Report 46.
______. 1973. Bedrock topography in southwestern Ontario: a progress report. Geological Association of Canada, Proceedings 25: 67-77.
______. 1974. Till statigraphy in parts of southwestern Ontario. Geological Society of America, Bulletin 85: 761-68.
______. 1984. Quaternary stratigraphy and history, Great Lakes-St. Lawrence region, in Quaternary Stratigraphy of Canada – A Canadian Contribution to IGCP Project 24. R. J. Fulton (ed.). Geological Survey of Canada, Paper 84-10. 137-53.
______, and A. V. Morgan. 1975. Quaternary stratigraphy of the Toronto area. Geological Society of America, Geological Association of Canada, and Minerological Association of Canada, Field Trip Guidebook. P. G. Telford (ed.). 161-79.
Moerner, N. A. 1971. The Plum Point Interstadial: age climate and subdivisions. *Canadian Journal of Earth Sciences* 8: 1421-23.
______, and A. Dreimanis. 1973. The Erie Interstade. Geological Society of America, Memoir 136. 107-34.
Prest, V. K. 1970. Quaternary geology of Canada, in Geology and Economic Minerals of Canada. R. J. W. Douglas (ed.). Geological Survey of Canada, Economic Geology Report 1. 676-764.
Saarnisto, M. 1974. The deglaciation history of the Lake Superior region and its climatic implications. *Quaternary Research* 4: 316-39.
______. 1975. Stratigraphical studies on the shoreline displacement of Lake Superior. *Canadian Journal of Earth Sciences* 12: 300-19.
Spencer, J. W. W. 1907. The falls of Niagara, their evolution and varying relations to the Great Lakes; characteristics of the power, and the effects of its diversion. Geological Survey of Canada.
Skinner, R. G. 1973. Quaternary stratigraphy of the Moose River basin. Geological Survey of Canada, Bulletin 225.
Taylor, R. B. 1913. The moraine system of southern Ontario. Canadian Institute, Transactions 10: 57-59.
Terasmae, J. 1960. A palynological study of the Pleistocene interglacial beds at Toronto, Ontario. Geological Survey of Canada, Bulletin 56: 23-40.
______, P. F. Karrow, and A. Dreimanis. 1972. Quaternary stratigraphy and geomorphology of the eastern Great Lakes region of southern Ontario. XXIV International Geological Congress, Field Excursion Guidebook A42.
Zoltai, S. C. 1965. Glacial features of the Quetico-Nipigon area, Ontario. *Canadian Journal of Earth Sciences* 4: 515-28.
Maps of Port Bruce re-advance and Mackinaw ice-split, after Chapman, L. J., and D. F. Putman. 1966. *The Physiography of Southern Ontario*. 2nd edition. Toronto: University of Toronto Press.
Map of moraines of southern Ontario, after Chapman and Putman, as above.

Latticework of Ecosystems

Map of forest regions of Ontario, after Hills, G. A. 1960, revised 1977. A ready reference Ontario Land Inventory. Ontario Ministry of Natural Resources, Toronto.
Table of characteristic forests of the site regions of Ontario, after Hills, G. A. 1959. A ready reference to the description of the land

of Ontario and its productivity. Ontario Department of Lands and Forests, Toronto.

Ice-Age Fossils and Vanished Vertebrates

Bell, R. 1898. On the occurrence of mammoth and mastodon remains around Hudson Bay. Geological Society of America, Bulletin 9: 369-90.
Bensley, B. A. 1913. A *Cervales* antler from the Toronto Interglacial. University of Toronto Studies, Geological Series No. 8: 1-3.
______. 1923. A muskox skull from Iroquois Beach deposits at Toronto: *Ovibos proximus*. University of Toronto Studies, Biological Series No. 23: 1-11.
Churcher, C. S. 1968. Mammoth from the Middle Wisconsin of Woodbridge, Ontario. *Canadian Journal of Zoology* 46: 219-21.
______, and R. R. Dods. 1979. *Ochotona* and other vertebrates of possible Illinoian age from Kelso Cave, Halton County, Ontario. *Canadian Journal of Earth Sciences* 16: 1613-20.
______, and P. F. Karrow. 1963. Mammals of Lake Iroquois age. *Canadian Journal of Zoology* 41: 153-58.
______, and P. F. Karrow. 1977. Late Pleistocene muskox (*Ovibos*) from the Early Wisconsin at Scarborough Bluffs, Ontario, Canada. *Canadian Journal of Earth Sciences* 14: 326-31.
______, and A. V. Morgan. 1976. A grizzly bear from the Middle Wisconsin of Woodbridge, Ontario. *Canadian Journal of Earth Sciences* 13: 341-47.
______, and R. L. Peterson. 1982. Chronologic and environmental implications of a new genus of fossil deer from Late Wisconsin deposits at Toronto, Canada. *Quaternary Research* 18: 184-95.
Coleman, A. P. 1933. The Pleistocene of the Toronto region (including the Toronto Interglacial Formation). Ontario Department of Mines 41: 1-55.
Crossman, E. J., and C. R. Harington. 1970. Pleistocene pike, Esox lucius, and Esox sp., from the Yukon Territory and Ontario. *Canadian Journal of Earth Sciences* 7: 1130-38.
Dreimanis, A. 1967. Mastodons, their geologic age and extinction in Ontario, Canada. *Canadian Journal of Earth Sciences* 4: 663-75. (Including map of mastodons in Ontario).
______. 1968. Extinction of mastodons in eastern North America: testing a new climate-environmental hypothesis. *Ohio Journal of Science* 68: 257-72.
Gadd, N. R. 1980. Maximum age for a concretion at Green Creek, Ontario. *Geographie physique et Quaternaire* 34: 229-38.
Karrow. P. F. 1984. Quaternary stratigraphy and history, Great Lakes-St. Lawrence region, in Quaternary Stratigraphy of Canada – a Canadian Contribution to IGCP Project 24. R. J. Fulton (ed.). Geological Survey of Canada, Paper 84-10. 137-53.
Peterson. R. L. 1965. The Lake Simcoe grizzly. *Meeting Place: Journal of the Royal Ontario Museum* 1: 82-7.
Russell, L. S. 1965. The mastodon. Royal Ontario Museum Series 6: 1-16.
Skinner, R. G. 1973. Quaternary stratigraphy of the Moose River Basin. Geological Survey of Canada, Bulletin 225: 1-77.
Sternberg, C. M. 1951. White whales and other Pleistocene fossils from the Ottawa Valley. National Museum of Canada, Bulletin 123: 259-61.
Sternberg, C. M. 1963. Additional records of mastodons and mammoths in Canada. National Museum of Canada, Natural History Papers No. 19: 1-11.
Terasmae, J. 1960. A palynological study of the Pleistocene interglacial beds at Toronto, Ontario. Geological Survey of Canada, Bulletin 56: 23-41.
Waddington, J. 1979. An introduction to Ontario fossil birds. Section 5. Pleistocene bird records from Ontario. Smithsonian Miscellaneous Collections 135: 1-11.

Rabies in Ontario Wildlife

Voigt, D. R. 1981. Rabies. *Seasons* 21: 33-7.

Passenger Pigeons – They Darkened the Sky

Mitchell, M. H. 1935. *The Passenger Pigeon in Ontario*. Toronto: University of Toronto Press. (Including map of colonies.)

Pembroke Swallows

Anon. 1987. Festival of the Swallows. A supplement to the *Pembroke Advertiser-News*.

Great Lakes as a Physical Environment

Table of Great Lakes shoreline, description, ownership, and use, after International Great Lakes Diversions and Consumptive Uses Study Board. 1981. Great Lakes Diversions and Consumptive Uses. International Joint Commission.

Manitoulin

Map, after Robertson, J. A., and K. D. Card. 1972. Geology and scenery, north shore of Lake Huron region, Ministry of Natural Resources, Toronto.

Acknowledgements

Over the years that this book moved from an idea to reality, many people and agencies enthusiastically helped it along. Initial impetus came from the late Gordon Garner, eastern sales representative of Hurtig Publishers, and later from Mel Hurtig. A grant to the editor from the Ontario Heritage Foundation (an agency of the Ontario Ministry of Culture and Communications) through its Natural Heritage League provided the financial means to begin. Costs also were defrayed by the donation of seventeen colour separations by the Federation of Ontario Naturalists.

Don Bonner of the Faculty of Environmental Studies, University of Waterloo, spent most of a year producing superb maps, and his skills and patience are reflected in the high quality of his work. He produced all but the seven maps of the physiographic features of the Niagara Escarpment, the two maps of the paths of cyclone centres, and the map of the distribution of Virginia meadow beauty, which were supplied respectively by the Niagara Escarpment Commission, Dr. F. Kenneth Hare, and Dr. P. Keddy. Drafts of the six climate maps were made for the book by the Atmospheric Environment Service of Environment Canada, courtesy of Dave Phillips.

The following people kindly read drafts of material in their fields of specialization written by others: Mike Cadman, Erica Dunn, Jim Gardner, Jim Ginns, Dick Harington, Dave Hussell, Bill Hutcheson, Harry Lumsden, Dave Malloch, Roger Macqueen, Rob McDonald, Gerry O'Reilly, John Riley, Sheila Thomson, Fred Urquhart, and Dennis Voigt.

The following people helped Bill Fox with the production of the most up-to-date map of the location of native tribes in Ontario yet published: Conrad Heidenreich, John Steckley, Grace Rajnivich, Thor Conway, and Rob McDonald. Steve Cumba of the National Museum of Natural Sciences provided C. R. Harington with the identification of seven new fish taxa from the Don Beds yet unpublished, including some North American records. J. Bruce Falls acknowledges the use in his article on territoriality of research contributions by Judith (Stenger) Weeden, Reto Zach, and James Jones.

The following agencies provided photos from their collections free of charge: Canadian Parks Service (Point Pelee National Park Collection), Ministry of Natural Resources (Algonquin Park Museum Collection), National Museum of Canada Photo Section (A. G. Austin Collection), Niagara Escarpment Commission, the Natural Conservancy of Canada, and the Royal Ontario Museum.

The following photographers, whose photos were previously published by *Seasons* (the magazine of the Federation of Ontario Naturalists), kindly provided free use: Hans Blokpoel, Mary Gartshore, Don Gunn, Betty Greenacre, Isador Jelkin, Phil Kor, Norm Lightfoot, Robert McCaw, Otonabee Region Conservation Authority, John Shaw, David Taylor, and Al Woodliffe. Advice on some of the photo captions was provided by A. G. McLellan, I. McKenzie, and Dan Schneider.

Elaine Theberge kindly proofread a draft of the entire manuscript.

The School of Planning (Sharon Adams and Mary Jane Bauer) and the Office of Research, University of Waterloo, provided administrative assistance.

Finally, the Chief Editor would like to thank his Associate Editors, all the authors, and the many people who submitted photos for consideration for their belief that Ontario's nature will benefit from this book.

John B. Theberge

About the Authors

Edward M. Addison, Ph. D., is a wildlife disease specialist with the Wildlife Research Section of the Ontario Ministry of Natural Resources. He received a B.Sc. from the University of Toronto, and a M.Sc. and Ph.D. from the University of Guelph. Since 1972, when he joined the Ministry, he has worked on parasites and diseases of moose, white-tailed deer, black bear, mink, lynx, beaver, otter, fisher, wolverines, ruffed grouse, and wild turkeys, and has published many scientific papers on these animals. Ed has served on the editorial boards of the *Journal of Parasitology* and the *Journal of Wildlife Diseases*, and been Secretary of the Parasitology Section of the Canadian Society of Zoologists. He is a former Vice President and Councillor of the Wildlife Disease Association.

Gary Allen, M.A., received both B.E.S. and M.A. degrees from the Faculty of Environmental Studies, University of Waterloo. He worked as an interpretive naturalist for three years at Point Pelee National Park and for four years was a district botanist with the Ontario Ministry of Natural Resources in Chatham and now is with the Ministry at Richmond Hill. Gary has a keen interest in the flora of Ontario, particularly Carolinian and prairie species, and in the establishment and management of natural areas. Currently, as a district botanist, he is responsible for plant inventories in designated Areas of Natural and Scientific Interest.

David Barr, Ph.D., is a biologist with the Royal Ontario Museum who has carried out systematic research (evolutionary and taxonomic studies) on various invertebrate animals including crayfishes, water mites, and army ants. His research techniques include comparative anatomy and behaviour simulations, and computer classification. He has carried out field work in all parts of North America as well as in Europe and Central America. In recent years he has worked primarily in the Canadian Arctic. Dave has written over forty interpretive publications to familiarize the public with insects and other invertebrates. Also cross-appointed to the University of Toronto, he has taught undergraduate and graduate courses on evolution and ecology. He has served as associate editor of *Seasons* magazine.

Irwin M. Brodo, Ph.D., has been Curator of Lichens at the National Museum of Natural Sciences for the past twenty-two years, and Chief of the Botany Division for seven. He received his B.Sc. from City College in New York, his M.Sc. from Cornell University, and his Ph.D. from Michigan State University. He has published over forty research papers, mainly in the fields of lichen taxonomy and ecology, including several monographs, papers on British Columbia lichens, and a book on lichens of the Ottawa Region. He has served as a President of the American Bryological and Lichenological Society, and was bulletin editor of the International Association of Lichenology for twelve years. More locally, he served terms as President of both the Ottawa Field-Naturalists' Club and the Ottawa-Hull Chapter of the National and Provincial Parks Association of Canada.

Michael D. Cadman, M.A., has worked since 1984 on Ontario's mammoth bird atlas project, and is senior author of the book, *Atlas of the Breeding Birds of Ontario*. He is currently a freelance ecological and natural areas inventory consultant.

Francis R. Cook, Ph.D., has been Curator of Herpetology at the National Museums of Canada for the past eighteen years. He holds B.Sc. and M.Sc. degrees from Acadia University, and a Ph.D. from the University of Manitoba. Under his direction the museum's collection of amphibians and reptiles has grown to become the largest in Canada. He has conducted field work in every province in Canada, and written extensively. In 1984 he published a definitive text, *Introduction to Canadian Amphibians and Reptiles,* through the museum. Francis is currently serving his second term as editor of *The Canadian Field-Naturalist*.

Robert J. Davidson, B.Sc., is the Earth Science Specialist with the Ontario Ministry of Natural Resources' Parks and Recreational Areas Branch, where he is responsible for efforts to protect significant earth science features. He is a graduate of the Department of Earth Sciences at the University of Waterloo. Bob's responsibilities have included overseeing the province's inventory of bedrock and landforms. He was actively involved in the incorporation of earth science features into the development of both the Ontario Provincial Parks Policy and the Niagara Escarpment Master Plan. More recently, he has been engaged in developing the Ministry's policy and program for Areas of Natural and Scientific Interest.

Darrell Dennis, M.Sc., is a waterfowl biologist with the Canadian Wildlife Service in London. His degrees are from the University of Toronto and University of Guelph. He started work with the Canadian Wildlife Service in 1965 as Canada Land Inventory Biologist in Sackville, New Brunswick. In 1967 he assumed duties as a C.W.S. habitat biologist in Aurora, Ontario, and in 1971 became a waterfowl survey biologist. He has published numerous articles on waterfowl in Ontario with emphasis on use of the Great Lakes shoreline marshes and population changes in southern Ontario. In recent years his research emphasis has focused on biochemical genetics and mate selection of black ducks and mallards. Darrell is the recognized authority on changes in the status of these species in Ontario.

Bruce Duncan, M.A., has a degree in psychology from Wilfrid Laurier University and in biology from the University of Waterloo. He was a resource interpreter at Taquamjah Nature Centre operated by the Grand River Conservation Authority and now works for the Hamilton Region Conservation Authority. He has banded hawks during spring and fall migrations for eleven years and has published numerous articles on hawk migration in Ontario. He is Past President of the Ontario Bird Banding Association.

Paul F. J. Eagles, Ph.D., is a professor of outdoor recreation and resource management in the Department of Recreation and Leisure Studies at the University of Waterloo. He received a B.Sc. in biology from that university, an M.A. from the University of Guelph, and a Ph.D. in Planning from Waterloo. He has extensive experience in applying the concepts of ecology to the management of land and specializes in the planning and management of parks and wildlands. He has pioneered techniques of identifying and managing environmentally sensitive areas in southern Ontario. He was instrumental in the genesis, data collection, and subsequent publication of the *Atlas of the Breeding Birds of Ontario*. He uses the study of birds as a lens through which he can determine changes in the health of the environment.

J. Bruce Falls, Ph.D., is a well-known ornithologist. He received both B.Sc. and Ph.D. degrees from the University of Toronto and has taught there since. He is recognized as an international authority on avian behaviour and communication, particularly on the role of bird song and territorial defence. Much of the work by Bruce and his students has been conducted in Algonquin Provincial Park, where he co-founded the Wildlife Research Station more than thirty years ago. Bruce is equally well-known for his work with conservation organizations. He has been President of the Federation of Ontario Naturalists, a long-time board member of the Nature Conservancy of Canada, and has served as Chairman of the Ontario Breeding Bird Atlas Committee.

M. Brock Fenton, Ph.D., is an international authority on the biology of bats. In 1983 he published *Just Bats* (University of Toronto Press), which was followed by two technical books, *Communication in the Chiroptera* (University of Indiana Press) and *Recent Advances in the Study of Bats* (Cambridge University Press) which he edited. He received a B.Sc. from Queen's University and M.Sc. and Ph.D. degrees from the University of Toronto. He worked for a number of years at Carleton University and is currently Chairman of the Department of Biology at York University.

William A. Fox, M.A., began his experience in Ontario archaeology as a high-school student in Hamilton. He obtained his M.A. degree at the University of Toronto in 1971 and subsequently worked for the Ontario Ministry of Natural Resources as regional archaeologist in north-central, and then in southwestern Ontario. He is presently stationed in Toronto with the Ministry of Citizenship and Culture as senior archaeologist responsible for policy and program development. Other research activities have taken him to France, England, the United States, and most recently Cyprus. His many years of field work in Ontario have enhanced his appreciation of this province's diverse natural heritage and his respect for native tradition.

Alan G. Gordon, Ph.D., is a research scientist with the Ontario Tree Improvement and Forest Biomass Institute, Ministry of Natural Resources, Sault Ste. Marie, as well as Adjunct Professor of Genecology at the University of Toronto. He graduated with a B.Sc.F. from the University of New Brunswick and a Ph.D. from the University of London, England. He is a specialist in the spruce genus (*Picea*), and is currently working on long-term spruce ecosystem studies in biomass, productivity, nutrient cycling, growth and nutrition, stand dynamics, and genetics. This includes attempts to produce new hybrids for tree improvement. He is an advisor to graduate students at several universities, to scientific review process for several journals, to the Canadian Forestry Service program reviews, and to the U.S. Environmental Protection Agency on acid precipitation and spruce-fir forest research in eastern North America.

F. Kenneth Hare, Ph.D., Professor Emeritus in Geography at the University of Toronto and Chairman of the Canadian Climate Program Planning Board, retired in June 1986 from the position of Provost of Trinity College that he had held since 1979. In the course of his academic career, he served as Director of the Institute for Environmental Studies at the University of Toronto (1974-79), President of the University of British Columbia (1968-69), Master of Birkbeck College at the University of London (1966-68), Professor of Geography at King's College, University of London (1964-66), and Dean of Arts and Science at McGill University (1962-64). His B.Sc. is from the University of London and his Ph.D. from the Université de Montréal. His publications include books, textbooks, articles in refereed journals, and many technical reports. One book *Climate Canada*, was written with M. K. Thomas. He is an Officer of the Order of Canada and a Fellow of the Royal Society of Canada, and he holds nine honorary degrees.

C. R. (Dick) Harington, Ph.D., born in Calgary, attended McGill University and the University of Alberta. He received a Ph.D. in zoology at the latter institution in 1977 for a thesis on Pleistocene mammals of the Yukon Territory. After working for geophysical companies in Alberta and for the Arctic Institute of North America in Ottawa, he spent a year on northern Ellesmere Island during the International Geophysical Year, 1957-58. Between 1960 and 1965 he worked on the Arctic islands as a Canadian Wildlife Service biologist, studying polar bears and musk-oxen. He then was appointed Curator of Quaternary Zoology with the National Museums of Canada, where he carries out studies on the ice-age vertebrates of Canada and Alaska, the evolution and distribution of Arctic and alpine mammals, and climatic change during the ice age. **Stewart Hilts, Ph.D.,** is a professor of Land Resource Science at the University of Guelph. He holds degrees from the University of Western Ontario and the University of Toronto. He is the author of numerous reports in the field of rural resource management and environmental planning, and is a co-author of *Islands of Green: Natural Heritage Protection in Ontario*. In recent years he has developed and co-ordinated a Landowner Contact Program and Natural Heritage Stewardship Award for Landowners to help protect designated Areas of Natural and Scientific Interest in Ontario. He is a Past President of the Guelph Field-Naturalists and an Honorary Life Member of the Federation of Ontario Naturalists.

Douglas Hoffman, Ph.D., is recently retired as the Chairman of the School of Planning, University of Waterloo. He still teaches, however, on a part-time basis at both Waterloo and York universities. Doug is a soil scientist, having conducted many of the first soil surveys in a wide variety of places in both northern and southern Ontario over a period of thirty-two years. He was responsible for the agricultural sector of the Canadian Land Inventory in Ontario. Prior to coming to Waterloo, he worked in the Department of Soil Sciences at the University of Guelph. In recent years he has focused his attention on land management issues in southern Ontario through consulting and participation on a wide variety of provincial or regional boards. He is a Past President of the Guelph chapter of the Agricultural Institute of Canada; the Soil Conservation Society of America, Guelph branch; Lambda Alpha; and the Canadian Mental Health Association, Guelph. An author of many papers and reports about Ontario soils and rural planning, he is a fellow of the Canadian Soil Science Society.

Michael Jones, M.Sc., is the Chief Naturalist at Pukaskwa National Park. Originally from Montreal, he graduated with a B.Sc. from St. Dunstan University in Prince Edward Island and an M.Sc. from Acadia University in Nova Scotia. He has served as an interpretive naturalist at national parks in the Maritimes, Saskatchewan, and Ontario.

Paul Keddy, Ph.D., holds a B.Sc. from York University and his Ph.D. from Dalhousie University. He studies theoretical plant ecology and its applications to plant conservation. He is currently an Associate Professor teaching plant ecology at the University of Ottawa where he coordinates a group of eight researchers. He has just completed a book on the role of competition in structuring plant and animal communities. He was founding President of the Halifax Field-Naturalists and is currently a Director of the Canadian Council on Ecological Areas. He is a member of the Scientific Advisory Committee of the World Wildlife Fund (Canada).

Alfred C. Lenz, Ph.D., is a specialist in invertebrate paleontology. He has been a Professor of Paleontology at the University of Western Ontario since 1975, before that working for industry. He received both his B.Sc. and M.Sc. from the University of Alberta, and a Ph.D. from Princeton. He is a member of several international committees on Silurian and Devonian stratigraphy, and is Canadian leader for "Project Ecostratigraphy." He is Past Chairman of the Paleontology Division of the Geological Association of Canada, author of many scientific papers, and supervisor of many graduate students in the paleontology of northern Canada and southern Ontario.

Harry G. Lumsden has recently retired as Senior Research Scientist, Wildlife Research Section, Ontario Ministry of Natural Resources. He served in the Royal Air Force as a pilot during the Second World War before joining the Ontario Department of Lands and Forests in 1948. He has published many papers on waterfowl and grouse, and he continues his work on the restoration of trumpeter swans to Ontario. He has been a Trustee of the Niska Wildlife Foundation and Kortright Waterfowl Park for five years.

John A. Livingston has been a Professor of Environmental Studies at York University since 1970. From 1962-68 he was the first executive producer of the CBC's *The Nature of Things*, and from 1955-62, President of the Audubon Society of Canada (now the Canadian Nature Federation). He has been President of the Federation of Ontario Naturalists, a founding member of the Board of Trustees of the Nature Conservancy of Canada, and a founding partner in LGL Ltd., environmental research associates. John has written nine books on natural history and natural philosophy, and is particularly well known for the challenging perspectives put forth in *One Cosmic Instant: A Natural History of Human Arrogance* and *The Fallacy of Wildlife Conservation*. As well, he has co-edited three books with Roger Tory Peterson, published numerous book chapters and articles, and written many television programs.

Roger W. Macqueen, Ph.D., is Head of Petroleum Geology at the Institute of Sedimentary and Petroleum Geology, Geological Survey of Canada, in Calgary. Previously he taught earth sciences at the University of Waterloo (1976-85), and is still an Adjunct Professor there. He has been President of the Geological Association of Canada, and has published more than sixty articles on regional geology, geochemistry, and the origins of lead-zinc deposits in sedimentary rocks. As well as teaching at the Universities of Toronto and Calgary, Roger has worked on geological projects in England, the United States, Europe, and the Middle East. At present, he and his colleagues are actively involved in research on the origin of the oil sands and heavy oils of the western Canada sedimentary basin.

Gerald McKeating, M.E.S., has been greatly influenced by the Lake Erie environment: he was "turned-on" to birds at Long Point, and had the thrilling experience of finding rare orchids at Rondeau. He spent a few years as a volunteer bird-bander with the Long Point Bird Observatory before becoming a manager for the Canadian Wildlife Service responsible for the Long Point Natural Wildlife Area in 1979. Prior to joining the Canadian Wildlife Service, Gerry received his M.E.S. degree from York University in 1976. At the same time, he was employed as Endangered Species and Non-game Biologist with the Ontario Ministry of Natural Resources. After spending two years in Ottawa, Gerry was posted to Edmonton in January 1986 as Head of Habitat Conservation for the Western and Northern Regions of the Canadian Wildlife Service.

Theodore Mosquin, Ph.D., was born on a small family farm in eastern Manitoba where, as a youth, he developed a deep interest in natural history. He received an honours degree in botany from the University of Manitoba in 1956 and a Ph.D. from the University of California in 1961. After teaching at the University of Alberta for two years he moved to Ottawa where he was a research scientist with Agriculture Canada for eleven years. In 1971 he became the first president of the Canadian Nature Federation and later its executive director. He established the federation's magazine, *Nature Canada*, and edited it for its first four years. Ted is currently President of the Canadian Parks and Wilderness Society, and has published numerous scientific papers and popular articles. He resides near Lanark in eastern Ontario, where he manages a successful consulting company, Mosquin Bio-Information Ltd.

Anita Payne, M.Sc., received her B.Sc. in ecology from the University of Guelph and her M.Sc. from the University of Western Ontario. She has been a research associate at the University of Ottawa for the past four years. She is the author of articles on endangered coastal plain species, and has studied and published about sand dune ecology.

Paul D. Pratt, B.Sc., received his degree in biology from the University of Waterloo in 1972. He is a naturalist for the City of Windsor, under whose jurisdiction falls the Ojibway Prairie. He was Regional Co-ordinator for the Ontario Breeding Bird Atlas Project, and was a member of the Ontario Bird Records Committee. Paul was a founding Director of the Friends of Point Pelee Co-operating Association. In 1985 he received the Lee Symmes Award of Excellence for environmental planning by a municipality. His present interests include the Ontario Herptofaunal Atlas, birding, and studying Ontario's dragonflies.

Paul Prevett, Ph.D., pursued an avid early interest in wild animals to formal studies in wildlife biology at the University of Guelph (B.Sc.) and the University of Western Ontario (Ph.D.). A fascination with the Arctic led to research on the family life of snow geese in the Northwest Territories for his Ph.D. thesis, and then to eight years of wildlife work in the Hudson Bay Lowlands with the Ontario Ministry of Natural Resources. He now works for the Ministry in London, Ontario, where he is involved primarily with endangered species and natural area protection.

James S. Pringle, Ph.D., is a plant taxonomist at the Royal Botanical Gardens in Hamilton.

Ron Reid, M.Sc., is a freelance writer and

environmental consultant living in Washago, Ontario. He was formerly Staff Environmentalist for the Federation of Ontario Naturalists, where he was foremost in promoting a wetlands policy for Ontario as well as being involved in a wide variety of conservation issues. He has published many conservation articles in magazines and newspapers, and with his wife Janet Grand, he is author of *Canoeing Ontario's Rivers*, a guidebook to some of the province's best canoe waters.

Mike Singleton, M.Sc., is a freelance conservationist. His initial fascination with reptiles led to a broader interest in natural history, and he trained in botany, zoology, geology, and paleontology. In twenty years of volunteer and staff involvement with the Federation of Ontario Naturalists, he has worked for the protection of wetlands, endangered species, parks, the Niagara Escarpment, and on other conservation issues. Author of a syndicated newspaper column and weekly radio features, Mike regards an appreciation of nature as the cornerstone of conservation.

Paul G. R. Smith, M.A., received degrees from the Department of Biology, University of Guelph, and the School of Planning, University of Waterloo. At Waterloo he wrote a thesis on planning for environmentally significant areas in the Northwest Territories. He later worked as a consultant on a project to identify and describe all the natural areas on the Canadian shores of the Great Lakes. He currently is employed by the Wildlife Branch of the Ministry of Natural Resources with responsibilities for wetland management.

Steve M. Smith, Ph.D., is a Professor in the Department of Biology at the University of Waterloo. He holds a B.Sc. and M.Sc. from McMaster University and a Ph.D. from the University of Manitoba. He is an internationally known expert in the biology of blood-sucking insects with special reference to blackflies and tabanids, having studied them in such diverse places as the eastern Canadian Arctic and East Africa. He has also studied the biology of lacebugs, and the biology of stream insects. He is Chairman of the Ontario Rabies Advisory Committee and a former editor of *The Canadian Entomologist*.

Barry Snider, M.Sc., is an Environmental Biologist with the Ministry of Natural Resources in Lindsay. He holds degrees from the University of Guelph and Lakehead University. After spending two years establishing a wildlife park in West Africa, he joined the Ministry of Natural Resources in 1973, working at White River and then at Terrace Bay. At Terrace Bay the Slate Islands fell under his jurisdiction. He has a special management interest in moose, white-tailed deer, and caribou.

Mark Stabb, B.E.S., received his degree from the Department of Man and Environment at the University of Waterloo. For the past three years, while a graduate student in the Faculty of Forestry at the University of Toronto, he has studied the southern flying squirrel. He has published many natural-history articles and was awarded the Ontario Forestry Association's 1987 White Pine Award for his contribution to conservation education. He is currently Provincial Co-ordinator of the Community Wildlife Involvement Program of the Ministry of Natural Resources in Toronto.

Dan Strickland, M.Sc., has worked in Algonquin Park since 1965 and has been Chief Park Naturalist since 1970. He was educated at the Universities of Toronto and Montreal. The subject of his M.Sc. dissertation – the ecology of the gray jay – continues to receive his detailed attention in a major ongoing study. Dan has written extensively on Algonquin Park's human and natural history in award-winning park interpretive publications, trail guides, and the park's summer newsletter, *The Raven*. He lives with his wife and two children just outside the park ("just this side of heaven," he claims).

John B. Theberge, Ph.D., is a Professor of Ecology and Resource Management at the University of Waterloo, where he has taught since 1970. He holds wildlife management and zoology degrees from the Universities of Guelph, Toronto, and British Columbia. John is best known for his research on wolves and their prey, having studied them in a variety of places: Ontario, the Yukon, Labrador, and British Columbia. He has published numerous scientific and popular articles and one book, *Wolves and Wilderness* (1975), about the ecology of wolves. He has promoted the establishment and protection of park and wilderness areas. In the Yukon, with colleagues and students, he directed ten years of identification and planning for environmentally significant areas. He was instrumental in the establishment of Kluane National Park and was editor-author of *Kluane: Pinnacle of the Yukon*, published in 1980. For his scientific work in the sub-Arctic he was elected a Fellow of the Arctic Institute of North America. He has served on the boards of directors and executives of the Canadian Parks and Wilderness Society and the Federation of Ontario Naturalists. The latter organization presented him with an Honorary Life Membership in 1984. He recently chaired a Task Force on Park Establishment for the federal Minister of the Environment. He is a member of the board of the Nature Conservancy of Canada and currently is directing a long-term study of wolves in Algonquin Provincial Park.

Mary T. Theberge is a freelance nature artist who portrays images of animals and nature to evoke feelings and respect for nature. She specializes in scratchboard art as well as watercolour and has illustrated two books, as well as many magazine articles and children's books. She promotes nature for children as an active Guider and District Commissioner. She is a competent naturalist and works with her biologist husband on field studies of large mammals in wilderness areas and parks.

Sheila C. Thomson is a former Assistant Curator of the National Mycological Herbarium of Canada. She produced a standard methodology for conducting mycological surveys for Parks Canada and, with a colleague, organized and supervised the first such survey in Canada, in St. Lawrence Islands National Park. A well-known Ottawa Valley naturalist, she is in demand as a lecturer up and down the Valley. She has published many articles on natural history, several books published by Reader's Digest, and scientific papers on morels. She is a Past President of the Ottawa Field-Naturalist's Club and of the Ottawa chapter of the Canadian Parks and Wilderness Society. In 1981 she was made an Honorary Life Member of the Ottawa Field-Naturalist's Club in recognition of her efforts to save the natural habitats of Gatineau Park.

Allan Wainio, M.A., was born in Toronto but raised in northern Ontario, near Timmins. He graduated from the University of Toronto with an M.A. in fisheries biology. Employed with the Ministry of Natural Resources since 1959, he has been responsible for fish-rehabilitation programs in the Great Lakes and other southern waters. He has published many articles on fish and is enthusiastic both in his research into lake and stream ecology and in his promotion of fishwatching as a naturalist pursuit.

Shan Walshe, M.Sc., a graduate of the University of Toronto with a B.A. in modern languages and an M.Sc. in plant ecology, has been Chief Park Naturalist at Quetico Provincial Park for sixteen years. Each summer he spends at least eight weeks canoeing and portaging in the Quetico wilderness. In 1980, after eight years of botanical investigations, he wrote *Plants of Quetico*, published by the University of Toronto Press.

Ron Weir, Ph.D., is an engineer, a scientist, and a Professor in the Department of Chemistry and Chemical Engineering at Royal Military College, Kingston. He studies low-temperature thermodynamics. By avocation, however, he is a naturalist, birdwatcher, and writer. His natural history articles have appeared in the scientific literature and the lay press, and he has written two books. Currently he is the Ontario editor of *American Birds*, and he writes the "Arrivals and Departures" column in *Seasons* magazine. He was the 1986 winner of the Federation of Ontario Naturalists' Conservation Trophy. He is a Past President of the Kingston Field-Naturalists.

Natalie Zalkind, B.E.S., received her degree from the Department of Geography at the University of Waterloo in 1981. Since then she has worked as an interpretive naturalist at St. Lawrence Islands National Park, Point Pelee National Park, and Gatineau Park, and as Head of Visitor Services at Sandbanks Provincial Park. Natalie has a special interest in environmental education and natural history. A fitness enthusiast, she spends her spare time bicycling, skiing, and teaching fitness.

INDEX

Page numbers of photographs and illustrations are in bold face.

DESIGN / *David Shaw (Bookends East)*

EDITORIAL CONSULTANT / *Sarah Reid*

COMPOSITION / *Trigraph Inc.*

FILM PREPARATION / *Colour Technologies*

MANUFACTURING / *D. W. Friesen & Sons Ltd.*